MOBILIZING CAPITAL
PROGRAM INNOVATION
AND
THE CHANGING PUBLIC/PRIVATE
INTERFACE IN DEVELOPMENT FINANCE

MOBILIZING CAPITAL

PROGRAM INNOVATION AND THE CHANGING PUBLIC/PRIVATE INTERFACE IN DEVELOPMENT FINANCE

Edited by
Peter J. Bearse

Elsevier
New York • Amsterdam • Oxford

HC 110
53
M6
1982

Exclusive Distribution
throughout the World by
Greenwood Press, Westport,
Ct. U.S.A.

Elsevier Science Publishing Co., Inc.
52 Vanderbilt Avenue, New York, New York 10017

Exclusive distribution throughout the world by
Greenwood Press
A division of Congressional Information Service Inc.
88 Post Road West, Westport, Connecticut 06881, U.S.A.

Library of Congress Cataloging in Publication Data
Main entry under title:

Mobilizing capital.

  Bibliography: p.
  Includes index.
  1. Saving and investment—United States—Addresses,
essays, lectures.   2. United States—Economic conditions—
Regional disparities—Addresses, essays, lectures.
3. Regional planning—United States—Addresses, essays,
lectures.   I. Bearse, Peter.
HC110.S3M6   338.973   82-1447
ISBN 0-444-00690-7   AACR2

Manufactured in the United States of America

To Jeanne MacFarland, late director of the Office of Economic Research, Economic Administration, who, if she had lived, would have continued to make significant contributions to the field of economic development and regretted the developments which are now adversely affecting the field.

Contents

Foreword

When the editor of this substantial volume asked whether I would write a foreword to this collection I was ambivalent. On the one hand my inclination is always to respond in the affirmative to any reasonable, and even not so reasonable, request of a younger associate with whom I have worked and whose scholarship I hold in high regard. On the other hand, I realized that the subject around which this collection of essays centered was far from the area of my expertise. I pondered briefly whether the second factor should outweigh the first, but decided that sentiment should win out over caution. I answered in the affirmative and now I must make at least a few pertinent observations about the central theme of this volume, the approaches followed, and about my views on public policy.

Bearse's introductory chapter provides a clue as to why he asked me to write the foreword. Bearse believes that certain structural transformations are characteristic of all advanced economies, particularly the U.S. economy. Among the most important of these transformations is the relative decline of manufacturing and the growth of services, with multiple consequences attendant upon this shift. In tracing out this transformation Bearse draws heavily on the research that the Conservation of Human Resources (CHR), Columbia University, which I direct, has devoted to illuminating the growth of services.

An earlier effort of CHR on *The Pluralistic Economy* (McGraw-Hill, 1965) addresses a second concern of Bearse, the increasing growth in advanced economies of the not-for-profit sector, that is government and nonprofit institutions, which we estimated as accounting in the mid-1960s for over 25% of GNP and between 33 and 40% of total employment.

To take the second proposition first, I believe that Bearse and his collaborators are definitely on the right track when they stress that the pluralistic economy offers opportunities for collaborative investments for infrastructure and other purposes involving all three parties—private, nonprofit, and government. The present volume offers multiple accounts and assessments of such recent collaborative undertakings.

The implications of the shift to services on investment opportunities are relatively muted in the contributions that follow. On the other hand, there are several illuminating treatments of the criticality of human resources for influencing locational decisions and for their effect on the potential profitability of the collaborative investments that are the central concern of this book.

Within the last year the National Commission for Employment Policy, which I chair, published its *Sixth Annual Report* which deals extensively with the interrelations between economic development policies and the employment of the structurally unemployed, a subject of concern to several of the contributors to the present volume. The Commission concluded that there were several opportunities for closer linkages between these two major governmental program areas, the one directed to the revitalization of declining urban areas, the other focused on improving the employability of the hard-to-employ. But the Commission and its staff were cautious in their appraisal of how much the two programs could be integrated given the "substitution" issue. In my view, substitution does not get the attention it warrants in subsequent chapters.

The funding that the government makes available via community or economic development grants and loans, which under the best of circumstances can result in the leveraging of private funds many times the amount advanced, still is not cost free. The assistance proferred Philadelphia, Newark, New York, or Buffalo means that somewhat fewer capital resources will be available for other communities. Whether or not targeting on the more or most strickened places makes sense for the short and longer term is a difficult inquiry to design and even more difficult to carry through. One of the virtues of the present volume is the rich materials that it provides which will surely help future students to improve their research designs and execution.

A word or two about European regional policies, the focus of Chap. XVI, a subject to which I have paid at least passing attention over many years. For a whole series of reasons, European governments have for a long time experimented with regional policies. Labor in Europe is much more immobile than in the United States and the housing market is much more constrained, which reinforces the disinclination of workers to leave their home area when the local economy goes into decline. My impression is that the German, Dutch, British, French, and Swedish regional policies that I have looked at do not commend themselves as clear-cut successes. Rather the reverse—they appear to have used considerable amounts of national capital with relatively small social returns.

What this suggests, at least to me, is not that we should turn our backs on using regional and other targeted investments but rather that we should recognize from the outset the multiple difficulties of launching and implementing such efforts in a way that they have a reasonable chance of succeeding.

The public and the private sectors have been mutually supportive during the heyday of laissez-faire. Note the pacification of the West by the U.S. Army and the role that the federal government played in the construction of the nation's railway network. More recently, consider the importance of federal and state infrastructure investments in highways and air travel. What Bearse and his collaborators are pressing for is a more realistic framework to speed development in an increasingly pluralistic economy characterized by serious infrastructure decay in older urban communities, the entrapment of these large numbers of poorly prepared minority members of the labor force, and the steady shift of the economy towards services.

The Reagan Administration, having nearly abolished the Economic Development Administration and cut back on other federal funding for community and economic development investments, is placing its bets on tax credits and subsidies to attract new enterprises and to encourage existing enterprises to expand in targeted urban areas which are sorely in need of rehabilitation and development. The extent to which the tax approach will work is moot. But what should be clear is that taxes alone will not add directly to the skills of the local underemployed and unemployed work force, lacking which few, if any, of these deprived areas will be turned around. The key capital in a service economy is human capital which today accounts for roughly 80% of national income. This has long been an area of governmental responsibility. If economic development is to be pursued aggressively in the years and decades ahead—as I feel sure it will—then we need improved linkages among the sectors not only with respect to the financial capital but also human capital markets. Bearse and his colleagues have made a contribution to the first. They, or others, must now write the counterpart volume focused on the accelerated development of human capital.

Eli Ginzberg, Director
Conservation of Human Resources
Columbia University
June, 1981

Acknowledgments

A few parts of this book originated with a conference on financing economic development which the editor convened in April of 1978 at Princeton University with support from the Economic Development Administration, U.S. Department of Commerce. Neither the Administration nor the University, however, are in any way responsible for the views or materials presented in this volume.

Contributors

Peter J. Bearse, Ph.D., the editor, is Director of Economic Development, Public/Private Ventures, Inc., Philadelphia. A professional economist, he is the author of many articles and reports on economic development issues and the co-author of another book, *Services: The New Economy* (Allenheld-Osmun, 1981). Previously, Dr. Bearse was staff director for the Governor's Economic Policy Council, State of New Jersey, and a lecturer and research associate, Woodrow Wilson School, Princeton University.

Arthur W. Bearse teaches finance and economics at Moravian College, Bethlehem, Pennsylvania.

Christopher Brennan is assistant director of the Bay State Skills Corporation. Previously, he served as special assistant to the Secretary of Economic Affairs, Commonwealth of Massachusetts.

E. Evan Brunson is Director of Intergovernmental Affairs, Southern Growth Policies Board, Research Triangle Park, North Carolina, and the author of several other articles on economic development in the South.

Jack E. Curtis, Jr., is a partner in McQuaid, Ludwig, Bedford and Curtis, a Washington, D.C. and San Francisco based law firm specializing in employee stock ownership programs. He was formerly Counsel to the Senate Finance Committee.

Belden Daniels is founder and senior principal of Counsel for Community Development, Inc.; lecturer at the Department of City and Regional Planning, Harvard University; and a leading consultant in the development finance field.

William O. Douglas is the late Justice of the United States Supreme Court who, at the time he wrote the article included in Chapter II, was the first Chairman of the Securities and Exchange Commission.

Eugene R. Eisman is a senior urban analyst in the Office of Urban Activities of the Federal National Mortgage Association in Washington, D.C. Before joining FNMA in 1979, he served as special assistant to the Secretary of Community Affairs of the Commonwealth of Pennsylvania (1971–1979). He has an M.S. in urban planning and policy development from Rutgers University and has published over a dozen articles on housing and community development topics.

Joel Freiser is Director of the Essex County (New Jersey) Department of Planning and Economic Development. From 1969 to 1980 he held various positions in the U.S. Department of Housing and Urban Development and was last responsible for coordination of the UDAG program in the State of New Jersey. During the mid 1970s, he was on loan to the City of Hoboken as Deputy Director of its Model Cities Agency and Director of Municipal Operations.

Diane F. Fulman is a consultant on urban economic development and public policy to the First National Bank of Boston. Among her recent projects, Ms. Fulman has designed a revolving loan fund for small businesses and authored training materials to encourage new lending relationships among commercial banks and community-based organizations.

Jeffrey R. Gates is Counsel to the United States Senate Committee on Finance. Prior to this, he provided the research input for Stuart Speiser's book, *A Piece of the Action*, and served as a consultant with Hewitt Associates, an employee benefits consulting firm.

Eli Ginzberg is A. Barton Hepburn Professor of Economics, Columbia University, and Director of Conservation of Human Resources, and until very recently was Chairman of the National Commission for Employment Policy.

Keith Hinman is a policy analyst in the United States Department of Energy. He received a Master's degree in Public Policy from the University of California at Berkeley in 1980, where the original version of his chapter was submitted as a thesis.

James M. Howell is Senior Vice President and Chief Economist, First National Bank of Boston; Chairman of the Council for Northeast Economic Action; and Chairman of the Massachusetts Private Industry Council.

David C. Jamison is Program Officer, United States Department of Housing and Urban Development. Previously, he served as Deputy Director of HUD's Office of Public/Private Partnerships, worked with HUD's UDAG program during its initation, and spent an equal number of years in the private sector.

James E. Jarrett is Director of the State Innovations Project, Council of State Governments, Lexington, Kentucky.

James Keefe is a staff member of the First National Bank of Boston, where he advises line lending divisions on neighborhood development issues and helps maintain the bank's compliance with the Community Reinvestment Act. Previously, Mr. Keefe was Director of Special Projects for the Massachusetts Department of Manpower Development, where he managed most of that agency's economic development initiatives.

Nancy Leifer is Chief of the Bureau of Economic Development, Department of Commerce, State of Montana, and a graduate of the Woodrow Wilson School, Princeton University.

Bruce W. Marcus is a consultant and an author of numerous books and articles on various aspects of finance, real estate, and economic affairs, including *Competing for Capital* (Wiley, 1978).

Richard J. Moore is Assistant Professor of Urban and Regional Policy, Woodrow Wilson School, Princeton University.

Michael A. Pagano is Assistant Professor of Political Science, Miami University (Ohio) and formerly senior policy analyst, CONSAD Research Corporation.

Mitchell Rosenberg is a staff member of the Technical Development Corporation, Boston, Massachusetts, who specializes in energy conservation and community development projects.

David Smith is Vice President of the Technical Development Corporation, Boston, Massachusetts and consultant to the National Center for Economic Alternatives.

Bernard L. Weinstein is professor of economics and political economy at the University of Texas at Dallas where he also serves as associate director of the Center for Policy Studies. Dr. Weinstein has published widely in the fields of economic development, public policy, and taxation. He has also worked for several federal government agencies and served as scholar-in-residence at the Southern Growth Policies Board.

Working Group on Community Economic Development Reform is a monitoring and advocacy group formed by the Center for Community Change, Washington, D.C. The prime concerns of both the Working Group and the Center are building the capacity of neighborhood and community groups, especially in disadvantaged or low income areas, to undertake economic development or influence decisions affecting their neighborhoods or communities. Paul Bloyd of the Center Staff was project director for the monitoring work reported here.

PART ONE

INSTITUTIONAL INNOVATION AND THE CHANGING PUBLIC/PRIVATE INTERFACE IN DEVELOPMENT FINANCE: OVERALL PERSPECTIVES

Institutional Innovation and the Changing Public/Private Interface in Development Finance: Overall Perspectives

Peter Bearse

Introduction

At this point in time, the nature of the relationship between the major institutional actors in the American economy, public and private, is the subject of intense debate and scrutiny. There is a significant body of opinion which, recognizing shortcomings in both big business and big government, holds the formation of new public/private "partnerships" as the solution to many socioeconomic problems and, perhaps, as the wave of the future. Yet, there is very little agreement on what form the new relationships or institutional arrangements should take. Although one could grapple with this problem in a variety of contexts, it is fair to say that recent debates on financing economic development have crystallized the issues involved more than any other single concern. Indeed, the waxing and waning of the debate on the appropriate relationship between public authority and private discretion has been one of the hallmarks of American economic history. The issue has never been long submerged, surfacing in the early days of the Republic, the late nineteenth century, during the Great Depression, and, not coincidentally, now, when the nation is in the midst of a major economic transition.

Thus, there would appear to be a timely raison d'être for this book. One might pause to ask why. Because the nature of the public/private relationship lies at the core of the American republic (indeed, any Western society), it has been the subject of countless treatises, from the standpoints of law, ideology, economics, sociology, and public administration. For example, George Lodge (1975) has provided a wealth of insights organized around the fundamental theme of ideology. Andrew Schonfield's (1965) treatise is something of a modern classic in examining the "changing balance of public and private power" cross-nationally. Recent books by Bell (1976), Walsh (1978), Shepard (1977), and Castells (1980) are all quite different, more or less relevant and quite apropos. With the exception of the book by Walsh, however, all these good examples discuss, diagnose, or dissect the issue at the level of ideas— concepts, theories, or ideologies. For someone who has been working in the field of economic development for some time, it has been frustrating to see the lack of a volume which, in a reasonably comprehensive way, presents and interprets actual experience with a variety of experiments which, at least as much as debates around concepts, may portend where the public/private relationship is going and the implications for American economic development for the remainder of this century. In contrast to a more European cast of mind, most Americans would still say, "actions speak louder than words" and "experience is the great teacher."

The purpose of this book, therefore, is to describe and assess a variety of institutional innovations which have recently arisen at several levels of the American political economy and which share three characteristics:

1. they are innovations designed to help mobilize or allocate capital for economic development;
2. they implicate changing public/private relationships in interesting or potentially important ways; and
3. they raise important questions concerning the replicability among areas or levels, and what institutional forms for public/private cooperation in economic development will ultimately take root.

Since the body of the book primarily focuses on experiences or concrete institutional arrangements rather than ideas, it is now the purpose of this chapter to provide at least some essential "ideological" or conceptual perspectives to crosscut the variety which follows.

The Transition to a Services Economy

The logic of this chapter rests on three major premises:

1. that the U.S. economy has, during the postwar period, undergone a major transformation;
2. that this transformation is not yet complete, i.e., the economy is still in the midst of a major transition; and
3. that there has been insufficient recognition of the implications of the first two points for development policy for the appropriate relationship between public and private institutions in pursuit of economic goals.

These premises are much more than mere hypotheses; a substantial amount of empirical evidence has accumulated, even to the point of fueling speculation in the popular press. How one weighs and interprets the available evidence is dependent on one's frame of reference. What is an appropriate theory for deciphering the stylized facts of the transformation? Once we have taken account of both "facts" and "theories," what are their implications for financing economic development and public/private relationships?

It is by now widely acknowledged that the United States has been transformed into a "post-industrial" society, though there is not widespread agreement as to what this means. The most familiar feature of this transformation is the shift from a goods to a services economy. This can be viewed in terms of the composition of output or employment. Over the postwar generation (1947–1977), goods-producing industry overall fell from 37.4% of output to 32.8%, while services industries rose from 62.7% to 66.1% of output. In terms of employment, the corresponding shifts (1948–1977) were: goods-producing, from 43.4% to 31.6%; services, from 56.6% to 68.4%.* (See Tables 1 and 2.)

The categories "manufacturing" and "services," however, only roughly represent the key categories of interest. A recent monograph characterizes the transformation along two dimensions: *what* is produced and *how* it is produced (Stanback and Bearse et al., 1981). The shift from manufacturing to services connotes a shift in the composition of output from tangible to intangible "goods," but this is only part of the story. An equally important part has been a tendency for services to become an increasing component of the value of manufactured goods. This is partly due to services being embodied via marketing, advertising, customer services, and other service functions needed to bring the goods to the final consumers. It is also due to the changing "how" of the production process. Abramovitz (1972), for instance, aptly characterized the latter as a shift from "hard-handed" to "soft-handed" work. In the employment statistics, this is reflected in a massive shift in the occupational composition of the work force from blue collar to white collar and from production workers to non-production workers. This has not only been a shift from firms classified as "manufacturing" to those classified as "services" but a very substantial shift, too, within the manufacturing sector itself (Fig. 1).

An important feature of the transition to a services economy, not widely recognized, is the rapid growth and increasing significance of what can be called "producer services." These are a wide variety of services which are provided primarily as inputs to business, in contrast to "consumer services" which are sold primarily to families and individuals. Producer services include such activities or industries as window cleaning, advertising, personnel recruiting, R&D, direct mail, and data processing. Consumer services include local barbershops, cleaning and recreational activities, and so on. These two major types of services differ radically in terms of firm size, rate of growth, productivity, types of jobs, and other indicators. The producer services component has been one of the most dynamic and fastest growing parts of the services sector.

---

*The *goods-producing* sector is here defined to include agriculture, mining, and manufacturing. The *services* sector includes all else. See Table 1.

Table 1. Percentage Distribution of Gross National Product by Sectors, 1947-1977 (in Billions of 1972 Dollars)

	1947		1969		1977	
	$	%	$	%	$	%
Agriculture, Extractive, and Transformative	175.1	37.38	388.3	35.99	437.4	32.81
Agriculture	26.1	5.57	33.0	3.06	38.3	2.81
Extractive and Transformative	149.0	31.81	355.3	32.93	399.1	29.94
Manufacturing	114.9	24.53	276.2	25.60	322.3	24.12
Services	293.6	62.68	690.9	64.03	881.1	66.09
Distributive Services	62.6	13.36	161.8	15.00	220.1	16.51
Retail Services	51.8	11.06	105.5	9.78	131.8	9.89
Non-Profit Services	12.5	2.67	38.6	3.58	53.8	4.04
Producer Services	72.6	15.50	197.0	18.26	268.2	20.12
Mainly Consumer Services	25.6	5.47	36.2	3.35	41.5	3.11
Government and Government Enterprises	68.5	14.62	151.8	14.07	165.7	12.43
Residual and Rest of the World	– 0.3	– 0.06	– 0.2	– 0.20	14.6	1.10
Gross National Product	468.4	100.00	1079.0	100.00	1333.1	100.00

Sources: U.S. Department of Commerce, Bureau of Economic Analysis, *The National Income and Product Accounts of the United States, 1929-74 Statistical Tables* (Washington, D.C.: USGPO, 1977), Table 6.2; "Gross National Product by Major Industry. Workfile 1205-02-03." Unpublished material provided by BEA.; and "U.S. National Income and Product Accounts: Revised Estimates, 1975-77," *Survey of Current Business*, July 1978, Table 6.2, p. 52. From Stanback and Bearse, et al. (1981).

Table 2. Distribution of Full Time Equivalent Employees by Industry, 1929 to 1977

	1929 Employee Number	Share(%)	1939 Employee Number	Share(%)	1948 Employee Number	Share(%)	1959 Employee Number	Share(%)	1969 Employee Number	Share(%)	1977 Employee Number	Share(%)
Agriculture, Extractive and Transformative	15,857	44.87	14,386	40.06	20,864	43.39	21,271	38.34	25,055	35.09	25,132	31.60
Agriculture	2,952	8.35	2,368	6.59	2,072	4.31	1,764	3.18	1,240	1.74	1,510	1.90
Extractive and transformative	12,905	36.52	12,018	33.46	18,792	39.08	19,507	35.16	23,815	33.35	23,622	29.70
Mining	993	2.81	832	2.32	993	2.06	709	1.28	610	0.85	810	1.02
Construction	1,484	4.20	1,219	3.39	2,278	4.74	2,761	4.98	3,452	4.83	3,641	4.58
Manufacturing	10,428	29.51	9,967	27.75	15,521	32.27	16,037	28.91	19,753	27.66	19,171	24.10
Services	19,481	55.13	21,528	59.94	27,226	56.61	34,205	61.66	46,350	64.91	54,403	68.40
Distributive services	5,535	15.66	4,634	12.90	6,512	13.54	6,742	12.15	7,832	10.97	9,034	11.36
Transportation	2,873	8.13	1,990	5.54	2,854	5.93	2,494	4.50	2,634	3.69	2,654	3.34
Communication	538	1.52	423	1.18	739	1.54	799	1.44	1,001	1.40	1,125	1.41
Utilities	493	1.39	445	1.24	528	1.10	594	1.07	651	0.91	734	0.92
Wholesale	1,631	4.62	1,776	4.94	2,391	4.97	2,855	5.15	3,546	4.97	4,521	5.68
Retail services	4,215[a]	11.93[a]	4,389[a]	12.22[a]	6,047	12.57	7,045	12.70	9,283	13.00	11,276	14.18
Nonprofit services	653	1.85	787	2.19	1,254	2.61	1,954	3.52	3,338	4.67	5,043	6.34
Health	429	1.21	522	1.45	825	1.72	1,366	2.46	2,375	3.33	4,128	5.19
Education	224	0.63	265	0.74	429	0.89	588	1.06	963	1.35	915	1.15
Producer services	2,068	5.85	2,094	5.83	2,912	6.06	4,566	8.23	7,162	10.03	9,515	11.90
FIRE	1,415	4.00	1,376	3.83	1,678	3.49	2,471	4.45	3,415	4.78	4,209	5.29
Other producer services	653	1.85	718	2.00	1,234	2.57	2,095	3.78	3,747	5.25	5,306	6.67
Mainly consumer services	3,806	10.77	3,452	9.61	3,689	7.67	3,592	6.47	4,108	5.75	3,966	4.99
Hotels and personal services	1,004	2.84	954	2.66	1,305	2.71	1,246	2.25	1,617	2.26	1,591	2.00
Auto and misc. repair services	59[b]	0.17[b]	58[b]	0.16[b]	349	0.73	360	0.65	520	0.73	685	0.86
Motion pictures, amusement, and recreation	395	1.12	345	0.96	461	0.96	394	0.71	504	0.71	676	0.85
Private households	2,348	6.64	2,075	5.78	1,574	3.27	1,592	2.87	1,467	2.05	1,014	1.27
Government	3,204	9.07	6,172	17.19	6,812	14.16	10,306	18.58	14,627	20.48	15,569	19.57
Public education	1,082	3.06	1,224	3.41	1,418	2.95	2,347	4.23	4,050	5.67	5,121	6.44
Domestic Industries	35,338	100.00	35,914	100.00	48,090	100.00	55,476	100.00	71,405	100.00	79,535	100.00

Source: U.S. Department of Commerce, Bureau of Economic Analysis, *The National and Product Account of the United States, 1929-74 Statistical Tables* and *Survey of Current Business*, July 1978.
From: Stanback & Bearse, 1981.
[a] Include auto services. [b] Exclude auto services

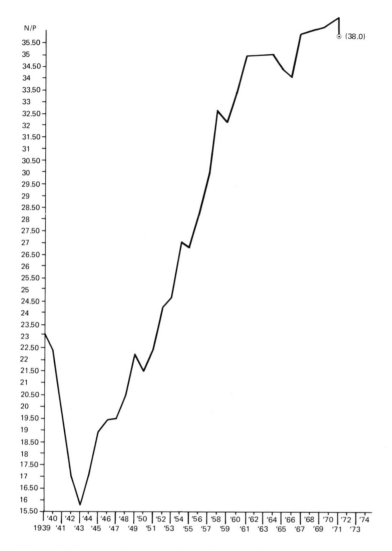

Figure 1. The increasing proportion of non-production workers in U.S. manufacturing.
SOURCE: *Delehanty (1968), Appendix Table A-1.*

By contrast, employment in consumer services has been declining. Yet popular perception views the manufacturing–services shift in terms of consumer services. This misperception has helped to obscure some of the most important features of the transformation of our economy. The point was made by Denison (1979):

The statement that the service share of employment has risen from 50% to 60% creates the impression that barbershops and laundries have replaced manufacturing as the mainstay of the economy and that the shift has been a general one.

A recent estimate is that, as of 1977, 25% of GNP originated in producer services, as much as the share of GNP resulting from the production of manufactured goods.* This remarkable statistic has arisen because producer services lie at the transformation in terms of *how* goods and services are produced as well as *what* gets produced. Many of these services are performed in-house as increasing amounts and specialized kinds of services are employed in the production of goods. The rapid rise of non-production workers within manufacturing substantially reflects increases in both the supply of and demand for producer-services-type personnel within manufacturing. The simple fact that producer services (and others) can be provided internally or externally (by purchase from another organization) is a fact of great consequence for development finance and the division of labor between public and private enterprise.

The other major, fast-growing components of the services (non-goods-producing) sector have been government and non-profit activity. The "non-profit" category includes health and educational services, private foundations, non-profit research organizations, and so on. Tables 1 and 2 show the different rates at which the various components of the U.S. economy, including the various services, have been growing. The non-profit category is especially important since its rapid rise connotes shifts in the organizational structure of the economy, in addition to the industry and occupational shifts already noted. Non-profit firms could also be termed semi-public or public/private hybrids since they perform many services that are performed in the public sector and the private for profit sector. The non-profit sector is largely a "private" producer of "public" services.

In fact, one is struck by the similarity of occupations and activities that go on within the fastest growing services categories—government, non-profit, and (private-for-profit) producer services. The similarity in their occupational makeup is revealed by Table 3. Note the large share of professional, technical, and kindred occupations in each case. This should be viewed in light of occupational statistics over time, which indicate these to be the fastest growing occupations in the labor force. One cannot avoid the inference that the services economy, in contrast to the goods economy, is one which, institutionally, is quite mutable. Economic activities are largely transferable across the three major types of economic organization— (public, private, and non-profit), so

---

*The 20% figure in Table 1 is simply the share of output originating in industries that are classified as producer service industries. The higher estimate arises when we recognize that a great deal of producer service-like activity goes on within manufacturing corporations.

Table 3. Shares of Employment (%) Within Industries and U.S. Economy, Average Earnings (in Thousands) with Intraoccupation Ranks: for Industry Occupation Cells, 1975ᵃ

	Profes-sionals	Techni-cians	Mana-gers	Office Clericals	Non-Office Clericals	Sales	Crafts-men	Opera-tives	Service Workers	Labor-ers	Avg. Rank
Mfg.	5.4	5.2	11.5	6.2	5.1	2.8	**14.9**	**42.2**	1.9	5.0	
$ Earning/Rank	17.4(3)	14.1(2)	16.1(1)	7.5(2)	8.8(3)	8.8(3)	11.2(2)	7.5(3)	7.2(2)	5.0(1)	2.2
Distributive Services	3.3	3.4	17.0	9.6	11.6	9.5	15.2	**21.3**	2.0	7.0	
$ Earning/Rank	17.6(2)	15.3(1)	15.5(2)	6.8(3)	9.2(2)	14.2(1)	12.8(1)	9.6(2)	7.4(1)	7.1(2)	1.7
Retail	1.3	0.7	**21.5**	6.2	14.1	**25.8**	11.1	9.1	2.9	7.4	
$ Earning/Rank	12.2(5)	9.3(5)	10.2(6)	5.2(6)	4.0(6)	4.5(7)	8.4(6)	5.1(7)	3.3(6)	4.0(5)	5.9
Producers Services	13.5	9.0	**17.3**	**21.3**	12.8	11.7	2.6	2.2	8.2	1.5	
$ Earning/Rank	18.2(1)	11.0(4)	13.2(4)	6.1(4)	6.0(4)	11.7(2)	9.7(4)	5.5(4)	5.1(4)	3.8(6)	3.7
Consumers Services	0.5	4.4	9.6	2.4	5.0	0.6	7.8	6.8	**58.6**	4.3	
$ Earning/Rank	11.2(7)	5.6(7)	9.3(7)	5.2(7)	3.6(7)	5.1(6)	7.3(7)	5.3(5)	2.7(7)	2.1(7)	6.7
Non-Profit Services	**36.0**	12.9	4.0	11.6	6.3	0.2	2.0	1.1	**24.8**	1.0	
$ Earning/Rank	12.1(6)	7.7(6)	12.7(5)	5.5(5)	4.3(5)	7.5(5)	9.1(5)	5.3(6)	4.4(5)	4.5(4)	5.2
Public Admin. Services	10.2	**25.1**	12.0	15.2	18.3	0.1	7.2	2.0	6.5	3.7	
$ Earning/Rank	15.9(4)	13.6(3)	15.2(3)	7.5(1)	10.5(1)	7.7(4)	11.0(3)	9.8(1)	6.4(3)	7.0(3)	2.6
Services	13.2	8.2	12.7	10.4	10.2	8.0	7.2	6.9	19.2	4.0	
Non-Services	4.4	4.1	15.6	5.2	3.9	2.0	20.7	31.3	1.4	11.3	
Total	10.3	6.9	13.6	8.7	8.2	6.0	11.7	15.0	13.3	6.4	

ᵃAgriculture-forestry-fisheries; mining and construction are not shown but are included in totals. Ranks are for average earnings among given occupations. Boldface is for emphasis.

Source: U.S. BLS (1975).

the degree to which the U.S. economy is "private" in the traditional sense will not be immune to the ongoing transformation of the economy.

In this context, there is also an important counterpoint to the current claim that it is the private sector which is the overwhelming source of job creation, not only of jobs overall but of "good" jobs. The employment growth statistics simply do not bear out this claim. Some perspective is provided by Ginzberg and Vojta (1981):

> It is difficult to understand how the national political ethos...continues to maintain that five out of every six jobs are created by the private sector. That was true in 1929, when government expenditures were about 10 percent of the Gross National Product. It ceased to be true, however, in the depression years and in World War II, and it is surely not true today.

In New York City during the 1970s, the non-profit sector was the greatest creator of jobs among the sectors, even more so than government (Armstrong, 1980). But for certain misclassifications, job creation within the government and non-profit categories would appear even greater than it is. For instance, Ginzberg and Vojta (1981) point to "the classification of such non-profit institutions as Columbia University, the Metropolitan Museum of Art and the Jet Propulsion Laboratory as private sector enterprises" (as well as) "categorizing the production of military aircraft by the Lockheed Corporation and nuclear submarines by the General Dynamics Corporation as private enterprise activity" (p. 51).

The fact that these services growth sectors are the locus of a large proportion of the "better jobs"—professional, technical, and other white collar occupations—has been viewed as the hallmark of the emerging socioeconomic order which Daniel Bell labeled "post-industrial." Some commentators have even gone so far as to announce the rise of a "new class." The post-industrial thesis has been that the transition to a services economy will bring about a generalized upgrading of work. There is an important sense in which this thesis is true and another, equally important but generally overlooked, in which it is not.* The sense in which this is true is that the transformation of our economy drives, and is driven by, a very substantial and continuous upgrading of the labor force in terms of its "human capital," human capacity augmented through the massive postwar investment in education and health as well as other forms of training. This investment in human capital is as much a characteristic feature of the services economy as the massive waves of investment in physical capital were characteristic of the industrial age. It is a feature which, along with complementary investments in basic and applied science and R&D activities, has caused some commentators to prefer the label "information economy" or "knowledge economy," rather than "services economy," to denote the stage of development we appear to have entered. Notwithstanding varying labels, the rising importance of human relative to physical capital

---

*A less sanguine view had been set forth earlier by Michael Young (1958).

investment in the economy has implications for our concerns with development finance and the public/private interface which need to be considered.

The "post-industrial" portrayal of changes in the occupational structure, however, overlooks some real and serious problems at the other (lower) end of the occupational spectrum. Specifically, recent analysis of the types of jobs arising through services growth indicates a bimodal distribution of jobs growth, with the highest percentages arising at both the high and low ends of the distribution in terms of either occupational status or employee compensation. [See Tables 3 and 4; also Stanback and Bearse et al. (1981), Chap. IV.] This pattern contrasts sharply with the distributional pattern of jobs created within manufacturing, which are largely "middle class." These data should at least alert us to a possible danger—that the transformation could create a highly stratified, partially dualized labor market. Even if this does not turn out to be the case, the growing population of white collar personnel in the labor force is not an unalloyed blessing from the standpoint of mobilizing capital and directing it to development objectives. The financial community has been challenged, and will continue to be challenged, to innovate and design new vehicles for tapping and investing the savings of new groups in the labor force.

Another feature of a services economy which is usually overlooked is that the fastest growing services are sufficiently interdependent (via input–output transactions, etc.) as to form a genuine industrial "complex," just as there have existed industrial complexes in manufacturing, such as petrochemicals and metalworking. This is itself an important feature of the economic dynamics of the transformation, especially when viewed in a spatial (locational) dimension. For too long now, crude "economic base" theory has held sway as a purported explanation of services growth: that the "basic" (jobs- and wealth-creating) sector is the goods-producing sector, and that services grow only in response to the growth of goods-production activity. The experience of the past 25–30 years, during which services employment has steadily risen while manufacturing employment has declined, should have disabused most people of such a simplistic relationship among the sectors. To the extent that producer, government, and non-profit services form a genuine complex, one can expect that the growth of the services economy will become increasingly less dependent on the manufacturing sector. Another implication is that services growth will be oriented to specific types of locations. As with so many other features of economic transformation, the transition to a services economy was first manifest in the largest cities. The replacement of factories and mills by office buildings and headquarters is the visible urban symbol of this transformation. Statistical analysis reveals that the proportion of urban labor forces employed in producer services, broadly defined, rises steadily with size of metropolitan area. [See Stanback and Bearse et al. (1981), Table I-4.]

In the course of this discussion, possible implications of the transition-to-services aspect of transformation have been implied but not specified. What might these be?

First, a services economy is likely to require some significant changes in the way capital is mobilized for development purposes. Greater reliance will have

Table 4. Earnings Distribution (%) of Job Increases in Employment, All Services[a]

	Job Increases	
	1960-1967	1970-1976
$12,000 and over	16.0	18.8
9,500-11,999	23.9	20.6
7,000- 9,499	11.6	12.4
4,500- 6,999	28.1	25.4
Below 4,500	20.4	22.8

[a] Job decreases are not shown, since they were relatively unimportant in services.

to be placed on public and semi-public channels, through the tax system and social insurance funds. This is likely to be a controversial claim. It rests only partly on features of the transformation that have been identified thus far, notably, the problems of productivity and inflation and the increasing significance of human capital and non-profit organization. It is more difficult for private investors to appropriate gains from investments in human capital and knowledge than from plant and equipment, Much will depend on the savings and consumption behavior of the new professional–technical elite, since the lower half of a (bifurcated) distribution will have little to add to investable funds.

Second, one can expect increasing controversy over how the transactions and adjustment costs of development activities are to be borne and who is to bear them. These costs are both real and financial. (Among the real costs are those personnel who provide the requisite services, and these can be lodged in the government, private, or non-profit sectors.) The incidence of the financial costs may or may not correspond, since the source of funds may be one sector to pay for services originating in another. How these allocations are resolved will influence development finance as well as the relationships and relative power among the sectors.

Third, the costs of adjustment in urban areas will continue to be a major problem, given both industry and geographic displacement of the lesser skilled portion of the urban labor force and the pent-up needs to refurbish urban infrastructure. Apportionment of these costs among the sectors will continue to be a major source of controversy and, hopefully, an impetus to innovation in development finance and public/private institutional relationships.

The Changing Institutional and Organizational Environment for Development Finance

The rise of the non-profit sector is but one of the salient institutional features of an economy which is being transformed in its organizational structure, not merely its industry composition. From the standpoint of this book, other key features of structural or institutional evolution are as follows:

1. Internationalization of the economy.
2. Continuation of secular trends towards increasing *firm-size* and increasing concentration in American industry.
3. Contrarywise (paradoxically?), increasing opportunities for *small business* and a resurgence of entrepreneurship.
4. The institutionalization of finance capital and increasing concentration in *the financial sector*; substantial restructuring of financial markets and financial institutions, including internalization of financial functions within non-financial corporations.
5. The increasing importance of basic networks, communications, transportation, and the nodes of these networks which are the system of larger cities. Great demand for network building and rebuilding in response to (a) new technologies and (b) deterioration of existing network links and nodes.
6. A changing role and scope for *government*, along with some realignment of responsibilities among levels of government.

It is impossible to do justice to the complex interwoven fabric of change within the scope of a single chapter. Let us consider each of these in turn, briefly— merely enough to permit some possible implications for development finance and public/private relationships to be drawn.

Internationalization

This aspect of the transformation is well documented and interpreted elsewhere (Gilpin, 1975; Cohen, 1977). The trend is now recognized by the public at large because of the increasing vulnerability of U.S. industries to foreign competition. This vulnerability has brought to the fore development finance and public/private questions around the issue of "reindustrialization." Questions in these areas are also under discussion because of the increasing interest in foreign institutional arrangements; e.g., the interwoven set of public/private relationships sometimes termed "Japan, Inc." Increasing foreign competition has raised the issue of to what extent the public sector should be involved in subsidizing the modernization of capital stocks in threatened industries or even in preventing their demise. This issue is the subject of Chapter XII, which analyzes the Chrysler case. The auto industry, however, is by no means a special case. Other basic industries are implicated, such as steel and, in the near future, basic chemicals and possibly even electronics. The "bailout" issue, in turn, is inseparable from another basic question in economic development: To what extent should development finance involving public capital assist investment in older, larger firms in contrast to newer, smaller firms?

Internationalization of the economy, moreover, is partly driven by the rise of the multinational on the corporate landscape. The increasing tendency of large corporations to make production and investment decisions on a world scale means that the opportunity costs of undertaking many types of investments domestically are increased and problems of capital outflows aggravated.

Firm Size

The increasing need to compete on an international scale has been only one of the factors behind the steadily increasing size of firms. Others include the need to diversify product lines and differentiate products, the need to innovate, and the cumulative improvements in communications, transportation, and the technology of management embodied in specialized producer services. The consequences, however, are problematic for development finance and public/private relationships. First, the larger the "private" firm, the more likely certain decisions will have "public" consequences, especially as corporate decisions are made in headquarters which view their strategic alternatives nationally and globally. The increasing controversy over plant shutdowns is illustrative, along with corollary debates on financing and ownership arrangements (e.g., ESOP's; see Chapter VII) which are designed to give more weight to worker or community interest in corporate decisions.

Second, as the largest corporations diversify they build up internal capacity to carry out a variety of specialized producer services functions, as indicated above. The next logical step, given the need to manage enormous retained earnings and diversification on a global scale, is for the non-financial corporations to acquire financial firms and, more and more, become their own financial intermediaries. This tendency has been very evident during the 1970s, e.g., ITT's acquisition of Hartford Fire Insurance (Cohen et al., 1980). As early as 1960, the possibility was already noted that large corporations could, in effect, create internal capital markets within their corporate networks. This points to a danger that capital markets will become segmented into "large corporate" and "other," with increased friction from the flow of investable funds to uses which do not reflect the priorities of corporations which control an increasing portion of those funds. Given the close relationships between large corporations and large banks and the high-risk aversion of institutional investors, this danger must be taken seriously.

Small Business

Paradoxically, small business entrepreneurship seems to be undergoing a resurgence even while increases in firm size and industrial concentration continue unabated. This is due largely to the emergence of new technologies, the increasing numbers of people with professional and technical training, and the increasing opportunities to provide specialized services for profit. Also, a proliferation of small businesses is not inconsistent with increasing dominance of the economy by big business. The literature on industrial organization has long recognized that big business "oligopoly" provides an "umbrella" under which a variety of small business can thrive in differentiated niches of the market, as long as they do not threaten the market share of the dominant firms (Modigliani, 1958).

Small business has also been enjoying a resurgence intellectually and politically. Intellectually, a set of reports appearing through the 1970s pointed to small business as a major source of economic development—in terms of new firms, employment generation, or innovation. [See, for instance, Birch (1979), SBA (1977), U.S. NSF (1973).] Politically, the crest of this wave of attention may not yet have been reached with the 1979 White House Conference on Small Business. A variety of legislation, some of it already passed, has addressed financial and regulatory impediments to entrepreneurship and small business growth. The latest of these was the Small Business Investment Incentive Act of 1980, which became law in October 1980. The small business issues are very closely related to parallel concerns with promoting new technology and innovation.

In an era of inflation and high interest rates, the resurgence or even survival of small business as a significant contributor to economic development is by no means assured. The access of small business entrepreneurs to capital is a major concern of various chapters in this volume (Chaps. II–VI, X). The question of access (and the *form* in which capital is made available) raises, as well, difficult public/private issues of exposure to risk and of public purpose in relation to private benefit, issues which also figure herein (Chaps. XII–XV).

The Financial Sector

The financial sector is evolving rapidly and it is by no means clear what structure will emerge. The sector is gradually being deregulated. During the 1980s one can envisage most of the regulatory fabric which has constrained competition among financial intermediaries since the New Deal being torn down or substantially altered. Simultaneously, there are two trends which will be reinforced by deregulation: increasing concentration and institutionalization. *Concentration* refers to the tendency for growth and diversification in the financial sector to devolve more and more upon the larger firms, while small firms fail or fall by the wayside. *Institutionalization* refers to the increasing concentration of investable funds in larger and larger pools of capital managed by professional investment personnel. The latter include pension funds, insurance plans, mutual funds, and federal, state, and local social security and retirement funds. In Europe, these are usually referred to as "social insurance" funds, since both the savings decisions which create them and the investment decisions which disburse them are collective in nature. The decisions involve a mix of public and private influences, not merely the preferences of discrete individuals.

Similarly, the matter of industry concentration in the financial sector implicates questions of competition and whether serving certain development finance needs will be met—questions which are appropriate concerns of public policy. For instance, in Chapter III, Daniels claims that both the above tendencies aggravate the difficulty of small business financing, as small broker-age houses familiar with local and regional investment opportunities go under with the creation of a national market system. The balance between the fiduciary responsibilities of institutional funds and legitimate public develop-ment finance objectives is also a matter at issue. The parallel concentration of business savings in corporate networks raises similar issues which were noted above.

Basic Networks

The quality and efficiency of communications, transportation, and urban networks are fundamental to economic development, as Pred et al. (1977) have demonstrated. Yet, urban infrastructure has been cannibalized during the postwar period and is in urgent need of improvement. Moreover, technological advances and the increasing services composition of economic activity will require the building of new networks or the rebuilding of old infrastructure to suit new requirements. The competition for capital for these purposes is sure to be a major influence on capital markets and economic development activities for the next generation. Basic issues will arise in discussion of financing, public/private allocation of costs, and institutional arrangements. The eco-nomic (and some of the political) issues are examined by Nelson (1976). In this volume, some of the issues are examined by Pagano and Moore (Chap. XVII).

Government

The appropriate role of government in the economy is in fact the core issue running through this volume. Provision of incentives? More or less regulation? Public development finance institutions? Decentralization? The spectrum of alternatives is considered in the sections to follow. The increased role of government in the U.S. economy is indicated by the increased government share of employment, 1948–1977, from 14.2% to 19.6% (Table 2). What is often overlooked, however, in the fanfare over "big government" is that a great portion of government activity is bearing costs which benefit the private sector. As Ginzberg and Vojta (1981) put it:

> The argument that (government) employment and expenditure are at cost to the "productive" side of the economy is belied by the historical record.

The private sector is also implicated in the growth of government in other ways:

1. private interest group demands and competition for public funds, which induces increases in government expenditure via "logrolling," etc.; and
2. the tendency of private enterprises to generate and then externalize social costs, which then usually end up being borne by some level of government in whole or in part (O'Connor, 1973).

Other Western advanced industrial democracies typically show governmental shares of gross domestic product which are significantly higher than in the United States. Sharewise, one is not likely to see any significant diminution of the role of government in the U.S. economy.

What is at issue in this volume, however, is less the share or the overall level of government activity in the economy than how this role is exercised. This "how" is a question both of the composition of public expenditure (how much for development purposes vs. how much for public services, rather than merely the level of expenditure) and of the appropriate institutional vehicles for allocating such expenditures. The development finance innovations or proposals featured in this volume are tantamount to a basic shift in the economic policy of government at all levels: a shift in focus away from the simple view of government as just an expender of funds or provider of services and toward a vision of government as also investor and creator of jobs—government with a public role in the mobilization of investable funds and a much broader and more strategic role with respect to the investment of those funds using *public* as well as private investment criteria.

The usual textbook economic model posits the dichotomy of investors versus consumers: The consumer spends and the investors invest. Most people think about the public and private sector roles in a similar way: Government spends and the private sector invests. We are moving away from that model toward one that includes a role for government as entrepreneur, risk taker, and institutional innovator. This suggests a new interface, a new working relationship between the public and private sectors in the planning and financing of economic development, as in hybrid institutions, joint ventures, and risk sharing. In a sense we may be returning to a more classical model characteristic of the early days of the Republic. The role of government then was very much the role of risk taker, of making those investments that would create the environment for private enterprise to come into areas where investments were needed for the development of the country.

Concepts and Theories

The profound post-war transformation of the U.S. economy puts to a severe test our prevailing ability to interpret what is happening in terms of concepts and theories. Interpretation will have profound implications for economic policy. Any attempt at it brings one very rapidly to a confrontation with the fundamental issues in economic development policy: What is "public"? What is "private"? What is "development"? What is the role of government in the private economy? and, What are appropriate public uses of private interest? The significance of concepts and theories in current economic policy debates cannot be stressed too strongly. It is apparent for instance, in current controversies between "Keynesians" and "supply-siders."

Even those who have a self-image of being "practical" and "hard-headed" operate within a system of ideas, often a mixture of ideology and lessons from experience which may be more second-nature than self-conscious. This was recognized by Keynes in his famous remark that (to paraphrase) "policymakers are often the slaves of some defunct economist." So, this section attempts to interpret the stylized facts of the transformation with an eye to the emerging institutional framework for economic development policy.

Lagging Perceptions of New Realities

Current economic theory is not a suitable framework for trying to explain a long-run, evolutionary process of development: It is static, equilibrial, and short-term in its time horizon, even though considerable progress has been made in the analysis of economic dynamics. The body of knowledge labeled "economic development" is still largely focused on explicating the transformations of the so-called "LDCs" (less developed countries), not those of advanced industrial economies. Partly as a result, attempts to explain the transformation of the U.S. economy are characterized by vague, descriptive language and the persistence of a number of "myths," including those pointed to earlier.

The non-rigorous, mythical flavor of many explanations, and the fact that these have stayed in good currency for so long in spite of contrary indications, is understandable if one realizes that the economy is either at or just past a threshold in a long-run transition. At such a historical juncture it is common for people to perceive what is happening in terms of the "models" or "mental maps" characteristic of the stage of development which is being superseded. Thus the discourse on the services economy has, so far, largely been obscured by concepts, models, and categories which were tailored to explain the behavior of an economy dominated by the factory.

This is even more a problem for economic policy than it is for economic theory. Once a set of interrelated ideas come into good currency in the world of policy, they take on a life of their own. This problem is understandable on the basis of what we know about behavior. People are generally averse to risk, and especially loathe uncertainty. At a time of transition, therefore, they will gravitate to familiar theories rather than face uncomfortable facts. The set of ideas associated with a dominant pattern of development, in diffusing through a society, becomes so ingrained that most people are not conscious of their intellectual heritage. Consequently, most people, including most intellectuals, feel only a vague sense of disquiet when the dynamics of development begin to suggest a pattern which is not quite congruent with the mental map they carry about in their heads. They will therefore continue to act and set policy on the basis of their mind-set as the new pattern of development comes only gradually into view.

This problem—the old policy remedies undermined by a mismatch between old theory and new patterns of development—is very much in evidence at the present time. One sees it in sub-national economic development policies which persist in focusing on manufacturing and ignoring services, policies grounded on a simplistic "economic base" theory of development. One sees it in shortsighted "Proposition 13" types of fiscal policies at all levels which, by taking a simple-minded "meat ax" approach to budgeting, ignore the potential for increasing the productivity of public services. One sees it in one of the last of the great "cottage industries," higher education, characterized by a lack of specialization in some respects and overspecialization in others, both detrimental to the advancement of knowledge. One sees it, too, in attitudes of the business community, which, by and large, has not been able to rethink an outdated, artificial division between public and private.

The task of reformulating economic policies at all levels is too urgent to wait until the theorists are through constructing a new framework to match a new reality. More likely, the obverse occurs: Scholars set about explaining a new reality only long after it has evolved. Ideally, the tasks of reconstructing theory, pursuing empirical investigations, and reconstituting policies should proceed in tandem, each feeding the other. The reformation of policy can provide useful hints for theory and investigation. In a period of transition, practitioners faced with concrete dilemmas will experiment with what might appear, superficially, to be ad hoc solutions to new problems. For observers whose minds are alert to the significance of innovations, however, these will provide valuable clues to the kinds of economic behavior and organization which are likely to emerge from the transition. Some of the clues are to be found in these chapters.

It has already been suggested that one of the basic impediments to understanding the transformation and transitional behavior of our economy is the static, short-term perspective of the economic theories which have come to dominate economic discourse during the post-war period. The main economic concepts—such as demand, supply, consumption, investment, capital, labor, elasticity, and so forth—are not necessarily static, but they have been used in a static way. Progress in reconceptualizing the transformation of the U.S. economy will only be made to the extent that investigators can delineate several dynamic processes and integrate them into an overall framework.

The key word here is *dynamic*, especially *disequilibrium*-dynamic. Static views provide snapshots of economic structure, unlike dynamic views, which trace changes over time. Even currently available dynamic models are limited in their ability to describe development processes because they are implicitly or explicitly grounded in assumptions of equilibrium tendencies—either balanced growth patterns or the specification of some equilibrium pattern towards which the economy is thought to be tending. Yet economic development is fundamentally a disequilibrium-dynamic process. There is no state of the economy one can specify, ex ante or a priori, toward which the economy is heading and will "end up" after some period of time. There is no ideal or hypothetical equilibrium state which is independent of the path of development. In other words, any future state of the economy, and the time of its development, depends on how the economy evolves; and that future state (whatever it may be) is unpredictable. By the same token, the process of economic development is irreversible and there is no state towards which, if left alone, the economy would return.

Fundamentally, development is a disequilibrium process because some of the most basic factors in that process are unpredictable and/or cumulative in nature. What is "development"? It is fundamentally a process of "social learning" [see Dunn (1971)] with two main features:

1. *Innovation and innovation diffusion*—institutional as well as technical.
2. *Capacity building*—expanding the supply (both quantity *and* quality) of basic resources (capital, labor, natural resources, knowledge, and information) and building the *networks* and systems by which these resources are transported and communicated, including the system of cities (urbanization).

Innovative events are quite unpredictable, though technical innovation is the single most important driving force in economic development. In theory, diffusion processes are predictable, but in practice mostly not, because they interact in complex ways and there is insufficient empirical understanding of even simple examples of this type. Barring major wars or catastrophes, capacity building is a cumulative process in any advanced industrial society. The steady advance of scientific knowledge, which has become fundamental to development during this century, is but the most obvious example [and it obviously feeds and conditions the processes under (1)]. Other examples include the gradual extension and improvement of transport and communications networks, steady increases in the education, training, and overall quality of the labor force, and steady increases in the stock of capital with which that labor force has to work through both capital broadening and deepening. Even so-called "natural" resources are not immune. There is no such thing as a stock of minerals or land, for example, which is independent of the state of technology or the stock of knowledge. Thus the extent of oil reserves and whether they are depleted (if ever) depend on technical advances and scientific knowledge, as well as a variety of strictly economic factors.

All these various "capacity" factors are cumulative: They feed and build on past achievements of capacity. The various fields and stocks of knowledge are also cumulative: Each increment of learning makes it easier for the next step to be taken. Economists have long recognized that there are significant economies of scale to be realized in building transport and communications networks. Network building is cumulative in other ways too (e.g., much of the early road system followed Indian and Buffalo trails). The dynamic cumulation of resources is also interactive, not just factor specific. Growth in stocks of information is accelerated by increases in the capacity of basic networks, as is urbanization (Pred et al., 1977). Scientific and technical progress feed improvements in the quality of the labor force and vice versa, as economists and others have increasingly recognized through the concept of human capital (Abramowitz, 1972). These examples highlight another reason why development processes are disequilibrium-dynamic—the mutually reinforcing nature of some of the main subprocesses.

How does this disequilibrium-dynamic way of thinking about development relate to the transformation of the U.S. economy discussed earlier and, in particular, to the evolving institutional framework for the pursuit of development objectives? First, it contrasts sharply with the modes of economic thinking that have come to dominate post-war economic policies at all levels. Often, the policy debates of recent years have been cast in terms of "Keynesians" vs. "monetarists," or "supply-siders" vs. "demand-siders." These labels are misleading, since the fundamental issues of economic policy are rather: static vs. dynamic, short-term vs. long-term, and equilibrium vs. disequilibrium, as per the developmental stance outlined above. In these terms, the currently dominant brand of thinking in the economic policy arena can be characterized as follows:

1. Overwhelmingly *static*—emphasizing narrowly defined efficiency considerations and, thereby, anti-developmental.
2. *Short-term*—in thinking in terms of time horizons of only a few years, similarly anti-developmental.
3. *Equilibrial*—by its heavy reliance upon equilibrium models and their corollaries, emphasizes forecasts, projects, and plans, rather than processes by which the economy dynamically adjusts, makes transitions, and is transformed.

Similarly, there is an inability to deal with discontinuities, like shocks, thresholds, major innovations, or institutional changes. The economic models are still "Newtonian" positing quick, marginal, continuous, low-cost adjustments, whereas the economy is "Einsteinian" revealing quantum jumps, transitions, and shifts requiring long-term, high-cost adjustments. This indictment pertains to both of the familiar levels of policy concern: "micro" and "macro." One cannot avoid the possibility that the diffusion of an economic science dominated by these terms of reference, spreading through the departments, ministries, and policy forums of virtually all the Western industrialized countries, must account in some small part for the signs of stagnation which are more or less evident among them.

At the micro-level, we see business school curricula, for instance, heavily influenced by the conventional textbook model of economic efficiency—short-term, resource allocation decisions. At the macro-level, we have seen, until very recently, emphasis on short-term demand management via both fiscal and monetary policy. The currently fashionable "supply-side" point of view appropriately criticizes the consumption (rather than savings and investment) bias in "Keynesian" policies. Yet, it is possible for supply-side policies to be as narrow and short-term in their prescriptions as anything promulgated by Keynesians. As Hinman notes in his chapter on Chrysler, the political pressures for short-term palliatives and the lack of any countervailing long-term developmental viewpoint are quite pervasive and do not respect party boundaries. The supply or conservative side of the policy debate is wedded at least as much to a narrow, short-term efficiency framework as the views of their political adversaries. A thoroughgoing supply-side framework *should* lead one logically to a long-term, dynamic view of the development process, but there is no assurance that this intellectual mutation will occur or survive in today's political environment.

For example, we have already identified "capacity" to be a fundamental concept in economic development. Among practitioners in the economic development field, this refers to the supply of appropriate organizational and human resources to undertake development activities, especially at sub-national levels. Capacity is a quintessential development concept, demanding a long-run perspective. It overlaps investment and innovation. Building the capacity of local organizations, for example, is an arduous long-term process demanding local entrepreneurship and, oftimes, institutional and financial innovations. [See Mayer and Blake (1980) and Chapter X.] One cannot seriously entertain the decentralization of money and power out of Washington, D.C., for almost any purpose, especially developmental, without giving serious consideration to the issue of capacity (whether it exists and how to create it). The Federal Office of Management and Budget (OMB), however, tends to undervalue and, therefore, underfund, capacity building programs. This is partly because it relies on short-term "results" and "efficiency" oriented evaluation measures derived form a narrow cost/benefit framework. There is no discernible concept of development guiding OMB decisions. This has been true for some time, regardless of which party is in the White House.

If federal funds for development were to come to state and local authorities in the form of block grants, the problem of capacity would be the ghost at the feast. Experience with the Community Development Block Grant Program (CDBG), as indicated in Chapter XI, suggests that much money would be wasted or misdirected, partly because of the lack of requisite capacity at the local level. If the vast expansion of development finance assistance authorized by the National Public Works and Economic Development Act of 1980 had in fact become a reality, a significant portion would have been wasted for the same reason. Similarly, if the Reagan administration attempts to increase funding for CETA Title VII ("Private Sector Initiative") programs, much money will be wasted if no account is taken of the very different capacities of Private Industry Councils and the need to build the capacity of those which are lacking (Public/Private Ventures, 1981).

The capacity issue is apropos of a number of development concerns which are likely to be denigrated or overlooked if the mind's eye is not equipped with the sort of dynamic developmental framework sketched above. The definition of an appropriate public/private relationship is, of course, one of these concerns. Neither the capacity issues nor institutional interface exist in the simplistic textbook model of a market economy in which the "market" is all of a piece, like a smoothly working machine with its movable parts all in synchrony. As unreal as this model is, one frequently hears the market described in these terms. In a more dynamic framework the issue comes squarely into view since building capacity of almost any sort, especially human resource, organization or network capacity, is a cumulative, sequential, long-term, learning type of process.

The issue also helps point to the problem of market structure. Far from promising a deus ex machina, the market economy is highly structured, providing differential opportunities contingent upon income, wealth, size, location, and so on. The differential capacity of individuals, firms, and communities to compete is a major aspect of structure. A corollary is that, in principle, a public sector role in helping to build capacity of "disadvantaged" market participants is a necessary and appropriate role for public policy.* For instance, Kieschnick's (1981) case for public intervention into the venture capital markets rests strongly on the observation that venture capital for business development is unavailable for many who could make productive use of it because of structural biases in the distribution of wealth. Lebergott (1959) makes an analogous but obverse argument, that access to capital resources through the financial markets is a significant influence on the distribution of income.

Attention to structure and to dynamics necessarily go together in development theory, policy, and institutional design. Dynamic behavior is conditioned by existing structures, and various types of dynamic interactions can gradually alter structural attributes. Wilbur Thompson's (1965) theory of urban economic development, for instance, highlights the significance of the initial advantages of cities, in terms of their infrastructure and services-base, as a major influence on the subsequent evolution of their industry structure. In a recent comprehensive study, Dunn (1980) documents how the structure of the U.S. Urban System has evolved in recent decades, in a way consistent both with Thompson's framework and with Dunn's own, which places heavy emphasis on the structure of basic networks. At the intraregional level, Bearse (1978) demonstrates the preponderant influence of structural features of "initial advantage" for the diffusion and development of new economic activities. These are only a few of the many studies which demonstrate the interrelationship between structural attributes and dynamic behavior.

Awareness of the connection between structure and dynamics provides a logical basis for asking: Has the institutional structure of the U.S. economy

---

*This inference, however, further rests on the premise that inequalities in the marketplace are not self-correcting but tend to be maintained or even aggravated in an advanced industrial or post-industrial economy. Evidence on the skewness and stability of income, wealth, and firm-size distributions makes the premise plausible.

become too inflexible? Is our economic malaise, our stagflation, due to institutional hardening of the arteries? Scitovsky recently made this claim in his 1980 Richard T. Ely lecture before the American Economic Association:

> With the passage of time, ... the joints of that once wondrously flexible (U.S.) economic structure are becoming more and more calcified and rigid; and the process seems hard to reverse, because it stems from so many different and diverse causes.

Among these "causes," Scitovsky specifically identified the role of government, affluence, improved technology, and the expanding size of firms, aspects of the transformation of the economy which were mentioned earlier in this chapter. Scitovsky warns: "Capitalism works when it's flexible, but self-destructs when it's not" (1980, p. 2), and points to several signs of growing non-adaptability in the economic system. These include the growth of government as a purchaser of goods and services, the "ever more pervasive regulatory powers of government," the lack of response to the rising costs of imports, government assumption of some of the risks of business enterprise, and increasing fragmentation of the economy. On one key point—the diminished response of prices to changing conditions—Scitovsky partly blames affluent consumers who, he says,

> are quite able and willing to bear the private cost of such behavior (meaning "ready to pay through the nose for maintenance of its living standards and status symbols"); they are unaware and unheeding of the social cost, which includes the diminished flexibility and viability of the system. (1980, p. 3).

The larger part of blame, however, is assigned to the growing organizational gigantism and bureaucratization of the American economy, both public and private. The problem of hardening institutional arteries is recognized as well in the organizational development literature, which refers to the phenomenon as "institutional entropy."

The age and size of organizations have been recognized as serious constraints to their adaptation to new circumstances. The concept of institutional age has little to do with calendar years. It relates, fundamentally, to the issue cited above: the ability to maintain dynamic, adaptive modes of behavior. A basic indicator of age is the extent to which organizations are overspecialized or overinvested in types of activity, technology, or capital stocks which were characteristic of an earlier stage of economic development. Another is the atrophy of entrepreneurship. Thus, their adaptability is highly constrained and/or lacks leadership. One observes, for instance, higher growth rates of new services and technology-based industries in cities which did not become overspecialized in manufacturing (Mollenkopf, 1979; Bearse, 1978). Similarly, a host of studies document that small or new business organizations are more innovative than large. Most large businesses have learned, sometimes the hard way, that overspecialization in a few maturing product lines spells serious problems some time in the future.

Scitovsky's argument that rising affluence fuels inflexibility is an insight worthy of further consideration. It suggests a statement of more generality— that rising affluence sets in motion forces which tend to erode that affluence. This is paradoxical, since economic development and productivity are contingent upon innovation and innovation is partly contingent upon the availability of largess in the form of slack resources. One line of argument is that rising productivity and its correlates, rising profitability and discretionary incomes, eventually dampen innovation and related sources of productivity growth because the incentives to innovate and use resources more efficiently are diminished. Incentives, however, do not exist in a vacuum, nor are they simply inherent in individuals; they are sensitive to institutional and organizational structure. The "affluence" argument, therefore, must have a structural, not merely an incentives basis.

Another hinge of the argument is suggested by the capacity concept noted earlier. The costs of continuing to increase productivity at a high rate will at some point begin to rise. There is just so much growth and differentiation that can be accommodated within a given structure of production before the structure itself must be altered. If capacity in the shape of new organizational forms must be created before we can realize the full potential of a services economy, then the process of transition or adjustment may take some time. In the medium term, reorganization of the economy will absorb scarce resources, but the reorganized structure will eventually serve as the basis for renewed productivity advance.

The chapters to follow suggest that one need not be apocalyptic in putting a premium on the need for structural changes. In a recent essay, Albert Hirschman (1980) identifies two types of attitudes toward flaws in the U.S. economy. One is complacent—that marginal adaptations or cosmetic improvements are all that are required. The other is "structuralist"—that the system is in deep crisis and needs fundamental remedies. The chapters in this book, however, seem to be consistent with the middle ground cliché that the truth is somewhere in between. Important institutional adaptations and innovations are going on at the margins and interstices of both the public and private sectors. Moreover, the many examples discussed in this book and elsewhere make suspect the recently fashionable tendencies to denigrate the public sector role and elevate the private-for-profit sector role in economic development and development finance. These tendencies are based on a grossly oversimplified public *versus* private image of the structure of the economy. Many of the developments discussed in the chapters to follow reflect initiatives which have originated in the public sector to assist the private-to-profit sector. Others have originated in what many commentators call the "third sector," private-non-profit organizations which assist both governmental and private-for-profit organizations with facets of the development process. Such developments belie the simple public/private dichotomy. Yet they raise again the question of flexibility posed by Scitovsky. At issue is the flexibility of institutional structures—their ability to adopt, adapt, and exploit institutional innovations.

Market Failure

A concept which has traditionally been used by economists to justify public intervention into the private sector is that of "market failure." This is a recognition that for a variety of reasons, the private market fails to function as efficiently and equitably as the textbooks or free enterprise rhetoric would have us believe. It is also a recognition, as indicated above, that "the market" is not in fact all of one piece, but is a highly (and hierarchically) structured system, with discontinuities, gaps, and imperfections among the levels and parts. Markets for many key resources that figure in development processes either are flawed or do not exist.

The key concept in the market failure diagnosis is "externality." Private market outcomes are faulty when social costs and benefits of market decisions are not adequately accounted for, thus being "external" to those decisions. Either benefits are conveyed by certain decisions which the price system does not reward or costs are imposed which the price system does not levy. For example, private firms frequently make investment/disinvestment decisions which burden communities with costs which are not reflected in costs to the firms. This is quite apparent in the growing body of literature documenting the effects of plant closings (e.g., Mick, 1975; Harrison and Bluestone, 1980). Another example, this time on the external benefits side, would be a private firm's on-the-job training of a work force which then proceeded to move on to another firm which could benefit from the training without incurring the cost [e.g., Baumol and Oates (1975)]. A frequent reaction to observed externalities are efforts to "internalize" the external costs or benefits. Regarding the first example, there has been a wave of proposals at both the federal and state levels to enact plant closing legislation that would impose certain costs on firms if they precipitously close down a large plant. With regard to the second example, once firms realize that other firms are "pirating" workers that they have trained, they will take steps, such as negotiating longer-term labor contracts, to ensure that they gain most of the benefits from the skills conveyed by their training. Economists' proposals to levy effluent fees or taxes on polluters is another example of an "internalize the externalities" strategy in response to market failures, one whose efficacy is increasingly being recognized in environmental policy (Baumol and Oates, 1975). The opposite, positive, counterparts of fees and taxes are incentive payments paid by government to private firms to induce them to undertake socially beneficial activities which, otherwise, they might not undertake. Fundamentally, a strategy of using fees or incentives to internalize externalities is a strategy which attempts to deal with market failures indirectly, via the price system. This strategy simply says: Shortcomings in the market system can be overcome if the system of prices can be adjusted to reflect actual costs and benefits more fully. This, however, is not the only possible strategy. Other more direct strategies of public intervention into the economy include:

1. regulation;
2. institutional innovation or adaptation, including public/private institutional hybrids;
3. public enterprise; and
4. bargaining arrangements and negotiated agreements between the sectors.

A clear way of visualizing the problem of market failure attributable to externalities was recently provided by Michelson (1979) through the four-way block diagram shown below (Fig. 2). The costs and returns of any organization can be categorized into one of the four. In each category, moreover, one can ask what behavioral objective pertains. The profit maximizing objective of private firms implies they will be striving to maximize monetary revenues which they can control internally and, similarly, minimize costs which affect their own balance sheet. This implies that costs or benefits arising in any of the other three (external or non-monetary) categories are either a matter of indifference or perhaps even of "passing the buck"—pushing as many costs and as few revenues onto the public sector as possible. This tendency is what O'Connor (1979) refers to as the "socialization of costs and the privatization of profits." Given our central concern for development finance, one of Michelson's (1979) remarks is apropos:

> What the perfect capital market would be perfect at is making decisions based on only one of the four categories, internal monetary cost. Just as obviously, what communities get upset about is external costs .... The conceptual difference between internal monetary cost and total cost creates the possibility that minimizing one does not minimize the other. (p. 7)

Yet, the application of market failure reasoning to the capital markets may not be entirely convincing. A good deal of economic theory and supporting empirical work indicate that capital markets most closely approach the

Figure 2.

economists' textbook ideal of perfect markets. Capital, already the most mobile among the factors of production, is becoming more so as financial institutions become larger and more international in scope and as improvements in communications and data processing reduce the costs of shifting capital among areas and alternative uses. Do these tendencies gainsay any case for public intervention or mixed public/private initiatives which may rest on the concept of market imperfections? By the same token, do they imply that a strategy of government acting to help "perfect" the market (by way of incentives, for instance) is the only strategy required, if any?

The answer to both of these questions is *no*. The reasons have a great deal to do with the concepts introduced thus far; that is, with a dynamic rather than a static view of how the economy works. As indicated earlier, the dynamic character of the U.S. economy is one of uneven development. It is an economy in transition that will continue to generate shifting patterns of opportunity, technological innovation, and investment decisions that mean prosperity for some, long-term distress for others. Investment shifts between sectors, industries, and regions spell major adjustments for affected people and areas. There are real and substantial costs to be borne if these adjustments are to be made efficiently and equitably. The adjustments take time, as in building new industry or retraining parts of the labor force. Observations suggesting increasing perfection of the capital markets are observations of *financial* markets. The underlying reality, as Thurow (1975, 1980) points out, is one of disequilibrium and continued imperfection in the adjustments of *real* capital stocks, including human capital resources.

Furthermore, there is a paradox: Not infrequently, market failure will be found to accompany market perfection. Perfection of financial markets at the national and international scale raises the opportunity costs of large institutions investing in local or regional projects. Then, too, the more perfect markets are at these (higher) levels, the more quickly shocks, innovations, and other impulses are transmitted to local and regional economies. Yet the ability of real resources to adjust in these areas is not quickened commensurately.

Barriers to dynamic adjustments in the economy are among the most significant sources of market failure. These include lack of information, uncertainty, high transactions costs, and high adjustment costs [see Vaughan and Bearse (1980) for further discussion of barriers to adjustment]. Also, if there are failings in markets for complementary factors, e.g., labor or energy, the operation of capital markets will suffer shortcomings as well. For example, instability in the markets for highly skilled labor may lead to underinvestment in industries which require new or sophisticated technology (Thurow, 1980). Similarly, barriers to transfers of ownership interests in local industry to employees or communities increase the likelihood of disinvestment (Stern and Aldrich, 1980).

The market failure thesis can be carried just so far, even in its dynamic form. Markets for some developmental resources do not even exist. Ultimately, questions of the appropriate roles of the public and private sectors involve ethics and values, not markets (Arrow, 1969). In any given situation, the relative significance of the various categories of market failure may be shifting. Some costs or benefits, formerly internal, become external, and vice versa. Non-monetary costs and benefits may be transformed into monetary entries on business accounting forms, but the converse can also happen. These shifts are not necessarily unidirectional nor are they determined by some sort of economic calculus. How society accounts for the various costs and benefits of economic development is fundamentally a matter of law, politics, and ideology. Steiner (1974) argues convincingly that the purely public and purely private goods or services are extreme cases. There is a broad range of goods and services which partake of both public and private characteristics.* It was suggested earlier that the transition to a services and information economy is increasing the range of this grey area. Also, as the interconnectedness of the various segments of the economy increases with urbanization and the articulation of increasingly sophisticated communications networks, there is every reason to believe that externalities are increasingly important and quite central to processes of development.†

Another major limitation of the market failure thesis is that, implicitly, it falls into the trap Peacock (1979) warns against: "the acceptance of the concept of impartial and omniscient government pervading so much of the economic theory of public policy," including a tendency to make "comparisons between real world market situations and unreal perfect governments" (p. 27). One must also recognize the possibility of "government failure" or "collective failure."

Government Failure

Reference to the Michelson diagram (Fig. 2) readily suggests that the public sector can generate externalities as well as the private. Each sector is the source of externalities which affect the other. There is by now considerable evidence that ill-conceived government laws, taxes, and regulations have adverse "spillover" effects on private business which are not simply justified by the social costs of business activity, or which have dynamic effects that outweigh static benefits.

The basic causes of the rise of government in the American economy have been frequently noted elsewhere: two World Wars, the breakdown of market economies during the 1930s, the movements for equity or equal opportunity, and so on. A feature and a consequence of this rise has been a reciprocal,

---

*Douglas (1979) even demonstrates a public or social dimension to those goods and services which, in the economist's view, are purely private—those devoted to consumption by families and individuals.
†By contrast, the textbook view is that externalities are a rather minor qualification to the vision of an otherwise efficient market.

intersectoral cause-and-effect type of relationship between public and private services. On the one hand, government has grown in response to the social costs and uncertainties of private enterprise. On the other hand, the growing influence of government has led to the growth of private sector services to deal with government and a competitive environment influenced by government.

Now that, due to the growth of government during 1930–1975, the public sector is not completely outsized by the private sector, a stably unstable relationship between the sectors is apparent, not unlike a relationship between duopolists. There is a dynamic tension between the sectors which, at least for several years, will cause the relative size of the sectors to ebb and flow, but within a narrow range. It is not at all likely that the size of the public sector in an advanced economy can be significantly diminished. There are powerful sources of stability in the public sector, generally recognized in the public finance and public administration literature.

The size and growth of government and its increasing influence on the economy have led to an intense wave of concern over the role of government in the economy. Yet simplistic "off the government" and "up the private sector" attitudes towards this issue are dangerously misplaced. One must be quite clear as to why, indeed, "government failure" as well as private "market failure" have been mutual factors in the lack of dynamism of the U.S. economy and how the two sources of failure interrelate.

First, most of the cliches about government are unfortunately true, and these are the lessons of experience, not economic analysis.* To quote from Bearse (1976):

> The left hand doesn't know what the right hand is doing. There is a marked lack of coordination among agencies. Government is characterized by excessive red tape, inefficiency, and bureaucracy. There is no such thing as an intelligent, overall policy that businessmen can depend on. Planning is boondoggling. Government is forever "reinventing the wheel." Studies and commission reports abound. Many are of questionable value, but even the good ones gather dust on library shelves because there is no systematic, enduring mechanism to translate analysis into policy into implementation. Governments do not have any economically meaningful control over their budgets; all they know how to do is spend. Government does not know how to transform itself. New programs, new forms, new laws are added on top of old and the structure grows more and more cumbersome and inefficient each year. Government likewise does not know how to adapt or respond creatively to changes in the larger economy or society. Programs are often established as a tardy, laggard response to some belatedly understood "trend." By the time the program has gotten off the ground and learned how to operate, the "trend" may have declined or disappeared, but the program lives on in the hearts of bureaucrats and the government budget. There is

---

*The author has served in government as staff director of the Governor's Economic Policy Council in New Jersey.

hardly any worthwhile program evaluation. Government does not know what information is important or how to use what it has.

A related symptom is the "crisis-response" syndrome. One of the characteristic symptoms of failure in government is its tendency not to consider a problem adequately until it has assumed crisis proportions, then respond to the crisis on an ad hoc basis. Separate crises are dealt with individually and responses are developed as independent additive actions. Large economic systems, however, are too interdependent to be dealt with under such a philosophy. In fact, such a philosophy at the government level is no more healthy than so-called "stimulus–response" patterns of behavior by individuals. Psychologists view the latter as severely neurotic.

Second, there is a pervasively short-term time horizon in government and the political system which substantially augments and aggravates the lack of any long-term developmental perspective noted earlier. Political and bureaucratic incentives are perverse in the sense of reinforcing tendencies to seek short-term gains, usually at the expense of longer-term objectives. These problems have recently been highlighted by two noted economists, one "conservative" and one "liberal":

> Because the political process does not reward or punish elected officials for the long-term consequences of their actions, there is little or no incentive for these officials to learn about such long-term effects. (Feldstein, 1980, p. 5)

> [There is a] lack of a systematic way of facing the future costs of present acts .... Capital investment is not distinguished from current consumption ... our system of local government(s) ... are fertile generators of external costs, duplicative and costly regulation and chronic neglect. If, as historians generally agree, Britain could not have carried through its Industrial Revolution without the great Victorian reforms of local government, we ought to be asking whether we can meet the emerging problems of our mixed economy without also facing up to the need for systematic local government reform. (Abramovitz, 1981, p. 13)

One might simply add to this: reform of government at all levels.

In a brilliant analytical synthesis of knowledge and experience entitled "The Working Bureaucrat and the Non-Working Bureaucracy," Michelson (1979b) identifies aspects of government failure that affect community economic development (CED). Specifically, he delves into the failures of the federal attempt to promote CED via the Office of Economic Opportunity (OEO) and its sequel, the Community Services Administration. The following failings stand out:

1. Too many, too vague, sometimes "contradictory or futile" objectives.
2. The wrong incentives in the bureaucracy.
3. Having agencies sponsor and supervise their own evaluations.
4. Just plain bad management.
5. More generally, "lack of the theoretical concepts of what the program is and how it should work. (pp. 585, 586)

The tendency for government agencies either to misunderstand or to discount the significance of "capacity" noted earlier is another symptom of the same sort.

A basic impediment to investment and economic development is uncertainty, which public policies have tended to aggravate rather than ameliorate. The emphasis of federal macro-economic policy on short-term stabilization objectives is one source of the problem. A lack of systematic economic planning is another source. Frequent shifts in funding or policy for economic development are a third. The tolerance of perverse incentives, or the inability to build appropriate incentives into government programs is a fourth.

The concept of "incentives" has appeared frequently throughout this chapter. It is fundamental but usually misused. Almost every conceivable economic development program has been referred to by somebody at some time as an "incentive" program. Yet incentives should only refer to those programs which attempt to affect development decisions through changes in prices or costs. These should be distinguished from another broad class of initiatives which can be termed "structural"—those which attempt to alter, through institutional innovation or adaptation, the institutional framework which underlies prices and costs. This distinction is fundamental. [See Vietorisz (1974) for an elaboration of this point and its various implications.]

The distinction helps focus a basic issue of current debate on the role of government in promoting economic development. Is it sufficient to simply provide or modify incentives for private enterprise? The new conservatives or supply-siders say yes; others, including the present author, say no. Oftentimes the argument is couched in terms of improving the economic "climate." *Climate* is a more general notion which includes, in addition to incentives, other factors conditioning the environment in which private enterprise is conducted, factors such as regulation and uncertainty. A focus on climate, like that on incentives, however, is a decidedly non-structural focus resting on the rather simplistic premises about the price system cited earlier. The currently fashionable "supply side" approach to economic policy is somewhat mislabeled, because it only deals with supply in terms of money and falls, thereby, into the climate and incentives school of thought. The assumption seems to be that "a dollar is a dollar is a dollar." Nothing is said about "supply" in the real, basic sense of institutional capacity, human capital, producers services, and so on. Thus, the emerging agenda for economic development policy debate in the 1980s is not (or should not be) as it is now cast, as "supply-side vs. demand side," but as a debate between alternative and very different versions of what "supply-side" economics is really about.

The "climate" point of view has nevertheless been ascendant, as illustrated by the quote below:

Urban decay need not be the immutable concomitant of American capitalism. The trend towards urban decay can be reversed by a regular influx of capital, labor, technology, and community services. The source of that influx need not—indeed, should not—be public monies. The bulk of entrepreneurial efforts can be left to the *natural dynamics* that are generic to a free enterprise economy, unfettered by the twin shackles of tax and regulation. [Emphasis mine; quoted from American Legislative Exchange Council (1981).]

Thus, we have very nearly come full circle. One's choice of policy depends on what one believes the "natural dynamics" of the American economy to be, and we cannot all be right. Contrary to the above quote, this chapter has indicated above that urban decay (or other externalities) may well be the concomitant of American capitalism, whether we view the dynamics as generating tendencies toward market failures *or* market perfection. The natural dynamics are disequilibrium dynamics and we are still in the midst of a major socioeconomic transition. Given this situation, there is no reason to believe that simple incentive or other climate-type remedies can succeed without also a considerable amount of institutional innovation, adaptation, and experimentation, some of which is reflected in this volume. "Incentives," after all, are contingent on "structure" (organizational and otherwise). This has long been recognized in Miles Law of Public Administration: "How one thinks depends on where one sits."

The real significance of government failure comes clearly into view if one accepts that it may not be sufficient for the public sector simply to improve the business climate. More direct institutional strategies may be needed to enable the public sector to deal with long-term change and structural problems in the economy. This requires at the very least, a much more creative, flexible, innovative—in a word, *developmental*—mode of governmental operation [as elaborated in Bearse (1976)]. A new economic development policy may also need to foster the formation of public enterprises which operate within and alongside the private market in a businesslike manner, but under *public* investment and accounting criteria. [See Smith (1979) for an excellent discussion of the latter point.]

A multitude of incentives, taxes, subsidies, tax expenditures, and regulatory rules either exist or can be designed to make the U.S. market economy work better. Certainly, it is important constantly to reexamine and refurbish these tools to ensure that their effects are as efficient and benign as possible. Yet it is important to recognize the inherent limitations of this class of policy options vis-à-vis more direct forms of public intervention or institutional innovation. There are essential differences, for example, between relocation allowances and CDCs as strategies to deal with problems of poverty areas, or between tax incentives and employee stock ownership plans as strategies for dealing with industry relocation. (See Chaps. XI and VII.) Relocation allowances and tax incentives—monetary tools operating at the margin—are not adequate to deal with the structural problems of a poor urban community or one stricken by a large plant shutdown.

An institutional innovation strategy can also help to bring the public sector to the point where it can deal with the private sector on more equal terms. At the state and local levels, there is substantial inequality between the sectors in terms of investment expertise and bargaining power. For example, most municipalities feel they must grant business demands for tax abatements or cost writedowns to "induce" investment in central cities. Most states feel they *must* offer tax incentives to "attract" industry. The fact that these options are so favored by states and municipalities owes very little to logic, for the economic analysis supporting these options is weak.* Without alternative organizational settings, the public interest factor in urban investment decisions will continue to be underrepresented.

Any idealistic view of the role of government in the economy, however, bumps sharply up against the sad reality recited earlier. The enormous gap between model and reality, even apart from any ideological considerations, leads many people to accept simplistic proposals to take a meat-ax to government budgets and programs, including some of those discussed in this volume. This policy, however, will not work in our advanced "post-industrial" economy. Private market failures and government failures cannot be dealt with in isolation: They aggravate each other, to the detriment of productivity and development in the economy overall. The notion, therefore, that one can promote the redevelopment of the American economy simply by "unleashing" private enterprise is a dangerous myth rooted in ideology rather than careful thought or observation.

Prevailing views concerning the relative roles of government and private enterprise are much too narrow. Many emerging markets are neither conventionally "private" nor "public" but an admixture. There are, therefore, increasingly subtle policy choices to be made since the mode of provision of many services is literally "up for grabs" with respect to legal forms of organization, incentives, financing, and other features. The role of government in the U.S. economy has never been as narrow as economic theorists conceived it to be (Witte, 1957) and will have to be broadened in future if the adjustment costs of the nation's continuing economic transformation are to be borne equitably and efficiently. Similarly, the role of private business, especially large corporations, is increasingly public in nature. One can easily envisage a shuffling and shifting of certain functions between sectors: government carrying out certain functions formerly thought to be the exclusive franchise of private business, and private business carrying out certain functions that were formerly thought to be peculiar to government.

The narrowly construed role of government as regulator and government as employer-of-last resort will to some extent have to be supplemented by government as investor, government as risk-taker, and government as en-

---

*Incentives have become an interstate, inter-urban competitive game, which, even though it has no winners, compels states and areas to match each other's moves.

trepreneur. On their part, the more sophisticated and alert portions of the private sector will find that there are many public markets for them to enter. It is obvious, as in areas of environmental protection and safety, that the interaction of public and private will continue to create new markets, following the old adage that one man's problem is another's opportunity.

A corollary is that there will be a continued need in both sectors to experiment with organizational forms which might incorporate the best features of public and private enterprise. The rapid growth of private, non-profit forms is itself witness to the growing grey area between public and private and to the failures of both sectors to meet supply or demand in certain areas of the economy.*

The financial sector, especially, is one area where the dynamic tension between public and private is apparent, and where one can look for some of the above tendencies to work themselves out. Recent debates over the Chrysler bailout, tax expenditures, the implementation of the Community Reinvestment Act, and federal credit policies are not merely episodic; they are symptomatic, as the following chapters indicate.

The new public/private organizational forms which are emerging, some of which are described and discussed herein, are perhaps the best indicator of the direction in which the U.S. political economy is moving. In many cases they are also the best examples of decentralized state or local initiatives to deal with the problems generated by the transformation of this economy.

Bibliography

Abramovitz, Moses (1972). "Manpower, Capital, and Technology," in Ivar, Berg ed., *Human Resources and Economic Welfare*. New York: Columbia University Press.

Abramovitz, Moses, and David, Paul A. (1973). "Reinterpreting Economic Growth: Parables and Realities." *American Economic Review* 63:428 (2).

Abramovitz, Moses (1981). "Welfare Quandaries and Productivity Concerns," *American Economic Review* 71:1 (March).

American Legislative Exchange Council (1981). "Enterprise Zones in the States," in *The State Factor*. Washington, D.C.: PUBL.

Armstrong, Regina (1980). *Regional Accounts*. Bloomington, IN: Indiana University Press.

Arrow, Kenneth (1969). "The Organization of Economic Activity: Issues Pertinent to the Choice of Market Versus Nonmarket Allocation." Washington, D.C.: Joint Economic Committee.

Baumol, William, and Oates, Wallace (1975). *The Theory of Environmental Policy*. New York: Prentice Hall.

Bearse, Peter J. (1976): "Government as Innovator: A New Paradigm for State Economic Development Policy," *New England Journal of Business & Economics* (Spring).

Bearse, Peter J. (1978) "On the Intra-Regional Diffusion of Business Services." *Regional Studies* 12 (December).

Bell, Daniel (1976). *The Cultural Contradictions of Capitalism*. New York: Basic Books.

*The view that the growth of the non-profit sector is largely attributable to failures in the public economy is set forth theoretically and empirically by Weisbrod (1972).

Birch, David (1979). *The Job Generation Process*. Cambridge, MA: Program on Neighborhood and Regional Change, MIT.

Bluestone, Barry, and Harrison, Bennett (1980). *Capital and Communities: The Causes and Consequences of Private Disinvestment*. Washington, D.C.: Progressive Alliance.

Castells, Manuel (1980). *The Economic Crisis and American Society*. Princeton, NJ: Princeton University Press.

Cohen, Robert (1977). *The Modern Corporation and the City*. New York: Conservation of Human Resources, Columbia University.

Cohen, Robert et al. (1980) *The Expanding Role of Services in Major U.S. Corporations: Hypotheses, Preliminary Findings & Cases*. New York: Conservation of Human Resources, Columbia University.

Delehanty, George (1968). *Non-Production Workers in Manufacturing*. Amsterdam: North Holland Publishing Company.

Denison, Edward (1979). "Explanations of Declining Productivity Growth," *Survey of Current Business* 59:1 (August).

Douglas, Mary (1979). *The World of Goods*. New York: Basic Books.

Dunn, Edgar (1971). *Economic and Social Development: A Process of Social Learning*. Baltimore: Johns Hopkins University Press, for Resources for the Future.

Dunn, Edgar (1980). *The Development of the U.S. Urban System*, Vol. I. Baltimore: Johns Hopkins University Press, for Resources for the Future.

Feldstein, Martin, ed. (1980). *The American Economy in Transition*. Chicago: University of Chicago Press, for the National Bureau of Economic Research.

Friedman, W., and Garner, J.F., eds. (1970). *Government Enterprise: A Comparative Study*. New York: Columbia University Press.

Gilpin, Robert (1975). *U.S. Power and the Multinational Corporation: The Political Economy of Direct Investment*. New York: Basic Books.

Ginzberg, Eli, and Vojta, George (1981). "The Service Sector of the U.S. Economy." *Scientific American* 244:48 (March).

Gurwitz, Aaron (1978). "The Economic Effects of Property Tax Abatement for Industry," *Proceedings*, National Tax Association—Tax Institute of America, 70th Annual Conference.

Hill, Christopher, and Utterback, James (1979). *Technological Innovation for a Dynamic Economy*. New York: Pergamon.

Hirschman, Albert (1980). "The Welfare State in Trouble: Systematic Crisis or Growing Pains?" *American Economic Review* 70:113 (2, May).

Johnston, T. L. (1963). *Economic Expansion and Structural Change: A Trade Union Manifesto*. London: George Allen and Unwin Ltd.

Kieschnick, Michael (1981). "The Role of Equity Capital in Urban Economic Development." San Francisco: Office of Economic Policy and Planning, State of California, mimeo (January).

Klein, Burton (1977). *Dynamic Economics*. Cambridge, MA: Harvard University Press.

Lancaster, Kelvin (1973). "The Dynamic Inefficiency of Capitalism." *Journal of Political Economy* 81:1092.

Lebergott, Stanley (1959), "The Shape of the Income Distribution," *American Economic Review* 49:328 (January).

Lodge, George (1975). *The New American Ideology*. New York: Alfred A. Knopf, Inc.

Mayer, Neil S., and Blake, Jennifer L. (1980). "Keys to the Growth of Neighborhood Organizations." Washington, D.C.: The Urban Institute, Report No. 1330-2 (February).

Michelson, Stephen (1979a). "Community Based Development in Urban Areas," in B. Chinitz, *Central City Economic Development*. Cambridge, MA: Abt Books.

Michelson, Stephen (1979b). "The Working Bureaucrat and the Non-Working Bureaucracy." *American Behavioral Scientist* 22: (5, May/June).

Mick, S. (1975). "Social and Personal Costs of Plant Shutdowns." *Industrial Relations* 14:203.

Modigliani, Franco (1958). "New Developments on the Oligopoly Front." *Journal of Political Economy* 66:215.

Mollenkopf, John (1979). "Paths Towards the Post-Industrial Service City: The Northeast and the Southwest." Program in Urban Studies, Stanford University.

National Science Foundation (1973). "The Role of New Technical Enterprises in the U.S. Economy." Cambridge, MA: MIT Development Foundation, for the National Science Foundation.

Nelson, James (1977). "Public Enterprise: Pricing and Investment Criteria," in William G. Shepard, *Public Enterprise: Economic Analysis of Theory and Practice*. Lexington, MA: Lexington Books.

O'Connor, James (1973). *The Fiscal Crisis of the State*. New York: St. Martin's.

Peacock, Alan (1979). *The Economic Analysis of Government, and Related Themes*. New York: St. Martin's.

Pred, Alan, et al. (1977). *City Systems in Advanced Economics*. New York: Wiley.

Public/Private Ventures (1981). "Public Initiatives and Private Sector Responses: A Report on the Private Sector Initiative Program." Philadelphia: Public/Private Ventures (April).

Schonfield, Andrew (1965). *Modern Capitalism: The Changing Balance of Public and Private Power*. New York: Oxford University Press.

Scitovsky, Tibor (1980). "Can Capitalism Survive?—An Old Question in a New Setting." *American Economic Review* 70:1 (2, May).

Shepard, William G. (1976). *Public Enterprise: Economic Analysis of Theory and Practice*. Lexington, MA: Lexington Books.

Silber, William L., ed. (1976). *Financial Innovation*. Lexington MA: Lexington Books.

Skidelsky, Robert (1979). "The Decline of Keynesian Politics," in Colin Crouch, *State and Economy in Contemporary Capitalism*. New York: St. Martin's.

Small Business Administration (1977). *Report of the SBA Task Force on Venture and Equity Capital for Small Business*. Washington, D.C.: PUBL.

Smith, David (1979). "The Public Balance Sheet," in Pat McGuigan and Bob Schaeffer, *Developing the Public Economy: Models from Massachusetts*. Cambridge, MA: Policy Training Center.

Stanback, Thomas, and Bearse, Peter, et al. (1981). *Services: A New View of the U.S. Economy*. Totowa, NJ: Allenheld Osmun, Universe Books.

Steiner, Peter (1974). "Public Expenditure Budgeting," in George Break, ed., *The Economics of Public Finance*, Washington, D.C.: Brookings Institution.

Stern, Robert N., and Aldrich, Howard (1980). "The Effect of Absentee Firm Control on Local Community Welfare," in John Siegfried, ed., *The Economics of Firm Size, Market Structure and Social Performance*. Washington, D.C.: Bureau of Economics, Federal Trade Commission.

Stigler, George (1967). "Imperfections in the Capital Market." *Journal of Political Economy* (June).

Thompson, Wilbur (1965). *Preface to Urban Economics*. Baltimore: Johns Hopkins, for Resources for the Future.

Thurow, Lester (1975). *Generating Inequality*. New York: Basic Books.

Vaughan, Roger (1980). "Capital Needs of the Business Sector and the Future Economy of the City." Washington, D.C.: Academy for Contemporary Problems Roundtable (March 14).

Vaughan, Roger, and Bearse, P.J. (1980). "Federal Economic Development Strategy: A Framework for Design and Evaluation." Washington, D.C.: National Commission for Employment Policy (October).

Vietorisz, Thomas (1974). "Economic Policy Design: Principles and Urban Applications. *Eastern Economic Journal* 1:66 (January).

Walsh, Annemarie Hauck (1978). *The Public's Business: The Politics and Practices of Government Corporations.* Cambridge, MA: MIT Press, for the Twentieth Century Fund.

Weisbrod, Burton (1972). "Toward a Theory of the Voluntary Non-Profit Sector in a Three Sector Economy." New York: Russell Sage Foundation.

Witte, Edwin (1957). "Economics and Public Policy." *American Economic Review* 67:1 (March).

Young, Michael (1958). *The Rise of the Meritocracy.* London: Penguin Books.

U.S. Bureau of the Census (1976). *Survey of Income and Education.* Washington, D.C.: U.S. Bureau of the Census.

\

PART TWO

THE ROLE OF CAPITAL IN THE ECONOMIC DEVELOPMENT OF U.S. REGIONS

II

Regional Finance

William O. Douglas

This chapter is an amalgam of three speeches given by William O. Douglas when he was first Chairman of the Securities and Exchange Commission under President Roosevelt. First published by Yale University Press in 1940 in a volume entitled *Democracy and Finance*, the essay is reprinted here with permission of the Press. Though the statistics in this essay are old, its theme seems as fresh and timely now as when it was written.

Regions and regionalism have presented one of the perennial problems with which this country has had to struggle. In these days, however, it is more and more an economic rather than a political problem. We know that there is no one–sided solution to the economic side of regionalism any more than to its other aspects. We need a reasonable amount of centralization. But we also must make the economic structure of our major regions complete and strong. Entire political philosophies and economic theories have been developed around the problem of regionalism, mainly under the title of centralization versus decentralization. I propose to keep away as far as possible from both and shall restrict myself to the one field with which I have been in daily contact but on which only very meager information on a regional basis has ever been collected—the capital market.

A historian would be needed to trace or even to summarize the development of the centripetal tendencies in our capital–market organization. In the early days, of course, whatever need there existed for borrowing and lending was met locally or, at best, regionally. As the nineteenth century progressed, however, long–term borrowing and lending, and the origination* and distribution of marketable securities became rapidly concentrated in three or four leading Eastern cities. Later, from about the 'seventies, the business gravitated more and more to New York. Many factors combined in this development. One of these was the stream of European capital which reached the United States through the intermediary of a few New York banking houses with European connections. For several decades, enterprises requiring large amounts of capital, such as railroads, were dependent on the cooperation of European capital. It was but natural that the small number of investment bankers who more or less controlled the distribution within the United States of capital imported from Europe (or who controlled huge sums under fiscal–agency contracts with foreign powers during the war) acquired a tremendous head start in building up an organization for the origination of securities and in cementing their current contacts with security distributors outside of New York into informal but very effective groups. More important still, American corporations came to look to these banking houses as their natural advisers and agents when they had to offer new securities.

The more important institutional investors† now control the great majority of new funds available for investment in securities, particularly in those of a fixed interest–bearing type. Some investment institutions raise and invest most of their funds locally; building and loan associations are good examples. Funds handled by these institutions frequently do not touch the central market at all. The same is true, of course, of the reinvested earnings of farmers and of small and medium–sized business enterprises. The largest institutional investors, however, collect their funds in many communities on a nationwide scale, but invest them mainly in the New York market. Insurance companies, investment companies, the investment departments of commercial and savings banks, and the trust departments of commercial banks and trust companies now operate, to a large extent, in this fashion. Probably only a small part of the large holdings of securities under the administration of these institutions is invested through the intermediary of local or regional capital markets.

The problem of financing small—or intermediate-size companies is primarily the problem of local companies which do not as yet enjoy national credit (or which may never enjoy such a credit because of size), no matter how good the risk and no matter how good the prospects. The problem is intimately tied up with the development of regional capital and securities markets. It is a problem of how to develop, with the help of local financial machinery, regional capital centers so as to keep local capital for local needs.

---

*"Origination" is the function performed by investment bankers in planning and bringing on the market new issues of securities.

†"Institutional investors" are institutions engaged in the investment of funds on a large scale—insurance companies, banks, investment companies, etc.

Granted the desirability and the necessity of having a great national market for capital funds upon which the whole country can draw, yet the dangers of leaving the small local enterprise without an adequate mechanism for obtaining adequate capital cannot be overlooked. It is a major national problem which presses for local solution in almost every community.

Strangely enough, many people fail to understand how extremely important small industry is to our whole economy. It takes no statistical analysis to indicate the enormous importance to our nation of the company employing from 100 to 200 men and women. Out of a total of 411,000 corporations reporting balance sheets and filing income–tax returns in 1934, 386,000 had total assets of less than $1,000,000. Thus, the corporations with less than $1,000,000 of assets were almost 95% of all the corporations. Large industry itself is to a great extent dependent upon the small company for its raw materials and for its markets. The small industry in most small cities and towns in the country is basic to our economic life.

Small business in this country has almost invariably been financed by plowing earnings back into the business, by commercial bank credit, and occasionally by private financing. The very high percentage of risk which is involved in many of the security offerings of small and unseasoned companies poses the question as to whether the public, and especially the small investor, should be urged to invest savings in this type of security. Commercial banks, whatever their attitude may be toward established companies, are chary about extending credit to a new and unseasoned business. But though the small company is seasoned it may still experience great difficulty in reaching the capital markets. There is thus a gap in the machinery of our capital markets.

There are throughout the country old, well-established companies which have given work to the citizens of their communities for years. Some have found that they can no longer compete with the larger ones unless they undertake extensive modernization. Such companies, and I have talked with the executives of many, must either restrict their activities to their most profitable lines on the present basis of operations—which of course means laying off men—or they must install up-to-date production methods. Others need capital to take advantage of new markets which lie at their doors. Looking at it broadly, this means that, while our national economic welfare rests on the welfare of small business, our national financial machinery is geared almost exclusively to big business. This is not a new problem. It is an old one. It is pressing at the present time especially because of the condition of our capital markets.

Why do we have a central capital market at all? Economists tell us that some parts of the country have more savings than they can put to profitable use, while others (in the developmental stage) do not have the resources to finance all needed investment. It is the economic function of the central capital market to match the surplus savings of some regions with the excess demand for new capital from other regions, in addition to tapping the national market for those issues which by size or nature have a national rather than a regional appeal. This function is necessary under existing conditions. If we had no central capital market, interest rates would differ much more between different parts of the country than they do now, and large parts of the country would be much poorer in capital equipment than they are. That is the theory. In fact, however, the central capital market does much more than match regional surpluses and shortages of long-term capital. It is not only the final clearing houses for surpluses and shortages which are left over after regional capital markets have attempted to match the supply of savings and demand for investment originating in their territory. Instead, the majority of the total supply of savings investable in new securities and of total new issues of securities go through the central market. That market combines to a large extent the function of a national clearing house with that of a dozen or so of undeveloped or underdeveloped regional clearing houses.

The real problem, then, is one of degree: To what extent could the matching of supply of, and demand for, long–term capital, which now flows to the central market, be done regionally without impairing the efficiency of our national capital market? This is a problem which obviously cannot be settled dogmatically. And it may be that it cannot be solved in the same manner in every region. Wherever a region has a very heavy excess of savings or a very large excess of demand for new capital, conditions for the development of a balanced regional capital market are not propitious. It would seem, however, that there are a number of regions in this country where both the supply of savings and the demand for capital are sufficiently large and sufficiently well balanced to permit the development of a sound regional capital market.

A wise man said long ago that figures might not govern the world, but that they did indicate how the world was governed. And figures certainly indicate to what extent the American capital market is highly centralized.

Of the nearly 7,000 brokers and dealers registered with the Securities and Exchange Commission (SEC), approximately 30% have their headquarters in New York. More significant is the fact that, of all underwritten issues of $1,000,000 or over registered under the Securities Act of 1933 between July 1, 1936, and June 30, 1938, 84% were managed by investment banking firms with principal offices in New York City, and that the underwriting participations of New York firms in the same issues aggregated 72% of the total, leaving but 28% for bankers or dealers in the provinces.* Most of our larger insurance companies, with policyholders in every state in the Union, are domiciled in New York and environs, and even those which are not conduct most of their

---

*"Underwritten issues" are security issues in which investment bankers are employed to "underwrite" the success of the offering. On a large issue an investment banker will commonly invite other banking firms to participate in underwriting the securities, or the offering of them, or both. A syndicate is formed and the original investment banker acts as "syndicate manager." The amounts of the issue taken by the various members of the syndicate are known as the "participations."

investment business through the New York market. About 70% of the total assets of our investment companies are held by companies domiciled in or around New York City, although their stockholders are spread over the entire country. Most of the larger investment counsel firms, which have been administering a rapidly increasing amount of funds of clients residing from Maine to California, have their headquarters in New York City. Even of the total security investments of all banks in the country, about one quarter is held by New York City banks. Similarly, of total trust funds under the administration of commercial banks and trust companies, it is estimated that between one-fourth and one-third are in the hands of about a dozen large New York institutions. And finally, a striking though well-known figure—of all stock trading on exchanges, about 95% takes place on the New York Stock and New York Curb Exchanges alone, leaving only 5% for the other 27 (registered and exempt) exchanges. If I were to lump together all of the available indicators, I should say that, at the present time, well over one half of our capital market, so far as it is represented by the current investment in marketable securities, is concentrated in lower Manhattan.

These developments all point the way to more adequate regional recognition, to greater regional development, to a larger degree of regional independence. Much work and study remains to be done. Some light is thrown on limited aspects of the regional problem by the following statistics.

The S.E.C. analyzed all the underwritten security issues of $1,000,000 and over which had been registered under the Securities Act of 1933 and offered for sale between July 1, 1936, and March 31, 1938. In dollar amount these totaled $3,418,820,000. There were $2,608,279,000 of bonds; $533,648,000 of preferred stock; and $276,893,000 of common stock. Then we examined the underwriting participations in these issues. Firms with principal offices in New York City had 74.05% participation in the bonds; 69.54% in the preferred stock; 64.72% in the common; 72.59% in all issues. Firms with principal offices in San Francisco had 1.18% participation in the bonds; 2.21% participation in the preferred stock; 1.42% in the common and 1.36% in all issues. Firms with principal offices in all of the Pacific Coast and Rocky Mountain States had only 1.48% participation in the bonds; 3.27% in the preferred stock; 2.59% in the common; and only 1.85% in all issues.

Another illustration may be found in the Fourth Federal Reserve District, located principally in Ohio. Although it covers only about 2% of the area of the United States, it represents, economically speaking, about 10% of the country. There is in the Fourth District about 9% of our population. It bought in 1935 $9\frac{1}{2}$% of all the goods sold at retail in the country. It accounts in good years for about 12% of our industrial production, and it pays about 9% of all Federal income taxes. The share of the Fourth District is, of course, much higher in a few large industries. Of rubber products, for instance, considerably over 50% is produced in the Fourth District, of steel and steel products about one third, and of stone, glass, and clay products, about one fourth. If statistics were available, comparable high percentages would be shown for a number of important but more specialized industries.

We may expect that a region of this importance and structure will also be an important source of savings funds and, at the same time, originate a large demand for new capital. Indeed, savings deposits in commercial and savings banks in the district aggregate, we estimate, nearly $2,000,000,000. Building and loan associations in the district have assets of over $1,000,000,000. The savings of residents of the district in the form of premium reserves with life insurance companies should amount to over $2,000,000,000, if population is an indicator. Interest in regional problems has in the past, unfortunately, been too small—and statistical difficulties too forbidding—to permit the citation of more exact and more comprehensive figures on the volume of saving and investment in the Fourth District. We know, however, that a considerable part of total new securities issued during the last few years was floated by companies whose plants are wholly, or in part, within the Fourth District. A rough calculation which I had made indicates that of total underwritten industrial and utility issues of over $1,000,000 registered under the Securities Act between July 1, 1936, and June 30, 1938, approximately 12% were of enterprises which may be regarded as domiciled in the Fourth District.

Is the investment–banking and capital–market machinery of the Fourth District commensurate with its economic importance, or its position as a source of savings and an originator of securities? I doubt it. Of course, there are a number of important investment banking firms domiciled in the district, some of which have more than regional importance. Statistics, however, indicate that of the more than 9,000 offices of registered brokers and dealers, less than 5% were located in the Fourth District. Similar relationships appear on investigation of the underwriting participations of firms domiciled in the Fourth District. Of underwritten issues of $1,000,000 and over registered under the Securities Act between July 1, 1936, and June 30, 1938, they took but 5.2% of the purchase group participations, and they managed only 2.7% of such issues, measured by the total dollar amount of offerings. This is to be compared with a ratio of about 12% of issues of Fourth District enterprises. There are only a few sizable insurance companies with head offices in the Fourth District. Commercial banks, of course, made considerable investments for their own and for trust accounts, but mostly, again, in securities issued or traded in New York. Finally, there are three of our twenty-seven securities exchanges in this district. But during the years 1936 and 1937 they accounted for not much over .04 percent of the total dollar value of the sales on all registered exchanges.

Undoubtedly, then, there is a considerable supply of funds available for long-term investment, and a large demand for long-term funds originating in the Fourth District. Much of this that might be matched regionally now goes to New York to be matched there. Suppose a part of these amounts were handled locally to form the basis of a regional capital market. What would that mean to the Fourth Federal Reserve District?

I hardly need to point out that it would mean more business for the investment bankers of the Fourth District, for the trust and registrar departments of its commercial banks, for lawyers and auditors of the district, and for printers of prospectuses. It would, indirectly, mean more business for the banks of the Fourth District, in the form of loans on new securities and wider opportunities for investment.

In these matters I do not wish to belittle the East. From the broad national point of view, as well as from a regional point of view, we need strong capital and securities markets in the East. There are national, as distinguished from regional, needs to serve. But the tangible and intangible values to the nation at large, and even to Wall Street, of regional development are as great as they are to the regions in question. In many instances in the past, the New York market, because of its greater financial and technical resources, has been able to render this service on terms with which the financial machinery of other communities could not compete. But this is not necessarily a permanent condition. Business and finance can will it otherwise. If the larger local enterprises were to patronize their local financial centers more extensively, those local financial centers could develop into healthy resorts for both small and large companies in need of financial assistance.

You know the industries in your community which need capital, and you know whether their need is deserving. Furthermore, you know to what extent the welfare of the entire community rests upon the welfare of the local industry. It may be that what is needed is a reappraisal of the standards upon which investment is made and loans are granted. It may be that the risks which lie in the backyards of cities throughout the country are just as good as the ones which have become glamorous because they have caught the fancy of the larger markets. In any case, we do know that our national economic welfare rests on the welfare of small or local business. Only regional facilities can care for that, for our national financial machinery is almost exclusively big-business machinery.

I believe there is a growing regional consciousness on all sides. It does not, and should not, take the form of economic barriers or trade walls. It merely recognizes that each region should stand more and more on its own feet, beholden to no outside economic power, dependent on itself for guidance and strength, and yet coordinated in its efforts with other parts of our national economy.

Small business must not be suffocated. In a capitalistic system dependent on individual initiative and freedom it must be served first. Can the ideal solution be found in the machinery of our capital markets? Can there be found or developed local reservoirs of capital for the legitimate needs of small business? Or, as a measure of last resort, should the Federal Government do the job? We need business statesmanship on this pressing problem. We know that the glib answer that the Securities Act of 1933 has caused this closure of the capital markets is not the correct one. For we know that these problems of the small business antedated that Act. In a sense they have always been with us. But their acuteness has been increased over the years with the growth of bigness.

Moreover, financing of small business is only one phase of the problem of development of local or regional capital and securities markets. There are seasoned local industries of a larger size which are constantly in need of adequate and healthy securities and capital markets, and which frequently can be well served locally. But there is the tendency of the larger local industries to go into the New York market when they are in need of financing. I realize the predicament of those industries when they have to obtain their capital through the available investment media. At times the local or regional capital machinery is inadequate. At other times it is wholly adequate. In any event the call is clear for recognition of a regional service which will keep control and capital at home. In recent days a prominent business executive took a strong position in favor of such decentralization. He is quoted as saying:

> I think New York would be better off with decentralization of management. We wouldn't have the load to carry here of justification of why there should be so much of the business of the country centered here. The advantages of moving back are obvious. The advantages to New York, I think, are equally obvious ... If your business is moved back you will be getting in with the local people. These local towns would have a stake in that industry. They would feel they had a greater stake than they have today.*

I heartily concur in that view.

Threads of this regional philosophy run throughout the statutes which are administered by the Securities and Exchange Commission. All national securities exchanges are its concern under the Securities Exchange Act of 1934. They are equal in the eyes of that law. It is the Commission's duty not to prefer one over the other. It is its task to aid and assist each to better serve its local, regional, or national, needs. From the viewpoint of some of the smaller exchanges, it is important to enable them to broaden their activities and to increase their resources. A strong local or regional exchange is symptomatic of local and regional financial strength and vitality.

Congress also expressed a local or regional philosophy respecting the utility industry when it enacted the Public Utility Holding Company Act of 1935. Under the much abused and misnamed death sentence in Section 11 of that Act, it is visualized that geographically integrated utility systems will be the pattern. Instead of far flung properties held together by remote control, there will be local or regional groupings of operating properties. This should result, more and more, in the disappearance of absentee management—in the return of the industry to its home region. So, when those at the S.E.C. concern themselves with these matters, they are not reading into the statutes their own economic and social predilections; they are expressing the implied or stated Congressional intent.

*From an address by Mr. W. Averill Harriman before the Bond Club of New York, as reported in the *New York Times* for January 29, 1938.

There are other indications that regional development is the modern trend. As I have traveled in New England, the Middle West, and the Far West, I have heard more and more of that philosophy. I once made the charge that certain legal devices were being employed merely for the purpose of corporate kidnaping.* But the term *corporate kidnaping* is not restricted to the endeavors of a small group to wrest control from the hands of the real owners of a company. It is likewise applicable to formal and informal arrangements for taking the actual control of a company away from the seat of its operations.

Absentee management, no matter how honest and able, cannot equal local management. Remote financial control may be rationalized as sound, but it is likely to be unresponsive to local needs. And it certainly does not sit well with labor, investors, consumers, and the communities back home. It is their industry and they should be in on it. Californian control of New England would be as bad as control by New York of California. I discern what I hope will be a decided trend to bring industry's headquarters back home.

The same philosophy is evident in a myriad of ways. An isolated example is taxation on dividends of companies in holding-company portfolios. This works for logical consolidations when that is possible, and for divestment when that is the more constructive way. Another is found in corporate reorganizations. I have been in touch during the last four years with many reorganization situations. A very large number of them involved companies and properties on the Pacific Coast or in the Rocky Mountain area. Most of them involved bonds issued under corporate trust indentures. In large numbers of cases the corporate trustee was located east of the Mississippi. In a smaller number of cases the trustee was located on the Coast. Close observers of the matter on the Pacific Coast have told me over and again what my own observation bore out, that the investors by and large fared better with a local trustee than with an absentee trustee. The difference lay in mobility of action and in the cost of operating from a distant point.

This is no disparagement of the trust institutions of the Eastern cities. It merely emphasizes the desirability of using local or regional trustees for the needs of local or regional business. This would result in the gravitation of other related business, such as paying agencies, registrarships, transfer agencies, depositaryships, and the like to the respective regions. By such use local facilities would be strengthened and improved. Regional financial facilities would grow. This would help regional independence to evolve. Such independence cannot be achieved if regional facilities are not given an opportunity. It can be achieved if regional facilities are allowed to fatten on regional business.

In sum, the development of regional financing should bring with it these conditions. First and foremost, it should bring simpler and more conservative finance, where finance is brought closer to the locus of business and where investors are brought closer to finance and investment.

---

*Before the Bond Club of New York.

Second, regional financing should produce better planned financing, since under that system there might be greater freedom from the scramble in the central capital market for the issues of temporarily popular industries.

Third, regional finance might be able to develop an adequate organization for the supply of long-term capital, particularly in equity form, to enterprises of moderate size.

Fourth, a reduction in absentee financing would result in a reduction of absentee ownership and management, with all the advantages which flow from keeping business at home for the home folks.

Finally, the development of regional capital markets would bring new capital and new brains into the investment banking industry and the financial management of local business. Regional capital markets of sufficient stature should help retain and employ the best of their own sons at home.

The development of regional capital markets seems to be eminently desirable but it will not come just by talking and writing. Regional capital markets, even under the best of conditions, can grow up only if local bankers and local businessmen want them. With local patronage, development of regional capital markets is possible. Without it, it is impossible. The problem therefore at this stage is largely in their hands.

III

Capital Is Only Part of the Problem

Belden Daniels

There is an urgent need for perspective on the problem of government intervention in capital markets to create economic development. The major message of this chapter is one of *limits*. There are four points which must be stressed: first, the limited importance of large business in the development process; second, the limited ability of capital to ensure economic growth; third, the limited availability of capital to small enterprise; and fourth, the limited ability of state and local development efforts to encourage economic growth in a context of national and international events.

Many of the comments in this chapter will challenge the current wisdom. It is important to note, however, that the current wisdom is still being tested. It is really only since 1964 that this nation has been seriously concerned with issues of regional and community economic development. There is much that still is not known about the role of capital in economic development. This chapter is an attempt to ensure that we use intelligently and creatively what we do know.

Let us now confront each of these four major points, in turn.

The Limited Role of Big Business

Economic policy in the United States has traditionally been formulated on the assumption that "bigger is better." Federal, state, and local development efforts have typically concentrated on fostering the growth of large-scale businesses—almost to the exclusion of small enterprise. Recent research has indicated how misguided this policy emphasis is. A growing body of literature suggests that small businesses

1. are the major source of new jobs,
2. are a major source of technological innovation, and
3. tend to be quite profitable.

Small Business as a Generator of Jobs

The most comprehensive research into the contribution of small businesses to employment growth has been conducted by David Birch and published in his book *The Job Generation Process* (1979). Using nationwide Dun and Bradstreet files for the years 1969, 1972, 1974, and 1976, Birch found that:

1. The migration of firms from one locality to another is a rare occurrence.
2. The rate of job loss due to the death or contraction of firms is 8% and is exactly the same in all regions of the country.
3. The birth of new firms and expansion of existing firms are the major source of employment growth in the country.
4. Firms with 20 or fewer employees generate 66% of net new jobs in the United States.

Research conducted by both the National Federation of Independent Businesses (1978) and the Urban Institute (1980) support these findings.

The nature of the small business sector's strength as a source of employment growth is, however, complex. In fact, the very dynamism of small business is the source of both its strength and its weakness as a job generator. Michael Kieschnick, in a particularly thoughtful analysis of Birch's work, points out that while the small business sector has *collectively* provided most of the net increase in our economy's employment, this increase has not resulted from the steady smooth growth of *each* small business (Kieschnick, 1979).

Two key reasons for small businesses' success in generating large numbers of new jobs suggest why the quality and duration of those jobs may be at issue in individual cases. First, small businesses tend to be more labor intensive than larger businesses. Thus, growth in the small sector results in more jobs while growth in the large sector often involves the substitution of capital for labor. Yet labor-intensive jobs tend to be lower quality jobs than those in which the introduction of capital leads to higher productivity which, in turn, leads to higher wages, more extensive benefits, and (perhaps) greater security. Second, smaller businesses tend to be younger, and thus are still in the growth stage, while larger firms tend to be more mature, and thus possess less absolute ability to grow. Yet, again this very dynamism which propels the growth of many young, small firms is the dynamism which makes the jobs they create of less certain tenure. Small firms are good at unmaking jobs as well as making them. In fact, research by Garn and Ledebur (1980) and Kieschnick (1979) indicates that employment in smaller firms tends to offer lower wages, fewer fringe benefits, and less stability than employment in larger firms.

Small Business as a Source of Technological Innovation

There is little disagreement about the important role that small businesses play in technological innovation. Various independent studies have pointed up the fact that small businesses have been the source of most significant technological breakthroughs in the twentieth century. A list compiled in 1967 of major innovations developed by small firms includes: xerography, DDT, ballpoint pens, the zipper, kodachrome, air conditioning, penicillin, and titanium, to name only a few (U.S. Department of Commerce, 1967). An updated compilation of this list would find it greatly lengthened with the contributions of small businesses in the fields of medical instrumentation, microelectronics, and energy technology. The research and development of solar technology is to date almost the exclusive province of small business. Further, all seven major innovations in the process of refining and cracking petroleum came from small firms and independent inventors (U.S. Department of Commerce, 1979).

Not only are small firms and independent inventors the main source of innovation, but they also innovate more efficiently and at a lower cost than larger firms. The National Science Foundation has reported that from 1953 to 1973, small firms produced four times as many innovations per research and development dollar as medium-sized firms, and 24 times as many as large firms (National Science Foundation, 1979). Scheirer (1977), in a study comparing innovative efforts in firms with less than 1000 employees to that in firms with over 1000 employees, reported that the ratio of innovation to sales is one-third greater in firms with less than 1000 employees. Moreover, the ratio of innovations to research and development employment is four times greater in firms with less than 1000 employees.

Small firms also tend to innovate for different reasons than large firms. For smaller, technically based firms, innovation plays a critical role in the economic viability of the business and is responsible for the creation of new products, new jobs, and new processes and markets. In general, smaller firms innovate to foster external development and growth while larger firms innovate to improve internal efficiency, cut costs, and substitute capital for labor.

The different reasons that motivate small businesses to innovate also explain, in part, their great success as innovators. Many analysts have pointed out that an entrepreneur who views a new product or process as her entry into the marketplace will be more oriented toward taking risks than a large well-established corporation. Further, the innovative process in small firms is not hampered by large bureaucracies or "standard operating procedures." At the corporate level, new ideas are "born by committee, run by committee, and killed by committee." In the small business, the lines of communication are clearer between the inventors or "idea people" and the operating units; indeed, the entrepreneur and the inventor are often one and the same.

Small Businesses are Profitable

As a whole, small businesses appear to be at least as profitable as large businesses, and perhaps more so. A recent study conducted by this author contrasted the percentage return to shareholders' equity of small and large businesses, using data collected by the Federal Trade Commission (FTC) (Daniels and Kieschnick, 1978). The data included a 100% sample of manufacturing firms disaggregated by asset size. The results of the study indicated that from 1958 to 1976 the after-tax profitability of manufacturing firms with less than $1 million in assets was .2% higher than the average for all firms. Over this 8-year period, firms with less than $1 million in assets were more profitable than all other firms except those with over $1 billion in assets. Even these largest manufacturers registered an average profitability that was only .5% higher than the smallest firms. During the most recent period, 1972–1976, firms with less than $5 million in assets registered profits on average that exceeded all other firms by at least 3%. All of these figures on profitability incorporate firm failure rates by asset size.

The high profitability of small businesses as a whole must be balanced, however, against the individual variability of return found within the small business sector. Small businesses tend to be more volatile than larger businesses. Of the hundreds of thousands of new businesses that are started each year, over half fail. Over the period 1969 to 1976, David Birch found that, regardless of age, businesses with 0–20 employees had a 58% probability of dying during that period. This was a far higher probability of dying than any other size group experienced, with the probability decreasing as firm size increased. Within each size group, Birch also found that the youngest firms— those of 0 to 4 years of age—had a far higher probability of dying during the period than any of the older firms within that size (Birch, 1979).

To reduce this volatility to terms of profitability, Michael Kieschnick measured risk as the year-to-year variation in rate of return for a 100% sample of manufacturing firms disaggregated by asset size (using the FTC data noted above). For the period 1958 to 1971, he found that risk was inversely related to size. Larger corporations, as a group, had more stable earnings than smaller corporations. For the period 1972–1976, however, he found no clear relationship between asset size and risk: All firms, disaggregated by asset size, experienced a variability of return of approximately 10%. For the overall period 1958–1976, as a general proposition, the smaller the firm size, the higher the variability of risk (Daniels and Kieschnick, 1978).

In Summary: The Role of Small Business in the U.S. Economy

Until recently, the role of small enterprise in the American economy has been overlooked. A growing body of research indicates how essential small enterprise is to the continued growth and strength of the economy. Small business is a net job creator, profit producer, and key innovator. Though the small business sector is relatively risky and may provide lower job quality and stability, it plays an important and insufficiently recognized role in the economic development process.

Public policy makers must realize the limitations imposed on any development effort that only attempts to attract large-scale industry to a region. What is called for is a public policy that recognizes the role in the development process of all different sizes and types of enterprise—and an end to the assumption that only large enterprise is worth supporting. Policies that emphasize equalizing the access to capital and the availability of technical support to all firms will foster far more economic development than those that are content to simply "chase smokestacks."

The Limited Role of Capital

In our overly money-conscious, Keynesian-dominated society, we have a great public policy tendency to believe that money solves all problems. In the development process, however, capital is a necessary, but insufficient, ingredient. It cannot make up for the lack of markets or management, or overcome the high costs of labor or land. In order to put capital in its proper development place, it is therefore necessary to understand the forces which drive economic activity from a demand and supply standpoint.

The Power of the Marketplace

The real forces which determine the location of economic activity are the enormous interregional and international shifts taking place in populations, purchasing power, labor supply, energy, and raw materials—in real goods markets—on a worldwide basis. The effects of these market changes are now visible in declining regions such as the Midwest and Northeast, declining cities such as Akron and Trenton, and declining neighborhoods such as South Boston and East Los Angeles.

In fact, it is important to understand that this is a national, not a regional, problem. As one analyst has noted, "There are many people in rural areas and disintegrating inner city neighborhoods in the Sunbelt who are still in the shade." These areas are competing in a worldwide goods market in which they are on the short end of both relatively declining markets (on the demand side), and relatively increasing costs and decreasing availability of key factors of production such as labor, land, and raw materials (on the supply side).

These profound market forces must first be addressed before looking to capital to bail out firms, regions, and neighborhoods. To put it in a nutshell, good money can never make otherwise bad deals good.

Behind the changing patterns of population and employment are the decisions by households about where to live and work, business firms about where to invest, and governmental units about where and how to tax and spend. These decisions, influenced by both social and economic factors, result in constantly changing growth and decline in all communities.

People or Jobs, Jobs or People

People choose where to live and work for a variety of economic, social, physical, and personal reasons: the quality of schools and neighborhoods, the availability of jobs, level of taxes, the climate and environmental quality, the nearness to friends and family, and many other reasons. Business firms, in deciding where to invest, respond both to shifts in the location of markets for their products and to changes in the cost and availability of the capital, labor, and land needed for production.

Although the preponderance of research shows that the movement of jobs and investments tends to follow the migratory patterns of people, there is some dispute among analysts as to whether people follow jobs or jobs follow people. In other words, has the growth in markets and labor supply due to population shifts been more important in determining business location than the availability of jobs has been in influencing people to move? Although there is some question about which is the driving force in the creation of markets, there is no question that areas with growing markets are attractive for business location.

People Shifts

There have been large changes in the distribution of population and employment in recent years. Since 1950, suburbs have grown faster than either central cities or rural areas. Up until 1970, it was also true that metropolitan areas were growing faster than were rural areas. Since 1970, however, this trend has reversed itself: Now rural places are actually growing faster than metropolitan areas. Indeed, central cities as a group have actually lost population absolutely (Bureau of Census, 1977; Birch, 1977).

Job Shifts

Along with these shifts in population have come changes in the interregional and intrametropolitan location of employment. There have been three types of movements: from industrial regions of the U.S. to less industrial regions, from metropolitan areas to rural areas within the same region, and from central cities of metropolitan areas to their suburbs. The Sunbelt has increased its share of employment faster than its share of population, while the Northeast and Midwest have experienced just the opposite. Rural area employment across the country has grown faster (or in some cases declined less) than metropolitan employment. Finally, within certain regions of the country, central cities have had absolute declines in employment between 1947 and 1972. This is especially true in the Northeast, while in the South and West even central cities have experienced substantial employment growth. On the other hand, regardless of regional location, the central cities of large SMSA's have held a declining share of metropolitan jobs (Bureau of the Census, 1974; Chinitz, undated).

These profound demographic and employment shifts in turn profoundly affect markets, and therefore the growth of economic activity.

The Relative Importance of Labor, Land, and Capital

While proximity to growing markets is the dominant consideration in location decisions for most firms, it is by no means the only important factor. For firms which export products nationwide or throughout the world, the relative cost and availability of land, labor, or capital may be the deciding factors in where to locate.

Most researchers see the location decision for large firms consisting of two steps: First, choosing an area based on broad considerations of market, labor costs, or availability of a key raw material; and second, choosing a specific site within the acceptable region based on the fine-tuning of such additional factors as transportation outlets and taxes.

For large established firms, the cost or availability of capital usually does not even enter the picture. For them, the relative importance of any one factor of production such as labor, land, or raw materials depends on the relative proportion of costs accounted for by that factor, and on the degree to which its cost and availability vary from place to place.

Labor costs appear to be important on both counts, as they are the largest single cost for most industries—66 cents out of each dollar of value added. Further, labor costs do vary from area to area, to a greater extent than capital costs or taxes (Cornia and Testa, 1978).

Land costs and availability, similarly, seem to vary substantially from place to place. Particularly in congested central cities, the lack of availability of large parcels of land seems to induce many firms to move, usually for a short distance, in search of space to expand (Schmenner, 1978). That short distance is usually less than 20 miles—often, from center city to suburb.

Capital, on the other hand, is not that significant a cost. Total annual capital costs generally range from only 6–10% of the total value of sales in manufacturing. And while data on interregional differences in capital costs are very limited, what we do know indicates that the differences are quite small. One study (Straszheim, 1969) shows that interest rates for the average business loan vary between North and South by less than one percentage point.

Differences in capital costs become important to the private sector only when geographic differences in markets and production costs are small. As we have seen, however, land and labor costs tend to vary dramatically with location, while capital costs tend to be constant across the country. Thus state development policies which attempt to improve a state's competitive economic advantage by subsidizing capital costs are targeted at a relatively insignificant factor on the corporate balance sheet.

The Impact of Federal Policies on Products and Markets

Policymakers concerned with developing an economically sound development strategy in low-income communities have to contend not only with the whole thrust of powerful worldwide market forces, but with the fact that federal government intervention in those markets through tax, expenditure, and regulatory policy has often had unintended and undesirable side-effects. That has been true in almost every major agency within the federal government. In virtually every federal cabinet post—including transportation, energy, education, labor, and housing—federal intervention has generally worked to reduce population and markets, and increase costs of production for those declining regions and inner cities of concern to us (Vaughan, 1977).

In general, the federal government's huge budget has one of two kinds of effects on economic development. It either affects the level and character of demand at different locations, or the cost and availability of human and material resources used by producers. It causes these effects by decisions as to who gets taxed how much where, who benefits from expenditures either directly (in contracts or loans) or indirectly (in new roads or sewer systems), or who is affected by regulation.

How federal policies shape the geography of economic growth in the United States has been catalogued in a recent major survey by the Rand Corporation (Vaughan, 1977). The most important of these policies and their effects are outlined below.

Federal policies that change the pattern of population migration and housing location have a powerful indirect impact on economic development. They influence both the market size and labor supply of regions. Policies of this kind, such as Federal Housing Authority (FHA) and Veterans Administration (VA) housing credit, highway construction, and low-priced energy have favored migration from the central city to the suburb, large metropolitan areas to rural areas, and older regions to younger regions.

Direct federal expenditures have tended to favor states in the South versus the old manufacturing belt. The Frostbelt has historically received much lower per capita public works and defense expenditures.

Specific fiscal and monetary policies vary in their effects. The investment tax credit has worked to the advantage of suburbs, rural areas, and younger regions since new plant construction, whose cost is reduced by the credit, tends to occur in these regions. The same is true of rapid depreciation allowance which shortens the apparent life of the depreciated asset less than its real life. In both instances, the employment redistribution away from historic manufacturing districts in central cities, larger metropolitan areas, and older cities is speeded up. In contrast, when the personal income tax rate is reduced, the old manufacturing belt benefits because of its still higher per capita money income.

Labor supply has been influenced in subtle and complex ways. Unemployment insurance and welfare have increased the cost and reduced the availability of unskilled labor in old, established industrial areas, where such payments are relatively high. Federal labor law has fostered the growth of trade unions, whose relative vigor in the old manufacturing belt has put this area at a labor cost disadvantage relative to the less unionized South.

The most important federal impact on the interregional cost of production has resulted from the development of an interstate highway system. These highways have opened up areas of the country (for firms using truck transportation) which otherwise would not have been potential industrial sites, particularly in Mountain and Southern states.

Similarly, Occupational Safety and Health Administration and Environmental Protection Agency regulatory policy is not neutral. The costs of the regulation weigh more heavily on, for instance, a Massachusetts industrial plant (which is 9 years older on average than that of the country as a whole) than on newer industrial areas such as Tucson.

In Summary: Capital and Economic Development

We must emphasize, again, that capital is a necessary but insufficient factor in the development process. The presence of capital cannot compensate for basic problems with markets, management, factors of production, or products. More important, policy makers have limited ability to deal with these more basic problems: National demographic changes, shifts in the labor supply, and contractions in the supply of energy are all factors over which local and regional administrators can exert little control.

Within this scenario of national and international events, it is understandable that policy makers attempt to utilize capital as a controllable factor. We must realize, however, that many other events compromise the ability of capital formation policies to influence the development process.

The Limited Availability of Capital

When capital does become the missing essential ingredient in an otherwise sound profitable venture, the issue is *not* the *cost of capital* — it *is* the *availability of capital*. As we have seen, on the one hand, capital is generally too small a part of the cost of doing business (6 percent to 10 percent for most firms, FTC, 1977) for its cost to make a difference. Reducing the cost of money is thus almost never sufficient to make up for real differences in markets, management, labor, land, or raw materials.

Since capital plays such a small part in the costs of doing business, it is easy to see why government programs that subsidize those costs make no sense. To make this key point vividly clear, a recent study showed that the guarantees proposed by Economic Development Agency (EDA) in the proposed National Public Works and Economic Development Act (NPWEDA) would decrease costs for the average U.S. firm by only $\frac{8}{10}$ of 1% and increase profits by only $\frac{1}{10}$ of 1%; that is, for the average firm receiving a guarantee on long-term debt, the firm's rate of return would increase from 10.6% to 10.7% (Daniels and Kieschnick, 1979). That difference is far too small to greatly affect any size firm.

On the other hand, the absence of capital can stop an otherwise good firm from being born or growing. Although good money cannot make bad deals good, the wrong kind of money can ruin an otherwise good deal, and the absence of money can keep the good deal from happening at all. For instance, a rapidly growing, highly profitable $50 million electronics firm in Massachusetts was recently told by its banker that there was a solution to its perennial money problems—stop growing! So when the Irish government financed its new plant, 300 new jobs were created there instead of in Boston.

Government must be careful, however, to intervene only when an otherwise profitable, growing firm is denied profitability and growth by the absence of capital. Large firms, for instance, have access to all the capital they need on the most favorable terms the market can supply. In fact, making government capital available to large firms is inflationary, as it merely substitutes public for private dollars. This is not to say that government policy cannot affect the investment and location decisions of large firms, but rather that neither the cost nor the availability of capital is a critical factor in location decisions for those firms.

Thus, capital market failings, while not a major factor at all in the success or failure of large firms, can have a critical impact on young, independent enterprises—the ones supplying at least half of the new jobs in our nation. In fact, more often than not, the absence of adequate sources of the right kinds of capital keeps these otherwise profitable and productive firms from generating income, profits, and jobs as they might.

While the problem of the lack of long-term funding for profitable, growing, new small corporations may not be associated with any particular region, its solution does represent a possible focus for targeted intervention in support of development in particular parts of the country. This is particularly appropriate in light of David Birch's findings that the fundamental difference in levels of economic activity from a declining area to a growing one is the rate of births and expansions of young, small firms. In essence, such a development policy begins by identifying that major source of job creation ignored by traditional development—capital access for small firms—and seeks to channel their growth in distressed areas.

History shows us that the availability of capital to innovative new firms from risk-taking investors can lead to whole new industries locating in specific areas. This is true for industries as diverse as tires in Akron, minicomputers in Boston, and tents in eastern Kentucky. Enterprising bankers, for example, played a key role in the location of the auto industry in Detroit and the tire industry in Akron. Differences in risk taking between financiers in New York and Boston as to which was willing to gamble in financing Western railroads finally gave New York the competitive edge in 1860 and 1870. More recently, a number of analysts feel the semiconductor industry located in the "Silicon Valley" of California because eager venture capitalists were ready and waiting to finance it in San Francisco and Palo Alto. More to our point, a dozen rapidly growing firms—a handful of which have national markets—now profitably flourish in the deeply distressed counties of eastern Kentucky because the Kentucky Highlands Investment Company (KHIC) is there to finance them. Several of KHIC's larger firms are now spinning off affiliates and markets for satellite firms. In each of these cases—from New York to San Jose to London, Kentucky—all the other necessary ingredients such as markets, labor, and land were present and the missing ingredient—capital to new, small firms—made all the difference.

The capital issue, therefore, for both the private market and government policy, is whether capital is *available* to profitable, growing, young, small firms. If not, how and when should government policy provide it?

There Is No Equity — or Long-Term Debt — for Young, Growing Firms

More often than not, small firms seeking financing from private capital markets find doors closed to them. Capital market failures and the constantly increasing concentration of assets in worldwide capital markets have tended to make capital availability much worse for small, young, growing profitable firms. Shocking as it may seem, it is not too strong to say that the poverty line in America begins at the level of $200 million in sales. Most major institutional investors today will not look at firms which are smaller than the threshold of $200 million in sales or $200 million in assets. This is in spite of recent evidence that the smallest manufacturing concerns, as a class, are more profitable than the largest multinationals.

Thus, we have major national problems in developing new industry, new products, and small industry *in any* location, let alone in those communities of greatest concern to us. As we have seen, firms as large as $50 to $100 million in sales still have difficulty raising equity or long-term debt for expansion capital. The problems in raising capital for profitable minority businesses and community enterprises, especially in declining neighborhoods, are even more extreme.

Far from the textbook ideal of organization and efficiency, the financing of most new enterprises is a hit-or-miss struggle against highly stacked odds. It is most often the owner's personal savings which provide the main source of start-up equity, supplemented perhaps with loans from friends and relatives, and maybe some limited indirect funds from commercial banks, venture capitalists, credit unions, finance and insurance companies (Fenstermaker, 1972).

The typical small venture will have more than a third of its capital in the form of debt—normally payable in the short or medium term (one to five years)—and virtually all as commercial bank loans rather than long-term bonds. This is because new and small enterprises generally face enormous barriers in acquiring funds in the long-term debt and equity markets—a difficulty that appears remarkably unjustified by differences in the rate of return and risk (Daniels and Kieschnick, 1978). At the same time, the 1976 report of the FTC notes that 76.1% of acquisitions were of companies with less than $1 million in assets, reflecting the paradox of very profitable firms which have no other way to obtain capital to grow. To grow, they had to be absorbed and cease to exist as an independent firm. We also know that when this happens, the absorbed firm tends to grow more slowly, generating fewer new jobs and less economic activity.

These trends of growing capital market imperfections and concentration of assets in a small number of very large financial institutions are powerful in equity and long-term debt markets, in private placements and publicly tended markets, in venture capital firms, investment banking houses, commercial banks, insurance companies, and institutional investors.

For example, in 1955, households owned 72.8% of all stock, but in 1976 they owned 53.8%—a decrease of 26%. In addition, the proportion of individual investors' assets held directly in equities dropped from 43.5% in 1965 to 26.7% in 1975. This increases market concentration, because there are now fewer investors, and risk aversion, as individual investors shift financial assets from equities to safer investments, such as fixed income securities. These increases in market concentration and risk aversion represent major obstacles to small firms in their search for capital.

Individual investors have left the equity market for two reasons. They want to avoid the risks they perceive in the stock market, and they feel they cannot compete with the institutional investors. Institutional investors have lower information and transaction costs because they have the advantage of research and lower commission rates. Loss of the individual investor is undesirable because it results in fewer investors to spread risk and places more importance on the investment decisions of the concentrated number of institutions.

Institutional investors have concentrated their investments in a small number of large stocks. Institutions limit the variety of their holdings because small companies cannot offer enough shares to interest them and because, as investment managers, they tend to act in unison so as to protect themselves from criticism. Institutions appear to statistically discriminate against small firms regardless of their profitability.

Currently, because of the investment decisions of individual and institutional investors, the new smaller companies have been cut off from much needed capital.

The increasing supply of funds to public capital markets through these large institutional financial intermediaries has had a serious impact on receptiveness of these markets to new and young companies. According to a report by the Small Business Administration (SBA) Task Force on Venture and Equity Capital, "It appears that the market value of a firm must be over $100 million to interest pension funds managers" (SBA, 1977).

Just as concentration on the supply side in public capital markets has produced problems for small and young businesses, so has concentration in the securities industry that serves as middleman in the flow of funds. Between 1965 and 1978, the number of brokerage houses fell from 646 to 505. This contraction has tended to be concentrated in those smaller "regional" or "specialty" houses which have historically been the principal source for underwriting the capital needs of young, small firms. Since 1973 the market share of the top 25 brokerage houses in terms of commission revenues has climbed from 37.5% to 57% (West, 1978). This bodes ill for smaller firms in several ways: Both the smaller regional houses and specialty or "boutique" houses often specialized in providing information to prospective investors. According to David Baker, an analyst at Drexel Burnham, approximately 500 companies have lost regular analysis and coverage by Wall Street researchers over the past two years. Smaller enterprises get dropped first because the smaller size of their bond and stock issues, combined with the biases of institutional investors, means the investment houses cannot make as much money making a market.

An equally serious manifestation of concentration in the securities industry is the absorption by giant brokerage houses of the smaller regional houses. These regional houses have historically had the best information available on regional companies since their principals often know regional company management and have followed those companies since birth. Securities and Exchange Commission (SEC) Chairman Harold Williams foresees the "danger that many regional brokerage firms which have historically served real purposes and helped smaller companies in their areas might disappear in great numbers" (*New York Times* 5/3/78).

On the other hand, the direct placement corporate bond market would appear to be more open than the public one to small- and medium-size enterprises. The average size of direct placements is one-third the average size of public offerings, and only about 20% of directly placed debt issues exceed $5 million (Brealy and Myers, 1979).

But the direct placement market imposes its own special burdens. Most important, from a public policy standpoint, is that while direct placement definitely serves a smaller size enterprise than the public bond market does, they are generally still fairly large companies. Many insurance companies will not give funds to an enterprise with less than $200 million in sales, at least 10 years of favorable operating experience, and a debt/equity ratio of no more than 0.6 (White and Light, 1979). This clearly excludes virtually 100% of those young, small firms which generate almost half of all new jobs and economic activity.

The enormous concentration and conservativeness of the life insurance industry is exemplified by John Hancock, a $15 million insurance company. In 1977, John Hancock invested $1 billion in the marketplace: Only 22 people worked on that portfolio. Those 22 money managers made only one loan to a firm with less than $100 million in sales—which also happened to control 65 percent of its world market in a market that cannot fail: the paper filing and storage business.

Corresponding to the direct placement market for debt dominated by insurance companies is a direct placement market for equity securities—the venture capital market.

Unfortunately, venture capital firms have been caught in the paradox that one of the major reasons it exists—the difficulty of small and young firms going public—is one of the main reasons it has trouble raising money from the directly placed equity it buys. Consequently, the direct placement equity market is not an adequate source of funds for small and young corporations. Its total assets have been estimated at only $1.7 billion (out of an entire capital market of several $1000 billions!) and annual investment at only slightly over $100 million. In 1975 only 5% of new investments went to start-ups of new enterprises and only 2% to first-round financings (SBA, 1977).

Generally, therefore, small and young corporations find themselves restricted to local banking markets to raise funds. For example, firms with total assets of $1 million or less receive about 90% of their loans from banks in the same SMSA (Griggs and Petty, 1970). These will tend to be smaller banks. A major reason for this is that the value of a loan to a small firm will not merit the requisite on-site inspection and negotiation on the part of more distant regional banks, nor does it merit the generalized publication of information about the business we also found absent in the public debt and equity markets. For local banks, however, the information and transaction costs are significantly less.

Unfortunately, local banking markets tend to be characterized by a high degree of concentration (Federal Reserve, 1978). In contrast, scores of large banks operating on an international, national, or regional scale compete quite aggressively among themselves, but only for those much larger firms which have lower information and transaction costs, and lower perceived risks.

Far more important is the effect of banking market concentration on the *availability* of capital. A large body of discussion and evidence has developed around the issue of *credit rationing* (Hodgeman, 1960; Jaffee, 1971; Baltensperger, 1978). Credit rationing occurs when loanable funds are allocated to borrowing firms not on the basis of the price they are willing and able to pay, but on the basis of the size of the loan and the risk of the borrower. Rationing mechanisms include the denial of loans, reduction in amount loaned, and reduction in maturity.

Market concentration also affects the risk-taking behavior of commercial banks to the detriment of small and young businesses. Gardner (1973) in a study of St. Louis, and Heggestad (1977) in a comparative analysis of several metropolitan areas, have found that banks in concentrated markets trade off potentially higher profits for reduced risk exposure. These urban studies are supported by evidence from rural isolated banking markets by Fraser and Rose (1972), Chandrose (1971), and McCall and Peterson (1977).

The Impact of Federal Policies on Capital

The growing imperfections and concentration of assets in capital markets is only made worse by current federal policy. Although these are often unintended secondary effects of well intended public policy, the cumulative effect of federal tax, expenditure, and regulatory policy is to reduce the availability of both equity and long-term debt to those small firms essential to job generation and economic development in low-income areas. Four striking examples involving the IRS, the SEC, and Employee Retirement Income Security Act

(ERISA) of 1974 show how well intentioned federal policy has cut off equity to small firms.

First, the Tax Reform Act of 1969 narrowed the gap between the tax rate on capital gains and on earned income. This was done to increase the horizontal and vertical equity of income taxation. Because capital gains and earned income are taxed differently, persons with the same real income can pay different taxes. Reducing this gap reduces this tax bill differential. Reducing the difference between tax rates also reduces the preferential treatment given to higher-income classes who benefit the most from reduced capital gains taxation. The gap between the tax rates for capital gains and earned income is intended to increase capital formation by rewarding risk takers. The Tax Reform Act of 1978 widens this gap to some extent (the top tax rate for capital gains is reduced from 36.5% to 28%), but not to the pre-1969 level (the maximum tax rate for capital gains was 25%). Reduction of the capital gains tax might especially help small companies that need equity capital. A capital gains tax reduction might be used to promote risk taking in small firms where equity capital is especially scarce. But it should be highly targeted to primary issues, and by size, and age of firm (which the 1981 reduction was not).

Second, since the advent of negotiated commission rates as required by the SEC on May 1, 1975, many financially stable brokerage houses have had to merge in order to raise capital they need to continue business. Mergers have significantly reduced the research capabilities of the brokerage industry because of both the cut of major research staff on Wall Street and the demise of many local brokerage houses who have traditionally provided the best information on regional companies. The resulting loss of research in effect has increased the information costs of following small and new companies which has hurt their equity capital raising abilities.

"May Day" has also increased transaction costs for individual investors who are much more inclined to take risk than institutions. The average retail commission rate has risen 20% since May 1975. On the other hand, institutional commission rates have fallen drastically.

Third, administrative costs in preparing a statement of registration under the Securities Act of 1933 may run from $50,000 to over $100,000. These costs of providing information and negotiating the transaction are in large part fixed; they do not vary much with the size of the issue. This means that the cost of raising a dollar in funds for a smaller and younger company, whose total debt or equity issue will be relatively small, will be greater than for a larger and more mature company which typically would be involved in a more sizable issue.

Finally, the powerful market forces which encourage pension fund managers to focus on the larger and more well-known enterprises seeking capital are intensified by their perception of legal responsibilities imposed by ERISA and other legislation. ERISA, as well as similar laws at the state and local level governing public pensions, was created to end unfair treatment of pension plan members and misuse of pension funds. Many observers believe, however, that these laws have also made pension fund managers excessively risk averse.

Small and young companies bear the brunt of intensified pension fund risk aversion since they tend to be the more risky investments. Nonetheless, a well diversified portfolio would hold shares in these firms and be rewarded with a higher rate of return. But if the "prudent man" rule is applied to each investment on its own, as a recent New York court ruling indicated, then pension fund managers cannot help but shy away from them. A survey conducted in July 1976 by the International Foundation of Employee Benefit Plans asked whether ERISA affected investment patterns. Of the respondents, 64% agreed either somewhat or strongly that "as a result of ERISA our trustees are less willing to invest in anything other than blue chip type investments" (SBA, 1977).

In Summary: Capital Markets and Development

Profitable, growing small firms are far too dependent on short-term bank credit and are virtually excluded from all long-term equity and debt markets. This is true both in public and private markets. Well-intended federal policies have further reduced the access of small businesses to capital by encouraging conservative investment patterns and by establishing expensive information and transaction requirements.

The Limited Role of the States

States can have very little impact on the creation of new economic activity. They do not create money, and they cannot impose tariff barriers. States have no control over the many macroeconomic factors that affect their competitive advantage. Once again, then, we must emphasize the limited ability of states to influence the development process: Regional policy efforts will be compromised, and even nullified, by international and national factors beyond their control.

Within these limitations, states can still design policies to encourage economic growth within their boundaries. Policy makers must first recognize that economic development is a long-term, comprehensive process that includes state tax, expenditure, and regulatory policy. Programs that exclusively focus on capital issues will not succeed without fully analyzing the positive and negative effects of personal *taxes*, infrastructure and education *expenditures*, and *regulations* that alter the location of markets and costs of production. More important, the traditional state economic development incentives of providing state corporate income and property tax subsidies have been shown to be relatively wasteful and ineffective methods for sponsoring development.

Given the constraints of markets, production costs, taxes, regulations, and expenditures, any state government can determine those key industries for which the state has a real comparative economic advantage. It is only within the context of a well-integrated economic development policy that policy makers can even begin to think about those limited uses of state intervention in capital markets which can, in fact, stimulate new economic activity.

Elements of a Comprehensive Development Strategy

When a state wishes to encourage economic development and small business formation, it has three strategies to choose from: chartering and regulation, economic incentives, and direct intervention. Each of the strategies increases the availability of capital by reducing the perceived level of risk or by reducing information and transaction costs. Regulation is the least costly and least risky; and intervention through the creation of new development finance intermediaries the most costly and risky.

Chartering and Regulation

As the charterer of state commercial banks, savings banks, savings and loan associations, insurance companies, and such public fiduciaries as state and local pension funds, the state can impose regulatory requirements which (a) increase or decrease the availability of capital to those financial institutions and/or (b) influence the nature of their investments. The state can regulate three aspects of financial institutions: liabilities (or sources of funds); assets (or uses of funds); and market structure (or entry and exit into the market).

Regulation can be passive in nature, consisting of bureaucratically administered rules, or active, involving the state directly in the pursuance of public purposes. Regulation can be negative, limiting the permissible uses of financial funds, or it can be positive, involving the state in helping to establish creative and flexible intermediaries or guiding them into innovative and useful forms of investments.

When correctly formulated, chartering and regulation allows the state to influence the cost and availability of capital while incurring only minimal costs. In the purest form of regulatory intervention, the state incurs only administrative costs. Several states have begun to move from passive–negative postures, whereby financial institutions are limited by bureaucratically administered rules, to active–positive regulatory efforts whereby the state acts as a "public entrepreneur" to harness the profit motive of the private sector to achieve designated public policy objectives. For a positive example of the use of regulation, consider the recent experience of Massachusetts and its $25 billion thrift industry. The state's list of legally acceptable thrift industry investments had been designed so that there was *only one* corporation headquartered in Massachusetts in which those $25 billion of assets could be invested. That firm was Gillette. A coalition of investment bankers, business owners, banking administrators, legislators, and savings bankers worked together to liberalize the investment list while still maintaining reasonable requirements. Now, every company in Massachusetts with over $25 million in sales is eligible for investment by the thrift industry if it meets a few simple criteria. The legal list of investments was immediately expanded to 30 Massachusetts based firms upon acceptance of the new regulations. It has been expanding ever since.

A second example of the use of regulation to encourage development can be found in the Massachusetts Capital Resource Corporation (MCRC). MCRC is a privately managed, publicly chartered investment company capitalized with $100 million in funds contributed by a consortium of eight life insurance companies headquartered in the state. The state agreed to reduce and restructure the tax liabilities of the insurance industry in return for the formation of the MCRC. The insurance industry agreed to lend MCRC funds to small businesses in accordance with carefully drawn state regulations.

Both of these models use capital market perfecting strategies to provide capital to small firms. The "legal list" is an example of a state removing well-intentioned but nonetheless unnecessarily conservatizing investment restrictions. MCRC minimizes individual investment risk by lending to a diversified group of businesses and then spreading the investment among the members of the consortium.

Economic Incentives

States can also use economic incentives to encourage financial intermediaries to channel funds to small businesses. The four most commonly used forms of economic incentives are interest subsidies, loan guarantees and credit insurance, secondary marketing techniques, and linked-deposit systems. Such strategies explicitly acknowledge the fact that pursuit of profit is the driving force in the private allocation of capital. Incentives aim to increase the marketability of riskier small business investments.

State development strategies have generally focused on *interest subsidies*. In most cases, however, subsidies are an inefficient and ineffective tool. Usually they

1. are too small to affect the profitability of smaller firms;
2. distort the market's decisionmaking process by either drawing otherwise profitable loans from the private sector or by allocating capital to otherwise unprofitable ventures; and
3. cost the state, in tax revenues, far more than the benefits they return.

State development planners offer *loan guarantees and credit insurance* to private lenders to induce them to lend to small businesses. Insurance is conceptually distinct from a guarantee. A guarantee exposes the state to an open-ended commitment to fund defaults. Insurance involves the purchase, by the borrower, of a premium which is used to make up a reserve fund. The reserve fund stands behind each loan in the pool but consists of a finite amount of money. An actuarially sound mortgage insurance fund is almost always preferable to an open-ended state guarantee—with insurance the state neither absorbs the risk nor funds the reserve from tax revenues.

The availability of a *secondary market* can drastically increase the availability of capital to potential borrowers and increase the lender's profitability.

Without a secondary market, an institution making a loan to a venture would normally hold that relatively illiquid loan as an asset. Its total ability to make loans would be diminished by the amount of capital it disbursed to that venture. With a secondary market, however, the institution could make that loan, and then sell the loan to an institutional investor. The lender is thus able to replace an illiquid asset (i.e., the loan) with a liquid asset (i.e., the cash it received from the sale of the loan). The lender can then make additional loans with the cash received from the sale, while the institutional investor obtains the illiquid asset which satisfies its investment needs.

Few states have attempted to use the incentive of a state-sponsored secondary market to induce fuller private market participation in their development. There are three possible roles that the state could play: one, as the broker who matches the lender and investor; two, as the lender who sells the loan; and/or three, as the investor who holds the loan.

Finally, *linked-deposit systems* have been established in several states as a means of influencing private market choices in the allocation of capital. With a linked-deposit system, a state government agrees to place its current account funds on deposit with a private financial institution in exchange for that private institution agreeing to make loans that fulfill publicly desired social or economic goals. In most states, linked-deposit systems have been relatively ineffective because the state's current accounts are too small to really influence the private institution's investment decision.

Direct Intervention

Finally, states can directly intervene in the financial marketplace through the creation of state development finance institutions. Such institutions often implement the previously discussed economic incentives. Further, they operate as publicly sponsored financial intermediaries by lending or investing in projects that do not have adequate access to *private* financial institutions. This last option is the most costly, risky, and aggressive form of economic intervention in the marketplace.

States have intervened to create both equity- and debt-providing public intermediaries. Currently, there are only four publicly chartered and capitalized equity institutions operating at the state level. Two of these are in Massachusetts: the Technology Development Corporation and the Community Development Finance Corporation. The two remaining institutions are the Connecticut Product Development Corporation and the Alaska Renewable Resources Corporation. All four of these institutions are charged with the general mandate of diversifying the economy of their respective states. Each, however, has different purposes, functions, and financial, legal, and management structures tailored to fulfill the specific needs of the state. The dearth of equity-providing development institutions in this country is in sharp contrast to European and Third World experience, where public equity institutions play an integral role in the development process.

Conversely, public debt institutions are present in almost every state. Public debt intermediaries are funded primarily in two ways. The first is tax financing, in which the intermediary receives funds directly from the state. These funds can then be used to leverage other state and federal funds. Because tax-financed institutions are funded independently of the private capital market, they are able to operate without the constraints that inhibit conventional lending. This freedom is balanced, however, by the conservatizing effect of financial dependence on annual appropriations from the state legislature. One of the largest tax-financed state lending programs is the Pennsylvania Industrial Development Authority.

The far more prevalent source of funds for public debt intermediaries is the sale of federally tax-exempt bonds to finance enterprise. Most states have established industrial development agencies authorized to issue revenue bonds. Tax-exempt revenue bonds capitalize on provisions of the federal tax code which allow states to confer their tax-exempt status on private financing efforts for rather broadly defined "public purposes." Industrial development has been found to fit this definition. Most states have been quick to capitalize on this incentive which occurs at the federal government's expense—and which is viewed as having no expense to the state.

Revenue bonds are secured by the lease payments in, or purchases of, developed land by the borrowing business. They are attractive to borrowers because their interest payments are significantly lower than taxable borrowings. Further, tax-exempt revenue bonds are attractive to investors in high marginal tax brackets because the tax-exempt interest compares quite favorably with taxable investments of similar risk.

Tax-exempt revenue bonds are susceptible to gross misuse. There are several problems. First, revenue bonds are basically a vehicle for subsidizing the cost of capital. As our previous discussion indicates, this reduction in the cost of capital is neither a very effective nor very efficient means of fostering development. Second, revenue bond use has hidden costs to the state. Because the demand for tax-exempt investment is limited, excessive issuing of revenue bonds can increase the interest that must be offered to attract sufficient buyers of the bond. Finally, because revenue bonds are secured by revenues from the borrowing enterprise, investors look beyond the issuing agency to evaluate the creditworthiness of the borrower. The conservative investment habits of individuals and institutions extends to their purchases of revenue bonds. Thus, tax-exempt revenue bonds offer capital at reduced rates to firms in which investors would normally be willing to invest. They seldom succeed in increasing the availability of capital to firms that find the private capital markets inaccessible.

An extreme example of the misuse of tax-exempt revenue bonds occurred in a small town in Valdez, Alaska, which coincidentally happens to be the end of a fairly big $10 billion pipeline. Six thousand people in Valdez floated a billion dollar bond issue in order to build a new port facility to get that oil from the pipeline to ships to market. It is obvious that if the oil companies could finance a $10 billion oil pipeline in the private capital markets—the largest single private financing in world history—they certainly could afford to finance privately a $1 billion terminal, especially if the terminal was essential to get the oil from the pipeline to market. The only reason for financing it through the municipal bond market was to receive a gift from the federal government—at the expense of taxpayers—of $50 million per year in interest subsidies.

Several techniques have been developed for solving these problems. Credit insurance (discussed earlier) places an actuarially sound reserve behind a bond, reducing the risk absorbed by the investor. A second innovation is the umbrella revenue bond.

Umbrella revenue bonds are a mechanism for increasing capital availability to firms normally excluded from private market financing. A pool of loans to several businesses is packaged into one revenue bond secured by the revenue stream and assets of each firm. Each borrower purchases mortgage insurance premiums to fund a reserve which stands behind each loan in the package, providing additional security to risk-averse lenders. The Connecticut Development Authority has been particularly successful in adapting the revenue bond mechanism to the needs of small business through such a program.

Recently, sentiment has increased among federal legislators to restrict the use of tax-exempt revenue bonds. In light of this, state planners might consider offering *taxable* bonds to support small business. These taxable bonds could be offered to institutional investors whose tax-exempt status makes tax-exempt bonds an unattractive investment. Since institutional earnings from all sources are tax-exempt, institutions prefer the higher yields of taxable investments. Taxable bonds, which pool loans to several businesses and reduce risk through the use of credit insurance and spreading techniques, would further increase the availability of capital to firms normally excluded from the private capital market.

Conclusion

The message of this chapter has been one of limits. We have made four important points.

Large businesses, the typical focus of most economic development programs, play a limited role in the development process. Small businesses, with their large capacity to generate jobs, innovate, and be profitable, are a more efficient target for public policies that attempt to stimulate economic growth.

Capital plays a limited role in the development process. Many other goods market factors—such as land, labor, energy, management, raw materials, and markets for the product—must be appropriately available to a business before capital can improve its viability.

Once a small business has solved its goods markets problems, the limited availability of equity and long-term debt capital threatens its very existence. Capital market failings and well-intended government regulations limit the accessibility of small enterprise to capital and challenges the ability of these otherwise profitable and productive firms to innovate and generate jobs and profits.

Goods and capital markets operate on a worldwide basis. Consequently, state and local development efforts have a limited ability to encourage economic growth that counteracts national and international trends. Well thought out economic development policies must attempt to build on the comparative economic advantage of a region to stimulate a diverse, growing economy.

The current debate over reindustrialization gives us an opportunity to present a concrete application of the many points discussed in this chapter. A wisely designed reindustrialization policy will focus on developing strong, new, viable sectors of our economy—not bailing out large, antiquated enterprise. This reindustrialization policy will also be designed to increase the availability of capital to small firms—and will deemphasize policies which attempt to decrease the cost of capital. Finally, a reindustrialization policy will be the stimulus for a stable, growing, diverse economy that capitalizes on the comparative economic advantages of this country.

Although it has not adopted a reindustrialization policy per se, the New England region accepted many of these points in its attempts to revitalize its economy. Over the last 15 years, New England has experienced the rapid decline of many of the industries that formed its economic base: shoes, textiles, and shipping. Generally, the region has suffered from

1. a declining role in international markets;
2. declining per capita income;
3. declining population;
4. increasing costs of production; and
5. a lack of natural resources, particularly energy resources.

When faced with its declining role in the international marketplace, New England, did not, however, shore up its declining industries. Rather, the region capitalized on its comparative economic advantage by supporting the growth of the high-technology industry. The region supported the development of small, new viable businesses rather than trying to lure large industrial firms to migrate to the area.

In many ways, the New England experience is a paradigm for this country's future. The United States is (and will be) suffering from these same problems: a declining role in world markets as compared to Japan, Germany, and perhaps even China, declining per capita income, population and energy resources, and increasing costs of production. While many may argue that these trends are the result of international events and cannot be reversed, it is clear that the United States could encourage a strong, stable, viable economy by capitalizing on its comparative economic advantage. When a reindustrialization policy is finally designed for this country, policy makers would be wise to adopt the principles presented in this chapter and follow the lead of New England.

Bibliography

Baltensperger, E. "Credit Rationing." *Journal of Money, Credit, and Banking*, May 1978.

Birch, D. "Regional Differences in Factor Costs: Labor, Land, Capital, and Transportation." Paper presented at a conference in Austin, Texas, September 1977.

Birch, D. "The Processes Causing Economic Change in Cities." Prepared for a Department of Commerce Roundtable on Business Retention and Expansion held February 22, 1978.

Birch, D. *The Job Generation Process.* MIT Program on Neighborhood and Regional Change, Cambridge, MA, 1979. Prepared for U.S. Department of Commerce, Economic Development Administration.

Brealy, R. and Myers, S. *Principles of Corporate Finance.* Unpublished manuscript (to be published by McGraw-Hill), 1980.

Chandrose, R. "Impact of New Bank Entry on Unit Banks in One-Bank Towns," 1971.

Chinitz, B. "Toward a National Urban Policy." Undated mimeograph.

Cornia, G., Testa, W., and Stocker, F. "Local Fiscal Incentives and Economic Development." Academy for Contemporary Problems, June 1978.

Daniels, B. and Kieschnick, M. Theory and Practice in the Design of Development Finance Institutions, 1978.

Daniels, B. and Kieschnick, M. Development Finance: A Primer for Policy Makers, Parts I, II, III. 1979.

Daniels, B. and Litvak, L. *Innovations in Development Finance.* Washington, DC: Council for State Planning Agencies, 1980.

Federal Trade Commission. Quarterly Financial Report. Washington, D.C., 1977.

Fenstermaker, V. "Sources of Equity Capital Used by New and Small Business Firms in Lousiana, Arkansas, Mississippi and Tennessee." Prepared for the Institute of Applied Business and Economic Research, University of North Carolina, under a grant from the Economic Development Administration, 1972.

Fraser, D. and Rose, P. "Bank Entry and Bank Performance." *Journal of Finance*, March 1972.

Gardner, C. "Banking Regulation and Urban Growth." The Rand Corporation, P-5057, July 1973.

Garn, H. and Ledebur, L. *The Small Business Sector in Economic Development.* Washington, D.C.: The Urban Institute, 1980.

Griggs, J. and Petty, W. Loan Practices of Commercial Banks and Economic Agglomeration. Economics Development Administration, September 1970.

Heggestad, A. "Market Structure, Risk and Profitability in Commercial Banking."*Journal of Finance*, September 1977.

Hodgman, D. "Credit Risk and Credit Rationing." *Quarterly Journal of Economics*, May 1960.

Jaffee, D. Credit Rationing and the Commercial Loan Market. Wiley, 1971.

Kieschnick, M. *Venture Capital and Urban-Development.* Washington, D.C.: Council of State Planning Agencies, 1979.

McCall, A. and Peterson, M. "The Impact of De Novo Commercial Bank Entry." *Journal of Finance*, December 1977.

Mullaney, T. "SEC's Fingers on Wall Street's Pulse." *New York Times*, May 3, 1978.

National Science Foundation. "Science Indicators," 1979.

76

Schmenner, R. "The Manufacturing Location Decision: Evidence from Cincinnati and New England." Economic Development Administration. U.S. Department of Commerce, March, 1978.

Statistical Abstract of the United States. Washington, D.C., 1974.

Statistical Abstract of the United States. Washington, D.C., 1977.

Steinnes, D. "Causality and Intraurban Location." *Journal of Urban Economics*, Vol. 4, no. 1, 1977.

Straszheim, M. "An Introduction and Overview of Regional Money Capital Markets." Economic Development Administration. U.S. Department of Commerce, 1969.

Talley, S. "Recent Trends in Local Banking Market Structure." Staff Economic Studies, Board of Governors of the Federal Reserve System, 1977.

U.S. Department of Commerce, Advisory Committee on Industrial Innovation. "The Effects of Domestic Policies of the Federal Government upon Innovation by Small Businesses." 1979.

U.S. Department of Commerce, Panel on Invention and Innovation. "Technological Innovation, Its Environment and Management." 1967.

U.S. Department of Commerce, Small Business Administration. Report of the SBA Task Force on Venture and Equity Capital for Small Business, #7. 1977.

Vaughan, R. *The Urban Impacts of Federal Policies*; Vol. 2, Economic Development. The Rand Corporation. R-2028-KF/RC, June 1977.

West, R. "Brokers' Fortune since 'May Day.'" *Wall Street Journal*, November 24, 1978.

Wheat, L. *Regional Growth and Industrial Location*. Lexington Books, 1973.

White, W. and Light, J. *The Financial System*. Homewood, IL: Richard D. Irwin, 1979.

IV

Capital Availability, Capital Cost, and Business Development in the Northeastern "Frostbelt" States

James M. Howell and Diane F. Fulman

The detailed findings of the survey discussed in this article were presented to the Economic Development Administration (EDA) as a source of new data on the pattern of spatial location, capital availability, and the asset structure and financing needs of business firms in the northeast.

Introduction

There has been considerable discussion during the past two decades concerning the issue of development banking. Demands have frequently been made calling for the creation of a new institution to satisfy a variety of perceived national or regional capital financing needs. Those who have argued for a new capital financing mechanism assume that gaps in capital markets—caused either by nonavailability or high cost—constitute one of the major impediments to the maintenance of a high growth rate in the national economy. Proponents of this view also maintain that a national development bank is needed to make economically distressed areas, where traditionally local financing sources have been inadequate, attractive to private investment.

Others have taken the position that there are far more compelling factors in business locational and spending decisions than capital availability/cost and, moreover, that financing can be obtained for any viable deal. The latter view is widely held within the banking community; namely, that all credit-worthy business deals receive financing and that only financially unsound firms are crowded out of capital markets.

This contemporary debate has had a major impact on national and regional economic policies, with policymakers receptive to the reasoning of development bank advocates. As a result, there have already been extensive changes in the development banking landscape (Vaughan, 1980). In effect a substantial number of mini-development banks have been created—public financing programs (or entities) that are designed to fill perceived capital gaps for business, especially in so-called distressed areas, which tend to be broadly defined. Indeed, at this writing there are now in operation at least 65 revolving loan funds funded through EDA Title IX and an additional 75 revolving funds financed through repayments from the Department of Housing and Urban Development's (HUD) Urban Development Action Grants (UDAG) program.* Yet, it is still unclear whether these and other financial mechanisms are filling verifiable gaps in existing financial markets rather than competing with the lending capacity of financial institutions.

In this paper, we address a number of issues affecting capital in the Northeast in the context of ongoing research undertaken by The First National Bank of Boston and the Council for Northeast Economic Action (CNEA). Over the past three years this research has centered on the capital needs of business firms, their locational preferences, and the relationship between these two issues. Essentially, the research addresses three fundamental questions:

Do specific capital market gaps exist, and if so, can they be empirically identified by credit type, industry, and location?

How important are the issues of capital availability and capital cost in the broader context of a firm's locational choices?

What role, if any, can a grant subsidy program play to encourage investment in distressed places?

We believe that these three questions constitute the critical cluster of issues to be addressed; consequently, we will devote the balance of the paper to providing at least preliminary answers to them.

Capital Gaps and the Operation of the Northeastern Capital Market

During the past year, the Council for Northeast Economic Action, in cooperation with The First National Bank of Boston, has been analyzing the results of a comprehensive survey of capital financing needs in the region.† While this analysis will continue for quite some time, we are now in a position to present some findings and conclusions.

*Urban Development Action Grants are discussed in Chapter XIII.
† This survey as well as the others referred to in this paper are described briefly in Appendix A of this chapter. Complete texts of the survey results are available from the Council for Northeast Economic Action, 100 Federal Street, Boston, Massachusetts, 02110. In this chapter, we have only completed the analysis of the Boston sample (the nine Northeastern states). Statistical tabulations are still underway for the remaining four regions surveyed.

Overall, the aggregate regional sample included 690 business firms representing both manufacturing and nonmanufacturing activity. The seven-page questionnaire contained 22 detailed questions concerning a wide range of capital financing and related issues. The purpose of this section is to briefly comment on the principal findings emerging from this study.

In this special survey, we sought to determine the extent to which there were unfilled gaps in short and long-term capital markets by measuring the demands for 14 different types of credits.* As a first approximation to describe the existence of these gaps we statistically identified those credits that satisfied two important criteria.

1. There was a strong capital market demand for the credit.
2. A high ratio of firms attempting to secure the credit were unable to obtain it.

We consider unmet credit demands as gaps only when the firms seeking the credit, but unable to obtain it, are financially viable. Here, "financially viable" is simply defined as a debt equity ratio greater than one.†

The capital gaps identified in our survey are shown in Table 1. Each dot represents a business credit demand that meets the two criteria cited above. The classification of credit demands is based on our professional judgement. None of the specific credit categories is deemed to be more important than any of the others.

Several observations emerge from the survey responses:

Unmistakably, three types of credit gaps dominate the unfilled capital demands—working capital, unsecured term credit 1–5 years, and secured term credit 6–10 years.

There seems to be a second tier of credit demand for which there is also a relatively strong unfilled demand—secured credit 1–5 years and, to a lesser extent, secured term over 10 years.

Finally, the demand for subordinated debt and equity capital does not show up as an unfilled need. To an undetermined extent, this may reflect the structuring of the questions on the sample survey itself. Specifically, we asked whether or not the firm attempted to obtain credit but found it either easy, difficult, or impossible to obtain. The capital gaps identified above only pertain to those firms that attempted to secure the credit but found it impossible to do so. The survey excluded certain firms; namely, firms with no recent experience with each of the credit categories, as well as those that

---

*One should bear in mind that there are always two sides to capital market issues: the unfilled demand for capital—which the survey attempted to measure—and supply side constraints (e.g., conservative lending practices regarding location and risk).

†The test of financial soundness was based on the capital structure of each of the firms. It was reasoned that if net worth were greater than the combined total short and long-term debt, the firm may be classed as financially sound. Clearly, we realize that other factors must be taken into consideration in judging the financial condition of a business firm. Managerial depth, cash flow, and market access for product are all important, but whenever the firm's net worth is considerably less than total debt, one must question the financial strength of the firm.

Table 1. Capital Gaps in the Northeast

Type of Credit	Manufacturing			Retail			Wholesale			Service		
	City	Sub.	Rur.	City	Sub.	Rur.	City	Sub.	Rur.	City	Sub.	Rur.
Short Term												
Working capital		○	○		○	○			○			○
Secured notes												
Unsecured notes												
Revolving debt												
Lease financing					○							
Intermediate Term												
Secured 1-5 years	○	○		○			○				○	
Unsecured 1-5 years	○				○			○	○	○		
Long Term												
Secured 6-10 years	○	○				○		○		○	○	○
Secured over 10 years			○			○			○		○	
Unsecured 6-10 years										○		
Unsecured over 10 years												
Subordinated convertible debt												
Preferred equity												
Common equity												

did not try to obtain the particular credit on the assumption that there was an extremely low likelihood of securing it. Subsequent surveys and analyses may well provide additional information on these firms.

Unquestionably, an important issue continues to be whether or not financially sound firms are demanding but unable to obtain these types of credit.* Although our analytical work is not yet complete, our survey clearly indicates that there are capital gaps among financially sound firms. Just how pervasive is this phenomenon—financially sound firms unable to obtain access to the credit markets? Our analysis supports the view approximately 0.5–3.0% of the total firms surveyed were in this position.† This conclusion is important in delimiting the magnitude of unfilled capital demand in the Northeast. Variations by credit type are noticeable, with the higher ratios most frequently associated with the unsecured credits. Shown in Table 2 are the preliminary estimates of capital gaps for financially viable firms in the Northeast by three most heavily demanded types of credit.

A number of conclusions may be derived from these data. First there are substantial differences in the frequency of demand for each type of credit. As expected, there is a strong demand for working capital (roughly one firm in two) but far fewer firms (approximately only one in eight) sought the intermediate 1–5 years, unsecured debt, and slightly more sought longer-term 6–10 years credit. Second, the success rate at which these credit demands were fulfilled in the money and capital markets also varies somewhat by type of credit. Here, two specific observations are helpful:

Note the generally high level of consistency. Businesses secured working capital in over 90% of the cases. This strongly suggests that the unmet capital market demand in this credit category is relatively small.

Note that only seven out of ten firms that attempted to obtain the intermediate unsecured credit were successful in obtaining it. This is important but not surprising for no other reason than the issue of debt collateralization.‡

*Another equally important issue, but one which was not addressed in the survey, relates to the equity capital needs of new business start–ups. Again, the nature of the survey was such that only businesses with a tract record in the lending market were included in the sample.

†One reaction to the size of these gaps may be that they are so small that financing them completely would be unlikely to have a significant impact on the economy. Nonetheless, it is important to keep matters in their proper statistical perspective. More specifically, a two percent unfinanced capital gap represents roughly 200,000 business firms, most of which are small and some of which have considerable inherent capacity to grow rapidly, creating substantial new job opportunities.

‡Unquestionably, one of the most important facilitating factors in any financial institution's credit decision is the availability of assets which can be claimed in the event that there is a failure to amortize the debt and/or bankruptcy. Indeed, unsecured long–term lending by banks and insurance companies is really the exception—not the rule. It is here that Federal/State chartered financing institutions can make a significant contribution to closing capital gaps; namely, in being willing to minimize the collateralization issue.

Table 2. Aggregate Ratios of Unfilled Capital Demand by Credit Type

	Working Capital	Unsecured 1-5 years	Secured 6-10 years
Total number of firms in sample	690	690	690
Total number of firms attempting to obtain credit	344 (50%)	84 (12%)	95 (14%)
Total number of firms that obtained credit	324 (94%)	59 (70%)	86 (91%)
Total number of firms unable to secure credit but were classed as financially sound	9 (1.3%)	14 (2.0%)	6 (0.8%)

Data at the level of aggregation which we have analyzed thus far are helpful for identifying capital gaps across the overall sample. However, a far more disaggregated analysis is needed to identify capital gaps by industry and by location. Accordingly, we undertook a highly disaggregated analysis of credit. The relevant statistical tabulations are shown in Table 3.

Again, a number of important statistical observations are evident.

First, it is obvious from these data that there are not substantial demands among the retail, wholesale, and service industries for working capital, unsecured debt (1–5 years), and secured debt (6–10 years). Specifically, note that among these sectors, credit demand, irrespective of location, falls within a very narrow range from a low of 0.1% (service and retail) to a high of 1.9% (retail). Furthermore, there appear to be no consistent industry location patterns. Finally, in 5 out of the 27 cases the survey showed no credit demand at all. In 16 our of the 27 cases all firms' credit demands were satisfied.

Second, it is equally obvious that the area of substantial unfulfilled credit activity is in the manufacturing sector.* The demand for working capital is the most actively sought credit among the three. At the same time, it is interesting to note the shifts in the demand for capital by credit type and location. Again, the highest ratios for firms unable to obtain credit were, as expected, concentrated in the unsecured credit type.

Third, there are generally stable patterns among the key credit demand ratios within the manufacturing sector. These patterns seem to suggest that there are stronger, yet unmet, capital financing needs among financially sound manufacturing firms in the central city vis-à-vis the suburbs and rural areas.

The final issue in the Capital Financing Survey that is relevant to this analysis relates to variations in capital market access with the size of the business firm.

*It should be noted that the strength of the manufacturing sector is especially important to local economies. Manufacturing offers a much higher wage base than service activity, thereby providing a more favorable income structure. Additionally, manufacturing companies are generally high value-added industries, producing a larger tax base vis-à-vis service firms or institutions.

Table 3. Unfilled Capital Market Demands by Credit Type

	Manufacturing			Retail			Wholesale			Service		
	City	Suburb	Rural	City	Suburb	Rural	City	Suburb	Rural	City	Suburb	Rural
I. Total Number of Firms Attempting to Obtain Credit [a]												
Working capital	12.9%	18.2%	9.2%	1.4%	1.9%	0.6%	1.4%	0.7%	0.2%	1.3%	1.0%	0.6%
Unsecured 1-5 years	3.3	4.3	2.1	0.5	0.4	0.1		0.7		0.3	0.1	
Secured 6-10 years	4.9	3.6	2.3		0.6	0.6	0.3	0.4		0.3	0.4	0.3
II. Total Number of Firms that Obtained Credit [b]												
Working Capital	93.3	94.4	93.7	100.0	100.0	75.0	100.0	100.0	100.0	100.0	85.7	100.0
Unsecured 1-5 years	69.6	60.0	80.0	100.0	100.0	100.0	100.0	80.2		100.0	100.0	
Secured 6-10 years	94.1	92.0	94.1	100.0	100.0	75.0	100.0	100.0		50.0	100.0	50.0
II. Total Number of Firms Attempting to Obtain Credit but Could Not Do So [b]												
Working Capital	6.7	5.5	6.3			25.0						
Unsecured 1-5 years	30.4	40.0	20.0					20.0			14.3	
Secured 6-10 years	5.9	8.0	5.9			25.0				50.0		50.0
IV. Total Number of Firms Unable to Secure Credit but Were Classed as Financially Sound [c]												
Working Capital	50.0	42.8	25.0			100.0						
Unsecured 1-5 years	71.4	50.0	33.3									
Secured 6-10 years	100.0		100.0			100.0						

[a] As percent of total sample
[b] As percent of total number of firms attempting to obtain credit
[c] As percent of total number of firms

In order to provide insight into this issue, we cross-tabulated the results by firm size and difficulty of obtaining capital. For the sample as a whole, the ratios in Table 4 are for secured and unsecured intermediate and long-term credits aggregated for all types of business in all locations.

These ratios demonstrate that the smaller the firm the greater the likelihood there will be difficulty in obtaining access to capital markets. Yet, it is often the highly leveraged small firm that has the greatest growth potential.

There are significant variations of employment and output among firms attempting to obtain access to capital markets, such that greater overall economic benefit is to be achieved by filling the capital gaps faced by small firms. Recent studies by the MIT Development Foundation and Data Resources Inc. provide ample empirical support to the view that the vast majority of new job creation consistently comes from the growth of the small high-technology related business firm [Flender & Morse (1975); Brinner (1978)]. Note that there is an important distinction between a small business per se and small high-technology related business firms. It is the firm in the latter category, especially during the highly leverage early growth phase, where marginal allocations of capital can produce extremely positive employment results. Finally, it must be recognized that not all small business firms grow up, so indiscriminant capital gap financing of all small businesses will not necessarily lead to widespread employment creation.

At the same time, it is important to recognize that the issue of the marginal productivity of capital and capital gaps is not limited to the technology-driven small business. If it were, matters of capital allocation to close gaps would be much more straightforward. There are many examples of lending situations where marginal increases in capital to close existing gaps can make a difference, even in low technology firms. This appears especially to be the case in central cities and rural areas confronted with limited investment opportunities. In these situations, capital allocation to close a gap may well be the only alternative to retain an existing business or to induce it to expand on its

Table 4.

Type of credit	Employment Size			All Firms In Sample (%)
	Less 25 (%)	25-49 (%)	50-99 (%)	
Secured debt capital Percent firms reporting impossible to obtain	25.4	17.1	5.4	8.8
Unsecured debt capital Percent firms reporting impossible to obtain	59.5	37.5	30.4	34.5

present site. In this sense, the marginal productivity of capital may be low per se, compared to the opportunity costs of investing elsewhere, but localized economic benefits may be quite significant.

This discussion of the marginal productivity of capital is important, but it necessarily must remain incomplete. Additional analysis must be undertaken in this area in order to provide urban and rural planners and developers with a more complete basis for understanding the opportunity cost tradeoffs inherent in funding capital gaps. To this end, additional empirical analysis is underway using the Council for Northeast Economic Action's Capital Financing Survey data to determine the capital–asset and capital–employment ratios of different kinds of business firms in different spatial locations.

We may summarize our analysis to this point by concluding that there are indeed empirically verifiable gaps in the region's capital markets. Our research reveals that the most sought-after, but generally most unavailable, type of financing is intermediate to long-term unsecured debt for small firms. Three to 5-year working capital is another major area of unfilled loan demand documented by our research. These gaps are concentrated in the manufacturing sector, and within this sector there appears to be noticeable differentiation by spatial location, with financially sound firms in central city locations having the most critical unmet gaps.

Capital Availability, Capital Cost, and a Firm's Locational Decision

Given the fact that there are identifiable capital gaps, a central policy issue that remains is whether filling these gaps is likely to make distressed areas more attractive as locational sites to business firms. On the basis of our research, it is our belief that capital availability and capital cost will, at best, have a marginal influence on business locational preferences. Detailed analyses of our Capital Financing Survey data provides support for this conclusion. It is evident from the survey results that the cost of capital is a relatively unimportant consideration in a firm's locational decision. In the Survey, the respondents were asked to rank 14 factors in terms of their overall impact on the business locational decision. This section offers summary comments from our analyses of this data.

Table 5 shows numerical ranking of the firms in the Boston sample (businesses in the nine northeastern states) in terms of an indicator of their financial soundness.* This is displayed for the aggregate sample as well as the small firms. The smaller the number, the higher the rank and the greater the significance attached to the factor as an influence in the locational decision.

*Financial soundness is defined here in a manner consistent to that in the preceding section. For details, see the footnote on page 79.

Table 5. We are interested in determining your attitudes about the following factors that impact on your business locational decision. (Rank 1 as most important; 14 as least.)

	Total Sample		Small Firms	
	Financially Sound	Financially Unsound	Financially Sound	Financially Unsound
Factors affecting product demand				
Access to market	4	4	2	2
Factors affecting labor input				
Labor availability	1	1	1	1
Cost of labor	2	2	3	3
Worker productivity	3	3	5	4
Factors affecting tax environment				
Personal taxes	9	12	9	9
Property taxes	5	7	4	6
Corporate taxes	6	6	6	13
Factors affecting governmental services				
Transportation system	7	8	7	10
State and municipal regulation	8	10	8	11
Crime control	13	13	13	12
Factors affecting capital financing				
Capital availability	12	5	11	5
Capital cost	11	9	12	8
Other factors				
Proximity to research	14	14	14	14
Quality of life	10	11	10	7

Careful analysis of these rankings reveals the following:

Labor availability, and its costs, and productivity, along with market access, are consistently singled out as the most significant determinants of location. These factors rank high irrespective of financial soundness and show no significant variations when small-sized firms are contrasted to the aggregate sample.

There are some minor variations across the four sample configurations, but issues in the tax cluster are rated about average in terms of their importance to business locational preferences. The lowest ranked issues are proximity to research, crime control, and, to a lesser extent, the quality of life.*

Quality of life designates community amenities, such as recreational, educational, and cultural facilities.

The most obvious swings across the sample categories, and of special interest to the issues being addressed in this paper, are the rather sharp differences in the importance accorded capital availability in making locational decisions. There is an a priori assumption in this study that a strong balance sheet means access to money and capital markets. For highly leveraged firms (both for the aggregate sample and for small firms alike) capital availability is accorded much greater importance, following closely behind the labor and market access clusters.

At this stage in our analysis, we may conclude that there is not a great deal of empirical evidence to support the view that capital availability and/or cost will have much, if anything, to do with a business firm's locational decision. Indeed, on the basis of the detailed analysis of the Northeast Capital Financing Survey, labor market and market access factors are overwhelmingly vital factors in the locational decision while capital cost is uniformly less significant even when variations by place, industry, and financial conditions are taken into account.

Admittedly, concern over the availability and cost of capital is a relative issue. Consequently, when interest rates accelerate to the point that they become a major factor in the cost–price structure of business, then capital subsidies through favorable financing terms may well become important, but to date there is simply inadequate empirical information on these shifts over the business cycle. When these surveys were carried out, interest rates were at far more manageable levels than they are at today.* Thus, interest rate subsidies could become more significant in locational preferences, especially for small firms which are highly leveraged and/or have cash flow problems.

This leads to our final question; namely, the relevance of a capital subsidy program to encourage investment in economically distressed places.

Capital Subsidies, Grant Programs, and Private Investment in Economically Distressed Places

In contrast to interest rate subsidies which provide marginal adjustments in the cost of capital, the impact of deeper capital subsidies on business locational decisions, such as those provided by grant programs, appears to be more important. Before we proceed with the analysis of this section, the concept of capital subsidy as provided by federal/state grant programs requires clarification.

In the remainder of this paper we use the phrase *capital subsidy* to refer to any government programs that lower the cost of doing business for private sector firms. Two specific examples will be helpful to develop an understanding of our usage of this concept. Urban Development Action Grants (UDAG) dramatically reduce the capital cost of a project, thereby permitting a capital

---

*From the period in which the survey was taken to the writing of this paper, the prime rate offered by most commercial banks increased from 12% to 20%.

expenditure to be funded that otherwise would be left outside traditionally functioning capital markets. Another example is the use of Community Development Block Grants (CDBG) funds to do site clearance and preparation and thereby facilitate a private sector capital expenditure in what otherwise would be an unattractive area for private investment.*

The critical point to keep in mind is that these federal/state grant programs, while representing a capital subsidy to business, act on a firm's balance sheet in direct and indirect ways. The UDAG example cited above impacts directly on the balance sheet, while the infrastructure preparation does not impact on the balance sheet in any way. But both impact in varying degrees on the cost of doing business.

The statistical evidence currently available to assess the impact of capital subsidies provided by grant programs is somewhat limited. This is not because such program subsidies have not been widely utilized. Rather it has to do with the nature and use of capital grants in the local development process and, in turn, their relationship to private capital formation.

Historically, federal grant subsidies, for instance, those provided by the Environmental Protection Agency (EPA) and the Economic Development Agency (EDA) as well as HUD's CDBG grants, have been mostly used in such a way that the public capital expenditure was not directly coupled to private sector investment. This was especially the case with EDA industrial park development and some HUD urban renewal programs. This absence of a clear linkage between public capital subsidies and private capital spending decisions has led some to believe that occurrences of these decisions, each type vis-à-vis the other, are more or less happenstance events. Yet selective use of grants can, and sometimes does, affect business locational decisions. Capital subsidies— either directly linked to a private investment project (such as UDAG) or indirectly leading private investment through infrastructure improvement (EDA Title IX)—can represent a significant portion of a total capital financing program. Deep subsidies, amounting to one-fourth to one-third of the overall cost of financing, can dramatically influence the cost of doing business in a particular location. This possibility places grant subsidies (and their accompanying leveraging capacity) into a category that is quite dissimilar from marginal cost adjustments through interest rate subsidies.

The CNEA's recently completed analysis of techniques to encourage private capital formation in older industrialized northern cities provides an important basis of support for these generalizations.† Increasingly, our experiences in northern cities are leading us to the conclusion that deep capital subsidies through the use of grants to assist financially viable firms offer an important

---

*Urban Development Action Grants, are discussed in Chapter XIII; Community Development Block Grants are discussed in Chapter XI. Both are administered by the U.S. Department of Housing and Urban Development (HUD).

†For specific details of this survey, see Appendix A.

technique to create job opportunities in economically distressed places where the market allocations in the capital market are inadequate to achieve desired employment levels.* In the CNEA 11-city project, the programmatic utilization of capital grants was analyzed in detail.

Specifically, we were interested in the extent to which private investment in 233 central city projects or deals involved the use of federal discretionary grant programs.† The analysis determined that there were 41 specific instances of indirect grants leveraging, 25 utilizing HUD programs, and 10 utilizing EDA programs. Overall, the utilization rates of 19 federal programs, representing four departments and three independent agencies were analyzed.‡ The specific grant usage rates for these programs and agencies are shown in Table 6.

The functional or operational usage of these federal capital grant programs is also of interest. Although the 41 cases of indirect leveraging related to five important types of infrastructure-related business problems, the most commonly cited use involved land clearance/site preparation. Specific uses are listed in Table 7.

The dominance of land clearance and site preparation reflects this chapter's focus on the leveraging of private investment in older Northeastern industrial cities. All 11 cities are of a relatively small geographical size, facing problems of downtown congestion and tightly drawn jurisdictional boundaries with their contiguous suburbs. Under these circumstances, a very important (in some cases, the only) technique to stimulate downtown private investment is site clearance for new commercial or industrial construction.

Clearly, additional work needs to be undertaken in the area of leveraging, especially expanding the composition of the city sample to include suburban and rural areas. Presumably, this would change the character of capital leveraging, but land clearance/site preparation still remains vitally important to "land-poor" cities. We may conclude that capital grants may be effectively used to stimulate and to retain private investment in economically distressed areas.§ Furthermore, grants are suited to play this role within the context of existing capital markets because they complement private sector financing, and they represent a deep subsidy in overall capital cost.

*For the purpose of this analysis we refer to these deep capital subsidies as indirect leveraging (i.e., the programming of public funds to provide infrastructure and investment related support). Direct leveraging, which is not analyzed in this section, refers to government funding that is part of an investment financing package.

†All the cities except Stamford, Connecticut were "distressed" cities according to then-current criteria.

‡These 19 programs were selected because of their impact on subnational economic development. For an elaboration of this point, see Wise (1976).

§The cost of doing business in economically distressed older central cities is 20–30% greater than in contiguous suburbs and rural areas. Part of this differential may be explained by infrastructure bottlenecks—inadequate building sites, transportation congestion, and worn-out waste–water treatment facilities are just a few of the impediments to investment. Capital grant subsidies are ideally suited to address these issues, and this at least partly explains why the UDAG grant program has been so successful in encouraging private investment in Northern cities.

Table 6.

Department/Agency	Number of Grant Programs Analyzed	Number of Times the Grant Program Was Utilized to Influence Business Locational Decisions
CETA	1	2
HUD	3	25
DOT	3	1
EPA	5	3
CSA	1	
EDA	3	10
USDA	3	
Total:	19	41

There is another dimension to the CNEA study that should also be mentioned. This pertains to the extent to which firms tend to expand at their existing site and/or relocate all or part of their operations within the state or region. We asked specific questions about this of the 233 firms in the CNEA study. Data on the relevant responses are shown in Table 8.

To the extent that these data are representative, and we believe that they are, they support the view that the most commonplace experience is expansion of existing facilities at the existing plant location. Two out of three investments are in this category. This indicates that capital subsidies should be concentrated on the retention of existing business firms.

Analytical Comments About Capital Availability, Interest Subsidies, and Locational Preferences

In this paper, we have discussed a number of factors that affect the functioning of capital markets and business locational decisions in the Northeast states. As is always the case in analyses of this nature, these factors—capital availability, interest subsidies, and site preference—are discussed as if they are discrete

Table 7.   Indirect Leveraging to Stimulate Business Investment

Business Problems	Number of Occurrences
Land clearance/site preparation	25
Sewer infrastructure improvements	4
Transportation access	2
Water pollution control	2
Other purposes	8

forces. For instance, for the purpose of analysis, we have assumed that the specific impact of an interest subsidy on plant location can be judged independently of the issue of capital availability. In the real world, matters cannot, of course, be so neatly compartmentalized.

The point here is that any capital financing package involves the interaction of a number of factors, and it is impossible to determine which one was singularly responsible for making the deal go. The importance of capital availability, financing terms, size of loan, and interest rates vary substantially with the size of a firm, its sector (manufacturing vis-à-vis service industry) and its financial viability. None alone is likely to dominate a business firm's locational decision, certainly not a decision to relocate a firm's operations. This will most likely be determined by the primary, or dominant, factors influencing locational decisions—labor market conditions, product market access, and property taxes, especially in central cities. These factors are of the utmost importance; indeed, their significance is of such magnitude that in the vast majority of cases, they are not likely to be offset by capital subsidies. Nonetheless, in a significant minority of cases, the depth of capital subsidy can make a difference in expansion and location decisions.

At this point, it is worth recalling that roughly two out of three private capital spending decisions represent expansions at existing locations. Thus, it would appear that capital subsidies, especially those that affect availability, can, and should, play a role in the retention and expansion of business at their present locations, especially in distressed areas.

Policy Implications

In reality, there is a broad spectrum of capital programming already in existence at all levels of government. However, many of these programs are launched without a financial analysis of business credit needs. Consequently, such programs may not be designed to meet unfilled capital market demands. The creation of capital financing programs in this manner represents a glaring "cart before the horse" government policy effort.

In the preceding analyses, we have demonstrated that capital gaps exist in short and long-term credit markets among what must be considered financially

Table 8. Characteristics of the Private Investment

Expansion of existing facilities	152
Relocation of operations from:	57
Within city (33)	
Within state (10)	
Within region (14)	
Not classified	24
Total:	233

viable firms as indicated by conservative debt-to-equity ratios. In addition, we have concluded in work for HUD that deep capital grants can dramatically influence the cost of doing business and, thereby, encourage firms to stay or expand in distressed areas.

Our findings suggest that, in the future, public officials designing and/or operating capital financing programs ought to focus their efforts in the following areas:

Producing a better match between credit opportunities available through their programs and the legitimate financing needs of businesses in the region. As a first step, a systematic analysis of the credit needs of businesses in each program's jurisdictional area should be undertaken. When completed, the CNEA Capital Financing Survey is an important step along the way, but clearly much more work needs to be done.

Targeting to firms with less than 25 employees. As our Capital Financing Survey revealed, a considerably larger percentage of small firms than medium and larger firms had unmet capital needs—for secured and unsecured intermediate and long-term credits, in particular. Moreover, as stated earlier, it is the rapid growth of small firms, especially in technology-related fields, that tends to contribute disproportionately to local job generation.

Singling out the manufacturing sector for special consideration. There are at least three reasons for doing so. First, it is the manufacturing sector that appears to experience the most difficulty in accessing certain segments of the capital market. Second, it is this sector that is most mobile. Third, the viability of the manufacturing sector is especially important to local economics, in terms of its more favorable income structure.

Emphasizing the retention (through in-site expansion) of existing business firms at their current operating sites. As we have seen, roughly two-thirds of all business capital investments fall into this category.

Involving the private sector in the operation of capital programs. The ultimate test of any kind of capital financing program must be its acceptance in the private capital financing sector. Unless the capital program is designed in such a way so as to fit into existing financing practices, it will most likely go underutilized. Thus, a role for bankers in program operation will help assure that the loan terms are consistent with private sector needs and capital market realities. Bankers can be involved in a variety of ways, although participation in loan review boards would assure an optimum use of their credit analysis skills and financial experience.

Working through local intermediaries with capital analysis and financing experience if the program is based at the federal or state levels. A local development corporation may well provide the most appropriate institutional structure to either deliver the capital program at the community level, or assist in packaging local business applications for loans. The weight of evidence for this view comes from the more than 150 revolving loan funds now in existence.*

Training program staff to improve loan and capital finance packaging. Our research showed that the possibilities for innovatively packaging capital assistance are substantial. One area that merits further consideration is the design of special bank/insurance credit and loan training programs for state and municipal employees involved in development finance programs. This may offer an expanded role for credit and loan training programs now operational at large regional banks as well as established business schools.

Finally, one policy issue requires brief elaboration: the extent to which public and private capital ought to be commingled. The relevance of this issue can be easily seen if we use an "orange box/apple box" analogy. The traditional view of the private financial sector is that public capital programs should not be indiscriminately mixed with private capital (i.e., the program should resemble an orange box with distinct compartments, one for public capital and one for private capital). Others generally prefer an "apple box" with no dividers, implying a commingling of public and private capital. While the ultimate resolution of this issue is far from clear, the dynamic of capital subsidy programming is pushing us into an "apple box" world. Whether this is the proper programming method is still a matter of some debate.

Turning to the research implications of our work, it is clear that research on capital market issues should be carried out on an ongoing basis, rather than as a special one-time analysis. Regular surveys on unmet capital needs should be undertaken, taking into account such factors as industry type, firm size, and location.

Moreover, additional research is needed which would differentiate between short-term credit gaps over the course of the business cycle, vis-à-vis long-term secular gaps. The identification of the same capital gaps in two radically different types of economic environments would confirm the existence of structural capital access problems requiring highly targeted programmatic solutions. To this end, it is interesting to note the strong parallelism in the conclusions reached in the CNEA Capital Financing Study and those in the T.A. Associates Capital Gap Study undertaken in 1975.† Both studies confirmed the existence of intermediate- to long-term unsecured lending as a capital gap.

Looking ahead to the 1980s, it would be misleading to assume that if we alleviate the remaining capital constraints we will unleash substantial economic growth and prosperity in the Northeast: That is simply not true. On the other hand, there is a potentially important role for development finance programs if

*See National Council for Urban Economic Development, *Using Revolving Loan Funds for Development*.

†See T.A. Associates, *Verification of Capital Gaps in New England*.

they are targeted to the unmet capital needs of business firms. Our research strongly suggests that this is clearly the time to closely scrutinize programs that already exist and determine how they can be used more productively to mobilize capital for the region's economic development.

Appendix A

The Council for Northeast Economic Action Capital Financing Survey (1979)

This special survey represents one of the most comprehensive investigations of capital financing needs of business ever undertaken. The programmatic conceptualization of the survey was designed by the CNEA with the survey assistance of The First National Bank of Boston, Continental Illinois National Bank, First Minneapolis National Bank, Mercantile Trust of St. Louis, and United Colorado Bank.

The sample was derived through a mail-out/mail-back survey beginning in the fall of 1979, running through the early winter of 1980. Although the final national sample configuration is not yet completely known, it will most likely represent 5000 responses from the five bank marketing areas, disaggregated by industry (manufacturing, retail, wholesale, and service), and by location (central, city, suburb, and rural). Sampling details permit additional analysis by financial soundness of firm and by size (either determined by employment or net worth).

The Northeastern regional sample includes 690 firms with the characteristics shown in Table 9.

The Council staff is now in the process of analyzing this important body of data on capital financing needs. It is anticipated that special reports/analyses will be periodically released over the coming year as new findings are completed.

Table 9. Characteristics of the Northeast Region Sample

	Firm Size by Location							
Firm Size	Total Sample		Central City		Suburb		Rural	
1-24	207	30.0%	65	30.2%	96	34.0%	36	23.8%
25-49	105	15.2	31	14.4	41	14.5	25	16.4
50-99	89	12.9	32	14.9	27	9.5	25	16.4
100-199	79	11.4	27	12.6	31	11.0	18	11.8
200-499	85	12.3	28	13.0	32	11.3	22	14.5
500-1000	42	6.1	12	5.6	17	6.0	9	5.9
Over 1000	66	9.6	16	7.4	30	10.6	12	7.9
Not input	17	2.5	4	1.9	9	3.1	5	3.3
Total	690	100.0%	215	100.0%	283	100.0%	152	100.0%

Table 10. Employment and Industry Characteristics of the Sample

Firm Size (Employment)	Manufacturing	Retail	Wholesale	Service	Totals
1- 24	9	1	5	8	23
25- 49	17	4	6	1	28
50- 99	31	3	6	10	50
100- 199	35	3	1	2	41
200- 499	20		1	4	25
500-1000	9	1	1	8	19
Over 1000	19		1	11	31
Not Classified	7	1	2	6	16
Total	147	13	23	50	233

Building Local Capacity to Leverage Private Investment (1980)

This investigation involved the detailed analysis of the sources of long-term capital financing for 233 private investments in 11 older, industrialized cities over the 5 year period ending in 1979, and determination of the extent to which state and federal discretionary grant funds were utilized in the private investment package. The characteristics of the sample are shown in Table 10.

The investigation was undertaken by the CNEA and funded by a grant from HUD. The 11 New England cities selected for intensive capital financing analysis were: Portland, Maine; Burlington, Vermont; Nashua, New Hampshire; Lowell, New Bedford, and Springfield, Massachusetts; Hartford, Stamford, New Britain, and Danbury, Connecticut; and Woonsocket, Rhode Island. The final results of this analysis are to be published in a Technical Report by the Council. Copies may be obtained by contacting the Council or HUD.

Bibliography

Brinner, Roger E., *Technology, Labor, and Economic Potential.* Data Resources, Inc., 1978.

"Capital Formation," Hearing before the Joint Economic Committee, U.S. Congress, June 9, 1976.

Evans, Michael K. "Long Term Forecast: The Next Ten Years, Inflation, Recession and Capital Shortage." Chase Econometric Associates, Inc., 1975.

Flender, John O. and Richard S. Morse, *The Role of New Technical Enterprise in the U.S. Economy.* M.I.T. Development Foundation Inc., 1975.

Hansen, Derek, *Banking and The Financing of Small Business.* December, 1979.

Hovey, Harold A., *Development Financing for Distressed Areas.* Washington, D.C.: Northeast Midwest Institute, June, 1979.

Jack Faucett Associates, Inc., *Effectiveness of Financial Incentives on Investment in the Economic Development Administration Designated Areas.* Prepared for the Economic Development Administration, Department of Commerce, June, 1976.

National Association of Securities Dealers, Inc., *Small Business Financing: The Current Environment and Suggestions for Improvement.* Washington, D.C., May, 1979.

Option Paper on Capital Formation and Retention, The White House Conference on Small Business, 1979.

T.A. Associates, *Verification of Capital Gaps in New England*, prepared for the New England Regional Commission, Boston, 1976.

Vaughan, Roger J., *Capital Needs of the Business Sector and the Future Economy of the City*. March, 1980.

Wheat, L., Regional Growth and Industrial Location, Lexington Books, 1973.

Wise, Harold F., *Conflicts in Federal Subnational Development Programs: An Analysis of Recommendations*, U.S. Department of Commerce, Economic Development Administration, 1976.

V

The Role of Capital in the Rise of the Sunbelt

E. Evan Brunson* and Bernard L. Weinstein†

Introduction

Assessing the role of capital in the rise of the Sunbelt‡ is similar to analyzing the regional impact of climate. Almost everyone agrees that climate and capital investment have been major contributing factors to the rapid postwar economic growth in the southern United States. Like climate, the role of capital in the rise of the Sunbelt has been inadvertent, a product of natural forces largely outside the control of large private or public institutions. Just as people have migrated to the Sunbelt seeking a milder climate, capital has flowed to the Sunbelt seeking its greatest prospective return.

While capital and climate have played major roles in the rise of the Sunbelt, the regional impacts of both are difficult to quantify, much less control. In undertaking this overview of the role of capital, it is our intuitive notion that, unlike climate, the role of capital in the economic development of the Sunbelt has not been different from its role in the development of any other region.

A review of the South's economic history since the Civil War suggests that "mobilizing capital" to finance the region's economic development has not been an issue. Indeed, the verb *mobilize* implies concerted action, (i.e., putting financial resources into movement or circulation, assembling, or making ready

*Director of Intergovernmental Affairs, Southern Growth Policies Board, Research Triangle Park, North Carolina.
†Professor of Economics and Political Economy, University of Texas at Dallas, Richardson, Texas.
‡*Note*: The focus of this paper is on the 14 southern states: Virginia, West Virginia, Kentucky, North Carolina, South Carolina, Georgia, Florida, Alabama, Mississippi, Louisiana, Arkansas, Texas, Oklahoma, and Tennessee.

for use). Mobilization does not imply spontaneity. Instead, it suggests a plan—the deliberate formulation and execution of a coordinated strategy, conceptualized and implemented by powerful public and private institutions.

The course of economic development in the South—in fact, in the entire Sunbelt over the past 40 years—does not support the notion that there has been a deliberate mobilization of investment capital. Instead, the Sunbelt's growth is primarily the result of economic fundamentals—of market forces that have been profoundly influenced by a series of seemingly unrelated factors. In short, the rise of the Sunbelt represents a reaffirmation of the marketplace. Capital has flowed to the region in search of high returns. As economic, demographic, and natural forces generated regional growth, a self-sustaining momentum was created, spurring new investment from within the region while accelerating investment from outside the region.

Of course, the invisible hand of the marketplace has not been the *sole* force in the rise of the Sunbelt. Since the Civil War, initiatives by both individuals and institutions have had an impact in mobilizing investment capital for southern economic development. However, economic fundamentals influenced by market conditions have been largely responsible for the success or failure of these initiatives.

An Historical Perspective

Proponents of an industrialized "New South" made a concerted attempt to mobilize investment capital for industrialization shortly after the Civil War. Such regional leaders as Henry Grady, editor of the *Atlanta Constitution*, not only called on southerners to become industrial entrepreneurs, they also urged capitalists from the industrial North to send their money South to invest in the region (Hackney, 1979). To attract this outside capital, Grady and others called on the South to create the conditions necessary to interest industrialists from the North. As Sheldon Hackney, President of Tulane University, recently noted, "industrialization became a veritable crusade in the 1880s" in the South.

While some outside investment occurred in the South between the late 1800s and the depression, the "New South's" early industrial promoters were largely unsuccessful. By 1930, the South was still dominated by agriculture. Where industrialization occurred, it was usually low-wage, low value-added industries that prospered where natural resources were abundant and labor was cheap. But in general, conditions were not favorable for the mobilization of capital to finance southern economic development between the Civil War and the Great Depression.

Subsequent attempts to encourage economic development in the impoverished South were more successful. The New Deal programs of the 1930s, particularly the Tennessee Valley Authority (TVA), pumped sizable sums of public capital into the South. However, it was not until the 1950s and 1960s, when market conditions were more favorable for southern economic growth, that the South began to reap the benefits from the large federal investments.

World War II, and the postwar increase in peacetime military spending, provided the initial stimulus for the rise of the Sunbelt. Hackney points out that "the South was launched on the road to economic modernization not by the self-conscious design of regional prophets, but by World War II" (Hackney, 1979). Some economists, most notably Donald Ratajczak of Georgia State University, contend that postwar federal military and space expenditures were the single most important catalyst to the Sunbelt's now booming economy. Here again, capital was mobilized not for regional economic development per se, but for the arms and space races. Regional development was an incidental side affect of the emergency of national defense policies.

The forces of change that began transforming the South and other parts of the Sunbelt accelerated slowly in the 1950s and 1960s. While some point to massive federal military, and later space, expenditures, a less visible phenomenon was to have a profound impact on the southern economy—the mechanization of agriculture. The results of mechanization are well chronicled— urbanization, the massive emigration of the rural poor, unemployment, and underemployment throughout the rural South.

The forces causing the vast dislocation of agricultural workers and small farmers in the South also contributed substantially to the economic maturation of the region. Mechanization of agriculture provided the labor force of the South's postwar industrialization. In addition to a massive outmigration from the region during and after the War, more than 3 million southern farm workers were absorbed by other employment sectors from 1940 to 1975 (Hodges, 1976).

Manufacturing provided the region's economy with a relief valve. The burgeoning rural labor surplus was absorbed by low-wage, labor-intensive industry—textiles, apparel, furniture, food processing, lumber, and wood products among others. Much of this new industrial growth stemmed from northern-based industry investing in the South to take advantage of low-cost, unskilled labor. By 1958, manufacturing had displaced agriculture as the leading employment sector of the southern economy. In the same year, McGraw-Hill estimated that the South received 60% of all U.S. capital investment (*South Magazine*, 1980).

By 1970, these seemingly unrelated events—World War II, the mechanization of agriculture, and the postwar shift in patterns of federal military and space spending—had propelled the region into a sustained growth phase and spawned the popular notion of a thriving and vibrant Sunbelt region stretching from Virginia to California along the nation's southern rim.

By the 1970s other forces were also contributing to the rising prosperity of the Sunbelt. Most notable was the dramatic population growth. Between 1970 and 1979, the 14 southern states had an estimated population increase of 8.6 million, or 14.9%. This accounted for over 51% of the total estimated U.S.

population increase during the 1970s. While the South experienced a birth rate higher than the national average, a phenomenal net immigration boosted the region's overall population growth. The Census Bureau estimates that the 14 southern states had a *net* immigration of almost 4.3 million persons from 1970 to 1979, accounting for almost half (49%) of the region's total population increase (U.S. Bureau of the Census, 1980).

Rapid population growth coupled with rising personal incomes created a vast new market for American business and industry, and spurred massive capital investment in new industry as well as in new housing and nonresidential construction. The following excerpt from an essay on southern economic growth published by the Federal Reserve Bank of Atlanta (1961) describes the dynamic nature of the growth of southern markets:

> To meet these new demands [for goods and services], retail establishments added more workers; some of them refurbished and enlarged their stores. National chains, always on the lookout for new opportunities to sell, opened outlets in the area [southeast], sales managers of firms with nationwide distribution, after seeing rising sales curves for their southern territories, found it worthwhile to establish distribution centers and area offices and to send experienced personnel from other parts of the county into the South. Some manufacturers, who had formerly met the demands for their products exclusively from factories outside the South, opened branch plants to supply the southern market. Bankers found the new high incomes of southern consumers a sound basis for increased consumer credit.

Rising personal incomes during the 1970s brought diversification to the economic base. As Donald Ratajczak has noted, beginning in the early 1970s, people moved South in search of increased opportunities while jobs followed the moving work forces (Atlanta Constitution, 1976). This massive growth of population and jobs could not have been sustained without a corresponding investment of private capital, much of which came from outside the region.

Other emerging forces supported this trend. The migration of retirees to the South not only contributed to the growth of housing and consumer markets, but brought a substantial transfer of savings and retirement income to be spent and invested in the region. The explosion of federal transfer payments in the 1970s, including social security, also contributed substantially to personal income growth in the Sunbelt. Finally, the energy shortages of the 1970s and the resultant increases in energy prices added new momentum to economic growth in parts of the Sunbelt. Texas, Oklahoma, and Louisiana gained billions of dollars in new capital investment for exploration, marketing, and distribution of petroleum products. Investment in industries that service oil and gas production also surged.

The Public Sector Impetus

While fundamental economic and demographic forces have been primarily responsible for the surge of capital investment in the Sunbelt, the public sector's role has not been inconsequential. In addition to the inadvertent regional impacts of military and space expenditures, and the massive flow of federal dollars to Sunbelt residents through transfer payments, federal public works and economic development funds have helped fuel the region's growth. The completion of the Interstate highway system has had a major impact on the industrialization of the South, particularly for the location of new branch plants in the region's smaller cities, towns, and rural areas. Federal funds from the Economic Development Administration (EDA) have financed the development of major industrial parks in the region's smaller and poorer communities, while federal grants and loans for water, sewer, and waste treatment systems have also facilitated growth. Federal investments for waterway development have spurred economic growth along the Tennessee, Arkansas, and Mississippi Rivers.

Southern state governments have typically taken an aggressive posture in promoting private capital investment. Almost all are considered by industrial location specialists to have a favorable business climate for private investment. State and local governments offer a plethora of inducements to encourage investment in new industry and expansion of existing business and industry. These inducements include tax exempt industrial development bonds, and a variety of state tax exemptions and reductions on land, machinery, buildings, inventories, and pollution control equipment. In many instances, state and local governments have provided new industry with services such as water and sewer, utility hookups, or access roads at zero or reduced costs.

An almost universal conclusion of research on the locational impacts of specific state and local tax incentives is that only in a few instances do they appreciably affect business location decisions (Advisory Commission on Intergovernmental Relations). This is especially evident when the broad regional implications of location decisions are analyzed.

There is other evidence, however, that the overall tax climate in the Sunbelt states has had more of an impact on investment decisions than specific locational incentives, especially when contrasted with high tax burdens imposed on business and high income families in many northern states. In particular, the level of personal and corporate income taxes in the southern states is thought to have a substantial but indirect impact on the overall cost of doing business. High personal taxes are often seen as an impediment to business growth since they force up salaries of executive, managerial, and technical personnel. In addition, the state–local tax structure in the South creates a subjective impression of a favorable business climate and thus influences investment and locational decisions. In short, the level of state–local taxes may be viewed as a barometer of the business climate, and thus can tip the scales one way or the other for a firm seeking a new location (Weinstein, 1978).

Both personal income and property tax levels in the southern states are generally ranked among the lowest of the 50 states. Many believe that economic gains in the South are directly related to these low taxes. Low tax burdens, coupled with fiscal conservatism and an official concern with economic and business development, have all played a role in attracting capital investment to the region. This pro-business climate has complimented and reinforced market forces, thus providing added impetus to the rapid economic growth throughout the region.

Business and Industrial Investment

The preceding review of southern economic growth suggests that capital has been readily available to accommodate the investment needs of the expanding southern economy. Market forces have allocated sufficient capital to finance growth. In the words of John M. Morris, a spokesman for the trust and investment division of Morgan Guaranty Trust Company of New York, "investment decisions are not geographical, we don't take that into account. We look for financial return" (*New York Times*, 1980).

Other studies have concluded that capital is a relatively insignificant factor in location decisions. Total annual capital costs generally range from 6–10% of the total value of sales in manufacturing. What's more, data on interregional differences in capital costs indicate that the differences are quite small, with interest rates for the average business loan varying by less than 1% between the North and South. One percentage of a point of a factor that accounts for only 6–10% of the costs of doing business is obviously not a deciding factor in regional location decisions (Daniels & Kieschnick, 1979). (For more on capital cost as a location factor, see Chapter IV.)

Historically, the most dynamic investment sector in the southern economy has been industry, and much of the region's industrial growth has been financed by capital from outside the region. These inflows of capital represent direct investments in property, plant, and equipment, and they have been drawn to the Sunbelt in the form of loans and purchases of debt and equity securities (Haywood, 1977).

An analysis of southern industrial development prepared in 1977 by the Federal Reserve Bank of Atlanta (Toal, 1977) found that "over the past 25 years, the South has transformed itself from a region of underinvestment to one that now garners a sizable portion of the nation's capital spending." In 1951, the states included in the sixth Federal Reserve District* received 6.8% of the nation's manufacturing sector spending. By 1973, the share was 12.2% of the nation's total. However, the region's share of the total national economy was larger than these percentages indicate. The study concludes that the southeast did not receive a disproportionately large share of manufacturing investment, and that in the past, there was "substantial underinvestment in southeast manufacturing."

---

*Alabama, Florida, Georgia, Louisiana, Mississippi, and Tennessee.

The same analysis found, surprisingly, that despite the region's large share of low-wage manufacturing, capital-intensive industries are investing proportionately larger sums in the southeast. In short, the region's manufacturing sector is now more capital-intensive than the nation's. The Atlanta Federal Reserve Bank concluded that the higher levels of capital spending per manufacturing worker in the southeast "imply future regional expansion and are a prime ingredient of the region's rapid economic growth." This high level of investment represents not only the recent growth of higher-wage, more capital-intensive industries in the South, but also the postrecession surge of capital investment by low-wage industries to improve productivity (Brunson, 1980).

A similar analysis of manufacturing investment in Texas in the mid-1970s showed that the state was leading all other states in the amount of manufacturing investment. Constant dollar investment spending in the state grew at an annual rate of 32.5% between 1974 and 1976, compared to 4.2% for the nation as a whole (Ekholm, 1978). The same study found that Texas' share of national manufacturing investment had surpassed the state's share of national manufacturing output for many years.

Data on total new capital expenditures reported in the 1977 Census of Manufacturers show that despite a slowdown in manufacturing in the mid-1970s throughout much of the South, 14 southern states accounted for 35.5% of total new capital expenditure in the U.S. between 1972 and 1977 (U.S. Bureau of the Census, 1979). These same 14 southern states had 26.7% of all U.S. manufacturing employment as of 1977. The increase in capital expenditures of manufacturing between 1972 and 1977 was 135.9% in the South, compared to 101.2% for the nation (Brunson, 1980). During this period, the South replaced the Midwest for the first time in the region of greatest new investment in manufacturing. And the *New York Times* reported recently that in total new capital investment in private enterprise, the South and West had a net gain of $17 billion a year over the Northeast and Midwest in 1977 as compared with 1972 (*New York Times*, 1980).

Overall then, private capital investment has been adequate to underwrite the growth of southern business and industry since World War II. This is not to suggest that capital markets have worked perfectly in the Sunbelt. Circumstantial evidence indicates that small businesses and small towns in the rural South have not had adequate access to capital. Branch plants of national companies with access to national capital markets have provided a major impetus to the region's industrial development. However, small businesses in the South have had to depend more heavily on regional or local sources of capital. Since the participation index of southern banks in financing business has been relatively low (Haywood, 1977), small business development in the Sunbelt has probably not played as strong a role as it did in the development of other regions.

It is also likely that much of the South, particularly the southeast, is a net importer of funds to support its capital spending for industrial development

(Toal, 1977). However, as Haywood points out, "in an economy where movement of financial resources is unimpeded by political boundaries and where financial markets and institutions have achieved high efficiency in the movement of funds, concern with regional sources of capital should not be carried to the point of preoccupation."

As regards the question of capital availability for small business, Haywood argues that "specialized knowledge is needed in lending institutions (mainly commercial banks) in order to make loans to new and different kinds of business. The low participation index of southern commercial banks in the business loan area may imply some deficiency in this area." State usury laws and banking laws that restrict statewide branching may also be obstacles to small business growth in the South.

In the final analysis, the lack of capital for small businesses and distressed rural areas in the South represents a problem of equity rather than efficiency. If so, this is a legitimate area of concern and responsibility for the public sector. The southern states and the federal government administer a multitude of grant and loan programs designed to foster small business and to finance investment in depressed areas. While these programs have not been entirely successful, there is no indication that these equity problems have substantially inhibited the overall performance of the Sunbelt's economy.

Housing

Rising per capita income levels combined with heavy net immigration have led to a strong demand for housing in the South, and this demand is expected to continue through at least 1990. Regional capital resources may lag behind such demand.

Capital for housing finance in the South is thought by some analysts to be subject to regional inefficiencies. One study tentatively concluded that while relatively large capital inflows (from outside the region) contributed to the expansion of housing in Florida, the rest of the South relied mainly on sources of capital from within the region during the 1970s.

Other studies tend to downplay the regional capital shortage for housing and other credit demands. A 1979 study published by the Federal Reserve Bank of Atlanta concluded that, in general, nontraded asset markets such as bank loans and mortgages "are fully integrated national markets." If so, the availability of capital for housing should be influenced primarily by national monetary policies. Consequently, the study concluded that there should be no reason to expect impacts of monetary policy to affect regions differently through the medium of credit markets (Keleher, 1979).

Public Facilities

Capital to finance the construction and expansion of public facilities in the Sunbelt has been readily available. The adequacy of public sector capital to date can be attributed to two primary causes: the fiscal conservatism of state and local governments in the region; and rising state and local tax revenues resulting from rapid economic growth. In those local communities not experiencing economic growth, federal grants and loans have helped finance public facilities.

Local governments in the South have been more pressed than state governments in financing public facilities to service rapid growth, primarily because local property taxes are not as responsive to economic growth as are state taxes. In most southern states, a relatively high proportion of state funds are used to finance local functions such as education, welfare, health, and highways. In other regions, these activities are financed primarily by local governments. Since the states finance a larger proportion of local functions in the South, local governments are able to benefit directly from some of the tax revenues derived from growth-sensitive income, sales, and severance taxes at the state level.

Still, the capital needs and capacities of local governments in the Sunbelt vary greatly. Cities and counties in fast-growing areas are finding it necessary to upgrade public services and infrastructure. Expanding business activity is also generating additional demands for public expenditures on water, sewerage, waste treatment, and highways—activities requiring large capital outlays. Many southern cities are raising local taxes to finance these demands; others are deferring spending for infrastructure expansion, thus risking the deterioration of their capital stock.

Neither alternative is desirable. To maintain the image of a "favorable business climate," local public officials are often obsessed with keeping tax burdens low and postponing needed capital improvements. But excessively tight controls on state and local taxes and spending may actually inhibit development, if governments cannot provide critical public services and infrastructure to new people and industry. Thus the dual challenge facing the public sector in the South during the 1980s is that of maintaining fiscal balance while at the same time responding to the needs of a growing population and industrial base.

Outlook for the 1980s

Financing the Sunbelt's continued economic growth is a subject of much discussion and concern among the South's business and community leadership. Dire predictions of a drying-up of investment capital for the region periodically surface. *South Magazine*, the premier journal of southern business, recently suggested that the trend toward more and more capital investment in the South may have peaked (*South Magazine*, 1980). The journal cited McGraw–Hill estimates that the level of investment in the South has been falling—from close to 60% of all investment in 1958 to 53% in 1980–1981. According to *South*, this indicates that "future capital investment in the region may be lower than expected."

James M. Howell, Vice President of the First National Bank of Boston, and Chairman of the Council for Northeast Economic Action, insists that the South faces a capital shortage as more funds remain in the Northeast to support a revival of that region's investment climate (Howell, 1978). Howell asserts that the recognition of economic stagnation in the Northeast has set off new policy initiatives to encourage business investment in the region. This economic revival will eventually lead to a smaller stock of capital for investments elsewhere.

Howell's bank has developed figures to back up his claims. From 1970 to 1979, it estimates that $12.8 billion in northeastern capital was invested as loans in the South. During this same period, the analysis concluded that the South experienced a deficit of $3.6 billion in its commercial development needs. From 1980 to 1984, Howell cites one bank estimate showing the North able to channel about $5.4 billion into the South to meet an expected capital shortfall of $7.4 billion. If the investment climate improves in the Northeast, however, the bank projects that the North would have only $1.1 billion to loan into the South, creating a substantial regional "capital gap."

To improve the investment climate in the North, Howell's bank and a coalition of northern business and government leaders are making a major effort to leverage private sector investment with public sector funds in distressed northeastern cities. Using such programs as federal Urban Development Action Grants (UDAG), SBA loans and guarantees, and federal grants and loans for infrastructure building, the northern states and their cities are attempting "to produce private sector capital formation in areas where markets have weakened or altogether overridden the underlying cost–price environment for private investment" (Council for Northeast Economic Action, 1980).

Howell's predictions of a regional capital gap in the South may be exaggerated. However, the approach being promoted by Howell and other northern leaders replicates to a large extent the successful development formula that has been pursued in the southern states. Stripped of its somewhat holistic aura, Howell's concept of leveraging simply means closer public–private sector cooperation in the North to promote and finance renewed economic growth. A better business climate would mean the end to the adverse nature of business–government relations that has contributed to the northeast's rapid decline in private sector growth. More significantly, it would mean that the northern cities will employ southern tactics—financial incentives for new business and industrial investment.

There appears to be little conceptual difference between a federal UDAG grant to support private investment in a large, distressed northern city and an industrial revenue bond or tax incentives to help finance a new industrial facility in a small town in the rural South. "Tandem" federal grants to assist new industry along the federally financed Northeast Rail Corridor, or intracity mass transit lines, would appear no different than a federal loan for a small town waste disposal system along a new federally financed Interstate highway in the South. The major difference is the role of the federal government, which is deliberately targeting urban grants to deteriorating northern cities. In short, the means are different but the hoped-for end results are the same. Leveraging public–private funds through targeted federal grants and loans represents a form of centralized economic planning to mobilize and allocate capital. Issuance of local industrial development bonds to attract new industries in the South suggests a more decentralized attempt to accomodate market forces.

While an improved business climate through closer private–public cooperation (liberally endowed with federal grants and loans) should make an important contribution to improved investment in the Northeast, the proposition that such changes will substantially alter the economic growth of the South is dubious at best. We would still contend that economic fundamentals will play the major role in attracting the capital to finance southern growth.

Admittedly, specific regional forecasts are hard to come by. In his overview paper on "Financing Growth in the South," Charles Haywood is mildly optimistic, at least concerning the business sector. Noting that projected rates of growth of personal income in the South through 1990 imploy "very large increases in capital spending and debt," he projected in 1977 that capital outlays in the South by 1990 will need to be two or three times the estimated 1977 level, assuming an inflation rate of 3–5% (Haywood, 1977). The need for creation of net new debt in 1990 was estimated to be three to four times its current (1977) pace.

In light of these projects, Haywood concluded that the South will still be a net importer of capital in 1990 by perhaps as much as $40 billion. His broad, aggregative analysis "provides some basis for believing that the availability of capital will be sufficient, in general, to support projected gains in personal income." Increased participation by southern banks in financing business, the development of larger banking organizations, and growth in the tertiary sector of the region's economy were seen by Haywood as increasing the "participation index" in the South, thus augmenting the access to national capital markets that many businesses in the South will continue to enjoy. The availability of commercial credit for the household sector was also reviewed as adequate to meet demand throughout the 1980s.

Haywood is much less sanguine about the future availability of capital to finance the demand for housing and public facilities in the South. These prospects take on an added dimension due to the fact that, in many parts of the South, deficiencies in housing and public facilities are substantial.

Many new financing innovations are now being tried at the state and local levels to deal with capital market imperfections (Litvak & Daniels, 1979). Some promising approaches include public issues of tax exempt mortgage bonds, variable rate mortgages, state "bundling" of local issues, state guarantee programs for municipal bonds, and state bond banks. In the South, some states are attempting to remove obstacles to capital investment by relaxing state usury laws and restrictions on statewide branch banking. Members of the financial community believe that interstate banking and relaxation of restrictions of the location of foreign branch banks are needed to increase the mobility of capital between and among states and regions.

Since financial innovations can be implemented more easily in a growing rather than a stagnant economy, the Sunbelt states should have ample opportunities to experiment with new approaches. However, open capital markets historically have served the region well, and there are substantial dangers inherent in excessive public sector intervention. Perceived problems of equity in the allocation of capital should not be allowed to obscure the overall efficiency of the marketplace. Intervention in the private market to remedy inequities often fails to achieve fairness while reducing inefficiency.

Policies for the Future

It seems likely that the Sunbelt will remain a net importer of capital during the 1980s. But because capital is mobile—flowing freely across state lines—the term "shortage" is probably a misnomer.

A more serious problem during the decade ahead may be the lack of institutional expertise in matching capital supplies to their most efficient uses. Several regional initiatives could help facilitate the efficient allocation of capital during the 1980s. These initiatives include reform of state banking regulations to allow branch banking in states where it is still prohibited, intraregional branch banking, and creation of state capital development programs.

Branch banking can facilitate economic growth because large, multi-branch banks have access to greater reserves and broader expertise. Arrangements to permit cross-state banking within the region, initially on a bilateral basis, could help the South's financial community prepare for the inevitability of nation-wide branching.

Some direct governmental assistance at the state and local level may also be in order. For example, municipal bond banks and umbrella bond programs could lower the cost of capital to small firms through pooling and tax exemptions. Product development corporations, a mechanism through which states become partners in new ventures, might also be considered.

While reforms in developmental finance offer some promise in overcoming inequities created by market "imperfections," the key to future economic growth in the Sunbelt will be the maintenance of a healthy business climate. Perhaps the single most important contribution southern state governments can make in this regard is to ensure that the growth of the public sector does not exceed that of the private sector.

The basic dilemma faced by several of the declining northeastern states is that their public sectors have become overdeveloped relative to their fiscal capacities. As a result, tax burdens are high and governments find themselves without the resources to deal with critical social and infrastructure needs. To avoid this dilemma, southern states should continue to pursue good fiscal common sense.

Of course, unsound monetary and fiscal policies at the national level could easily undermine continued expansion in the Sunbelt as well as economic revitalization in the North. Since 1973, inflation has constrained expansion of total real personal income, and this in turn has inhibited national savings and investment. Federal tax cuts to stimulate private investment coupled with reduced federal deficits are essential requirements for an improved growth climate in both the South and the nation.

In closing, we reiterate our view that market forces have served the Sunbelt well in the postwar era. While new public sector interventions may be necessary to correct minor capital market imperfections, the South must not lose sight of its basic competitive advantages that tend to accommodate national market forces. If the region as a whole maintains a healthy business climate and controls the growth of state and local government, market forces should continue to provide the Sunbelt with the capital necessary to finance economic growth through the 1980s.

Bibliography

Advisory Commission on Intergovernmental Relations, *Interregional and Interstate Tax Competition*. Washington, D.C., May 18, 1979. See also Lawrence Litvak and Belden Daniels.

Atlanta Constitution, "Facts Refute Senator Jackson on Dixie Labor." April 28, 1976.

Brunson, E. Evan, "Structural and Spatial Trends in Southern Manufacturing; Implications of the Eighties." Paper prepared for the Southern Growth Policies Board Task Force on the Southern Economy, July, 1980.

Council for Northeast Economic Action, *Building Local Capacity to Leverage Private Investment*. Boston, May, 1980, pp. 113–114.

Daniels, Belden H. and Kieschnick, Michael, *Development Finance: A Primer for Policymakers*, Part I, p. 21. The National Rural Center, 1979.

Ekholm, Art, "Manufacturing Investment Booms in Texas." *Voice of the Federal Reserve Bank of Dallas*, November 1978, pp. 8–15.

Federal Reserve Bank of Atlanta, "Consumption, Saving and Southern Economic Growth." in *Essays on Southern Economic Growth*. May, 1961, p. 21.

Hackney, Sheldon, "Past as Prologue." A Speech Delivered at the University of Virginia as part of the lecture series "Southern Business: The Decades Ahead." September 24, 1979.

Haywood, Charles F., "Financing Growth in the South." Southern Growth Policies Board, September 1977, p. 21.

Hodges, Luther H., "The March Toward a Truly New South". Remarks to the Southern Industrial Development Council, Nashville, Tennessee. October 25, 1976, p. 4.

Howell, James M., "Meeting the Capital Requirements of Business in the 1980's: New Challenges for Regional Cooperation." Remarks presented as Chairman, Council for Northeast Economic Action, to the 1978 Annual Meeting of the Southern Growth Policies Board, Atlanta; December 1, 1978.

Keleher, Robert E., "Regional Credit Market Integration: A Survey and Empirical Examination." Working Paper Series, Federal Reserve Bank of Atlanta, February, 1979.

Litvak, Lawrence and Daniels, Belden, *Innovations in Development Finance*. Washington, D.C.: The Council of State Planning Agencies, 1979.

South Magazine, Vol 7. No. 7. "Has Capital Investment Peaked". July 1980, p. 9.

Stevens, William K., "Pension Funds' Flow to Sunbelt Spurs Shift of Investment Capital." *New York Times*, May 20, 1980.

Toal, William D., "Southeastern Industrial Investment." *Economic Review*, Federal Reserve Bank of Atlanta, May/June 1977, pp. 63–68.

U.S. Bureau of the Census, "Annual Estimates of the Population of States: July 1, 1970 to 1979." Series P-25, No. 876, February, 1980.

U.S. Bureau of the Census, 1977 Census of Manufacturers, "Selected Statistics for States: 1977 and 1972." Preliminary Statistics, December 1979.

Weinstein, Bernard, "A New Look at State and Local Tax Incentives for Economic Development." Paper delivered to the Western Economic Association Annual Conference, San Francisco, June 28, 1978, p. 8.

PART THREE

GOVERNMENT AS INVESTOR: PUBLIC ENTREPRENEURSHIP AND PROGRAM INNOVATION

VI

State Initiative to Foster New Technology-Based Enterprise: The Case of the Connecticut Product Development Corporation*

James E. Jarrett

The Need for a Product Development Funding Mechanism

It is one of the happy incidents of the Federal System that a single courageous state may, if its citizens choose, serve as a laboratory and try novel social economic experiments without risk to the rest of the country.

Supreme Court Justice Louis D. Brandeis

Summary

Small companies have always experienced difficulty in obtaining capital. This is especially the case if small companies seek financing to develop new products. Because development of new products is risky and because smaller enterprises often lack collateral, traditional lending sources rarely will finance new product development. For various reasons, other sources of financing also are unavailable to small companies which are attempting to diversify and expand. The inherent investment bias against high-risk ventures of small manufacturers hinders industrial expansion and creation of new private sector jobs.

To help smaller companies overcome their difficulties, Connecticut officials established a Product Development Corporation. This corporation's primary aim is job creation, which occurs when products developed with state financial assistance subsequently are manufactured and sold. Connecticut's Product Development Corporation provides companies with *risk capital* (not loans or

*An earlier version of this chapter was published as a report by the Council of State Governments with support from the National Science Foundation. This article reflects the views of the author and not necessarily those of the National Science foundation or the Council of State Governments.

grants) for expenses associated in developing a new product, device, technique, or process which can be exploited commercially. In most situations, a private company incurs 40% of development costs and the Product Development Corporation supplies the remaining 60%. State funds may be expended only for costs associated with developing and exploiting specific inventions and products, not for operating expenses, basic research, equipment, land, or buildings. Use of the corporation's funds in no way replaces private financing since state aid is provided only to companies which cannot reasonably obtain financing from commercial sources. In fact, conventional lenders are encouraged to work with companies which have built a product prototype and are seeking financing for full-scale production.

Because the Product Development Corporation provides risk capital, the corporation may lose its entire investment if a company's product is never commercially sold. When this occurs, the company has no obligation to repay the corporation's funds. When a product is successfully developed and marketed by the company, the corporation is paid a royalty on each product sold. Commonly, the royalty rate is 5% of the product's gross selling price, and royalty returns to the corporation do not stop once the corporation has recouped its original investment. Rather, as compensation for having taken a risk, the corporation continues to receive royalties until it has obtained five times its original investment. In some cases, the payback can be less than this amount if the royalties are generated quickly.

Connecticut's Product Development Corporation was established by the state legislature as a "quasi-public instrumentality" with direction provided by a seven-member board of directors. Funding for the corporation's activities and investments is provided by issuing state general obligation bonds. Originally, the issuance of $10 million in bonds was authorized. The Legislature reduced the authorization to $6 million in its 1980 session on the basis that only $1.6 million had been committed by the corporation up to that time. By law, the corporation may be required to repay the bonds, with interest, and is expected to become self-sustaining. Royalty income derived from the sales of successfully developed products is placed in a revolving fund which is used to pay the corporation's minimal operating expenses.

During the corporation's six years of operation, approximately $3.5 million has been invested in joint ventures with 36 Connecticut companies. For fiscal year 1981, royalties of more than $218,000 have been collected. Investment outlays and royalty returns are lower than anticipated at this stage for two principal reasons: unanticipated legal and administrative obstacles had to be resolved at the outset, and the task of making the corporation known to businesses in the state was greater than expected. Most companies which have received funds are relatively small manufacturing or electronics firms. To date, only seven ventures have been written off as failures; most of these were relatively small investments. A product development corporation is a promising device for stimulating economic activity and job creation, and seems especially applicable to many states and large cities that have a substantial base of small manufacturing businesses. It is still premature to assess the corporation's long-term performance; however, to date, it has shown a steady growth in jobs created and royalty income.

The Problem

Small companies in the United States have always experienced more difficulty in obtaining capital than larger companies. For many types of financing, the major problem is simply one of differentials in the cost of obtaining capital. As long as credit is freely available, however, both smaller firms and larger companies can obtain some financing. But in attempting to finance development of new products, the situation is radically different. Whereas larger companies often can obtain necessary financing either from conventional lenders or from their internal retained earnings, small firms generally cannot. Conventional lenders usually do not lend money except where secured by collateral. Unfortunately, smaller companies have fewer assets to use as collateral or their assets already are serving as security for a loan. Also, the cash flow of small firms does not normally generate sufficient internal funds for product development.

Development of new products is a risky enterprise because there are so many steps at which a product could stumble. Translating an idea into a successful commercial product involves engineering design and other technical processes, tooling up for prototypes and production, actual manufacturing and, of course, marketing. There are significant uncertainties at each stage of the multiyear process, and the averages are not favorable—rarely do more than 10% of product ideas become successfully marketed, although the figures vary considerably by industries and companies. When the uncertainties of new product development are compounded by the inherent financial and entrepreneurial problems of many small firms, it is easy to understand why securing adequate financing is difficult.

A typical situation is illustrated by the following example paraphrased from Fournier (1978):

> There is a small manufacturing company which employs 6 to 10 people, and has annual sales of less than $500,000. This company has been in existence for from one to three years. In the true spirit of American enterprise, the company was founded by one or two individuals, who had become disenchanted with the thought of working for someone else the rest of their lives.
>
> This company, as with almost all small companies, can be classified as a single-product company. Most often, the company's single product was developed by the company's founders. This is a particularly vulnerable time for any young company. Should the market for the company's single product be lost or experience a severe decline, the company has no back-up product.
>
> Having successfully operated the company for a period of time, the founders recognize their excessive vulnerability as a single-product company and decide to

try to lessen this vulnerability. Normally, the owners of the company begin by exploring the possibility either of broadening their product line through the addition of other products, or by diversifying into a complementary line of other products. Unfortunately, the company soon discovers it is not generating sufficient funds from its daily operation to provide the funds required to undertake the contemplated product development project. Consequently, the company must go outside the company to obtain the requisite funding.

The first place a company's owners often turn to obtain product development funding is the company's own bank. Often, this avenue proves fruitless for several reasons. First, the bank usually will want collateral for any loan; however, the company has no collateral to pledge. Typically, the company leased facilities, so it has no real property to pledge. Likewise, production equipment, if new, is unpaid for or, if used, has little market value. Lastly, the founders of the company already have pledged their own personal assets as collateral on loans to found the company. Without such collateral, therefore, the company's likelihood of obtaining bank loan funding is minimal.

Secondly, assuming the company is not prevented from obtaining a bank loan because of a lack of collateral, the next stumbling block the company normally encounters in dealing with a bank is an unwillingness on the bank's part to provide funds for product development. In most instances, it is difficult to interest a banker in funding the development of a new product which, at the time the funds are to be made available, may only exist in the form of a pencil sketch. In such cases, the banker often tells the company to come back when it has a prototype of the new product to show. This suggestion may be of no help to the company if the company lacks the funds to build the prototype to show to the banker.

The next avenue a company commonly will explore is that of the venture capitalist. Here, too, the company most often will come up empty-handed and, again, there are several reasons. First, because the company is virtually in a start-up situation, it is not particularly attractive to a venture capitalist.

Secondly, the venture capitalist, if he decides to put money into the company, may want input to the operation of the company in order to minimize the chances of losing the investment. To accomplish this, many venture capitalists seek working control of the companies in return for investments. On the other hand, the founders of the company probably are not prepared to relinquish company control. Consequently, no funds flow to the company from this source.

To this example could be added a fourth possible, and generally inadequate, source of funds—the Small Business Administration (SBA). In addition to the normal criticisms that SBA requires too much paperwork and cannot act quickly, many small company officials believe that SBA has been and continues to be oriented to small service ventures, not financing for new product development.

A Response: Connecticut's Product Development Corporation

In 1971, in response to a high level of unemployment and unsatisfactory industrial activity, former Connecticut Governor Thomas J. Meskill initiated a

Statewide Task Force for Full Employment. Eleven subcommittees were formed to analyze the state's economic problems and to propose mechanisms and programs to stimulate economic development and employment. One subcommittee examined industrial research and development. After analyzing both national and local conditions impeding new product development, the committee concluded that the inherent investment bias against high risk ventures by small manufacturers was hindering industrial expansion and creation of new jobs. Furthermore, the situation seemed unlikely to change without some form of state government action.

A Connecticut businessman, Joseph F. Engelberger, chaired the task force, and through prior business ventures in England, had become familiar with England's National Research Development Corporation (NRDC). The NRDC was established in 1948 to aid the postwar economic recovery effort in Great Britain. From its inception, NRDC helped develop new industries such as the Hovercraft and helped create and apply new technological forms. NRDC participates in joint ventures with private corporations and provides funds for independent projects not involving major companies. Sometimes NRDC recovers it investments through equity participation, although more often NRDC owns all or a portion of the patent rights and regains its investments through royalties from patent rights and patent licenses. Since 1967, NRDC's income has exceeded expenditures and it has a current income of more than $20 million per year, the bulk of which is provided by pharmaceutical licenses. Mr. Engelberger believed the NRDC mechanism could be applied to Connecticut's situation, and NRDC was used as a model for the Connecticut Product Development Corporation (CPDC).*

While NRDC served as the inspiration for CPDC, Mr. Engelberger and other members of the task force subcommittee realized that substantial modification would be necessary. Quite early, the task force realized that a corporation designed to produce new technology and entirely new industries might be successful on the national level but would be less feasible for a state government than concentrating on new product assistance. Financing new product development also would be a surer and faster route to creation of new employment as well as being more attuned to the needs of existing small companies in the state.

Other major changes were made. Instead of adopting NRDC's normal practice of assuming an equity position in start-up companies it was aiding, task force members believed that a payback in terms of royalties on successfully developed and marketed products would be preferable. Another major alteration was that financing in Connecticut would be limited almost solely to the developmental phase; once a prototype or several prototypes has been

---

*More information about NRDC, the National Research Development Corporation which in July 1981 was merged with the National Enterprise Board to form the British Technology Group, is presented in Appendix C.

built, financing would cease. This was in contrast to NRDC's approach of providing working capital for actual production of the new product. And, whereas Britain's NRDC placed considerable emphasis on ownership of patents related to their funded projects, the Connecticut program would be focused on the royalties from product sales, with any patents remaining the property of the firm. As a precautionary move, however, the Connecticut legislation was written quite broadly and permits CPDC to own patents and to acquire an equity position.

The task force recommendation for creating a state product development corporation was accepted by both the governor and the state legislature. In 1972, shortly after the task force report, the Connecticut Product Development Corporation Act was passed by the legislature with virtually no opposition. (Public Act 248 is contained in Appendix A.)

Implementing the Concept

Key Legislative Provisions

Public Act 248 specifies that CPDC will help stimulate the development of new products and creation of new jobs through the use of financial aid to companies which could not reasonably obtain financing from commercial lenders. The corporation was established as a "quasi-public instrumentality" with tax-exempt status, and six gubernatorially appointed directors comprise the board of the public corporation. (Four of the directors must have "favorable reputations for skill, knowledge, and experience in the areas of the development of technological invention.") Recently, the board was expanded from six to seven.

The CPDC board of directors is empowered to make venture agreements with Connecticut firms, on such terms as the board may decide, and the board is given broad powers over the execution of agreements. General guidelines for determining how projects would be evaluated were contained in the legislation and are described later.

Many different types of venture agreements are possible under the legislation, although the act specifies that funds may be disbursed only for developmental expenditures and expenditures associated with exploiting the invention or product. This provision excludes companies' operating expenses as a legitimate area for financial aid. Also excluded are funds for basic research, land, buildings, equipment (except perhaps for a testing facility needed for the product), start-up capital, and for costs already incurred by a company in developing a specific product. The original statute authorized the State bond Commission, composed of the governor and several department secretaries appointed by the governor, to issue up to $10 million bonds to operate the corporation. The legislation did not specify if the funds were to be transferred immediately to the CPDC or whether they would be distributed after the corporation and the bond commission approved individual agreements with companies. Through an amendment passed in 1980 (SA80-41, Section 66) the authorization ceiling was reduced to $6 million. This amount includes both the corporation's operating expenses and funds for the companies. This change will not affect CPDC operations for two or three years.

The law provided for the corporation to eventually repay the $6 million under terms which may include a forgiveness of interest, a holiday in the repayment of interest or principal, or both. It was, and is, intended that the corporation become completely self-sustaining at some future time. No specific dates were set for these actions.

Since the original legislation was enacted, there have been two amendments in addition to the authorization ceiling reduction and the increase in the number of directors. In 1974, the state legislature placed the CPDC under the state's Department of Commerce (now the Department of Economic Development) for budgetary and administrative purposes only. This change was made for administrative reasons and has not significantly affected either the intent of the original legislation or CPDC's activities. Additionally, an act was passed in 1980 (PA 80-267) which requires that CPDC give priority to defense-dependent companies that wish to diversify into nondefense products and to companies in areas of the state which have been seriously and adversely affected by cancellation or cutbacks of defense contracts.

Initial Problems

Implementation of the Connecticut Product Development Corporation was not a smooth or speedy process. The lack of controversy surrounding the enactment of the CPDC statute in 1972 stands in sharp contrast to the political, financial, and legal problems which delayed effective implementation of the program for three years. An initial problem became apparent in 1972 when the State Bond commission did not construe the legislation to mean that the bond appropriation should be granted in one block to CPDC. Instead, the commission was ready to approve funding for projects as they arose. A funding request of $500,000 for two CPDC approved projects, administrative costs, and initial capitalization was being processed when a major legal issue arose.

Legal counsel for the State Bond Commission refused to approve the bonds on the basis that Public Act 248 was of uncertain constitutionality. Resulting legal problems continued for 18 months, postponing CPDC activities until the State Supreme Court decided the case in August 1974. The court, in a unanimous decision, concluded that Public Act 248 did not violate the state's constitution. An analysis of the case is presented in Appendix B.

During the period of controversy, CPDC was at a virtual standstill. The two projects which had been approved by the CPDC board could not be funded. More importantly, because no operating funds had been appropriated by the state, the corporation was facing possible dissolution. Only the timely availability of federal assistance from the Economic Development Administration of the U.S. Department of Commerce prevented CPDC's termination. This federal agency was interested in the CPDC concept and its potential from the outset, and supplied approximately $300,000 for operating expenses during the early years of the Corporation's existence. In return for this federal assistance, the corporation contractually agreed with the U.S. Department of Commerce to supply information on its operations for five years and to allow the department to monitor and evaluate its activities.*

Following resolution of the constitutional questions, CPDC staff prepared to commence actual operations. Due to the governor's opposition to the use of state bond funds to pay operating expenses, however, CPDC's budgetary situation still needed clarification. Finally, in late 1974, an appropriation of $85,000 was made for CPDC's operating expenses.

Management

Because the Product Development Corporation has the form and status of a quasi-public corporation, the board's directors essentially serve as trustees of the corporation and have authority and responsibility concerning its operation. Just as with a private corporation, the minutes of board meetings serve as the official record of CPDC and constitute the evidence of the decisions and actions of the board. By legislation, broad powers have been granted to the board including authority to expend funds, forgive repayment of money provided to companies, hire staff, and purchase and sell property. Yet, the corporation remains a public entity and its funds are public funds. Therefore, CPDC's expenditures are postaudited by the state auditor's office as if these expenditures were those of any other state agency.

In addition to the seven voting directors who have been gubernatorially appointed, the Commissioner of Economic Development is an ex-officio, nonvoting director. All directors have extensive experience in some aspect of the product development process. The directors have included an inventor businessman, a patent attorney, an administrator of a university-based material sciences institute, an engineering professor, a retired business executive, an insurance company economist, and individuals with strengths in strategic planning, marketing, and financial analysis. Directors fulfill their duties on a part-time basis, meeting formally 11 times per year. All directors serve without compensation but may be reimbursed for necessary expenses.

By law, the board appoints a president of the corporation, and the president appoints other staff members. Currently there are three professionals, who are in the state's unclassified service, and one secretary. A variety of outside consultants are also utilized for detailed technical and financial reviews on some applications.

The corporation's annual budget is determined by the board of directors and has not been subject to legislative or executive changes. Recently, the annual

---

*Another unit within the Commerce Department, the National Bureau of Standards, also provided financial support ($300,000) for investment in projects. This award was made in early 1974 and initial funds were committed in 1975.

operating budget has been approximately $170,000, about three-quarters of which has been devoted to salaries and outside consultants. Operating funds are authorized by the State Bond Commission and operating funds are part of the $6 million limiting appropriation. During fiscal year 1981 (July 1980–June 1981), royalties more than covered all operating expenses.* In previous years, a combination of Federal funds, bond proceeds, and royalties defrayed administrative expenses.

The Joint Venture

What is important to the CPDC is not that technological or product innovation be spawned, but rather that jobs be created. In line with this purpose, restrictions on the kinds of companies and projects which may qualify for CPDC funding have been deliberately minimized. For instance, a "new" product or commercially salable process is defined as one which is new to the company making an application, not new to the world. CPDC conceivably might enter into a joint venture for development of a product already being manufactured by an in-state company although this possibility is most unlikely because of the product's seemingly low potential for market penetration. There are two basic criteria which must be satisfied:

1. Products must be developed within the state and
2. the applicant company must have been unable to obtain reasonable financing from traditional commercial credit sources.

But even given these two conditions, there may be some latitude depending on each applicant's circumstances.[1]

Applications are encouraged and have been received from a variety of business which were in existence prior to CPDC involvement. Almost all of the approved applications have emanated from small and medium-sized companies. Large companies, those with annual sales exceeding $20 million, are not the primary beneficiaries of CPDC for several reasons:

1. These companies are better able to secure financing from private sources or to generate internal funds.
2. Most CPDC development projects are under $200,000, an amount which is often not sufficient for a larger company's needs.
3. These companies are reluctant to enter into a royalty payback arrangement if company officials can secure cheaper financing based on their perception that the product will be a success.

Applications from "basement" inventors are discouraged because of most inventors' relative lack of prior business skills and background, their inability to raise matching funds for the venture, and their lack of an existing produc-

---

*No bonds specifically earmarked for the corporation have yet been sold. Connecticut operates on a common cash basis so the disbursements from the State Bond commission to the CPDC have been either from the treasurer's general fund or from excess proceeds from other bond offerings.

tion facility and sales network. Consequently, individual inventors have not been CPDC's main clientele.

At any given time, 10 to 20 applications will be pending. (The application fee is 0.25% of the amount requested from CPDC, or a minimum of $100. All but $100 is refundable if an application is withdrawn prior to action by the board.) Many applications eventually will be withdrawn prior to formal action by the board after the qualifications and requirements for CPDC participation are explained. Each application is initially evaluated by the staff and then by the directors. Evaluation essentially consists of examining the company's past and present financial condition and the capability of its management, and analyzing the proposed product, including an assessment of its technical feasibility and market potential. No point system or other formal weighting are placed on any of these components; nor must a project be capable of eventually generating a minimum number of new jobs. Preference is given, however, to products, devices, and processes which potentially could generate many new jobs and large sales revenues.

While the expertise of staff and directors is considerable, it is obvious that they do not possess the capability of evaluating the technical feasibility of each proposed product. This limitation is recognized, and the evaluation process has been adjusted accordingly. Emphasis is placed on the company's financial health, its management, and on the business plan for the new product. If the staff and directors ask the proper questions of management, they feel that they can determine if the venture is sound from an entrepreneurial viewpoint, and, that any major potential technical weaknesses of the product also can be elicited through proper questioning. CPDC relies increasingly on outside consulting help in technical and financial areas in its evaluations.

Applications acted upon by the board may require three to four months for the application and review process. Most board decisions are unanimous. Once the board has approved the applications, the project is placed on the agenda of the State Bond Commission's next monthly meeting. So far this step has been a formality but it is necessary that the bond commission approve the allotment of the funds to each project before CPDC can enter into a contract with the company.

The Terms

Any special provisions of a venture are, of course, worked out during the application phase. A contract, putting together these specific provisions and standard terms, is prepared as soon as the CPDC board has approved the project. CPDC provides risk capital, not outright grants or repayable loans. In most cases, CPDC will provide 60% of the product's developmental costs and the company is responsible for the remainder. (CPDC's share cannot be used for any costs which had been incurred by the company prior to the contract agreement. However, because CPDC's share can be 60% of *total* project costs, in some cases CPDC's share will appear to be larger than 60%.) Officials of CPDC do not specify from what source the company will find its 40% share. Normally, the company will use internal funds, often in-kind contributions, such as overhead, although funding from a third party has also been used.

Because CPDC provides risk capital, as opposed to a loan, CPDC may lose its entire investment if the product is never commercially sold. (The provision of risk capital does not constitute debt to the company so CPDC funding adds no encumbrances to the company's balance sheet.) If a product is not successfully developed, the company has no obligation to repay CPDC.

When a product is successfully developed and marketed, however, CPDC receives a return on its investment in the form of a royalty on product sales. Commonly, the royalty rate is 5% of the product's gross selling price. As previously mentioned, royalty returns to CPDC do not stop once CPDC has recouped its original investment. In most recent contracts, the company will continue to provide royalties until either CPDC has obtained five times its original investment, or the company can substantiate that the royalty is hurting sales, or the product is discontinued. Sometimes, a company will not have to pay back five times the initial CPDC share. As an incentive for early payback, CPDC recently decided that the following schedules also were acceptable:

1. If the payback within five years is $2\frac{1}{2}$ times CPDC's investment, then the royalty would drop to 1% of the sales price for the next five years.
2. If the payback within seven years is $3\frac{1}{2}$ times CPDC's investment, then the royalty would drop to 0.75% for the next seven years.

Companies generating royalties must remit them regularly since most contracts stipulate that any royalties will be sent to CPDC no later than 30 days after the close of the company's fiscal quarter.

Each contract also contains certain provisions deemed necessary to protect against possible abuses. For example, CPDC may hire an auditor to check the company's financial records to ensure that the correct amount of royalties has been remitted. In extreme cases, CPDC may terminate a contract for cause. If this occurs, CPDC has the legal right to obtain the technology package developed by the company (such as engineering drawings and production specifications). Also, the contracts normally contain provisions which grant CPDC the residual rights to the product. CPDC staff indicates that these safeguards will be exercised only when a venture is terminated for cause. Otherwise, the company's documents and product materials will be considered proprietary information and, as with all information which is provided by the company, will be maintained in confidence to prevent competitors from acquiring it. Each contract also provides that the venture may be terminated at any time by the mutual assent of the company and CPDC.

The contract may be signed by the company as soon as it is satisfied with its terms; however, CPDC will sign only after the Bond Commission has made the funds available. The signed contract is then submitted to the state's Office of Policy Management and the attorney general's office for final reviews. Approval by these agencies usually take two or three weeks, and can, with special handling, be accomplished in less time.

Following final approval by the attorney general's office, funds actually become available to the company. CPDC retains the funds until the company submits invoices on a monthly basis. Normally companies are reimbursed within seven days after the invoices are received. There is no requirement that the company actually expend what has been obligated to the project. If, at any time during the development of the product, the company decides that CPDC funds are not necessary, they can choose not to utilize CPDC financing. Because companies with successful products are required to pay back five times the amount of CPDC funds which they actually used, there is obviously an incentive not to use all the granted CPDC funds unless necessary.*

Once the product development phase has begun, there is continual monitoring by CPDC staff. At each monthly board meeting, there also are reviews of each project's status. On several occasions, board members themselves have conducted site visits to assess progress. In all cases, however, board members and staff are careful not to become an undue influence on the project's progress. CPDC board members do not sit on the company's board of directors; nor do they become actively involved in the day-to-day operations of the company.

CPDC officials see no reason to interfere with the company's internal activities. They view their role as helping private companies through the riskiest phase of product development and assisting companies with their financial, managerial, and technical expertise. Over the long term, they feel this will result in new products, industrial expansion, and more permanent jobs for Connecticut residents.

The Corporation's Record

Projected Benefits

Before CPDC was implemented, 10-year estimates were made of its revenue and cash flow conditions and its potential impact on employment. These projections were based primarily on the experiences of Britain's National Research Development Corporation, data on economic development in Connecticut, and a series of assumptions about the state's joint ventures.

Among the most important assumptions for the cash flow projection, illustrated in Figure 1, are the following:

1. Project sizes (CPDC's share) will range from $20,000 to $500,000, with the average being $100,000.

*At any time after a project commences, the board of directors may adjust downward the royalty payback arrangement or allow a company to delay paying its royalties. According to CPDC staff, these actions will occur only under extraordinary circumstances.

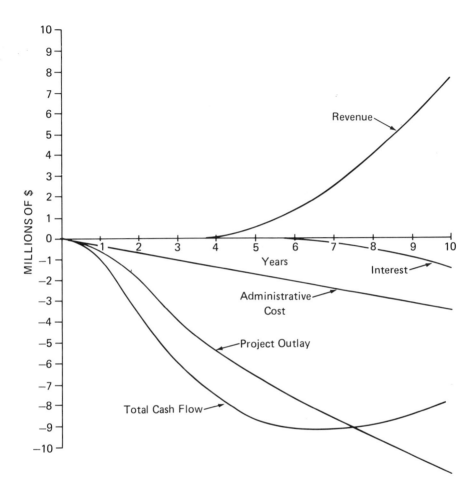

Figure 1. CPDC cumulative cash flow projection.

2. Twenty percent of all projects will be total successes and pay back five times CPDC's initial investment, while another 20% will terminate before products are marketed, and the remaining 60% of the projects will contribute some royalties.

3. Successful projects, on the average, will produce no revenue for two years, produce small royalties for the next three years, and then produce royalties at a constant mature volume for six more years before decreasing.

4. The sales volume at maturity for each successful project will be 10 times the total project expenditures and CPDC will receive 4% of the product's selling price.

Based on these parameters, it can be seen from Figure 1 that CPDC would not achieve a cumulative positive cash flow within 10 years and that the cumulative negative cash flow would reach its maximum around the fifth and sixth years, at which time revenues in the form of royalties would begin. (Total project outlays, of course, would continue to show a negative pattern since additional projects would be financed by the revenues from other projects' royalties.) Three important items not shown in Figure 1 are these annual estimates: new state tax revenues of $400,000, local government tax revenues of $280,000, and an estimated $43,000,000 of new product sales by the companies. These figures were predicted for the 10th year of CPDC's existence.

Employment estimates also were made based on the following assumptions:

1. direct employment of one person for every $20,000 of new product sales;
2. one research and development employee per $25,000 in loans;
3. two new service jobs for every three newly created manufacturing jobs; and
4. employment by subcontractors of 12% of direct employment resulting from new product sales.

With these figures, it was calculated that at the end of 10 years, 3400 new Connecticut jobs would result from CPDC's efforts.

Progress to Date

After nearly six years of operation, it is apparent that the originally projected benefits cannot be achieved on schedule because project outlays have been significantly less than anticipated. According to the original projection, approximately $7.5 million was to have been invested in projects by the end of the sixth year. Actually, about $3 million, or less than one-half of the projected amount, will have been invested. However, project outlays have increased smartly, reaching $742,000 in fiscal year 1980 and $1,363,000 in fiscal year 1981. Outlays in future years are expected to be approximateely $1 million each year.

Royalty returns also have been behind schedule because of the lower project outlays. While nominal royalties were received as early as September 1975, as of July 1980 only $68,000 in royalties had been received. Yet the prospects are anything but bleak. Royalties for the 1981 fiscal year have reached $218,000. With a host of new products coming to market during 1981–1982, royalties are projected to increase again, perhaps dramatically. It seems unlikely that the $8 million in royalties which had been projected by the 10th year can be achieved but this figure is still within the realm of possibility.

The lower-than-expected project outlays suggest that the corporation board has taken a cautious approach in its joint ventures. Indeed, this has been the case, although there are other reasons for the lower project outlays. Problems arose very early in reaching potential companies and informing them of CPDC's existence and purpose. A mass mailing to 600 small companies in the state produced little response; CPDC officials attribute this to their credibility problem (being part of state government and also trying to help business) and to the fragmented nature of the small business sector. Because relatively few small manufacturers belong to business groups such as local chambers of commerce, there was no easy way to reach the intended audience as a group.

As a result of these communication difficulties, the number of serious applicants representing established firms did not reach expected levels. Considerable interest has been shown by "basement" inventors but few of their proposed ventures have been seriously evaluated. Over the past two years, however, CPDC has become better known through referrals from client companies, bankers, and officials in other state agencies.

Also, a sustained public information program was instituted in 1979. Because of this campaign and an increasing number of private referrals, the number of high-quality applications has increased. This in turn has led to greater project outlays than in previous years.

Funded Projects

As of May 1, 1981, CPDC had become involved in 36 joint ventures.* Table 1 provides information on the projects and products which had been developed or were in the process of being developed as of July 1, 1980. Most firms have annual sales of less than $5 million although one firm approaches the $20 million annual sales level.

All of the firms have been based in the state for several years. Inquiries have been received from out-of-state companies regarding a possible relocation to Connecticut, contingent upon CPDC financing. Such inquiries are treated skeptically by CPDC staff, who believe that if a company relocated to Connecticut because of product development financing, the company would move away if another state provided greater incentives. CPDC staff encourages such companies to apply for financing *after* they have moved into the state.

To illustrate the role of CPDC in financing new product development, three actual cases are presented below. Each company's situation is different but they are generally representative of the funded projects.

Abbott Coin Counter Co., Inc.

This company supplies equipment to the retailing and banking industries and has undertaken development of a new line of products which would represent major advances compared to existing products now on the market. When Abbott officials first approached CPDC in 1975, the company had about 45 employees and annual sales of approximately $2.5 million. CPDC provided $320,000 for development costs.

In attempting to secure financing for development of its new lines of equipment, Abbott's management discovered that the company's existing financial condition overshadowed its potential market penetration with the

---

*This involvement included more than one project with a few companies. Note that several of CPDC's earliest ventures were funded with assistance from a similarly innovative program at the federal level—the Experimental Technology Incentives Program (ETIP). This program is discussed and evaluated by Britan (1981).

Table 1. CPDC Funded Projects

Company	Town	Product	Project Start Date
ETIP Funded Projects			
6 Misc. Projects	Various	Various	3/75-1/78
Anders, Inc.	Simsbury	Vibratory Control Unit	7/29/75
ECD Corporation	Plainville	Electrochemical Deburring	5/08/75
Automation Systems, Inc.	Brookfield	Laser Inspection Equipment	10/26/76
Batrow, Inc.	Branford	Tooling for Irrigation Controller	12/17/79
Total Federally Funded Projects			
Connecticut Bond Funded Projects			
TIE/Communications, Inc.	Shelton	Kay Telephone Systems	6/11/75
Abbott Coin Counter Co., Inc. Co., Inc. I			
Abbott Coin Counter Co., Inc. II	Stamford	Currency Handling Equipment	5/07/75
Abbott Coin Counter Co., Inc. III			
Raymond Engineering, Inc.	Middletown	Torque Wrench	1/12/77
TR Systems, Inc. (PECO)	Bloomfield	Thermal Reduction Systems	4/29/77
E&L Instruments, Inc.	Derby	Microcomputer System	4/29/77
Four Data, Inc.	Southington	Program Tape Editor	3/07/77
DeVar, Inc.	Bridgeport	Electronic Temperature Transmitter	5/27/77
Indicon, Inc.	Brookfield	Electronic Pipette	1/05/78
Batrow, Inc.	Branford	Irrigation Controller	3/01/79
Automation Systems II	Brookfield	Laser Inspection Equipment	5/02/79
Electrostatic Equipment Corp.	New Haven	Automatic Coating Machine	9/24/79
Altman Associates, Inc.	Stamford	Printed Circuit Verifier	9/24/79
Engineered Wire & Cable, Inc.	Winsted	Fire Resistant Wire Coating	2/25/80
Widder Corporation	Naugatuck	Pipe Cutting Machine	4/28/80
Solar Energy Structures, Inc.	Southbury	Solar Heat Panel Forming Machine	4/28/80
Organization Change Inc.	Bloomfield	Human Resources Software	5/27/80
Total State Funded Projects			
Grand Total			

Source: Connecticut Product Development Corporation, Annual Report, FY 1980–Figure 3, Project Summary.

Amount	Royalty Start Date	Status 7/1/79	Royalties Paid	Royalties Expected	
154,672	8/75	3 terminated; 3 inactive	33,202	none likely	
43,869	3/77	product on market	12,223	$ 50,000	(7 years)
23,841	12/75	product on market	1.852	uncertain	
60,000	12/77	product on market	13,740	$ 120,000	(7 years)
9,500		product on market	–	$ 47,500	(10 years)
291,882			61,017	$ 217,500	
192,500	8/79	product on market	26,532	$ 950,000	(5 years)
⎧	10/78	product on market	13,471	$ 900,000	(7 years)
320,000 ⎨		in development		$ 270,000	(7 years)
⎩		in development		$ 330,000	(7 years)
22,000	–	in development	–	$ 110,000	(8 years)
150,000	9/78	product on market	25,249	uncertain	
75,000	–	in development	–	$ 375,000	(7 years)
42,000	9/79	product on market	336	uncertain	
30,000	–	in development	–	$ 150,000	(9 years)
44,000	–	in development	–	$ 600,000	(10 years)
44,400	8/79	product on market	2,427	$ 250,000	(10 years)
60,000	–	in development	–	$ 300,000	(10 years)
255,000	–	in development	–	$1,275,000	(7 years)
141,870	–	in development	–	$ 700,000	(5 years)
81,000	–	in development	–	$ 405,000	(10 years)
120,000	–	in development	–	$ 600,000	(6 years)
90,000	–	in development	–	$ 450,000	(5 years)
45,000	–	in development	–	$ 225,000	(7 years)
1,712,770			68,115	$7,890,000	(10 year potential)
2,004,652			129,152	$8,107,500	(10 year potential)

new products. Because of rejections from conventional lenders, and because of insufficient internal research and development funds, management turned to CPDC.

Management's reaction to CPDC can be summarized as terrific. Processing of the application took only several months, which was considered very fast, and CPDC staff and board members were given high marks for their expertise in evaluating the products' potential and the company's financial needs. A company official indicated that the paperwork involved with the contract was not unnecessarily long and would have been prepared for internal purposes in any case. Furthermore, CPDC promptly reimbursed the company after its suppliers' invoices were forwarded. No concerns were expressed regarding the possible breach of security about details of the new products.

Company officials believe the 5% royalty share is no bargain but they consider the terms to be "very fair." They saw no real problems with CPDC's role or its operation and felt improvements were unnecessary. Even with hindsight, management indicated it would have made the same arrangement with CPDC.

Marketing of the first product of the new line began late in 1978 although the major sales are just now beginning. One of the products alone probably will produce $2.5 million in sales, thereby doubling the company's annual sales. Company employment has risen already and further increases are likely if market acceptance reaches expected levels.

Vibrametrics

This small (15-person, $400,000-in-annual-sales) company produces instruments to measure and analyze vibration in rotating machinery. With the instruments, it is possible to perform structural analysis of machinery and detect possible failures and necessary machinery maintenance. Because the company was already highly leveraged and undercapitalized, outside financing for development of a new vibratory control unit could not be secured.

As with Abbott officials, a company officer indicated that CPDC was a great concept and had been well implemented. In particular, this manager said the CPDC procedures for reimbursement were very businesslike and not at all onerous. Also, the individual noted that the monitoring activity of CPDC was strict enough to prevent any abuse of taxpayers' funds but not overly tight that it interfered with normal company practices. CPDC funds of $44,000 allowed internal research and development resources to be redirected to other product lines.[2]

CPDC project funds were expended but sales of the product by Vibrametrics did not occur. The company manager indicated that the company's continuing undercapitalized position prevented manufacturing numerous prototypes, building up inventory, and undertaking a marketing campaign. So, after searching government agencies such as the Small Business Administration and Economic Development Administration for working capital for manufacturing, the company sold the product to Anders, Inc., another Connecticut company.

According to a Vibrametrics officer, the inability of CPDC to provide working capital in addition to development funds is CPDC's major weakness. Otherwise, CPDC is given a very favorable assessment. Management would consider using it again and would recommend that other small firms explore CPDC financing. While management thinks the royalty arrangement is generally fair, he also thinks CPDC money will be "expensive" money. In this case, CPDC money proved to be quite inexpensive, from the company's perspective.

TIE/Communications, Inc.

This company is producing a number of new telephone equipment products and has begun market penetration into highly regulated industries. Although its annual sales exceeded $10 million at the time, the company could not obtain conventional financing for development of its new family of equipment systems. CPDC became involved after the state economic development agency suggested the company contact them for possible financing.

The joint venture has been highly successful. With a $3.85 million revenue bond approval by the Connecticut Development Authority, the company constructed a new 70,000-square-foot manufacturing facility. Approximately 100 employees from an out-of-state site were brought to Connecticut when the facility was completed.

CPDC was evaluated favorably in all regards—the expertise of the board and staff, their protection of confidential information, and their speed in granting approval to the application. The contract terms were considered fair by the company official.

As for the future, the company does not foresee the need for utilizing CPDC again. Because of the company's rapid expansion, new product development will be financed primarily by retained earnings and other means. In the spring of 1981, the company's financial strength and growth allowed it to sell a bond issue nationally. Royalty payments to CPDC are anticipated to be $1.85 million. With some justification, this company's growth is pointed to by CPDC officials with a sense of pride.

Additional Assessments

Assessments of CPDC by managers involved with the corporation generally parallel the evaluations given by management for the three cases just presented. CPDC operating procedures are not viewed as onerous or restrictive on companies' activities. CPDC staff's assistance in other areas, such as helping companies secure capital for manufacturing from conventional lenders, locating other state government programs oriented to land acquisition and building construction, and providing expertise on patent rights, also received favorable assessments. (For one company, $60,000 in CPDC project funds enabled it to attract $200,000 from a small business investment company and $300,000 from a local bank backed by an SBA guarantee.) In fact, the high quality of CPDC staff and board of directors has been viewed as the most important factor in CPDC's successes to date.

On several other matters, CPDC also has performed well and has avoided potentially troublesome issues. For instance, there have not been any major problems with elected officials attempting to influence decisions on particular applications from companies. Nor has there been criticism from conventional lenders that CPDC is a competitor. Legally, CPDC can provide funds only to companies in "situations in which financial aid would not otherwise be reasonably available from commercial sources." This requirement has been interpreted to mean any company which would not otherwise have conducted the new product development at this time. While this interpretation might permit CPDC to finance nearly all development projects, CPDC for all practical purposes only will arrange projects with companies which cannot meet private lenders' collateral requirements. Finally, CPDC has not been and cannot be criticized as being unaccountable to the electorate. All funding decisions must be approved by the State Bond Commission which is composed of the governor and several gubernatorially appointed cabinet officers.

Still, there have been critical comments on three points. First, CPDC is not known well enough throughout the state's business community, particularly among its potential clients. Because this situation is changing, this criticism will become less important. A second and potentially more troublesome point is that CPDC fills one void in financing but cannot help bridge the other void—working capital. Without being able to guarantee that working capital will be available for the postproduct development phase, CPDC's activities are seen as less than completely fruitful. Another aspect of this argument is that many more small businesses could be aided by CPDC if it were permitted to provide capital to firms which were selling services as well as new products.

A third issue relates to the riskiness of the board's project decisions. Critics of CPDC feel that the board has been overly cautious. If CPDC supplies funds only for the least risky projects, is CPDC really helping as many firms as need assistance and is it doing its best to create new industry and employment opportunities? If, however, CPDC takes extraordinary risks and many projects fail, critics understand that taxpayers will voice their disapproval. Clearly, there is no objective method of resolving this issue since screening must be tough enough to exclude weak companies but sufficiently lenient to help marginal firms develop their promising new products. So far, seven of the approved projects have been written off, which is about what had been anticipated.

Current Issues and Possible Modifications

One operating procedure has required a change and another has yet to be solved. Problems in obtaining quorums for the board plagued CPDC for several years before the board was enlarged by one person. One issue still needs clarification: When will CPDC begin paying interest on funds obtained from the bond commission? Because of the time horizon on royalty paybacks and because of the less-than-expected amount of project outlays to date, there has been no compelling need to resolve the issue. With more than nominal royalties beginning to be repaid, however, decisions regarding the mechanics of the revolving fund will be necessary.

Possible modifications in CPDC's funded projects principally relate to the size of projects and the financial arrangement between CPDC and the firms. The board has already relaxed its informal policy of restricting most projects to a maximum of $200,000. By doing so, CPDC has increased its potential number of clients. Such a move also would allow CPDC to increase its impact on the state's employment conditions.

New types of financial arrangements, other than the standard 5% royalty figure, have been discussed. If CPDC invests more than $300,000 in one or more projects, the board may decide that the larger risk might require an equity position in lieu of, or in addition to, the royalty payback. The legislation does not prohibit CPDC from assuming an equity position. Board members have not expressed strong interest in broadening the standard financial arrangement but neither have they indicated that an equity position would never be taken. Because each firm's request is judged independently, there may very well be a situation during the next few years in which the board and the company's officers believe that an equity position would be the best course of action.

Other major modifications in CPDC's procedures are unlikely at this stage. Now that CPDC has established a good reputation, any major changes could damage its stable and businesslike image, an image which is still being formed by its clients, the financial community, and state officials.

Is CPDC a Useful Model?

Market Needs

Increasingly, the role of industrial and technological innovation in stimulating economic development is being recognized. A recent report from the U.S. Commerce Department indicated that technological innovations accounted for nearly half (45%) of the nation's economic expansion from 1929 to 1969. During 1957–1973, high-technology companies created jobs 88% faster than other types of businesses. [See *Business Week* (1981) for further discussion.] Even though not all of CPDC's clients could be categorized as high-technology firms, most companies are developing either electronic products or highly sophisticated mechanical products. CPDC, then, seems to be focusing its resources on firms which, in the aggregate, show the most potential for rapid expansion.

The distribution of technologically oriented firms throughout the United States is, however, quite uneven. This fact suggests that not all states would need, or would benefit, from a state-financed product development corporation. Connecticut has a large number of small firms producing sophisticated mechanical and electronic products, and a ready supply of experienced managers and entrepreneurs. In states with agriculturally based economies, there may be less need for a CPDC. The industrialized and urban areas of such states may generate a sufficient number of possible clients, but that would need careful evaluation.

A CPDC also may prove most useful in areas with a skilled labor force, highly diversified suppliers, and well-developed capital markets (Katzman, 1976); but again, CPDC's utility does not seem restricted only to jurisdictions with these characteristics. CPDC may be needed most in precisely those areas with underdeveloped capital markets and may be quite successful if working capital and production financing arrangements also were possible. (Where there might not be a large number of existing small businesses, a corporation similar to CPDC might focus on helping start new companies.)

It is possible that a CPDC mechanism could be modified to prove beneficial for nearly any type of new economic development enterprise, in any geographical area. The key questions are:

1. How many profitable opportunities are being missed or postponed in the state because capital is unavailable or cannot be located at the proper time? and
2. For how many of these opportunities does the potential for significant job creation outweigh the risks?

While these questions cannot be answered conclusively until after a CPDC has been established, there may be only a few states in which a product development corporation would be completely unnecessary. Where ventures capitalists are few, where the financing needs of companies are too small (under $250,000) to be attractive to venture capitalists, where credit is not readily available, and where there are several newer, smaller firms oriented to new products, the potential seems the greatest. In such areas, the number of possible clients and applications will either require large funding or will permit the corporation to choose applicants with outstanding potential and lessened risks. In other areas, the corporation may be forced to choose products and companies which are more risky. The amount of risk involved is really the key—not whether there need be a CPDC at all.

Identifying the potential need for a product development corporation is only the first step. There may be legal obstacles to creating product development corporations in other states and these obstacles must be analyzed and overcome.

Potential Constitutional Obstacles

As is explained in Appendix B of this article, the Connecticut State Supreme Court had little difficulty in upholding the CPDC in *Wilson v. Connecticut Product Development Corporation* (355 A.2d. 167 Conn. 111). The Connecticut court found that a specific state constitutional provision against the use of public money for private purposes had not been violated because the CPDC had been established to serve a legitimate public function of increasing employment in the state. Other states with different constitutional provisions and varying court interpretations may find the legal obstacles to the implementation of such a mechanism to be at least as serious as those present in Connecticut. (As an example of another state's situation, see Appendix E by Peter Buchsbaum on the constitutionality of a New Jersey Product Development Corporation.)

Both specific state constitutional restrictions on the use of public funds and general common law "public purpose" requirements were developed primarily during the 19th century. Many states placed "public purpose" requirements similar to that of Connecticut in their state constitutions. Other states without specific "public purpose" language in their constitutions have imposed such limits by judicial action. In fact, the requirement that state expenditures have a public purpose has been found by the United States Supreme Court to have a federal basis in the due process requirements of the 14th amendment to the United States Constitution. The public purpose doctrine arose before the spread of several specific prohibitions on the use of state funds which are now in effect in nearly half the states. Historically, the general requirement of a "public purpose" is distinct from the specific prohibition clauses which were adopted later by many states. It seems likely that to establish a product development corporation in many states might require both that there be a judicially recognizable "public purpose" and also that any existing specific constitutional prohibitions not be violated.

The specific constitutional prohibitions which may be faced are of several types. Most states have a prohibition against lending state credit to private enterprise, although specific wording varies from state to state. Approximately one-fourth of the states have specific constitutional language prohibiting the gift or loan of public money to private persons or enterprises.

In states where specific constitutional strictures exist, or where general "public purpose" requirements offer a means of challenging a mechanism like CPDC, courts have available to them several means of avoiding a holding of unconstitutionality. Barring unusual court interpretations, a general requirement that public expenditures have a public purpose will not pose a serious obstacle in most states. Judicial interpretations of public purpose generally are quite broad, with the functions of increasing employment and economic progress likely to satisfy any judicial requirements. Specific constitutional prohibitions on loans and gifts have been more troublesome to state courts but, here also, various devices and interpretations have been developed to avoid constitutional strictures. Prohibitions on the lending of public credit might be avoided by a judicial finding that the public credit had in fact not been pledged. In addition, where the device of a public corporation (such as CPDC) or other form of once-removed public entity is used by a state, it may be easier for a court to determine that actions which would be impermissible for a state are unobjectionable when performed by a quasi-governmental unit. The fact that CPDC is a public corporation and not an ordinary state agency was noted in *Wilson v. CPDC* as a reason not to find that the "public purpose" doctrine was violated.

Finally, and most importantly, some states may find specific limits on the use of public funds have not been violated merely if a "public purpose" to the expenditure can be found. As noted above, there is legal authority to suggest that the general public purpose requirements are in addition to, and separate from, any specific constitutional strictures existing in a state. Yet several courts have in recent years concluded that such specific limits may be satisfied by a public purpose even when the specific language of the constitution seems to have been violated. Although it seems likely that combining the two forms of tests into one will not soon be accepted by all states, where it is available, this judicial interpretation may be a useful means of circumventing apparent constitutional limits.

Obviously, the resolution of legal issues surrounding the use of a product development mechanism in a state cannot be predicted. Where such issues arise, their seriousness will depend upon the many factors present in the legal environment of a particular state. It is suggested here, however, that the variety of existing state constitutional restrictions often will make the legal issues of aid to industry into important threshold questions for state officials interested in the CPDC concept.

Why Risk Capital?

If state officials believe that a product development corporation might be applicable to their state and would not be prevented by legal restrictions, they may wish to consider alternative financing methods to promote product development. Because the financial relationship between state government and the potential firms is so important, it deserves considerable study. A brief discussion of the strong and weak points of several alternatives follows. [Also, see Daniels (1977b).]

Grants

One possible method of helping companies with their product development is simply to provide nonmatching grants. These grants could include a requirement for payback in successful development situations, or a decision could be made that no paybacks would ever be required, on the rationale that:

1. the companies could utilize the "state funds" for production and marketing costs, or
2. the state will achieve its return on successful developments in the form of additional tax revenues and higher employment.

Nonmatching grants, with or without immediate payback provisions, seem unwise, however. First, product development is, as has been suggested, a minefield of risks. Company officials would be tempted to apply for funds for their most risky products, and a CPDC probably would be flooded by applications for "free money." Clearly, placing all the considerable risks on the taxpayers would be unacceptable. Also, without a requirement for payback, CPDC's revolving fund would need periodic injections of general fund revenues.

Tax Credits

This form of assistance seems a more viable alternative than outright grants, at least initially. As is well known, foregone revenue collections or tax credits require no major additional state government activity or personnel and private sector managers retain decision-making authority over the allocation of these resources. With regard to a product development corporation, these advantages are more than equaled by significant disadvantages.

First, estimates of foregone revenues are frequently imprecise,thereby creating the likelihood that the amount of incentive will be more than was anticipated or planned. Second, corporate tax situations are quite diverse and it is difficult to predict accurately how the incentive will affect the operations of numerous smaller firms. Third, past experience with tax credits has shown that larger firms utilize the credits to a larger degree and more quickly than smaller companies. Even by restricting the credits to smaller firms, there is no assurance that the credits will be used, or that the cash flow benefits will come at the proper time. Fourth, tax credits may not be used for new product development at all. Some firms may use the funds for cash flow purposes. Others might use the funds for higher salaries. Perhaps more importantly, even if the retained funds are used for product development, state officials will have no role in selecting which product development situations appear most promising. Finally, because tax credits are diffuse and product developments require several years before any returns are achieved, state legislators and executive officials will have almost no information on which to evaluate whether the policy is effective. Isolated examples of successful product development might be obtained but overall there would be almost no information on which to evaluate the results.

Tax credits may be useful as a tool for promoting general economic measures but they will be a poor device for directing funds for the specific purpose of product development.[3]

Other Financial Arrangements

Because of the risks in new product development, some state officials may seek more security for taxpayers than does Connecticut's Product Development Corporation. Requiring collateral would seem appropriate because that is how traditional lenders operate. According to CPDC officials, a collateral requirement would be self-defeating. Many of the firms could not meet this requirement as they are already either highly leveraged or severely undercapitalized; that is a major reason why traditional lenders have rejected their applications for financing. In addition, a collateral requirement may impact negatively on the firm's cash flow. CPDC money has a major advantage of not adding further encumbrances to the firm's balance sheet.

Another possibility would be a requirement for an equity position in the firm (albeit a much smaller position than that of a venture capitalist), conditional upon a successful product development. Besides the possible political and legal problems of state government entering into such an arrangement, this alternative has the negative consequence of tying up part of the state's funds. While this latter problem could probably be resolved without undue difficulty, the royalty payback feature clearly is more advantageous.*

In sum, the risk capital financial arrangements currently in use by Connecticut's PDC seem very appropriate, given that the goal is product development. The other possible financing methods discussed in this section may be successful economic development tools in other contexts; but for new product development financing, they appear not to offer significant advantages over CPDC's current procedures, which allow limited state government resources to be highly focused through the use of risk capital only on the most promising product development opportunities.

Suggestions

If officials outside Connecticut decide that a product development corporation may be applicable to their state or city's economic conditions and economic development plans, the following suggestions may prove helpful:

1. Determine if there are significant, legal, fiscal, and operational advantages in establishing the product development unit as a separate, independent legal entity. The arguments for a separate entity include: (a) perhaps avoiding potential legal problems mentioned earlier; (b) allowing the unit to move quickly in making business decisions and circumventing normal government delays caused by rigid and formal procedures; and (c) freeing the unit from undue executive and legislative branch influence on business decisions. Independence also has its drawbacks since additional support services would be needed, and there may be an additional credibility problem if the corporation is portrayed as being separate from the state government when almost all the funding is provided by state government. Regardless of how this issue is resolved, the product development unit should be self-supporting within a maximum specified period of time.

2. Consideration should be given to providing an initial appropriation for the corporation's operating expenses along with the authorization for a specific amount of bond money which will be used solely for investments. In

---

*Ownership of patent rights and licenses is another aspect of the equity issue. CPDC officials indicate that most patents are difficult to sell and, therefore, there has been no move in this direction. CPDC does control residual rights and nonexclusive rights on the patents, as protection against any firm which might furtively attempt to sell the product which CPDC has helped finance.

addition, consideration might be given to making a one-time appropriation of funds for both internal operating expenses and investments, with the major portion of the funds being invested by the appropriate state investment official until these funds would be obligated for product development.*

3. The legislation should not be unduly restrictive about the corporation's internal operating procedures. For example, there may be no need for a law to prohibit contracts with firms that were not specifically rejected by traditional lenders. While the large majority of companies will have been rejected, in some cases the board of directors might decide that a contract would be beneficial in speeding up development of a product which otherwise would have been postponed indefinitely.

4. Particular attention should be given to existing statutes regarding conflict of interest, and disclosure of personal investments by staff employees and members of the board of directors. Current provisions may not be adequate to cover this new state activity.

5. Existing freedom of information statutes and regulations ("sunshine laws") also must be scrutinized. Because new product development involves sensitive technical information, there may be a need for a specific provision which excludes the public from perusing information on the product and the firm's financial condition except in court cases involving possible malfeasance or criminal charges. There may also be a need to hold closed meetings when the board discusses the merit of an applicant's proposed project.

6. A nonpartisan board of directors should be appointed and be composed of individuals with financial and technological expertise. The board should have members with backgrounds in the areas of engineering, patent law, and finance as well as management experience. To ensure that there is coordination between the corporation and existing and proposed economic development assistance programs of relevant state agencies, one or more state economic officials should be members of the board. Because the primary clients will be applicants from smaller businesses, one or two board members should be current managers from such firms. As with most other boards, continuity should be encouraged by providing for staggered terms.

7. Operational details should not be overlooked once the corporation has been established. Personnel requirements include one professional member for each 10 active projects, based on the experience in Connecticut. While it is important that staff be familiar with financial issues, it is more important that staff have technical backgrounds supplemented by experi-

---

*Another alternative is to issue nonvoting stock to be held by the state treasurer and financed by general obligation bonds. This was the approach planned for the Massachusetts Technology Development Corporation.

ence in product development, patents, or manufacturing. Normal state practices probably will determine if staff will be state employees but the matter should be given some study to determine if highly qualified staff can be attracted by state-compensation levels. Because of the nature of the enterprise, perhaps staff could be eligible for lump-sum, year-end bonuses for outstanding performance and better-than-expected financial returns on the investments.

8. Because the number and quality of applicants' proposals will depend to some extent on the corporation's ability to reach its intended clients, early emphasis should be placed on advertising and publicity efforts. Furthermore, because firms whose applications have been approved will normally wish to proceed rapidly with development, any bottlenecks in the contract-approval should be rectified quickly. The application and evaluation process should be as nonbureaucratic as possible until the quantity of applications requires more formalized evaluation procedures for ranking proposals.

9. The board of directors should decide at an early date if it is advisable to limit the size of projects and the number of projects with any one firm. The extent of risks which will be tolerated probably will be decided on a case-by-case basis, yet an intentional decision can be made that low risks will be the normal practice until significant royalty returns permit more risky ventures.

10. Before the corporation is established, a thorough review of the corporation's achievements and activities should be mandated at some specific future time. This review will assess the corporation's progress in terms of royalty returns and job creation. Equally as important, the review will address possible modifications in the activities and scope of the corporation such as: (a) placing increased emphasis on management assistance for smaller firms, (b) allowing risk capital to be used for the second-stage financing needs of inventory build-up and marketing, (c) permitting capital to be used for a wider range of new products and for service-oriented firms, (d) providing direct funding for project feasibility studies and helping to completely finance new enterprises along with private investment participation, and (e) establishing a special investment account similar to a mutual fund in which the states' citizens and private firms could directly invest their money in new product development situations.[4] The review also could determine, of course, that the corporation was not successful or no longer filled a void in the capital market.

What Impact Should Be Expected?

A product development corporation is a promising device for stimulation of economic activity and job creation. Yet is must be remembered that a CPDC mechanism is essentially a small program and its impact will be limited.

Clearly, the aggregate number of jobs which will be created by a CPDC will seem low in comparison to a state's total employment in the manufacturing and service sectors. (As of July 1981, the number of jobs created by CPDC financing was 160. This number has started to rise rapidly and would be greater still if suppliers' new jobs were included. Still, the number will seem relatively small.) In all likelihood, the number of CPDC-generated jobs will be low in comparison to the number of new jobs in the state which resulted from normal expansion of industry. Nor will a CPDC mechanism make any discernible impact on unemployment levels.

To achieve a very significant impact of thousands of new jobs, it is obvious that scores of larger projects would need to be funded. There is no conclusive information that such a large-scale effort is needed or would be successful.

CPDC's long-term potential remains great, involving thousands of jobs within a decade. Even if the corporation only produces one or two thousand jobs, it will have proven successful. Of course there is no precise way of determining if CPDC's impact in terms of its own rate of return and newly created jobs would surpass the rate of return on the funds which state officials could have invested in alternative investment instruments or the return which might have been realized from other economic development efforts, such as a job training or retraining programs. If all projects were failures or if the rate of royalty payback were very low, obviously funds should be reallocated to more traditional investment instruments, Perhaps in another three years it will be possible to compute both the direct and indirect rate of return on CPDC's investments and determine whether its own balance sheet will be as good as it appears to promise.*

Perhaps equally as important, there is the issue of opportunity costs. While CPDC may be creating identifiable new jobs, what if the state government had not extracted $3 million from the capital markets? Would an equivalent number of new jobs have been created in other firms had they not been deprived of capital? Arguments advanced in a prior section on tax credits suggest that a CPDC mechanism probably will produce more jobs—but this question can never be conclusively answered.

Some elected and appointed officials no doubt will see only the potential problems failures of a CPDC device. To be sure, there are potential problems which must be avoided. However, as long as CPDC funds are not displacing or competing with private capital sources, and as long as CPDC is achieving a satisfactory rate of return and helping to generate new jobs, there is no compelling reason not to initiate a product development corporation elsewhere. If, at a later time, private firms become more interested in supplying risk capital to smaller firms, perhaps there will be no need for a CPDC; but then its replacement by the private sector would be another indication of its success.

---

*Computing the real rate of return would be complex because computations would be needed for new tax revenues, foregone interest payments, and alternative investment returns. Some reasonable estimates probably could be calculated within another few years.

142

Concluding Comments

The strong appeal of the CPDC concept is demonstrated by its continued existence and current growth, despite the serious problems faced in the first few years of the corporation's life. It is important to note that the availability of federal funding at crucial points in the history of CPDC was responsible for its survival. A clearer initial conception of the manner in which the organization would be funded and would operate on a daily basis could have helped greatly in overcoming unnecessary problems and in increasing program success.

It is premature to assess CPDC's long-term success. While CPDC appears on the road to accomplishing its objectives, progress has been slower than anticipated. Still, as for those products which CPDC is financing, benefits from CPDC's activities will occur over the longer term, and it is solely from a longer-term developmental perspective that it should be judged.

State officials should view creation of a CPDC as an investment in their state's economic future. As with most important investments, immediate returns should not be expected. Given this perspective, the recent decision to reduce CPDC's bonding authorization is disturbing, perhaps indicative of a tendency to adopt a time horizon which is too short-term for the pursuit of economic development objectives. If a short-term orientation is adopted by elected officials, board and staff members of a product development corporation probably will be forced to adopt a similar orientation. While a balanced portfolio of short-term successes and long-term successes is not necessarily bad, the danger is the potential sacrifice of good, long-term projects for small short-term gains.

A CPDC mechanism in conjunction with traditional economic development efforts offers decision makers some tools for launching industrial and technological innovation and for promotion of economic development. Despite the annoying bond authorization reduction in Connecticut, CPDC's outlook remains quite promising. Perhaps equally as important, nothing which has occurred with Connecticut's Product Corporation suggests that similar mechanisms would not work in many other state or large local governments.

Notes

[1] Products developed by parent companies in the state might be manufactured elsewhere or manufactured at both an in-state and out-of-state location. Nothing in the legislation would absolutely prevent this or would prevent licensing and franchising to other locations. The law, however, stipulates that agreements be conditional "on contractual assurances that the benefits of increasing employment and tax revenues shall remain in this state and shall accrue to it." Under appropriate circumstances, the board might be receptive to such an arrangement although that question has not yet arisen because most of the firms have no subsidiaries. As to the second possibility, there is a matter of interpreting what is meant by a reasonable financing arrangement and whether the company must be rejected formally by a conventional lender. To date, the board has taken the position that it would consider applications for products which otherwise

would not be developed by a company at this time. It is the applicant's task to convince staff and directors that product development could not and would not be undertaken without CPDC funding.

[2] The fact that internal research funds can be redirected to other projects is not the only way companies are assisted with their cash flow situation. Most contracts permit royalties to be paid to CPDC 30 days after the close of the fiscal quarter. This, of course, allows companies to use these funds in the interim. Also, all CPDC funds are "drawn down" by a firm only when they are needed. If a firm decides not to use all of its allotted funds, there is no requirement that it do so. When this occurs, the firm will be required to pay back royalties only on the amount actually used.

[3] Federal tax law changes in 1978 and 1981, which affect capital gains taxes and venture capital, injected more funds into product development situations. These changes do not seem to have obviated the need for a CPDC. Many small firms are reluctant to work with venture capitalists because they normally demand a major equity position; and in many cases, venture capitalists are reluctant to become involved with small product development projects—particularly for those under $300,000. As a result, most research and development managers and economic developers working with smaller firms believe the supply of available capital is still not close to filling demand.

[4] This idea is different but has similarities to the general stock ownership plan being studied by Alaskan officials. Under that plan, every state resident would hold stock in a state-chartered corporation which would invest in major private business ventures, such as the proposed natural gas pipeline and existing oil pipeline. Residents would receive annual dividends once all expenses had been paid. Key differences between the proposed Alaskan corporation and the suggestion in the text are: (1) participation would not be automatic or equal by virtue of being a state resident; (2) private businesses also could invest money; and (3) the investments would be restricted to new products rather than existing companies and planned, massive ventures. For more information about the Alaskan proposal, see *The Washington Post* (1978).

Bibliography

Alaska House Special Committee on the Alaska Permanent Fund (1978). "The Role of the Permanent Fund in Alaska's Future," and "A Proposal for the Alaska Permanent Fund." Juneau, Alaska: Alaska House of Representatives.

Britan, Gerald M. (1981). *Bureaucracy and Innovation: An Ethnography of Policy Change.* New York: Sage.

Charleswater Associates, Inc. (1976). "ETIP Experiment No. 78: Data Collection Summarization and Interpretation for ETIP Project Connecticut Product Development Corporation." Semi-Annual Report Draft prepared for the Experimental Incentives Technology Program of the National Bureau of Standards, Washington, D.C.: U.S. Department of Commerce.

Colosimo, D.D., et al. (1974). "The State Development Foundation: Meeting Societal Needs Through Centers of Innovation." Columbus, Ohio: Ohio Department of Economic and Community Development.

Connecticut Product Development Corporation (1980). Annual Report, FY 1980.

Daniels, Beldon H. (1977a). "Models and Options for the Alaska Permanent Fund: Functions, Regionalization and Accountability." Paper prepared for the Alaska House Special Committee on the Permanent Fund (September).

Daniels, Beldon H. (1977b). "Thinking About the Alaskan Permanent Fund: A Cautious Approach for Alaskan Policymakers." Paper prepared for the Alaska House Special Committee on the Permanent Fund (July).

Fournier, Jr., Arthur (1978). "Capital for New Technology," in Peter J. Bearse (ed.) *Mobilizing Capital for Economic Development*, Princeton, NJ: Woodrow Wilson School, Princeton University (October).

Institute for Innovative Enterprise (1976). *Incentives for Innovation: A Study of Innovation in Maine Industry*, University of Maine at Portland-Gorham, Portland, Maine (July).

Katzman, Martin (1976). "New Incentives in State Economic Development Promotion: New England Prototypes," Discussion Paper D76-1, Department of City and Regional Planning. Cambridge, MA: Harvard University (January).

Katzman, Martin (1975). "Toward a Positive-Sum Strategy of State Economic Planning: Reflections Upon Two New England Regional Commission Studies," Discussion Paper D75-8, Department of City and Regional Planning. Cambridge, MA: Harvard University (November).

National Council of Urban Economic Development (1977). "Update: States and Urban Development," Information Service Newsletter Number 11, Washington, D.C. (August).

National Research Development Corporation (1977). *28th Annual Report and Statement of Accounts 1976-77*. London, England.

National Research Development Corporation (1978). "World of Venture Capitalists Becomes More Complicated," by Bradley Graham (October 1), pp. M1–M2.

The Washington Post (1978a). "Something's Happened to Yankee Ingenuity," by Bradley Graham (September 3), pp. G1–G2.

The Washington Post (1978b). "Alaska, Inc., an Economic Experiment," by William Greider (October 22), pp. A1, A15.

Appendices

Appendix A:
Public Acts No. 248

An Act Creating the Connecticut Product Development Corporation.

Be it enacted by the Senate and House of Representatives in General Assembly convened:

Section 1. This act shall be known as and may be cited as the "Connecticut Product Development Corporation Act."

Section 2. It is found and declared that there exists in the state a great and growing need for industrial and commercial development and activity to provide and maintain employment and tax revenues; that assistance and encouragement of industrial and commercial development to provide and maintain such employment and revenues is an important function of the state; that the availability of financial assistance is an important inducement to industrial and commercial enterprises to remain or locate in this state; that there exists in the state a serious shortage of venture capital to promote the development and exploitation of invention and products; that this shortage has resulted and will result in a serious decrease in the development of new business enterprise and job opportunities in Connecticut; and, further, that providing state financial assistance for the development of products, innovation and invention for industry in this state will assist in the creation of new products and industry in this state, resulting in increased employment and public revenues; and, therefor, the necessity in the public interest and for the public benefit and good for the provisions of this act is hereby declared as a matter of legislative determination.

Section 3. As used in this act, the following terms shall have the following meanings unless the context clearly indicates another meaning and intent: (1) "Corporation" means the Connecticut Product Development Corporation as created under section 4 hereof; (2) "financial aid" means the infusion of risk capital to persons for use in the development and exploitation of specific inventions and products; (3) "invention" means any new process or new technique without regard to whether a patent has or could be granted; (4) "person" means any individual, partnership, corporation or joint venture carrying on business, or proposing to carry on business, within the state; (5) "product" means any product, device, technique or process, which is or may be exploitable commercially; such term shall not refer to pure research but shall be construed to apply to such products, devices, techniques or processes which have advanced beyond the theoretic stage and are readily capable of being, or have been, reduced to practice; (6) "venture" means, without limitation, any contractual arrangement with any person whereby the corporation obtains rights from or in an invention or product or proceeds therefrom in exchange for the granting of financial aid to such person.

Section 4. (a) There is hereby created a body corporate to be known as the "Connecticut Product Development Corporation." Such corporation is constituted a quasi-public instrumentality and the exercise by the corporation of the powers conferred in this act shall be deemed and held to be the performance of an essential public function. (b) The corporation shall be governed by a board of six directors to be appointed by the governor, at least four of whom shall be knowledgeable, and have favorable reputations for skill, knowledge and experience, in the areas of the development of technological invention. On or before May 1, 1972, the governor shall so appoint six members of said board, two to serve for two years, two for four years and two for six years from July 1, 1972. On or before May 1 of the even-numbered years thereafter, the governor shall so appoint directors to succeed those whose terms expire for terms of six years from July 1 in the year of their appointment and until their successors have been appointed. A director shall be eligible for reappointment. The governor shall fill any vacancy for the unexpired term. (c) The directors shall annually elect one of their number as chairman and one as secretary. The board may elect such other officers of the board as it deems proper. Members shall receive no compensation for the performance of their duties hereunder but shall be reimbursed for necessary expenses incurred in the performance thereof. (d) Each director of the corporation before entering upon his duties shall take and subscribe the oath or affirmation required by article eleven, section 1, of the constitution. A record of each such oath or affirmation shall be filed in the office of the secretary of the state.

Section 5. The corporation shall have perpetual succession and shall adopt, amend and repeal bylaws and regulations for the conduct of its affairs. Such succession shall continue until the existence of the corporation is terminated by law, provided no such termination shall affect any outstanding contractual obligation of the corporation to assist any person and the state shall succeed to the obligations of the corporation under such contract. Upon termination of the corporation its rights and properties shall pass to the state.

Section 6. The powers of the corporation shall be vested in and exercised by the board of directors. Four members of the board shall constitute a quorum and the affirmative vote of a majority of the members present at a meeting of the board shall be necessary and sufficient for any action taken by the board. No vacancy in the membership of the board shall impair the right of a quorum to exercise all the rights and perform all the duties of the board. Any action taken by the board may be authorized by resolution at any regular or special meeting and shall take effect immediately unless otherwise provided in the resolution. Notice of any meeting, whether special or regular, shall be given by telephone or orally, not less than forty-eight hours prior to the meeting. The board may delegate to one or more of its members, or its officers, agents and employees such powers and duties as it may deem proper.

Section 7. The board shall appoint a president of the corporation who shall not be a member of the board and who shall serve at the pleasure of the board and shall receive such compensation as shall be determined by the board. The president shall be the chief administrative and operational officer of the corporation and shall direct and supervise administrative affairs and the general management of the corporation. The president may employ such other employees as shall be designated by the board of directors; shall attend all meetings of the board; keep a record of all proceedings and maintain and be custodian of all books, documents and papers filed with the corporation and of the minute book of the corporation and of its official seal. He may cause copies to be made of all minutes and other records and documents of the corporation and may give certificates under the official seal of the corporation to the effect that such copies are true copies, and all persons dealing with the corporation may rely upon such certificates.

Section 8. The purpose of the corporation shall be to stimulate and encourage the development of new products within Connecticut by the infusion of financial aid for invention and innovation in situations in which such financial aid would not otherwise be reasonably available from commercial sources, and for this purpose the corporation shall have the following powers:

(1) To have perpetual succession as a body corporate and to adopt bylaws, policies and procedures for the regulation of its affairs and conduct of its businesses as provided in section 5 of this act;

(2) To enter into venture agreements with persons doing business in Connecticut, upon such terms and on such conditions as are consistent with the purposes of this act, for the advancement of financial aid to such persons for the development of specific products, procedures and techniques, to be developed and produced in this state, and to condition such agreements upon contractual assurances that the benefits of increasing employment and tax revenues shall remain in this state and shall accrue to it;

(3) To receive and accept aid or contributions from any source of money, property or labor or other things of value, to be held, used and applied to carry out the purposes of this act, subject to the conditions upon which such grants and contributions may be made, including but not limited to, gifts or grants from any department or agency of the United States or the state;

(4) With the approval of the commissioner of finance and control, to acquire, lease, purchase, manage, hold and dispose of real and personal property in the state of Connecticut and lease, convey or deal in or enter into

contracts with respect to such property on any terms necessary or incidental to the carrying out of these purposes;

(5) To borrow money to the extent permitted under this act;

(6) To hold patents, copyrights, trademarks or any other evidences of protection or exclusivity as to any products as defined herein, issued under the laws of the United States or any state or any nation;

(7) To employ such assistants, agents and other employees, who shall be state employees in the unclassified service, and to engage consultants and appraisers as may be necessary or desirable to carry out its purposes in accordance with this act;

(8) To make and enter into all contracts and agreements necessary or incidental to the performance of its duties and the execution of its powers under this act;

(9) To sue and be sued, plead and be impleaded, adopt a seal and alter the same at pleasure;

(10) With the approval of the state treasurer, to invest any funds not needed for immediate use or disbursement, including any funds held in reserve, in obligations issued or guaranteed by the United States of America or the state of Connecticut and in other obligations which are legal investments for savings banks in this state;

(11) To procure insurance against any loss in connection with its property and other assets in such amounts and from such insurers as it deems desirable;

(12) To the extent permitted under its contract with other persons, to consent to any termination, modification, forgiveness or other change of any term of any contractual right, payment, royalty, contract or agreement of any kind to which the corporation is a party;

(13) To do anything necessary and convenient to render the bonds to be issued under section 10 hereof more marketable;

(14) To do all acts and things necessary and convenient to carry out the purposes of this act.

Section 9. All applications for financial aid shall be forwarded, together with an application fee prescribed by the corporation, to the president of the corporation. The president, after preparing necessary records for the corporation, shall forward each application to the staff of the corporation, for an investigation and report concerning the advisability of approving the proposed financial aid for such company and concerning any other factors deemed relevant by the corporation. Such investigation and report shall include, but shall not be limited to, such facts about the company under consideration as its history, wage standards, job opportunities, stability of employment, past and present financial condition and structure, proforma income statements, present and future markets and prospects, integrity of management as well as the feasibility of the proposed product and invention to be granted financial aid, including the state of development of such product as well as the likelihood of its commercial feasibility. After receipt and consideration of the above report and after such other action as is deemed appropriate, the corporation shall approve or deny the application. The applicant shall be promptly notified of such action by the corporation. Such approval shall be conditioned upon payment to the corporation, within such reasonable time after notification of approval as may be specified by the corporation, of a commitment fee prescribed by the corporation.

Section 10. The state bond commission shall have power in accordance with the provisions of section 3-20 of the 1969 supplement to the general statutes to authorize the issuance of bonds of the state in one or more series and in principal amounts not exceeding in the aggregate ten million dollars to carry out the purposes of this act. The principal and interest of said bonds shall be payable at such place or places as may be determined by the state treasurer and shall bear such date or dates, mature at such time or times, bear interest at such rate or different or varying rates, be payable at such time or times, be in such denominations, be in such form with or without interest coupons attached, carry such registration and transfer privileges, be payable in such medium of payment and be subject to such terms of redemption with or without premium as, irrespective of the provisions of said section 3-20, may be provided by the authorization of the state bond commission or fixed in accordance therewith. The proceeds of the sale of such bonds, after deducting therefrom all expenses of issuance and sale, shall be paid to the corporation. When the state bond commission has acted to issue such bonds or a portion thereof, the treasurer may, pending the issue of such bonds, issue, in the name of the state, temporary notes in anticipation of the money to be received from the sale of such bonds. In issuing the bonds authorized hereunder, the state bond commission may require repayment of such bonds by the corporation as shall seem desirable consistent with the purposes of this act. Such terms for repayment may include a forgiveness of interest, a holiday in the repayment of interest or principal or both.

Section 11. On September 1 of each year the corporation shall report on its operations for the preceding fiscal year to the governor. Such report shall include a summary of the activities of the corporation and a complete operating and financial statement. The corporation shall be subject to examination by the state treasurer. The accounts of the corporation shall be subject to annual audits by the state auditors of public accounts.

Section 12. The state of Connecticut does hereby pledge to and agree with any person with whom the corporation may enter into contracts pursuant to the provisions of this act, that the state will not limit or alter the rights hereby vested in the corporation until such contracts and the obligations thereunder are fully met and performed on the part of the corporation, provided nothing herein contained shall preclude such limitation or alteration if adequate provision shall be made by law for the protection of such persons entering into contracts with the corporation.

Section 13. The powers enumerated in this act shall be interpreted broadly to effectuate the purposes thereof and shall not be construed as a limitation of powers.

Section 14. To the extent that the provisions of this act are inconsistent with the provisions of any general statute or special act or parts thereof, the provisions of this act shall be deemed controlling.

Section 15. The corporation shall be and is hereby declared exempt from all franchise, corporate business and income taxes levied by the state, provided nothing herein shall be construed to exempt from any such taxes, or from any taxes levied in connection with the manufacture or sale of any products which are the subject of any agreement made by the corporation, any person entering into any agreement with the corporation.

Section 16. This act shall take effect from its passage.

Appendix B

Wilson v. CPDC: A Case Summary

The case ultimately decided by the Connecticut Supreme Court (*Wilson* v. *Connecticut Product Development Corporation*, 355 A.2d. 167 Conn. 111), was brought by two Connecticut residents in their status as taxpayers. Named as defendants were the CPDC and two companies whose applications for financing had been approved prior to the bond counsel's decision. The plaintiffs relied upon two constitutional arguments. They concluded that the CPDC legislation was unconstitutional in that it violated the requirement in Article I of the state constitution that "no man or set of men are entitled to exclusive public emoluments or privileges from the community." The plaintiffs contended that CPDC assistance was such a public emolument granted to private individuals without a legitimate public purpose and was, therefore, in violation of Article I.

Plaintiffs argued, however, that even if the CPDC financing were not devoid of a legitimate public purpose, that the act was unconstitutional because of the legal principals relating to the delegation of legislative powers to executive branch agencies. They contended that the CPDC legislation failed to provide adequate standards to guide the discretion of the CPDC officers in making their decisions regarding the financing of particular projects and was, therefore, unconstitutional as an unrestricted delegation of the power of the legislature to perform the legislative function of distributing public monies.

The Connecticut Supreme Court responded to the plaintiffs' two major arguments in direct fashion and was able to unanimously conclude that the CPDC legislation in fact did not violate the constitution of the state. In responding to the plaintiffs "public emoluments for private purposes" argument, the court found that there was indeed a public purpose behind the legislature's establishment of the Product Development Corporation. The court first noted that in a declaratory judgment action the presumption falls necessarily in favor of the constitutionality of the act being challenged. They then further observed that the modern legal trend is to broadly construe the meaning of "public purpose" and that if the act promotes the welfare of the state it serves a legitimate public purpose, and was not a public fund for only private benefit. Plaintiffs had argued that the benefits of the legislation were "speculative" but the court said that this argument only disputed the policy judgment of legislature and did not argue that in fact there was no public purpose behind the enactment. The fact that the employment benefits of CPDC might not be direct effects of the act was discounted as irrelevant—if the act was passed with those potential benefits in mind then the requirement of a public purpose was served. The nature of the CPDC as a quasi-public corporation and the role of the state bond commission as a potential restraining influence on CPDC decisions were also cited by the court as reasons to conclude that the public had been protected by the act from use of the CPDC funds for purely private purposes. The court concluded their response to the first of plaintiffs' arguments by noting that a public purpose was clearly present.

The plaintiffs' second constitutional argument was disposed of by the court in a similar manner. The modern trend of the law on questions of delegation of legislative powers was explained by the court as being to find the delegation constitutionally unobjectionable if the standards provided by the legislature for the exercise of the powers granted are described as explicitly as is "reasonably practicable" under the circumstances. The court then proceeded to find that the act set forth clearly the objectives of increasing employment and public revenues in the state through the development of new products and industry. The requirements that most of the corporation directors have expertise in the area of technological innovation and the requirements of staff reporting on applicants and statutory criteria for financing awards were all listed by the court as being standards for the operation of the CPDC. Detailed standards were found to be unnecessary, and those contained in the act were held to be clearly sufficient.

Appendix C

Great Britain's National Research Development Corporation

The National Research Development Corporation (NRDC) of Great Britain points to its involvement in several new industries and products as evidence of the corporation's success. Yet critics of the NRDC say the "profits" since 1967 and NRDC's involvement in successful industries and products does not necessarily indicate that the corporation has enjoyed success commensurate with the nation's investment. They argue that since NRDC has not paid interest on money borrowed from the treasury to finance its projects, that the true costs and benefits of the corporation have not been weighed. They contend that although income exceeds expenditures, that if interest had been required the balance sheet might not have been positive. In addition, critics speculate as to whether the public money invested through NRDC would have resulted in less or more technological innovation and economic growth if it had been invested directly by private industry without public involvement.

Regardless of the level of success which NRDC ultimately reaches, it seems clear that the concept of a government-funded development corporation of the NRDC type is an attractive one for Britain and other nations as well. Since the first execution of the concept in England, similar mechanisms have been created in France and Sweden and about 10 other nations.

More information about NRDC is available from Jim Jarrett at the Council of State Governments, John Phillips, President of Connecticut's Product Development Corporation, or by contacting the NRDC's Manager of Public Relations at Kingsgate House, 66-74 Victoria Street, London SW 1 E 6SL.

Appendix D

CPDC Operating Expenses for 1980

Account Description	Budget	Actual	Favorable (Unfavorable)
Salaries	$ 99,971	$ 90,701	$ 9,270
Lump sum	100		100
Overtime	416		416
Fringe benefits	25,018	22,775	2,243
Advertising	900	781	119
Printing and binding	1,200	1,585	(385)
Dues and subscriptions	200	12	188
Fees	800	15	785
Travel-in-state	2,700	1,709	991
Travel-out-state	800	257	543
Telephone	2,700	1,913	787
Rent	12,000	11,903	97
General repairs	400	6	394
Motor vehicle repairs	200		200
Sundry operating expenses	2,545	2,014	531
Outside professional services	10,200	24,250	(14,050)
Non-professional services	1,700	710	990
Motor vehicle rental	810	1,030	(220)
Postage	520	86	434
Lease personal property	2,430	2,345	85
Utility services	1,000	274	726
Maintenance supplies	200		200
Office supplies	1,290	1,171	119
Educational supplies	220	86	134
Miscellaneous	100	233	(133)
Equipment	3,630	2,701	929
TOTALS	$172,050	$166,555	$ 5,495

Source: Connecticut Product Development Corporation 1980 Report to the Governor.

CPDC Balance Sheet

	June 30, 1979	June 30, 1980
Assets		
Cash		
On deposit in bank	$ 32,214.37	$ 20,956.66
In custody of State Treasurer	(962,829.24)	(1,262,346.12)
Petty cash fund	63.94	35.38
Investment in State Treasurer's short-term investment fund	43,000.00	5,000.00
Grant funds receivable from U.S. Dept. of Com merce Economic Development Administration Act	20,000.00	20,000.00
Accrued interest on investment	158.48	39.60
Accrued royalties receivable	33,458.80	29,630.05
Due from corporate funds	86.06	86.06
Investments in product development projects	1,061,841.18	1,302,602.06
Equipment	4,444.59	7,782.47
Future borrowings authorized	1,483,900.00	2,262,770.00
TOTAL ASSETS	$1,716,338.18	$2,386,556.16
Liabilities, Reserves, and Fund Balances		
Accounts payable		373.38
Accrued salaries and wages payable	2,322.43	6,934.27
Accrued fringe benefits payable	583.16	1,865.17
Due to general fund	86.06	86.06
Allotments in force		
For projects	300,570.60	665,358.97
For administration expenses	594.57	49,888.37
Liability for petty cash fund	100.00	100.00
Reserve for investment in product development projects	1,061,841.18	1,302,602.06
Reserve for equipment	4,444.59	7,782.47
Reserve for uncollected royalties	24,900.00	29,100.00
Reserve for future borrowings authorized	1,483,900.00	2,262,770.00
Fund balances	1,163,004.41	1,940,304.59
TOTAL LIABILITIES, RESERVES & FUND BALANCES	$1,716,338.18	$2,386,556.16

Source: Connecticut Product Development Corporation 1980 Report to the Governor.

Appendix E

Memorandum on the Constitutionality of a New Jersey Product Development Corporation

Peter Buchsbaum, Esq.

Warren, Goldberg, and Berman, Princeton, NJ

A question has been raised in New Jersey as to whether a state development finance entity similar to the Connecticut Product Development Corporation (CPDC) would be approved by New Jersey Courts. This memorandum argues that it is quite likely, though not certain, that a New Jersey entity incorporating the essential principles of the CPDC would be sustained in New Jersey. To summarize: the New Jersey constitutional provisions and legal precedents cited below imply that it should be possible for the state legislature to establish a state development finance vehicle to provide risk capital for new technologies in the form of equity or royalty financing, with little danger that the legislative work would be undone by legal challenges.*

The essential features of the Connecticut entity, which would presumably be carried through in New Jersey, are (1) the use of State funds derived from appropriations or bond proceeds to provide venture capital for new businesses engaged in the development of new kinds of products, technologies and projects, (2) a series of legislative standards explaining which businesses qualify for assistance and limiting assistance to persons doing business in New Jersey, and (3) administration of the legislative standards by a Board of Directors and staff which are required to have technological and financial expertise and are required in addition, to undertake some investigation or analysis of each proposed venture prior to its being funded.

The New Jersey State Constitution of 1947 contains a number of provisions which restrain State assistance to private business entities. Article VIII, Section II, Paragraph 1 declares that "the credit of the State shall not be directly or indirectly loaned in any case." Aside from this restriction on use of the State's credit, there are restrictions on the use of appropriated money for private benefit:

> No donation of land or appropriation of money shall be made by the State or any county or a municipal corporation to or for the use of any society, association or corporation whatever. N.J. Const. 1947, Article VIII, Section III, Paragraph 3.

Further, Article VIII, Section II, Paragraph 2 provides that appropriations

---

*A legal challenge to the CPDC was not sustained before the Connecticut Supreme Court. See 167 Conn. 111, 355A.2d72 (Sup. Ct., 1974).

pursuant to law be "for the support of the State government and for all other State purposes."

Despite the absolute language of these provisions, they have never been interpreted literally. State appropriations to private individuals have been allowed where they promote a public purpose and engender only incidental private benefit.

The leading case is *Roe v. Kervick*, in which the Court sustained the constitutionality of the Area Redevelopment Act. In that case, the State Treasurer challenged the constitutionality of the Act insofar as it authorized a loan of $500,000 from State funds to the Area Redevelopment Fund under which the Act was to be financed. He also challenged the legitimacy of loans from the newly created Area Redevelopment Authority to local area redevelopment agencies for the purpose of assisting privately sponsored redevelopment projects. The Treasurer argued that these provisions violated the constitutional prohibitions against loans of State credit and appropriations of State funds to corporations. In response, the Court stated that the test was whether public money or credit was being given or loaned for a private as distinguished from a public purpose. Further, and most crucially, it defined public purpose in extremely broad and flexible terms:

> The concept of public purpose is a broad one. Generally speaking, it connotes an activity which serves as a benefit to the community as a whole, and which, at the same time is directly related to the functions of government. Moreover, it cannot be static in its implications. To be serviceable it must expand when necessary to encompass changing public needs of a modern dynamic society. Thus it is incapable of exact or perduring definition. Roe v. Kervick, 42, N.J. 191, 207 (1964).
>
> In addition, the Court found no significant difference, in determining whether a public purpose was involved, between a loan of credit or an actual appropriation of money.

The Court went on to hold that the purpose of the Area Redevelopment Assistance Act, the relief of unemployment, was clearly a public one. The legislature clearly had the power to devote public funds to direct relief of the unemployed or to establish public works projects utilizing the services of the unemployed, 42 N.J. at 217. It concluded that the legislative decision to achieve relief of unemployment through a new means, area redevelopment projects, could not be invalidated by a court:

> It seems to follow, therefore, that if the purpose of a statute be public, as it clearly is here, the means of accomplishing it laid down thereby ought to be regarded as a matter of valid legislative policy so long as the means are restricted to the public end by the legislation and contractual obligations. 42 N.J. at 217.

Having determined that unemployment could be relieved through State assistance to private enterprise, the Court then asked whether the statute in question sufficiently ensured that the public money would indeed be used to promote the public purposes. The answer to this question was held to depend on the imposition on the private entity of a contractual obligation to carry out the public purpose and the primacy of public as contrasted with private benefit from the transaction:

> Obviously the funds of the State or a county or municipality could not be loaned to a private agency to be used as the agency pleased. Clearly the constitution would stand in the way. But when the loan is granted for an obvious public purpose and its use confined to the execution of that purpose through a reasonable measure of control by a public authority by means of contractual stipulation, statutory and administrative regulation, the private agency takes on the form of a special public agent for the paramount purpose of devoting the money to relief of unemployment. 42 N.J. at 222.

The Court ultimately found that given the public interest as broadly conceived and the existence of assurances that the loan recipients would actually provide employment, the Area Redevelopment Assistance Act could not be deemed inconsistent with the "gift" and "loan of public credit" requirements of the State Constitution.

The later cases have largely adhered to the principles laid down in *Roe v. Kervick*. Thus in *Clayton v. Kervick*, 52 N.J. 138 (1968), the Court sustained an appropriation of $100,000.00 in start-up money to the New Jersey Educational Facilities Authority which was established to issue revenue bonds for the construction of dormitory facilities at private as well as public educational institutions. The Court found the furtherance of higher education in New Jersey to be a public purpose. It also found the requirement that loan recipients actually build dormitory facilities sufficiently ensured advancement of the public interest by the private grantee. It therefore sustained the statute. Similarly, in *New Jersey Mortgage Finance Agency v. McCrane*, 56 N.J. 414 (1970), the Court again dealt with the refusal of the State Treasurer to release appropriated start-up monies on the ground of constitutional doubt as to compliance with the public purpose requirements of the constitution. The issue in *McCrane* was the validity of the New Jersey Mortgage Finance Agency which was to issue revenue bonds, the proceeds of which would be in turn loaned to private financial institutions which would then be obligated to make mortgage loans. The Court found this measure to be a reasonable means of dealing with the State's housing crisis through the creation of an additional source of funds for the purchase of housing. It further found that the bank's obligation actually to use the monies for the making of mortgage loans ensured that the private sector would indeed implement the public purpose of the legislation. On these grounds the Mortgage Finance Agency legislation was sustained.

These cases establish two essential principles governing State loans and appropriations to the private sector: the State funds must be used for public purpose, and implementation of this public purpose must be ensured through a contractual relationship with the grantee which requires it to carry out the public purpose and subordinates private gain to the interests of the public. It is against these twin measuring rods that a New Jersey Product Development Corporation would be evaluated.

It seems clear that such an entity would at least theoretically serve recognized public purposes. The enhancement of new and innovative business enterprises in New Jersey would be designed to generate employment and thus come specifically within the public purpose endorsed by the Court in *Roe v. Kervick*. In addition, such new businesses would also generate additional public revenues which is also the legitimate end of government. Clearly, in line with *Roe v. Kervick*, the legislature could not be second guessed if it chooses to increase the public treasury through the enhancement of private activity rather than through simply raising tax rates or adding additional taxes.

However, judicial approval of such a scheme would require more than these simple assertions of promotion of a public benefit. In each of the cases discussed above, the Court made specific reference to legislative findings or study reports indicating that a serious public problem existed and that public assistance to private enterprise was a reasonable method of addressing that problem. Thus, in *Roe v. Kervick*, the Court quoted the legislative findings concerning unemployment. In *Clayton*, the Court relied on the report of a committee which discussed the need to enhance the status of higher education in New Jersey and which recommended an authority to increase the student capacity of New Jersey colleges. Finally, in *New Jersey Mortgage Finance Agency v. McCrane*, the Court adverted to public reports and information concerning the housing scarcity in New Jersey.

By analogy, the case for a product development corporation would depend in part on the existence of a legislative record or executive report(s) indicating that New Jersey lags in the development of new kinds of products, technologies, etc. and that public assistance in the form of venture capital is needed to help produce the tax and employment benefits which could be engendered by the stimulation of innovative enterprises. It is to be noted that *Wilson v. Connecticut Product Development Corp.*, the Connecticut decision sustaining the CPDC explicitly referenced a study and recommendations of the Governor's strike force on full employment. See 355 A.2d at 74, 76.

The further question would be the inclusion in the scheme of adequate standards to ensure that the public benefit is achieved. This requirement does not necessarily mean that assisted ventures must succeed. Certainly nothing in *Roe v. Kervick* required that redevelopment projects actually make money. Rather, all that should be required is that the legislation obligate the Board of the corporation to select only those projects which have a reasonable chance of producing employment and tax revenues and further, that the businesses selected actually carry out the projects for which they are being financed. The requirement that the projects be conducted locally will also help to ensure that the public funds actually enhance the public welfare of the State rather than simply add to the net worth of the grantee corporation. In this context, the comment of the dissent in *Clayton v. Kervick* is noteworthy—Justice Hall complained that the educational facilities program there sustained, did not even specifically require private colleges to increase their enrollments when they obtained a loan from the Educational Facilities Authority. Despite this comment, however, the legislation was sustained on the ground that the law at least required colleges to build projects for which the money was being loaned. Similarly, a requirement that an enterprise develop a technology which is likely to engender employment and tax revenues should be sufficient to sustain a statute even if there can be no assurance that the technology will actually produce the end result sought. As was stated by the Connecticut Court in the *Wilson* case, "the strong presumption of the Act's constitutionality will not be overcome simply because the plaintiffs' economic forecasts differ from those of the legislature." Thus, assured effectiveness of State venture capital assistance in promoting employment and tax revenues is not required. 355 A.2d at 76.

It should also be noted that there appears to be no significant difference between a loan mechanism and an equity mechanism from a constitutional standpoint. The Court in *Roe v. Kervick* stated that the constitutional tests were the same regardless of whether the concerned were over an appropriation of funds or a loan of public credit. 142 N.J. at 208. Further, the acceptability of a scheme depends on its fulfillment of the public purpose, not on repayment of the public funds. See *Roe*, 42 N.J. at 218. Finally, each of the three major New Jersey cases has involved the constitutionality of appropriations as well as of loan mechanisms and in all cases both direct appropriation and the loan procedure have passed. Therefore, there is no inherent reason to believe that an equity program would be subject to a different standard of review than a loan program. This is not to say that the acceptability of a venture capital scheme might not be assisted in some fashion by the imposition of a method for recovering the cost of the initial State investment where enterprises are successful. A State role in management could also be required legislatively as a condition of a capital grant. Nonetheless, such requirements, while helpful in any constitutional test of a new venture capital scheme, would probably not be dispositive. The New Jersey twin test of public purpose could probably be met without them.

Comparison with Connecticut and Massachusetts

Brief mention was made above of the Connecticut case, *Wilson v. Connecticut Products Development Corp.* The reasoning in the Connecticut case is very similar to that employed by the New Jersey precedents. Like New Jersey, the Connecticut constitutional ban on grant of public funds to private entities has been interpreted to prohibit only those grants which do not serve a public purpose. 355A.2d at 74. Connecticut also used the strong presumption of statutory constitutionality which means that the legislative judgment as to public purposes and the means of furthering them will ordinarily be sustained unless the private benefit aspect of a statute is clearly apparent. See language quoted above with respect to differing economic forecasts. Further, the Connecticut court, like New Jersey's Courts, looks to the legislative record for facts underlying the statute in supporting the claim that it furthers a public purpose.

The Connecticut Court also requires that the means chosen for advancing the public purpose ensures that public rather than private interests predominate. In *Wilson*, the issue was said to be the insufficiency of standards to prevent public giveaways or to guide the discretion of the CPDC's officers in the administration of the program. 355 A.2d at 76, 77. The Court noted a number of restraining aspects of the legislation such as intervention of the CPDC itself as a buffer between the legislature and the recipients of financial support, the right of CPDC to withhold funds from projects found not to be in accordance with the goals of the Act, CPDC's right to obtain royalties or other advantages from a product line it assists, and the additional requirement that the State Bond Commission approve any bonds issued by CPDC. The Court further noted that assistance was limited to products and corporations in Connecticut and that the majority of CPDC directors and its staff were required to have expertise in determining the appropriateness of potential projects. These facts are similar to the ones looked to by the New Jersey Courts in evaluating various finance schemes which it has had to review. Thus, while New Jersey Courts have focused on the term adequate public contractual consideration rather than on lack of legislative standards sufficient to guide administrative discretion, the ultimate test behind the differing language appears to be rather similar. Further, since the reasoning of the Connecticut Court is similar to those in New Jersey holdings, it can be expected that the *Wilson* case would have a considerable influence on the New Jersey Supreme Court when and if it has to evaluate the constitutionality of a New Jersey Products Development Corporation.

In contrast, the Massachusetts Supreme Judicial Court appears to have adopted a stricter view of its State's constitutional prohibition against the loan of public credit. The Massachusetts Constitution, Article 84 provides:

> The credit of the commonwealth shall not in any manner be given or loaned to or in aid of any individual or of any private association, or of any corporation which is privately owned and managed.

This language is almost identical to Article VIII, Section III, Paragraph 2 of the New Jersey Constitution which forbids political subdivisions from assisting corporations and is certainly no more absolute in its phrasing than Article VIII, Section II, Paragraph 1 of the New Jersey Constitution which forbids the State's credit to be "directly or indirectly loaned in any case." Nonetheless, the interpretation adopted by the Massachusetts Supreme Judicial Court in Opinion of the Justices, 369 N.E. 2d 447 (Sup. Jud. Ct. 1977), is not the same. In that case, the Court evaluated the constitutionality of the Massachusetts Community Development Finance Corporation. This entity was empowered to invest in publicly controlled, local community development corporations which would use the investment proceeds to provide financial assistance to private projects that would otherwise be unable to obtain such aid. The opinion's first section evaluates this scheme in terms of a public purpose concept that is as flexible as that employed in Connecticut and New Jersey. However, the second part of the opinion focuses not on whether the means chosen adequately advance the public purpose, but much more literally on whether the community development corporations which will directly benefit from assistance under the Act are technically private associations or corporations which are privately owned and managed. 369 N.E. 2d at 450. Thus, while the operative New Jersey question would be whether the private entity is actually required to be an agent carrying out the public purpose, the Massachusetts approach appears to bar any direct assistance to a private corporation no matter how tightly its discretion is confined. Based on this observation, it can be concluded that a Product Development Corporation, involving direct capital grants to businesses as per the Connecticut model, would probably not receive approval in Massachusetts.

The Massachusetts decision can be criticized as being insufficiently flexible. Further, the Court's opinion is silent as to the ultimate disposition of funds by the local community development corporation: It nonetheless held that the local development corporations validated the scheme since they were publicly controlled. The Court thus seems to have adopted a double intermediary test requiring (a) that State funds first pass through a public corporation such as the CDFC and (b) be granted to a local publicly controlled corporation before (c) they could actually be invested in private development projects. There would seem to be no logical reason for requiring that public funds pass through two intermediaries before being expended on a private entity. It can be assumed that the Massachusetts Court adopted this approach only to imbue its rigid "private association" test with some flexibility without abandoning the letter of the test. Nonetheless, so long as the test remains in formal effect, it can be expected that the Massachusetts Court would not approve a products development corporation even though the Connecticut courts have and the New Jersey courts probably would.

VII

ESOPs—An Emerging Technique for Development Financing

Jeffrey R. Gates and John E. Curtis, Jr.

An employee stock ownership plan (ESOP) is an employee benefit plan that may be used as a technique of corporate finance. An ESOP has two basic purposes. The first is to enable employees to acquire stock in their employer. The second is to provide a tax-favored means of corporate finance.

ESOP financing has been used to accomplish a variety of corporate objectives. This chapter will illustrate how an ESOP may be innovatively structured to assist in development financing. For example, ESOP financing has been used to accomplish the following corporate objectives:

Motivate employees with stock ownership

Finance new capital

Refinance existing debt

Acquire other companies

Acquire outstanding shares

Divest subsidiaries

Recover taxes

Provide a market for closely held stock

Plan for estate liquidity

Quality for additional tax credits

This chapter provides an historical overview of ESOP-related legislation and a capsule summary of the philosophy behind the ESOP concept. The basic mechanics of implementing an ESOP are also discussed, including an indication of several different methods for structuring ESOP transactions. Many of the limitations and considerations confronting any potential ESOP company are also covered, along with a treatment of common problems and pitfalls. Also provided is a summary of how a company can qualify for additional tax credits with an employee stock ownership plan. In addition, this chapter summarizes two case histories of federally-assisted ESOPs and reviews the results of several recent studies of ESOP companies.

ESOPs—An Historical Sketch

Although widespread interest in ESOPs began only in the mid-1970s, the basic ESOP idea dates from 1921. At the time, there was no Social Security. The U.S. income tax was just a few years old. World War I had only recently ended, and the Congress was considering the Revenue Act of 1921.

Legislators were looking for a method by which U.S. industry could "attract and retain" qualified employees. They settled on the idea of profit-sharing plans and stock bonus plans. The 1921 Act first granted tax-favored status to those two types of employee benefit plans. Interestingly, it was not until five years later that federal legislation granted this same tax-favored status to pension plans.

The 1921 legislation is significant because profit-sharing plans are similar to ESOPs and, more importantly, because stock bonus plans form the nucleus of ESOPs. In fact, ESOPs are actually a special type of stock bonus plan. It should be kept in mind that these types of plans are not intended so much as retirement plans as they are intended to be "ownership participation" plans. As the Internal Revenue Service points out, stock bonus plans are intended "to give the employee-participants an interest in the ownership and growth of the employer's business."

Legal authorization for the first so-called "leveraged ESOP," however, dates from 1953. In that year, the Internal Revenue Service ruled that an employee trust (such as a stock bonus plan) could be used to borrow funds for investment in the stock of the sponsoring corporation. It was under this ruling that the first "leveraged ESOPs" were established.

Most commentators, however, trace the birth of the ESOP to 1973. That was the year Congress debated the financial fate of several of the nation's troubled railroads in the Northeast and Midwest, the bankrupt Penn Central being the best known of the lot. In the Regional Rail Reorganization Act of 1973, Congress required that ConRail (as that consolidated group of railroads is now known) evaluate an ESOP before it qualified for government assistance. ConRail did not implement an ESOP, at least not in 1973. ConRail was back again in 1978, however, for another $1.2 billion in federal aid. Under the Regional Rail Reorganization Act of 1978, $162.5 million of that amount will now be funded through an ESOP.

It was in the 1973 ConRail legislation that Congress first characterized the ESOP as a "technique of corporate finance that uses a stock bonus trust in connection with the financing of... capital requirements of the corporation." That language was repeated the following year when ERISA (the Employee Retirement Income Security Act of 1974) formally recognized the ESOP as an employee benefit plan and established criteria for its adoption and use. For financing purposes, the most important aspect of ERISA was its "ESOP loan exemption" from the otherwise "prohibited transaction" rules of the 1974 Act.

ERISA generally prohibits loans between an employee plan and a "party-in-interest" (for example, the employer, a plan trustee, company officers or directors, shareholders owning 10% or more of the stock, and others). Thus it is the "ESOP loan exemption" that makes ESOP financing possible. (The actual mechanics of ESOP financing are explained in a later section, "ESOP Implementation.")

The third piece of ESOP-related legislation was the Trade Act of 1974 which expanded the President's power to negotiate trade agreements. The Act also permits the granting of federal loan guarantees for companies in foreign trade-impacted industries. In assessing such loans, the Commerce Department was directed to give preference to corporations agreeing to finance 25% of the loan principal through an ESOP. The Trade Act also described the ESOP as a "technique of corporate finance."

The fourth and fifth pieces of ESOP legislation introduced a new type of ESOP—one funded not with tax deductions but with tax credits. The Tax Reduction Act of 1975 established the availability of an additional 1% investment tax credit for employers who adopt a specially defined type of ESOP (also known by its acronym "TRASOP"). The Tax Reform Act of 1976 then amended the 1975 Act to permit an employer to claim yet another .5% investment tax credit, provided employees contribute a matching amount of cash to the plan. The Economic Recovery Tax Act of 1981 further amended this type of ESOP. After 1982, the tax credits available for funding ESOPs will be based on payroll instead of investment. The tax credit ESOP is discussed in the "ESOP Implementation" section of this chapter.

The Revenue Act of 1978 and the Technical Corrections Act of 1979 simplified many of the provisions relating to ESOPs. In 1978, legislation was also enacted authorizing government funding for the Delaware & Hudson Railroad, mandating the creation of an ESOP as a condition of federal assistance. The federal government's financial assistance to the Chrysler Corporation was also linked to the establishment of an ESOP as part of the Chrysler Corporation Loan Guarantee Act of 1979.

The year 1980 saw the enactment of a Small Business Administration (SBA) bill containing several ESOP-related incentives. A principal provision specifically provides that the SBA may lend to ESOPs (lending previously denied because ESOPs were not considered small businesses). The Act is designed to promote the ownership of small businesses by employees, including a means by which employees can purchase their companies when their employer might otherwise be closed, liquidated, or relocated. SBA loan guarantees may now be extended not only to ESOPs but also to trusts which seek to purchase 51% of the stock of a small business.

The ESOP Concept — A Philosophical Overview

The basic idea behind the ESOP is to provide a financial vehicle by which more people can acquire stock in the companies for which they work. Congress has cited many reasons why broadened stock ownership might prove beneficial.

An oft-recurring theme is one of basic fairness. Many senators and congressmen have questioned the equity of a system in which the bulk of the nation's corporate stock is owned by a small group of people. A 1975 study by the Joint Economic Committee of Congress indicated that 50% of the personally held corporate stock in the United States is owned by less than 1% of the U.S. population. Six percent, it was found, own over 80%. In addition, the Committee found that 46% of corporate dividends flow to 1% of the population. The Committee's figures also indicate that working nonprofessionals—comprising some 76% of the U.S. workforce—own but 19% of the capital stock.

This question of equity also has a more pragmatic side. The U.S. economy is presently suffering from a severe decline in productivity. During the decade 1967–1977, the United States had the lowest productivity gains of any major industrial nation in the western world. Over that ten-year span, non-farm productivity increased only 27%, the same as in economically-troubled Great Britain, but less than half as much as in France, West Germany, and Italy, and less than a quarter as much as in Japan.

New capital investment is a must. For the 25 years prior to 1973, capital spending added 3% per year to the economy's capital base, that has since slowed to 1.75%. And whereas from 1945–1970 the economy enjoyed an average annual growth rate of 3%, by 1977 that rate was cut in half. By 1978 it was 0.4%. And for 1979 the United States recorded its first decline in productivity since we began to keep such statistics more than three decades ago.

That is economic reality. Although economists seldom agree, the vast majority of them acknowledge that as a nation we must somehow increase our productivity and that to do that we simply must have more investment and capital formation. The political reality, however, is that proposals encouraging capital formation almost always involve reducing taxes for wealthy taxpayers and increasing taxes for less wealthy taxpayers. And packages weighted too heavily in that direction are simply too heavy to sail legislatively.

The political pragmatics of this situation are perhaps best summed up by Senator Russell B. Long, ranking Democratic member of the Senate Committee on Finance, who explains:

> For our economic system to survive, its proponents must be able to win elections.
> This is so for the simple reason that if a system cannot win elections, in time, an
> unfriendly administration will inflict grave damage and, eventually, destroy that

system. The best way to guard against this is to make sure that when we orate about the virtues of capitalism and free enterprise, there are enough capitalists among those listening to help win the elections. For capitalism to have meaning as a workable, defensible system, it must have meaning to the average American worker.

The ESOP concept proposes to broaden ownership by encouraging capital formation in such a way that it will be paid for out of the future earnings that the newly-formed capital produces. Financially, the ESOP is intended to tap the financial logic of the modern corporation. For example, modern corporations generally will not approve financing for capital expansion plans unless those plans are supported by financial projections indicating that the project will pay for itself out of future earnings.

Through the ESOP, Congress is also providing tax incentives for corporations to finance their transfers in ownership in such a way as to create more stockholders.

The debt-financing (or "leveraging") aspect is meant to do more than provide a rapid infusion of cash to the corporation. It is also meant to resolve a financial "Catch-22" facing employees desiring to buy stock in their employer. Without the ESOP, such employees would be required to pay for the stock "up front" out of their own savings. For most employees (and particularly in these economically troubled times), that often effectively forecloses the possibility of ownership. But the leveraged ESOP enables the employee group to acquire employer stock over time, with earnings of the employer being applied to pay for the stock. In no sense is the stock a "gift" to the employees. Instead, the corporation, through the ESOP, is encouraged to use its credit to acquire for its employees a stock ownership interest at today's stock prices. The employee–shareholder thereby gets the chance to reap the benefits (and run the risks) of leveraged stock ownership.

This ownership psychology is also intended to have an effect on work motivation and, thus, on productivity, profitability, job satisfaction and the quality of working life. (This is discussed in a later section, "ESOPs—Impacts and Implications.")

The ESOP concept is also intended to provide employees with a supplemental source of income, a dividend income to supplement the wages from their labor. In a technologically-advanced market economy it has been argued that the working man needs more than his labor as his "stock-in-trade." Left with only his labor, he finds himself in the position whereby if he wants to raise his standard of living he must insist on a higher wage, a wage not necessarily related to increased input or increased productive power but related instead to his need or to his desire for more purchasing power. To the extent that this increased purchasing power is not backed with increased productive power, we fuel inflation.

It has been suggested, therefore, that we begin to more closely match purchasing power to productive power through the use of ownership-broadening financial techniques. This idea is the conceptual heart of the ESOP, and is also the primary reason that the legislative history consistently refers to the ESOP as a "technique of corporate finance." As ownership is broadened, corporations, it is hoped, would begin to pay out the bulk of their earnings, financing future growth with depreciation allowances and ESOP-type debt rather than with retained earnings. Those earnings, if distributed untaxed, could generate a sizable second income to a steadily broadened base of stockholders.

Implementing an ESOP

An ESOP is an employee benefit plan designed to operate in such a way that it satisfies certain requirements of the Internal Revenue Code; such an ESOP is said to be "qualified" under the Code. It is the plan's continuing qualification that enables both the employer and the employees to realize the two primary tax benefits of the plan: employer contributions to a qualified ESOP are tax-deductible to the employer (within limits set by the Code); and employees are not taxed on their stock in the plan until distributed at some future date (upon retirement, for example, when they are likely to be in a lower tax bracket). Qualification also enables employees to receive certain favorable tax treatment on their distribution from the ESOP.

An ESOP is designed to invest primarily in employer stock. To accomplish that purpose, the plan may "leverage" the purchase. That is, the plan may borrow the funds necessary to purchase employer stock. The stock may be acquired either from the corporation itself or from its shareholders. Stock acquired by the ESOP is held in trust for employees and is distributed to them after termination of employment.

Purchases of employer stock may be financed through loans to the ESOP directly from the employer corporation. In addition, the leveraged acquisition of employer stock by an ESOP may be financed by an existing shareholder through an installment purchase of that shareholder's stock by the ESOP.

Fundamental Plan Requirements

In order to be a qualified plan, an ESOP must be operated under rules regarding eligibility, participation, vesting, reporting and other aspects of the plan which comply with the provisions of both the Code and ERISA.

An employee's nonforfeitable interest in an ESOP is called a "vested benefit," and the provisions in the plan which determine each employee's vested benefit are called the "vesting schedule." These schedules are generally set so that the longer an employee stays with the employer, the greater the vested benefit becomes. When an employee terminates for any reason other than retirement (or in some cases death), the vested benefit is determined by how many years the employee has worked for the employer.

Benefits in which the employee does not have a vested benefit are forfeited. Forfeitures are generally allocated among the ESOP accounts of remaining employees on the same basis as employer contributions, that is, on the basis of relative compensation. Thus, for example, if a participant's compensation is $10,000 and the total compensation of all participating employees is $1 million, his account would be credited with both 1% of all employer contributions and 1% of all forfeitures.

The Code also imposes an annual limitation on the amount that may be allocated to each participant's account. That amount generally may not exceed the lesser of 25% of covered compensation or $25,000 (as adjusted for cost-of-living increases since 1974), plus loan interest and forfeitures. If the employer also maintains a pension plan, a combined limitation applies.

Distributions for former employees from an ESOP may be made in either cash or employer stock. However, the employee generally has a right to insist that the distribution be made in employer stock. If the employer's stock is not publicly traded, the participant is entitled to a "put option" on the stock (i.e., the right to demand that the employer, or at the election of the ESOP, the plan itself, purchase his stock). This ensures that each former employee has a market for his shares of a closely-held corporation should he wish to sell.

A closely-held ESOP company may attach a "right of first refusal" to its stock distributed from the plan. This is an optional plan feature intended to protect such a company by preventing the stock from being acquired by outside parties and to protect the company from violating any federal law as a result of having its stock sold when it does not satisfy certain government rules concerning the regulation of securities. The employer or the ESOP may exercise this right and purchase the employer stock at its fair market value before a participant (or beneficiary) may sell it to a third party.

It is important to note, however, that the plan may not be obligated in advance to purchase employer stock, e.g., via a buy-sell agreement. This is because it may be imprudent for the plan to make such a purchase at that future date.

Certain voting rights also apply to ESOPs. If a leveraged ESOP acquires publicly traded employer stock, the employees must be entitled to direct the plan trustee as to the voting of employer stock on all corporate issues. If closely held employer stock is acquired by an ESOP, employees must be entitled to direct the trustee as to the voting of such stock on all corporate issues which (by state law or corporate charter) must be decided by more than a majority vote. Such issues typically include matters such as mergers, acquisitions, or a sale of substantially all of the employer's assets.

The Code imposes an annual limit on employer contributions to a leveraged ESOP of 25% of the compensation of plan participants, plus interest on the loan. If for any year an employer makes a contribution of less than the permissible 25%, the Code permits the unused deductible amount to be carried forward to succeeding years to be added to the tax-deductible contribution for those years, provided the deductions do not exceed 25% for any year. This carry-forward amount is usable until exhausted.

Thus, if an ESOP has borrowed money from a lender and the employer has guaranteed repayment of the loan to the ESOP, the employer's debt repayment schedule generally would be planned so that its loan payments are within the deduction limitations of the Code.

Dividends on employer stock in the plan may be used to repay ESOP indebtedness or may be paid out to ESOP participants on a current basis.

ESOP loans for the purpose of acquiring employer stock are themselves subject to several requirements. The interest rate must be reasonable and the terms of the loan must be similar to those that might prevail between independent parties dealing at arm's length. Also, the proceeds of the loan may be used only to acquire employer stock or to repay a prior ESOP loan. The loan must also be for a specific term. Thus, an ESOP loan may not, for example, be used to finance an open line of credit.

The only assets of an ESOP that may be pledged as collateral are the employer securities acquired. In the event of default, however, only collateral of sufficient value to pay the default may be forfeited. Stock acquired with the proceeds of an ESOP loan is placed in a suspense account and "released" for allocation to participants' accounts as loan payments are made. The number of shares released and allocated each year is generally proportional to the annual amount of principal and interest paid.

Because an ESOP loan from an outside lender is generally secured by an employer guarantee, a pledge of stock is usually unnecessary. In fact, in the event of default on the loan, the employer stock would be of questionable value to the lender, who would likely prefer the status of a corporate creditor to that of a stockholder with unsellable shares. And in the case of a publicly traded company, such a pledge of stock may raise problems under the margin rules of the Federal Reserve Board. A pledge of stock often unnecessarily complicates the loan transaction and is generally no more necessary than in the case of a conventional loan to the sponsoring employer from an outside lender.

The ESOP as a Financing Vehicle

The use of a leveraged ESOP for the financing of new corporate capital is typically structured as illustrated in Figure 1.

Example. Company A wants to raise $1 million to finance capital expansion. The company's bank has agreed to provide a $1 million term loan, either directly to the company or to an ESOP established by the company. The loan will be repayable over a five-year period, with interest at 15% per year. Payments of principal will be approximately $200,000 per year, and payments of interest, we will assume, will be $150,000 per year. The company has 300 employees with an annual payroll of $4 million.

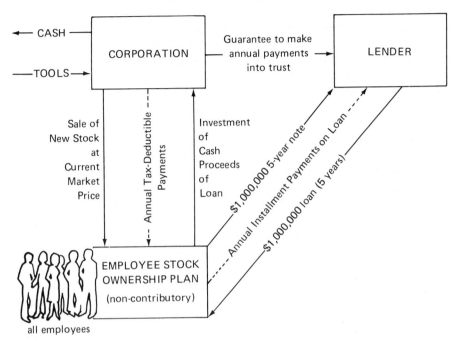

ESOP FINANCING
(New Capital Formation)

Figure 1.

Step 1. The company establishes an ESOP.

Step 2. The company arranges for a $1 million loan to the ESOP. The ESOP gives its note to the bank and the corporation provides its guarantee of the loan.

Step 3. The ESOP invests the proceeds of the loan in company stock, providing $1 million of new capital to the company. The stock may or may not be pledged as security for the loan.

Step 4. The company makes annual cash contributions of $350,000 to the ESOP for the five-year period of the loan. To the extent permitted under the Code, the company will receive a deduction for its annual contribution. The contributions will be applied by the ESOP to repayment of principal and interest on the loan. Dividends on stock held by the ESOP may also be used to repay the loan.

Step 5. On an annual basis, shares of the company stock are "released" from the ESOP's "suspense account" and allocated to participants' accounts in the plan.

With the consent of the lender, existing corporate debt may be refinanced through an ESOP so that it is repayable with pretax corporate dollars. For example, an existing debt may be assumed by the ESOP, with the debt repayment guaranteed by the employer. The corporation would issue new shares to the ESOP equal in value to the principal amount of debt transferred to the ESOP. The new shares may be pledged as collateral for the indebtedness, or assets of the employer may be pledged as additional security for the loan. From the lender's viewpoint, the debt should be more secure because loan repayments are now made with pretax rather than aftertax employer dollars.

ESOP financing may also be used to finance the acquisition of other corporations. Outside lenders may provide the funds for financing the acquisition. Employees of the acquired corporation may be included as participants in the ESOP; this would create a large compensation base which would increase the amount of tax-deductible contributions that may be made each year to the ESOP to repay the debt. In addition, the pretax earnings of the acquired corporation are available for debt repayment.

ESOP financing provides an alternative method for raising capital for closely held corporations that are either unable or unwilling to raise funds through a public offering of stock. Thus, an ESOP may be an appropriate alternative for corporations that wish to avoid the expense of a public underwriting (including SEC registration) and the additional costs of operating as a publicly traded company. In addition, existing owners and management may prefer to build ownership into employees rather than to create ownership by those outside the company.

For publicly traded corporations, ESOP financing provides an alternative to the expense of a secondary offering of securities. Also, the use of an ESOP to acquire stock for the benefit of employees may restrict (and possibly eliminate) public trading of its stock. For example, an ESOP could make a tender offer for all or a portion of the company's outstanding shares, financing the acquisition through loans either from outside lenders or directly from the company.

ESOP Financing of Transfers of Ownership

ESOP financing may also be used for the purchase of employer stock from existing shareholders. Such purchases may be financed with loans from outside lenders to the ESOP or through loans directly from the employer corporation. Also, the sale may be structured through a cash (i.e., nonleveraged), transaction, or on an installment basis. A sale of stock to an ESOP generally enables the selling shareholder to realize capital gains treatment on the proceeds of the sale.

Thus, the ESOP creates an "in-house" market for the acquisition of employer stock offered for sale by existing shareholders during their lifetime, upon their retirement from the business, or in the event of death. For example, an ESOP may be used as a vehicle for financing the transfer of ownership from a retiring shareholder to the employees of the corporation. Although the employees as a group may be the logical successors in ownership, it may be difficult or impossible for the employees (or the management group) to finance the purchase with personal aftertax dollars. An ESOP enables the employees to finance the acquisition with the future pretax earnings of the corporation. The use of an ESOP for the financing of transfers of ownership is typically structured as illustrated in Figure 2.

Example. Company B is 50% owned by Mr. B. Mr. B. wishes to transfer a portion of his ownership to the employees over the next five years. Mr. B. also wants cash from the company for other purposes. The company is valued at $4 million. The company has 250 employees, with an annual payroll of $4 million. The company has no existing qualified plans of deferred compensation.

Step 1. Company establishes an ESOP.

Step 2. Bank loans $1 million to ESOP. The ESOP gives its note to the bank and the corporation provides its guarantee of the loan. (Alternatively, the

Figure 2.

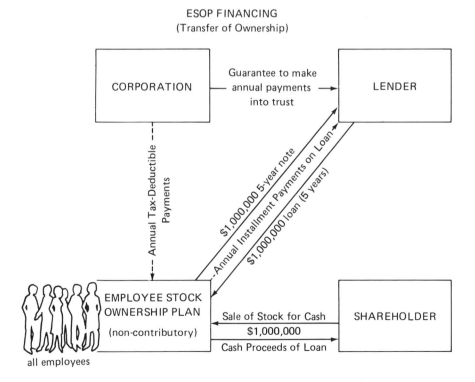

ESOP FINANCING
(Transfer of Ownership)

purchase of Mr. B's stock could be structured on an installment basis, i.e., Mr. B would act as "lender.")

Step 3. The ESOP uses the loan proceeds to purchase company stock from Mr. B.

Step 4. The company makes annual cash contributions of $250,000 to the ESOP for the five-year term of the loan. To the extent permitted under the Code, the company will receive a deduction for its annual contribution. The contributions will be applied by the ESOP to repayment of principal and interest on the loan. Dividends on stock held by the ESOP may also be applied to repay the loan.

Step 5. On an annual basis, shares of company stock are "released" from the ESOP's "suspense account" and allocated to participants' accounts in the plan.

Step 6. If Mr. B then wishes to sell additional stock to the ESOP, the steps set out above would be repeated.

Similarly, ESOP financing may be used in the divestiture of a corporate division or subsidiary to its employees. For example, the stock of a division (or the stock of a new corporation established to acquire the business and assets of a division) may be sold to an ESOP. The ESOP's acquisition may be financed with third-party loans or through an installment purchase. If necessary, any debt financing may be guaranteed by the seller corporation as well as by the acquiring corporation.

For example, assume Company C wishes to divest itself of Division X but is having difficulty locating a buyer willing to pay the full purchase price of $5 million. The company is, however, able to find a purchaser (Company P) willing to pay half that amount, provided Company P has majority control. Company P organizes a new corporation, Newco. And just prior to Newco's purchase of Division X, Newco establishes an ESOP.

The Newco ESOP borrows $2.5 million from a bank on the guarantee of Company P. Immediately prior to the acquisition, Company P transfers $2.5 million to Newco and the ESOP likewise transfers $2.5 million. Newco then pays $5 million to Company C for the assets of Division X. The ESOP then repays the loan with the annual contributions of Newco.

Nonleveraged Acquisitions

An ESOP may also be utilized to provide employee stock ownership on a nonleveraged basis. As explained earlier, cash contributions would be made directly to the plan and would be used to acquire employer securities from existing shareholders. This could be done on an annual basis.

In addition, direct contributions of employer stock can be made from the employer corporation. This would create tax deductions (without any cash outlay) equal to the fair market value of the stock as of the date of the contribution. Thus, an employer could use a nonleveraged ESOP to "tax shelter" its repayment of a traditional loan by making annual contributions of stock to the plan equal in value to the payments of loan principal. As with the leveraged ESOP, contributions to the plan are tax deductible only to the extent permitted by the Code.

Of course, the nonleveraged approach would not permit an immediate purchase of a large block of employer stock. Thus, if such a purchase is called for, the only solution may be leveraging. With a leveraged ESOP, plan participants are credited with any growth in value of the stock (due to the "up front" purchase). In contrast, with a nonleveraged plan, it would take the employer several years to contribute an equivalent amount of stock. Conversely, should the employer's stock lose value from the first year of the plan, participants will sustain less of a loss with a nonleveraged than a leveraged plan.

ESOP Financing — Problems and Pitfalls

ESOP's are not simple. At best, we can provide but an overview of the considerations facing an employer contemplating an ESOP. This section reviews two of the most common problems accompanying the adoption and maintenance of an ESOP: valuation and liquidity.

The Code authorizes ESOP financing under a special ESOP loan exemption. This exemption is provided, however, only so long as the amount that an ESOP pays for employer stock is no more than "fair market value." In the event that more than fair market value is paid, an excise tax (plus possible penalties) may be levied on the seller.

Thus, the proper valuation of employer stock is of critical importance. Where there is a generally recognized market for the stock, fair market value is the price prevailing on a national securities exchange (if applicable), or the offering price established by current bid and asked prices quoted by independent parties. Otherwise, fair market value must be determined by an independent appraiser experienced in valuing closely held corporations.

Certain aspects of an ESOP may require compliance with the rules and regulations of the Securities and Exchange Commission (SEC). For publicly traded companies, this should create no problem, since such an employer is already satisfying SEC requirements. For a closely held employer, however, the expense of SEC compliance can be a costly and troublesome burden. Fortunately, the SEC has not required registration where employees do not contribute money to the ESOP or are not otherwise called upon to make an investment decision.

Certain liquidity requirements accompany an ESOP adopted by an employer whose stock is not publicly traded. As explained earlier, an employee's benefits in a ESOP may be distributed in either cash or stock. The participant generally may, however, insist that a distribution be made in the form of employer stock. In addition, once the participant receives this stock, the company or the plan must have sufficient cash available to permit the repurchase of the stock if the participant exercises his "put option" under the plan. Adequate cash should also be available to permit the plan to exercise the "right of first refusal" (if utilized) should the participant desire to sell the stock to a third party. Thus, an ESOP should be operated so as to provide adequate liquidity to meet the plan's cash requirements.

Tax Credit ESOPs

The leveraged ESOP described above enables an employer to claim a tax deduction for its contribution. Thus, for corporations with more than $100,000 in taxable income, a $100 contribution generates $46 in additional cash to the company (i.e., the tax that would have been levied on the $100 deduction).

With a tax credit ESOP, however, a company can qualify for a credit against taxes for its contributions to a specially defined type of employee stock ownership plan. A credit, of course, generates a dollar-for-dollar reduction in taxes that would otherwise be paid. Consequently, a tax credit is more than twice as valuable as a tax deduction.

An employer with a tax credit ESOP is currently permitted to claim an additional 1% investment tax credit, i.e., 11% versus 10%. The employer can also qualify for an extra tax credit of up to 0.5% if participants contribute to the plan an amount equal to the additional credit and the employer matches their contributions.

Because the additional tax credit is based on qualifying capital investments (i.e., expenditures for certain depreciable property such as machinery and equipment), the tax credit ESOP has been most attractive to capital-intensive employers. Beginning in 1983, however, an ESOP company will be permitted to claim a tax credit based on a portion of its payroll. The Economic Recovery Tax Act of 1981 terminates the investment-based ESOP credit for equipment placed in service after 1982. In its place, for 1983 and 1984 companies may claim an ESOP credit of 0.5% of covered payroll. This payroll-based ESOP credit increases to 0.75% for 1985–1987.

Tax credit ESOPs are now quite prevalent in capital-intensive industries. A 1980 Hewitt Associates survey of the Fortune 1300 indicates that their prevalence since 1977 has grown from 12.7% to 32.4% among such companies, with another 8.8% considering implementation. Four major capital-intensive industries have a particularly strong record of TRASOP implementation: utilities; petroleum refining; mining and crude oil production; and paper, fiber and wood products.

ESOP Case Histories

Case History I — South Bend Lathe, Inc.

The year 1975 saw the beginning of the use of government grants, loans and loan guarantees to promote employee stock ownership through ESOPs. The first of these was South Bend Lathe in South Bend, Indiana, some 90 miles east of Chicago. At the time, South Bend Lathe's parent company was Amsted Industries, Inc., which was planning to liquidate the South Bend facility. This plant closing would have resulted in the loss of over 500 jobs.

Instead, South Bend Lathe's management found a way to use an ESOP to acquire the company. They turned to the Economic Development Administration (EDA) of the Commerce Department. The EDA has funds available under the Public Works and Economic Development Act of 1965 that are to be used "to alleviate conditions of substantial and persistent unemployment and underemployment and to establish stable and diversified economies." Title IX of that Act permits the Secretary of Commerce to make grants to certain "eligible recipients" to alleviate unemployment, expected unemployment, or other long-term economic deterioration.

Title IX does not permit grants to private profit-making companies. Rather, the "eligible recipient" must be a state, a political subdivision (e.g., a city), or a private or public nonprofit organization representing a redevelopment area. Redevelopment areas must have established an overall economic development plan consistent with the purposes of the 1965 Act. The vast majority of areas in the United States have now done so.

The EDA has a mandate to use means which are "anticipatory and innovative" to alleviate pockets of unemployment. The South Bend Lathe facility occupies a corner of the 570-acre former Studebaker Corporation complex, which was located in an area of South Bend which had 33% unemployment at the time. At the same time, the City of South Bend itself was experiencing a 7.4% unemployment rate.

To create the necessary "eligible recipient," the city of South Bend enacted an ordinance establishing a trust agreement with a local bank and agreeing to comply with the terms of a $5,013,000 Title IX EDA grant by depositing the funds upon receipt in a "revolving fund" established and governed by the trust agreement. The stated purpose of the trust was to promote and finance the use of ESOPs or for other industrial purposes consistent with Title IX. The trust is governed by a board of directors and fund committee consisting of the trustee and local industrial development and human resource personnel. This committee determines loan applicant eligibility with guidelines creating a preference for ESOP-type financing.

The ESOP buyout was accomplished with three loans. The first of these was a loan of $5,013,000 from the "City of South Bend Industrial Revolving Fund." The term of the loan was 25 years at 3% interest. South Bend Lathe secured the loan with its guarantees, and with a second mortgage on its real property. The proceeds were used to purchase 1000 shares of common stock of the company. Subsequently, there was a 10:1 stock split, giving the ESOP a total of 10,000 shares. The second loan was an extension of credit from the parent corporation to purchase $2.3 million in accounts receivable. Amsted Industries, Inc., financed this loan, without interest, for the 60- to 90-day period it took to collect the accounts.

The third lender was a consortium of three private-sector lenders which provided a loan commitment of up to $4 million. South Bend Lathe borrowed $2.258 million on this line of credit, of which $2.2 million was used to purchase additional assets from Amsted and $58,000 was retained for working capital. The loans were for five years at an average of several points over prime and were secured by first mortgages on all South Bend Lathe property, equipment and current marketable assets.

These loans enabled South Bend Lathe employees to purchase their company and related assets from Amsted Industries, Inc. The price was $9,571,500. The sum of $5,013,000 was put up by the ESOP, $2,258,000 was borrowed, and $2,300,000 was from receivables.

As of September of 1980, South Bend Lathe had a record of five profitable years (after a string of unsatisfactory years as a division of Amsted). Profits have improved each year, with net sales growing from $13.8 million in their initial year as an ESOP company to more than $24 million for fiscal 1980.

Its commercial loans were repaid in 1977 and, at present, it has no bank debt. The company does, however, have $903,000 of industrial revenue bonds (used to build a new 30,000 square foot office building and acquire new equipment). Equity/debt ratio has steadily improved and as of June 1980 was 4.1 to 1. Earnings per share increased from $20.30 in their first year to $69.48 for the third fiscal year, and as of June 1980 stood at approximately $55.00.

South Bend Lathe has made a contribution of 15% of salaries and wages to their ESOP for each of the five years for an average annual contribution of approximately $2,300 per employee (roughly 2.5 times the average contribution to pension plans in the machine tool industry). Those employees who were with the company when it was acquired as of June 30, 1975, now have an average of $12,500 in company stock credited to their ESOP account. The overall average is $10,700 per employee.

Case History II — Jeannette Sheet Glass Corp.

Jeannette Sheet Glass Corp. is one of the latest of more than a dozen employee buyouts financed with federal financial assistance. The corporation was formerly a plant owned by ASG Industries, Inc., of Kingsport, Tennessee, and Fourco Glass Company of Clarksburg, West Virginia. In November of 1978 Fourco, which had recently purchased controlling interest in ASG, decided to close down the glass operation located in Jeannette, Pennsylvania, 25 miles southeast of Pittsburgh. The decision left 435 people (in the community of 12,000) without jobs.

However, the employees put together a buyout arrangement that reopened the plant for production early in 1980. First, 350 of the employees put up $2,000 apiece to buy 20 shares in the new company. A local bank stood ready to grant personal loans for that amount to anyone who needed it. The employees also agreed as a cost-cutting measure to substitute an ESOP for a traditional pension plan.

With the help of a 90% EDA loan guarantee, a local bank agreed to a direct loan of $2.812 million for working capital and fixed assets. The Pennsylvania Industrial Development Agency (PIDA) also granted a low interest loan of $720,000 to buy the real estate. The PIDA loan was in the form of a grant to the Greater Greensburg Industrial Development Corporation which, in turn, made the loan. The new company then established an ESOP, issuing $720,000 of stock to the plan and taking back a note. The stock is to be allocated on a per capita basis over a five-year period.

The parent corporation also took a note for $600,000 as part of the purchase price. A crucial piece of the financial puzzle was supplied by an agreement with General Glass International Corporation of New Rochelle, New York, to buy 85% of the new company's production. General Glass also extended, through their bank, a $1.2 million line of credit.

The sum of $1.4 million was paid to the parent company for the land and buildings and $600,000 for the machinery, equipment, tools, etc. Two million dollars was spent renovating the plant and replacing their outdated and inefficient furnace (a chief cause of the shutdown). Five hundred thousand dollars was set aside for working capital and start-up expenses, and $200,000 was reserved for miscellaneous expenses.

The initial equity in the new company is $1.5 million, one-half of which is owned directly by the employees (via their $2,000 contributions), and one-half of which is employee-owned through an ESOP. In December of 1979, 125 employees began the refurbishing. And in March of 1980, production resumed.

ESOPs—Impacts and Implications

Over the past few years, several surveys and studies have been conducted of ESOP companies and of companies in which employee ownership is a significant factor. The first of these dates from December 1977 when five students at UCLA Graduate School of Management (as part of the requirement for an MBA) conducted a survey of 180 ESOP companies. The results of this survey appear in outline form below:

I. *CHARACTERISTICS OF 180 ESOP COMPANIES*
  1. Average age of the plan is 3 years.
  2. Average number of shareholders ranges from 2 to 5.
  3. 12.2% of the companies are publicly traded.
  4. 33 states are represented, with a range of 1 to 8 responses from each state. The exception: California, with 58 responses or 42% of the sample.
  5. 26% of companies have at least one union.

6. *Sales Range*

Percent of Companies	Sales Range
8.3%	0–$ 1,000,000
28.7%	$ 1,000,000–$ 5,000,000
19.5%	$ 5,000,000–$10,000,000
28.4%	$10,000,000–$30,000,000
15.4%	Over $30,000,000

7. *Number of Employees* (ranges from 1 to 44,000)

91% of the companies had 650 or fewer employees
82% of the companies had 200 or fewer employees
62% of the companies had 100 or fewer employees
40% of the companies had 50 or fewer employees

8. *Types of Industries Represented*

Percent of Companies	Type of Industry
28.9%	Manufacturing
17.2%	Wholesale
11.7%	Financial
10.0%	Construction
9.4%	Service
6.7%	Retail
6.1%	Professional
10.0%	Other

II. PLAN DESCRIPTION

Type

85% were stock bonus plans.

15% were stock bonus and money purchase pension plans. (7 were TRASOPs).

Conversions & Combinations

30% were the result of a conversion from a previous plan.

27% were combined with another benefit plan. (45% of which were profit-sharing plans.)

Leveraging

16% were currently leveraged.

Vesting

85% ranged from 3 to 12 years with 55% providing 10% per year for 10 years.

10% require the statutory maximum of 15 years.

5% (mostly TRASOPs) had immediate vesting.

Type of Stock

93% held common stock.

7% held preferred stock.

Some also held debentures, cash & other marketable securities.

Distribution
Generally in lump sum with cash for fractional shares.

III. *PROFESSIONAL ADMINISTRATIVE SERVICES*
   Trustee

Individual	23%
Committee	39%
Institution	38%

   Provider of Legal Services for Plan

Corporate Legal Department	13%
Outside Corporate Counsel	63%
Independent Attorney for plan only	20%
Other	4%

   Provider of Administrative Services

Internal	38%
Outside Administrators	45%
Combination	17%

   Costs

	Range	*Average*
Plan Installation	$500–$125,000	$12,204
Annual Maintenance	$500–$150,000	$ 5,766

IV. *BENEFITS OF THE PLAN*
   The following were most commonly cited as "important:"

	% of Companies
Improved employee motivation	70%
Tax advantages	64%
Cash liquidity of company	43%
Market for closely held stock	41%
Estate Planning	35%

V. *PROBLEMS WITH THE PLAN*
   The following were most frequently cited as "important:"

	% of Companies
Changing governmental regulations	64%
Administrative complexity	45%
Employee reaction	26%
On-going costs	25%
Dilution	13%
Loss of confidentiality	5.4%

Interestingly, while the single most important advantage cited by companies was improved employee motivation, employee reaction also ranked high in the problem areas. Many companies indicated no difference in the level of employee motivation. Of these, the majority claimed that the complexity of the plan and the difficulty of making an intangible benefit appear real was responsible for the apparent indifference or confusion on the part of employees.

The survey findings go on to point out:

> The effect of the ESOP on employee motivation seems to be a distinctly individual phenomenon, which is related more to the company's prior condition than to the event of ESOP installation. Further, the more closely involved the employee is in the outcome of the operation of which he is a part, the more interest he will have in the plan.
>
> Even in those companies where perceived employee response was considered good, management stressed the importance of an on-going educational program to sell the ESOP concept. As employee understanding of the plan was rated fair to poor by 71% of the companies responding, the need for better communications is further underscored.

The findings also report a mixed reaction on the ESOP's ability to attract or retain personnel in comparison with other benefit plans. One explanation "may be that most of the plans have not been in effect long enough for a trend to be identified."

> The ESOP's effect on employee motivation appeared to depend on the individual company. The better the ESOP met the needs of the employees, the more value it held for them. It did not seem that the ESOP by itself measurably improved employee morale or motivation unless the work atmosphere and employer/employee communications were good to begin with. Where no esprit de corps exists, an ESOP cannot be expected to create it.

The majority of responses to the survey indicated a "high degree of satisfaction with ESOPs. Most respondents felt the plan was important to the company and that it was living up to expectations. The great majority of respondents also said they would install an ESOP again if given the choice."

The Survey Research Center

Another study of ESOP companies was conducted in 1978 by the Survey Research Center of the Institute for Social Research at the University of Michigan. Several aspects of performance are analyzed in the 98 companies interviewed, including motivation, productivity, job satisfaction, and the quality of working life. Sixty-eight of the firms had ESOPs, while 30 had direct employee ownership. Their median size was approximately 350 employees; 17% had less than 100 employees and 25% had 1,000 or more. Roughly half of the companies had sales of $25 million or more in the year preceding the study. In about three-quarters of the companies, employees owned at least half of the equity. In 60% of the ESOPs, however, employees owned less than 25% of the equity.

Because profit data were supplied by only 30 companies, the statistics reflecting the impact of employee-ownership on profitability cannot, the report acknowledges, be regarded as statistically significant. Nevertheless, the study suggests that "the employee-owned firms are above average in profitability for their respective industries." The study also concludes that "it is the amount of equity owned by workers that appears to be most often associated with profitability." On the other hand, the report continues, "employee ownership is more likely to be reported to have positive effects on profit where such ownership is direct, rather than through a Trust."

The study included interviews with both employees and managers. While conceding that the findings are only preliminary, the study suggests some "tentative conclusions." Managers see employee ownership as having a positive effect on productivity and profit. They also assess the industrial relations climate as being quite good. Managers are more satisfied with the plan where ownership is direct rather than through an ESOP. They also appear happier with plans where employee participation is widespread, even though this may involve only a small fraction of the company's equity. They also see an ESOP as having a substantially positive effect on the attitudes of employees, though this response is less positive where workers have representatives on the board of directors than where they do not.

Managers offered a number of reasons for having established an ESOP. The incentive that it provides to employees and the tax advantage that it affords the company were among the most prominent reasons given. Reasons relating to the creation or maintenance of employment were also mentioned by several ESOP firms, but employment-related reasons were more frequently offered by managers of firms in which employees own stock directly.

An Employee-Owned Firm

The study also included a survey of employee attitudes and perceptions in one ESOP company, South Bend Lathe. (A summary of the South Bend Lathe ESOP appears as a case history in this chapter.) The data were collected from interviews with 51 randomly selected persons in the company. The interviews were conducted approximately 18 months after the ESOP's acquisition of the company. Data from company records provided information about profit, worker productivity, absences, grievances, injuries, and other indicators of company performance.

Performance at the company has improved in recent years. According to company personnel (both workers and managers), at least some of the improvement is attributable to the change in ownership and to the employee stock ownership plan. The interviewers acknowledge, however, that the causes of this improvement cannot be determined with certainty from this preliminary analysis.

According to the report, "practically all the workers and managers whom we interviewed indicated that the company had changed for the better since the ESOP was introduced." Improvements fell into several categories. First, about half of the workers and managers mentioned that the relationships between people had improved and that people worked better together now that they all owned stock in the company.

Second, nearly three-quarters of the managers and close to half of the workers felt that morale had improved and that people were more conscientious about their jobs. One manager cites "a feeling of personal pride among the workers," while a worker responded, "The guys are more conscientious about their work. They feel they've got to put out a much better product now because that's what's going to make more business for us. They do a little better work now than they did before."

A third category of favorable comments, cited somewhat more by the workers than by the managers, concerns benefits and working conditions, which were perceived as improved. Reduction in waste and absenteeism was also mentioned by several respondents. A fifth category of responses concerns the future of the company, which according to several workers and managers looks promising, one commenting, "There's much more confidence in the future."

Finally, the report notes that a small number of respondents mentioned that employees had more of a voice in the company, while a few indicated that some workers were still suspicious or that communications were not good. Negative comments of this kind were rare.

Employee Attitudes

The study also asked managers and workers to comment about changes in the attitude of employees toward management. A majority of both groups felt that employee attitudes had improved. Forty-five percent of workers and managers reported that working relationships between the two groups were improved in that better communication, more confidence and respect for managers and improved teamwork prevailed. Another group (18% of the managers and 8% of the workers) felt that workers were taking on increased responsibilities or that management was more conscientious.

Also included in the report was a survey of employee attitudes toward their work. Both workers and managers reported an improvement in motivation, morale and commitment to the success of the company. A high percentage of both groups (36% of the managers and 50% of the workers) mentioned that workers were more interested in their jobs because they felt they were working for themselves or that company success was a result of their efforts. One manager claimed, "They feel a little bit more responsibility for quality workmanship, being it is their own company." Some of the workers made similar comments. Regarding the feeling of ownership, one stated, "I seem to think I want to get it out better than I did because I know it's for me."

The survey also questioned managers and workers as to whether there had been any change in the way decisions that affect them are made. The majority (68% of workers and 55% of managers) felt that there had been no change. Eighteen percent of both groups felt that they had more say, and that they were consulted about major decisions. Ten percent of the workers reported that the attitudes of management seemed better.

When questioned about their general opinion of the ESOP, 82% of the managers and 77% of the workers made positive comments. A number of the South Bend Lathe employees went out on strike during a portion of the summer of 1980.

The ESOP Association Survey

In mid-1979 another survey was conducted, this time by the ESOP Association of America, a trade association. A survey form was distributed to ESOP companies who were members of the association. The stated purpose of the survey was to compile information that would be helpful in influencing favorable ESOP-related legislation. The results were released in the form of a profile of a typical ESOP company. The following profile was constructed from 72 ESOP companies:

At the time of the ESOP installation, which typically took place three years ago, their average ESOP company had been in business 24 years. Over the three years an average of 7% of the ownership of the company was transferred to the ESOP each year until the plan now holds 20.6% of the company stock.

During the three years from pre-ESOP to post-ESOP, annual sales rose from $19,596,000 to $33,780,000, an increase of 72%. The number of employees increased from 438 to 602, representing an increase in employment of 37%. Pre-ESOP, sales per employee stood at $44,700; the post-ESOP figure shows an increase of 25%, to an average of $56,000 per employee. The average profit in years with an ESOP was $2,039,000, an increase of 157% over the $794,000 of profit generated in the same number of years prior to installation of the ESOP. Prior to the ESOP, the typical ESOP company reported taxes paid of $312,000. According to the survey, that has since risen to $780,000, an increase of 150%.

GAO Study

In contrast to these findings, the General Accounting Office (GAO) concluded from a study of 16 ESOPs implemented by government contractors that "research to date is inconclusive about the impact of ESOPs on employee motivation and productivity." The GAO report (released June 20, 1980) reports that they "could not determine whether ESOPs improved employee motivation and productivity."

ESOPs—The Legislative Outlook

Since 1973, Congress has passed, and four presidents have signed into law, 15 separate pieces of legislation designed to encourage employers to provide stock ownership for their employees. (See the Historical Sketch at the beginning of this chapter.) In addition, several state legislatures have adopted legislation focusing on ESOPs as a favored form of development financing.

Legislative developments at both the federal and state level indicate a trend toward the promotion of employee stock ownership through financial assistance from both federal and state agencies.

Several ESOP-related provisions are currently under consideration by the Congress. One is an amendment permitting companies to deduct the expense of dividends paid out to employees on their ESOP stock. This provision is intended to encourage companies to use these plans to generate a "second income" for employees. It is also hoped that this ownership income will stimulate employee motivation and commitment to the company.

In addition, it is proposed that an ESOP be treated as a charitable organization for income, estate and gift tax purposes. This, it is hoped, will encourage individuals, by gift or bequest, to leave stock in their company to an ESOP or a TRASOP. Another suggested change would provide for the tax-free rollover of the proceeds from the sale of a small business to an ESOP where such proceeds are reinvested in another small business within 18 months.

State Initiatives

Several states have also been active in the ESOP area. The first of these, Minnesota, in 1974 became the first state to enact a law designed to promote the use of ESOP financing. The statement of legislative intent, which serves as a preamble to the Minnesota statute, describes that state's view of the potential value of ESOP financing:

> It is the intention of the legislature in defining and allowing for employee stock ownership trusts that (employee) participation in... enterprise through the use of employee stock ownership trusts would benefit all the people of Minnesota by:
> 1. Renewing and enlarging a sense of the worth of human effort;
> 2. Recognizing the interdependency of human effort and the ownership of the productive assets with which people work;
> 3. Providing direct economic advantage to employees from increased productivity;
> 4. Reducing differences in the real interests of labor and capital and
> 5. Relieving a primary cause of social tension and alienation.

One innovative feature of Minnesota's ESOP law characterizes qualified ESOP trusts as charitable organizations for purposes of state estate and gift tax laws. Thus, this charitable contribution deduction offers to owners (who might otherwise give their stock to private foundations or other charitable organizations) the alternative of transferring their stock to employees instead.

More recently, Maryland enacted legislation in 1979 supportive of ESOP financing as a matter of state policy, providing in its resolution that "broadening the ownership of capital should be a twin pillar of economic policy, along with achieving full employment." After further study of the ESOP concept, Maryland enacted legislation early in 1980 requiring state economic development agencies to include in their annual reports a discussion of their efforts to comply with the policy statement set forth in their "Broadened Ownership Act." In June of 1981, Delaware enacted similar legislation.

Michigan now provides technical assistance to employee groups wishing to utilize an ESOP (e.g., to prevent a plant closing or relocation). Similarly, the state of New Jersey has directed its Department of Labor and Industry to study the use of ESOPs as an alternative to plant closings.

Conclusion

A host of considerations confronts any company contemplating an ESOP. ESOPs are designed to promote a corporate financial structure that will benefit both the employees and the employer. Thus, for example, if an ESOP is to be the company's only deferred compensation plan, the company should carefully consider whether an ESOP is the benefit vehicle best designed to achieve that purpose. A defined benefit pension plan may be more appropriate.

The company should also consider the effect on other shareholders, including the dilution effect when additional shares are sold to an ESOP. In addition, the pass-through voting requirement raises the question of whether the company is prepared to welcome its employee group as shareholders and treat them as such.

ESOPs are neither simple nor inexpensive. In addition to meeting the complex requirements of the Code and ERISA, an ESOP company should also be prepared to incur the expense of an ongoing communications program. For nonpublicly traded companies, the initial and annual costs of valuation are also an added expense. And, of course, any leveraged ESOP should be well-designed to meet the company's objectives. This should include an evaluation of the plan's ongoing liquidity requirements.

Despite the complex nature of ESOPs, they often can be the most appropriate means for structuring development financing. And in today's inflationary environment, the ESOP's capacity for leveraged pretax financing provides an innovative method for accomplishing development financing that might otherwise prove infeasible.

VIII

Investing the Energy Windfall in Resource-Rich States: The Montana Coal Tax Trust Fund

Nancy Leifer

Montana has been called the last frontier. Today, state policy makers are standing on the edge of a new frontier, expanding the boundaries of knowledge about public investment at the state level through a new form of investment fund—a general-purpose, natural-resource, severance-tax trust fund.

The potential of the fund for discretionary investment in-state is particularly attractive to states like Montana which have economies largely based on primary production of raw materials. These states, like Alaska, Wyoming, Montana and Idaho, have long felt themselves to be colonies of the rest of the country. A natural resource trust fund promises capital for in-state investment to foster economic diversification and a lessening of dependence on world markets for economic stability.

Two key questions remain to be answered. Is a natural resource severance tax a viable source of monies for such a fund? What mechanisms and criteria should a state use to direct investment of the fund? This chapter examines these questions in the case of Montana's Coal Severance Tax Trust Fund.

The Setting

In order to appreciate the significance of the Coal Tax Trust Fund to the people of Montana, it is necessary to review briefly the historical development of the state's economy. Montana became a state in 1889, meeting requirements for statehood because of the influx of people seeking their fortunes in gold diggings and silver mines. Today, the central and western portions of the state are dotted with the ghost towns left behind as the gold ran out, federal policy on the silver standard changed and people picked up their hopes and moved on.

Copper provided the stimulus for the next economic boom. Butte, termed the "richest hill on earth," has seen millions of dollars in minerals taken from its mines beginning about 1880. These riches flowed out of the state to add to the capital resources of such companies as the Hearst Newspaper Chain, Standard Oil, and, later, the Anaconda Company.

Little of these riches benefited the State of Montana or its people. Governor Joseph Dixon took steps to boost the state's revenues in the early 1920s by supporting passage of a nominal severance tax on minerals. It was no easy undertaking as all but one or two of Montana's newspapers were owned and controlled by the Anaconda Company. Governor Dixon succeeded in establishing the tax. He was not re-elected.

Today, Butte's downtown sags with abandoned buildings and empty streets. The introduction of open pit mining, followed by a recession in the world demand for copper, has cut employment drastically. Less than 25,000 people remain in what was once a thriving community of over 40,000.

Agricultural development has a similar history of unstable development. The Homestead Boom swept across the Northern Great Plains from 1910 to 1920, riding on high wheat prices and abnormally wet summers into what had become known as the "Great American Desert." Population growth in Montana's central and northeastern counties mushroomed, aided by the efforts of J.J. Hill, a railroad tycoon. Hill combined the services of his railroad with those of local land office dealers into homesteading packages which were promoted to the farmers of the Midwest and of Scandinavia. The promise of rich farmland for one's own was very appealing.

The promise didn't last long. Post-World War I depression in wheat prices and the onset of a hard drought turned the dreams of many into nightmares as it became impossible to make payments on equipment and buildings. By 1920 an exodus of population from these countries was in full swing and continued all through the 1920s and 1930s. Some eastern counties are still shrinking, reflecting the difficulties of making a living in the semi-arid Great Plains. Hill took his promises elsewhere, investing the profits from his Montana operation into railroad building in China.

The harvest of timber and the production of lumber and wood products became of major importance to the economy of the western portions of the state. As with copper, fluctuations in world timber markets have had a significant effect on the well-being of counties in western Montana. The future promises even greater instability as harvestable timber supplies run out. Western Montana's short growing season and fragile reforestation capability is unlikely to permit the current rate of harvest to be sustained indefinitely. While estimates vary, timber reserves will very likely run short before the end of the century.

Montana's economic development up to the early 1970s has been based on the production of primary goods: copper, wheat, timber products and cattle. These products are characteristic of a colonial economy dependent upon international markets over which it has no control. Montana's small population (760,000) and geographic location have increased its economic dependence because it cannot support many indigenous consumer goods industries. National and worldwide movements toward corporate agglomeration have further eroded the proportion of economic activity purely endogenous to the state. While Montana's economy is very dependent on the rest of the nation, economic indications through 1970, such as unemployment rates and per capita income, show that the state has consistently been on the losing side of the national averages.

Now Montanans are wrestling with the latest arrival in the series of natural-resource-development schemes: coal. One-quarter of the U.S. domestic coal reserves are in eastern Montana. These reserves could well become instrumental in reducing dependence on foreign energy sources. Once again, the promise of natural-resource riches is attracting a new generation of immigrants to the state.

By 1975 coal development in southeastern Montana had created problems for the local population in the mining areas. Historically a sparsely populated region of cattle ranches and small communities, the area lacked the ability and resources to absorb the sudden inflows of population which accompanied the first strip-mining operations. Undesirable effects of boom development such as overcrowded schools, insufficient water and sewer systems, and escalating crime rates, began to appear.

In light of these problems, the state policy makers in 1975 passed into law the Montana Coal Producers' Severance Tax. It was designed with two purposes in mind: to insure that the additional costs of public services in the impacted areas would be borne by the coal developers and the consumers of the coal; and to insure that, this time, the state's population would gain some lasting benefit from the loss of its nonrenewable resources. Then, in 1976, the voters of Montana passed a constitutional amendment by a margin of two to one, putting a portion of the coal tax into a permanent fund.

Perhaps the best way to capture the passion and intent of Montanans in supporting the Coal Severance Tax Trust Fund is to quote the words of supporters of the amendment published in a pre-election pamphlet for voters:

Montana has estimated coal reserves of 108 billion tons—25% of the nation's coal supply and over 10% of the world's coal supply. Montana has 52% of the nation's low sulphur coal reserves. Because of the importance of coal, it is an extremely valuable resource both for the state of Montana and for the United States.

Coal is irreplaceable. What will we have to show for this valuable resource once it is all mined and gone? We once had fabulous copper reserves but now we have very little to show for our copper resource. We should not make this mistake again.

Another area of the country is known for its fabulous coal resources. This area is Appalachia. Appalachia is also known for the poverty of its people. The Montana legislature was determined that the fabulous wealth underlying Eastern

Montana should not be translated into poverty of Eastern Montanans and that the state of Montana should have something to show for this valuable resource once it is gone. Thus, they levied the highest coal tax in the nation on coal mined from strip mines in Montana.

Setting aside 25% (50% after 1980) of coal tax revenues in a permanent trust fund is a sound way to manage Montana coal revenues. We should not be shortsighted and spend all our tax income as rapidly as we earn it.

Further, [if] we become addicted to all coal monies in support of the state's day-to-day operations, our decision makers will be biased in favor of more and more coal mining. They will lack the independence they now enjoy to decide what is best for the people, the air, the water, and the land in the coal-rich areas of the state. Then, too, if we are directly dependent upon all of the coal revenue to support our day-to-day expenditures we will be severely punished financially on the day when the coal no longer exists or has value.

The last session of the Montana legislature, by an overwhelming vote, has placed this proposition on the ballot. Legislators know how tempting it is to dip into the coal tax monies with this and that "worthy project" until in the distant future there is nothing to serve as a revenue generating investment base. The proposals for use of coal tax revenues have already started mounting and pressures will be placed on the next session of the legislature to carve out more and more of the tax revenues for all sorts of "worthy projects." By passing this amendment we will guarantee an endowment for the future and avoid temptations to spend it now.

This proposal is one of the most forward looking proposals ever presented to the people of this state. It will demonstrate to future generations of Montanans that we chose to share the riches of this state's nonrenewable resource heritage with them (Office of the Secretary of State, State of Montana, 1976).

What makes the investment challenge of the Coal Severance Tax Trust Fund so exciting is that a state government rarely finds itself the possessor of a substantial block of funds expressly set aside with no other considerations than investment in the state's future. States have found themselves responsible for pension funds and single-purpose trust funds, and they are increasingly aware of the need for professional fund management. These types of funds traditionally have been treated with the same constraints in the public sector as apply to private sector investments, so that in-state economic development objectives have become secondary to private financial considerations in making investment decisions.

The taxation of nonrenewable resource development to provide investment funds to be used for in-state economic growth is a very recent development. Thus far, only Alaska and Montana have opted to create permanent investment funds from the proceeds of resource development taxation. The Alaskan fund is based on oil revenues.

The case of Alaska is the most striking, for not only is the projected tax revenue to the fund substantial (conservative estimates place it as $2 billion), but also the state's non-oil economic base is very limited. A great deal of thought and research has already been directed to the design of appropriate investment strategies for the Alaskan Permanent Fund. This work, which is referred to in the Bibliography (Daniels, 1979; Daniels et al., 1980; Daniels and Katzman, 1976; Institute of Social and Economic Research, 1977), also raises questions relevant to Montana and other states.

Other states, like Pennsylvania, for instance, are beginning to watch the Alaskan and Montanan experiences carefully to assess the effectiveness of this form of taxation and investment. Several key questions have to be answered. Is the taxation of resource development a viable source of public funds for an investment fund at the state level? What fund investment mechanisms can be used to help shape the state's economy, yet also supplement the private investment community, not undermine it? What constitutes responsible stewardship of a public trust? The remainder of this chapter examines the Montana experience, to focus attention on these questions and to derive at least preliminary answers to them.

Source of the Trust Fund: Montana's Coal Producers' Severance Tax

Montana's Coal Producers' Severance Tax is unique in several respects. It is the only coal severance tax to be based on the Btu content of the coal. The tax rate is either 20% or 30%, the higher rate applying to coal with higher Btu content. Current provisions for establishing the amount of the tax are based on the contract price of the coal f.o.b. mine and include a 20,000-ton exclusion per year. This method of valuation allows the tax to be graduated in keeping with the most salient feature of the coal, its energy-producing capability. A comparison figured by one state analyst found that, per Btu, the tax is not out of line with severance taxes levied elsewhere on oil resources. Table 1 shows the evolution of coal severance tax rates in Montana since 1920.

Another unique feature of Montana's Coal Severance Tax is that it is more than twice the rate of the next highest state mineral severance tax in the country. (Oil is not included as a mineral.) The power of states to use mineral severance taxation is well established legally. It is the rate of the Montana tax that has become highly controversial.

During 1980, the Montana State Supreme Court heard a suit brought by 11 out-of-state public utilities operating in the midwest and southwest and several companies which mine coal in Montana. The original suit consisted of four counts, one of which asked for an injunction to prevent the disbursement of the taxes collected. This count was separated from the suit and dismissed by a lower district court.

The remaining three counts claimed the tax was unconstitutional on the following grounds:

1. It constitutes an undue burden on interstate commerce.
2. It substantially frustrates Congressional purposes to increase coal production as a substitute for oil.
3. It distorts the compromise between the federal government and the states

Table 1. History of Montana Coal Taxes

1921—June 30, 1971
5¢ per ton; 50,000 ton exemption
July 1, 1971—June 30, 1973
4¢ per ton for 6,000 Btu or less
6¢ per ton for 6,001 – 7,500 Btu
8¢ per ton for 7,501 – 9,000 Btu
10¢ per ton for 9,000+ Btu
July 1, 1973— June 30, 1975
12¢ per ton for 7,000 Btu or less
22¢ per ton for 7,001 – 8,000 Btu
34¢ per ton for 8,001 – 9,000 Btu
40¢ per ton for 9,001+ Btu
July 1, 1975 —Present
12¢ per ton or 20% of Contract Sales Price (whichever greater) for 7,000 Btu or less.
22¢ per ton or 30% of Contract Sales Price (whichever greater) for 7,001 – 8,000 Btu.
34¢ per ton or 30% of Contract Sales Price (whichever greater) for 8,001 – 9,000 Btu.
40¢ per ton or 30% of Contract Sales Price (whichever greater) for 9,000 + Btu.

Source: Compiled by the Energy Division, Montana Dept. of Natural Resources.

by appropriating a major part of the "economic rents" attributable to coal extraction (*Commonwealth Edison Company, et al. v. State of Montana*; *Lake Superior District Power Company, et al. v. State of Montana*).

The Montana Supreme Court ruled in favor of Montana. The case then went to the U.S. Supreme Court, which also ruled in favor of Montana. If the State's ability to tax is going to be reduced, Congress will have to pass new legislation. Such legislation would affect all states' rights in the area of taxation.

The argument underlying this controversy is that, because the rate of the tax is so high, Montana coal is unduly expensive for use in the midwest and southwest and the development of Montana's coal resources for these markets is thereby constrained.

The argument can be broken down into two separate questions. The first question is, on what basis should the tax rate be figured? It is the differential between Montana's tax and the other states' tax rates that causes it to appear as an undue burden. On what grounds were these other tax rates based? Are they reflecting the full costs of mining development borne by the citizenry of their respective states? In light of increasing knowledge about the social effects of boom development and the environmental effects of strip mining, especially in the semi-arid West, Montana's tax may prove to be insufficient.

A recent study commissioned by the Old West Regional Commission addressed this question. It concluded that measurement of the damage from coal development is beyond present economic analysis techniques:

The evidence is overwhelming that large uncertainties are inherent in even the most refined estimates of social overhead costs, particularly as they are reflected in forecasts of net fiscal impacts on state and local governments. Moreover, present economic analysis techniques are unable to quantify the costs of a large number of important externalities in any meaningful way. For example, it is widely conceded that in areas of intensive research, such as the health effects of air pollution, total economic costs continue to be significantly underestimated. While the value of the external diseconomies generated by coal development is intuitively important...perhaps dominant...in comparison to that of the net fiscal effects (resulting from increases in social overhead costs), no methods exist by which that value can be meaningfully quantified.

In sum, the social overhead costs of coal development cannot be determined with any certainty, while the potentially more important external costs cannot be meaningfully estimated at all. Thus, benefits criteria cannot practically be used to establish appropriate levels for coal taxes (Mountain West Research, Inc., 1979).

The second question focuses on the economic factors that go into a utility's decision to burn Montana coal. Is the amount of the cost increase attributable to the severance tax the significant decision factor? Or are there other factors which are operating simultaneously and with greater impact to lessen demand for Montana coal? While 30% sounds like a sizable figure, it is 30% of the value of the coal at the mine, not at the point of use. This price is significantly lower than the price of the coal to the consumer, which includes the transportation costs of getting the coal to the midwest or southwest. Thus, it does not constitute a 30% increase in costs to the consumer.* The severance tax, furthermore, contributes less to consumers' cost of energy than do sales taxes which states typically levy on utility bills. These sales taxes add 2 to 9% to utility bills in the midwest, whereas the severance tax contributes only 0.2 to 1.9%.

Transportation costs and stability of supply are major concerns for utilities seeking coal supplies under long-term contract. The city of San Antonio, Texas, for example, has found that while Wyoming coal is initially cheaper per ton, it is less expensive to buy coal from South Africa or Australia once shipping charges are added. This has caused the city to initiate a suit against the rail lines for collecting too large a portion of the economic rent from coal. Montana is not as well served by rail lines as is Wyoming. Montana has only one east-west rail link, while Wyoming has access to several transportation routes. The probability of blockage along one line is fairly high and could affect the ability of coal to be delivered from Montana on time. In this respect, Wyoming coal is more attractive among Western supplies.

The fact is, demand for Montana's coal has been much less than anticipated by state officials and mining companies alike. Mining companies have been

---

*Furthermore, as any standard economics text will demonstrate, the burden of a tax on the consumer is less (and on the producer, more), to the extent that demand is elastic.

producing more coal than they can sell. One company invested millions in a gigantic dragline operation that has been sitting idle. Is Montana's coal tax solely to blame for this situation, or have the coal companies miscalculated the market?

According to a series of articles carried in the May 1980 *Washington Star*, the entire coal industry is in a slump, in Appalachia as well as in the West. For example, a May 5th article, based on interviews with the president of the National Coal Association, had this to say:

> The industry is still waiting for the boom in domestic coal that President Richard Nixon promised would come under his Project Independence plan of 1973. In the last year a dozen mines have closed, and the United Mine Workers of America estimate there are now 20,000 of their rank and file drawing unemployment checks in Ohio, Indiana, and West Virginia, with others working three-day weeks. Coal, which sold for $31 a ton two years ago, now is going for $22 a ton.

It appears that Montana coal operations are not alone in having difficulty finding markets for their coal.

A number of other factors could be cited to explain the lower demand for Montana coal, some of which have contributed to the industry slump as a whole. Lower growth rates in electrical consumption have reduced the expected demand for utility power generation from coal-burning plants, both existing and planned. At the same time, confusing and often contradictory federal regulations have slowed the rate at which existing oil-burning plants are being converted to coal, another source of expected demand that has not yet materialized. Other federal regulations have had special impact on western coal, reducing its desirability over eastern coal. Recent changes in Environmental Protection Agency regulations have replaced absolute sulphur emission standards with treatment-equipment requirements for all new facilities. Under the old standards, low sulphur coal from the west could be burned to meet emission standards without certain pollution control devices being necessary. Under the new standards, all emissions must be treated with pollution control devices, erasing the possibility of substantially reducing treatment equipment costs by burning low sulphur coal. Eastern coal has a high sulphur content and requires the use of pollution control devices under both new and old standards.*

To the extent that the law suit reflects the frustrations of coal companies in dealing with these various disappointments, it must untangle the effects of all of these factors. Montana's Coal Severance Tax should not serve as a scapegoat for unfortunate investment decisions.

However successful the opponents of the severance tax may ultimately be, it is only the tax rate, not the right to tax, which is in question. If the existing rate is struck down, a lower rate will be put in its place. The trust fund itself is not in jeopardy. It will continue to receive 50% of the coal tax revenues at whatever rate they accrue.

*The Clean Air Act could, however, be substantially altered by proposals now under consideration.

The magnitude of the trust fund account does affect the degree to which it can make a significant contribution to Montana's future generations. If the rate is sustained, other states may enact similar taxes. If the practice becomes widespread, state governments could become significant actors in the area of investment, a third party at the macro-economic level in the balance between federal economic policy and private investment.

How large is Montana's Coal Tax Trust Fund? State government officials, like coal company officials, had expected more rapid development of coal to take place. Early projections by the state's financial analysts put the Trust Fund at nearly $1 billion by the end of the century. These estimates have been revised dramatically downward as it became clear that coal development was falling far short of expectations. The projections in Table 2, as of June 1, 1979, present a more realistic picture (Cohea, 1979).

The balance in the Coal Tax Trust Fund as of June 30, 1981, was $74,527,000, which reflects the fact that by law, only 25% of the Coal Tax Revenues went into the fund through December 31, 1979. Thereafter, 50 percent of the tax's revenues are earmarked for the trust fund, as reflected in the figures above. Table 3 shows the disbursement of the tax revenues which do not go into the fund.

The fund will grow in proportion to the amount and value of coal developed over time. While the balance may not reach $1 billion by the end of this century, the coal reserves are there to support such a figure at some later date. Policymakers should bear this in mind in setting up investment mechanisms for the trust fund.

Initial Investment Provisions for the Coal Tax Trust Fund

What mechanisms have been established to invest the Coal Tax Trust Fund? How is Montana grappling with the question of investment strategies for these public funds? State policy makers began to address this question during the 1977 session of the legislature. In accordance with the Constitutional Amendment passed in 1976 creating the Trust Fund, the 1977 state legislature passed Senate Bill 44 to establish a new distribution schedule for the coal severance tax revenues and to specify procedures for the investment of the trust fund monies. Responsibility for management of the Coal Tax Trust Fund was given to the State Board of Investments to be invested according to the provisions of the board's Unified Investment Program.

Table 2.

Fiscal year	Tons (000)	Weighted average price	Value (000)	Tax (000)	Trust fund (000)
1980	33,027	4.804	$158,663	$47,599	$23,800
1981	36,329	5.044	$183,243	$54,973	$27,487

Table 3.   Disbursement Formula for Montana's Coal Severance Tax

Trust Fund	Until 1980*	After 1980 (Jan. 1)
	25% of all tax revenue; the remaining 75% apportioned as follows:	50% of all tax revenue; the remaining 50% as follows:
Counties with coal-mining activity	2% of taxes on coal paid in county	0%
Alternative energy development	2.5%	5%
Local impact and educational trust fund	26.5%–7/11 local 4/11 educational	37.5%–7/15 local 8/15 educational
Coal area highway impact	13%	0%
State equalization aid	10%	10%
County land planning	1%	1%
Renewable resource development	2.5%	2.5%
Parks acquisition	1.25%	0%
Parks trust	1.25%	5%
General fund	50%	38%
Library commission	0%	1%

*The percentage figures in the left hand column add up to more than 100% because they represent the maximum percentages observed over four years, given variation in the Fund's composition over that period.

The Unified Investment Program itself has only been in existence since 1971. Its creation was a major advance in the handling of state funds, for it replaced a fragmented hodge-podge of accounts and funds scattered throughout four departments of state government. In addition to pulling these various accounts into one place, the Unified Investment Program provided for a special staff and policy board to replace the mixed quality of management the funds had been receiving. The policy board, called the State Board of Investments, consists of five people, chosen by the governor on the strength of their financial expertise, to serve four-year terms.

By 1977, the Unified Investment Program had proven itself qualified to carry the responsibility of investing the Coal Tax Trust Fund. For example, the fiscal year 1976 Annual Report stated that the annualized, time weighted overall rate of return on common stock holdings of Montana was 19.08%, compared to 8.07% for the A.G. Becker Median and 14.03% for Standard and Poor's 500. By these traditional methods of financial measurement, the Unified Investment Program was proving to be a highly successful innovation.

As part of the Unified Investment Program, the legislature established investment policy guidelines in keeping with generally accepted legal principles regarding the management of investment funds. These guidelines consist of a "modified prudent man rule," typically found in public investment programs. The "prudent man" portion exhorts the board to undertake only those investments that a prudent man would consider justifiable in terms of both risk and return. There are three principle characteristics that have been attributed to "prudent" investments by U.S. courts and that pertain to Montana's investment program (Cohea, 1977):

1. A trustee must use more care in making public investments than he would if he were investing his own money.
2. A stricter standard of care and skill applies to a body of professional trustees than applies to individual, non-professional trustees.
3. The trustee has a duty to use "reasonable care" in making each investment on a number of criteria. One of these criteria is the earning capacity of other assets in the fund, thus allowing some balancing of risk and return in varied investments grouped into portfolios.

A "modified" portion of the prudent-man rule is also common practice, and refers to a list of permissible investments outlined by the legislature. Enabling legislation indicates which types of investments may be made outside of the strict confines of traditional prudent man investments. Montana's list of permissible investments is found in Section 79-310 of the state statutes, and includes the following provision particular to Montana:

4. The state board of investment shall endeavor to direct the state's investment business to those investment firms, and/or banks, which maintain offices in the state and thereby make contributions to the state economy. Further, due consideration shall be given to investments which will benefit the smaller communities in the State of Montana. The state's investment business will be directed to out-of-state firms only when there is a distinct economic advantage to the State of Montana.

It should be noted that the above provision for investment business directed to in-state investment firms and/or banks includes banks located in Montana that are owned and operated by out-of-state banking firms. Over 50% of the bank deposits in Montana reside in banks controlled by out-of-state concerns.

The board has several activities aimed at increasing its portfolio of in-state investments. The board holds its monthly meetings in different cities around the state and invites local bankers to attend for the express purpose of explaining the investment procedures of the board, especially the mortgage program. The board also buys certificates of deposit or savings certificates with two-to-five-year maturities on a bid basis from Montana financial institutions.

Purchase of Montana mortgages and certificates of deposit are the primary vehicles for in-state investment of state funds. As reported in the fiscal 1979 final report, these two programs accounted for $139.9 million of the total state investment funds of $891.9 million. Thus, in-state investment amounted to less than 16% of total state investment funds.

The initial provisions set down by the 1977 state legislature for investment of Montana's Coal Severance Tax Trust Fund made no special provisions for its investment, leaving it, therefore, to be handled in the same manner as other trust fund accounts. However, this was only the beginning of a continuing debate. The 1977 legislature saw the introduction of numerous bills proposing various investment schemes for the Coal Tax Trust Fund.

Two of these bills, authorizing the expenditure of the interest from the fund, were passed and signed into law: (1) to match federal funds for a weatherization program, and (2) to purchase a masterpiece by Montana artist C.M. Russell.

The other bills, all of which failed to pass, covered a broad range of ideas on investment policy. They included bills to establish a market-price bid process for investment of the Coal Trust Fund in-state; to use coal tax funds to broaden investment in residential mortgages for below-average-income families; to finance energy conservation measures by local governments and businesses; to encourage entry into farming; to create a state bank; and to retain all interest and income in the fund until the year 2000.

This plethora of bills containing conflicting investment policy prescriptions made apparent the need for careful study. In recognition of this need, the 1977 legislature adopted two joint resolutions. Each called for an interim study of investment strategies and the preparation of draft legislation for the next session of the legislature. The resolutions specified several general areas to be covered by the investment research: "to promote good quality middle and lower income housing and other Montana investment"; and "to help people get a start in agriculture or business." As the Montana State Legislature meets only every other year, the interim study was to be ready for the 1979 session of the legislature.*

Three Views of Public Investment Policy

One key dimension along which people differ regarding the proper investment of public funds is the degree to which they believe the capital needs of the state's economy are being met by the existing financial institutions. In the case of Montana, this dimension is tempered more by belief than fact. An analysis of capital flows was completed late in 1980. The degree to which such an analysis can capture the dynamics of capital needs at the state level is always open to question because of the difficulty in pinning down capital flow information inside a state boundary or across state lines. Until such time as a thoroughgoing analysis is possible for a single state, it should be acknowledged that any person's views, invariably drawn from limited experience, may be tempered by a dose of belief about what ought to be, not what is.

---

*It was at this point in the debate that the initial version of this paper was written to provide Montana policy makers with a framework for discussion and debate of the tradeoffs involved in various approaches to public investment.

Another dimension along which people differ in determining the proper mechanism for Coal Tax Trust Fund investments is the degree to which they think differences between public and private ownership of funds provide legitimate reasons for the two to be treated differently. For example, there are potentially significant differences, both in theory and in practice, with respect to time-horizon, risk aversion, scale, and the characteristics of the beneficiaries of investment decisions. From the standpoint of theory, the literature of public finance implies significant public-private differences. From this standpoint, public sector investment behavior, relative to private, should permit longer time horizons, less aversion to risk (or, if similar aversion, then a greater ability to offset perceived risks), larger scale of investments, and more inclusive definitions of potential beneficiaries. Observed behavior differences between public and private sector investors in practice, however, may or may not correspond to any a priori theory. For instance, it has been observed that public sector investors in many state economic development authorities or investment boards seem to behave in a way which, in its revealed preference for risk, is scarcely distinguishable from the behavior of conservative local commercial bankers (Kieschnick and Daniels, 1978). Unfortunately, the analysis of experience at the state level is much too limited to provide a basis from which to draw firm conclusions. Indeed, the actual existence of public sector experience relevant to the concerns of this chapter is too limited. Montana's Coal Tax Trust Fund is an example of a new species of financial creature whose public-private characteristics have yet to be determined. In considering potential investment policy for such a fund, the overlap between its potential beneficiaries and political boundaries argues for a broader definition of investment returns than private sector mechanisms would typically allow. The latter requires that we first distinguish "real" from purely financial aspects of investment.

Financial investment is an exchange of money and paper documents, such as loans, stocks or bonds, that involve a stream of cash over time, usually in the form of interest and principal. Real capital investment is the conversion of that cash into tangible goods, such as buildings, machines, and inventories. Returns on the financial portion of investment are measured by the return cash flow, and are independent of the geographic location and type of activity being financed. Returns on the real portion of capital investment are likewise measured by the cash flow generated from the use of the buildings, machines, etc. In addition, however, real capital investment adds to the infrastructure, employment, and tax base of the area in which it is located.

In terms of public ownership as contrasted to private ownership of funds, Montana's Coal Tax Investment Fund presents a special case. All private investment funds and most state public funds, like pension funds and special purpose trust funds, have specific beneficiaries that are identified by who they are, rather than where they are. Certainly this is true of private beneficiaries and pensioners who receive benefits even when they have moved out of the state in which the fund is located. While it is true that special purpose trust funds require beneficiaries to live in the state to receive benefits, once state residency is taken as a given, the nature of who you are is still the determining characteristic in receiving benefits. For example, if one is to benefit from the library trust fund, one must be a user of libraries. The managers of the library trust fund must be able to take the returns earned by the fund and transfer them into library services if the proper beneficiaries are to benefit.

The salient feature of all these beneficiaries, private, pensioners and public alike, is that the return on investment of these types of funds must be purely financial so that the benefits can be targeted to the specific purposes and/or people they were meant to serve. As long as the beneficiaries constitute a subset of the state's population, or are free to move beyond the borders of the state, return on investments must be geographically mobile. Financial returns have this characteristic of spatial transferability, whereas real returns in the form of facilities, tax base and employment do not. Therefore, while it may be adequate or appropriate to measure the returns from the former types of investments solely by their financial yields, it may not be so for the returns from the latter types.

In the case of Montana's Coat Tax Trust Fund, the definition of beneficiary is the present and future population of the state. Given the coincidence between political boundaries of state jurisdiction and the spatial boundaries of beneficiary populations, the location of the real portion of the investment is clearly relevant. Complete coincidence of beneficiaries and boundaries permits the state, which is a political subdivision with taxing powers, to capture and count as return on in-state investments both the financial returns and those aspects of real returns that contribute to public benefit. These include increases in tax base, employment and incomes, direct and indirect, plus increased diversification and stability of the state's economy. Over the long run, a more stable, diversified economic base can reduce the risks of boom/bust development cycles and cushion the state against swings in world timber, grain, copper and cattle markets. These real returns accrue to the resident population of the state, who are simultaneously the beneficiaries of the trust fund itself. The need for restricting the measure of return to the financial portion is eliminated because the real returns from in-state investment are targeted to the beneficiaries, too, without requiring spatial mobility.

This suggests that, contrary to private investment practice in which the nature and location of the real activity being financed is irrelevant, the location of real investment is very relevant to capturing the full rate of return for beneficiaries. State policymakers should take a close look at mechanisms for investment of Montana's Coal Tax Trust Fund which distinguish between in-state and out-of-state investment and attempt to measure the full returns of each.

What effect would this have on future Montanans, who are also beneficiaries of the fund? The principle means by which a state can redistribute wealth from one year to the next is through taxes and state expenditures. The Coal Tax

Trust Fund proposes to do this by easing the tax burden on Montana taxpayers in both the middle and long run. In the middle run, this will be accomplished by not allowing state expenditures to grow enormously through spending all the coal tax revenue now, for to do so would expand the tax burden that will fall on future taxpayers when coal revenues are no longer sufficient to meet these increased expenditures. In the long run, investment of the fund now will result in greater income to the state in the future, thereby offsetting part of the tax burden of future Montanans with increased revenues from the investments.

Offsetting future tax burdens with the returns from the fund's investments, however, can occur regardless of whether the real investment that results is in Montana or not. If high interest rates can be captured elsewhere, out-of-state investment can have the effect of importing capital over time. If, on the other hand, high rates of inflation are sustained above the interest rates being earned, future generations might be better served by the infrastructure, tax base, employment and diversified economic base generated by real investment in-state than by relying on financial interest rates alone. In an inflationary environment, inflation adjusted rates of interest will be far below actual market rates and could be negative.

The three views of investment policy that follow differ along the dimensions outlined at the beginning of this section (i.e., the degree to which each believes existing capital needs are being served by existing institutions and the degree to which each believes public funds may be used in more flexible investment mechanisms than is traditionally in keeping with investment of private trust funds). As a result, they differ in the degree to which they seek to encourage real investment within Montana using state funds. Investment policy for the Coal Tax Trust Fund could include aspects of any or all of these views, which are summarized in Figure 1.

Figure 1.

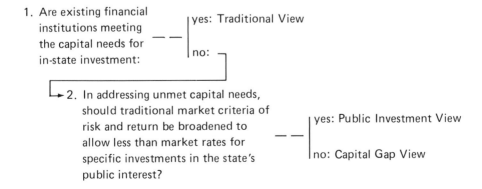

Decision Criteria for Investment Policy

1. Are existing financial institutions meeting the capital needs for in-state investment:
   — — yes: Traditional View
   no:

2. In addressing unmet capital needs, should traditional market criteria of risk and return be broadened to allow less than market rates for specific investments in the state's public interest?
   — — yes: Public Investment View
   no: Capital Gap View

Traditional View

The traditional view of investment policy focuses attention primarily on the financial portion of investment. This view relies on existing private market mechanisms and financial criteria for investment. It assumes that the existing financial institutions are functioning well, so that all the in-state ventures that are acceptable according to reasonable risk and profitability criteria have been able to find financing. There are no viable opportunities unable to obtain the capital they need. Conversely, if an investment opportunity is not funded, then it is not "viable" and should not be funded. These presumptions, furthermore, rest implicitly on a set of assumptions about the private marketplace:

1. Perfect or nearly perfect information—that private institutional decision-makers are fully informed on available investment opportunities.
2. Transactions costs—that the various transactions costs, information gathering, accounting, business planning, negotiations costs, etc., necessary to bring deals to market are not worth undertaking unless, over and above these costs, private rate of return targets can be met.
3. That there are not other constraints or impediments, such as imperfections in other private markets or government regulations, that bias private decisions.
4. That private investors' perceptions of risk, discount rates and opportunity costs are fully appropriate standards for assessing investment projects.

No attempt is made to distinguish the effects of real investment in-state. Therefore, Coal Tax monies should be invested through the existing market, going first to opportunities in Montana that meet these private investment criteria, with the remainder being invested out-of-state.

The traditional view of investment approximates existing investment policy implemented by the State Board of Investment for all state investments, including the Coal Tax Trust Fund. The amount of funds invested in-state depends on market demand, and is facilitated through both the certificate bid process and the mortgage loan program currently offered by the State Board. The fact that more money is available for bid than is being sought by Montana financial institutions indicates that all opportunities for in-state investments are being served. Therefore, investment of the remaining funds out-of-state contributes to the state's economic base by importing funds over time through interest on investments. This interest will reduce the tax burden of Montana citizens in the future. Again, in-state investment in fiscal year 1979 amounted to almost $140 million, which is less than 16% of the state's investable funds of $892 million. This figure measures the investment funds in bid certificates and mortgages, the principal mechanisms for in-state investment.

As mentioned above, the traditional view of investment measures return to the state only through the private financial rate of return. If net additions to tax revenues result from in-state real investment, the combined income returned to the state would be higher than the market measure of financial return would indicate.

Capital Gap View

The Capital Gap View of investment policy assumes that there may be ventures in the state that meet reasonable criteria for risk and profitability but have not been able to find investment funds because of gaps in the structure of the existing financial markets. These gaps limit the flows of capital to certain sectors, areas or types of firms and thereby constrain economic development.* Designing innovative public investment programs to fill the gaps, at fair market rates of return, will not compete with the private market and will enhance the amount of real investment in the state. Therefore, Coal Tax Trust Fund policy should include periodic review of financial capital needs and availability and develop special programs to channel investment funds where needed. The remainder should be invested out-of-state according to the Traditional View outlined above.

All investments would be judged and measured by private market criteria. Administrative and information costs would likely be higher since, if studies done elsewhere are any guide, capital gaps mainly impede the growth of new, young or small firms (see below). While in-state investment would take priority, such investments would have to stand on the merits of their financial returns alone. Any viable opportunity currently having difficulty in locating the capital it needs would be served, thus guaranteeing as much in-state investment as is economically sound using these criteria.

Montana has never had a systematic analysis of its financial availability and needs. Recent research on capital markets in the New England States revealed that, while there was no shortage of capital funds overall, certain categories of potential real investment were systematically cut off from existing sources of capital funds (Daniels and Katzman, 1976). Researchers found, for example, that major lending institutions had ceased to consider loans to firms of less than $2 million in sales. Firms too small to meet this standard, but too large for programs like the Small Business Administration, were caught in a capital "gap." Other studies, including Chapters III and IV, above, and items referenced there, also indicate gaps of various types affecting small business.

The absence of comprehensive data on Montana makes it difficult to see if gaps exist here as well. It is difficult to analyze capital flows at the state level in part because capital is meant to flow freely between states, and in part because much information on the banking sector is confidential. It is interesting to note

---

*The concept and causes of capital gaps are discussed at length elsewhere. For an especially clear and thorough treatment, see Section II of Kieschnick and Daniels (1978).

that while 31% of the banks in Montana are owned by out-of-state interests, they control 52.6% of total deposits in Montana banks (as of December 31, 1978).

Recent conversations with economic development people at the state and local level revealed widespread perceptions that Montana does indeed have some problems with capital flows. Several types of problems were mentioned. Venture capital for the establishment of new businesses is difficult to find as Montana has no venture capital firms. Recently established businesses have encountered difficulties in obtaining loans for operating and inventory expenses. This has become particularly acute for businesses whose creditors are changing payment schedules to meet the high costs of inflation. Montana businesses in general suffer from a shortage of equity as a percentage of assets, thus making it difficult to get credit on reasonable terms, if at all. While there appears to be a sufficient amount of capital in the state, it seems there are types of capital needs that are going unmet.

As a concept, the notion of capital gap allows of some ambiguity. It is never clear a priori which among several potentially causative factors may explain observations that certain investment demands are going unmet. The mix of causes and the mix of demands are likely to vary by city, state and region. Only careful empirical studies of regional capital markets can give practical content to the concept. At the conceptual or theoretical level, however, there should be no ambiguity as to the implications. The concept of capital gap implicates the structure or mechanics of the capital markets at the regional level; it does not imply that there is, in some sense, a "shortage" of capital overall. The structure/mechanics of the system include information channels, the existence or capability of institutions to enable risk pooling, risk preference biases due to institutional structure, and so forth. In the case of Montana, we noted two problematic features—concentration and domination by out-of-state institutions, and the lack of venture capital firms. The precise implications of these, plus the identification of other structural/mechanical anomalies, need to be systematically explored before specific implications can be drawn.

One should also understand that the concept of capital gap does not confuse capital "needs" with "demands," although there has sometimes been some careless commentary leading to confusion of this sort. It is unquestionably an economic concept grounded in the concept of demand, that is, that investment projects or capital requirements are being brought to some portion of the market, but that the market is not cleared. Again, this may be due to a number of factors at work singly or together—lack of information, high transactions costs, inability to pool risks, institutional bias in risk perception or risk aversion, et al.

It is important to be quite clear on this point because there is also a class of "needs" that may not get translated into demands. That is, there may be a number of types of investment projects that do not get formulated to the point where they can be taken to the financial marketplace, a number of types of business activities that do not get sufficiently organized, or a number of deals that do not get put together, because of a more deeply rooted problem of a lack of capacity to do economic development. By "capacity" is meant the availability of specialized skills, management and entrepreneurship. These are especially likely to be lacking in rural states like Montana.* And it is the explicit recognition of this lack of capacity as a key part of the economic development problem, plus the willingness to do something about it, which helps to distinguish the "public investment view," following, from the views which have been discussed thus far.

Public Investment View

The public investment view of investment policy places primary emphasis on the state's ability to use whatever investment funds it has to benefit the state through real investment, consistent with the principles of investment responsibility to fund beneficiaries. Investment mechanisms should be designed and implemented to fill capital needs unmet by existing financial institutions. The differences between public and private investment imply a more active role for the state, not only in supporting certain demands, but in identifying investment needs and helping translate them into viable demands. This role allows the state to invest funds in ways that offer capital at lower than market rates for in-state investments that are financially sound but unable to carry a loan at a market rate of interest. It may also include direct financing of ventures that are either too large or for which the payback period is too long from the standpoint of the risk preferences, or capacity of private investors.

It is apparent, therefore, that natural resource trust funds like that of Montana bring two unconventional assumptions to the forefront of debate on investment policy. One assumption is that, when the owners of the investment are geographically defined, the location and type of real investment being supported is relevant to the investment's rate of return. The financial rate of return should not be used alone in judging the potential payback of an investment. Rather, the extent to which financial yields and real wealth are jointly created must be assessed in defining acceptable rates of return. This assumption, if reasonably correct, can justify a decision to invest in a project whose financial rate of return is less than the market rate, but which offers returns through increased employment, tax base diversification and stability of the state's economy. In making this determination, the costs of the proposed project in terms of public services must also be accounted for as offsets to its gross real returns. The duration of return flows should also be considered. Returns from the real investments may continue long after financial returns have ended. For example, the interest paid on a loan to build new capacity for

---

*For further discussion of this important point, see Bannerman and Daugherty, 1980; Jones, 1980; and the discussion of problems of rural cooperatives in Chapter X of this volume.

a plant ceases when the loan is paid back, while the employment and growth potential made possible by the added capacity may continue.

The other assumption relevant to general purpose natural resource trust funds has to do with the definition of public values. Private investment theory, from which rates of return are derived, is based on the use of prices as a surrogate for direct measurement of the value people place on a particular thing. The beauty of the theory lies in its ability to derive collective values from the actions of people expressed individually. The result, a market rate of return for a particular investment category, then becomes the decision criterion for investment that takes all these individual values into account.

Public investment should also be based on criteria that reflect the collective values of its owners. Where these owners are geographically determined, it becomes possible to define public values directly through the political process. The public investment view assumes that direct measurement through the political process is a more accurate reflection of public values and therefore should be included in investment criteria. This assumption has considerable support in the public finance literature.

Guidelines for Investment Implementation

Guidelines and criteria for sound investment consistent with the Capital Gap and Public Investment views are very much in formative stages. Montana policy makers can profit from advice already given to Alaskan policy makers on the subject of limits to the potential for investment (see Daniels, 1977; Daniels et al., 1980). While Montana's economy is larger and more diverse than Alaska's nonoil economic base, it has some limit to the rate at which it can absorb capital in profit-making ventures. As mentioned above, one of the biggest constraints on rural development is lack of capacity and, though the "public investment" standpoint encompasses capacity building as a necessary part of the economic development process, it is not an activity where tangible benefits will appear soon. In fact, a strong case can be made for the establishment of a separate capacity-building and transactions-cost reducing intermediary institution, as in Massachusetts.* Thus, the State Board of Investments, though subject to a mandate to account for a full range of real benefits in its assessment of investment opportunities, would not be placed in the awkward and perhaps compromising position of having to originate the deals it then needs to evaluate. Enthusiasm for in-state investment should not be allowed to cloud sound distinctions between long-term viable opportunities and ventures that will continue to operate in the red regardless of how

---

*Reference here is to the Community Economic Development Assistance Corporation, a public corporation financed with the Massachusett's governor's 4% discretionary money under CETA. This was established partly in response to the fact that an agency previously established to finance "real" investments by community development organizations was faced with a lack of adequately prepared investment opportunities.

"socially desirable" they may seem. Investment monies cannot create real economic activity; they can only support those for which a genuine market and effective management exists (Bivens, 1977; Daniels, 1977).

Investment policy for the Coal Tax Trust Fund could involve aspects of any or all of these three views of investment. The following section outlines various steps that can be taken to implement each policy in Montana. Included also are some examples of public funds investment programs elsewhere as illustrations of relevant experience which does exist.

Implementation of the Traditional View

Initial provisions for investment of the Coal Tax Trust Fund as part of the Unified Investment Program of the State Board of Investments embodies the investment philosophy of the Traditional View. Therefore, there is little that needs be done to further implement this policy. More can be done to monitor the effects of in-state financial investments, particularly with regard to the bid process for two- and five-year-maturity certificates. The purpose of such monitoring would not be to improve the financial rate of return, for that is determined by the market, but rather to determine the effects of the real investment it engenders.

The State of Alaska conducted an in-state investment program with oil tax revenues from 1969 to 1971. The program was later evaluated by the Institute of Social and Economic Research of the University of Alaska (Institute of Social and Economic Research, 1977).

Their findings revealed, among other things, that several structural factors in the banking system were preventing the funds from being used as they were intended. For example, one condition of the loans required they be backed by U.S. Government obligations which were not committed as collateral for other deposits. In fact, uncommitted U.S. Government obligations were in short supply, thus limiting the amount of funds that state banks could use. This restriction was modified in 1971. Careful monitoring of Montana's in-state investment loans would help determine if similar problems are artificially constraining Montana's existing loan bid program.

Implementation of the Capital Gap View

A decision to pursue this philosophy of investment for the Coal Tax Trust Fund requires as a first step a thorough survey of capital needs and availability in the state. Once this has been done, areas needing financial investment funding, if any, will be apparent and programs designed to meet these needs can be developed. Such programs are consistent with the policies governing the Board of Investments, as prudent man principles and market rates of return would remain qualifying criteria. However, as this constitutes a more innovative use of public monies, it may be legally desirable to pass legislation specifically removing the Coal Tax Trust Fund from the more general trust fund category, and adding a special provision specific to the Coal Tax Trust

Fund. Additional staff and funding may be necessary for the Board of Investments to carry out any special programs.

British Columbia and North Dakota offer examples of how capital markets can be improved. If the problem is geographic (i.e., that some regions in the state are unable to meet capital needs because their reserves are too small), British Columbia offers an example of the creation of a new network to mobilize and distribute capital funds. The 186 credit unions in British Columbia banded together many years ago to pool their assets and form their own "Central Bank" which is then able to raise additional funds in Toronto, New York, and in international markets. The British Columbia Central then provides liquidity loans, rediscounting and loan participation to the member credit unions. While no such credit union's union exists in Montana, a further look at their operations might reveal something of use in distributing investment funds more broadly across the state.

The Bank of North Dakota is an example of how comprehensive circulation efficiency of a rural state's capital resources can be achieved. North Dakota has the oldest state-owned and managed commercial bank in the country, established in 1919. The bank has three main responsibilities: to promote the agricultural, commercial and industrial sectors of the state; to manage and provide financial services to state agencies and state funds; and to provide professional help to organizations that will promote the economic well-being of North Dakota.

The bank is four times the size of any other bank in the state, and has been very successful, earning 3% on its assets (compared to the next highest bank earnings in the country, 1.2%). Its actual role is that of a trustee and clearing house for commercial banks in the state, especially the small ones. The bank is prohibited from lending to individuals (except to farmers) and instead lends directly to other financial institutions and engages in secondary market operations to increase the liquidity of the in-state capital market. The bank lends directly to municipalities and is the chief underwriter of bond issues. Finally, the bank has a variety of agricultural finance programs including one for young, small farmers to develop irrigation.

If, for example, it is found that municipalities are having trouble finding underwriters for their bond issues, a program to invest in these with public monies such as is done in North Dakota would ease this capital problem. Implementation of something as comprehensive as the Bank of North Dakota would require major expansion of the existing State Board of Investments, and passage of more comprehensive enabling legislation than that which currently governs its actions.

Implementation of the Public Investment View

In the above two views of investment policy, fair market demand determined the areas and amount of financial investment. By contrast, public investment policy reflects a conscious decision to include other criteria in determining sound investment decisions, areas and amounts. The first step in implementing a program of public investment should be the formulation of long-range development goals for Montana. If one purpose of the investment view is to encourage real investments that Montanans value more highly than the private market, it behooves state policymakers to determine what these values are. Direct measurement of people's values and preferences through a political goals formulation process would identify what areas of investment ought to be encouraged to respond to these values.

Policymakers must also be cognizant of general problems in public investment. One of these is attempting to use dollar measures and market rates of return for social values. The science of public benefit measurement is uncertain, inelegant, and difficult to apply in a way which is either sufficient, precise or comparable to traditional financial analysis. Direct measurement through the political process helps to set goals and directions in keeping with social values, but measurement of progress toward these goals is still problematic. Managers of Montana's investment monies should bear these limitations in mind when trying to evaluate public investment decisions.

Another problem is locating the necessary financial expertise to distinguish a good loan from one likely to default. One way to circumvent the lack of expertise in the public sphere is to channel public investment through private capital institutions containing the appropriate expertise. This also permits closer knowledge of the local situation than can be possible from a centralized public agency. Reliance upon traditional expertise does have its drawbacks, however, for it introduces an inclination toward financial conservatism that can overpower the original public goals for which the program was intended. Often the goals and guidelines creating the program are too indefinite to be binding. Few programs have succeeded in resolving the tension between public accountability to the electorate and professional accountability to the financial community. One factor that can help is well defined program goals and criteria for evaluation.

Some observers of the State Board of Investments feel that professional financial interests have come to dominate the decisions of the board at the expense of Montana investment opportunities. The allure of high rates of return from out-of-state investments has dampened the interest of the board in the lower return but low-risk financial paper of the Farmer's Home Administration and Small Business Administration. These observers feel that the state legislature had a broader social role in mind for the board when it was created in 1971. They argue that a more aggressive role could be taken by the board within its existing mandate to increase its Montana portfolio.

Legally, new legislation removing the Coal Tax Trust Fund from the provisions of the Unified Investment Program would be necessary to implement any program involving less than market rates of return. While not required by law, it may be advisable to also create a new board to oversee any such programs, as the current Board of Investments has indicated an unwillingness to embrace such programs. In a memo to the Coal Tax Oversight Committee, dated September 17, 1977, Dean Albert, Chairman of the Board, wrote the following:

> We ask of you to understand the responsibility we bear in performing our duties with the funds entrusted with us. The study which you have undertaken is the direct result of legislation which was introduced last session to direct the investments of the Coal Tax Trust Fund. Most of the bills would have directed us to employ those funds into subsidy programs and/or various social programs. We do not consider or envision our operation as encompassing those types of programs. We are trustees of investment funds and in the capacity we act as professional investors and money managers. We do not have the expertise or staff support for programs other than prudent investments.

Two examples of public investment programs, one dealing with business expansion and the other with farming, illustrate the kinds of programs that have been undertaken elsewhere. In May 1972 Connecticut became the first state to help bear the high risk of new product development through creation of the Connecticut Product Development Corporation (CPDC). The CPDC expects returns on 20% of its projects and, based on the experience of the National Research and Development Council in Britain, this should be enough to cover its losses. The CPDC doesn't deal with individual entrepreneurs, but encourages them to find existing businesses with which the CPDC then shares the costs of new product development, usually 60–40. New Product means any product new to the firm. Repayment is made completely through royalties. Those projects that fail repay nothing while those that succeed pay until five times the value of the original loan is returned. This program is particularly useful for small, new companies which have established themselves in a limited market and wish to expand to additional products, but find their credit position weak due to their newness and their high debt/equity position. Policy makers in Connecticut see this program as an innovative approach to job creation. Rather than short-term, make-work employment, new productive jobs are created via the private sector. (See Chapter VI for further details.)

The Saskatchewan Land Bank Commission is also of particular interest as it is directed primarily at the problems of the family farm. The Land Bank has three main purposes: to offer an alternative to farmers not wishing to commit themselves and their resources to a lifetime of investing in the land; to facilitate the transfer of family farms between generations; and to help people begin farming without substantial family assistance, thereby helping to maintain rural communities.

The bank buys land at market prices and leases it at a rate of 5.5% of the purchase price for the first three years, then at 5.5% of the market value per year, figured on a three-year moving average. So, for example, a farmer wishing to retire can receive the value of his land and know that it will be leased to a new farmer or his own children at prices they can afford. Or, if a farmer needs to free up some of his capital for expansion, he can sell all or part of his land and have the money to work with, then lease it back from the bank. In all cases, the lessee has the option to buy the land after five years, although financing must be arranged through other sources.

The bank began in 1973 with $100 million in borrowing power, funded by providing treasury bonds sold over 20 years. Interest on this money is paid with lessee fees. As the land is sold, the bonds will be retired. The Land Bank Commission expects to be solvent in 50 years. As of 1977 it was managing about 700,000 acres.

The Debate Continues: Actions of the 1979 Montana State Legislature

Meanwhile, back at the Montana Legislative Council, the interim study of investment policy requested by the 1977 Legislature had been looking into a number of investment mechanisms to fit Montana's needs. From their ranks, five pieces of legislation were drafted for the 1979 session. Three bills and two joint resolutions were introduced:

S. 244. A bill for an act entitled: "An Act to create the Montana Product Development Corporation, a public corporation to provide financial aid for products and inventions and to appropriate $2 million for the operation of the Corporation for the biennium ending June 30, 1981." This money is to be appropriated from the Coal Tax Trust Fund.

S. 158. A bill for an act entitled: "An Act to establish preference for investment of certain state funds in Montana securities." This bill excludes retirement funds but allows other funds including Coal Tax Trust Funds to be invested in securities issued by Montana corporations and political subdivisions even if they will produce up to 1% less annual income than out-of-state investments.

S. 248. A bill for an Act entitled: "An Act to create the Montana Homestead Land Program, devoted to the acquisition, lease, and eventual sale of agricultural land, and to appropriate funds for the initial expenses of the program." Funds are to be obtained through the issue of bonds, with the Coal Tax Trust Fund to stand as a capital reserve for the bonds.

S.J. 4. A Joint Resolution of the Senate and the House of Representative of the State of Montana urging the Board of Investments to participate with the Farmers Home Administration in farm ownership loans.

S.J. 5. A Joint Resolution of the Senate and the House of Representatives of the State of Montana urging the Board of Investments to purchase more Small Business Administration guaranteed loans.

An additional piece of legislation was introduced independently of the Interim Study in the House of Representatives:

H. 667. A bill for an Act entitled: "An Act to allow the Board of Investments to give preference to Montana securities and other investments that contribute to a stable state economy when investing the Coal Severance Tax Trust Fund while at the same time insuring the safety of the Trust's principal." This also authorized investment of said fund at less interest than investment in comparable out-of-state securities.

All four of the bills reflect the Public Investment View of investment policy. All four simultaneously tie their investment mechanism to the Coal Trust Tax Fund and/or specifically exclude state retirement funds from the proposed policy. This indicates an increasing appreciation among state policymakers of fine distinctions of public investment theory. This knowledge is a necessary first step toward the evolution of investment mechanisms that meet appropriate standards of financial security while carving out new responsibilities in keeping with the capital needs and long-range goals of the State of Montana.

The two joint resolutions reflect the Capital Gap View of investment policy. Neither distinguish the Coal Tax Trust Fund as the special focus of the proposed policy, but apply it to the whole of the state's investment funds. This is in keeping with the Capital Gap View which accepts market rates of return as the standard, thereby making the sources of the funds irrelevant. The introduction of these resolutions marks the first time, since 1971, that state policymakers have addressed the broader question of investment policy for all state assets. As an expression of concern over in-state investment, these resolutions also evidence increased understanding of financial mechanisms as well as a desire to broaden in-state involvement of the state's funds.

The fates of these pieces of legislation varied. S. 158, establishing preference for Montana investments at 1 percent less than the market rate, died in the Senate Taxation Committee. S. 244, the Montana Product Development Corporation, was indefinitely postponed after second reading in the Senate, a procedural way to bury a bill alive. H. 667, establishing a separate account for the Coal Tax Trust Fund and allowing it to be invested in-state at less than market rates, was killed outright on second reading. S. 248, the Montana Homestead Land Program, was so altered and amended that proponents of the bill helped to kill it in the second reading in the House. Many who opposed these bills saw them as contributing to the growth of socialism.

The joint resolutions shared the opposite fate. Both were passed in the flurry of activity that marked the closing weeks of the session. Whether they will affect the investment decisions of the State Board of Investments remains to be seen. One possible explanation for their passage may be the fact that they carry very little clout. Within the framework of the enabling legislation, which contains the language governing any exceptions to "prudent" investment behavior, policy for investing state funds is solely a matter of the discretion of the State Board of Investments. Passing joint resolutions has no effect on the enabling legislation. The legislature merely has gone on record with an expression of its wishes, which the State Board of Investments is free to consider or, based on its own judgment, reject. Observers of the current state board predict rejection.

There is an odd irony underlying the debate over investment policy for the Coal Tax Trust Fund. While policy makers continue to debate the criteria by which investment of the fund ought to go to opportunities in-state, existing investment of the Coal Tax Trust Fund, as of the end of fiscal year 1979, was entirely out-of-state. Table 4 presents the figures for investment of the fund. As can be seen from the table, more than one-third of the total went to out-of-state utilities. It was only by chance that none of it had been invested in the very same utilities that brought the suit against the Coal Producers Severance Tax.

The way in which one reacts to the absence of in-state investment of Coal Tax Trust Funds can serve as a litmus test to determine which view of investment policy one holds. Those who accept the traditional view of investment policy will accept this fact as incidental. According to the traditional view, neither the particular source of the investment funds nor the nature of the activity in which they are invested are relevant beyond the requirements for risk and return. More state funds are available through the bid process to in-state financial institutions than they can use. Therefore, the 16% of state assets currently invested in-state is meeting all capital needs of the state's economic development. The fact that the coal tax is not represented in this 16% is irrelevant to whether the fund is being invested with the best interests of the beneficiaries in mind. The only relevant concern is the fund's long-term growth rate.

If, for example, investment in utilities produces a high rate of return, it is good investment policy to invest coal tax monies in utilities. This is especially true if the investment is used by the utility to finance coal-burning equipment for Montana coal. Such investments lead to increased fund growth through increased tax revenues from expanded coal production in addition to high interest from the investment itself.

If one is outraged by the fact that this investment capital for the state's future is going entirely to out-of-state concerns, one's underlying assumptions must be that viable uses of that capital exist in Montana and are being cut off from the capital they need. In a situation of capital shortage, the state should be adopting whatever policies it can for the more discretionary Coal Tax Trust Fund to ensure that capital needs at home are met before capital funds are exported. Control of capital itself is a precious resource, especially as Montana is trying to broaden and diversify its predominantly "Colonial" economy.

Feelings of outrage at pure out-of-state investment of the fund are appropriate to both the Capital Gap View and the Public Investment View. They can be distinguished from each other by whether one feels cheated at the prospect of a Montanan paying less interest into the fund than would a similar borrower out-of-state. The Capital Gap View requires interest rates to be comparable. The Public Investment View is willing to consider criteria other than interest rates alone as legitimate for investment decisions.

Final authority for investment policy for the Coal Tax Trust Fund lies with the State Legislature. The actions and debate of the 1979 session evidence a shifting predominance of views from the Traditional to the Capital Gap. By adopting the two joint resolutions calling for more state participation in Small Business Administration and Farmers Home Administration loans, policy-

Table 4. FY 1979 Investment of the Coal Severance Tax Trust Fund

| Security | Permanent Coal Trust Fund | | | | | |
	Par Value (000)	Interest rate	Maturity date	Cost	Market value	Yield
Corporate bonds						
Industrial						
Borden	500	9.375	06-15-09	500,000	503,750	9.375
Continental Oil	500	9.375	04-01-09	498,759	506,850	9.400
Dana Corporation	300	8.875	11-15-08	298,530	288,750	8.923
Diamond Shamrock Corp.	500	8.500	04-01-08	490,413	460,000	8.690
Dow Chemical Co.	200	8.625	02-15-08	198,471	187,080	8.700
Hershey Foods	300	9.500	03-15-09	298,886	303,000	9.538
Montgomery Ward Credit	300	9.375	05-15-84	299,332	296,220	9.438
Shell Oil Ust Atlantic PP	444	9.300	03-07-02	444,327	442,149	9.300
Studebaker Worthington	300	9.350	11-15-03	300,000	297,090	9.350
Texaco Inc.	200	8.500	04-01-06	197,378	187,740	8.630
Subclass total	3,544			3,526,096	3,472,629	
Banks and insurance						
American General Insurance Co.	500	9.375	12-15-08	496,318	495,000	9.450
Crocker National Corp.	500	8.600	12-01-02	497,653	449,400	8.648
Subclass total	1,000			993,971	944,400	
Other financial						
Beneficial Corp.	200	8.350	02-15-88	200,000	187,740	8.350
Beneficial Corp.	100	8.350	02-15-88	100,000	93,870	8.350
Ford Motor Credit Notes	200	8.375	05-01-84	199,516	192,500	8.439
National Rural Utilities	500	9.750	04-01-09	497,619	502,500	9.800
Subclass total	1,000			997,135	976,610	
Utilities						
Arkansas Louisiana Gas	200	9.100	10-01-98	200,000	191,500	9.100
Baltimore Gas & Electric	300	9.375	07-01-08	300,000	292,500	9.375
Duquesne Light & Power	500	10.125	02-01-09	494,435	505,000	10.244
El Paso Electric PP	500	9.950	05-01-04	500,000	495,300	9.950
General Telephone Co of California	200	8.875	04-01-08	197,515	186,500	9.000

Idaho Power Co.	500	9.000	08-15-08	500,000	467,500	9.000
Iowa Power & Light	500	9.750	01-15-09	495,267	494,400	9.849
Mountain States Tel. & Tel.	500	8.625	04-01-18	495,155	467,100	8.710
Pacific Gas & Electric	500	10.125	08-01-12	498,751	508,750	10.149
Pacific Tel & Tel	500	9.875	02-15-16	500,000	502,100	9.875
Public Service Co Colorado	100	9.250	10-01-08	100,000	97,130	9.250
Public Service Electric & Gas	300	9.375	11-01-08	302,212	293,910	9.299
South Carolina Electric & Gas	500	10.125	04-01-09	495,028	510,000	10.231
Southern California Edison Co	500	9.625	11-01-03	496,585	498,100	9.700
Southwestern Public Service	150	8.750	03-01-08	150,000	139,875	8.750
Texas Electric Service Co	500	9.500	02-01-09	496,539	503,400	9.571
Utah Power & Light Co	300	9.125	05-01-08	300,000	286,140	9.125
Virginia Electric & Power	200	9.625	07-01-08	200,000	193,860	9.625
Subclass total	6,750			6,721,487	6,633,065	
Canadian						
Bell Telephone of Canada	400	9.000	01-15-08	400,000	371,000	9.000
British Columbia Hydro & Power	500	9.625	06-01-05	494,094	489,350	9.750
Subclass total	900			894,094	860,350	
Security total	13,194			13,132,783	12,887,054	
Government agencies						
US Government Agencies						
Federal National Mortgage Association	500	7.500	10-13-87	500,000	456,250	7.500
Federal National Mortgage Association	500	8.550	09-12-88	498,750	482,500	8.580
US GG Ship Financing Bonds LNG Arles	500	8.200	12-13-02	500,000	460,250	8.200
Subclass total	1,500			1,498,750	1,399,000	
Security total	1,500			1,498,750	1,399,000	
Other holdings						
Short-term investment pool[a]	2,276	.000	00-00-00	2,275,889	2,275,889	
Subclass total	2,276			2,275,889	2,275,889	
Security total	2,276			2,275,889	2,275,889	
Fund total	16,970			16,907,422	16,561,943	

Source: FY79 Report, State Board of Investments.

[a] A portion of this is invested in short-term Montana securities.

makers were expressing their dissatisfaction with the State Board of Investments' performance on in-state investments, for the first time since the board's creation in 1971. One thing is certain—the State Legislature will be watching the level of in-state investment very closely over the next few years.

One other factor is certain. The minority of legislators who supported the four bills on investment policy in the 1979 session will not let the debate stop here. A great deal of work is going into the preparation of legislation and arguments for the 1981 session. They are optimistic about the potential for change.

Very little of the disagreement over Montana's Coal Tax Trust Fund investment policy is currently a matter of fact. Comprehensive data on capital flows and needs within the state do not exist. Proven examples of other states' investment strategies tailored to meet specific capital needs are few and grew out of experiences not necessarily transferable to the Montana situation. Until the current suit is settled, it is difficult to know whether the magnitude of the fund will even justify the time spent in debate.

In light of such uncertainty, it is the spirit of Montana people that will determine the outcome. The analogy of the pioneer is appropriate. Early settlers to the state had to take risks in the face of the unknown. They also had confidence in their knowledge, knew its limitations, and learned from their mistakes.

Changing the Coal Tax Investment Policy away from the Traditional is a step toward the unknown. It will involve risk, but the risk can be calculated from existing knowledge of public investment. It will likely involve mistakes, but they can be corrected and in the process provide new knowledge for the future.

Maintaining the existing Traditional policy is analogous to settling down once the unknown is beyond the horizon, security is paramount, and risk is minimized. It remains to be seen how settled Montanans have become.

Bibliography

Bannerman, Charles D. and Daugherty, Scott R. (1980). "NPWEDA Capital Market Issues—Needs of Rural Areas." Prepared for the Conference on Development Finance, Washington, D.C. (Jan. 4).

Bivens, William E., III. (1977). "State Development Strategies for Rural Communities." State Planning Series 6. Council of State Planning Agencies, National Governor's Association (October).

Cohea, Teresa O. (1977). "Research Memoranda #1 to the Coal Tax Oversight Committee on Investment of State Funds." Montana Legislative Council (June).

Cohea, Teresa O. (1978). "Report of the Coal Tax Oversight Committee to the 1979 State Legislature." Montana Legislative Council (November).

Cohea, Teresa O. (1979). "Research Memoranda to the Coal Tax Oversight Committee on Background for June Meeting." Montana Legislative Council (June 11).

Commonwealth Edison Company, et al. v. State of Montana.

Daniels, Belden Hull (1977). "Thinking About the Alaska Permanent Fund: A Cautious Approach for Alaskan Policymakers." Department of City and Regional Planning, Harvard University, Cambridge, MA (July).

Daniels, Belden, et al. (1980). "An Overview of Alaska's Development Finance." Confidential Draft to the Honorable Russ Meekins, Chairman, House Finance Committee (February 11).

Daniels, Belden Hull and Katzman, M. (1976). "Development Incentives to Induce Efficiencies in Capital Markets." New England Regional Commission and International Center for New England, Inc. Revised.

Gay, Lance (1980). "Return to Coal." *The Washington Star* (May 5–8).

Institute of Social and Economic Research (1977). "The Permanent Fund and the Growth of the Alaskan Economy—Select Studies." University of Alaska (December).

Jones, E. Walton (1980). "Rural Development—A Continuing Challenge." Prepared for the Conference on Development Finance, Washington, D.C. (January 4).

Kieschnick, Michael, and Daniels, B. (1978). "Theory and Practice in the Design of Development Finance Institutions." U.S. Economic Development Administration (November).

Lake Superior District Power Company, et al. v. State of Montana.

Markusen, Ann R. (1978). "Class, Rent, and the State: Uneven Development in Western U.S. Boomtowns." *Review of Radical Political Economics*, Vol. 10, No. 3.

Mountain West Research, Inc. (1979). "Mineral Fuels Taxation in the Old West Region." Billings, MT (October).

Office of the Secretary of State (1976). "Voter Information for Proposed Constitutional Amendments." State of Montana (November 2).

IX

Innovative Uses of CETA for Economic Development

Christopher Brennan and James Keefe

The fundamental equation in economic growth is usually written: capital plus labor equals production. Other chapters of this book have given significant treatment to the capital side of this formula. This chapter, in addressing innovative uses of CETA for economic development, will give some attention to the labor side. As we do, it will become apparent how meaningless the conventional capital/labor distinction can be in urban economic development. Money, after all, can be used for many purposes, and seed money for a new enterprise can be used to pay for either wages or equipment. Thus, "labor" subsidies are potentially as important as "capital" subsidies in starting up a business or initiating any other type of economic development activity. As policy makers and planners begin to recognize that the work experience, technical skills, and education embodied in a labor force represent crucial forms of capital, *human* development programs such as CETA will begin to figure more prominantly in economic development strategies.

In Massachusetts, CETA has been used to further economic development efforts at the state and local levels. It has contributed to the retention and growth of small businesses, and the more dramatic growth of our high technology industries. Moreover, as we shall explain, it has been a catalyst in furthering small-scale, neighborhood-based economic development objectives. Furthermore, CETA has played a supporting role in the State's much publicized urban revitalization program by fostering the growth of jobs in economically depressed cities.

We do not suggest that CETA has been the single most important contributor to all of these efforts; rather, it has been creatively woven into the existing fabric of many ongoing programs and ventures. While this metaphor is often used to excess, it serves the purpose of this article (and indeed, this book) very well. We maintain that the effective economic development planner, especially now in the advent of budgetary cutbacks in several economic development programs, will have to combine resources, package them and achieve a whole greater than the sum of its parts. CETA—as the primary tool in developing human resources—should not be overlooked in this process.

CETA—the Comprehensive Employment and Training Act—is a program to aid the unemployed, underemployed and economically disadvantaged. This aid comes in the form of training and job opportunities. The program is divided into eight separate titles, three of which have a direct bearing on economic development. In *Title II* of the law, primary attention is given to the structurally unemployed. Under this title, there are provisions for training (either in the classroom or on the job), retraining, and/or public service jobs. *Title VI* of the law is geared more to the cyclically unemployed, and thus resources within this title are directed principally to providing public service jobs. *Title VII*, the centerpiece of the CETA reauthorization in 1978, is aimed at establishing better links with the private sector. Finally, again under *Title II*, the Law allows for a significant pool of funds to be made available for discretionary purposes. Each of these resources can stand by themselves, or, as we shall point out, they can be used in concert with one another (Massachusetts Department of Manpower Development, 1979a).

CETA Programs and Economic Development

The CETA program offers a range of resources through the above-mentioned titles which can accommodate and indeed stimulate a number of economic development activities. What follows is a short description of how each activity under CETA can be effectively applied.

Classroom Training (Title II – B) (Federal Register, 1979)

This type of training is normally conducted in an institutional (classroom) setting. It is designed to provide individuals with the technical skills to obtain a specific job or group of jobs. Classroom training can also serve to enhance the employability of individuals, by offering courses in English as a second language (ESL) or by preparing trainees for high school diploma equivalency exams (GED). CETA subsidizes 100% of the cost of instructors, materials, etc., and also provides trainees with a small stipend.

Example. A major high-technology company in Massachusetts decided to locate a multimillion dollar manufacturing plant in a deteriorated neighborhood in Boston. One factor which led to the firm's decision was the agreement by the local CETA program to train neighborhood residents as electronic hand assemblers and test technicians. The training not only reduced the overall cost of the locational decision, it also guaranteed the company a trained workforce once the plant was brought on line.

On-the-Job Training (Title II – B) (Federal Register, 1979, Section 676.25 – 2)

On-the-Job Training, or OJT, is suited primarily to smaller firms or firms seeking to hire relatively few employees in any one occupational category. Using an OJT format, a company agrees to hire one or a number of CETA-eligible participants at the outset. In return, CETA will reimburse the employer as much as 50% of the participants' wages for as long as it takes the trainees to become trained and productive employees of the firm. OJT can also be linked up with classroom training or public service employment activities.

Example. A community organization in Boston's Dorchester neighborhood sought to reopen a supermarket after it, and several others, had been closed by a national supermarket chain. After three months of negotiations, the group was able to buy the building, purchase $120,000 in inventory and hire back 30 employees to run the new venture. A loan under favorable terms from the Massachusetts Community Development Finance Corporation (CDFC) and a Small Business Administration (SBA)-backed conventional loan were major factors leading to the reopening. However, the viability of the business plan was further strengthened by $50,000 in CETA on-the-job training subsidies for six new employees. In a business where profits represent only one percent of gross revenues, this was a substantial injection of additional capital.

Retraining (Title II –C) (Federal Register, 1979, Part 677, Subpart C)

Retraining under CETA is a relatively new activity within the law, added in the reauthorization of 1978. With this provision, CETA can provide subsidies to equip individuals with new skills when their old skills are found to be obsolete. To qualify for retraining, workers must be faced with an imminent layoff, and there must be no demand for their existing skills within the local labor market. If these conditions exist, currently employed workers can be retrained via the classroom training or OJT activities mentioned above.

Example. A manufacturing company in Eastern Massachusetts dealing in precious metals was extremely hardpressed as a result of the recent spiraling cost of gold and silver. The company, caught with a bloated inventory and few cash reserves (as a result of the decrease in sales), sought retraining assistance from CETA. In this situation, the company was faced with only two alternatives: it either had to lay off a majority of its workforce or move them into a new production line, manufacturing cheaper, more competitive goods. CETA was the primary resource for pursuing the latter alternative.

Public Service Employment (Title II – D and VI) (Federal Register, 1979, Section 676.25 – 3)

Public service employment programs provide cyclically and structurally unemployed people with an opportunity to earn a salary and gain valuable work experience. The salaries of PSE workers are 100% subsidized by CETA, up to a maximum of $10,000 a year. While employed in CETA, PSE workers can provide a range of public services, including the winterization of low-income housing, housing rehabilitation, neighborhood crime and clean-up efforts, services to the elderly and disabled, etc. While the above-mentioned activities (classroom training, OJT, etc.) are geared primarily to the needs of private, profit-making institutions, public service employment is conducted exclusively through public agencies and nonprofit community-based organizations.

Example. One frequent barrier to economic development planning is the lack of accurate, detailed and up-to-date information. The Chamber of Commerce in Lowell sought to overcome this difficulty by gathering economic base data and providing concise listing of available land and buildings. Seven CETA workers developed a complete listing of properties, by building type and square footage, for an area where the city was intensifying commercial rehabilitation. As a result, the city was much better organized in its marketing of developable properties, and potential industrial or commercial tenants could use this information to narrow and simplify their search for an appropriate location.

Another example. Valued in the millions, clams are the most important economic resource for Essex, Massachusetts. However, for a time, some local clam flats were yielding far fewer clams than expected. Eleven CETA workers, eight of whom were local unemployed clammers, were employed to restore and conserve this economic resource. Their work included predator and disease control, habitat management, and the rehabilitation of currently barren flats. During the winter months, when no outdoor work could be done, the participants built fences, repaired tools and did research and laboratory work. The research activities were particularly helpful because no systematic research on clam growth and habitat had been done in over 60 years. This public service employment project helped to reverse a trend which could have significantly damaged the local economy.

Private Sector Initiatives (Title VII) (Massachusetts Department of Manpower Development, 1979, Part 679)

The Private Sector Initiatives Program (PSIP) was another major product of the reauthorization of 1978. The primary aim of this title is to increase the involvement of the business community in the planning, design and implementation of CETA-funded employment and training programs. This increased involvement is achieved through the establishment of Private Industry Councils, or PIC's, comprised in the majority by representatives from private businesses. While most activities mainly take the form of OJT and/or classroom training, as much as 30% of Title VII funds can be used for "employment generating" programs. PIC's enjoy a great deal of flexibility under this category of funding, and can finance a number of economic development initiatives as long as they result in new job opportunities for the unemployed.

Example. An economically depressed city in Southeastern Massachusetts is using Title VII money, within the employment generating category, to provide resources and staff to a local advocacy group which promotes economic growth in the region. The model takes the form of a local development cabinet, where the group serves as the central coordinating arm for the local block grant program, the industrial development staff, the CETA agency, and the mayor's office. The group conducts economic and labor market research, brings in consultants on a project-by-project basis, and coordinates all marketing activities for the city and the region. To date, the organization has been successful in securing several major federal grants for the city and in attracting a number of large employers.

Governor's Four Percent Discretionary Fund (Title II) (Federal Register, 1979, Part 677, Subpart d)

Four percent of all Title II training money entering a state is allocated to the Governor for "discretionary" purposes. In Massachusetts, this has amounted to nearly $2.5 million a year for the past five years. Similar to employment generating funds in Title VII, 4% money is extremely flexible, and as long as it is spent within federal guidelines it can be used to finance a wide variety of activities serving the needs of the CETA-eligible population. In addition to financing statewide economic development activities, these funds can be used to develop innovative programs on a demonstration basis. Once the value of these projects has been determined, they can be permanently financed through other titles in CETA, or through other federal, state and local programs.

Example. The Massachusetts Community Development Finance Corporation (CDFC) was established to provide capital to business ventures owned and operated by local nonprofit community development corporations. In this way, CDFC makes higher risk investments with public dollars in economically distressed communities, in businesses employing local residents. However, in its first two years of operation, CDFC only financed two ventures, and one of these failed. With $140,000 in CETA 4% funds, a parallel organization was established to provide assistance to CDC's in developing specific ventures and in packaging projects to be funded by CDFC. This new agency, the Community Economic Development Assistance Corporation (CEDAC), has assisted in the development of six new business ventures funded recently by CDFC. This assistance included training the leadership of these organizations, financing market studies, and arranging for business consultants to develop and finalize business plans.

CEDAC has been instrumental in generating CDFC-funded business ventures, and with a proven track record behind it, is much better able to secure permanent financing to continue its important function.

In the above sections, we have attempted to give the reader a general understanding of how CETA monies can be fitted into successful economic development strategies. In the remainder of this chapter, we shall elaborate on three especially creative uses of CETA, uses which display both the program's complexity as well as its inherent potential.

The Massachusetts Experience:
Innovative Uses of CETA

For purposes of discussion, let us describe our experience in Massachusetts in terms of "traditional" and "nontraditional" economic development. Traditional economic development involves larger scale public works improvements such as road, sewer or transit construction. Although for the most part federally funded, it is carried out by mayors or governors in citywide or statewide jurisdictions. The general intent of these programs is to improve the infrastructure upon which private businesses can expand, create new jobs, purchase additional goods and services, and thereby increase the aggregate income of residents in the region.

In Massachusetts, while emphasizing traditional economic development programs such as this, a number of initiatives have been taken which represent an entirely different approach to economic development. This "nontraditional" approach, consisting primarily of community based economic development activities, seeks to foster job creation activities in urban and rural areas experiencing higher levels of poverty and unemployment. The underlying assumption to this approach is that even with proper infrastructure development, growth will continue to bypass these areas. Community economic development strives to ensure that other factors in economic growth are available, such as entrepreneurship, management and capital, and that these are employed in the direct start-up or retention of specific business ventures. Furthermore, whereas its traditional counterpart is carried out by municipal or state officials, community economic development is usually accomplished by incorporated neighborhood groups known as Community Development Corporations, or CDC's, under the guidance and supervision of residents and merchants of the target areas. CETA's link to community economic development should be obvious; they both share the same goal of creating job opportunities for the unemployed and economically disadvantaged.

Nontraditional Economic Development:
CETA Job Creation

A major task we began nearly three years ago—the CETA Job Creation Program—sought to test the notion that limited-duration public service employment funds could be used to foster self-sustaining community-owned businesses. As an example of the concept we tried to advance, consider the SEVCA wood stove manufacturing venture.

SEVCA, The Southeastern Vermont Community Action program, began its wood stove manufacturing business to help low-income residents of Southeastern Vermont cope with dramatically rising home heating costs. The idea was so successful and the demand for the product so strong, that they began to meet orders from middle- and upper-income consumers. With the revenues generated from these sales, they were able to expand their capacity, and further subsidize the cost of the stoves purchased by low-income people on a sliding fee scale basis. The venture was originally capitalized by a grant from the New England Regional Commission (which covered the cost of materials, equipment, and operating expenses) and CETA public service employment (which covered the wage and fringe benefit costs for 12 employees). The critical factor in the viability of this enterprise, to be sure, was in its ability to capture a growing market and generate profits with which to meet future capital costs and operating expenses. When the Department of Labor discovered that CETA workers were being employed in this type of activity, they ordered the CETA workers to be withdrawn from the project. The Labor Department was principally concerned about the following three issues:

1. the legality of allowing CETA public service employment funds to generate and retain program income,
2. the legality of continuing CETA projects beyond the 12-month limitation which was in effect at that time, and
3. the legality of allowing CETA projects to "produce goods" or engage in similar activities that are not considered a traditional service of state or local government.

In May of 1977 the Massachusetts Department of Manpower Development sent a proposal to Ernest Green, Assistant Secretary of Labor, requesting his assistance in clarifying the above three issues and soliciting his support in our efforts to expand SEVCA-like projects, thereby creating self-sustaining businesses from CETA public service employment funds (Massachusetts Department of Manpower Development, 1977). From a CETA standpoint, we argued that projects like this, which provide a needed product to low-income people, are excellent vehicles to provide good skills training and good jobs. Furthermore, a small-scale cooperatively run project promotes a feeling of self-respect and job satisfaction, and CETA workers who realize they have the potential to convert their temporary jobs into permanent jobs will be more highly motivated than their counterparts in strictly limited-duration projects. In terms of economic development, SEVCA had the potential for facilitating the transition of 12 previously unemployed or economically disadvantaged people into permanent, unsubsidized jobs. Further, where the wood stoves would be increasing the disposable income of many residents in the region and in particular the poor, we would expect to see increased economic activity as a result of these monies purchasing additional goods and services in the local economy.

After a thorough review by the Department of Labor's Solicitor's Office, the response to our request was negative. The Employment and Training Administration, while generally supportive philosophically, did not feel there was sufficient latitude in the law to allow for this unusual activity. In addition, they raised concerns about the potential of federally subsidized businesses competing against private, unsubsidized businesses. We formulated a contingency to address this issue, namely by providing for the sign-off on all of our proposed projects by private companies doing similar activities. In fact, turning to the SEVCA example, we pointed out that private manufacturers in the region actually welcomed the SEVCA project, as it provided them with a steady flow of trained personnel.

Working with groups such as the National Governors Association and the Massachusetts Law Reform Institute, we were able to make statutory changes in the CETA law when it was subject to reauthorization in the Fall of 1978. The new CETA law,* and the current CETA regulations (Federal Register, 1979, Part 676, Section 676.36) allow public service employment projects to both generate and retain income when it is used to advance the purpose of the project. The other two questions were addressed in the new law and in the Senate Report accompanying the new law. Although an 18-month limitation was placed on the time a *participant* could be enrolled in CETA PSE, no limit was placed on *project* duration. With the possibility (allowed by the new Act) of "piggybacking" a year of training onto a year-and-a-half of PSE, this limitation on enrollment and project duration was no longer a problem. Finally, the issue of manufacturing, while not specifically addressed in the statute, is mentioned explicitly in the Senate Report accompanying the new law (Senate Report No. 95-891: May 15, 1978, p. 23). Thus, the new CETA law of 1978 paved the way for us to embark on our job creation experiment.

In March of 1979, the Commonwealth of Massachusetts implemented a demonstration *CETA Job Creation Program* to explore the feasibility of developing ongoing public service enterprises from Title II–D and Title VI PSE projects. A total of $55,000 from the Governor's 4% Discretionary Fund was awarded in grants ranging from $10,000 to $20,000 to four already operating PSE projects located throughout the State. The program provided potentially self-sustaining projects with additional administrative support that would be key to the development of a new venture. This support included, but was not limited to, the purchase of additional supervision, expertise, training and/or technical assistance. The support also could include help in preparing a business plan, feasibility study, or marketing strategy. The state identified numerous examples of potentially self-sustaining projects, including solar retrofit, recycling, housing rehabilitation, child care, and home care for the elderly, and chose to fund four of these that demonstrated the capability to take full advantage of our injection of additional capital. We funded a day-care center in Plymouth, a housing rehabilitation program in Lawrence, a theater

*Public Law 95-524, Section 123h.

group in Greenfield, and a community newspaper in Springfield (Massachusetts Department of Manpower Development, 1980).

LaVoz is perhaps the best example of one of our Job Creation projects. The Spanish American Union (SAU) in Springfield, Massachusetts, received a Job Creation Grant in support of its CETA-funded bilingual newspaper, *LaVoz/The Voice*. Begun as a CETA Youth Project, *LaVoz* was continued under Title VI, employing six full-time staff. With a circulation of 5,000 to 7,000, the weekly newspaper served the inner-city Hispanic population of Springfield. Because of the newspaper's role as a vehicle for communication within the Hispanic community and between the Hispanic and non-Hispanic communities in Springfield, SAU sought Job Creation funding to continue indefinitely the publication of the newspaper. They identified two critical needs: a professional advertising consultant to train their CETA-funded advertising person and a market study to determine the nature and extent of the market throughout Greater Springfield. The Job Creation Grant included funding for both of these needs, as well as for the purchase of used office furniture. With the results of the market study in hand, and the trained advertising person in place, SAU will be seeking permanent financing from the Massachusetts Community Development Finance Corporation in the near future.

While some ventures, such as energy audit businesses, need less capital than others, most businesses need a substantive, primary source of capital for equipment, operating capital, and other major start-up costs. The wages paid by CETA to people in public service employment projects are in fact a very significant subsidy, especially if the project is labor intensive. Also, because training can be a heavy cost in new or expanding businesses, CETA resources, creatively and effectively applied, could be the difference between a bottom line in red or one in the black. As a conscious first step in starting a community enterprise, therefore, CETA can be an important resource for building organizational capacity, identifying and establishing a market, training new employees or, most important of all, providing the community entrepreneurs with sufficient time to secure more permanent financing. Although as of this writing it is too early to determine the final outcome of our Job Creation projects, they all—especially *LaVoz*—have advanced our understanding of the approach and convinced us of the basic need.

Nontraditional Economic Development: BIC–NET

Another major nontraditional program we have undertaken in Massachusetts is known as BIC–NET. A BIC—or Businesses Information Center—is a community-based agency designed to provide technical assistance to small businesses. They are usually staffed by one person, who offers local business persons assistance in a variety of areas, including the writing of business plans, the preparation of cash flow and market studies, locating sources of federal, state and local assistance, etc. The essential ingredients in the BIC concept are problem identification and the application of common sense. The BIC–NET program is a network of these BIC's throughout the state, 21 as of January 1980, designed and developed as vehicles to deal directly with the problems of small businesses.

Though the dimensions of the small-business problem are large and complex, very few programs deal directly and systematically with the needs of small business. Dunn and Bradstreet data show that nearly a third of all new businesses fail within the first year, and more than half fail within five years. Unfortunately, from a public policy perspective, the high failure rate is attributed to the ebb and flow of market forces. A closer analysis reveals a more complex explanation.

Because small businesses, by definition, employ a limited number of employees, there is very little staff capacity available beyond the primary production activity around which the business is structured. Thus, the small business has little time to do strategic business planning. Moreover, because of its limited financing capabilities, a small business can ill afford to make mistakes in tapping new markets and in exploring new production techniques. Furthermore, because many small businesses typically lack the management sophistication and expertise enjoyed by larger counterparts, they tend to emphasize one aspect of a business (e.g., production, at the expense of other equally important aspects, e.g., accounting, marketing). Thus, where adverse market forces may explain part of the small business problem, they by no means explain it all. Too many businesses are stagnating or failing even though they have significant growth potential.

The BIC–NET program, therefore, was established to help foster some of this unrealized growth. As an integral component of a statewide community economic development strategy, the potential impact is enormous. For example, of the more than 122,000 businesses in the state, 113,000 (93%) employ less than 50 workers, and 105,000 (86%) employ two workers or less! If just 10% of these smaller businesses could expand their operations by only two employees, this could mean a growth in employment of 21,000 jobs, a figure comparable to half the growth of high technology employment in our state over the past two years.

The BIC–NET program was initiated with a combination of CETA Title II 4% and Title VI resources. The 4% money financed a small central and regional staff working out of the Massachusetts Department of Commerce and Development, and Title VI monies were used to pay the wage and fringe benefit costs for the coordinators themselves. Ironically, it was the program's close association with CETA which brought about the most serious barrier to implementation. Many observers were somewhat skeptical about prospect of using CETA workers, who themselves are unemployed, to provide services to small-business persons. This perception was countered on two fronts. First, it was continually emphasized that BIC–NET was only working with the smallest of small businesses, where the steps to good business planning are relatively simple and straightforward. And second, out of the total universe of the CETA-eligible population, there were many who had a solid foundation in mathematics and accounting, and some who had had business experience. Nonetheless, this perception was never entirely eliminated.

The single most important reason for the program's success is the originator of the concept itself, Dr. William Osgood. Formerly the Director of Urban Affairs at the Federal Reserve Bank of Boston, Dr. Osgood now serves as the Director of the statewide BIC–NET program. His formula for success is quite simple; after embarking on an intensive screening and selection process, he would train the CETA worker (usually a Title VI participant) for five weeks in the mechanics of small business planning. He placed the BIC trainee in an on-the-job training environment for another five weeks, where they could further explore and develop those skills learned in the classroom. Finally, the BIC Coordinators were stationed in a local Chamber of Commerce, a community development corporation, or a similar local setting. Once situated in this type of location they then begin establishing contacts with local bankers, merchants and other business persons. Through this entire process, Osgood and his staff played an instrumental role in selecting and training the coordinators, getting the BIC's started, and in making themselves available for those instances where additional expertise was required.

To data, 37 coordinators in 21 separate locations have provided in-depth business planning assistance to over 800 small businesses throughout the State. An important measure of the BIC–NET program's effectiveness is the amount of new loans obtained through the assistance of the coordinators. Since April of 1979, 39 business plans and loan packages have been completed and approved by various conventional lending institutions and the Small Business Administration. Approximately 20 additional packages are presently in various stages of preparation. Secured loans amount to over $1.8 million in new investment, more than tripling the amount of CETA dollars initially invested in the program. But most important of all, as a direct result of these secured loans, over 100 new jobs were created and more than 700 jobs were retained (Massachusetts Department of Commerce and Development, 1979).

The potential impact of BIC–NET has other implications for community development. While the economy of Massachusetts has undergone substantial growth over the past four years, most of this growth has tended to bypass inner-urban and rural areas. In fact, depressed urban neighborhoods are usually characterized by a blighted commercial district, where there is a high business failure rate in spite of a potentially fertile market within walking distance. BIC–NET—with its economic development objectives—can help rejuvenate these commercial areas. BIC's have been instrumental in organizing merchant associations, a critical factor in the viability of a commercial district. BIC's have helped these groups win designation as Local Development Corporations (LDC's) under the SBA's 502 program. BIC's can also help merchants initiate cooperative insurance, security, trash removal, market analysis, and marketing endeavors, which serve to reduce the cost of doing business, while making the district more attractive to nearby shoppers. By providing this centralized staff support to all businesses in the commercial district, these areas will be on much more equal footing with competing malls and shopping centers in the suburbs. Equally important, the availability of a Business Information Center in several communities has greatly enhanced their capacity to develop community-owned ventures such as those funded in our CETA Job Creation program mentioned above. Thus, in a manner similar to our Job Creation endeavors, we have structured a program using limited duration federal funds which serves as a major revitalization tool, an incubator of new and healthier businesses, and a source of more and better jobs.*

Although we have developed other nontraditional models for economic development, we shall now consider a more traditional model. The key distinction to be made between the following model and the previous two is that it is carried out by a state agency, and not a locally based group; it is primarily directed toward larger, private, profit-making institutions and, although it has an urban emphasis, its resources are available to urban and suburban areas alike. However, in terms of providing real and valuable job opportunities for the State's poor and unemployed, it has equal if not greater significance.

Traditional Economic Development: Regional Skill Training Centers

Many states, South Carolina in particular, run very successful statewide manpower training programs. They have developed this capability as one of many incentives for encouraging companies to locate and/or expand within the State's borders. Massachusetts, until recently, had been lagging far behind other states in developing such a capacity. Two events occurred, however, which served to enhance our state's efforts in this area:

1. the reauthorization of CETA with its new Title VII, the Private Sector Initiative program, which included within CETA (as mentioned previously) a mandate and resources for making the law more relevant to the needs of the local economy and private business; and
2. the state's economy had virtually turned around, from being one of the most hard pressed in the United States in September of 1975, to being one of the healthiest by February of 1980.

This second factor was especially significant. Leading the way in this rapid turnaround was the explosive growth of our high technology industries, which between 1976 and 1978 accounted for nearly 47,000 of the more than 200,000 jobs that were created during this period. Service and health occupations were

Editors note: As the book went to press the BIC–NET program had been cut back due to the reduction of CETA funding in the federal budget. It still exists, though on a smaller scale.

also expanding, followed by rapid growth and turnover due to retirement in our machine occupations (Massachusetts Department of Manpower Development, 1979b). These trends caused certain labor pools to dry up, and employers, especially in the fastest growing industries, found it increasingly difficult to obtain sufficient numbers of trained personnel to meet their expansion needs. Many began to talk less about the State being "Taxachusetts," a reference to the tax burden perceived by some to be quite large in the State, and more about what they called the "human factor." In their view, this human factor had supplanted taxes as the primary impediment to growth in the State. Whatever the case may be, we were faced with an unprecedented opportunity for gearing CETA programs more to the needs of the private economy.

In the Spring of 1979 the Commonwealth of Massachusetts produced a manual which would serve as a blueprint for change in the State's CETA program. Called *Putting Massachusetts to Work*, the manual outlined a number of initiatives to be taken to better serve the needs of employers and unemployed alike. Yet the primary emphasis of *Putting Massachusetts to Work*, in addition to improving the responsiveness of the system, was to enhance the capacity for *skills* training in Massachusetts—skills urgently needed by high-growth Massachusetts employers. This expansion would be achieved largely through the development of Regional Skill Training Centers.

Why Regional Training Centers? Although the Commonwealth of Massachusetts has an enormous amount of investment in its community college and vocational education system, these institutions were falling short of meeting the needs of the CETA-eligible population and the skilled labor needs of private employers. Few programs were equipped with the necessary supportive environment to suit the needs of trainees who had motivational problems, handicaps, language barriers, or little or no education. What few there were that could accommodate these needs, could only offer programs in the afternoon or evening, after the students for whom the facilities were built (high school and community college age students) had gone home. These systems were also tied into various units of state and local government, and with the tenure and inherent inflexibility of government institutions, they were and remain today hard pressed to keep pace with changing demands within the private sector.

Several of the larger local CETA programs, faced with reliance upon existing public institutions as the only alternative, began to run training programs themselves. This would often require building acquisitions and modifications. In these instances, precious administrative monies as well as monies which otherwise would have been used for training were being diverted to making expensive capital improvements. The smaller programs, unable to support these expenditures, were faced with a logistical nightmare, as they had to subcontract with various public and private prevocational and vocational programs offered throughout the region. For example, a CETA trainee would receive GED training at one location on two nights a week, and heavy-equipment operator's training on the other three nights at another location thirty miles away. This drove up transportation costs for both the participant and the program operator, further diverting resources away from direct training activities. More important, many CETA participants found leapfrogging around the counties of Massachusetts a disincentive (at best) to taking full advantage of training opportunities within the program. It was little wonder to us that many CETA training programs were only achieving modest success.

In this environment there were a few notable exceptions. One of the exceptions was the Hampden District Regional Training Center in Springfield, Massachusetts. The key to the "Skills Center" in Springfield was its flexibility and its ability to house all aspects of employability development. In other words, assessment, counseling, prevocational, vocational, and job development services were all located within the same facility. In addition, its location on a major bus route and its on-site day-care center were essential complements to the program. Unlike other CETA programs in the state, where the delivery of services were often fragmented, the Hampden County Center was highly successful in orchestrating the services so as to reinforce one another. Another feature of the Hampden County Center was its emphasis on individual development. In sharp contrast to the more formal and rigid method of teaching one class at a time, its open-ended system trains people as individuals and not as groups. Such a system allows for individuals to enter and exit the training programs based upon their own needs, aptitudes and achievement. From an administrative standpoint it allows the job developer, a person who tries to find employment for the trainees, a chance to deal with a steady and manageable flow of people exiting the program, instead of handling them in blocks of 30.

The Springfield Skills Center has a primary emphasis in training both high technology and machinist occupations. In both of these areas, trainees are given basic training, and depending on their aptitude and motivation, are allowed to rise to increasing levels of capability. For example, a trainee might start out as an electronic (hand) assembler, but from there could rise to be a test technician or even a computer programmer. Accordingly, the basic skill might gain for the trainee an entry-level wage of between $4.00 or $5.00 an hour. The more sophisticated training will enable the participants to obtain jobs in excess of $6.00 per hour. For former unskilled and unemployed workers, some of whom were on public assistance, this is a remarkable achievement. The Springfield Center, in addition to having completion and placement rates of 93 and 90% respectively, had all the ingredients we were looking for. The centerpiece of *Putting Massachusetts to Work*, therefore, was replicating throughout the state the innovation and success of the Springfield Skill Center.

Early in the summer of 1979, we initiated scores of meetings with city mayors and managers, community and economic development directors, as well as local CETA directors from around the state. We encouraged them to

regionalize and to plan for a skill center that could address regional employment and training as well as overall economic development needs. In other
words, we were aiming to coordinate and consolidate more than twenty local
CETA programs (Prime Sponsors and Subgrantees) into four or five regional
centers. Instead of running these separate machinist training programs, for
example, with each requiring its own instructor and equipment, four or five
programs would be operated. In this way, more resources would be available
for planning, operation, and evaluation. Also, with the economies of scale to be
achieved, programs could run more efficiently and greater numbers of clients
could be served.

As can be expected, many cities began to actively compete for site designation, viewing the regional training center, particularly in light of pending labor
shortages, as an asset for industrial expansion and as a magnet for attracting
major employers to their cities. Although the competition generated a good
deal of political posturing and controversy, it was by and large healthy to the
overall development of the program. The local business and labor communities, as well as the Chambers of Commerce, took an active role in winning site
designation. Mayors and other public officials began talking more and more
about the relationship between the proposed skill center and the possibilities of
improving the community's ability to attract new jobs and tax revenues. Much
of this found its way into the newspapers and, while it made our decisions
more difficult, it also did a great deal to educate the public as to the
interrelationship between human resources and economic growth. In November we submitted a grant application to the Federal Economic Development
Administration for $8 million to develop four regional training centers in
Lowell, Worcester, Fall River and Boston through the rehabilitation of existing
structures in each of these older urban areas (Massachusetts Department of
Manpower Development, 1979c).

The skill center program took on a number of economic development
objectives. First, each skill center would have the capacity to train between 700
and 1,500 people a year, primarily in occupations experiencing acute labor
shortages. Secondly, each of the recommended sites were in older urban areas
with unemployment rates several percentage points higher than the state's
average. There was an internal policy debate as to whether we should locate
the centers where the new jobs were being created, in that part of the state
known as the 128–495 belt, a largely suburban area, or in the central cities,
where the highest concentration of unemployed persons resides. Since part of
the skill shortages of these growing companies could be attributed to their
suburban locations, and to the lack of decent public transportation at a time
when gasoline prices were skyrocketing, we opted to locate the centers in
central city locations and to do this as part of the overall program in
Massachusetts to make cities more attractive for private investment.

Deciding upon an urban location raised yet additional possibilities. Our
model called for adaptive reuse of existing buildings of between 70,000 to

100,000 square feet. As an important factor in each city's request for site designation, we asked them to discuss at length how the skill centers would be woven into existing downtown and community revitalization strategies. The results were truly exciting: in Worcester, the development of a skill center would trigger another $2.5 million in public investment, making substantial improvements to nearly two acres of land within that city's central business district. In Lowell, the skill center would be part of a $40 million national park complex where 100,000 square feet of a million square feet of vacant mill space would be used as the training site. The city believed the remaining 900,000 square feet could be more successfully marketed to business and industry with a skill center as part of the total complex. The center would guarantee a trained workforce for potential tenants, and with 10% of the facility modernized and rehabilitated, it would allow a potential developer a glimpse of what the entire mill would look like fully restored. Our final proposal to EDA called for the rehabilitation of four buildings, three of which were in arrears for back taxes, and two were of "architectural and historical importance." Since the announcement of the recommended skill center sites, private developers have obtained options on two of the locations, and are now in the process of securing commitments from tenants.

Along these same lines, we decided to take an urban focus for another important reason. As mentioned previously, the state's high-technology industries are growing dramatically. While this is good for the state's economy as a whole, not enough of this growth is occurring in our older urban areas with surplus labor and underutilized or unused plant facilities. Many firms have virtually exhausted the labor supply in peripheral areas, thus forcing them to pay exorbitant costs to recruit people from outside the region and star competitors.

Meanwhile, major nearby cities are being bypassed by all this prosperity. By developing regional training centers with strong high-technology skill components in surplus labor areas, we hope to reinforce the energy, labor, and other factors now working in favor of cities and achieve a more equitable distribution of this growth. Instead of moving to or expanding in another state in search of a trained labor force, we hope to encourage them to move to Fall River, for example, where unemployment is 6.5% and high technology accounts for only 1% of all employment. We believe when all of these factors are considered, that the development of regional skill training centers in urban locations may tilt the direction of growth away from areas where it is not needed, to areas where it is.

EDA has already approved funding ($1.125 million) for one of the centers (in Lowell) and reportedly is waiting for its reauthorization to make a commitment on the other three.* Construction is set to begin in June 1980 in

---

*Editor's Note: Because EDA is slated for elimination by the Reagon administration by FY 1983, this source of funding is unlikely to come forth.

Lowell, and because of an aggressive development strategy, is scheduled to be completed in September of 1981. We are hopeful that the other three sites will follow shortly thereafter, and that the effort of "Putting Massachusetts to Work" will be well on its way.

Caveats

Although our experience and examples indicate considerable potential for imaginative uses of CETA in economic development, there are also considerable constraints and difficulties which may impede the realization of this potential. Congress giveth and Congress taketh away. On the one hand, as indicated above, Congress expanded the potential use of CETA for economic development under the 1978 reauthorization by liberalizing the retention and use of revenues which might be generated from CETA projects. On the other hand, in a poor compromise at the same time, Congress effectively lowered the wages or salaries which could be paid to CETA workers. Moreover, in subsequent appropriations, Congress severely cut back the amount of funds available for CETA public service employment, from $7 billion nationally in 1977 to $1 billion in 1980 and to zero by October 1, 1981. These Congressional actions have significantly diminished the extent to which CETA dollars can be imaginatively used to enhance job creation in economically depressed communities.

Consider first the effects of the average annual wage requirement. Although the ceiling paid to any individual participant remains at $10,000 per year, a national average CETA wage of $7,200 per year now cannot be surpassed, by statute. In practice, this rule is applied to each prime sponsor, and it dictates a strict trade-off between the number of higher and the number of lower wage "slots" in any CETA program. Higher wage slots must be offset by lower wage slots in such a way as to ensure that the average CETA wage does not exceed $7,200 (plus or minus a few hundred dollars, since the applicable wage can vary somewhat by state and region). Because the applicable average wage requirement is often below prevailing entry level wages or other established wage scales in public and private agencies, many project sponsors are either unwilling or unable to administer programs consistent with this requirement. The minimum salary in Massachusetts state government, which had employed as many as 1,500 CETA workers at one time, was $143.00 a week, or $15 more than the average wage of $128.00 required in many areas throughout the state. Many of the state's cities and towns pay wages which are somewhat higher than the state's, so the constraints were even greater at the municipal level. As a result, prime sponsors in Massachusetts recently returned $20 million in unexpended CETA funds for reasons directly attributable to the average wage issue. This dilemma was not unique to Massachusetts or to the industrial Northeast; it was experienced by state and local governments throughout the country.

Many observers in Washington hoped that community-based organizations could pick up the slack in hiring left by state and municipal governments. Unfortunately, this did not occur. Many CBO's had established wage scales which were consistent with those of other public agencies and thus they too were higher than prescribed wage levels. Also, many CBO's were philosophically opposed to creating what they viewed as low-wage, dead-end jobs. Still others lacked the fiscal and administrative capacity to productively employ the number of PSE workers they were expected to hire. For all of these reasons, community-based organizations, where many of the creative programs in CETA have been developed, were as hamstrung in dealing with the average wage issue as other public agencies.

The negative effect of these constraints has been aggravated by the severe cutbacks and then elimination of CETA PSE appropriations. This means that, even if the average wage constraints and trade-offs can be managed in some areas, the number of relevant experiments that can be mounted will be far less. The matter of roller coaster Congressional behavior with respect to economic development-related appropriations is a general concern, not limited to any one program. If the Congress wants to promote economic development, then appropriations for these purposes must have more certainty and longer time horizons than Congress seems able to provide within the yearly budget cycle.

New enterprises for community development will not be planned or put in place if one's only reasonable expectation is that Congress might "pull the plug" and change the rules of the game next year. Congress will have to decide, consciously, whether and to what extent CETA and other jobs programs should serve economic development (rather than just temporary, contracyclical objectives) and then what three-to-five-year funding pattern is consistent with such objectives. Clearly, in the private sector initiatives (Title VII of CETA), Congress has made a declaration of purpose—that manpower programs should be integrated with economic development programming and that effective public sector/private sector relationships through PIC's, et al., are instrumental. But private sector involvement could languish if businessmen sense that public sector intent, as revealed by erratic budgeting and naivete about requisites for enterprise development, is not to be taken seriously.

Liberalization of the rules with respect to revenue-generating CETA subsidized enterprises has not been an unalloyed blessing. Throughout the country, there exists a great deal of confusion in the interpretation of the new regulations. The basic question still remains: how far can one go in the use of revenues generated by CETA projects to help build a self-sustaining business or community enterprise? CETA regulations state: "The recipient or subrecipient may use program income... during the grant or agreement period and for two years thereafter to carry out any CETA activity authorized under the former grant or agreement" (Federal Register, 1979).

Although we received a positive response by DOL in Region I, the response by DOL has varied from region to region, reflecting a certain degree of arbitrariness and inconsistency. Here again, a satisfactory resolution of unresolved issues is contingent upon Congress being clear and consistent about its concept of economic development.

It is also likely that the potential role of CETA in new enterprise development will be insignificant or largely unsuccessful unless there exist state or local development agencies which stand ready to take new ventures past the start-up phase once CETA resources are phased out. In Massachusetts, we have two such agencies in the form of the Massachusetts Community Development Finance and Community Development Assistance Corporations. Lacking second stage financial, technical and managerial assistance to assist the successful continuation of a CETA-initiated enterprise, one is forced to view them as enterprises whose output is primarily trained labor, rather than permanent jobs.

Conclusion

In the design and implementation of economic development programs, CETA should be considered as a potentially important component among several development-related resources. While it is a significant program in and of itself, it is even more useful when it is considered part of a larger, more comprehensive endeavor. CETA employment monies are most effective when they are linked with other sources of funds, such as Community Development Block Grants. Similarly, CETA training resources are better employed when they are used within a total development portfolio, which might also include an Urban Development Action Grant, an EDA loan, a state financing incentive and/or a local tax abatement. In these situations, public and private resources serve to strengthen one another, making for a much more broadly financed proposal. The economic development specialists who can build a viable CETA component into their plans will be more successful over the long run in getting proposals funded and creating jobs.

As mentioned at the outset, CETA deals exclusively with the labor aspects of production. Indeed, this chapter has tended to focus on what we would call the "human dimension" of economic development. We feel that this has too often been missing in economic development strategies. All too often, people view economic development and revitalization in terms of brick sidewalks, access roads to industrial parks, sewer pipes and promotional brochures. Yet, as economists long ago discovered, investment in "human capital" is an essential component of development and is as important a form of capital as these physical manifestations.

Finally, a ballplayer was once asked to comment on the prospects of his team winning the following day's baseball game—the seventh and last game of the World Series. His short reply was, "You gotta believe." This represents our closing sentiments exactly. The CETA program is at a very important crossroad. In recent months, many observers have been critical of the manner in which the program has been implemented, and these criticisms have become more intense as the wave of tax revolt and budget cutting fever sweeps across the nation. Many of the charges against CETA have been accurate, but others have been largely inaccurate. The emphasis on CETA's problems has had an adverse effect on the public's image of the program and this had tended to "turn off" those people who otherwise might have been able to make a positive contribution to the program (particularly private businessmen). This being the case, such criticisms, particularly those that are unfounded, only result in a self-fulfilling prophecy. If CETA is to work, people have to believe in it enough to *make* it work. The models and examples given above are testimony to the fact that it can work. More economic development administrators must learn how to recognize CETA as an important source of capital, and as the critical means of developing human resources. To do this, however, they must do what the man said: "You gotta believe." It is our hope that this chapter has given the program a measure of the credibility it clearly deserves in the formulation of overall economic development strategies.

Bibliography

Federal Register (1979). Comprehensive Employment and Training Act Regulations, 20 CFR Section 676.25-1 (April 3).

Massachusetts Department of Commerce and Development (1979). *Business Information Center Network: Program Report* (December), p. 7.

Massachusetts Department of Manpower Development (1977). Letter from B. J. Rudman to Ernest Green (May).

Massachusetts Department of Manpower Development (1979a). *Introduction to CETA: A Handbook for Non-CETA Administrators* (September).

Massachusetts Department of Manpower Development (1979b). *Defining "High Technology" Industries in Massachusetts*. Policy and Evaluation Division (September), p. 12.

Massachusetts Department of Manpower Development (1979c). *Enhancing Skills Training for Economic Development*. A Proposal to the U.S. Department of Commerce, Economic Development Administration. Office of Special Projects (November).

X

The Self-Help Development Fund: Will Its Promise Be Realized?*

David Smith, with Mitchell Rosenberg

The passage of the National Consumer Cooperative Bank Act represented a significant advance for the consumer movement and for that relatively new group of cooperative organizations throughout the country providing food, medical care and other critical services to members across the country. The Bank was designed to provide access to capital for consumer and other cooperatives.

Yet to those most concerned with community economic development, the important innovation was less the bank itself than the Self-Help Development Fund, authorized in Title II of the Act. The Fund offers a unique combination of flexible financing capacity and extensive technical assistance designed to help overcome the enormous start-up problems which have historically hampered cooperatives and other organizations attempting to do development work in low-income areas.

The cooperative movement has a long tradition in the United States, beginning with agricultural efforts in the mid-west, and including the development of large-scale consumer cooperatives during the 1930s. Yet, outside of the agricultural south, there has been very little cooperative activity in poor communities; and despite the growing number of community development efforts undertaken by these communities over the last two decades, the

*Many people assisted in the thinking which underlies this paper, and I am grateful for their contributions. Mitch Rosenberg of the TDC staff contributed substantially to the initial formulation of the proposed Fund strategy. Lee Webb and Michael Freedberg of the Conference/Alternative State and Local Public Policy have labored valiantly to ensure that the Fund would indeed be used as an instrument of serious economic development in low-income communities, and Phil Primack helped translate often obscure prose into a readable form.

cooperative form has seldom been used. There are many possible explanations for this absence of coop activity in poor American communities, not the least of which is the enormous difficulty of raising the required member equity and sustaining a sufficiently high level of participation among women and men already burdened by very difficult day-to-day life circumstances. The cooperative form of organization itself presents problems as well as advantages. The problem of mobilizing capital for development is more difficult because cooperatives can only share the economic fruits of their enterprise with their members; therefore, they cannot raise capital by seller shares to outsiders. This is also a (mixed) advantage in that returns are entirely retained among the membership. The advent of the Self-Help Development Fund offers an unmatched opportunity to use cooperatives both as a means to reduce the cost of living and to build locally controlled production enterprises. The Fund has the tools that are needed: the capacity to do significant planning and pre-deal organizing; the ability to provide sustained technical assistance; sufficiently flexible and concessionary financing; and other features associated with a well-conceived development bank.

However, it remains unclear, now that the initial euphoria has settled, whether these capacities will actually be used by the Fund to fulfill its real, much needed potential. In fact, many of the initial plans for actual Fund operations would have turned the Fund into a soft loan window for the Bank proper.

This chapter explores in detail some of the issues which are central to the Fund's potential being realized. Most of the chapter was prepared after the legislation establishing the Bank passed, but prior to the Bank starting operations. Thus some specific references may seem dated, and many of the propositions discussed in the paper have been adopted by the Bank and now represent Title II policy. Nonetheless, the jury is still out and many important operating questions are yet to be resolved. In what follows we describe what the Fund might become and propose a strategy for realizing that opportunity.

Background

While the cooperative movement in America has had significant successes, low-income communities have been mainly left out of the coop process. Yet developments in recent years have indicated increased awareness of the coop potential in low-income areas. With enactment of the National Consumer Cooperative Bank Act in 1978, this process received a new and potentially historic spur.

One of the main features of the Bank, which survived a rocky three-year odyssey through Congress, is a specific commitment to the needs of low-income cooperatives. The general purpose of the Act is "to encourage the development of new and existing cooperatives eligible for assistance by providing specialized credit and technical assistance." To assure that low-income groups and communities have full chance to participate in this "new and exciting" development, the Bank (NCCB) is obliged to try to spend at least 35% of its assets on low-income cooperatives.

Congress, recognizing the problems and particular needs of such enterprises, established as Title II of the Act a Self-Help Development Fund authorized to spend up to $75 million over three years in equity grants and interest subsidies to low-income coops which are otherwise unable to benefit from the Bank itself.* The Self-Help Development Office also includes provisions for technical and other forms of support to low-income cooperatives.

The NCCB in general and the Self-Help Development Fund in particular could become a catalyst for low-income community development; or the Fund could end up becoming just another financial institution, albeit one with good intentions towards the poor. The factors which will determine the outcome are not primarily financial; basic policies, more than dollar expenditures, will be influential.

Lending Policies and Financial Strategy

The Fund, or for that matter any institution geared mainly to low-income needs, must above all recognize that just being another bank will not be sufficient; it must seek to structure both its financial services and other forms of assistance so that they clearly respond to the persistent problem of an absence of equity capital and front end development resources. The Fund itself is prohibited from providing actual equity to low-income cooperatives. What it must do, then, is pursue lending policies and a financial strategy that amounts to the delivery of equitylike financial resources.

Case histories of low-income coops indicate consistently that one of the major obstacles coops face in maintaining and expanding operations is the lack of equity in their capital structure. Equity is the financial contribution members make to a coop (conventionally: owners to an enterprise) to participate in the benefits of ownership. The money is not lent. Rather, it is retained by the enterprise as long as the member/owner participates. The significant features of equity for the management of the enterprises are that it carries no interest cost or fixed repayment terms, which allows a great deal of flexibility in the timing of its use and the purposes to which it is applied. The major uses of equity are (a) to cover short-term interruptions of cash flow caused by fluctuations in costs or availability of supplies, or small, one-time plant and equipment expenditures which the coop does not want to or cannot finance, and (b) to leverage debt financing of large fixed assets, the cost of which can only be recovered if amortized over the long term.

The problems low-income coops face in obtaining equity capital arise from two features shared by all such enterprises. First, due to organizational form, a coop cannot distribute surpluses on the basis of capital contributions alone.

---

*The 96th Congress actually only appropriated $40 million and this was cut further in the Reagan FY '81 budget.

Therefore, it cannot attract capital from central, profit-oriented sources, individual or corporate. Still, a coop, like any enterprise, needs a cash reserve to cover the contingencies involved in starting up, expanding or improving service. It must, however, rely on its members for equity. Since by definition, low-income coops serve relatively poor people, the pool of capital available to them is small.

Low-income coops, then, require a type of financing which, in cost and terms of repayment, resembles equity. The Fund, logically, should provide financing of a type not available from other sources. Within its statutory constraints, it can provide equity-type financing.

The major purpose of the National Consumer Cooperative Bank as a whole is to "encourage the development of new and existing cooperatives eligible for its assistance by providing specialized credit and technical assistance." (NCCB Act, Sec. 101)

The Office of Self-Help Development is specifically directed to provide such assistance to coops by two alternative provisions. The first provision defines an eligible applicant as one whose "initial or supplemental capital requirements exceed its ability to obtain such capital (from the Bank)." This passage should be interpreted to mean that the eligible coop cannot qualify for credit under the regulations and lending practices of the Bank or other sources. The Bank and most other sources are constrained by statute and the structure of their capitalization to provide term loans carrying market interest rates and fixed repayment terms, and they must structure their credit evaluations accordingly.

The second provision defines eligible coops as those having memberships consisting of (or otherwise servicing) low-income persons. Conventional credit analysis standards need not be applied; however, the Fund must determine that repayment is possible within a 30-year term. It is reasonable to assume that the sets of coops defined by the two provisions will substantially overlap.

In making credit decisions, the Office has only to determine that the applicant can repay an advance over a period of thirty years. Section 203 is similarly unrestrictive in specifying lending terms. The Board, which sets major policy for the Bank as a whole, is obliged only to set some interest rate, which may be "lower than the rate applicable to loans by the Bank (proper)." [NCCB Bill, Section 203 (c)] There are no restrictions governing the structure of repayment schedules. Using this flexibility to charge nominal interest rates and structure repayment schedules so as to defer credit costs in the early years of the term, the Fund can and should provide financing which, in terms of the repayment burden imposed on users, resembles equity funding.

Finally, a decisive feature of the legislation supporting the adoption of an equity-type financial policy is the Fund's capitalization. The Fund's loan resources are to be provided by an appropriation from Congress of $40 million over a three-year period. These funds need not be repaid.* They should be

---

*See the postscript at the end of this chapter regarding the radical change in outlook for the Fund under the FY '81–82 (Reagan) budget.

sufficient to support an equity-type financing policy long enough to provide the Office with sufficient operating experience to explore and evaluate the usefulness of the institution. Cash flow calculations supporting this assertion appear later in this chapter.

While the Fund's charter clearly calls for the adoption of such equitylike financing, some of the procedures being considered are inconsistent with that strategy. The Task Force set up to design the Fund explicitly recommended in one of its drafts that loss rates "be considered in setting interest rates," implying that interest receipts should cover all or part of portfolio losses.

If pursued, this is the sort of direction which could lead the Fund or any such effort into becoming just another bank; the credit standards which would then have to be employed would make it impossible for most low income or community development focused cooperatives to participate. Government credit agencies which have dealt with enterprises similar in some ways to the Fund's intended users have experienced losses ranging from seven to twenty percent. So the above recommendation implies charging a substantial interest rate to Fund users. This is indicated by Table 1. A subsequent policy statement also implied regular repayment schedules should be the norm, though perhaps modified on a case-by-case basis.

Recognizing the burdens such an interest policy would impose, various devices have been suggested for use in individual loan agreements to ease the repayment burden. This list is not comprehensive, but it indicates that solutions to this problem can be found.

"Progressive" Interest Rate Charges

One suggestion is that interest rates charged to Fund users should increase over the term of the advance, presumably starting at some nominal rate and rising to a conventional rate. The justification for such a scheme is that the coop's cash flow is expected to increase as it gains experience, allowing for larger debt service payments. Also, as interest rates on the Fund's advance approach those charged by other sources, Fund users would be induced to refinance those advances, thus making that money available to the Fund for relending.

While the basic outline of such a proposal is sound, some details must be specified if in the long run it is to be consistent with the principle of providing equity-type financing. Most important is the repayment schedule. Coops are

Table 1. Loan Loss Rates of Comparable Institutions

Program	Failure Rate	Portfolio Loss as Percentage of Capital Invested	Source
CSA special impact	7.6%	17%	Abt SIP evaluation
Minority enterprise SBIC	12.3%	–	Abt SIP evaluation
SBA equal opportunity loans	–	20%	2nd draft report
SBA 7A loan guarantee	–	10%	GAO evaluation

likely to encounter most cash flow contingencies in the early going as membership, markets, supply and production procedures are developed. During this stage, debt burdens should be kept to a minimum. Therefore, all but nominal interest payments should be deferred for some period, after which interest rates should begin to rise and regular retirement of principal should be required. If the coop is successful and able to refinance its advance, the Fund will have lost relatively little in total interest receipts by using this system of deferment. If the coop encounters difficulties which could lead to the curtailment or termination of activities, a large debt burden in the early going will only reduce the chance of its attaining stable operations.

Periodic Renegotiations of Terms

In early deliberations over Fund policy, periodic review and renegotiation of lending terms as a regular feature of lending contracts was specifically rejected. The reasons were that such a policy would complicate planning for both the Fund and its users and that a contractually specified renegotiation would be viewed as a call date by outside creditors.

An additional problem, addressed further on in this chapter, is that the Office was given insufficient staff to carry on such activity. If a lending policy calling for substantial interest payments and conventional repayment schedules were implemented, the incidence of renegotiations would likely be rather high, further reducing field staff time which should be devoted to more productive uses.

Subordination to Other Credit Sources

Subordination of repayments to the Fund to those owed to other sources merely establishes the priority by which operating income is allocated to the claims of various sets of creditors. The proposed order is: other lenders, the Fund, members. This provision might enable coops to obtain conventional loans even if their cash flow is only marginally sufficient to meet total credit obligations. It should, therefore, be included in loan contracts. For those coops whose only external financial liabilities are to the Fund (this would include most new and existing coops), this provision would have no effect on the timing or the incidence of their debt payments.

Loan Contract Structure

Some have suggested that capital advances could be provided in the form of preferred stocks and loans. The issue of ownership raised by stock purchase is best avoided since these obligations are not likely to be traded in a secondary market or bought by coop members. The advance, then, should be made as a loan whose contract contains features desirable for both the coop and the lender, whether it be the Fund or some other public or private source.

The following suggested features of a loan contract help protect coops and at the same time help minimize administrative effort involved in servicing the advance. They also provide an incentive for the mature coop to refinance its advance.

1. *Low average interest rate*. The average annual effective interest rate (truth in lending rate) should be considerably lower than that charged to standard borrowers.

2. *Minimal debt payments in the first years*. During the first three to five years, debt payments should be set at zero or a minimal interest rate of, say, 1%. All principal repayments should be deferred to the end of this period. The choice of three to five years is not arbitrary. Representatives of the New England Food Cooperative Organization have stated that most food coops tend to suffer cash flow problems from inadequate capitalization during the fourth or fifth year of operations, as cash reserves generated during the initial membership drive run out. Abt Associates' 1973 study of 18 low-income rural coops funded by the Office of Economic Opportunity determined that most of the coops required organizational development activities lasting an average of four years before they could begin to operate profitably. A second evaluation of the Special Impact Program collected business data on enterprises sponsored by community development corporations which, in view of the amount of community organizing involved, the unfavorable market conditions encountered, and the use of equity finance, resemble the Fund's most likely constituency. Those enterprises which were operating profitably took an average of 28 months to reach breakeven cash flow.

3. *Progressive interest rates*. Loan contracts should specify that, after the initial "grace" period, interest rates will be increased at regular intervals and repayment of principal will begin. This is perhaps the most effective and easiest way to induce a Fund user to seek refinancing through the Coop Bank or another institution. Knowing debt obligations in advance will also simplify planning for the coop.

    Another device which has been suggested to ensure that coop borrowers refinance their advances is a mandatory call provision which would take effect when the coop demonstrates stable operations and can approach more traditional lending sources. While this notion may seem attractive, it creates problems. For one thing, it would take a great deal of administrative time on the part of the Fund. Secondly, as long as the Fund's lending terms are significantly better than those offered by other sources, the borrower is likely to resist refinancing. Besides, it would not be possible in all cases to arrange for timely take-outs in advance.

4. *Contract restrictions on use of advances*. Certain restrictions on the use of advances should be written into the loan contract. One obvious restriction is

that the advances should not be used to refinance obligations previously incurred. In order to reinforce the importance of business planning, the uses of funds should be restricted to those specified in the documents supporting the loan application. In order to monitor compliance with these provisions, annual audits should be required and checked against the loan contracts.

Since the Fund faces few statutory constraints on its lending practices, the suggestions made here are technically within its capacity. It is required only to find that an applicant can repay a capital advance over a period of thirty years in order to approve the advance. The Consumer Coop Bank Board, which sets major policy for the Bank as a whole, is obliged to set some interest rate, but it may be "lower than the rate applicable to loans by the Bank (proper)" Sec. 203). There is no statutory language governing repayment schedules.

In fact, however, the Fund is limited by the size of its staff and appropriation. Congress to date may appropriate only $40 million of the Fund's three-year $75 million authorization.* This raises a basic question of the Fund's ability to maintain a positive cash balance while undertaking the financial strategy described here.

Cash flow projections using the $40 million figure were prepared by the Technical Development Corporation (TDC). They assumed financial policies and administrative facts based on real operations of various coops. The results show that under a wide range of assumed levels of initial capitalization, the Fund can maintain a lending policy of the type set forth above. Loan funds will not be exhausted before the Fund can gain sufficient operating experience to establish itself and thus be able to seek further appropriations from Congress.

A cash flow analysis makes this case in the section to follow. Its methodology and numbers, while immediately applicable to the Fund, help to make the case for similar major ventures to aid low-income coops. But though the numbers are reasonable, a broader point must not be lost: while the concern that the Fund may run out of money is proper, it must not become the all and all. If the Fund or any similar venture becomes preoccupied with trying to become wholly self-supporting, it will quickly become useless to low-income groups by adopting overly conservative financing terms.

The following numbers show that liberal financing terms nearly tantamount to equity can be provided by the Fund without exhausting its capital.

Cash Flow Analysis

The cash flow projections are based on three sets of assumptions. The *rate of lending activity* is controlled by staff size and capacity, as adapted from the experience of other institutions. The *composition of the portfolio* is based to some extent on an examination of requests for advances to date. In addition,

---

*See the postscript to this chapter.

TDC has incorporated its own judgments concerning the mix of deals the Fund should affirmatively seek to achieve if it is to play a developmental role. The size of advances is based on relevant experience. The terms for repayment reflect an aggressive development policy. *Repayment* is based on the experience of institutions financing organizations similar to the Fund's target group. The two sets of projections differ only in the assumed rate of lending activity. In the first set, the rate of lending is much higher than the Office can reasonably hope to achieve. These figures are designed to show just how far the office can go with $40 million. The second set reflects a more realistic assessment of the level of activity the staff can sustain.

Rate of Lending Activity

First Projection

There are ten field offices and 24 staff allocated to the Fund's General Office. Of the latter, 12 are presumed to be primarily responsible for loan development and origination. It is also assumed that each of the field offices and each of the 12 D.C.-based staff will develop 10 loan applications per year suitable for consideration by the Advance Committee.

These assumptions lead to 220 completed applications submitted annually to the Advance Committee. Assuming that the Committee approves 80% of these applications, 176 loans will be made per year. These numbers imply a constant and furious level of activity for both the staff and Advance Committee. The Committee would have to review 18 applications every month and approve 14 of them to keep up the pace. This is clearly impossible, given the membership of the Committee and the many other operating responsibilities allocated to the staff.

The record of organizations similar to the Office provide some basis for a more realistic projection of lending activity. The Massachusetts Community Development Finance Corporation (CDFC) has consummated only 14 deals in $2\frac{1}{2}$ years, with an average staff of three persons. The Southern Cooperative Development Fund, as a matter of policy, allows each of its loan officers to maintain an active portfolio of no more than five coops in any one quarter. It seems reasonable then to cut the number of deals closed by one-third in the second projection. This means that each staff person would generate six or seven completed applications each year, and that the Committee would approve around 113 advances.

Composition of the Portfolio and Repayment

For purposes of this projection we have assumed that the Fund portfolio will be composed of four types of deals. The first two, interim financing for housing coops and term loans to commercial consumer and producer coops to acquire plant and equipment, dominate the current crop of applications. In line with our hypothesized lending strategy, TDC has included two other types of loans in the portfolio. The first consists of what for lack of a better term are called "development loans." They will primarily be used to pay for staff and the organizational cost required to help "new pre coops" develop an organization capable of acquiring and profitably using physical assets. The second consists of more speculative "venture capital" type lending.

Table 2 shows a hypothetical yearly addition to the Fund's portfolio, under the two assumed levels of total lending activity. Each type of deal implies somewhat different average loan size and terms. Each is characterized by different expectations concerning likelihood and timing of repayment. These assumptions follow.

Housing finance. Judging from the housing finance applications the Fund has received so far, two basic types of advances can be expected in this sector. The first is interim construction financing; the second financing of upfront planning and legal costs. Once a housing project reaches a stage where it can use permanent financing, it should be able to solicit a mortgage from the Bank or a conventional lender. In the projections, advances to projects which successfully negotiate this development are assumed to be rolled over into permanent financing and out of the Fund's portfolio.

For construction finance, assume an average loan size of $1 million, though this is high (The two housing advances approved so far total only $295,000; pending applications average $42,000.): To facilitate development, assume the Fund charges concessionary rates of 5%. Finally, suppose that two of the projects financed each year encounter difficulties and are not completed. In the projections, the successful projects repay their advance with interest when they are rolled over—after one year. The Bank will have to attempt a work out of the unsuccessful projects. This is represented in the calculations by the Fund's recovery of half the principal two years after the advance is made.

Advances to cover planning costs are assumed to average $100,000, and will be offered on the same terms as the construction advances. Assumptions concerning the timing of recovery and failure rate are the same. However, it is unlikely the Fund will recover any of the advances to projects which do not reach the construction stage.

Commercial loans. Currently, the average size of applications for term loans to acquire plant and equipment is $29,000. In keeping with the high-demand scenario, $40,000 is the projected average size for such advances.

Table 2. Yearly Lending Activity for the SHDF

Level	Housing Construction	Planning	Commercial	Development	Venture	Total
High	8	10	100	50	5	173
More likely	5	7	64	32	5	133

The terms used in the projection are: The repayment period is 20 years, payments are deferred for the first two years, after which Fund users pay only interest for two years; the interest rate is progressive, starting at 5% and rising by 1% each year over the time covered by the projections.

The portfolio loss rate is based on the experience of other organizations lending to businesses in low-income areas. Table 3 provides a summary of this experience. These figures are estimates by staff or accounts of the proportion of the organization's investments which will not be recoverable even if the borrowers continue to operate. Thus the write-offs incorporate failures. The highest figure—20%—has been chosen for these projections. In the calculations, losses on the current portfolio are subtracted from "volume outstanding" for the next year. Receipts are thereby reduced in subsequent years.

The experience of CDFC is that many users need to restructure their capitalization after a few years of operation. Usually, this requires a further injection of capital in the second or third year. These projections assume one-third of the commercial loans will require restructuring during the third year, with an additional contribution from the Fund of $20,000, on the same terms as the initial loan.

Development loans. These loans will be used primarily to finance organizers and the acquisition of technical expertise for one year prior to a coop's purchase of plant and equipment. The average amount of these loans was set at $15,000. These are modest but high risk loans which can be expected to show a significant loss rate.

Of each year's batch, 50% will not pan out; 25% will be recovered after one year without interest; and, after one year, the remainder will be rolled into commercial loans at the rates described above.

Venture capital financing. The Fund's flexibility allows it, unlike the bank proper or any other conventional leader, to use debt as venture capital. New sectors (such as cable TV), acquisitions and new product development opportunities cannot be effectively exploited in the absence of high risk front end financing. In order to take advantage of these opportunities the Fund must develop an investment strategy akin to the venture capital industry and must

Table 3.

Program	Portfolio Loss as Percentage of Capital Invested/Year	Source
CSA special impact	17%	Abt Evaluation
SBA equal opportunity	20%	2nd Draft Report
SBA SA loan guarantee	10%	GAO Evaluation
CDFC	7%	Staff Estimate

develop deal structures which allow it to participate in the financial benefits of those which succeed.

Recovery of large multiples of the original investment may be possible when there is a large influx of long-term members or the acquisition of a valuable asset based on the successful completion of the speculative activity. Legal mechanisms for doing this may include joint ventures between the Fund and users, issuance of convertible debentures, or other types of securities.

The projections in Tables 4 and 5 assume that the Fund makes five such investments in each year at an average size of $100,000. TDC assumed that all but one of the investments in each year fail, with no recovery. On those which

Table 4. Self-Help Development Fund Cash Flow Projections[a]
Higher Level of Lending Activity

	1981	1982	1983	1984	1985
Balance forward	40	25.75	19.03	13.08	7.29
Total advances	14.25	14.25	14.91	14.91	14.91
Housing const.	8.0	8.0	8.0	8.0	8.0
Housing plng.	1.0	1.0	1.0	1.0	1.0
Commercial	4.0	4.0	4.0	4.0	4.0
Development	.75	.75	.75	.75	.75
Venture	.50	.50	.50	.50	.50
Loan receipts	–	7.53	8.46	9.12	9.31
Housing const.	–	6.30	7.30	7.30	7.30
Housing plng.	--	.84	.84	.84	.84
Commercial	–	–	.13	.29	.48
Development	–	.39	.39	.39	.39
Venture	–	–	.30	.30	.30
Year end fund balance	25.75	19.03	13.08	7.29	1.69
Begin volume outstanding	–	14.25	19.55	22.41	24.40
Housing const.	–	8.0	10.0	10.0	10.0
Housing plng.	–	1.0	1.0	1.0	1.0
Commercial	–	4.0	7.20	10.06	12.05
Development	–	.75	.75	.75	.75
Venture	–	.50	.60	.50	.50
(Portfolio losses)	–	1.77	3.11	3.98	4.38
Housing const.	–	–	1.0	1.0	1.0
Housing plng.	–	.20	.20	.20	.20
Commercial	–	.80	1.14	2.01	2.41
Development	–	.37	.37	.37	.37
Venture	–	.40	.40	.40	.40
Advances	14.25	14.25	14.25	14.25	14.25
(Principal repaid)	–	7.18	8.28	8.28	8.28
End volume outstanding	14.25	19.55	22.41	24.40	25.99

[a] In millions of dollars.

succeed, the Fund recovers its investment plus a premium of 200% after two years.

Results

High Lending Activity Assumption

At the end of the period 1981–1985, the Fund has advanced $73 million to 866 projects. Of these, 265 have failed, and the Fund has had to write off $13,150,000 in bad debts and lost equity. Over $13 million remains in the Fund balance, and almost $18 million in portfolio value.

Table 5. Self-Help Development Fund Cash Flow Projections[a]
Lower Level of Lending Activity

	1981	1982	1983	1984	1985
Balance forward	40.0	30.76	25.45	21.10	17.30
Total advances	9.25	9.25	9.66	9.66	9.66
Housing const.	50.0	50.0	50.0	50.0	50.0
Housing plng.	.70	.70	.70	.70	.70
Commercial	2.56	2.56	3.06	3.06	3.06
Development	.48	.48	.48	.48	.48
Venture	.50	.50	.50	.50	.50
Loan receipts	–	3.93	5.31	5.44	5.54
Housing const.	–	3.15	4.15	4.15	4.15
Housing plng.	–	.53	.53	.53	.53
Commercial	–	–	.08	.21	.31
Development	–	.25	.25	.25	.25
Venture	–	–	.30	.30	.30
Year end fund balance	30.76	25.45	21.10	17.30	13.18
Begin volume outstanding	–	9.25	13.39	15.45	16.76
Housing const.	–	5.0	7.0	7.0	7.0
Housing plng.	–	.70	.70	.70	.70
Commercial	–	2.56	4.61	6.25	7.56
Development	–	.48	.48	.48	.48
Venture	–	.50	.60	.50	.50
(Portfolio losses)	–	1.35	2.76	3.09	3.35
Housing const.	–	–	1.0	1.0	1.0
Housing plng.	–	.20	.20	.20	.20
Commercial	–	.51	.92	1.25	1.51
Development	–	.24	.24	.24	.24
Venture	–	.40	.40	.40	.40
Advances	9.24	9.24	9.66	9.66	9.66
(Principal repaid)	–	3.74	4.84	4.84	4.84
End volume outstanding	9.24	13.39	15.45	16.76	17.81

[a] In millions of dollars.

In some cases, the assumptions behind the projections vary significantly from the Fund's actual experience and practice. First, the terms of investment are a great deal more lenient than those the Fund has given users to date. Secondly, the volume of lending is a great deal higher than the Office can reasonably expect to achieve at current staffing levels. Still, the Fund balance remains positive at the end of the fifth year. Having assumed "worst case" loss and failure rates, the Fund's portfolio still contains over 430 going enterprises.

What this exercise demonstrates, then, is that the Fund can utilize the maximum flexibility the statute allows to encourage the growth and development of the Fund's low-income coop users. In a broader sense, this further shows that if a problem exists with providing aid to such coops, it is not primarily a financial one. Rather, the underlying issue is one of policy.

Staffing and Technical Support

Even if all parties agreed that money was no issue at all or that Congress would simply appropriate everything needed, the Fund or any similar venture is doomed to failure unless it pays careful attention to the non-financial needs of its clients. The provision of adequate technical assistance during initial planning and early operations of Fund users and other coops is as much a foundation for a successful development project as capital.

Documented experience shows that low income coops need such assistance most. They can seldom draw on their membership for badly needed professional or technical skills, or the resources with which to purchase them.

The experience of existing coop assistance organizations such as the Southern Cooperative Development Fund (SCDF), the New England Cooperative Training Institute (NECTI), and TechniCoop, Inc., which offer help to agricultural, food and housing coops, respectively, indicates that extensive on-site involvement and considerable expense are often needed to complete organizing tasks and provide coop staff and members with the skills required for on-going, self-sufficient management. On the other hand, many technical assistance operations can be considerably less intensive. Organizations which currently lend to coops, including the Southern Cooperative Development Fund and the New England Cooperative Loan Fund, report that practically all applicants need help in accounting and business planning in order to complete loan applications.

On this score, the Fund is insufficiently staffed to offer the wide range of services its coop clientele will require. With only ten authorized technical assistance field staff and an annual operating budget of $2 million, the Office will neither be able to provide such services directly nor to sufficiently subsidize the purchase of necessary services by individual users. Existing coop support groups report that at least three-fourths of their clients require more than cursory assistance in conjunction with borrowing. Where a project is complex and the level of required technical and organizational skills among members is low, as in the conversion of a low-income tenant housing project to a cooperative, large amounts of professional time and money are needed to provide adequate planning and management assistance.

Edgar Jordan of the SCDF reports that the process of completing the supporting documents for a loan application requires 60 days' work from a loan officer whose entire active portfolio is limited by management directive to five cases per quarter. Most groups coming to NECTI for assistance have already completed the organizational development stage of coop building. Still, the program of technical assistance leading to the establishment of a storefront food coop generally takes one year. Not until the end of that year are the assisted coops ready to take a loan to finance plant and inventory.

There is no reason to believe that applicants to the Fund will not require similarly intensive staff involvement in project development and loan processing, and this the limited staff of the Fund cannot fully offer. The Fund's loan processing procedure itself constitutes a full workload for the field staff of fifteen, supported by five specialists in the central office. The operation proceeds in three stages: screening and evaluation, negotiation of terms leading to the credit decision, and loan servicing. Each of the 20 loan officers participate at two or more of these stages, undertaking in the process no less than a dozen conceptually separable tasks. Some of these require travel between the field and the central office. With such a small number of staff performing such a diversity of functions, it appears unavoidable that bottlenecks will develop. In view of these burdens, it is unlikely that each loan officer will close more than one deal per month. Yet the volume of applications anticipated for the Fund, divided through by an average loan value considerably higher than that reported by the officers interviewed, implies a productivity of three deals closed per loan officer per month from the day the Fund office opens its doors. This is clearly impossible, yet it is on the basis of this projection of lending activity that the Fund appears to be formulating its lending policy. Again, the issue here is the number of deals the Fund will have to examine before finding those which can actually be closed, and the care with which screening and deal preparation are done. The Fund is not and cannot be a financial assembly line. If its staff cannot spend adequate time assessing deals, staff will operate a bad Fund and Fund purposes will not be met.

Hopefully, these operational problems can be dealt with so that the Fund can perform the sort of comprehensive technical support services that would make its lending policies both meaningful and practical. On a case-by-case basis, the technical assistance component of the Fund or, for that matter, any agency similarly seeking to aid low-income and other coops, will have to

1. assess the type of aid it needs;
2. choose and formulate contracts with consultants; and
3. arrange whatever financing is necessary to pay for these services.

In order to fulfill this responsibility, the office will need to compile information on services already available from public and private organizations, including the location, capacity and fees of the listed contractors, and supply this information to the field. Where certain problems arise frequently in predictable form, such as in structuring accounting practices to fit standardized loan forms, the central staff should prepare instructional materials and programs which could, to some extent, substitute for direct staff involvement. Experience of existing organizations suggests that this involvement must, at a minimum, cover the following areas.

Assessment of Need

Coop assistance organizations generally assess a client's need for technical assistance in conjunction with evaluation of a loan application. The prospect of receiving credit becomes a stimulus for systematic business planning and for determining which managerial tasks need to be accomplished with outside assistance. At the Southern Cooperative Development Fund, the technical assistance and lending staff work together with the applicants at this stage to formulate a development program of which a loan may be part. The New England Cooperative Loan Fund Board, which has only one part-time staff person, specifies which tasks are to be performed before a preliminary loan application is reconsidered. In both cases, sponsors and staff of the assisted coop participate in determining the type of technical assistance to be sought.

Some types of cooperative development require extensive assistance before they are ready to use a loan. This is particularly true of housing coops formed by organizing tenants of an existing rental project. TechniCoop, Inc. and the Foundation for Cooperative Housing have provided on-site assistance to coop conversions of low-income rental projects. Jonathan Zimmer (1977) reports on their experience in *From Rental to Cooperative*. The ten cases he documents demonstrate a fairly consistent organizing process.

The projects at which TechniCoop and the FCH undertook conversions had suffered high rates of turnover, vacancy, rent delinquency and vandalism. The housing coop organizers found it necessary to take over the management of the project for a period of months before soliciting and selling coop shares to residents. This was necessary to retain current tenants and induce them to participate in the coop.

Where necessary, architectural and engineering studies were commissioned so that the nature of the good to be provided and the cost of the project could be accurately represented to prospective housing coop residents. In an area where coops were not common, it was difficult to convince low-income tenants to take on the financial and management responsibilities of coop membership, even though downpayments were low ($350–700). Once 70–80% of the units had been sold, subsidized mortgage financing was sought. The final step for the organizers before withdrawing from the site was to find reliable permanent staff and help members establish a workable ongoing organization.

The organization of worker coops to buy out existing industrial plants requires similarly extensive involvement by technical experts. In cases where such service is needed, the financing of technical assistance itself becomes a crucial factor in the ultimate success of the enterprise; it must be included in the financial planning of the project as a whole. In all cases, whether assistance consists of one or more discreet tasks or whether it consists of on-site involvement from organization development through project completion, the assessment of technical assistance need and the prescription of specific measures cannot proceed apart from the negotiation of financial arrangements.

Choosing and Contracting with Consultants

Where necessary, the technical assistance representatives should help client coops find and negotiate terms with contractors. One of the major weaknesses of community development organizations is an inability to identify, select and effectively employ consulting assistance. As a result, a great deal of technical assistance money has been wasted in the past* and could also be wasted by Fund clients unless due care is exercised. This will require extensive central office support in the form of a directory of technical assistance resources including the location, capacity and fee schedule of potential contractors.

Financing Technical Assistance

Client coops should be obliged to pay for as large a portion of technical assistance as possible without threatening the financial viability of the project. This is desirable not only to conserve the small pools of funds available to the Office for subsidizing technical assistance costs for individual coops but to also assure that the coops exercise some care in choosing and overseeing the work of contractors as well.

The proportion of technical assistance costs which the coop itself can pay out of its own reserves depends upon the extent of the assistance required and the nature of the project; this must be determined on a case-by-case basis. Even coops operating in the same sector with memberships of similar socioeconomic characteristics may require different degrees of subsidy.

The cases reported by Zimmer, for example, TechniCoop and FCH, generally worked on a contingency basis; i.e., if a conversion project was successfully completed, their costs, which ranged from $20,000 to $50,000 per case, were reimbursed out of the mortgage loan. That these costs were recoverable, however, was the result of a conscious decision by the organizers to concentrate on large projects requiring few physical improvements. Thus, development costs were small in relation to the mortgage value of the properties. This was not the case in tenant conversions in New York City involving small deteriorated buildings. There, and in worker coop buyouts as well, front-end costs must be covered by planning grants, individual equity contributions or volunteer labor.

---

*For instance, there are many complaints from people in the community development field about the quality and usefulness of technical technical assistance from the network of support organizations funded by the Community Services Administration (CSA).

When a coop's membership is comprised of extremely disadvantaged people, technical assistance requirements tend to be extensive and the costs are seldom wholly recoverable. In a 1973 study of 18 OEO-funded rural coops, Abt Associates found that the expenses of organizational development and member education accounted for 15–20% of the sampled coops' financial requirements. In most cases, these expenses were not recovered, even after the coops achieved sufficient net operating income to pay off land and equipment loans. SCDF has provided technical assistance directly through its own staff and by sub-sidizing the salaries of experienced coop members hired on behalf of the members. The direct services are provided by a staff of eight specialists in various sectors which are financed by $500,000 in grants. Little of the $160,000 expended as salary subsidies has been recovered.

Resource Constraints

The Office's technical assistance (TA) program faces severe limitations both in the size of its staff and in the amount of money available to subsidize the fees of TA contractors. The process of assessing TA needs, locating appropriate contractors and planning for their payment are all time-consuming tasks requiring specialized technical knowledge in many cases.

Many observers have remarked that the level of the technical assistance authorization to the Fund is inadequate. Given the plans for the use of that money and the number of individual requests for technical assistance which can reasonably be expected, the size of the authorization will prove to be an additional constraint on overall Office operations. Use of the same funds to commission research with wider applicability or to finance demonstration service delivery programs may also be necessary and appropriate, but they subtract from the pool available to provide timely assistance to individual projects.

Judging from the experience of coop federations, the demand for the remainder of the authorization is likely to be huge. These groups report that upwards of 75% of their constituents, regardless of the background of their members, require more than cursory assistance at some stage of their develop-ment, particularly when applying for credit. Using the earlier projections of lending activity, it could be expected that at least 135 (180×.75) successful applicants to the Fund would apply for technical assistance subsidies. Since, in many development situations, technical assistance must be provided before a loan is made, many groups which do not subsequently achieve bankable operations will also request technical assistance subsidies.

If the Fund is unable itself to provide full technical assistance and informa-tion, it has another option. It could call upon other agencies or individuals to offer assistance, and put appropriate coops in contact with them. This is essential to overall Fund success, and not just for technical assistance. It should be a general policy of the Fund to use its own scarce resources, insofar as possible, to leverage participation or contribution of resources from outside sources. After all, to fully succeed, the Fund or any similar effort must have a working system of external relations to arrange alternative or later stage funding. It is this need which the next section discusses.

Coordinating Outside Activities

A close working relationship at the Fund with the larger Consumer Coop Bank is mandatory for the success of both. The Fund must also actively seek the participation of other public and private agencies in providing financial and technical assistance to coops, perhaps to the extent of delegating some administrative prerogatives. Such a strategy is necessary not only to overcome the constraints presented by the Fund's resources, but to broaden and strengthen the web of organizations politically committed to and technically capable of assisting coops.

The kind of support which external agencies might most immediately and effectively offer falls into two main areas.

1. *Provision of Technical Assistance.* In the case of most individual projects the Fund finances, outside consultants or organizations will be the direct providers of technical assistance. The Office should catalogue the kind of services available in various regions it covers and provide that information to loan officers who have direct contact with potential Fund users. In the past, private, nonprofit organizations and federal agencies such as CSA and the Department of Agriculture have provided the largest share of funding to groups assisting low-income coops. The Office will have to expend some organizational effort to ensure that this level of effort is maintained and expanded.

2. *Arranging for Financial Participation.* Soliciting the financial participation of other government agencies and private institutions in individual projects will be important, not only to stretch the Fund's capital, but to align whatever political influence these institutions may have behind the Office's efforts. There will be two basic modes of arranging financial participation.

   a. *Take-outs.* When Fund users achieve sufficient stability and cash flow to take on term-debt commitments, the Office should seek to arrange for an outside agency or the Bank to put out the remaining principal and refinance the advance according to their own regulations. The Bank has a complimentary motivation to undertake such transactions in that it is legislatively required to make its best efforts to maintain a fairly high proportion of loans to low-income coops in its portfolio. Other agencies and programs have similar motivating statutes, regulations and program guidelines.

   b. *Joint Ventures.* Joint ventures differ from take-outs in that the participation of the outside organization is negotiated before the deal is made. Such transactions will be time-consuming to arrange. Since coops seeking joint funding are likely to have a shorter credit history than those seeking take-outs, it may be difficult to convince venture participants to commit Funds. On the other hand, such a transaction would, in most cases, obviate the need for later negotiations and align outside support at an early stage in the assisted coop's development.

A number of cash and in-kind grant sources already exist. The brief recitation below cites just some of the possible sources which the Fund or even individual coops might pursue to finance actual development or to receive other forms of technical assistance.

Sources of Cash Grants

Foundations. The Ford Foundation, the Campaign for Human Development and the National Institute of Mental Health have all been active in providing finance to coop development groups.

Community Services Administration. CSA has provided major financial support to the Southern Cooperative Development Fund. Cooperative development could also be sponsored by CDCs under the Special Impact Program.*

Urban Development Action Grants. UDAGs are available to severely distressed cities under Section 119 of the Housing and Urban Development Act of 1977. Cities would be able to distribute such grant funds to coops if they are shown to be part of "a concentrated urban development action program setting forth a comprehensive action plan and strategy to alleviate physical and economic distress through systematic change." Among the criteria for HUD approval of such grants are the projected impact of the UDAG program on the special problems of low and moderate income persons and minorities, and the extent of the financial participation of other public or private entities. Fund-supported low-income coops are likely to rate well in these respects.

In-Kind Grants

VISTA. VISTA has provided money to the Boston Food Coop to hire and train butchers to run an expanded meat section. It is hoped this service will broaden the coop's market. Such assistance could not only be useful to the direct beneficiaries; it could also help to build a pool of trained coop managers. The Older American Volunteer Program of ACTION could be another source, particularly for the free aid of experienced older people.

---

*CSA is slated for elimination by October 1, 1981. Some of its functions are to be transferred to the Dept. of Health and Human Services. To the extent any funding will be available at all for coops, it will be through community services block grants.

CETA. Under the Comprehensive Employment and Training Act, NECTI and its affiliates in New Haven have received several year-long subsidized staff positions.

Conclusion and Summary

The statute and legislative history are clear. A major purpose of the National Consumer Cooperative Bank is to "encourage the development of new and existing cooperatives eligible for its assistance by providing specialized credit and technical assistance." Congress clearly anticipated that Office of Self Help Development would have the primary responsibility in this regard and would pay particular attention to the development of cooperatives in low-income communities. This emphasis on the role of the Office of Self-Help Development is made even more dramatic after an examination of the capital structure and the lending constraints of the bank proper. The debt burdens placed on the bank, the requirement that the Treasury capital be retired, and the obligation to meet market rates of interest make it extremely unlikely that the bank itself will be able to provide developmental support to low-income cooperatives. It is therefore especially important that the guidelines established for the activity of the Office of Self-Help Development reflect an understanding of the particular problems facing low-income cooperatives.

Documented experience demonstrates that four principal and recurring problems face low-income cooperatives in the early stages of operation: an inadequate capital structure growing from members' inability to make substantial equity contributions, a resulting lack of access to working capital, inadequate organization and project definition growing out of an inability to afford appropriate front-end planning expenses, and a need for especially intensive management assistance. If the *Office of Self-Help Development and the Self-Help Development Fund are unable to be responsive to these needs, it is extremely unlikely that the statutory obligations will ever be met.*

Therefore a number of crucial decisions must be made in the early stages of establishing the Fund.

1. Interest rates and lending conditions must be designed so that capital advances have the effect of equity investments. This requires extremely low interest rates, a substantial moratorium on principal repayment, and a willingness for the Fund to take risks normally associated with venture capital rather than lending institutions. An important corollary is full and clear recognition that the Fund is neither a bank nor under any statutory obligation to be self-sufficient.

2. Recognizing the substantial inadequacy of the Funds authorized for operations and technical assistance, the bank must establish a work flow which ensures that serious professional attention can be paid to each deal. The

demand for Office assistance will outstrip the staff capacity long before the resources of the Self-Help Development Fund are exhausted. Staff and participating cooperatives must resist the temptation to trade sloppy work for more lending activity through over extension.

3. Leveraging the resources of the Fund and the Office is necessary if even minimal technical assistance requirements are to be met. The Office must structure itself to aggressively seek joint ventures with other financial institutions, including private sector institutions, a systematic take-out arrangement with the bank proper, and provisions to work closely with other technical assistance providers in both the public and private sectors.

The Office of Self-Help Development has the statutory authority and administrative flexibility to move in each of these directions. This chapter demonstrates that the Fund can operate successfully in accordance with these principals. It is also clear that such operations are consistent with the statute and they reflect congressional intent. But while intent and even statutory authority may be clear, implementation is a problematic link between hopeful promise and proved accomplishment.

This chapter has focused on some of the issues facing the Fund, proceeding from the premise that any development finance effort must link comprehensive development and appropriate lending policies. In principle, the Fund should be able to do this. But its limited capacity will have to be utilized if the Fund is to help address the most difficult challenge of all in the development field—to foster new economic enterprises in low-income areas. It would be easy for the Fund, however noble its inspiration, to become just a bad loan window for the Consumer Cooperative Bank. If that happens, it will be remembered not as a breakthrough for low-income economic development, but as just another in a string of failed efforts.

Low-income development institutions face enormous hurdles. The Fund has the capacity to help overcome some of these. It remains to be seen whether it will succeed.

Postscript

As this chapter was being written during 1980, the National Consumer Cooperative Bank was just getting underway as a development financing vehicle of considerable promise. As this chapter demonstrates, the Bank's most innovative component, the Self-Help Development Fund, had the potential to palpably and beneficially assist the development of consumer cooperatives in low-income communities, even if the amount appropriated by Congress was, at $40 million, significantly less than the $75 million originally authorized. As of the beginning of FY 1981–82, the outlook has radically changed. Though the Bank still exists, federal budget cutting is likely to mean that the promise of the Fund will not be realized. There is no capital contribution to the Fund per se.

The Congress has made a "final," one-time contribution of $65 million to the Bank. This is not an equity contribution; the U.S. Treasury must be repaid. As this book goes to press, it is unclear whether the Bank would capitalize the Fund, and only a carryover amount of about $9 million remained in the Fund. There is no operating appropriation for the Bank or the Fund; operations are sustained only from cash flow. At this point, therefore, the promise of the Fund seems effectively eliminated.

Bibliography

Abrahamson, Martin (1976). *Cooperative Business Enterprise*. New York: McGraw Hill.

Anderson, Glenn M. (1972). *A Better Way*. Common Bond, Inc., Minneapolis, Minnesota.

Case, John and Taylor, Rosemary C.R. (1979). *Co-ops, Communes and Collectives*. New York: Pantheon.

Dublin, B. (1975). *Credit Unions: Theory and Practice*. Cooperative League, U.S.A., Washington, DC.

Lundberg, W.T. (1978). *Consumer Owned: Sweden's Cooperative Democracy*. Palo Alto, California: Consumer Cooperative Publishing Association.

National Economic Development Law Center (1978). *Organizing Production Cooperatives*. Berkeley, California.

National Economic Development Law Center (1979). *Community Development Credit Unions: A Self-Help Manual*. Berkeley, California.

Schaaf, Michael (1976). *Cooperatives at the Crossroads: The Potential for a Major New Economic and Social Role*. Exploratory Project for Economic Alternatives, Washington, DC.

Schaars, Marvina (1970). *Co-ops: Principles and Practice*. University Center for Cooperatives, Madison, Wisconsin.

The Co-op Handbook Collective (1975). *The Food Co-op Handbook*. Available from the North American Student Cooperative Organization.

Zimmer, Jonathan (1977). *From Rental to Cooperative*. Beverly Hills, California: Sage Publications.

Zwerdling, Daniel (1980). *Workplace Democracy*. Available from Conference on Alternative State and Local Policies, Washington, DC.

XI

Targeting Public Funds for Community Development: Lessons from the CDBG Program

The Working Group for Community Development Reform

Background and Summary of Findings

From the late 1970s through 1980, the federal government focused increasing attention on economic development, greatly expanding the resources available for programs designed to create or retain jobs and to stimulate local economies. In particular, the Department of Commerce greatly expanded programs under the Economic Development Administration and redirected them toward urban revitalization, while HUD established the Urban Development Action Grant program and expanded it very rapidly.

This new emphasis has been clearly reflected in the Community Development Block Grant (CDBG) program as well. The CDBG program was enacted in 1974 to replace and to consolidate several HUD categorical programs, such as urban renewal and water and sewer facilities development, which had been administered independently up to that point. The main intent of this consolidation was to provide flexibility at the local level so that effective governmental response to local needs would be enhanced. The CDBG statutes were amended in 1977 with the purpose of adding clarity and strength to the legislative guidelines for the application of CDBG funds. These amendments, which were largely the result of pressure applied by citizen's organizations and several congressional representatives, were aimed at increased targeting of CDBG funds to projects primarily benefiting lower-income people as well as improving overall the methods used to encourage citizen participation.

The 1977 amendments to Title I opened eligibility under the CDBG program to a variety of economic development activities which previously had not been allowed. In that same year HUD began to stress the importance of expanding local spending on economic development. HUD's estimate is that approximately one-third of all communities allocated CDBG program funds to economic development activities in all of the first four program years (HUD, 1979, p. VII-1). Expenditures on such program activities ranged from 10 to 13% of annual allocations in the first year of the program, and these percentages were expected to increase (HUD, 1979, p. VIII-3).

The Working Group for Community Development Reform is a national organization, with over 75 member organizations, which is dedicated to increasing the availability of CDBG funds for programs that would benefit and involve lower-income people. The Working Group received a three-year grant from the Community Services Administration (CSA) so that it could sponsor selected local citizens' organizations throughout the nation to monitor local CDBG programs. CSA is mandated under Title IX of its enabling legislation to evaluate the impact of non-CSA programs upon the poor. Thus was launched the National Citizens' Monitoring Project on CDBG, which is a special project of the Center for Community Change—itself a member of the Working Group.

Because of growing emphasis on economic development, the Working Group decided to select such programs as one of the first subjects for local monitoring and evaluation. Therefore, during the first year of the Project, 12 monitors prepared in-depth case studies on local economic development projects which were funded in whole or in part with CDBG entitlement funds. The programs are described in summary form in Tables 1 and 2. These 12 projects alone account for over $37 million in planned CDBG expenditures.

Of the local jurisdictions represented in these case studies, all but one had significant minority populations. Most have higher than nationwide unemploy-

Table 1.

Project Type	Number of Cases
Neighborhood Projects	
Strip revitalization	6
Industrial Park	3
Technical assistance to local neighborhood development corporations	1
Comprehensive economic development project	1
CBD Projects	5
Downtown shopping mall	2
Comprehensive downtown redevelopment	3
Citywide Project	1
Project Uses	
Commercial	7
Industrial	1
Commercial and industrial	1
Commercial, industrial, residential	3

Note: Based on information available to local monitors, it appears that at least 10 of the 12 projects included more than one category of specific eligible CDBG activities (e.g., acquisition, clearance, relocation, etc.).

Table 2. Summary Descriptions of Specific Economic Development Projects

No.	Jurisdiction	Project Name	Summary Description
1	Bergen County, New Jersey	Hackensack Center City Complex	Downtown redevelopment for office, parking and retail
2	Chicago, Illinois	Business Area Improvement Program	Public improvements and parking in selected neighborhood commercial areas
3	Cleveland, Ohio	Assistance to Local Development Corporations	Funds for planning, design, operation and related improvements in selected areas
4	Detroit, Michigan	Woodward Avenue Mall	Creation of restricted traffic covered downtown street mall
5	Indianapolis, Indiana	Concord Industrial Park	Site preparation for neighborhood Industrial Park
6	Los Angeles, California	North Hollywood Commercial Revitalization	Planning for new and rehabilitated commercial development in an NSA
7	Newark, New Jersey	Newark Economic Development Corporation	Funds for part of operating expenses of city-wide economic development agency
8	New Bedford, Massachusetts	Waterfront Historic District Revitalization	Public improvements and commercial rehabilitation and restoration
9	New York City, New York	Brooklyn Fulton Mall Project	Utilities, surface improvements and commercial rehab on street mall
10	Rochester, New York	Neighborhood Commercial Development	Public improvements and commercial rehabilitation in selected neighborhoods
11	San Francisco, California	Yerba Buena Center Project	Acquisition and site preparation for large, multi-use redevelopment downtown
12	Westchester County, New York	Port Chester Redevelopment Project	Site preparation, residential and commercial rehabilitation, parking and retail development as part of downtown redevelopment

ment averages, particularly among youth, minorities, and working women.* Six projects are located in the eastern United States, four in the midwest, and two in the west.

These 12 projects were selected for study by the local monitors for a variety of reasons. Some were the only significant CDBG-funded local economic development activities, or the only ones sufficiently underway to be studied (Bergen County, Chicago, and Cleveland). Some were the largest CDBG-funded local economic development activities in the jurisdiction (Detroit, New York City, and Westchester County). Some had received significant local citizen attention in design or implementation (Indianapolis, Los Angeles, New Bedford, Rochester, and San Francisco). Finally, some were still at a stage where the project could be improved through citizen study and recommendations (Los Angeles and Westchester County).

What has been the impact of these programs? Who has reaped their benefit? Perhaps the most important finding of the Project's monitoring of economic development projects is that it is extraordinarily difficult to answer these questions because of the pervasive failure of local governments to set clear, specific project goals which can be the basis for measuring progress and benefit. The monitors found:

a complete lack of quantifiable, specific goals, especially in the area of job creation for low- and moderate-income citizens, a key criterion for judging the eligibility of economic development projects under the Act.

a lack of specific targeting of project benefits to low- and moderate-income citizens'; for example, in none of the cases studied was there evidence of contractual requirements placed upon the developers, retailers, or industries who benefit from the expenditure of CDBG funds with regard to hiring low- and moderate-income persons for jobs that result from the project.

a lack of minority hiring and contracting requirements, despite the fact that federal law requires affirmative action in minority hiring and contracting in CDBG-funded projects.

strong indications that these compliance problems and the lack of specific project goals were evidence of a larger problem of poor quality in overall project planning and implementation.

Monitors found seventeen instances in which applicants were in violation of statutory or regulatory requirements. In addition, the monitors raised serious questions about whether several of the projects could quality as eligible economic development activities because HUD requirements state the such activities are eligible "only if HUD finds that they are likely to produce certain results" (HUD, 1978) and the project descriptions provided insufficient detail to give HUD a basis for making such a determination.

---

*Refer to Appendix D of the June 1980 report by the Working Group from which this chapter is derived.

How Does Economic Development Fit Into the CDBG Program?

Local jurisdictions are not required to include economic development activities in their Community Development plan. However, HUD encourages them to develop such programs as well as a broader economic development strategy. The CDBG Regulations state

> Grant assistance may be provided for the following development activities, which are directed toward the alleviation of physical and economic distress... through stimulation of private investment, community revitalization and expansion of economic opportunities for low- and moderate-income persons and handicapped persons, and which are necessary and appropriate to implement the applicant's strategy for economic development.

Eligible economic development activities include the acquisition of real property; acquisition, construction, reconstruction, rehabilitation, or installation of commercial and industrial facilities; or real property improvements and public facilities improvements otherwise eligible for assistance.*

If a local government decides to use CDBG funds for economic development, it must include an economic development strategy in its application to HUD. That strategy must contain

1. a description of major needs for economic development, including those of identifiable population groups experiencing unemployment or underemployment;
2. a description of the activities proposed to further economic development and attract private investment;
3. the number and types of permanent jobs expected to result from the activity, particularly jobs for unemployed or underemployed and low- and moderate-income persons, and the extent and nature of any job training programs for such persons; and
4. evidence of commitments or interest by developers of new or expanded employment facilities.†

Economic development projects do not have to principally benefit low- and moderate-income people. They may instead be justified as preventing or eliminating slums or blight,‡ or meeting particularly urgent needs.§ If, however, they are justified as being of principal benefit to lower-income people, they must

> provide direct employment opportunities for permanent jobs, the majority of which will be for low- and moderate-income persons if the persons expected

---

*24 CFR S570.204 also lists other economic activities which are eligible if carried out by certain nonprofit entities. Since none of the projects discussed in this chapter were carried out under that subsection, such activities have not been listed in the text.

†24 CFR S570.304 (b) (3).

‡24 CFR S570.302 (e).

§24 CFR S570.302 (f).

to be employed are defined as low- and moderate-income prior to employment (it is not necessary that the incomes of persons employed by economic development projects be low and moderate after the project is completed); or

be designed to attract or retain neighborhood commercial facilities which provide essential services to residential areas which have a majority of low- and moderate-income residents.*

On economic development projects as well as other CDBG activities, the local government must comply with Section 3 of the Housing and Urban Development Act of 1968. It must, in short, provide opportunities for training and employment to lower-income residents to the maximum extent feasible, while giving similar priority to contracts for local businesses.† Finally, all jurisdictions must take affirmative action with regard to employment, upgrading, and training.‡

Do the Economic Development Projects Have Clear Goals?

Under the Block Grant program, local officials have taken on the obligation of defining their jurisdictions' needs, their goals for meeting those needs, and their program plans and strategies. If these locally set priorities comply with statutory requirements, they are accepted by HUD and later used as the basis for judging whether the local government's performance has been satisfactory. In stressing enforcement of locally set goals, the authors of the legislation hoped to see an improvement in the capacity of local governments to plan and execute CDBG programs. In the words of a report from the House Subcommittee on Housing:

> The success of this approach depends on how well the statute is administered by these (local and federal) decision makers. In this sense, they have a larger responsibility for assuring that local programs developed by CDBG are meeting statutory purposes than they had under the categorial programs (U.S. Congress, 1977).

HUD is to review proposed economic development projects to assess whether they are "necessary or appropriate to implement the applicant's strategy for economic development."§

The activity should be one which is likely to produce the results claimed, and the results should be significant in relation to the applicant's needs and

---

*24 CFR S570.302 (d) (2). In evaluating projects to see if they meet the "benefit test," HUD will look at (1) their appropriateness, given the needs of low- and moderate-income citizens in relationship to the general needs and conditions of the applicants; (2) whether they have income eligibility requirements; and (3) in the absence of income requirements, whether it is demonstrated that a majority of the beneficiaries will be low- and moderate-income residents.

†24 CFR S570.370 (m).

‡24 CFR S570.307 (1) (5).

§24 CFR S570.203.

conditions. This assessment requires a judgment as to the reasonableness of the cost in relation to the anticipated benefits. The more speculative the proposed undertaking, and the most costly, the greater is the necessity to ensure the activity is appropriate to meet the applicant's needs and accomplish its strategy.*

The Monitoring Project's Survey of economic development projects raises serious questions about how well these responsibilities are being carried out. In only three of the twelve projects studied by monitors were program goals made specific enough to provide a basis for determining whether the activity is likely to produce the results claimed, or significant results, or results which are reasonable in relation to cost. In the other nine the goals were also too vague to provide a basis for later measuring project success.

Many of the projects had no specific stated goals, other than a list of physical activities to be undertaken. Where project objectives were stated, they ranged from "improve a deteriorated neighborhood, improve the city's tax base, and create new jobs" to a repetitive 23-point list of project components, activities, and expected benefits.

For its CDBG-funded Fulton Mall project, New York City's application fails to provide a concrete statement of goals. The project's stated goals are: to strengthen the retail character of downtown Brooklyn, to generate private investment, and to increase tax revenue. The application goes on to provide a pleasant-sounding description, without very clear goals and plans:

> The mall will include a widened pedestrian walkway with amenities such as street furniture, information and vending kiosks and decorative paving from building line to building line. A two-lane bus transitway and new subway entrances will create a mass transit-oriented environment. The mall will strengthen the retail character of the area, generate private investment and increase tax revenues for the city.

Los Angeles furnishes an example of how a program which was originally justified with very vague goals continues to flounder years later. Into its third year of CDBG funds, the Commercial Revitalization Subcommittee in Los Angeles released the following statement about the commercial development program:

> Last discussed were the ideas, concerns and procedures on how to create various opportunities for the revitalization of the downtown commercial strip. Among the goals of this phase of the project are: (1) to bring money back to North Hollywood; (2) to entice the Universal Studio tourists to come here to eat and shop; (3) to bring new people into the area who can find housing, jobs, leisure activities, shopping and banking within the core area. Suggested ideas for the design include a Westwood Village/Farmers Market-style shopping center, and a high-rise complex that would house apartments, stores, businesses and restaurants in one building.

*HUD Notice PD 78-9, p. 9.

In Detroit, while the CDBG economic development project had no estimated numerical job benefits of its own, the city attributed jobs from a nearby proposed UDAG activity to the CD-funded project.

Such a failure by HUD to require quantitative or otherwise clearly defined goals and the failure of local governments to develop such clarity on their own calls into question whether HUD is carrying out its responsibilities with regard to economic development. It also raises questions about the federal government's ability to evaluate program progress or to monitor compliance with economic development benefit requirements. Finally it indicates that local mayors, councils, and citizens do not have sufficient benchmarks upon which to base a local evaluation of the effectiveness and impact of these major programs.

Two related points strengthen these concerns. The grantee performance reports still do not require any information with regard to job benefits from economic development—or other—projects. And HUD's Annual Report to Congress gives no substantial attention to job-related issues. In the *Fourth Annual Community Development Block Grant Program Report*, HUD devoted the following six lines to reporting on the employment impact of CDBG.

> The CDBG program creates close to 300,000 jobs yearly.... Over one-half of these jobs are in central cities and about 52,300 are in suburban areas. Nearly 50,000 person-years of employment were created for minority employees. CDBG jobs paid nearly $3.7 billion in wages. Of this total, close to $2 billion went to employees in central cities (HUD, 1979—HUD cited no data source.).

The local monitors evaluated the twelve economic development projects against the jurisdictions' own stated goals, despite their vagueness. The difficulty of this task is reflected in the following observations drawn from the case studies:

> General goal of "physical revitalization" of a historic district commercial area is consistent with performance, but performance against the goal of job creation for low- and moderate-income persons cannot be assessed because the goal was not quantified, conditions regarding job provisions were not imposed, and no data are available on the nature and recipients of the jobs produced.*

> For reasons not reported, 43% of the project's commercial rehabilitation activities have been outside the city's Primary Target Area, while the project's annual stated goal focused entirely on the target area.†

> Downtown revitalization goals, while quantified overall to some extent, were not specific to this project and were dependent on all downtown projects from whatever fund sources. Half of the physical activities for this project were shelved because of a conflict with the design for a nearby proposed UDAG project which, however, is not yet approved for funding.‡

*New Bedford, Massachusetts, Waterfront Historic District Revitalization.
†Rochester, New York, Neighborhood Commercial Development.
‡Detroit, Michigan, Woodward Avenue Mall.

The lack of quantified, specific project goals indicates that the results accruing from at least three-fourths of the projects studied cannot be effectively assessed against the purposes which provided the basis for the projects' original approval by the local jurisdictions and HUD. Furthermore, HUD's approval of such vague proposals for economic development and its failure to require a clearer basis for postaudits and performance review raises serious questions about HUD policies and procedures.

Do CDBG Economic Development Projects Benefit Low- and Moderate-Income Persons?

Since the National Citizens' Monitoring Project has a special concern with lower-income benefit as part of its broader concern with the overall effectiveness and accountability of the Block Grant program, the local monitors looked in particular depth at the benefit of the economic development program for low- and moderate-income people. Monitors asked whether programs had been targeted to specific geographic areas or income and ethnic groups; whether specific commitments from employers or developers were required for participation in the program; and the nature and extent of job creation and training programs.

The findings of this aspect of the monitoring are particularly interesting in light of HUD's own assessment of benefit from economic development programs. In its *Fourth Annual Report* the Department estimated that 71% of the benefit from economic development projects accrues to low- and moderate-income *areas*. "At present, economic development is the strategy which targets the second highest percentage of funds to low- and moderate-income *areas*" (HUD, 1979). Such statistics raise serious questions concerning HUD's current method of calculating benefit. HUD assumes that a project located in an area with low- and moderate-income residents will benefit those residents. This clearly is often not the case.

With the wide range of funding sources available for economic development, CDBG funds should be seen as unique among all of a city's economic development resources because of its statutory and regulatory connection to lower income needs. While CDBG funds may be used for economic development activities that are directed toward the alleviation of physical and economic distress or the economic development of a new community, it is *also* to include expansion of economic opportunities for low- and moderate-income persons and handicapped persons. This is not an alternative; it is a stated requirement for eligibility of economic development projects for CDBG funding.

Yet in seven of the twelve cases studied, the project was in no direct way targeted to benefit low- and moderate-income residents. In the remaining cases, evidence of specific targeting was available but weak at best.

Employment Opportunities

Enhanced employment opportunities are the most obvious potential benefit of CDBG-assisted economic development programs (though by no means the only one) for low- and moderate-income citizens. Furthermore, job creation is the only area where the HUD regulations specifically require jurisdictions to meet quantitative goals and maintain numerical records. Section 570.304 (a) (3) (iii) states that an economic development strategy must include "the number and types of permanent jobs expected to result from economic development projects, particularly jobs for unemployed or underemployed population groups and low- and moderate-income persons...."

Thus, the monitors paid special attention to measuring program achievement against objectives with regard to jobs. They concentrated especially on analyzing the means through which localities would expand employment opportunities for low- and moderate-income residents.

The results were both revealing and disturbing:

Only five of the projects included job creation or retention as a stated goal.

Only one specifically targeted these jobs to low- and moderate-income persons.

None of the projects listed specific numbers of new or retained jobs for low- and moderate-income persons as a stated goal.

None of the cases showed any evidence of contractual requirements upon developers, retailers, or industries who would benefit from the project, concerning the hiring of unemployed or underemployed or other low- and moderate-income persons, for temporary or permanent, new or retained jobs which were likely to result from the project.

None of the projects were linked with specific employment and training efforts (such as local CETA programs) to help ensure the identification, hiring, training and advancement of local unemployed and lower-income persons in the projects.

In two cases, New York City and Detroit, jurisdictions used city ordinances to impose mandatory hiring goals upon contractors and subcontractors. The City of Detroit used the Economic Development Administration's 10% contracting set-aside for minority-owned business enterprises to achieve a high level of minority contracting in the project.

On the whole, however, the monitors found great weakness in the projects' attention to the jobs question, as the following comments from their reports demonstrate:

> The project itself contains no projections of permanent jobs for low- and moderate-income persons. City justifies project as principally benefiting lower-income persons by claiming it as essential to other downtown projects which do carry job projections.
>
> The project plans contain no projections of numbers of jobs for lower-income persons, project operations contain no mechanisms to ensure the provision of such

jobs or essential services, and city data on jobs created lack information on types of jobs or nature of the recipients.

Program goals make no mention of creation or retention of jobs for lower-income persons, and no data are available indicating actual results in this area. Goals include no specific attempt to provide essential services to lower-income areas, and nearly half of the program's commercial rehabilitation has been outside the Primary Target Area.

Final assessment is not possible, but plans do not specify numbers of jobs for low- and moderate-income persons, nor essential services within majority lower-income areas.

While the project has been involved with creation of jobs and generation of new business, there is evidence that working conditions for many of the jobs created have been negative, low-paying, and seasonal, so that the net effect of the activity overall and in relation to lower-income persons is in question.

Project contains no specific job goals for lower-income persons, no mechanisms nor guarantees for retention or production of such jobs, and no workable strategy for relocation or provision of new housing for lower-income area residents.

Essential Services

In addition to the provision of employment opportunities for low- and moderate-income persons, HUD regulations state that an economic development project may be regarded as benefiting low- and moderate-income persons when it is designed to attract or retain neighborhood commercial facilities if they provide essential services to residential areas which have a majority of low- and moderate-income persons.

Monitors rarely found goal statements for these economic development projects that would indicate the jurisdiction's intention to meet this objective. Because the goals and objectives stated were so broad and vague, it is, however, difficult to know whether the applicants considered the provision of essential services to be among the potential outcomes of these projects.

HUD fails to give any definition or clarification of what is intended in its regulations by the phrase "essential services." However, the monitors viewed two factors as indications of whether these economic development projects would provide essential services. First, whether the jurisdictions identified what services would be provided, and, second, whether there was any assessment of service needs as part of the planning and programming for these projects. Monitors report:

> In New Bedford, Massachusetts, local needs as defined by the different portions of the public sector cover a wide spectrum. Defining the phrase "local needs" on a general level means determining priorities of services that are needed to help those who need the services most. In the case of CD [Community Development, or CDBG], "local needs" should address the needs of low- and moderate-income residents of the entitlement area. This is specifically where the Waterfront Historic District falls short. This specific problem is not addressed.

In San Francisco, California, even as designed, the project's projections are open to the usual questions. There is every reason to believe that the private development so long hoped for may, because of national economic forces, never fully materialize. Indeed, the plan offers very little to the City's urban environmentalists and neighborhood planning forces who had viewed Yerba Buena Center as an opportunity to explore new concepts and approaches to revitalizing inner cities through mixed commercial, industrial and residential uses that would be designed to meet the articulated needs of the city's existing residents.

In Rochester, New York, the monitor notes that one final issue which appears to be left out of the city's neighborhood commercial strategy is the location of necessary services such as food stores, postal stations and drugstores convenient to low-income neighborhoods. A strategy to persuade these types of retail stores to locate in city neighborhoods should be pursued. Large competitive grocery stores multiply business for nearby commercial establishments, so that if one does elect to locate in a neighborhood commercial area, it would undoubtedly boost neighborhood establishments also.

The monitor in Los Angeles, California, notes that none of the planning documents take into account what essential services are required for the current North Hollywood population, especially low- and moderate-income residents. This question is not specifically addressed in the consultant's methodology. However, the CRA's community liaison officer said, "The shopping center will be planned for current residents. Obviously you couldn't put a Bullock's Wilshire in North Hollywood, but you could put a Zody's."

With two exceptions—one which provides assistance to local development corporations and a second which states as its goal the improvement of a deteriorated neighborhood—the goals of the twelve projects were generally directed to redevelopment and revitalization activities. They are largely projects which attempt to make areas economically or commercially viable, leaving the potential objective of providing essential services to a neighborhood to be, at best, served accidentally. For instance, monitors report:

In Bergen County, New Jersey, the redevelopment project in Hackensack is part of a larger program to revitalize downtown and enable it to hold its own vis-à-vis the large shopping centers and to continue its role as government and banking center. Compacting the retail district into the area north of the railroad tracks is intended to ensure the future viability of that area, while doing away with the more marginal retail operations in the redevelopment area.

The revitalization of the Waterfront Historic District was one of the original CD-funded programs for the City of New Bedford, Massachusetts. The stated goals of this program were originally to initiate the restoration and revitalization of the Waterfront Historic District through building rehabilitation and associated public improvements to complement the city's continuing attempt to promote economic growth and commercial revitalization while preserving and maintaining its historic flavor.

Finally, the jurisdictions' lack of intention to provide essential services as a component of the economic development projects was evident from their failure to concentrate on specific areas where such services, if provided, could benefit low- and moderate-income persons. Monitors noted not only the failure to target activities to low- and moderate-income areas, but also the diversion of such activities from the projected target areas, and even the displacement and relocation of neighborhood businesses and residences so that these CDBG-funded projects could proceed.

> In Chicago, Illinois, the monitor states that there are no clear criteria for how locations for business area improvements are selected. The city apparently feels justified in allocating as large a portion of its money to this program as it does because it gets so many requests from Chambers of Commerce and business associations for improvements. Requests may have no relationship to needs. The city has not designed this program to meet certain criteria or certain conditions. Rather, judgments are made based on the opinion of the staff that the area is viable, has a fairly strong base, is located in a fairly decent residential area, has potential for continuing as a viable commercial area and has active business organizations requesting assistance.

Are Minorities Served by CDBG Economic Development Projects?

All CDBG activities are covered under Title VI of the Civil Rights Act of 1964 and Executive Orders 11246 and 11375, which prohibit discrimination by government contractors and require an affirmative action program to promote equal employment opportunities. As noted above, they are also covered by Section 3 requirements. Eleven of the twelve communities analyzed for the case studies had significant minority populations.

Several monitors evaluated the extent to which CDBG-assisted economic development programs served minorities in their jurisdictions. Out of twelve projects, they identified two projects with strong minority hiring requirements and one with a strong minority contracting requirement. For the most part, however, jurisdictions studied by the monitors appeared not to be taking their affirmative action obligations seriously.

In Westchester County, New York, the monitor found that, while minorities comprise 80% of the target area population for Port Chester's economic development program, minorities have been excluded from the citizen participation process, and the sponsoring jurisdiction has failed to provide guarantees of employment for lower-income, minority persons in the target area. In Bergen County, New Jersey, 50% of Hackensack's total CDBG allotment has been earmarked for an economic development program. That jurisdiction's population is 17% black and 7% Hispanic. Yet the monitor observes:

> The project appears to be at odds with Section 3 because of the city's failure to take any affirmative steps to secure minority or project area employees or contractors for the project, nor to try to attract minority business enterprises as final occupants.

Some local monitors presented specific information concerning possible discriminatory treatment in the location and impact of projects. Monitors cited alleged discriminatory treatment of workers in new jobs created, disproportionate negative impact on minorities as a result of displacement by the project, and selection of project sites in white areas rather than minority areas.

Chicago, Illinois, which is at least 34% minority, has allocated more than $7 million in its fifth year CDBG program to revitalize neighborhood commercial shopping strips. The monitor found that the majority of these projects are located in white neighborhoods and that the completion rate of projects under the program is much greater in white than in minority areas. There is no apparent effort under the program, the monitor observes, to involve minority contractors, nor has the city developed any quantifiable job retention or creation goals for any target group or target area.

Are the CDBG Economic Development Programs Effectively Administered?

Many of the local monitors presented evidence that the apparent lack of concern with lower-income benefit and civil rights requirements is part of a larger problem of overall project design and implementation. These problems together raise questions of the capacity of many local governments to plan and carry out economic development projects. Some aspects of administrative performance related to economic development are discussed in this section.

Timely Performance

Title I of the Housing and Community Development Act of 1974, as amended, makes plain that applicants must carry out their programs in a timely manner. Section 103 (d) requires the HUD Secretary to review programs against this standard: "The Secretary shall, at least on an annual basis, make such reviews and audits as may be necessary or appropriate to determine... whether the applicant has a continuing capacity to carry out in a timely manner the approved Community Development Program."

Yet, in at least nine of the 12 projects studied, the monitor reports significant delays in completion and implementation. Three of the projects are still in their early planning stages two years or more after initial project approval. In seven of the 12 projects, information on the overall percentage of work actually completed was simply unavailable.

In Detroit, Michigan, the monitor summarizes the circumstances for slow performance:

> The plan was modified after construction had begun on the overhead enclosure because of the announcement by a major downtown retail establishment that its facilities adjacent to this project would be demolished, and that a new store for the company might be built in a planned suburban-style shopping mall nearby. Funding is still not firm for the latter, and the final form of the Woodward Avenue Mall depends upon whether the shopping mall project is constructed.

The monitor in Westchester County, New York, reports that little progress has occurred on the Port Chester economic development project. In the making since 1975, with an initial public hearing in 1977, a full staff has not yet been assembled and a relocation plan still needs to be developed. Due to the long delays, internal fiscal problems, and community opposition, the first cash drawdowns were not effected until May of 1979. Of the $110,000 spent the first year, $67,000 has been for administration, planning and property appraisal.

The reasons reported for delays indicate other deficiencies in the projects' design, implementation, and administration:

Lack of specific goals or plans at the time the application is submitted;

Faulty technical data and lack of coordination with nearby projects or activities;

Inadequate number and quality of city or county staff;

Changes in policy after project initiation; and

Legal challenges initiated by citizens objecting to original project design.

Available information indicates that nearly all of these delaying factors could have been anticipated during initial project design.

HUD's estimate of the timeliness of economic development projects is in striking contrast to local monitors' findings. HUD has stated that the "majority of (all) projects (of all types) are on or close to schedule and have achieved a satisfactory level of impact" (HUD, 1979, p. 2). HUD also found that "neighborhood commercial and Central Business District projects move somewhat faster than the average CDBG project" (HUD, 1979, p. IV-11). Eleven of the twelve projects surveyed in this study were neighborhood or CBD projects and thus should, according to HUD's evaluation, have been proceeding in a timely manner.

Cost – Benefit

Another important standard for judging effective administration is whether project benefits have an appropriate relationship to costs. This standard was explicitly set forth in a HUD issuance on review of economic development projects (HUD, 1978). Does the net effect of a project justify the financial and other costs? Are negative impacts of projects upon lower income residents addressed by the jurisdiction through mitigating actions, as required in HUD benefit regulations?

In general, the lack of uniform and specific objectives for these twelve projects prohibits any specific analysis of cost in relation to benefits based on the original project designs. Moreover, no jurisdiction was reported to be planning to undertake such an analysis. Therefore, it appears that the net effect of these projects in relation to their costs either will not or cannot be assessed by the local jurisdiction, and that it will be very difficult for others to conduct such an evaluation.

Availability of Information

Another important standard is that information regarding programs be readily available to the public. While only one local monitor reported outright refusals by the jurisdiction to provide program information, six others reported that important information on the projects being examined either did not exist or was not readily available.

Monitors requested, but were unable to get financial data free of discrepancies, and information on project impacts (such as characteristics of displacees, jobs produced, job recipients, and impacts on business operation, retention and creation). Given our other findings, it can be assumed that the unavailability of much of this information reflects the jurisdictions' failure to gather it themselves as the basis for setting objectives and conducting project evaluations.

Citizen Participation

Local monitors found that at least seven of the twelve projects studied were apparently not in compliance with HUD citizen participation standards. Most monitors observed that lower-income people and minorities were either not represented or only minimally or inadequately represented on Citizens' Advisory Committees or Boards, or project area advisory committees, or the Board or Commission with oversight for the project. Moreover, nearly all of the projects were designed primarily by city or county staff, with citizen involvement limited to business representatives and some public officials.

Some monitors observed projects where virtually no opportunity for citizen input had been afforded throughout the history of the project or activities in the area. The monitors cited instances in which modifications in the project came about only through lawsuits directed to such issues as relocation, financing and environmental impact.

How Could CDBG Economic Development Projects Be Improved?

The monitors made a total of thirty-six recommendations to local officials, citizens, and HUD concerning these twelve projects. The largest number of these recommendations pertained to issues of program design, strategy and problem analysis. Others suggested organizational improvement.

Two recurring themes in the monitors' recommendations are:

1. CDBG-funded economic development projects need to be more tightly designed overall and with respect to low- and moderate-income benefits; these projects should include quantified goals and mechanisms for ensuring lower-income benefits and timeliness.
2. Cities and counties should use their powers to condition the use of CDBG

economic development funds for the achievement of specific project goals by public agencies, contractors and other participating business enterprises. Such conditioning could include the following kinds of requirements:

a. adherence to specific goals for lower income permanent job benefits;
b. priority for jurisdictions' own residents to receive jobs created;
c. linkage to CETA-funded employment and training efforts;
d. achievement of significant minority contracting and hiring goals;
e. emphasis on commercial enterprises which provide essential services to lower-income persons;
f. use of minority-owned financial institutions and community banks and credit unions for handling project monies; and
g. reinvestment of project profits in community institutions.

Finally, implied throughout the monitors' analyses of these 12 projects is the need for increased HUD direction concerning various aspects of CDBG-funded economic development activities. These twelve case studies provide ample evidence that local governments are having great difficulty planning and mounting effective economic development programs. They are having trouble setting local goals, developing the capacity to meet those goals, and then evaluating their own progress so that they can establish increasingly effective and useful programs. Because of these deficiencies, local mayors—as well as city councils, citizens, and HUD—often do not have the basic information they need to know what is happening with the money and to ensure that it is spent in ways which meet local goals and national objectives.

Equally seriously, these reports indicate that many projects which are classified by local governments as benefiting lower-income people—and approved by HUD as doing so—are not, in fact, having such an impact. The lack of effective measures to require that jobs be targeted and that such beneficial impact be shown raises serious questions about both HUD estimates with regard to the benefit of such activities and the wisdom of HUD's current emphasis on using CDBG funds for economic development.

The Monitoring Project's findings with regard to economic development, housing, benefit, and other aspects* of the Community Development program also suggest the issues and problems one can expect to arise in even more aggravated form as the Reagan Administration "block grants" a much broader range of development, job training, and community service programs per the CDBG model. There is a need for new measures which will greatly toughen HUD's insistence on adequate performance, and which will give local governments another opportunity to demonstrate that they do, in fact, have the capacity that will be needed to mount an effective community development program.

*The Monitoring Project also included a careful assessment of housing and other aspects of Community Development assisted by CDBG funds, and the conclusions and recommendations reflect this other work.

Bibliography

HUD (1979). Office of Community Planning and Development, *Fourth Annual Community Development Block Grant Report*. Washington, DC: U.S. Government Printing Office (September 7).

HUD (1978). "Review of Entitlement Applications for Fiscal Year 1978." HUD Notice PD 78-9, #6504.1 (April 28), p. 9.

U.S. Congress (1977). *Community Development Block Grant, Staff Report*. H.R. Reg. No. 83–516. 95th Congress, 1st Session (February), p. 6.

PART FOUR

THE NEW PUBLIC/PRIVATE RELATIONSHIP IN DEVELOPMENT FINANCE

XII

Lemon Capitalism?
An Analysis of the Chrysler Bail-out and the Desirability of Federal Loan Guarantees to Private Firms

Keith Hinman

Executive Summary

This chapter investigates the merits of granting federal financial assistance to the Chrysler Corporation and discusses some of the ramifications of such aid for future policy and our economic and political institutions. The questions raised by the Chrysler Affair are interesting in their own right as well as being important as precedents if the Chrysler case turns out to be a harbinger of things to come in other industries. The questions addressed are whether a federally guaranteed loan program is an appropriate policy for dealing with the problems of Chrysler, and whether such loans establish a desirable policy precedent.

Chrysler's problems are the result of a series of management errors over time, exacerbated by rapidly shifting consumer tastes in the auto market and by the 1980 recession. With losses of over $1 billion in both 1979 and 1980, the firm is a likely candidate for bankruptcy if left to its own resources. Arguments that the government should bail Chrysler out because the company's problems are not its "fault," however, are found to be disingenuous or irrelevant. The regulatory "burden," often painted as the villain, is found to account for but a small portion of Chrysler's losses.

The case for aid rests primarily on the potential impact of a corporate liquidation on jobs and output, particularly in the Detroit area. This potential economic trauma, primarily a short-run effect, can be regarded as a "market failure" in which private markets fail to serve the social welfare during a period of transitional adjustment. The probable impact of a "worst case" bankruptcy and liquidation is indeed projected to be potentially severe in the short run. Longer-run impacts are possible in the Detroit area, the region hardest hit by a Chrysler shutdown.

Bankruptcy followed by liquidation is not the only alternative to federal aid, however. There was (and is) the possibility of attracting a merger offer from a healthier company or of declaring bankruptcy and undergoing a successful reorganization under Chapter II of the bankruptcy laws. Indeed, even with federal assistance, significant reorganizing and economizing must take place. Federal aid can underwrite and perhaps cushion the regional and employment impacts of Chrysler's reorganization, but cannot prevent these social losses entirely.

Moreover, the short-run economic costs of a Chrysler failure must be balanced against the long-run economic cost of using society's resources inefficiently and against the precedential "cost" of granting aid. On balance, the costs of aid are found to outweigh the benefits.

Policy alternatives and lessons for the future are discussed briefly. The economic impact and political visibility of possible similar occurrences in the future make it advisable to consider policies other than direct loans to firms and laissez-faire "benign neglect." The proposed reinstitution of a Reconstruction Finance Corporation to institutionalize large corporate bail-outs is considered by this author to be undesirable, potentially combining the worst features of capitalistic and planned economies. Given the undeniable public importance of large private firms; however, it seems clear that some creative re-thinking of the public/private relationship is in order. Two broad directions are possible: public policies to ameliorate the undesirable social side effects of a fundamentally private economy; or active public policies to plan and direct an economy which, according to economic or sociopolitical criteria, is judged to be failing.

Introduction

During its highly publicized financial crisis in the latter half of 1979, the Chrysler Corporation mounted an aggressive drive on Washington in pursuit of federal assistance. This marketing blitz was aided by fears of massive job losses and economic devastation, and it culminated on December 21, 1979, with the enactment of an extraordinary federal loan guarantee program. This legislation (P.L. 96–185) authorized a specially created Loan Guarantee Board to issue up to $1.5 billion in federal loan guarantees for private loans. These guarantees, contingent on Chrysler's obtaining additional financial commitments of $2 billion from a variety of other sources, would allow Chrysler to borrow money at low interest rates, whereas previously it had been unable to borrow at any price.* Each issuance of loan guarantees[†] is contingent upon a finding by the specially created Chrysler Loan Guarantee Board that Chrysler has a "viable" recovery plan and, less formally, that other involved parties are taking a reasonable share of the risk. Congress has ultimate veto power.

---

*A federal loan guarantee is essentially a pledge to a private lender that the U.S. government will repay any portion of loan and/or interest on which a private debtor (beneficiary of the guarantee) defaults. This effectively removes the risk from a loan for the private lender, with the

Unfortunately, interest in many of the broader issues raised seems to fade whenever the immediate problem recedes. This study seeks to extend the dialogue on some of those issues. For instance, the Chrysler Affair spotlighted the uneasy role of the federal government in a mixed public and private economy. To many, the bail-out amounted to changing the economic rules in the middle of the game, a poor precedent which would demoralize efficient firms as well as impede the efficient operation of the economy. Growth, productivity and employment could all suffer in the long run, these people argued. Aid supporters, on the other hand, pointed to the possibly dire consequences of withholding aid, and to the success of an earlier federal loan guarantee to Lockheed Corporation in 1971.

The federal government's role in economic policy has traditionally stopped short of aid to particular firms; when such aid has been awarded, it has usually been directed at whole industries (e.g., the loans to steel companies by the Economic Development Administration) or depressed regions (e.g., programs administered by the Department of Housing and Urban Development) and has been limited to small firms (e.g., the programs operated by the Small Business Administration). Federally supported assistance for a giant private firm such as Chrysler (or Lockheed) is a relatively novel form of government intervention.

Bringing such economic decisions into the public area is an important precedent with potentially significant effects on our political and economic institutions. Moreover, most economists agree that the next decade will be a difficult time, and that there will be further calls for federal assistance.

Problems in the U.S. Economy

Since World War II, the U.S. economy has undergone a dramatic transformation; manufacture of goods is now a smaller proportion of national output than provision of services. In addition, several technological "revolutions" have radically altered a number of sectors, through the widespread application of electronic equipment, miniaturization techniques, computer and information systems, etc. The historic U.S. lead in high-technology industries is now being challenged, particularly by the Japanese. At the same time, some of the more

---

government assuming that risk. Moreover, Treasury backing makes possible very low rates, because of the government's impeccable credit rating, thus further benefiting the borrower. While the government puts out no money initially, it essentially assumes a risk equivalent to that of a direct lender, since it may be called upon to pay loan plus interest at some future date. If the loan guarantee is successful, the government charges an administrative fee and makes a small profit.

In Chrysler's case, guarantees are issued by the Chrysler Loan Guarantee Board, which oversees the loan legislation. Before issuing guarantees, they must find that equal matching funds have been obtained from other sources, and that the government's loan is adequately secured by collateral. The first $500 million in guarantees was approved by the Board in May 1980. Chrysler is actually raising the money by issuing its own notes on the money markets, rather than obtaining it through the banks, because of current high interest rates at banks.

[†]As of March 1, 1981, $1200 million in guarantees had been approved and issued.

mature "core" manufacturing industries in the United States are saddled with aging, inefficient plants and are increasingly vulnerable to import competition. Labor costs in some industries are high enough to constitute a disadvantage in international markets—a situation which is worsened by stagnating productivity growth in the United States. Thus, many people fear that foreign competition threatens to "export jobs." Moreover, the changes in the types of economic activity have had a regional impact, causing relative economic power, as well as population, to begin shifting away from the northeast and midwest, formerly the heartland of industrial production. This development has led to increasing concern over the possible decline of the "frostbelt" and special concern over the fate of the northern industrial cities.

Some Industries in Trouble

For all these reasons, it is feared that, increasingly, vital industries will find themselves in trouble, and that other large firms may fail without some form of assistance. Foreign auto makers continue to increase their share of the U.S. market. The steel industry is not cost-competitive with Japanese manufacturers and must comply with expensive air emissions requirements; yet domestic steel interests seem content to rely on import protection rather than attempting to modernize their plants. Railroading continues to be a troubled industry. Much of the airline industry is highly leveraged (has high debt) and a number of large airlines suffered losses in 1980. Even some relatively young, healthy industries may have difficulties in the decades ahead. The aluminum industry, built on cheap energy in the Northwest, will have to adjust to a new era of high energy prices. The high-technology semiconductor industry faces increasingly tough foreign competition (Schwartz and Choate, 1980).

One financial consulting firm has attempted to develop a system for ranking companies according to their financial vulnerability. Their system, which weights seven key financial ratios, indicates that 5% of Standard & Poor's 400 could be especially vulnerable to a recession or a credit crunch. The list includes a number of large airlines and a variety of other companies (*Business Week*, 1979, 1980).

Loan Guarantees in the Future?

The more strident forecasts of apocalypse just around the corner are no doubt overly pessimistic; an economist would point out that the average bankruptcy is not a total economic loss, since a defunct firm's physical resources continue to exist after the firm itself has failed. Nevertheless, despite the assertions by a number of Congressmen that the Chrysler loan guarantee plan was "not a precedent" (U.S. Congress, 1979a), it appears quite likely that other large corporations and even entire industries will ask for government assistance in the years to come. The possibility that assistance will be granted more and more in the future raises concern that the United States will slide into a system of "welfare for large corporations," but "capitalism for the man on the street."

This analysis will examine the need for a Chrysler bail-out and the desirability of federal loan guarantees for accomplishing that end. The primary focus will be on the broader question of direct federal financial assistance, rather than on the nuances of various financing mechanisms (i.e., direct loans, loan guarantees, etc.). A framework will be developed for weighing the costs and benefits. The various arguments used to justify aid to Chrysler will be scrutinized, and the strengths and weaknesses of existing analyses discussed. The political process surrounding the passage of the legislation will also be examined briefly, and some policy implications inferred.

Finally, some thoughts on future policy, suggested by the Chrysler analysis, will be discussed. These policies include possible conditions to be attached to loan guarantees, bankruptcy as an option, and the proposed institutionalization of a quasi-public lending agency to deal with such situations in the future.

As a caveat, it should be noted that this analysis is written while the Chrysler story is still unfolding. Thus, while some sections are now history, others will no doubt prove embarrassing under the harsh glare of hindsight.*

Chrysler's Plight: A Brief History

Industry-Wide Problems

Chrysler is not unique in the domestic auto industry in experiencing difficult times. Ford Motor Company, for example, lost about $1 billion in 1979 on its domestic operations; because of booming overseas sales, however, it was profitable overall. All the auto companies, however, suffered substantial losses in 1980, as detailed in Table 1. A number of factors have played a part in bringing Detroit to its current precarious position, including costs incurred in meeting regulatory requirements for safety, pollution control and gas mileage; a *nolo contendere* attitude by domestic auto makers toward import domination of the small-car market (until recently); high labor costs; and, more recently, a buying slump caused by the 1980–1981 recession and high credit costs.

By far the most devastating blow to the domestic auto industry was dealt by OPEC; however, American auto makers failed adequately to anticipate the massive shift by the buying public towards a preference for small cars. The inexorable rise in gasoline prices since 1973 and the two gas "crunches" of 1974–1975 and 1979 have made small-car believers out of traditionally gas-guzzling Americans. Even while Detroit auto makers were complaining loudly that government-mandated corporate average fuel economy (CAFE) requirements were forcing them to build cars smaller than consumers wanted, the public's taste swept by them. From 1979 to 1980, for instance, the market share of big cars (full-sized and intermediate) dropped from 42% to 33%

---

*This paper was originally written in May 1980. Where appropriate, facts and figures have been brought up to date as of January 1981. While the underlying economic analysis has not been altered, it is now apparent that the auto industry has failed to recover as quickly as was expected in May and that Chrysler's prospects for survival may be worse than indicated in this article.

Table 1. Historical Market Share and Profits, U.S. Auto Market

Company	Market Share (percentage of U.S. market)						
	1974	1975	1976	1977	1978	1978	1980
GM	41.8	43.4	47.5	46.1	47.7	45.9	46%
Ford	25.0	23.0	22.3	22.8	22.8	20.1	17%
Chrysler	13.6	11.5	12.9	10.9	10.1	9.3	7%
Imports	15.8	18.3	14.8	18.6	17.7	22.0	27%
	Profits ($ millions) ( ) = loss						
GM	950	1151	2902	3337	3507	2900	(763)
Ford	361	323	983	1673	1589	1200	(1600)
Chrysler	(52)	(260)	423	163	(205)	(016)	(1700)

Sources: NHTSA study, Chrysler Operating Plan; Motor Vehicle Manufacturers' Association.

(*Business Week*, 1979, 1980). From 1968 to 1979, the market share of domestic small cars (compacts and subcompacts) rose from 15.6% to 35.1%; imports (mostly subcompacts) rose from 10.7% to 22%. In 1980, the import share ran at about 27%—before 1979, the peak penetration of imports had been 18.5% (National Highway Traffic Safety Administration, 1979). A large part of the reason for this was simply a lack of capacity by domestic manufacturers to meet the demand.

Most industry analysts, moreover, believe that the shift in demand is permanent, not merely an aberration as in the previous small-car boom in the years following the Arab oil embargo.* For one thing, gasoline prices will very likely continue to increase, from about $1.25 today to at least $2.00 by the end of 1983. General Motors, for one, has become a convert and plans to accelerate its shift to production of front wheel drive cars (the most practical design for increasing fuel efficiency while preserving interior space) by two years, to 1983 (*Business Week*, 1979, 1980). Indeed, some analysts predict that consumers will demand an average fuel economy of 27.5 mpg by 1982 (mandated for 1985), and will want 40 mpg by 1990 (*Business Week*, 1979, 1980).

Detroit thus finds itself with a set of products poorly matched to its market; it has significant excess capacity in some market segments, but has too little production capability in the more popular segments. It is reduced to playing a game of catch-up with foreign auto producers who already produce the types of cars Americans want. The industry as a whole plans to spend a whopping $75–80 billion from 1980 to 1985, and perhaps $150 billion over the next 15 years (*Business Week*, 1979, 1980), largely to improve fuel economy. This level of capital spending would constitute an increase of about 50 percent over the historical industry levels. Chrysler's original 1980–1985 Operating Plan called for aggregate capital expenditures totaling $13.6 billion, but that has since been scaled back to $12.5 billion and finally $11.2 billion, as of May 1980

*Maryann Keller, statement before the Senate Banking Committee, October 10, 1979.

(Chrysler Loan Guarantee Board, 1980)—while further revisions to the Operating Plan have been made, the details have not been made public because of the potential adverse publicity caused by projections which fail to be realized. Even with such a massive retooling effort, however, changeover is slow, and imports will very likely keep a 25–30% share of the market through 1985 (*Business Week*, 1979, 1980).

The retooling effort is complicated by the profit structure of domestic manufacturers. Although U.S.-based auto makers produce significant numbers of small cars, their profits are traditionally made on large cars (primarily because of the effective competition of imported cars in the small car segment). One industry observer estimates that GM makes $1,000 profit on a large car, but only $200–300 on a small car (*Business Week*, 1979, 1980).

While big car sales held up, the auto manufacturers could finance their capital expenditures out of big car profits. With the bottom dropping out of the large car market, however, all the auto makers have suffered serious losses in profits and in working capital. Unusual capital spending requirements, coupled with declining in-house cash, are forcing auto makers to borrow significant amounts of money. At least one industry analyst thinks they may have difficulty getting it (Keller, 1980).

The industry's problems have been further exacerbated by high interest rates, tight credit and the 1980 recession. Even under more normal conditions, the auto industry is highly sensitive to shifts in the economy. In an industry with such high capital needs and fixed costs, however, such volatility can be a serious problem. Auto sales in the U.S. market in late 1979 and early 1980 ran at a reasonably healthy level of about 8.3 million units per year. However, the normal spring buying surge failed to materialize, and sales for 1980 as a whole have plummeted to a dismal 6.6 million units, the worst in over a decade (see Table 2). By mid-1980, the industry had shut down indefinitely six of 47 assembly plants and by January 1981 it idled 236,000 workers.

Table 2.   Sales of Passenger Vehicles in the U.S. Auto Market

	1979		1980	
	No. of Units (millions/ yr.)	Percentage of Market	No. of Units (millions/ yr.)	Percentage of Market
Domestic auto makers	8.3	78%	6.6	73%
Foreign auto makers	2.3	22%	2.4	27%
All sales to domestic market	10.6	100%	9.0	100%

In the long run, most industry experts expect auto sales to continue to grow more or less at their historical rates, with all sales increasing to about 12 million units annually by about 1985. There is a danger, however, that domestic manufacturers will be unable to dislodge the foreign competition even after tooling up to produce small cars, since consumers may continue to believe that foreign cars provide better gas mileage or are better made.

The Problems of the Chrysler Corporation

The Chrysler Corporation is the weak sister in a troubled industry. Its problems are more severe than those of Ford and GM, and are, in some respects, unique. While regulatory requirements have cost all auto makers some R&D and retooling effort, Chrysler has claimed that such regulations have had a disproportionate impact on it because of its smaller size and that they are a major cause of its present troubles.

However, a look at Chrysler's history reveals that many of its problems date from before the period when the industry became heavily regulated (Keller, 1980). Long known for its outstanding engineering, the firm shifted its emphasis to marketing and sales in the 1950s. Troubles began in 1953, when Chrysler introduced new model lines which were unpopular. In 1955, Chrysler began a major program of plant improvement and expansion, and attempted to diversify its nameplates so as to compete product-for-product with GM and Ford. This strategy also proved unfortunate, as Chrysler found that its lack of size and vertical integration prevented it from competing on an equal basis. By 1957, the company had borrowed enough to give it a debt-to-equity ratio of .29, as compared to .07 for GM and .09 for Ford.

In the 1960s the company carved out a strong position in the compact car market, as well as in the light truck and van segment. At the same time, however, Chrysler attempted to follow the lead of Ford and GM into the international market, but only succeeded in purchasing unsuccessful foreign operations which were a net financial drain. While all three domestic auto makers used the profitable U.S. market as a cash "cow" to finance foreign investments, Ford, in contrast to Chrysler, was successful enough that foreign profits are currently earning enough to "carry" unprofitable domestic operations.

In the 1970s Chrysler introduced several ill-timed new models, worsening its position: updated intermediates were introduced in 1971, as demand shifted back to full-size cars; new large cars were introduced in 1974, at the height of the energy crisis; and new intermediates came out in 1975, while the market was swinging back to full-sized cars. In 1974–75, Chrysler laid off 30% of its work force and 80% of its engineering staff, which led to a large number of problems and recalls with its new Volare/Aspen model. By 1975, Chrysler's debt–equity proportion had reached .44. Despite the increasing debt and declining profits, Chrysler continued to pay dividends until the third quarter of 1979, long after dividends were financially justifiable.

Thus, Chrysler's decline is largely due to a series of management errors and poorly timed product introductions. One oft-cited example of outdated management technique has been Chrysler's practice of building autos without explicit dealer orders. This practice (recently abandoned) resulted in a company inventory in 1979 of 90,000 unwanted vehicles, worth over $700 million (*The Wall Street Journal*). Chrysler's attempts to go multinational and to compete product-for-product with the other auto manufacturers have undermined its financial structure and its manufacturing efficiency. Chrysler has delayed modernizing its domestic plants, so that it now has significantly higher production costs than Ford or GM. Most of these extra costs are not due to any inherent lack of economies of scale, although a lack of vertical integration has played a part.

With a $1 billion loss in 1979 and large projected losses for 1980, Chrysler was unable to persuade its bankers to extend it new credit. Indeed, many banks had written off their previous loans as losses. Without large infusions of capital, however, Chrysler would have been unable to modernize so as to compete effectively in the marketplace of tomorrow. Thus, it was argued, federal aid was (and is) needed to avert a potential catastrophe.

Should the Federal Government Bail Out Chrysler?

The Market Failure Rationale for Government Intervention

Arguments abound as to why the government should bail out Chrysler. Aid supporters point to past government regulation, potential U.S. job losses, subsidies to foreign auto makers and many other possible rationales for public action. As a threshold question, however, it may well be asked why the government should even consider bailing out a private firm. Are not private markets supposed to allocate resources to their most efficient use? The usual economic rationale for overruling the decisions of "the market" is to point to some sort of "market failure" or situation in which private decisions may not reflect the best interests of society. Market failures may involve social externalities or public goods, or they may exist because of other institutional imperfections such as poor information, factor (labor or capital) immobility, monopoly or union power, taxes, regulations, etc. In such cases, government intervention can often promote efficiency. Distributional equity is another important social goal and rationale for intervention, quite distant from economic efficiency considerations.

Most of the rationales proposed to justify intervention to salvage Chrysler can be interpreted as one or another allegation of market failure. For instance, it may be that private financial markets are not allocating credit optimally in the case of Chrysler, perhaps because the banks are risk-averse and fear the consequences of such a large corporate failure. Subsidization of imports by foreign governments could also be a source of inefficiency, justifying some sort of compensatory action by the United States.

A body of literature holds that firms often do not face the true social and economic consequences of plant closings, which may devastate a community; thus firms may close down plants too readily.* Moreover, since, in practice, capital and especially labor are not perfectly mobile, the collapse of a giant firm such as Chrysler would inevitably lead to a potentially severe economic dislocation until the economy finds ways to reabsorb the idled workers and capital. Traditional static equilibrium analysis tends to downplay such costs. Further, even if the economy as a whole recovers, some regions, such as Detroit, may be unable to attract replacement industries and thus could sustain much longer-term losses.

Finally, Chrysler may be involved in the production of a public good, so that its collapse would entail greater social than private loss. For instance, it could be argued that the United States would suffer a national security loss if it became dependent on foreign sources for supply of a vital transportation link.

Many of the arguments used to justify federal aid to Chrysler postulate some sort of market failure that is alleged to have *caused* Chrysler's near-bankruptcy through no fault of the firm's. We will turn now to an examination of those purported market imperfections. We will then examine more closely the possible *consequences* of a Chrysler collapse.

The Causes of Chrysler's Plight: Who "Lost" Chrysler?

In the (often fruitless and irrelevant) debate over who "lost" Chrysler, several leading arguments emerged as to why the company itself was not at fault and therefore deserved assistance. These included:

The Regulatory Burden Argument

The "Energy Burden" Argument

The Capital Market Failure Argument

The Import Subsidization Argument.

The Regulatory Burden: Government to Blame?[†]

Chrysler President Lee Iacocca contended in testimony that government regulations were an important reason for Chrysler's financial troubles, saying they were "tremendously expensive" and that "the smaller company...must bear a heavier per unit cost than its larger competitors." If Chrysler had indeed been injured more by regulation than other firms, there might be an equity argu-

---

*For a more detailed consideration of the market-failure argument for public intervention, see Vaughan and Bearse (1980).

[†]See Appendix 2, available from the author, for a more extended discussion of the regulatory issues; also see relevant articles listed in the Bibliography.

ment for equalizing the burden. However, Chrysler failed to demonstrate any such disproportionate impact despite company-sponsored studies which argued (without data) that such a regulatory "penalty" existed. Since all auto makers, including importers, are required to meet substantially the same regulatory standards, there is little reason to provide aid to Chrysler on this basis.

Moreover, federal regulations on safety, pollution and fuel economy embody a public decision to pursue certain goals; given the public's decision to correct for certain private market failures, the cost of social externalities are properly charged to the producers of those social costs. Further, the idea that regulatory compliance costs can account for any large portion of Chrysler's losses is absurd. Even using Chrysler's assumptions, the differential burden of regulation could have totaled only $137 million in 1979; yet Chrysler sustained losses of $1.1 billion. Most other firms are not compensated for the expenses incurred in meeting safety or pollution requirements.

It has been charged that the federal government exacerbated the auto industry's plight by maintaining a system of petroleum price controls which encouraged large-car purchasing and thus interfered with an early wave of attempted small car introductions in 1973–1974. It is not clear, however, that controls have actually been successful in depressing prices at the pump. Even if controls did lower gasoline prices, they certainly did not insulate consumers entirely from OPEC price increases. Thus, the impact of price controls on automobile demand is rather unclear.

A somewhat different argument charging government culpability for the auto industry's problems is that federal monetary policies have resulted in high credit costs, thus depressing auto sales. This policy, however, is undertaken for the long-term benefit of the economy, including the auto industry. Many business men would decry (and perhaps be injured financially by) a looser monetary policy, although lower interest rates would probably aid the auto industry in the short run.

If the government is called upon to aid Chrysler as a form of redress for past injuries, it should be noted that many government policies and regulations have benefited the auto industry. Indeed, it can be argued that federally mandated Corporate Average Fuel Economy (CAFE) requirements, strongly resisted by the auto industry, have placed the U.S. auto manufacturers in a better competitive position than they would otherwise have been in. The multibillion dollar Highway Trust Fund, as well as state highway programs, constitute a huge indirect subsidy to the auto industry. The highly concentrated auto industry has not been the target of antitrust proceedings, although equally concentrated industries have been less fortunate. Finally, it is important to realize that an argument which justifies government aid on the basis of real or imagined past injury is essentially an equity argument. It says that the government "owes" aid to Chrysler, not that such aid is a sound or intelligent investment of public monies.

The Energy Burden: Nobody to Blame?

It was sometimes argued that a special "energy burden" made it necessary for the federal government to step in to help beleaguered companies with the "one-time" cost of transition. Aid opponents, on the other hand, reversed this argument, charging that Chrysler had long had its head in the sand and should have anticipated the market shifts.

From a policy perspective, it is irrelevant whether Chrysler's troubles were of its own making or whether the company was a victim of circumstance. Insuring a firm against any failure which, according to some determination, was not its "fault," is carrying government responsibility to an absurd extreme. Anticipation of future market conditions is a central aspect of any business and the government would only interfere with the efficient functioning of the marketplace if it prevented the failure of firms which guessed incorrectly. Since the government is not alleged to have caused the energy crisis, no equity argument for aid equivalent to the regulatory burden argument can logically be made. Moreover, acceptance of the "victim of circumstance" argument could have very broad implications throughout the economy and would tend to promote inefficiency, reward incompetence, and discourage sound planning and decision making by private firms. Such a rationale for aid to Chrysler must be rejected as spurious and disingenuous.

Failure of the Capital Markets?

Is it possible that the banks have made a mistake in not properly appreciating Chrysler's potential? Alternatively, are they excessively cautious because of the large risk or perhaps unable to lend because of a general credit shortage?

The first argument is unpersuasive. Informed observers agree that Chrysler's horizon is cloudy at best. A number of reputable auto analysts (e.g., Maryann Keller of Kidder Peabody & Co., and David Healy of Drexel, Burnham, Lambert, Inc.) are pessimistic about Chrysler's prospects even with a loan guarantee and advise their clients not to invest in the company. Chrysler's own optimistic recovery plan, first submitted in 1979, has been radically revised several times due to the bearish 1980–1981 auto market.

The notion that Chrysler's bankers are deterred by the sheer size of the risk is also unconvincing because of the extensive risk-pooling arrangements among Chrysler's banks. As of December 1979, Chrysler Corporation's debt of over $1.1 billion was shared among a total of 176 banks; Chrysler Financial, a subsidiary considered sounder than the parent, had an additional debt of $1.9 billion spread among 143 banks. Chrysler's lead bank, Manufacturers Hanover Trust, had only $30 million outstanding in loans to Chrysler. No bank was endangered by a Chrysler collapse.*

Nor does the "credit crunch" argument explain Chrysler's forlorn situation. Chrysler was first denied credit in mid-1979, before there was a real credit

---

*John McGillicudy, testimony before the Senate Banking Committee, October 10, 1979.

squeeze. In addition, Chrysler has access to world capital markets and can thus circumvent any regional tight credit situation, as is demonstrated by its European and Japanese lines of credit.

Thus a failure of the capital markets does not explain Chrysler's inability to obtain credit. The company was simply a poor risk by any standard. As John McGillicudy, President of Chrysler's lead bank, said, "[banks] aren't in the business of lending money when we don't expect to get paid back."

Foreign Subsidization the Culprit?

Foreign governments, it is argued, subsidize their auto manufacturers, making it necessary for the United States to preserve jobs through countervailing subsidization. It is indeed ironic that some European auto manufacturers only exist today because they were protected by their governments from an export-minded Detroit earlier in the century. The most cogent argument against reviving such policies of trade protectionism is the danger of retaliation. If all countries pursue neo-mercantilist tariff and subsidy policies, it results in economic losses for all.

Government promotion of its national industries, moreover, presents real difficulties in an age of multinational corporations. Chrysler imports many of its best-selling autos from Japan's Mitsubishi and buys all the engines for its popular Omni/Horizon line from Germany's Volkswagen. Volkswagen has opened a second auto assembly plant in the United States. Honda and Nissan of Japan have both announced plans for U.S. assembly plants. A consistent policy of promoting U.S. industry would have to discriminate against Chrysler imports and Omni engines, while favoring domestic operations of foreign-based companies.

Chrysler's own behavior provides an illustration of the inherent problems in thinking of multinationals as "national champions": even as the 1979 Congressional debates over aid were reaching their most frenetic pitch, and Chrysler was in the process of phasing out several U.S. plants, the company announced plans to build a new engine plant in Mexico. In an even more striking display of *panache*, Chrysler's ubiquitous President Iacocca has called for tariffs on imports, *excepting* Chrysler's own Mitsubishi imports. Such policies have no consistency, except insofar as they would serve Chrysler's interests. They aid neither American consumers nor American workers and they interfere with energy conservation efforts.

Nevertheless, despite attempts by the OECD countries to promote free trade through the General Agreement on Trades and Tariffs (GATT), and despite the inconsistencies inherent in subsidization policies, many international trade experts think that protectionism is on the increase (*The Wall Street Journal*). The large Japanese auto makers operate in concert with their government in the unique Japanese government-business "partnership," which has come to be called "Japan, Inc." Although there are no subsidies one can point to, the system does provide favored businesses, such as exporters Toyota and Nissan, with banking privileges and other advantages.* In any meaningful sense of the word, these advantages constitute a form of subsidy. Can the United States afford to ignore such pressures? The answer depends upon the consequences of subsidization policies.

Subsidization of our imports by foreign governments benefits U.S. consumers in the short run. The only real dangers of such policies arise if the U.S. economy is too inflexible to adjust, and jobs and output are lost, or if foreign producers once established are able to secure and exploit a position of market power by charging monopoly prices and blocking entry by new firms. Job losses and overweening market power are potential problems whether or not they are caused by foreign subsidization; they will subsequently be explored at great length.

Public Policy Should Be Based on Potential Consequences of a Chrysler Collapse

While some of the preceding arguments point to possible market failures, none of them can justify government intervention to aid Chrysler. The economic perspective on public policy suggests the irrelevance of sunken costs for decision making. Blame or responsibility for Chrysler's situation is unimportant, except insofar as it provides guidance as to what to expect in the future. The relevant policy question is whether or not the outcome determined by private market forces is socially disadvantageous. While the answer to this question depends on the existence and magnitude of private market failures, it focuses our attention on the consequences, rather than the causes, of the problem. Upon examining the consequences of granting or withholding federal aid, another set of potential market failures emerges that turns out to be much more central than the alleged market failure "causes" in evaluating the federal aid question. We turn now to an examination of the impact of a possible Chrysler bankruptcy.

The Consequences of a Chrysler Bankruptcy: A Cost/Benefit Approach

The merits of granting aid to Chrysler rest on the likelihood and the potential consequences of a Chrysler bankruptcy, as well as on the likely effectiveness of a loan guarantee program. The important efficiency, distributional, and development issues can be examined through a social cost/benefit framework, which evaluates the opportunity cost of a loan guarantee by projecting the consequences of the various possible alternatives. To develop this "expected utility" evaluation of the desirability of loan guarantees, we will adopt an explicitly national perspective. We will then turn to an examination of the likelihood of bankruptcy and liquidation without the loan and of the likelihood that a federal loan will succeed.

*John Wilson, Vice President for Economics, Bank of America, personal interview.

Finally we will make a direct evaluation of the probable social cost of a Chrysler collapse, as well as of the social cost of the government loan guarantees. This latter section will examine a number of potential market rigidities and externalities which might cause a Chrysler collapse to have a greater impact than it would in a more "ideal" economy. In examining the costs of *granting* a loan guarantee we will examine the potential long-run impact on efficiency and development as well as the short-run budgetary effects. Finally, we will combine the estimates of costs and benefits with the rough probability estimates already developed and generate an estimate of the "expected social utility" of a loan guarantee program.

Analytic Perspective

What constitutes a cost or a benefit depends on one's frame of reference. At least three points of view have been implicitly or explicitly advanced during the debate over Chrysler, defining whose interests ought to be considered in this decision. All three perspectives—government, regional, and national—are important and will be considered in this analysis. No one perspective, however, should be viewed in isolation.

A cost/benefit approach from the point of view of the federal government was one of the more common perspectives used. For instance, it was maintained by aid proponents that the cost to the federal government, in the event of a Chrysler bankruptcy and liquidation, was likely to be far greater than the amount of aid being contemplated. One widely quoted statistic was the projection by the Federal Pension Benefit Guaranty Corporation (PBGC) that it could be liable for as much as $1.1 billion in unfunded pension obligations to Chrysler employees, in the event of a shutdown. This amount, however, could have been financed through increased employer premiums rather than general revenues.* Another major cost to the federal government in the event of a shutdown would have been an estimated $1 billion in increased unemployment benefit payments in the first year. Increased unemployment benefit costs would also have placed many State Trust Funds, already in debt to the federal government, in severe financial straits. Potential federal tax loss was estimated to be as high as $500 million in the year following bankruptcy (Department of the Treasury, 1979). A fairly realistic estimate of total federal losses in the first year of bankruptcy was the $2.75 billion figure calculated by the Department of the Treasury (1979).

Moreover, since the federal government has preferred creditor status, it is unlikely that it will actually lose money by guaranteeing loans to Chrysler. The loan guarantee, completely off-budget and unlikely to result in federal losses, might thus appear an attractive investment to government budgeters. Government cost, however, is not synonymous with social cost. Pension, unemployment and welfare expenditures, which appear as costs on the government's books, are in fact only transfers of wealth from a broader social perspective.

*Statement by Robert Nagle, Executive Director of Pension Benefit Guaranty Corporation, Senate Banking Committee, October 10, 1979.

A regional perspective was another point of view which informed a number of the analyses done on the potential impact of a Chrysler collapse. A study by the Northeast/Midwest Institute emphasized the disproportionate effect on the northern states (Tropper and Adams, 1979). Witnesses before the Senate and House Banking Committees described the dramatic effect a bankruptcy might have on Michigan and on Detroit in particular. Chrysler lobbyists exploited this concern by circulating lists of Chrysler and "Chrysler-dependent" workers to members of Congress whose districts might be affected.*

From a national point of view, regional impact is important primarily as an equity consideration. Thus, while it is important to safeguard the federal purse and to note potentially severe impacts on particular regions or groups, it is only through a comprehensive national perspective that such effects can be properly weighed and placed in context. The analysis to follow will employ such a perspective.

Forecasting the Future: What Will a Loan Guarantee Buy?

Evaluation of the costs and benefits of a loan guarantee requires a projection of the two alternative scenarios—loan and no loan. One should not conclude too readily that government aid will ensure Chrysler's survival, or that a lack of aid would lead inevitably to a total shutdown.

Bankruptcy Likely Without a Loan

Much of the Congressional discussion assumed that if the government were to deny the loan request, Chrysler would inevitably go bankrupt, put its assets on the auction block and turn its employees out on the street. There were, however, other potential options:

Cut the Fat

Despite its $1.1 billion losses in 1979 and 1980, its outdated facilities and high debt load, Chrysler still possesses a number of unencumbered assets, potentially valuable to other firms, which could be sold to finance its capital investment and pay off its debt. In 1979 and early 1980, Chrysler sold off many of its assets, including its Marine Division, Chrysler of Australia and Chrysler of Argentina; negotiations for the sale of Chrysler Finance Co. have so far come to naught. However, Chrysler has additional salable assets, including profitable domestic plants. Of course, selling off its most attractive assets is a dubious way for a company to regain its profitability. Whether or not such auto-cannibalism would enable Chrysler to survive is not clear.

Chrysler critics contend that the company's best course would be to pare back its operations and concentrate on producing only a few types of vehicles. Chrysler's spokespersons respond that such plans are unrealistic (Chrysler

---

*Senate Testimony, Hearings before the Banking Committee, October 10, 1979.

Corporation, 1979d). Small cars alone, they argue, do not produce enough profit because of their low margins. Large cars alone would run afoul of federal (CAFE) fuel economy standards (although it would now appear that anemic large-car demand rules this option out in any case). Trucks, they maintain, are a large and profitable segment of their business (although demand has softened considerably recently). Dropping truck production, moreover, would sacrifice the substantial cost benefits resulting from the interchangeability of parts between cars and trucks.

Dubious industry analysts, however, point out that helmsman Iacocca's reputation is based on product development and marketing skill, not management or finance. Automotive management consultant Robert J. Orsini believes that Iacocca has failed to make the cuts necessary in excess parts and assembly capacity (*Business Week*, 1979, 1980). Many observers note that Iacocca is so wedded to the idea of Chrysler as a full-line producer that he would very likely quit rather than manage the company through a radical reorganization and cutback (*Business Week*, 1979, 1980). Yet it is inevitable that, with 1979 losses of $1.1 billion and greater losses in 1980, serious cutbacks will have to be made even with federal loan guarantees

Merger Not a Live Possibility

Another possibility short of bankruptcy would be merger with a foreign auto maker. A cash-rich foreign manufacturer would be able to finance Chrysler's ambitious modernization and retooling plans, while benefiting from Chrysler's existing marketing network and brand loyalty. In January 1980, Treasury Secretary Miller (head of the Chrysler Loan Guarantee Board) stated his belief that Chrysler must, in the long run, attract a merger or takeover offer if the firm is to avoid failure.

Does Bankruptcy Necessarily Mean Liquidation?

It appeared in December 1979 that bankruptcy would be a likely eventuality without a loan. The depressed auto sales of 1980, had they been anticipated, would have made bankruptcy a near certainty. Even if Chrysler had declared bankruptcy or been forced into it by creditors, however, it was not certain that liquidation would result. An alternative would have been to attempt a reorganization of the company under Chapter 11 of the newly revised bankruptcy statutes. The new laws are supposed to make it easier for a company to survive. Experts such as professors Vern Countryman of Harvard, David Epstein of the University of Arkansas* and Attorney Murray Drabkin, a Washington bankruptcy specialist (*Business Week*, 1979, 1980), pointed to the significant advantages of a Chapter 11 reorganization: old debt is subordinated to postbankruptcy debt, making capital easier to obtain; disadvantageous

---

*Testimony before the Senate Banking Committee, October 10, and House Subcommittee on Economic Stabilization, October 18–26, 1979.

contracts can be rejected; and the prebankruptcy management may even be retained. The procedure is intended to make it easier to restructure and pay off debts while holding off creditors.

Proceeding with a bankruptcy would have the further advantage, according to some, of forcing Chrysler to undertake the drastic retrenchment which it really needed. Countryman and Epstein, moreover, both recommended that the government allow bankruptcy to proceed and provide loan guarantees after bankruptcy, if necessary. This was the government's role in the Penn Central bankruptcy.

An equally distinguished cast, however, agrees with the official Chrysler position that a bankruptcy would almost inevitably result in the company's liquidation.* The nature of the automobile as a product, they argue, would make it impossible for the company to survive under the cloud of bankruptcy. Automobile purchasers buy with the expectation of many years' access to service, parts and company backing; lack of consumer confidence in Chrysler's continued viability would, so the argument goes, cause a precipitous decline in sales and thus doom any reorganization effort. Partial evidence for this view was supplied by the deterioration of Chrysler's sales in the last quarter of 1979, when its financial troubles became widely known. Chrysler's market share in this period dropped from 12% to under 9%.

On the other hand, it may have been that Chrysler's customers had already discounted the value of its merchandise, so that sales would not necessarily have dropped precipitously if bankruptcy had been declared. Until and unless a bankruptcy occurs, the outcome must remain problematic. Thus the bankruptcy/liquidation scenario, while not necessarily the inevitable or even most likely consequence of withholding a loan guarantee, cannot be ruled out as a possible worst case.

Bankruptcy Possible Even with Aid

In the long run, demand for Chrysler cars will determine the company's fate. While Chrysler's market share has been slipping for years, the company's recovery plan predicts an optimistic resurgence, from 9% to 12% of the domestic market. In 1980, moreover, the entire market has taken a plunge worse than that during the auto recession of 1974–1975. Chrysler's declining share of a declining market bodes ill for its recovery prospects. Can it survive and regain its market share in the years ahead?

Booz, Allen, and Hamilton, management consultants, performed a sensitivity analysis of Chrysler's plan, varying Chrysler's assumptions of total demand, small car market share, Chrysler market share and projected variable margins per car (Booz, Allen, and Hamilton, 1979). This analysis, which concluded that Chrysler's projections left too little room for error or adversity, was a major basis for expanding the size of the loan package from $1.5 billion to $3.5

*See, for example, "Expert Testimony before Senate Banking Committee," October 10, p. 355.

billion.* Booz–Allen projected that Chrysler would need $2.1 billion in outside funding, and recommended contingency funding of an additional $700 million, for a total requirement of $2.8 billion. With the benefit of hindsight, it can be seen that Booz–Allen's "downside risk" estimates for 1980 have proven *too optimistic*, thus casting increasing doubt on Chrysler's continued viability even with a loan. Table 3 presents some of Chrysler's and Booz–Allen's projections, some comparative historical data and projections for 1980, based on the first 4 months of the year.

On the other hand, the Loan Guarantee Board, in approving the issuance of federal guarantees in May 1980 (more recently than the Booz–Allen study) concluded that Chrysler's survival prospects were reasonable, despite the dismal 1980 auto sales. The board noted the changing auto market structure, with GM enjoying strong sales and good profit margins on its X-car (Chevy Citation), similar to Chrysler's K-car, which was marketed in late 1980. The board members, however, acknowledged in testimony that their finding as to Chrysler's long-run viability was a "close call."†

Thus, the $1.5 billion loan guarantee is no assurance of Chrysler's long-term survival. The company will still have to repay its heavy debt load, although it will benefit from lower interest rates on the government-insured portion of its debt. Moreover, it inspires little confidence in the stock market or in the financial markets, who do not wish to lend Chrysler additional money even with the federal government insuring part of the risk. In sum, Chrysler could quite conceivably go bankrupt within a few years; in that case, the loan guarantee would have bought, at most, a more orderly transition—and, at the least, a mere delay of the event.

The Costs of a Chrysler Collapse

In a textbook economy, the bankruptcy and liquidation of a single firm would be practically costless because the firm's valuable resources would be quickly reallocated to other uses. In the real-life economy, however, the collapse of a giant firm is an economic shock that can cause severe short-run losses in the form of higher unemployment and lower output. These losses result because resources are slow to move to new uses and laborers and capitalists are slow to adjust their behavior. This inflexibility can be regarded as a type of market imperfection potentially justifying public intervention. There may, in addition, be longer-run economic costs if, for example, new capital investment fails to come into the affected area and laborers are unwilling or unable to migrate to areas where jobs are more plentiful. Thus, the major potential costs to be examined are the following:

---

*The original $1.5 billion package would have included federal loan guarantees of $750,000, and equal matching funds from other sources. The final plan increased the government share to $1.5 billion, to be contingent on an additional $2 billion from other sources.

†Chrysler was in an even more marginal financial situation in January 1981, as the Loan Guarantee Board considered granting another $400 million in guarantees.

Table 3. Market Size and Market Share Assumptions (Chrysler; Booz–Allen; Actual)

Source	1977	1978	1979	1980	1981	1982	1983	1984	1985
				Market Size—Millions of Passenger Vehicles Sold in U.S.					
Chrysler operating plan				10.5	11.1	11.2	11.4	11.7	11.9
Booz–Allen contingency				9.0	11.0	12.1	10.8	11.7	12.3
Actual	11.0	11.1	10.4	9.0					
				Market Share—Percentage of U.S. Market					
Chrysler: 1980–1985 operating plan				10.2	11.1	11.6	11.8	12.1	12.4
Booz–Allen contingency				10.0	10.8	11.2	11.7	11.6	11.8
Actual	10.9	10.1	9.3	7.0					
		Historical					Projection		

Sources: Booz-Allen Historical Study, Chrysler Operating Plan, WSJ, Motor Vehicle Manufacturers' Association.

Loss of output and employment, including

short-run transitional effects,

long-run costs, and

distributional and regional impacts.

We will also examine some social externalities and public goods which society might lose if Chrysler were to liquidate. These potential social costs include

loss of competition in the auto industry,

loss of production vital to the national security, and

loss of socially valuable research and development (R&D) work.

Output and Employment

The consequences of a Chrysler collapse have often been exaggerated. It was assumed that the loan guarantee, if it ensured Chrysler's survival, would virtually guarantee the jobs of Chrysler's employees. Many aid boosters failed to acknowledge that Chrysler would be forced to cut costs even with a loan, and insisted on comparing Chrysler, as of mid-1979, with the stark specter of a total collapse. In truth, Chrysler would have been forced to lay off workers and close some facilities with or without the loan. In December 1979, at the height of the frenzied official debates over the loan guarantee, Chrysler had already laid off about 30,000 workers out of a total work force of 140,000. By January 1981 the number of Chrysler workers employed had dropped to 75,000, with about 47,000 on indefinite lay-off. Nevertheless, estimates of the benefits of bailing Chrysler out continued to be based on studies which assumed that Chrysler's continued operation meant continued full employment. Such comparisons clearly overstated the benefits of a loan.

Moreover, the more pessimistic projections tended to ignore the reemployment which would take place at Ford and GM in the event of a Chrysler collapse. The domestic auto industry as a whole had laid off 237,000 workers (31% of the 1978 work force), either indefinitely or temporarily, as of January 1981 (*The Wall Street Journal*). This figure actually understates the loss in employment, because a certain number of workers is dropped from the lay-off rolls after a period of time and become officially unemployed with no chance of recall. Most of these *are* Ford and GM workers. An equivalent excess of plant and capital equipment exists in the industry. Thus, if Chrysler were to shut down, the rest of the industry would be capable of filling the void—especially if demand remains at its lethargic 1980 levels. Chrysler workers themselves would probably not be rehired, since laid-off workers of other firms would have priority for any new jobs at those companies.

Which firms (and workers) stand to gain business from a Chrysler failure? Most of the slack would be taken up by other domestic manufacturers, who produce the same sorts of autos that Chrysler does. The major exception would be in the subcompact market segment, where domestic capacity is limited and foreign auto makers could be expected to fill the gap. Table 4 details the excess

Table 4. If Chrysler Shut Down, Could Ford and GM Pick Up the Chrysler Segments of the Market?[a]

Market Segment by Chrysler Body Size (small, large)	Chrysler Sales Mid-1979 (in thousands)	Excess Capacity at Ford and GM in These Segments	Any Leftover Units, Which Would Not Be Picked up Domestically?
L-Body (Omni)	307	81	226
F-Body	302	287	15
M, SX	263	430	
R-Body	134	514	
Pickups	154	814	
Vans	93	368	

[a] 1979 figures; see Anderson *et al.* (1979).

capacity at Ford and GM in the various Chrysler body sizes in 1979; with production way down in 1980, excess capacity was even greater than this table indicates.

It may be objected that demand for autos would not remain constant, but would decline if Chrysler were to go bankrupt. However, even if all Chrysler workers were to lose their jobs in the short run, the effect on national output would not be significant. With aggregate demand little changed, it is unlikely that demand for autos would be much affected either. Demand for autos may be quite sensitive to aggregate economic shifts and to energy prices, but is unlikely to be greatly affected by the failure of a single corporation.

Can we be sure that other auto makers would gear up quickly to meet the demand? While there might be some delay or hesitation by manufacturers who waited to see what happened to the market, such delay would probably not be significant (perhaps only a matter of a few months). Most importantly, excess capacity currently exists in many market segments, and little start-up time would be required. Idle plants and laborers are an expensive drain on the resources of auto manufacturing firms, only too gladly dispensed with if production were to be justified by demand. Moreover, increased cash flow is badly needed by domestic manufacturers, so as to help finance the industry's large capital investment needs (*Business Week*, 1979, 1980).

Thus the major effect of a Chrysler collapse would be to shift unemployment around, rather than to create more of it. So long as an industry has excess capacity which cannot be transferred easily to other uses, the existence of idle resources is not necessarily evidence of waste.

The economic impact of a Chrysler collapse would also be somewhat mitigated by the likely continued operation of certain facilities which are profitable on their own and thus attractive to other auto makers. A study by the Transportation Systems Center of the Department of Transportation identified two to four such plants (out of 40-odd), employing 6,000 to 12,000 workers, which fall into this category as of 1979 (Anderson et al., 1979). As time goes on and Chrysler modernizes its physical plant, more of its facilities will become attractive to potential purchasers. The reason that more plants might not be attractive to other automakers is that many facilities are integrated across product lines (i.e., one plant makes transmissions for several different lines of cars), thus making it difficult to operate a single plant profitably without operating the entire network. Additionally, many Chrysler facilities are outdated and need to be retooled. Many auto manufacturers might find it more attractive to build a new plant from scratch than to purchase and renovate a 50-year-old Chrysler plant. On the other hand, many plants possess value merely as sites, and could attract auto or other industrial manufacturers on that basis alone (Anderson et al., 1979). Thus, there is unlikely to be any long-term "capital cost" associated with a Chrysler collapse.

Several analyses were conducted to identify the short-run costs of a Chrysler collapse.* These studies compared the macroeconomic effects of a Chrysler failure with a baseline case in which Chrysler survived. All the estimates made some assumption as to the amount of direct output and employment lost, estimated an additional level of secondary "multiplier" effects on the economy and made some assumption as to the amount of time required for capital to be reallocated and labor reabsorbed. These projections are summarized in Table 5.

Unfortunately, three of the four studies assumed unrealistically optimistic "base cases" (no bankruptcy).† In addition, the studies concentrated on providing point estimates or best guesses, with little indication as to the likely range of error. The most widely quoted study, by Data Resources, Inc. (DRI), is almost certainly too pessimistic with its projection of unemployment losses of 500,000 and GNP losses of $8 billion resulting from a bankruptcy (Data Resources, Inc., 1979). The DRI study assumed that Chrysler survival would result in continued direct employment of 137,000 persons, while failure would result in a total shutdown. In fact, Chrysler, throughout most of 1980, employed fewer than 80,000 active workers, and at least 6,000 to 12,000 of these would probably continue working even if liquidation took place; by early 1981, Chrysler employment had slipped slightly to 75,000 workers. The multipliers, of course, magnify these errors.

The study conducted by the Department of the Treasury can be regarded as a reasonable "best guess" of the effects of a bankruptcy and liquidation. This study assumed that the only net output loss results from that portion of Chrysler production captured by overseas producers (as well as secondary multiplier effects). Unemployment loss was calculated via a simple Okun's Law relationship between GNP and employment (a 1% increase in unemployment

---

*Four studies: Anderson, Treasury, Chase, and Data Resources, Inc.
†Appendix 4, available from the author, details these studies and their assumptions.

Table 5. Summary of Economic Forecasts of Chrysler Shutdown[a]

Forecaster	Scenario	GNP loss ($ billions)			Employment loss (thousands of workers)		
		1979	1980	1981	1979	1980	1981
DRI[b] (GNP in 1972 $)	Survive (Baseline)	1412.5	1429.7	1482.0	96,500	96,900	98,900
	Fail (Loss)	−2.0	−8.0	−5.3	0	−500	−400
Chase[c] (GNP in 1972 $)	Survive (B.L.)	1415.7	1410.9	1457.3	88,390	88,220	90,070
	Fail (Loss)	−0.4	−1.7	−0.7	−50	−170	−90
Transp. Systems Ctr., DOT[b]	Fail (Loss)		−33.0			−290 to 345	
Treasury[b]	Fail (Loss)		−4.0	−6.0		−75	−100

[a] Appendix 4, available from the author, provides detailed assumptions.
[b] Assumed full shutdown.
[c] Assumed partial shutdown.

corresponds to a 3% decrease in GNP). It is possible that this approach underestimates the cost of transition somewhat, since the adjustments by other domestic auto makers would probably not be immediate. On the other hand, it is quite possible that some manufacturer could purchase Chrysler's Belvidere assembly plant, which produces subcompact Omnis and Horizons, and resume production of subcompacts within a short time—perhaps six months or a year. In this case, there would be little effective increase in import penetration and losses to the U.S. economy would be lower than estimated.

Finally, it should be noted that the longer bankruptcy is staved off, the less severe are its effects in any one period. As Chrysler streamlines and modernizes its operations, plants are inevitably closed and workers laid off—permanently. At the same time, improved facilities geared to today's market become more attractive to potential purchasers. Thus bankruptcy of a smaller Chrysler, with less dead weight, is easier for the economy to absorb if it should still occur. While the direct economic impacts of such a phase-out would be no less than in the immediate bankruptcy scenario (they would merely be spread out more over time), it is possible that the economy would be able to adjust more easily to it, thus lessening the total indirect macroeconomic impact. Arguments can also be made, however, that macroimpacts are *reduced* by swallowing the bitter pill all at once.

Distributional Effects

Who would bear the economic and social costs of a Chrysler collapse? Unfortunately, Chrysler facilities are heavily concentrated in a few communities. The impact on Detroit and on some smaller "one-factory" towns is likely to be acute.

The Transportation Systems Center study painstakingly attempted to estimate these local effects. This study used two somewhat different approaches in analyzing the effects of a liquidation: a head count of workers and communities affected, and a regional multiplier analysis which estimated the indirect job loss for all direct manufacturing job losses. Both approaches yielded much the same result (see Table 6). However, this study has several flaws which bias its estimates upwards. It, too, calculated impacts assuming a nonbankruptcy base case which was overly sanguine.*

Moreover, the study ignores compensatory reemployment by other auto makers. This is too strong an assumption, even for an estimation of regional and local effects, since Ford and GM employ people in many of the same areas in which Chrysler has plants (see Table 6). For instance, a cause for particular concern is the potentially severe impact of a shutdown on Detroit. While it is true that Chrysler is more concentrated in and around Detroit than the other two large auto makers, GM actually employs more people than Chrysler does

---

*The study calculated impacts on the basis of full employment of 140,000; actual employment in May 1980 was 78,000. The study noted that, even as of August 1979, 24,000 workers had been laid off, but used the 140,000 figure to calculate impacts, on the theory that the 24,000 workers were receiving "full layoff benefits." Such benefits are properly viewed as transfers, however, not productive economic activity.

Table 6. Employment by Big Three in Areas Where Chrysler
Is Concentrated

Location	Employment (number of workers) as of January 1, 1979		
	Chrysler	Ford	GM
Detroit–Central City	27,343	6,409	41,270
Detroit–SMSA	49,354	72,400	101,402
St. Louis, Mo.	8,900	3,175	9,100

Source: Transportation Systems Center Study.

in Detroit proper and both Ford and GM employ more people in the Detroit area (SMSA) than Chrysler.

Nevertheless, the impact of a shutdown could be serious for individual Chrysler workers, and in some regions (Anderson et al., 1979), particularly in Michigan, but also in Indiana, Ohio, and Missouri. The effect would be most severe in the Detroit SMSA, with the DOT/Transportation Systems Center study estimating that a Chrysler shutdown would have caused a rise in unemployment from 8.7% to 16–19%.

A liberal estimate of the potential regional (and local) impact of a Chrysler collapse, employing the DOT study's regional multiplier analysis, but with actual 1980 employment statistics, yields an estimated unemployment figure for all regions with Chrysler plants of about 157,500 workers. Michigan alone, by this estimate, would suffer a total employment loss of 92,750.* These numbers overstate the potential impact, because they do not allow for potential reemployment by other auto manufacturers in the same regions. While somewhat lower than the estimates by the Transportation Systems Center, these figures nevertheless represent 2.5% of the employment in Michigan and over 5% of the employment in Detroit.

Minority Impact

Blacks and other minorities would bear a disproportionate share of the cost of a Chrysler bankruptcy. Fifty–four percent of Chrysler's 27,000 central Detroit work force is minority (mostly black). Thirty-three precent of Chrysler's blue-collar employees are minority workers. When operating at full strength (early 1979), Chrysler employed 36,400 blacks; the "black payroll" totaled

*Chrysler work force as of May 1980 is 88,200, of whom 60,800 are hourly workers (another 40,600 hourly workers are on indefinite layoff); 10,200 hourly workers are on temporary layoff, while a company-wide reduction of 6,900 of the 27,400 white-collar workforce was announced on April 22, 1980. At least 6,000 to 12,000 workers would remain at work even in the event of a liquidation. Thus regional effects in all areas: $(60,800-600) \times 2.5 = 137,000 + (27,400-6,900) = 157,500$. Effects in Michigan (largely in Detroit area): 53,000 total blue-collar force $- 24,000$ indefinite layoffs $= 29,400$; $29,400 - 1200$ retained at Introl plant $= 28,200 \times 2.5 = 71,250 + 21,500 = 92,750$.

$800 million, or 1% of the estimated "black economy" in the United States (Chrysler Corporation, 1979a).

Will Regional Impacts be Long-Term?

Even if the aggregate economic impacts of a Chrysler failure "wash out" after two to four years (as was predicted by the DRI and Treasury studies) it is possible that some communities would suffer much longer-term damage. The Transportation Systems Center study contends that this would be the case for the majority of communities affected, but makes no estimate of the duration of such effects. Local impacts are significant both from an equity point of view and because there are significant external social costs that can accompany long-term unemployment: alienation, hopelessness, crime, illness and other concomitants of unemployment that can fray the social fabric. Thus it is important to ascertain whether local, regional and minority impacts are likely to be temporary, with economic adjustments and replacement industries moving in to fill the economic void, or whether the effects are likely to be long-term.

Perhaps the most troubling aspect of the Chrysler aid question is the doubt that Detroit's economic base possesses sufficient diversity and flexibility to adjust to the trauma of a major corporate collapse. Would high unemployment become endemic? One optimistic counterexample is provided by the experience of the Seattle–Everett area (Department of the Treasury, 1979). When the aircraft-dependent local economy experienced a severe decline in 1968 due to the cancellation of the SST project, 60,000 manufacturing jobs were lost and the unemployment rate in the metropolitan area jumped from 2.9% in 1968 to 12.4% in 1971. By 1978, however, area unemployment had dropped to 5.3%, below the national average. Significantly, this recovery took place largely through diversification of the economic base, rather than through a recovery of the aircraft industry. While there are, of course, many differences between the two situations, it is interesting to note that Detroit's economic base has also showed a shift away from dependence on heavy manufacturing in recent years, as the economic future of big cities generally is moving away from heavy manufacturing. The long-term impact of a Chrysler collapse on Detroit depends on complex demographic and economic factors. It is a major area of concern that, as of this writing, poses many questions and no answers.*

The Effects on Credit

Costs and benefits can be analyzed from either the credit or the real resource side of the economic ledger. Since credit represents command over real resources, this amounts to much the same thing. As already detailed, risk-sharing among Chrysler's bankers indicate that the firm's bankruptcy would not cause a financial panic. As another possible "credit" effect, various economists

*The aspect of the Chrysler issue is inseparable from on-going debates on the issue of plant closings. See Chap. VII on employee stock ownership.

have argued that giving Chrysler preferential credit treatment amounts to placing it at the front of the line of borrowers, thereby (implicitly) displacing some other marginal firm at the tail end of the line.*

Normally, the effect of providing a guaranteed loan would be to raise the interest rate other firms must pay for funds, rather than denying any firm credit altogether. With physical resources unchanged, this raises the cost of doing business to all borrowers. How serious an effect is this? Overall, there is little doubt that federal loan guarantees substantially affect the shape and direction of the economy. In a $2.3 trillion economy which raised about $400 billion in new credit in 1979, the value of outstanding federal loan guarantees was over $350 billion and new guaranteed credit about $40 billion.† In this context, $1.5 billion more to Chrysler is but a drop in the bucket, and would probably have no detectable effect on interest rates. However, the important effect of reallocating credit is to reallocate real resources in the long run. We turn next to an examination of this effect.

Long-Term Effects of a Chrysler Collapse

It is unlikely that a Chrysler bankruptcy would have any long-run depressing effect on the national economy. Loan supporters made the claim that a Chrysler collapse would result in "permanent" job loss, and that federal aid to Chrysler would therefore yield permanent benefits. This claim was partly based on a misreading of the macroeconomic forecasts, which showed continuing unemployment and GNP effects through 1981. As Sinai (of DRI) noted, however, if the DRI model had continued to run for two more years, all such effects would have washed out and the Chrysler-depressed economy would have returned to the same level as the untraumatized baseline economy.‡ The macroeconomic forecasts, then, lend no credence to the permanent job loss thesis; indeed, even the pessimistic DRI forecast predicts a relatively short-term dislocation of two to four years.

Nevertheless, it can reasonably be argued that foreign importers, with 22% of the market in 1979 and 27% in 1980, are well positioned to grab a permanently larger share of the market should Chrysler collapse. In fact, they are capturing an increasing share of the auto market without the benefit of Chrysler's formal demise. It is quite possible that Japanese importers will build up a body of consumer loyalty that will make it difficult for American manufacturers to reclaim lost market share, because of the foreign cars' reputation for superior quality and gas mileage.§

It is not clear, however, that such an outcome can or should be avoided. If Japanese producers really are able to build cars more cheaply, American consumers benefit thereby. On the production side of the equation, a perma-

---

*For example, testimony by Alan Greenspan, Senate hearings, October 10, 1979.
†Ed Dale, House Subcommittee on Economic Stability, telephone interview.
‡Dr. Allen Sinai, testimony, House hearings.
§Articles supporting this view: *Business Week* and *The Wall Street Journal*.

nently higher level of imported autos does not necessarily mean a long-term loss in employment by Americans. A continuing balance of payments deficit should result in a depreciation of the dollar, making imports more expensive and exports cheaper to foreign buyers, thus correcting itself in the long run.

Moreover, there is no reason to believe that the United States is somehow doomed to be uncompetitive on the world market. The U.S. economy has significant export strength, as is demonstrated by the small balance of payments deficit in 1979 (about $3 billion) and the $5.5 billion current accounts surplus in 1980 (Department of Commerce), despite a huge oil import bill.* The economists' case for allowing productive resources to flow to those sectors where there is a cost or technical advantage is thus buttressed by the evidence. On the other hand, humility becomes economists and other prognosticators; in our real and very imperfect world, there can be no certainty that Chrysler's collapse would have no negative long-term effects. Therefore, we turn next to an examination of some of the other potential externalities and social diseconomies involved in a Chrysler collapse.

Loss of Competition from a Chrysler Collapse?

Aid proponents charged that a Chrysler collapse would threaten competition and decrease the number of firms in the already highly concentrated auto market. Alfred Dougherty of the Federal Trade Commission testified that, historically, Chrysler has been a valuable source of competition in the large car segment of the market.[†] The significance of this role may be lessened, however, by the recent drastic decline in large car sales. Moreover, the industry's profit structure, in which large cars earn large profits while small cars essentially break even, casts some doubt on the effectiveness of Chrysler as a competitive force. Large profit margins in the segment of the market which is most concentrated suggest a pattern of price leadership, with large car profits subsidizing bare knuckle market warfare in the small car segment. Short-run profits are improved by allocating a disproportionate share of the corporate-wide fixed cost onto the product in the less competitive market, and pricing accordingly (thus avoiding the need to idle plants and pay expensive fixed costs). In the long run, the company hopes that the low-profit sector will earn profits on its own, thus rewarding the expensive strategy of protecting market share.

This situation points up the really effective source of competition in the domestic auto market: foreign imports. The highly competitive small car market is likely to remain competitive whether or not Chrysler is a market force. So long as the auto market effectively remains a world market, no one firm (or group of firms) is likely to gain enough market power to dominate. Important multinational auto manufacturers exist in Japan (currently No. 1),

---

*The United States, however, did incur a trade deficit of over $34 billion in 1980.

[†] Testimony by FTC chairman Alfred Dougherty to the Senate, October 10, 1979.

the United States, Italy, France, Germany and the United Kingdom,* with national subsidiaries springing up in places like Brazil, Argentina, Mexico, Spain, Taiwan and Australia. With such a diversity of firms, collusive price fixing is unlikely in the foreseeable future. Since many of the companies are aggressively export-oriented, agreements to divide up the market also seem unlikely. The record thus far is one of vigorous international competition. The majority of innovations in recent years has also come from abroad. The stagnation of the U.S. domestic auto industry is testimony to the past lack of meaningful competition in domestic auto markets. See Klein (1977) for an elaboration of this point.

Moreover, to the extent that small cars are substitutes for large cars, or that foreign manufacturers threaten to invade that market also, the competitive benefits of free trade may spill over into the large car segment of the market as well. Foreign auto makers have shown in the past a tendency to build larger and larger cars for the U.S. market as they become attuned to mainstream American tastes. Of course, if market demand continues to shift in their direction they will have no need to build larger cars.

Thus a policy of free trade promises to be far more effective in promoting competition than would the preservation of Chrysler, especially if that preservation involved import barriers. The very success of import competition can lead to protectionist pressures, however, as is revealed by a look at the history of the textile, oil, steel and, most recently, auto industries. Suppose that domestic demand for automobiles rebounds to historical levels, as most industry analysts believe it will, and rises to levels of 11 to 13 million units per year in the 1980s. Suppose further than increasing penetration by importers leads to tariff protection or "gentlemen's accords" limiting imports and effectively insulating the U.S. market. Would it not then be folly to allow Chrysler to liquidate, when in only a few years there would be room for a third major auto manufacturer who added competition to the industry? In this case, it could be argued that a loan guarantee is a small price to pay to prevent the dissolution of Chrysler as a corporate entity and a diaspora in which its skilled workers, its organizational and engineering talent and its corporate experience are scattered to the winds. The cost of rebuilding such an organism could well be enormously greater than the cost of nursing it through hard times.

It should be noted, however, that a partial "brain drain" is already occurring, as those employees with the most options (and the least loyalty) desert a company that has such an uncertain future, and as Chrysler lays off or fires managerial and engineering staff. By January 1981 Chrysler had cut its salaried work force to a bare-bones level of 24,400, or only 56% of the white collar work force employed on January 1, 1979 (*The Wall Street Journal*). Thus the value of what is to be saved should not be overestimated.

*Datsun, Toyota, GM, Ford, Chrysler, Fiat, Peugeot-Citroen, Renault, Volkswagen, British Leyland.

Moreover, since Chrysler plans to retool and modernize the majority of its plants by 1985, it is arguably engaged in building a new company "from scratch" already. Some idea of the magnitude of the task can be gleaned from the figures: Chrysler, with paper assets of $7 billion, a net worth of less than $2 billion and a market value of only $600 million, planned capital investments of $11.2 billion over the five years 1980–1985 as of May 1980. These investment plans are over 50% higher than past levels, largely because so much of the existing plant is essentially worthless until it is retooled.

The main force of the "preservation for competition's sake" argument, however, depends primarily on the barriers to entry which will exist in the future auto market, since monopoly power cannot be exercised if other firms can enter the industry easily; the salvage value of Chrysler is less relevant to this question than an evaluation of the start-up costs (or other entry barriers) which would face a potential new entrant to the American market.

Start-up costs are indisputably large in an industry with such significant economies of scale. A huge multinational corporation can orchestrate world-wide operations, planning for the world market and taking advantage of regional variations in production costs. Indeed, GM is consistently more profitable than Ford, which in turn is more profitable than Chrysler. American Motors, although profitable at times in the 1970s, is financially strapped in 1981 and plans may be in the works for a merger with a foreign manufacturer. Thus, if American experience is any guide, economies of scale are quite large in the auto industry.

In any case, future competition is not likely to come from a new company starting from scratch, but from an existing manufacturer, probably a foreign multinational. What would it cost a foreign auto maker to locate in the United States so as to circumvent trade barriers?

Recent Volkswagen experience provides some relevant data. Volkswagen built an integrated assembly plant in Pennsylvania with a capital investment cost of approximately $300 million—plus an estimated $40 million in tax breaks and incentives from the state (*The Wall Street Journal*). This plant has a yearly capacity of about 225,000 vehicles and employs about 5,700 workers. Engines and many parts are still imported. Volkswagen has announced plans to build a second assembly plant, with a capacity of about 200,000 units yearly, in Ohio; projected investment for this plant is also about $300 million, employment about 4,000 (*The Wall Street Journal*). Such plants are large enough to capture the relevant economies of scale in assembly. Economies of scale in engine production are slightly greater, with minimum efficient scale being reached at a level of 300–500,000 units per year (National Highway Traffic Safety Administration, 1979).

The Volkswagen experience suggests that U.S. production costs are competitive with those in Germany, and it may be that other European auto makers will follow suit in building U.S. assembly plants, if sales warrant it. Honda and Nissan of Japan have all announced plans to build U.S. assembly plants, although this may be due as much to political pressure as to cost considerations (*Business Week*, 1979, 1980).

Thus, only if protectionist barriers are raised will it be necessary to "build a new Chrysler" to preserve competition and diversity in the auto market of the future. U.S. assembly is already cost-competitive for some foreign manufacturers, and will no doubt become increasingly common as import sales rise and political pressures mount to limit imports. No huge new start-up cost need be incurred. Importers can start with a small beachhead which is integrated with a large existing international structure, and gradually expand their operations within the United States. Competition will not decline if Chrysler goes bankrupt, as some claim.

Chrysler Important to the National Security?

National Defense

The national defense argument was important in justifying loan guarantees to Lockheed in 1971. Is Chrysler similarly involved in the "production" of national defense (or another public good) which would be endangered by the firm's collapse? While Chrysler does produce tanks for the Federal Government, this operation is easily separable from the main automotive line and could readily be sold off and continue in operation in the event of a corporate collapse. Thus Chrysler's collapse would not endanger the national defense.

Chrysler Autos Vital to the Infrastructure?

It is also difficult to argue that Chrysler autos are vital to the national security in the same way that oil, steel or merchant ships are felt to be. Many people contend that these goods are vital links in the nation's economic infrastructure, and that it is therefore unwise to become critically dependent on foreign sources for their supply. Such arguments have been a powerful rationale in justifying federal aid to these industries and others. However, dependence on uncertain foreign auto suppliers is unlikely to be a security problem because significant domestic auto-making capacity would exist even if all Chrysler plants disappeared overnight; and the United States is so saturated with automobiles that if new car purchases ceased tomorrow, it would be years before serious transportation bottlenecks appeared.

Federal aid to railroads has usually been justified, not on the ground that the United States would have become dependent on foreign services, but on the argument that, without federal aid, vital services to individuals and businesses would cease altogether. This argument, too, is inapplicable to Chrysler, since close substitutes for Chrysler products are readily available from other sources.

Socially Valuable Research and Development

Private R&D work may benefit society more than the company which engages in it; indeed, one study estimates the social rate of return for R&D work to be twice the private rate (50% compared to 25%) (National Science Foundation, 1977). Does Chrysler perform valuable research or provide leadership in innovation? For many years, Chrysler had a reputation for excellence in engineering. More recently, however, Chrysler has contributed little to the industry, preferring to copy the models of other auto makers. The automobile industry has not been notable for its innovativeness over the last three or four decades (Klein, 1977). Basic engine designs are remarkably similar to those in the days of the Model T, with the only recent innovation coming from Mazda of Japan. All American auto makers are essentially copying the front wheel drive configurations and space-saving interior body designs from abroad. The most notable recent American innovation, the catalytic converter, was developed by GM.

Nevertheless, due to the changing energy situation, there may be significant new work to be done in developing lightweight materials and new power plants.* Given its lackluster record, however, and the fact that the financially strapped company will be unable to devote many resources to research or experimental new designs, it is unlikely that a Chrysler collapse would greatly hamper the industry's progress.

The Costs of Federal Loan Guarantees

Thus far we have dealt largely with the short- and long-run costs of a Chrysler bankruptcy. We have seen that the major costs of bankruptcy are the short-term transitional cost, and a severe, potentially long-term, regional impact. What is the other side of the coin: the cost of granting loan guarantees?

Even if Chrysler survives, the social return on loan-guaranteed dollars will be lower than it would be in other uses. If private capital markets are functioning adequately (and there is no reason to believe they do not—at least for larger firms), Chrysler's negative rate of return to capital, its poor credit rating and its low stock market valuation (about $600 million in 1980) (Department of the Treasury, 1979) indicate that the firm is a much worse-than-average investment. This means that resources devoted to Chrysler produce less valuable output, on average, then resources elsewhere in the economy.

What exactly are the reallocative effects of granting aid in this case? If aid has the intended effect of rescuing Chrysler, it will have a near-term influence on resource allocation three to four times the size of the $1.5 billion loan because of its leverage effect on other resources: private loan monies, existing Chrysler assets and Chrysler workers. Chrysler workers and physical assets, instead of being idled and gradually reabsorbed, will be kept in production, but they will yield a lower return than similar resources used elsewhere. New loan infusions (both public and private) will also yield a lower social return than they would if invested elsewhere in the economy.

*Peter Gagnier, Chrysler, phone interview.

In most cases, the actual alternative uses of Chrysler resources cannot be predicted with any accuracy, although many existing capital assets would undoubtedly be purchased by domestic or foreign auto makers. On the other hand, a number of plants are valuable as sites and could well be purchased by nonautomotive manufacturers. The next-best use of public and private loans would probably also be outside the auto industry.

The costs of this resource allocation only become clear over the long term. An estimate of the magnitude of these costs can be made by comparing likely Chrysler performance with the performance one might expect from those same resources in an "average" use in the U.S. economy. Table 7 details the results of such a comparison. Output and employment are first estimated for a hypothetical base case in which Chrysler collapses and liquidates in 1980, with the economy recovering in three to four years. A second base case projects the much lower social cost of a successful Chapter 11 reorganization. These scenarios are then contrasted with four possible alternative cases, all of which assume Chrysler is granted federal aid. It should be cautioned that such comparisons of necessity rely on guesswork about the future. Thus the figures should be interpreted as rough rather than precise estimates.*

"Bail Out" Case 1 is the most optimistic projection of Chrysler's future with aid. It assumes a full recovery by 1985, with Chrysler performance improving to the point that it achieves a rate of return to capital commensurate with that of the average company. Case 2, on the other hand, projects the possibility that Chrysler might survive but never achieve an average level of profitability. This might be due either to continuing industry problems or to Chrysler's unique problems: high debt, little vertical integration, etc. Case 3 forecasts a possible future in which Chrysler succeeds in its current recovery operation, only to be faced with a new financial crisis in 1985. This might occur if there were a need to embark on a second massive retooling effort, due to the continued evolution of the auto market towards greater fuel efficiency. Finally, Case 4 projects the possibility of a bankruptcy, deferred to 1986; a deferred bankruptcy might take place for a number of reasons, including a shift in the automobile market. A bail-out followed by a near-term bankruptcy is not included, not because such an event is unlikely, but because the impact of this most pessimistic scenario is very similar to that of Base Case 1: Bankruptcy and Liquidation without federal aid.

Future streams of output and employment for all these cases are estimated and compared. The estimates of short-run bankruptcy costs (already developed) are included, with the Treasury Study's figures being used as a "best guess" of those costs. A net present value of output produced over time indicates whether the Chrysler aid package is likely to yield a social surplus or a net loss under the different assumptions.

The results indicate that benefits clearly outweigh costs if a full recovery takes place with aid, and if bankruptcy and liquidation would have occurred

---

*Details on assumptions and methodology are given in Appendix 5, available from the author.

Table 7. Long-run Costs and Benefits of Loan Guarantees Under Various Assumptions[a]

	Bail-out Case 1 Full Recovery	Bail-out Case 2 Subnormal	Bail-out Case 3 New Crisis in 1985	Bail-out Case 4 Bankruptcy in 1986
Output				
Present discounted value,[b] in $ millions, of output over/(under) — Base Case 1				
— (Liquidation)	$ 9,000	$ 2,600	($ 19,140)	($ 22,000)
— Base Case 2				
(Reorganization)	300	(6,000)	(27,800)	(30,700)
Employment				
Total number of job years[c] (undiscounted) over/(under)				
— Base Case 1	136,700	(78,000)	(744,000)	(797,000)
— Base Case 2	(21,300)	(235,000)	(903,000)	(966,000)
Number of jobs more than/(less than) Base Case 1 in				
— 1980	75,000	75,000	75,000	75,000
— 1989	(3,000)	(11,600)	(53,100)	(67,200)
— 1999	(5,500)	(34,500)	(94,400)	(84,000)

[a] See Appendix 5, available from the author, for derivation and expanded treatment.
[b] 5% discount rate, 20-year period.
[c] 20-year period.

without federal aid. On the other hand, very substantial losses could be realized if Chrysler undergoes a second financial crisis, resulting in either poor performance (Case 3) or bankruptcy (Case 4). The marginal example is Case 2 which shows small net social benefits when contrasted with liquidation (Base Case 1), but losses when compared to the possibility of reorganization. In both instances, the subnormal performance scenario results in fewer jobs overall in the long run than do the Base Cases in which aid is denied. The job loss, however, is far more evenly distributed over time than would be the case with a bankruptcy which occurred today.

The results are fairly sensitive to different discount rates and time horizons. A shorter time span and a higher discount rate tend to make the case for a bail-out appear stronger. On the other hand, a greater emphasis on the overall employment effect tends to make the case against aid appear stronger. The weight one places on employment as opposed to efficiency considerations will influence one's view of the problem. The more important parameter, however, is the probability which one attaches to the various scenarios themselves.

Integration of these results with the other components of the cost–benefit analysis is now discussed.

Chrysler Loan Guarantees: Weighing the Costs and Benefits

How can the costs and benefits of issuing loan guarantees be summed up in a manner useful for decision making? First, it will be noted that the initial list of potential costs and benefits has been whittled down to a few seminal items, primarily the output and employment losses which can result from a significant economic shock (if bankruptcy is allowed to occur) or from a misallocation of resources (if aid is granted). Output loss is a good proxy for the more theoretically precise concepts of social surplus or welfare cost. Unemployment effects are important because job loss carries with it significant externalities which are probably not captured in the output calculation alone.

The major potential costs are summarized in Table 8. If government aid is denied, there is a likelihood of bankruptcy followed by liquidation, resulting in significant transitional costs in output and employment (although lower than is commonly believed), as well as severe regional impacts in Michigan which are potentially long-term. If government aid is granted, on the other hand, it may result in a long-term loss in efficiency, it may have unfortunate impact as a precedent and it may not be effective.

A decision on the merits of the question requires some educated guessing as to the future and a relative weighting of various social objectives. Bankruptcy, followed by a successful reorganization (without federal aid), would be the most desirable outcome, on efficiency, employment and equity criteria. Yet the liquidation scenario, with its higher-social costs, cannot be rejected as sufficiently improbable to justify its being ignored. Alternatively, if one could predict with confidence that government aid would avert bankruptcy and lead

Table 8. Summary of Social Costs and Benefits of Federal Loan Guarantees to Chrysler

Costs of a Bankruptcy/Liquidation	Costs of a Loan Guarantee
Output & Unemployment	
Short-run dislocation $4–6 billion output and 75–100,000 jobs lost in first two years, declining to nothing in four years.	Long-run efficiency loss Inefficient resource allocation, lowers future output and employment; estimates range from $9 billion benefit (PDV) to $30 billion loss.
Regional impact Loss of up to 170,000 jobs in first year; long-term effects unknown.	Possible later bankruptcy
Minority impact Loss of about 25,000 direct jobs.	Behavioral inefficiencies Induced by awareness of government as lender of last resort; increasing demands on public monies in future?
Loss of competition Unimportant	
Loss of national security Unimportant	
Loss of R&D Unimportant	
Government Budget Impact Approx. $8 billion over four years in tax loss, unemployment insurance increases, etc.[a]	$0–2 billion of bankruptcy prevented; much higher cost if bankruptcy occurs anyway.

[a] From Treasury Study estimate: $2.75 billion loss in first 2 years, declining thereafter.

to full recovery, then the benefits of aid would clearly outweigh the costs, and the decision would be easy in that case too. Unfortunately, it is all too likely that Chrysler will decline or fail, even with federal assistance.

One way to approach the problem might be to make a decision based on "expected utility" or likely social benefit. Based on available information, none of the scenarios considered in the previous section seems particularly unlikely. One might therefore guess that reorganization and liquidation are equally likely without aid (probably too pessimistic an assumption), and that each of the alternative "Bail Out" scenarios is equally likely with aid. (Note that this approach may be slightly biased in favor of granting aid, since the possibility of a *near*-term bankruptcy is discounted.) Using a 5% real discount rate and a 20-year-time horizon, denying aid would then be the superior choice. Even if one assumes that liquidation is inevitable without loan guarantee assistance, the expected utility outcome is still better if aid is denied. Indeed, one can even drop one of the most pessimistic bail-out cases (3 or 4) and denial of aid still remains the better choice. If one makes similar calculations with respect to expected unemployment, the case against aid is even stronger. If Chrysler experiences significant difficulties or goes bankrupt in the 1980s, the decision to bail out Chrysler now could result in a long-term loss on the order of 740,000 to 900,000 jobs.

Use of a higher discount rate or shorter time frame improves the case for aid, since the benefits of current output and jobs are more heavily weighted. Taken together, a 13% discount rate and a 10-year-time span are sufficient to shift the case in favor of federal assistance. Such an approach, however, places too little weight on future needs and long-term considerations. A more pessimistic appraisal of the effects of a bankruptcy also improves the case for federal aid, but not enough to shift the balance by itself. On balance, the cost/benefit analysis leads one to deny aid, both on efficiency and employment grounds.

One should not, however, ignore considerations that cannot be quantified as output or employment effects. What are the equity considerations and potential intangible costs associated with the loan guarantee decision? An important argument made against aid for Chrysler is the potential importance of that action as a precedent. Granting aid to Chrysler, it is argued, could vitiate private firms' incentives to operate efficiently and usher in a new era of political pork-barreling for corporations, with serious, long-run debilitating effects on the economy. On the other hand, aid to Chrysler might be seen as a first, groping step towards more active economic management, perhaps leading to a new form of public-private partnership.* Clearly, the decision's ultimate impact as a precedent—whether good or bad—will depend largely on what is to follow, and particularly on future perceptions of the success of the Chrysler bail-out. On balance, the precedential impact of the ban guarantee is probably negative, pleasing neither to free market advocates nor to proponents of a more active government economic role.

Another troubling consideration not captured in the cost/benefit calculation is the equity issue. While the U.S. economy and even the auto industry would probably recover fairly quickly from a Chrysler bankruptcy, the effects would be particularly acute, and perhaps much longer lasting, in Detroit and other areas of the Midwest. A case can be made that the city lacks the ability to attract replacement businesses, and that the area would suffer a long-term depression, with attendant social cost.

Indeed, regional economic development programs within HUD and the Department of Commerce provide incentives to firms to locate in economically depressed areas, often in aging city centers. Viewed in this light, aid to Chrysler might be seen as a form of urban relief. However, Chrysler is under no obligation to continue operating particular plants; indeed, three Detroit-area plants were closed down in 1980. Perhaps the most that should be expected of

*For example, it might be seen as the harbinger for a latter-day version of the Reconstruction Finance Corporation, one of the experimental agencies of the New Deal. This possibility is discussed subsequently.

federal assistance is that the aid will slow this ineluctable trend, allowing jobs to be phased out more gradually and with a less devastating impact on the communities involved. It may even be that federal aid to prop up Chrysler will only impede a necessary and desirable diversification of Michigan's economic base, delaying the day of reckoning and possibly aggravate the underlying economic problems.

Moreover, if the policy is to be justified on distributional or equity grounds, it has some troubling inconsistencies. Aid to Chrysler provides a windfall both to shareholders and to workers (who are among the highest-paid factory workers in the country). It is financed by the taxpayer who, on average, is poorer than both. Furthermore, implicit in the reallocational effects of providing loan guarantees is a redistribution of jobs away from unknown workers to Chrysler and Chrysler-dependent employees. The equity argument, then, while carrying some weight, is a two-edged sword.

Thus, while critical uncertainties and intangible considerations make it impossible to resolve the Chrysler aid question with certainty, the weight of the evidence and analysis clearly falls on the side of a denial of aid to Chrysler. The long-run costs of a loan guarantee on jobs and output, the uncertainty that the loan guarantee will be effective, and the possibly far-reaching precedential implications of such aid outweigh the possible short-run costs of a Chrysler collapse. While the potential regional effects of such a bankruptcy could be severe, these effects are better dealt with via targeted economic development assistance to diversify the area's economy.

The Political Context of the Chrysler Loan Guarantee Plan

Thus far the analysis has proceeded as if the Chrysler aid question could be decided in a political vacuum. In truth, of course, political realities were far more important than economic analysis in deciding whether or not to grant aid. It is undoubtedly appropriate for such an important and relatively novel issue to be decided by elected representatives; however, the decision-making process raises many questions. Was the outcome inevitable, or would it have been different with slightly different timing, conditions or loan "packaging?" Was the "public interest" adequately protected or were our political institutions more receptive to some interests than to others? Is Congress likely to approve such guarantees again in the future; if so, on what does such approval depend?

Perhaps the most interesting aspects of the political story were the broad-based support for the legislation, which cut across traditional party and ideological lines, and the equally striking lack of vigorous opposition.* Moderate and liberal Democrats, such as Representative Moorhead, Senator Biden and President Carter, generally supported the powerful United Auto Workers

*See Appendix 1 available from the author for more detail on the legislative history.

Union or feared the impact on urban areas and blacks. Conservatives were wooed by arguments that Chrysler was a victim of overregulation. Congress members from Michigan (such as Representative Blanchard and Senator Riegle) were instrumental in guiding the legislation through Congress. Even members from states which would be relatively unaffected, such as Senator Tsongas of Massachusetts, turned a sympathetic ear, perhaps mindful of the possibility that their states could face similar problems in the future. Organizations such as the NAACP, the Urban League and the U.S. Conference of Mayors all favored aid. Even General Motors and Ford came out in favor of aid, albeit half-heartedly.

Chrysler itself orchestrated a high-powered lobbying campaign involving the law firms of Thomas Boggs, Jr., and William E. Timmons, as well as former Representative Garry Brown (R-Mich., 1967–1978) (National Journal, 1979). Chrysler lobbyists distributed lists of Chrysler-related jobs and businesses by Congressional District, and induced dealers and suppliers to contact their representatives. UAW lobbyist Howard Pastor and President Douglas Fraser also worked the Hill.

Opposition, by contrast, was scattered and disorganized. The Congressional debates generated little correspondence from the general public. Members of Congress, in the main, preferred not to see the Chrysler loan bill an important precedent. Rather, in the words of the House Banking Committee report, "[Your committee] has dealt with the Chrysler problem on a one-time, pragmatic basis in recognition of a unique situation…" (U.S. Congress, 1979a). Active Congressional opposition to aid was confined to legislators of the Don Quixote ilk, such as Guardian of the Fisc William Proxmire (D-Wis.) and free market proselytizer David Stockman (R-Mich), now Director of the Office of Management and Budget. While several organizations, such as the Business Roundtable, the National Taxpayers' Union and the National Association of Manufacturers announced their opposition to a federal aid package, they made little effort to oppose it actively. Indeed, the only active opposition lobbying was conducted by Howard Symons of Congress Watch, who found himself an unlikely bedfellow of The Wall Street Journal.

Why was Congress so receptive to Chrysler's request, when analysis indicates that the merits of the question are far from clear? One reason is that Congress, like other political institutions, tends to represent best those constituencies which are organized and visible. Many of the groups which stand to benefit from aid are politically powerful. Conversely, any costs will be borne by a diffuse public or by sets of businesses and which are diverse and hard to identify.

Another important reason for widespread support was the sympathy of those legislators who could foresee the need for similar favors to their constituents in the future. They may have wished to keep the door ajar and avoid setting a precedent which would block future aid efforts.

It is probably a mistake to conclude that the outcome was inevitable, however. The mood of Congress changed during the latter stages of the debate, with opposition to the loan legislation stiffening considerably. The shift in the political wind suggests that many legislators were uncertain about their beliefs and groping for a position. While support was broad, it may not have run very deep.

The gut issue which decided the question for many was jobs. If the Chrysler aid bill had really been perceived as a mere corporate bail-out, without socially redeeming effects on employment, the bill would have stood little chance. The other powerful determinant of the outcome was the successful experience with Lockheed, the ghost at the feast. Similarly, success or failure of the Chrysler experiment will be an influential, perhaps overriding, factor in future deliberations over loan guarantee requests.

Barring a conspicuous failure of one of the large bail-out recipients (Lockheed, Conrail, New York City and now Chrysler), Congress and the administration are likely to continue to be receptive to such requests. It may even be that they are truly representing public opinion in providing succor to those faced with possible calamity. One may be forgiven the suspicion, however, that our political institutions are perhaps too responsive to short-term needs and highly visible interests, possibly to the detriment of society's long-term interests.

Some Considerations for Future Policy

What are the lessons to be learned from the Chrysler experience? Opinion is divided as to whether the Chrysler story is a harbinger of things to come. The more pessimistic soothsayers point to a variety of problems in the heavy manufacturing "core" industries of the Midwest and Northeast and infer a general pattern of decline.

According to this view, one would expect to see an increasing number of firms become candidates for government assistance. These future supplicants will generally be located in the northern industrial regions and in mature industries. They will complain of foreign subsidization and the export of American jobs. They will point to government regulation or other policies as a source of their troubles. Some firms will be viewed as vital to the national defense (e.g., Lockheed) or to the economic infrastructure (e.g., oil, shipping, railroading). The most important argument for aid, of course, will be the potentially devastating human cost of a large bankruptcy, particularly in certain regions. According to this point of view, government intervention is needed to revitalize the faltering economy itself. Active government policies to provide loans and assistance to firms and communities may be called for, perhaps coupled with federal economic planning directed at regional and/or sectoral problems.* This approach would address long-run problems with long-run solutions, rather than short-run palliatives.

It may be, however, that the so-called problems of the industrial sector are confined largely to the steel and auto industries. According to this point of view, problems in these industries are mere growing pains experienced by an evolving economy and generalizations about a general economic decline are greatly exaggerated. Institutionalized policy responses to such problems would be inappropriate and possibly self-defeating. The best policy, according to this perspective, would be to avoid interfering with what are essentially necessary and desirable economic charges. Interventionist government policies might still be desirable to alleviate the social cost of economic changes on individuals, communities and regions—but not to interfere with the basic direction of change.

The highly political nature of the Chrysler issue, which brought a traditionally private event into the public arena, is another important factor to be considered in designing future policies. It remains to be seen whether similarly eclectic, broad-based support would coalesce around a future seeker of aid. Such support will no doubt depend upon the particular circumstances, the economic and political climate at the time and the success of the Chrysler experiment. Almost certainly, however, the employment issue will be paramount, and powerful political forces will support federal aid if many workers are likely to be affected. If the Chrysler experience is representative, information will be poor and analyses will be used largely as propaganda. Anticipation of such effects has led some people to propose the creation of a quasi-public agency to finance troubled private firms, thus "de-politicizing" the process. The powerful political support likely to be attached to a request for federal aid suggests that a fruitful approach might be to accept the inevitability of some form of aid but to consider ways of shaping that aid so as to mitigate its drawbacks.

We turn now to an examination of possible alternatives to the approach used in the Chrysler case.

Modifying Loan Guarantees to Attain Social Goals

One policy approach might be to build on past experience with loan guarantee programs by continuing with that form of aid, while paying greater attention in the future to structuring aid packages so as to maximize attainment of social ends. In the Chrysler case, a consensus existed that the major issues were job losses and possibly long-term regional impacts; yet the aid bill was remarkably free of conditions ensuring Chrysler's conformance to public purpose objec-

---

*A somewhat different rationale for a high level of government intervention in and direction of the economy is the argument that private market institutions, even though economically "healthy," fail to serve important human and social needs. Policies based on this premise would be directed not at improving economic performance or competitiveness in the usual sense, but at restructuring the economy so as to serve the desired social goals.

tives relating to these concerns. The Chrysler Loan Guarantee Act contains few conditions, apart from specifying financial contributions required from other parties. In the future, the following conditions might be included:

Plant-closing requirements. Plant-closing legislation already exists in a few states and is mainly aimed at giving workers and communities advance notice of a permanent plant closing [see Bearse (1977) for more on this]. Alternatively, the government could negotiate an actual plan with the company for a given number of years, specifying which plants could or could not be shut down. Penalties could be exacted for breaking a commitment.

Requirements to locate new plants in the United States.

Severance taxes. These could go to the communities affected, the workers, or both.

Retraining and/or relocation assistance. Displaced workers could be aided in moving to new plant locations, or given new skills which would enable them to obtain work in a "replacement industry." Special unemployment benefits, such as Trade Adjustment Assistance, could be linked to participation in retraining programs.

The object of inserting such requirements is not merely to compensate displaced workers, nor to prevent or penalize plant closings, but to affect the firm's decisionmaking by altering the relative prices it faces in closing down a plant and to encourage workers to exit from declining industries.

While a loan of this sort confers windfall gains by its very nature, steps can be taken to minimize private profits. Conditions could include requiring sacrifices and financial contributions from parties who stand to gain. An attempt to require sharing of the risk and sacrifices was in fact incorporated into the Chrysler aid bill, which specified the contributions to be made by various parties.

Since there is a strong prior suspicion that by providing the loan guarantee the government is encouraging inefficiency, it might be appropriate to encourage modernization and increase efficiency by fiat to the extent practicable. The Chrysler loan bill requires a viable recovery plan and an "energy-saving plan" as conditions for the loan. There were suggestions that Congress go beyond this vague language and require Chrysler to go into the mass transit business or build prototypical safe, fuel-efficient autos. Such detailed specifications, however, could well prove to be impractical when imposed by outsiders ignorant of engineering or marketing realities. As Congress member Blanchard wryly remarked at one point before the bill's passage: "I just hope we stop short of designing tail fins." An alternative, however, might have been to award part of the aid in the form of a government contract for the autos desired.

One obvious drawback to most of the above requirements is that they hamper the firm's ability to make cost-saving changes and return to profitability.

"Don't tie their hands," was a common sentiment. Moreover, if the firm, saddled with government requirements, continues to decline, it has a much better case when it returns for a second round of help. This consideration, along with a distaste for any more federal involvement than absolutely necessary, was undoubtedly an important reason for leaving such conditions out of the Chrysler legislation. This judgment may prove sound. On the other hand, the government's status as a creditor gives it the right to impose conditions on the loan and to demand some assurance that its aims in granting aid are realized. Furthermore, the more onerous the conditions imposed, the less likely it is that other firms will attempt to seek government aid.

Institutionalizing Loan Guarantees: Create a New Reconstruction Finance Corporation?

Some people have suggested that the major lesson to be drawn from the Chrysler story is the need for a new institution to deal with such cases. Felix Rohatyn of New York's Municipal Assistance Corporation has called for the creation of a special financing agency, patterned along the lines of the Reconstruction Finance Corporation (RFC) of the New Deal era (*The New York Times*). This agency would be capitalized initially with general revenue funds, and thereafter financed through a tithe on large firms. It would have the authority to lend or invest in large but failing enterprises, including manufacturing firms and perhaps banks. Proponents of this idea argue that such an institution would allow experienced, trained financiers to evaluate a firm's problems and prospects away from the political hurly-burly of Capitol Hill. This arrangement would supposedly result in more rational, dispassionate decisionmaking.

However, much of the preceding analysis casts doubt on the wisdom of such an enterprise. The tax on large firms would not necessarily shift the financing cost of the agency away from the taxpayer, since higher costs are likely to be passed on in large part to consumers. Moreover, the real economic cost of supporting inefficient firms will ultimately be borne by both consumers and workers in the form of higher prices, lower wages and lower productivity.

More importantly, it is naive to believe that a new, independent, quasi-public lending agency would be immune to the political pressures surrounding a major corporate collapse. Powerful forces would almost certainly lobby for aid in any large bankruptcy. Equally inevitably, other groups would accuse the agency of making biased or arbitrary decision, or with showing some form of favoritism. The original version of the RFC was better able to deal with such pressures than a new one probably would be, partly because it was led by a strong and charismatic chief, Jesse Jones, with close ties to President Roosevelt, and partly because it was one of the flagship agencies of the New Deal.

If the government is going to enter into a new financial partnership with major private institutions, a good argument can be made that the arrangements should be worked out by directly elected representatives in the full light of day. If Congress were of a mind to delegate such authority to an agency, it would seem advisable to lodge that authority within a powerful existing entity, such as the Department of the Treasury.

Another reason for avoiding the creation of an independent agency concerned primarily with preventing large private bankruptcies is that a large corporate bankruptcy will inevitably involve many considerations cutting across a wide range of jurisdictions. An agency with too narrow a purview could work at cross purposes with other important government objectives, such as the reduction of international trade barriers and competition in domestic markets.

Another question is, to what end will the agency's financial experts be free to make their "objective" evaluations? If the Chrysler experience is any guide, there will be no mistake by the private financial institutions which are refusing credit. Application of standard loan criteria would almost certainly lead the government to refuse aid, too. If additional criteria are to be used to justify aid, what are those criteria?—the potential number of jobs involved? the probable impact on particular urban areas or other regions? the strategic value of a particular industry or firm? How are the difficult distributional and equity questions to be decided? These "public purpose" considerations are fundamental in any decision to lend public monies to a private company. There is no reason to believe that private financial experts are the appropriate people to decide such matters, or that they would be particularly good at it. If more reliable information and greater financial expertise is needed (and judging by the Congressional debate over Chrysler, it is), the Congress could develop its own expertise in the Congressional Budget Office or the General Accounting Office. This would allow Congress to take advantage of more reliable information without final decisionmaking power.

Potentially far-reaching institutional and behavioral effects also militate against the RFC idea. Thus far, the very trauma and difficulty of going to the government to obtain a loan has probably mitigated, to a large extent, the desire of other firms to try the same thing. If the process were streamlined or if a federal lending agency were felt to be sympathetic, the floodgates could burst. Moreover, private banks might be encouraged to abdicate any "responsibility" for providing high-risk loans if the government were ready as a back-up lender in any case.* The mere existence of such an agency could greatly expand its business. Furthermore, beyond the potential efficiency loss of such aid lie equity and morale problems which could undermine the economy in the long run. What will be the reactions of the efficient firms, which are penalized, and the small firms, which are left out altogether?

---

*This tendency has been noted in some European situations; also domestically, in banks' involvement with SBA loan guarantees. See *Business Week*, June 30, 1980, p. 142.

It is clear from the above arguments that a grant of loan guarantees to a large corporation, and, even more, the institutionalization of that form of aid, is as much macroeconomic as microeconomic policy. Long-run efficiency, employment, productivity and sectoral and regional growth may be affected. Instituting a mechanism to influence such matters without first diagnosing the problem and making the tough policy choices required would be putting the cart before the horse.

An examination of the history of the original RFC reveals that it was not created in isolation, but was a piece of a larger federal effort to spur recovery from the Great Depression. The economic problems of those times were very different from our own. During the New Deal, the RFC could play a role merely by stimulating aggregate demand. A few bad loans might be considered unimportant when compared to the benefit of increased economic activity overall. Today, however, the economy suffers a different malaise: the coexistence of high inflation and high unemployment. A policy which indiscriminately promotes inefficient activities could well exacerbate the problem by decreasing productivity and increasing inflation.

The above arguments are not meant to suggest that the Federal Government should necessarily refrain from economic policies, like institutional innovation, which intervene directly in the marketplace. Regional or sectoral growth policies may well be an appropriate weapon for attacking difficult structural problems in the U.S. economy, and the loan guarantee mechanism could prove a valuable tool for this effort. Diverse organizations and individuals have called for such an active federal role. Brock Adams, former Secretary of Transportation, urged that the Chrysler debate be used as a forum for developing an "Economic Plan for the '80s" (Adams, 1979); California Governor Jerry Brown, columnist Joseph Kraft (in "The Reindustrialization of America") and others have called for a "reindustrialization" program. Assorted think-tanks and private organizations have urged an active sectoral (Schwartz and Choate, 1980) or regional* growth policy. The evidence, however, suggests caution in pursuing such policies.

Japan's corporatist economy is perhaps the best example of how government can intervene actively and successfully in individual sector and firms. Protectionist policies at home and active support for exports have helped Japan attain the highest sustained growth rate, in this century, of any industrialized country. Japanese policies indicate the importance of pursuing sectoral policies within the context of an overall economic plan and of retaining the ability to allow the weakest companies to fail during hard times. The Japanese economic "miracle," however, has also benefited from the society's system of cooperation between important leaders in business and government, as well as from the traditional cooperativeness of its labor force.

*For example, see publications of the Northeast/Midwest Institute.

Government involvement in particular industries has met with far less success in the United Kingdom, a country much more akin to our own in its history and institutions. In 1968, the British Government decided to rescue British Leyland, the troubled auto conglomerate, at a projected cost of 1 billion pounds sterling. Since that time, however, the firm's market share has fallen from 40% to 20% of the British market, and it is now requesting another 200 million pounds. Indeed, according to auto analyst Maryann Keller, most European auto makers are far less efficient than competing subsidiaries of GM and Ford (Keller, 1980). Government ownership or control of these firms is a major reason; for example, their ability to lay off workers is highly constrained.

Thus foreign experience with active sectoral or firm-specific economic policies yields mixed reviews. More study is needed to determine the applicability of such programs to the United States.* The United States does operate some programs to promote economic development in particular industries or regions, but the programs are rather small and are not guided by a coherent overall strategy.

The federal agency most involved with such policies is the Economic Development Administration (EDA) within the Department of Commerce. The EDA administers a variety of programs, including loans and technical assistance to depressed rural and urban areas, public works grants, trade adjustment assistance grants to workers displaced by imported products (for which laid-off auto workers are eligible) and a recently completed $550 million aid program for the steel industry. The Department of Housing and Urban Development (HUD) also administers loans and grants to promote economic development in urban areas. These programs may provide valuable experience if the United States decides to embark on a larger sectoral or regional economic program.†

However, there are a number of ways in which the small loans administered by the EDA and HUD are generically different from large loans à la Chrysler. The entire EDA budget for 1979 was about $1.8 billion,‡ as compared to the $1.5 billion guaranteed to Chrysler, a single firm. The economic significance and political importance of any one EDA loan is relatively slight. This means that learning costs are fairly low and outside political pressures fairly weak. Large loans to large firms, on the other hand, have consequences which are potentially much greater and generate much more political heat. An EDA-style agency might therefore be a poor organization to administer a larger loan program.

The EDA is also largely reactive in its policies. It attempts to arrest the decline of industries and regions, and to compensate and retrain displaced

---

*For more on this matter, see Chap. XVI on "European lessons."

† These are also threatened with extinction in President Reagan's FY '82 budget.

‡Ed Dale, House Subcommittee on Economic Stability, telephone interview.

workers. If the federal sectoral role is to expand, a more disciplined forward-looking strategy would be advisable. The institution of an RFC without coherent economic plans and priorities would be an expansion of the federal economic role without the vision and discipline which should accompany that expansion. It would in truth be the worst of two worlds: a welfare state for corporations.

Allowing Bankruptcy to Proceed

An alternative policy route would be to deny future government aid to Chrysler or any other firm seeking aid and allow events to take their course. This strategy would have the advantage of encouraging the ailing firm to seek a merger or undergo bankruptcy and reorganization under Chapter 11 of the Bankruptcy Code. Either option would lead to a corporate reorganization, perhaps with a change of management, without any federal intervention. The government, if it desired, could even make financial aid available to the firm after bankruptcy, rather than before. This possibility, recommended by several expert witnesses before the Congressional committees considering aid, would help to ensure that all feasible steps to economize and reorganize had been taken and that federal aid was truly necessary.

Even if the worst-case scenarios of bankruptcy and liquidation were to come about, the government might better address the situation by providing various forms of emergency impact assistance to affected individuals and communities, rather than to the affected firm. These would include special unemployment benefits, retraining programs for displaced workers, economic development loans to communities, and special incentives to induce new businesses to locate in depressed areas. Such programs can assist people at risk without impeding necessary processes of economic transformation and adjustment.

Conclusion

Several important conclusions emerge from the preceding analysis. The paramount lesson for politicians and government officials is that they must avoid too myopic a view of the problem. In evaluating the desirability of various alternative programs for addressing a situation like Chrysler's, it is difficult to stress too highly the importance of looking at the potential long-run effects of government actions. By taking a short-run view of the situation, as well as by focusing on budgetary impact rather than social cost, Congress concluded that the Chrysler aid package was a good investment. The potentially high near-term cost of denying aid, however, should be weighed against the long-run cost of allocating resources inefficiently and impeding the (re)development of the U.S. economy. Only then does it become clear that the cost of the loan guarantee is not the potential loss of government funds, but the probable loss of productivity, output and, ultimately, future jobs and living standards. Similarly, there is a need to consider long-run remedies which may prevent a Chrysler-type problem from reaching crisis proportions.

Another troubling aspect of the entire Chrysler affair has been the failure to define a defensible public policy rationale or a generic rule on the appropriate public/private distinction. This is due partly to the complexity of the problem and partly to the inadequacy of traditional attitudes and beliefs. Easy, conventional distinctions between the public and private sectors or between the political and economic spheres of activity provide little help in thinking about Chrysler. While nominally a private firm, any institution as large and important as Chrysler is inevitably "public" in its effects on society. When the imminent collapse of such a private firm can wreck such havoc, responsive political institutions are usually going to be sympathetic to the demands for help of those who stand to be hurt. This blurring of the public/private distinction requires open-minded rethinking of the nature of our institutions rather than the disingenuous excuse that aid to Chrysler is merely an exception to an otherwise comfortable division between things public and things private.

Recognizing the long-run nature of the problem and the essentially public characteristics and responsibilities of any large institution are only the first steps in developing a more useful intellectual framework for policy making. Although it is the judgment of this author that the granting of aid to Chrysler was an unfortunate mistake, it does not necessarily follow that a pure laissez-faire approach would have been the best alternative. Creative analysis of some promising alternative policies would be a logical and invaluable next step in designing policies for potential future Chryslers.

The best policies will take a long-run view of the problems being addressed, including an awareness of the possible long-run ramifications of government policies. While the best policy will depend on the particular circumstances involved, there are at least two generic types of alternatives. One approach would be to allow private market forces to take their course, while directing public action at ameliorating "distress." The other possibility would be to adopt a program of active economic policies designed to encourage growth in particular regions and industries, on the assumption that private market forces are failing to direct the economy efficiently or to serve basic social needs adequately. Retraining and relocation assistance are programs of the former type, while a subsidy program to the steel or auto industry would be representative of the latter. Some programs, such as loans to communities, plant severance taxes or incentives to invest in depressed areas, fall under either category. The types of programs selected will be determined by one's view of the ability of the economy to function efficiently and to fulfill human needs. A number of the possibilities identified earlier on in other chapters of this book appear to be potentially superior either to adopting a cold-blooded laissez-faire policy or to backing into a system of "lemon capitalism" for large corporations.

332

Bibliography

Adams, Brock (1979). "First Chrysler—and Then?" *The Washington Post* (September 9).

Anderson, Martin, Bryon, George, and O'Donnel, John (1979). "Employment and Economic Effects of a Chrysler Shutdown or Major Reduction in Business: Preliminary Data and Analysis." Cambridge, MA: Transportation Systems Center (August 1979).

Bearse, Peter (1977). "Plant Closings: Prescription for Legislative Action." *New Jersey Magazine: A Journal of Public Affairs* (March).

Booz, Allen, and Hamilton, Management Consultants (1979). "Analysis of 1980–1985 Operating Plan" (October 22).

Business Week (1980). "The Economic Case Against Government Bailouts"; "U.S. Autos—Losing a Big Segment of the Market Forever?" (March 24).

Business Week (1979). "Could Bankruptcy Save Chrysler?"

Chrysler Corporation (1979a). "Analysis of Chrysler Corporation's Situation and Proposal for Government Assistance" (September).

Chrysler Corporation (1979b). "Chrysler Corp. Facilities Fact Book" (August).

Chrysler Corporation (1979c). "Report to Shareholders" (September 30).

Chrysler Corporation (1979d). "Chrysler 1980–1985 Operating Plan" (November).

Congressional Budget Office (1978a). *Loan Guarantees: Current Concerns and Alternatives for Control.* Washington, DC: U.S. Government Printing Office (August).

Congressional Budget Office (1978b). "Transportation Finance Choices in a Period of Change" (March).

Congressional Budget Office (1979). "U.S. Trade Policy and the Tokyo Round of Multilateral Trade Negotiations" (March).

Congressional Research Service (1978). "The Concept of a Sick Industry." Washington, DC: Julius Allen (July).

Data Resources, Inc. (1979). "Chrysler and the U.S. Economy: A Simulation Study." Lexington, MA: Terry Glomski and Allen Sinai (August).

Department of the Treasury (1979). "Treasury Staff Analysis of Economic Impact of a Shutdown of the Chrysler Corporation" (November 7).

Economic Development Administration (1978). Annual Report.

Findings of the Chrysler Corporation Loan Guarantee Board (1980). Reprinted by the House Committee on Banking, Finance and Urban Affairs, Washington, DC (May 12).

Green, Mark, and Waitzman, Norman (1979). "Business War on the Law. An Analysis of the Benefits of Federal Health/Safety Enforcement." Corp. Accountability Research Group (Nader).

Jones, Jesse H. (1951). *Fifty Billion Dollars: My Thirteen Years with the RFC (1932–1945)*. New York: Macmillan.

Keller, Maryann (1981). *Business Week* (March 24).

Moe, Ronald C. (1979). "The Reconstruction Finance Corporation, A Brief History." Washington, DC: NHSTA (November).

National Journal (1979). Issues, October–December.

National Highway Traffic Safety Administration (1979). "The Effects of Automobile Regulations on Industry Competition." Washington, DC: NHTSA (November).

National Science Foundation (1977). "Relationship Between R&D and Economic Growth/ Productivity" (November 9), p. A-7.

Schwartz, Gail, and Choate, Pat (1980). "Revitalizing the US Economy: A Brief for National Sectoral Policies." Washington, DC: Academy for Contemporary Problems.

Shuber, Sandra. "Problems in Detroit—How Much Effect on the Economy?" *Chase Econometrics.*

Tropper, Peter, and Adams, Amy (1979). "The Regional Impact of the Crisis at Chrysler." Washington, DC: Northeast/Midwest Institute (December).

U.S. Congress (1979a). House of Representatives, House Report 96690, "Chrysler Corporation Loan Guarantee Act of 1979" (December 6).

U.S. Congress (1979b). "Chrysler Corporation Loan Guarantee Act of 1979," Conference Report. Washington, DC: U.S. Government Printing Office (December).

U.S. Congress (1979c). House Committee on Banking and Currency, "Hearings on Chrysler Corporation Loan Guarantee Act of 1979." Washington, DC: U.S. Government Printing Office (December).

U.S. Congress (1979d). Senate Committee on Banking, Housing and Urban Affairs. "Hearings on Chrysler Corporation Loan Guarantee Act of 1979." Washington, DC: U.S. Government Printing Office (December).

Vaughan, Roger, and Bearse, Peter (1980). "Federal Economic Development Strategy: A Framework for Design and Evaluation." Washington, DC: National Commission for Employment Policy (October).

Vernon, Raymond. *Big Business and the State.*

H.C. Wainwright & Co., Economics (1979). "The Impact of Government Regulations on Competition in the Auto Industry" (May 4).

The Wall Street Journal. Numerous issues, July 1979 to the present.

XIII

The Urban Development Action Grant Program

Joel Freiser

"Be ready to do business." This was the rather straightforward formula for success offered to public officials by a private developer. "Doing business" was the theme of a conference on urban economic development sponsored by the New England Municipal Center late in 1979. George Slye, a Boston-based developer, offered the conferees a private-sector perspective for building successful public–private partnerships. But doing business in the public sector is a phrase that local elected officials understand but find difficult to master. Mr. Slye focused upon an element of successful public–private relationships by observing, "Time and interest rates are the enemy of the private sector. Uncontrolled, time tends to inflate costs and erode profitability. For elected officials, time is traditionally measured in budget cycles, appropriations, and revenues. Time, in particular, has been a factor which, in public life, is seemingly in endless supply."

Public–private partnerships for economic development in cities founder when conflicting premises and definitions of time collide. Past and current failures to forge successful public–private economic development projects are often casualties of mismatched perceptions of timing and goals by private and public entrepreneurs. The availability and mobilization of capital alone does not always guarantee success.

As George Slye addressed New England mayors in late 1979, visions of federal "sugarplums" danced in their heads. The "sugarplum" both public and private organizations seek these days is known as UDAG, or Urban Development Action Grant. UDAG has emerged since 1978 as an effective economic development tool. A recent federal initiative, it is widely used by local government to stimulate private investment in distressed cities. Across the

United States it has generated private investment and job creation. In each case, a public–private partnership is forged to accomplish economic development objectives. UDAG marks the latest chapter in federal urban policy since urban initiatives gained momentum during the Depression. Its full impact will not be felt until most projects are complete. Early indications of success have attracted wide interest.

Key Problems to be Addressed

UDAG represents the changing nature of the public–private relationship in a variety of ways. It may foretell the direction of economic development policy.

This chapter treats UDAG as a program and process that highlights the complex interactions of many public and private actors. It shows UDAG to be a policy tool that can harness the dynamism of swiftly changing economic opportunities. In a discussion of the program's organization we shall see how it joins simplicity, performance, and economy of design.* We shall identify conflicts among many of the key actors' goals, and then see how the program's rules are designed to fashion mutually acceptable goals even though some actors will not get all they want in the way of public or private gains. In short, we want to understand UDAG as a mechanism for making a "deal."

This chapter shall then turn to UDAG's antecedents and contrast UDAG with previous approaches to the public stimulation of private economic development. We shall see that previous attempts at urban problem solving did not give sufficient emphasis to the interactive nature of multiple actors, causes and effects. The character and level of public–private sector participation will be reviewed to highlight its emerging role and the problems it poses for future efforts. By examining UDAG's pattern of implementation, we shall see how regional trends and comparative economic advantages have shaped the type and location as well as the impact of projects. This is of topical interest because it will show the UDAG seems best used to complement and exploit established or emerging economic trends. This is a feature of some significance to public officials struggling to develop local economic development strategies. Review of the program's implementation problems may alert both public and private participants to potential blind alleys and more productive program designs.

A deeper understanding of the UDAG program leads to a more sophisticated understanding of economic development as a subtle and complex design process. By viewing development activities in this light, the UDAG program and its participants may come to realize a greater degree of sensitivity and greater control over a host of often unpredictable elements. By observing the

---

*Considerations suggested by Christopher Alexander's *Notes on the Synthesis of Form* (Alexander, 1964).

interactions among the variety of key actors in the UDAG process, both reader and participant can become better able to design and utilize this economic development tool. By noting points of potential dissonance or conflict among key actors, especially along the public–private interface, perhaps more effective teamwork can be encouraged.

The difficulty of the matter at hand is considerable. We are attempting to characterize a universe of key actors across a spectrum of sometimes conflicting interests and objectives. Implicit in this effort is a set of principles expressed by Erich Jantsch in *Design for Evolution*:

> Life is a gift and a predicament. It is the same gift for all creatures alive, but the particular human predicament differs in an important way from the general predicament inherent in life within the order of a natural ecosystem. The human predicament is regulation—not only living in accordance with, but *designing* forms of regulation which will ensure the steering of a viable course. There are many forces acting in the stream, pulling and pushing from all sides, sometimes mutually enhancing or cancelling out, but more often conflicting with each other in complex ways.

Thus, in examining UDAG, we shall be looking at the various forces influencing the urban economic development process.

Description of the UDAG Program

The UDAG program is a financial incentive; in effect, a capital subsidy designed to stimulate private investment in distressed urban areas. In this respect, it is similar to previous Federal capital investment programs for declining cities or distressed areas. The urban renewal program of the 1950s is the best known example. In contrast to urban renewal, UDAG funds flow to both public- and private-sector agencies and the public-sector agencies assume a more direct role in the development process. UDAG projects are designed to assure a more predictable outcome than did urban renewal. Formally negotiated partnership agreements govern both the plan and outcome of a UDAG program.

In actuality, actors in the UDAG program set in motion a dynamic process to do far more than the simple provision of financial incentives.

As a *program*, UDAG endeavors to:

leverage private financial commitments with federal, state, and local resources;

strengthen local tax bases by generating increased local revenues;

create new permanent jobs and retain jobs for low- and moderate-income persons; and

respond to local economic development opportunities while they are viable possibilities.

As a *process*, UDAG enables:

public and private officials and professionals to negotiate feasible economic development initiatives;

utilization of diverse financial and technical resources;

unique and complex proposals to be structured and refined for funding on a quarterly calendar basis; and

timely funding and completion of increasingly complex public-private initiatives.

Once an approved UDAG is in place, private profit and public benefit are defined by written contract. For the private sector, profit takes the traditional forms common to economic development: tax shelter, cash flow, depreciation of real property improvements, operating income, and other revenues. For public sector, increased business activity generates employment and increased tax revenues. Payback of UDAG loans provides a source of on-going local economic development capital. Public improvements strengthen and improve the attractiveness of an urban setting. New permanent employment for low- and moderate-income persons revitalizes individuals, families, neighborhoods.

UDAG is a development finance tool which offers flexible and attractive financing arrangements to urban developers. UDAG bridges the gap between available private capital and total development cost. The financial flexibility of UDAG allows the gap to be filled in a variety of ways. Sometimes it is used for direct public investment in physical infrastructure. Sometimes it is used to provide secondary financing on flexible terms for the private sector. This flexibility is multidimensional. Small as well as large projects can be financed. Complex as well as simple initiatives can be launched. Commercial, industrial, neighborhood, and energy-related economic development projects are eligible. This broad scope means wide applicability.

In recognition of UDAG's wide appeal, Congress increased annual funding from $400 million to $675 million annually from FY 1979 to FY 1981.* Its popularity is reflected in the volume and variety of projects submitted. This popularity may also be grounded in a belief by municipal officials and others that UDAG financing will have a palpable "output effect" on urban economies. If a UDAG capital subsidy brings about investment which might not otherwise take place, total output in the local economy should expand and, as output expands so might employment; this is the output effect (Jacobs and Roistacher, 1979). Whether or not there is a genuine "output effect" is an open question. The question is equivalent to the question of whether public incentives or assistance for private investment leads to a "substitution effect"—the substitution for public or private capital—or whether the private sector

*As of this writing, the UDAG program has been retained at a funding level of $500 million for FY 1982. The odds are good for its continuation past FY 1982.

investment represents a net increase in private investment over and above what would have been forthcoming anyway. From an analytical or methodological point of view, this question has not yet been satisfactorily addressed, though we will see further on how UDAG attempts to address the issue administratively.

Since a private financial commitment is essential, UDAG draws the government, from the federal level on down, into new roles. Government becomes facilitator, underwriter, and investment analyst. Federal stewardship operates principally on behalf of local government, and augments a locality's often limited capacity to structure such initiatives. The private sector now finds itself dealing with federal and local officials as both regulators *and* partners. The public–private partnership must, therefore, strike a working balance between these two conflicting roles and responsibilities. The regulatory role of the public–private relationship is the mold within which an initiative is structured. The private sector must work within a public planning framework and be prepared to integrate specific public objectives. On its part, the public sector must recognize the dynamics and incentives of the market. It is the harmonious integration of public and private objectives which ideally result in a feasible UDAG project. Conflicting goals abound. It is, however, the UDAG negotiation process which, when successful, enables a mutually beneficial solution to emerge.

UDAG is a project-specific economic development tool. It is meant to help distressed cities and urban counties reclaim deteriorated neighborhoods or revitalize their economic base. It is HUD's first economic development program with job creation as a key objective. Action grants were authorized at $400 million per year for FY 1978–1980 by Section 110 of Title I of the Housing and Community Development Act of 1977. The 1978 amendment to the Act increased the annual appropriation to $675 million. Accounting for the recent annual inflation rate, this increase in funding may be close to 50% in real terms. The program is mainly focused upon larger cities. Twenty-five percent of the fund is allocated by law to small cities below 50,000 population which are not central cities of Standard Metropolitan Statistical Area(s). (The other, larger cities will be referred to as "metropolitan cities.")

A recitation of official program statistics provides at least an initial impression of the scope and impact of the program. As of July 16, 1980, a total of 766 projects had received preliminary approval. The total amount of federal assistance using UDAG funds amounted to $1,487,000,000. A total of $8,420,000,000 in counterpart private commitments had been generated. A total of 228,377 new permanent jobs was projected. The estimated number of jobs retained was 95,232. UDAG activity generated a total of about 176,000 construction jobs up to mid-1980. In housing development and rehabilitation, UDAG was responsible for generating 22,000 new housing units. Rehabilitation totaled 24,912 housing units. In terms of project type, a total of 244 neighborhood projects received UDAG funding for a total of $419 million.

Industrial projects accounted for a total of 261 approvals for total UDAG funding of $336 million. A total of 261 commercial redevelopment projects was approved for UDAG support of $732 million. In all, metropolitan cities received 442 UDAG approvals while 324 projects were approved for small cities.

This enumeration of UDAG approvals suggests that something noteworthy has occurred. The public sector has stimulated private investment in distressed urban areas on an unprecedented scale. The UDAG Program was set in motion in early 1978 and has operated for a relatively short period of time.* The public sector has been able to channel the economic leverage of the private sector at least somewhat in the direction of public policy objectives. By further examining the qualification and application process, we hope to highlight some of the conditions contributing to these results. The failures, difficulties and shortcoming are also instructive.

Having targeted distressed urban areas, the UDAG application and negotiation process becomes the framework for designing and negotiating fundable projects. (Refer to Figure 1.) Units of general-purpose local government are always the official applicant. A successful economic development program calls upon a combination of professional skills. These talents and their deployment greatly influence the product. Larger, more complex undertakings require a blending of talented leadership and technical resources. Every project requires essentially the same set of key actors. Local government capability to plan and manage economic development activity is paramount. Unfortunately, the correct combination of technical, financial, and political resources are not always available. This places less prepared elements of the public sector at a distinct disadvantage. Larger cities, usually over 100,000 population, enjoy the advantage of a larger pool of leaders who have at their disposal some funds and professional assistance. Even sizable populations and local financial resources are not enough to mitigate often immense socioeconomic problems of poverty and disinvestment. We shall examine further on the impact that city size has upon its ability to marshall key actors and implement complex undertakings.

Small cities often suffer the greatest disadvantages. Marshalling local public and private sector resources is also an important problem for them. When it comes to attracting *industrial* investment to distressed nonmetropolitan areas, however, we shall see that small cities enjoy a distinct advantage.

Large and small cities must always orient their use of UDAG toward achieving statutory economic development objectives. The degree to which this occurs is an index of the quality of individual projects and proposals. At worst, the federal selection procedures can be a somewhat impressionistic assessment. At best, it assures that only the most promising proposals are funded. Future research efforts will, no doubt, yield more definite evaluations.

---

*A total of 36 months since 1/78, when the first round of applications began, to 1/81, when this chapter was drafted.

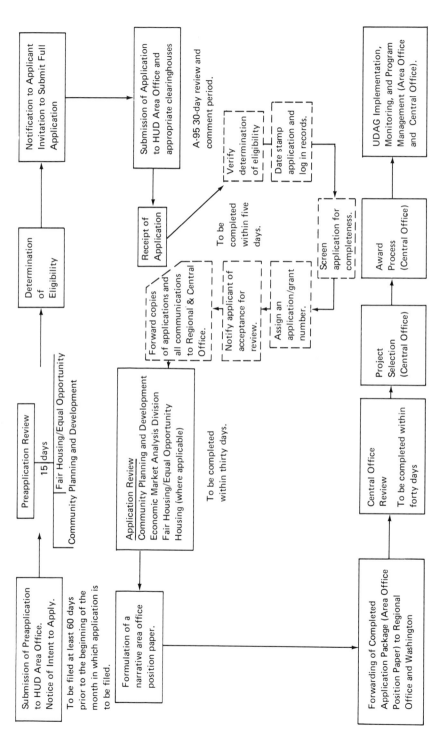

Figure 1. Flow chart of UDAC application process.

Each UDAG application must explain how it meets statutory and programmatic objectives. The question of the actual necessity of the grant is crucial. This requirement and the others challenge federal reviewers to make difficult determinations. The range and type of initiatives fundable by UDAG is unlimited. Commercial, industrial, and neighborhood development initiatives of varying complexity, necessity, and feasibility can be considered. The ability to properly assess and separate the "wheat from the chaff" is certainly a challenge to public decision making.

In some detail, each proposal must demonstrate how it will

1. alleviate physical distress,
2. alleviate economic distress,
3. provide fiscal improvements to the local government,
4. have impact upon special problems of low- and moderate-income persons and minorities,
5. plan to assure that private sector jobs are available to the unemployed,
6. demonstrate the local government's capacity to carry out the project based upon its prior accomplishments.

A series of simple charts in the applications show the number of jobs contemplated, and all key financial transactions. Detailed narratives fill in where necessary. Private sector participants must provide statements of financial conditions, credit references, and a *pro forma* of the proposal. All private financial disclosure is treated in confidence. A UDAG proposal calls for basically the same degree of disclosure as any complex or even simple economic initiative brought to a private financial institution for assistance. All these elements play an instrumental role in the funding process. As a competitive and discretionary public grant program, HUD/UDAG operates in many ways as an investment banker. The UDAG selection factors enable public managers to assess financial feasibility and the degree to which a proposal meets other public investment criteria. HUD must be prepared to assess a potentially vast array of development ideas and proposals. Each proposal is usually part of a unique local setting.

UDAG places the federal government more heavily in the development banking business. It falls short of the comprehensive plan for a National Development Bank, as proposed by the Carter administration in 1978, but essential elements of the National Development Bank proposal can be seen in the UDAG program. It provides capital assistance in amounts up to 25% of total development cost. The actual amount varies according to the nature of each proposal. It emphasizes the piggy-backing and integration of other federal resources. Most prominent among other federal resources have been direct loans and guarantees from the Economic Development Administration and the Small Business Administration. The ceiling on the total cost of project financed by tax-exempt Industrial Revenue Bonds is raised to $20 million when UDAG is used. Most importantly, perhaps, management of the UDAG program's hundreds of proposals and project approvals has resulted in increased professional capacity within the federal establishment for assessment and negotiation of complex development initiatives through public–private partnerships.

A key determinant of funding feasilbity is the adequacy and firmness of the private sector's financial commitment. Without a private financial commitment, the UDAG program cannot work. Nonfinancial considerations also carry weight, as we shall see.

UDAG's Antecedents in Federal Programming and Policy

The UDAG program is the lastest in the lineage of Federal urban renewal programming whose antecedents lie in the New Deal. Urban housing and public works projects of the depression era highlight these origins.

The period after World War II was marked by a series of contradictory federal policies—simultaneously encouraging slum clearance and urban renewal while passively encouraging the decline of urban areas in favor of suburban development. This decline was accelerated through inexpensive Veterans Administration and Federal Housing Administration mortgage lending programs. At the same time the federal government created national interstate highways while neglecting the need for urban mass transit systems. The history of contradictory and self-defeating federal policies affecting the viability of urban areas is considerably longer than this but these sufficiently illustrate the point.

The Urban Renewal Program illustrates a federal policy designed to stimulate the elimination of slums and blight through making available at low cost land prepared for productive use. In many cities urban renewal created a virtual "sea" of vacant lots or parking areas, with little of the hoped-for revitalization. Urban renewal efforts occurred at the same time that the suburban exodus was at its height. It enjoyed a strong federal financial commitment at the front end. However, it suffered from a serious flaw at the rear end. Federal funds and publicly guaranteed notes were floated to provide cities money to acquire and clear blighted acreage, relocate individuals and businesses, and install public improvements. All this was in preparation for the marketing and disposition of land for private development. Proceeds from the sale of development parcels would partially liquidate the initial federal investment. Urban Renewal policy assumed that the so-called land write-down would be sufficient encouragement; especially when the renewal site offered attractive locational advantages. More often than not, especially in the older cities of the Northeast, large numbers of cleared renewal sites never realized any appreciable private investment. By the time land became available for actual development, the supporting market of middle income families and essential facets of the social infrastructure were gone. The middle class and the more upwardly mobile moved to the suburbs. While sound in concept, the urban renewal program failed to account for local, regional, and national market forces. It foundered amidst a sea of uncontrolled patterns of urban and suburban development.

The decades of the 1950s and 1960s comprised a period of economic expansion, cheap energy, and quietly growing social upheaval. The Vietnam War, the Civil Rights movement, and economic distress for disadvantaged minority groups contributed to the context of this period. The promise of the Urban Renewal era faded as social turmoil exploded in American cities. The failure of Urban Renewal became evident. The program came to be known as "minority removal." Urban Renewal was designed to address the problems of physical decay in cities but during the 1950s, conventional wisdom did not admit to the underlying social and economic causes resulting in American urban decline.

The 1960s found the nation focusing upon the social and economic distress of the poor in cities and rural areas. Indeed, the rhetoric of the Kennedy and Johnson administrations as well as the federal War on Poverty attest to government's effort to respond to social unrest and aspirations in distressed areas. Important advances were made in Civil Rights legislation and in federal domestic programming. Head Start, VISTA, Model Cities, Public Service Careers Programs, and other initiatives poured hundreds of millions of public dollars into stabilizing and sometimes even advancing the economic status of the poor and disadvantaged.

The Model Cities Program, in particular, was a federal effort to institutionalize a comprehensive approach to solving urban problems in local governments. By concept and design it recognized the interactive nature of urban distress. It called for cities eligible for assistance to prepare comprehensive programs to solve or at least make progress toward solving the problems of poverty in urban areas. It attempted to assure that all the key facets of urban distress be addressed. Education, child care, environmental protection, housing, economic development, manpower development; these and other problems were examined and, to some degree, were addressed. For six years, Model Cities funds were funneled into so-called "Demonstration Cities." In retrospect, much of the money went into human capital investment. Some of it was wasted, noteworthy advances were made in many areas, but the overall problem was far from being solved. While the funds provided were sizable, they were not sufficient to the task. Underlying causes of economic and social distress were not effectively engaged. Coupled with continued social unrest in American cities, disturbing trends of disinvestment continued unabated. The era of Urban Renewal faded into the era of Model Cities. This too faded as instruments for stimulating urban reinvestment were not adequate to the overwhelming task at hand.

Urban Renewal's shortcoming resulted from a complex of reasons. The program failed to provide a mechanism for encouraging private investment in cities beyond the provision of cleared land prepared for development in accordance with traditional urban planning concepts. The eruption of urban violence and civil disorder in the 1960s made urban private investment even more unattractive. Among the numerous other disincentives to urban investment were counterproductive federal and state tax policies and large numbers of poor people ill-equipped socially and educationally for productive participation in the urban economy. Sadly, the same problems continue to confront us today.

The Urban Renewal Program foundered along until 1968. Its official demise occurred when the Nixon administration began to implement its "New Federalism." From 1968 to 1970 Urban Renewal grants become known as the Neighborhood Development Program or NDP. NDP provided financial assistance in yearly increments for accomplishing what could be completed in one calendar year. NDP signaled the official end of Urban Renewal and the beginning of the present era in federal urban policy and programming using the so-called block grant.

Through the decades of Urban Renewal, Model Cities, and the War on Poverty, private investment in urban revitalization was limited. The attraction of private capital was mainly the result of developers identifying and utilizing a very limited number of profitable opportunities in certain urban areas. Many larger cities do enjoy areas of revitalization as a result of land cleared for development under the Urban Renewal Program. In New York, for example, the emergence of Lincoln Center for the Performing Arts and the West Side as desirable areas are due, in large measure, to the use of Federal Urban Renewal funds. Showcase examples of development exist in many American cities. In the final stages, however, private development capital was the essential ingredient for success, but success was elusive. The aging and distressed cities of the northeast and northcentral regions of the United States still suffer from underinvestment, disinvestment, and deterioration.

Out of the social and political maelstrom of the 1960s, federal policy shifted again. The game plan shifted from categorical funding to combat urban social and economic problems to "block grant" funding under greater local control. Instead of federal review of detailed local urban renewal plans, communities gained greater local discretion in selecting and treating problems of physical decay, abandonment, and redevelopment. Federal urban development policy began to limit the social programming and public service activities of the Model Cities and War on Poverty era. Federal guidelines began emphasizing physical infrastructure and housing, especially rehabilitation.

With the start of the Carter administration in 1976, it was recognized that the absence of private investment in urban areas should be addressed directly. The challenge to find ways to channel private investment toward distressed cities began. Enactment of the Urban Development Action Grant program in 1978 is the prime example of current initiatives to encourage private investment in sick cities.

A description of the UDAG program and the process by which it operates will illustrate the changing nature of the relationship between the public and private sector of our economy. UDAG places the public sector in the novel (for the American economic system) position of entrepreneur on behalf of the public interest. At the same time it seeks to channel the productive energy of the private sector toward the economic revitalization of distressed American cities. UDAG is somewhat the obverse (other side of the coin) of the recent federal loan guarantee extended to the Chrysler Corporation. Chrysler management approached the public sector in response to its deteriorating market and financial position. With UDAG, the public sector of "distressed" areas is approaching the private sector with a similar stance. Both situations entail significant risks. (See Chap. XII on risks in the Chrysler case.)

The Urban Development Action Grant Process

The UDAG process begins with the over 300 cities which meet federal criteria of distress. The program is targeted to localities with declining tax bases, population outmigration or stagnation, aged housing stock, and job lag or decline. Minimum standards for physical and economic distress for small cities, metropolitan cities, and urban counties are established and revised annually by the Department of Housing and Urban Development.

On the local level, the UDAG process begins in the minds of local elected officials facing economic distress in their communities. It also begins in the minds of the development community. In fact, each key actor in the economic development process plays a role in bringing specific proposals to the "marketplace" as well as playing a key role in bringing them to constructive fruition. Conventional opportunities for economic development usually result in a developer, financial institution, and associated professionals (accountant, lawyer, architect, and engineer) assessing, planning, packaging, and marketing their joint initiatives. Before UDAG, the role of the public sector in conventional development opportunities was limited to encouragement or discouragement through traditional planning or zoning techniques.

Especially in distressed cities which are UDAG-eligible, one or more development plans have often been on the shelf for several years or more. Some are remnants of planning completed during the Urban Renewal years of the 1950s. In other localities, recent plant closings have precipitated major unemployment and economic dislocation. In either event, local elected leadership is prompted to take some form of constructive action to alleviate distress. Especially in the northcentral and northeastern regions of the United States, state and local promotional efforts though industrial commissions have attempted to attract industry or commercial activity. In contrast to the sunbelt region, the declining regions continue to suffer from plant closings, business failures, and relocations. In the UDAG program, local governments and private sector partners have a tool with which to forge legally binding plans and financial arrangements for specific industrial, commercial, and neighborhood initiatives via uniquely tailored combinations of private and public financial resources and incentives.

Once a UDAG proposal is reduced to a complete application package, its elements comprise a series of firm financial commitments and transactions. From this point, federal and local officials refine the proposal together with their private sector counterparts. Great emphasis is placed upon getting the best deal for the local economy. When UDAG funds are used as a secondary loan to the private sector, repayment plans are fashioned to provide the best possible payback to the locality. In some instances, local government is able to realize additional revenues from private profit beyond a set minimum. In other instances local government becomes a partner in the enterprise.

By accepting and funding UDAG applications on a quarterly basis, the time-honored tradition of bureaucratic delay and uncertainty are significantly reduced. Proposals that have merit but lack essential elements can be held over for further consideration in upcoming quarterly funding rounds. This preserves promising yet incomplete proposals.

The heart of the UDAG process is the interaction of the key players. During the formative stages of specific projects local government, federal UDAG reviewers, and the private sector refine their objectives and desired outcomes. The interaction of public and private economic forces creates a dynamism. Just as dynamics is a branch of physics dealing with forces and their influence on the motion of bodies, the fashioning of a UDAG economic development project sets in motion private developers and public officials. An equilibrium of forces results in a fundable UDAG project. By examining the key actors in this dynamic process, some insight into UDAG and the nature of the emerging outline of public–private partnerships will be gained.

First of all, there is the developer. This could be just about anyone. Frequently, the developer is an experienced professional with a successful track record. Often, developers specialize in particular types of projects. More recently, development has been attempted by nonprofit organizations such as community development corporations. As the key entrepreneur, the private developer's objective is profit. It is accomplished through acquiring, improving, and selling a development. Sometimes it is accomplished by also managing a completed development as well. Syndications, limited partnerships, and joint ventures provide developers with the vehicles for marketing developments to investors.

So-called conventional development opportunities are mainly found in the growing market sectors of the economy. The sunbelt region is typical. Industrial, commercial, and residential developers are attracted to growth areas by relatively ample availability of capital and market demand. Financial appreciation from the skillful orchestration of professional and capital resources is the essence of the developer's goal.

Development in older urban areas, especially in regions experiencing economic decline, present special problems to the private developer. Special risks, problems, and complexities add uncertainty to successful completion and operation of development projects in old cities. It is these special risks that the UDAG program was designed to address.

Less often, the developer role is undertaken by nontraditional entities. Local nonprofit economic development corporations and community development corporations fill the gap created by the absence of the private developer in many of the most distressed urban areas. Frequently lacking professional experience, the local, community-based nonprofit development corporation presents special problems of capacity building. In an effort to build local development capacity in the public sector, HUD and nonprofit organizations such as the National Development Council have embarked upon a demonstration program to build these skills within local government and community-based organizations. In selected cities, the National Development Council is providing technical assistance and training to create a local cadre of economic development professionals. Equipped with special set-asides of HUD resources, e.g., Section 312 commercial rehabilitation loans and Section 108 loan guarantees, and targeted funding by the Federal Economic Development Administration and Small Business Administration, local economic development corporations are marketing and packaging their services. To date, the National Development Council claims to have facilitated over one billion dollars in public and private commitments for distressed cities. Growing numbers of public, nonprofit,* state economic development authorities and urban development corporations provide key resources for economic development.

The second major actor is the lender. As the major source of debt financing for economic development, various members of the financial community play this role. For interim or construction financing, commercial banking institutions continue to be a traditional source for this type of capital. Long-term debt financing is often secured through institutional investors such as insurance companies. The lender's goal is clearly a secure and credit-worthy risk. For the interim lender, project completion, permanent financing, and repayment of principal and interest are essential goals. For the long-term lender the goal is a secure income stream and cash flow to service the debt obligation. In the UDAG program, financial commitment initially, and evidence of legally binding commitment after preliminary approval, are critical to success. Without lender commitments, a feasible project is not possible.

The equity investor is another important actor in the development process. He is usually also the same person or group as the developer. The cash put into the typical development venture is likely to be a small percentage of the total development cost. If a venture is in the $10 million range, the cash equity can often be as high as $1 million. If shares in the project are syndicated, the equity risk is spread among more than one individual. Under the UDAG program, local government becomes an equity investor. HUD grants UDAG dollars to a

---

*Definitions of profit appear, per force, to be evolving as we realize the generation of public revenues in partnership with private capital. With this phenomenon, public investment criteria change as well.

locality. In turn, the locality lends these funds to the developer. A local government's return on its investment is the repayment of interest and principal on this loan.

The next key actor is the professional. This includes legal, financial, marketing, and design specialists. All or some of these specialists may be part of the developer's organization. Their objective is to support the developer's technical requirements.

The contractor, builder, building inspector, and permit official are yet another class of key actors in the economic development process. Their contribution to a development effort is essential but often difficult to orchestrate. Timely completion of a project during the construction phase is dependent upon this class of actors. Active cooperation between permit officials, construction inspectors, and contractors is essential to assure that interim financing for construction is not exhausted before completion of the project.

Unquestionably, the role of local government officials in economic development is an evolving one. Competition among cities for development is fierce. It thrusts upon mayors, county officials, and other local leaders the need to compete for public and private resources. They must attract developers to translate proposals into projects. Their goal is to strengthen the economic base and create new employment. The role of local top officials is becoming more entrepreneurial (see Goodman). To succeed, local government executives must be able to formulate and shape development strategy. They must also be able to provide aggressive leadership in its pursuit. Their contribution is among the most difficult and challenging. Personal leadership qualities, public brokerage and marketing skills must be able to reconcile diverse and conflicting interests. It is to be expected that conflicting public and private interests will surface when initiatives are incubated, planned, and implemented. They must align political forces in support of economic development proposals and be able to bargain effectively in the public interest for their adoption. Political and managerial leadership of local elected officials is in itself a difficult and complex process. It depends upon the ability of the local chief executive to maintain the unity and control of the local governing body. It is essential to assure adoption of public actions authorizing official commitment of personnel and resources (Banfield, 1965).

Indeed, all UDAG projects require the authorization of local governing bodies to permit the chief executive to submit an application. Where local political partisanship is intense and divisive, elected chief executives will have great difficulty in negotiating economic development initiatives. When economic development proposals involve condemnation or changes in land use, the generation of political support is further complicated by the opposition of residents, property owners, and other organized groups. To repeat: bargaining in the public interest by local chief executives is a key element in the success of any economic development program. Highly questionable outcomes can arise if local political and development officials have little sense of either long-range development strategy or the nature of the public interest. Some observers are now tempted to say that UDAG is just another "give away" to private interests. Given the capacity of local government to deal in the development arena, one would be very surprised if this were not true to some extent. But to whatever extent it is true, it is because governmental officials at all levels, especially local, have not formulated a development strategy which balances both long-term and short-term objectives and have not learned to strike hard bargains in the public interest.

The next important class of key actors is nongovernmental organizations. Their influence can be crucial to the adoption or rejection of an economic development project. When in support of an initiative, their voices add stature and indicate broader local commitment. When raised in opposition, their criticism often delays if not cripples the initiative. Especially in neighborhood economic development programs, nongovernmental organizations can serve as nonprofit developers. UDAG regulations provide two important opportunities for nongovernmental organizations to participate in the economic development process. Community Development Block Grant regulations provide that nongovernmental organizations may receive public funds to undertake projects (24 CFR 570.204) (*Federal Register*, 1978). Local governments applying for UDAG must assure that they have provided opportunities for citizens to participate in the planning of programs and have convened two public hearings in accordance with Federal Register Regulation 24 CFR 570.456 (c) (11) (i) (A), (B), and (C). Solicitation of the views and proposals of nongovernmental organizations and individuals, therefore, is built into the federal regulatory process. It provides a channel for identifying the needs and goals of low- and moderate-income persons.

Finally, the federal government is the remaining key actor in the urban economic development process.* This is nowhere more evident than in the role it plays in the management of the UDAG program. Through review and assessment of UDAG proposals, federal managers actively participate in fashioning public–private partnerships. In the process of reviewing and negotiating specific projects, HUD plays a facilitative role. Rather than finding reasons for disapproving applications, the federal review posture is to facilitate the structuring of "fundable" projects. This does not mean that all "fundable" project applications can, or would be approved. It means that when applications are ranked and placed in competition with one another during a quarterly application review cycle, those scoring most highly on selection factors will likely be approved within available funding.

The objectives of the Federal management process are:

1. to assure feasible projects are proposed,

*Whether, under the Reagan administration, this role will be supplanted by a state role via a system of block grants remains to be seen.

2. to produce desirable levels of job creation, revenue improvement, and urban revitalization,
3. to assure maximum impact of related federal and other public financial and programmatic resources.

These goals are consistent with the National Urban Policy statement issued by the White House in 1978 (see *A New Partnership to Conserve America's Communities: The President's Urban and Regional Policy Group Report*).

Structuring UDAG proposals for maximum impact on local economies is accomplished through a variety of means. Some of the methods result in UDAG funds being "injected" into a local economy and earmarked for continuous recycling. In many instances, UDAG funds are lent to private developers. These are subsequently repaid to the local government, entering into revolving funds which recycle the money into other economic development programs which are eligible under UDAG regulations and the Community Development Block Grant program. In other instances, an economic return is assured by factoring the local government into a project as a partner so that financial returns are based upon the long-term viability of the venture.

Financial and related investment, social, environmental, and consumer issues must be factored into a deal properly to assure the best prospects for success. This demands a high level of professional involvement and public management ability. Federal UDAG staff provides a diverse array of professional specialists in public and business administration, real estate, banking, and related disciplines. Many have been private developers, bankers, or attorneys. Many have extensive experience in the management of local economic development programs.

In March 1979 the General Accounting Office (GAO) issued a report which voiced several criticisms of the UDAG program. The basis of funding decisions was found to be deficient, so that independent auditors could not identify the rationale for judgments on various criteria.* Corrective actions by HUD followed. These included staff additions as well as several steps designed to effect a more disciplined management operation. Since then, the volume of applications has continued to rise. The applications process has become more competitive and the average leveraging ratio of public to private financial commitments has been forced upward in response to increasing demand.

The UDAG private–public negotiation process is a progressive series of interactions. Within it, public and private social, physical, and economic benefits are assessed. Trade-offs are made to satisfy, even if not to maximize, the goals and objectives of the key actors. The desired outcome is a public–private partnership consisting of a legally binding agreement to assure that the negotiated objectives are fulfilled. The common goal of each actor is a fundable project.

---

*Including the basis of decisions on the important "but for" criterion described in the following paragraphs.

The public investment management capacity demanded by the UDAG program calls for the federal government to play several key roles. First, it must serve as agent on behalf of local government and the public. Additionally, it must stimulate private initiative and investment. In so doing, federal officials must determine that "but for" the UDAG funds, a project would not be feasible. It is upon this determination that the issue of capital substitutability merges. Sometimes the nature of a proposal makes the "but for" decision straightforward. For example, without UDAG funding for a parking structure, commercial development of a downtown parcel may clearly not be financially feasible. In most cases, however, the determination is far more difficult.* More clear-cut are those cases where significant private investment has apparently been planned for some time. There are cases where new corporate investment may have been considered for some time and where a municipality and corporation have decided, jointly, to apply for a UDAG using the corporate commitment as a lever. There are also projects where small amounts of UDAG funds are supposed to "leverage" private investments in excess of $10 million. In the latter cases, HUD scrutinizes the "but for" justification to determine if the proposal is designed simply to "trigger" a jump to a $20 million total project cost for the use of tax-exempt industrial revenue bonds.† Such projects show leveraging ratios of public to private financial commitments which can be unbelievably high. To forestall this tactic, HUD requires that the UDAG grant request be no less than 5% of the private investment. In such cases, wherever possible, the UDAG should be paid back in no more than five years with a market interest rate. The minimum ratio is 1 to 2.5.‡

Especially in those proposals where local government requires support to negotiate with private developers, UDAG staff will not only point out pitfalls but also recommend promising strategies for greater return on investment or project structure. The process is necessarily a balancing act. If "fundability" is not achieved, the "deal" will fall apart. HUD may withdraw from a poorly conceived proposal by disapproval. The private developer may withdraw. The local government may dissolve it. Cities with local capacity in managing economic development are usually able to present ambitious proposals with clear economic and social objectives by the time an application is submitted to HUD.

The inauguration of the UDAG process also signals the arrival of federal officials with actual private sector development experience at the working level. Indeed, the first director of HUD's UDAG office in Washington was David Cordish, formerly a private developer in the Baltimore area. Federal UDAG staff are a blend of talented public and private sector managers. During its

---

*It is no less difficult, even within other terms of reference, for the academic program-evaluators who have not yet found satisfactory methodologies to analyze the substitution issue.

† The lack of any apparent justification for approvals in such cases was one of the points raised in the GAO critique.

‡ This ratio, at first an informal guideline, was formalized in late summer 1980 (see Proposed Rule, 24 CFR 570.459(b)(2), May 12, 1980).

initial two years of existence, the UDAG office developed a fund of practical policy and experience in reviewing, approving, and managing a portfolio of over 750 public–private partnerships. Presently in the form of policy memoranda, this portfolio offers a basis for the codification of public investment management practice into a body of procedures and guidelines. The job of codification should be expedited for, when complete, it may represent an important "first" for the emerging public/private political economy in the United States.

Already, a modest body of knowledge on urban economic development practice has been generated by practitioners at the National League of Cities, National Association of County Officials, and other national public interest groups concerned with urban economic development. The production and dissemination of materials reflecting their knowledge and experience has been financed by HUD's Office of Community Planning and Development and Office of Policy Development and Research under legislation authorizing the provision of technical assistance to states and localities. Through HUD's Office of Neighborhoods, Voluntary Associations, and Consumer Protection, local nongovernmental organizations are encouraged to provide local leadership for neighborhood-level revitalization efforts. UDAG and its companion program, the Community Development Block Grant, are key tools in this local revitalization process. Building the local capacity of neighborhood-level nongovernmental organization is one of the key objectives of these programs. The HUD Office of Neighborhoods also assists neighborhood organizations to build their capacity to better utilize the resources of the UDAG program to address problems in their own communities.

These goals and major approaches of UDAG are shared by several federal agencies.* The Department of Commerce, through the Economic Development Administration is an important federal actor in the UDAG program through its loan and guarantee programs. In nonmetropolitan areas, the Business and Industry Program of the Farmers Home Administration is an important source of loans and loan guarantees for UDAG. Through the Federal Home Loan Bank, Federal Reserve Bank, Office of the Comptroller of the Currency, and other banking and credit regulatory authorities, the provisions of the Community Reinvestment Act are stimulating local financial institutions to direct more credit toward the revitalization of distressed urban areas. (See Chap. XIV.)

The UDAG program and the dynamic management and development process it has generated is a singular approach to public investment management for distressed American urban areas. It highlights federal efforts to integrate public and private resources. It accomplishes this by flexibility and feasibility in concept and structure. It also reflects new levels of interdependency between the public and private sector which appear to be giving a distinctive coloration to urban economic development in the early 1980s.

---

*This paragraph is still valid, though the financing capacities of the agencies cited have been severely reduced by the Reagan administration.

354

Implementation Patterns

Implementation patterns in the UDAG program are revealed in Table 1. Metropolitan cities have captured more UDAG funds for commercial projects than for any other type. Small cities succeed in developing more industrial projects using UDAG. The greatest degree of leveraging private investment has occurred in industrial rather than commercial types of projects. Leveraging ratios have been lowest in neighborhood projects which have emphasized new housing units or rehabilitation with little or no appreciable net fiscal return to the local government. Regionally, UDAG funds flow more to the north than to the south. This is largely because the greatest concentration of decline in urban areas exists in the northcentral and northeastern United States. 1978 amendments to the UDAG legislation provide funding to "pockets of poverty" in otherwise nondistressed localities. This provision enables such areas to secure UDAG assistance for their "pockets of poverty," as long as the nondistressed cities provide a portion of the cost from their more robust economic bases. Establishing eligibility for pockets of poverty depends upon the ability to document in some detail the social and economic conditions in neighborhoods, as well as those in the surrounding municipality. The pockets of poverty regulation and methodology are contained in Federal Register 24 CFR 570.466.

The jobs impact of UDAG falls into three categories:

1. construction jobs,
2. new permanent employment,
3. jobs retained.

New permanent jobs targeted for low- and moderate-income persons are the most desired employment goal of the program. Job retention is sometimes almost as important, especially when a UDAG project will assure retention of a major local employer. In some instances, a plant closing can be averted. For example, the Universal Folding Box Company of Hoboken would have moved to a suburban location to expand its facilities. Subsoil conditions at its Hoboken location required pilings to add more plant capacity. The UDAG grant, provided to Universal as a secondary loan, made financing for the added cost of expansion available. In this case, the retention of some 50 jobs resulted in the creation of nearly 30 new permanent jobs. In Waterloo, Iowa, the Rath Packing Company received preliminary approval of a UDAG to permit the creation of an employee stock ownership plan for the ailing firm.

The job impact of UDAG in nonmetropolitan areas, involving mostly industrial projects, is generally higher than the impact in metropolitan areas, involving mostly nonindustrial projects.* This reflects the continuing advantage that distressed nonmetropolitan areas enjoy over metropolitan loca-

*Whether one talks in terms of job "creation," "impact," or some other term is really a matter of semantics since the substitution issue is being begged here.

Table 1. Urban Development Action Grant (Program Totals to Date)ᵃ

	Small Cities	$(Millions)	Metro Cities	$(Millions)	Total	$(Millions)
Number of projects	324		442		766	
Neighborhood	76	65	168	354	244	419
Industrial	159	151	102	185	261	336
Commercial	89	68	172	663	261	732
Number of cities	294		192		486	
Leveraging ratio	6.8		5.4		5.7	
Action grants approved		284		1,202		1,487
Private funds committed		1,936		6,484		8,420
Other federal financial commitments		82		243		325
State/local financial commitments		86		551		637
Total investment		2,388		8,480		10,868
Property tax revenue increase		26		121		148
Other tax revenue increase		14		90		104
Tax revenue per action grant		.09		.10		.10
Action grant per job	$ 4,374		$ 7,359		$ 6,509	
New Permanent jobs	65,011		163,366		228,377	
Low income jobs	37,357		92,085		129,441	
Retained jobs	15,794		79,438		95,232	
Construction jobs	43,481		132,627		176,108	
All housing	7,192		39,482		46,674	
New housing	5,463		17,102		22,565	
Rehab housing	1,729		23,183		24,912	
Low income housing	3,257		19,587		22,844	

ᵃNote: data derived from applications announced for preliminary approval.

Sources: Data Systems and Statistics Division, Office of Community Planning and Development, HUD, Washington, DC, August, 1980.

tions, especially for manufacturing activity. On average, it appears to be more expensive to create new jobs in metropolitan areas. Job retention, especially among larger inner-city businesses, is likely to lead to long-term expansion. The variety of spin-off effects of UDAG in a local economy can be considerably more than appears at first glance. Secondary, tertiary, and other indirect economic effects of UDAG are acknowledged in the preliminary research of Jacobs and Roistacher (1979).

The effects are both quantitative and qualitative. While quantitative increases in employment are essential, the qualitative effect of even modest job creation often sufficiently changes adverse perceptions of local economic climate enough to generate further private investment on its own. Having achieved initial success in securing a UDAG, local perceptions of each of the key actors in the process is altered. All have participated in the process of molding a public–private partnership. Each has helped to forge and fit together a diverse set of elements. All are left with added confidence necessary to generate the process again and again, with or without UDAG. The emergence of professional local capacity with the skills and confidence to generate local economic development is a vital outcome of the UDAG program. It exposes all the key actors to a shared experience with a successful outcome.

Implementation Problems

Implementation problems in UDAG usually center upon failure of a key private financial commitment at some point after preliminary approval by HUD. Local controversy before or after UDAG approval can also be another source of implementation problems. Proposed UDAGs and even committed UDAGs fail and cannot be replaced. At risk, too, may be the federal financial interest.

As indicated earlier, most implementation problems cluster around environmental, relocation/displacement, equal opportunity, historic preservation, and citizen participation issues.* When any or all of these issues surface during the UDAG application review period, an opportunity is created to address and resolve them. Often, these issues are symptoms of weak planning and local capacity. Sometimes they result from insufficient involvement of neighborhood groups in UDAG project areas. In New Brunswick, New Jersey, for example, the development of a major downtown hotel/conference facility using UDAG was delayed by residents of the adjacent Hiram Market historic area. In New Brunswick this conflict appears to have stemmed from insufficient involvement of the neighborhood groups in the planning process carried on by the local government and the major financial interests in the project, Hyatt Hotels, and Johnson and Johnson.

*Proposed Rule, 24 CFR 570.450 through 463, May 12, 1980, Clarification and Changes to UDAG Requirements, adds a new section in order to protect residential and nonresidential tenants who are displaced by an action grant. Citizen participation and public hearing requirements are also amplified.

In other instances, citizen participation controversies may be related to a poor local record in equal opportunity for low- and moderate-income persons and minorities in employment and housing. It appears especially true where localities have experienced rapid demographic changes and economic stagnation without compensating changes in the composition of local elected government leadership. The emergence of this type of problem frequently stalemates promising economic initiatives. Where controversy of this type emerges, it forces local government leadership to pay closer attention and expend greater energy toward building community and neighborhood support in more tangible and directly beneficial ways. These types of implementation problems may prompt local elected leaders to deal, often for the first time, with social, political, and racial issues which have been festering beneath the surface.

Linkages with Other Federal Assistance Programs

Selection criteria 24 CFR 570.457(f) and (g) give consideration to the extent of financial participation to be made available by the state as well as the nature and extent of financial participation by other public entities. These provisions point to the important role played in public–private economic development by "linkages." Projects which include financial assistance from the state will receive more favorable consideration. One of the most widely used sources of state and local financial participation has been the tax-exempt industrial revenue bond issued by state and local economic development authorities. Projects which receive financial assistance from other public entities will also receive more favorable consideration. Other public resources may be provided by matching other federal grants or by firm commitments of other federal or local resources, such as those from the Economic Development Administration, the Small Business Administration, the Urban Mass Transit Administration, or from the local government applicant's own general purpose funds or municpal bonds. Beyond providing local government with incentives to link together state, federal, and local public funding sources for triggering private investment, through UDAG, another important series of linkages is encouraged with the Federal Comprehensive Employment and Training Act (CETA).

During the Carter administration, "Employment Initiatives" task forces of federal agency representatives attempted to identify and link economic resources which would be supportive but were not initially included by local government applicants. In particular, the Employment Initiatives program was designed to link UDAG proposals with CETA Prime Sponsors who would provide trained CETA-eligibles for employment resulting from a UDAG or other federally funded proposal for local economic development.* CETA Title

---

*This program begun in March 1980, is currently being implemented on a demonstration basis at 14 sites nationwide as the Targeted Jobs Demonstration Program. The evaluation of the program, to be conducted by a HUD contractor under terms of reference in HUD RFP 6540, will reveal to what extent jobs in UDAG-assisted projects have gone to CETA eligibles.

VII Private Industry Councils composed of local business, labor, and public leaders augment these efforts. Under the Reagan administration, the Employment Initiatives effort has languished at the federal level, but the interest in effecting linkages continues at state and local levels.*

Recapitulation and Outstanding Questions to be Addressed

This chapter has reviewed the UDAG program as a recent and extensively used approach to fostering partnerships between the public and private sectors for economic development. In addition to generating impressive levels of public and private investment for industrial, commercial, and neighborhood projects, UDAG has established federal and local elements of the public sector in the difficult role of developers and entrepreneurs representing the public interest. Of course, the definition of the public interest is subject to the political ideology and national policy framework within which the program operates. Future research on UDAG, as on other public programs, must cope with the question of neutrality and advocacy in policy research along the lines discussed by Harold Orlans and others [see Orlans (1975) for an example].

Although the net effect of UDAG may be negligible in the ebb and flow of national and international economic forces as they impact upon urban economic ills, it has demonstrated the efficacy of a new approach to public decision making. At its essence, it is probably the dynamic tension between the public and private entrepreneurial actors which provides the momentum for more innovative and efficient economic development initiatives. Another question to be answered is how to assure that all key actors in the economic development process are given the opportunity to have their goals factored into initiatives without fatally damaging the final outcome. There is the continuing danger of reconciling all differences at the cost of sacrificing the forward momentum needed for creating effective public–private partnerships. In the long term, the test of this experiment in public–private partnerships will be the extent to which disadvantaged segments of our society are able to fulfill their economic aspirations.

Evaluations of the UDAG Program

Given the controversial, dynamic and evolving nature of the public/private relationships in UDAGs, the program will continue to be the subject of lively assessment for some time to come. Several evaluation conferences have been held. One such conference was sponsored by Princeton University's Urban and

---

*Additionally, a few states are considering bond issues to provide state "mini-UDAG" program funds.

Regional Research Center on November 1 and 2, 1979. Another was held at the Urban Institute in Washington consisting of UDAG recipients making presentations before evaluation juries of developers and public officials. A critical report on the UDAG program by the U.S. General Accounting Office (March 30, 1979) resulted in tightening of review procedures and additional staff for HUD's UDAG office. Most assessments give the program good marks. All question the actual need for UDAG assistance where private investment was believed likely to occur anyway. But none is able to convincingly suggest more effective alternatives to the present approach of using UDAG. In a significant number of cities, UDAG resources have been instrumental in hastening the disposition and redevelopment of long-dormant Urban Renewal sites.* By increasing the ceiling on the total project where UDAG is utilized, a sizable number of industrial projects have been implemented which might otherwise not have been undertaken in distressed urban areas.

The program has also resulted in the federal government developing professional capacity in public–private investment management. It marks the entry of the federal government more deeply into the investment banking role as partner with the private sector in support of local economic development. By acting, when requested, as a local government's surrogate in UDAG negotiation with private developers, the federal government is fashioning and refining a fiduciary capacity which promises to play an increasingly important role in public decision making during the coming decade. In the process, local economic development management capacity is developing as more and more local governments become experienced in its practice. Appreciative of the balance of private and public forces which must be fostered though the UDAG process, the federal government has entered new and strange waters with, so far, very few mishaps.

In the coming years, the role of the public sector as entrepreneur will undoubtedly evolve in response to the demands of "plotting a viable course." The often wrenching economic dislocations resulting from escalating energy costs are being felt in recessionary and inflationary spirals. Public policy tools like UDAG offer approaches to communities for reducing or even helping to reverse long-term economic distress. Hopefully, UDAG will make a solid contribution to mitigating urban economic and social challenges facing the nation in the coming decade. It will be from the creative interaction of public and private elements of our economic and social systems that tools such as UDAG will continue to evolve. It should enable the local government to participate in the economic development process by compensating for its weaknesses and building upon its strengths.

---

*The question of how well UDAGs will fare when the supply of urban renewal sites dwindles is a question which has been asked (by Richard Nathan) but not yet answered.

Appendix

Ten Questions on the UDAG Program

1. What Criteria Are Used to Determine Whether a UDAG Is a Loan or a Grant?

UDAG assistance takes the form of a loan to the private sector when the financial assistance will accrue to the benefit of the private sector and the funds will be used for improvements which remain in private ownership. When UDAG funds are used for direct investment in public infrastructure, i.e., roads, sewers, etc., assistance is provided on a direct grant basis. Of course, direct grants assistance for infrastructure or improvements which remain in the public domain must be integral to the private sector investment for which the UDAG was awarded in the first place.

2. Are Local Economic Development Corporations Technically and Legally Equipped to Handle Revolving Funds and Sons of UDAG?

As UDAG recipient, the unit of local government is usually responsible for observing the provisions of UDAG grant agreement(s) with regard to revolving funds or "sons" of UDAG. The legal and technical capacity for local economic development corporations to administer revolving funds must be determined on a case-by-case basis. Technical capacity of local economic development corporations is usually established upon a record of demonstrated accomplishment in the course of the UDAG application process. Legal capacity is dependent upon the legal powers enumerated in its certificate of incorporation as well as the nature of the legally-binding agreement(s) by and between it and the unit of local government in connection with a particular UDAG project. In summary, the answer is yes, in light of the foregoing.

3. How Is It Determined Which Local Agency Handles These Revolving Funds?

The local agency which handles revolving funds resulting from UDAG is determined by the applicant (i.e., the unit of local government).

4. Are UDAG Criteria and Review Still Used for Sons of UDAG or Can the Local Development Corporation Use These Funds as They Wish?

Unless otherwise specifically authorized or required at Exhibit A of the UDAG Grant Agreement, all Grant Revenues received by the Recipient, or by any Participating Party, after completion of all UDAG Funded Activities, shall be used by the Recipient, or by the Participating party subject to the approval of the Recipient, for community or economic development activities which would be eligible for assistance under Title I of the Act. (This is pursuant to Section 2.04 of the standardized UDAG Grant Agreement format.)

5. Why Do UDAG Funds Go First to a Local Development Agency and Then to a Developer?

Since the Act provides UDAG assistance to eligible units of local government, the municipality is always the initial Recipient of funds which then pass through its hands to the Participating Party (the developer).

6. One Negotiated Point is the Return of "Excess Profits" to the Municipality. How Is the Amount Determined? Does This Requirement Deter Private Commitment? Can the Municipality Use Those Funds in Any Way It Wants?

The return of "excess" profits to the municipality is determined by the amount of the net cash flow to the developer after deducting

1. expenses,
2. debt service,
3. real estate taxes.

This requirement may deter private commitment but since the UDAG is essential to the viability of the proposal, a developer is usually receptive to an equitable distribution as long as his criteria for a "reasonable" return on investment is achieved. The municipality can use those funds pretty much as it wants in light of Section 2.04 of the Grant Agreement (see answer to Question No. 4).

7. In Order to Be Effective, What Skills Should a Local Development Corporation Have? What Powers Should They Have? Should Decisions on Deals Be Made by a Municipal Board Consisting of Representatives of the Public and Private Sectors?

In order to be effective, a local development corporation must be skilled in "team building" within and among the key actors in the public and private sectors, financial analysis and loan packaging, and marketing/promotional activities. Local development corporations would have the power to undertake activities as described in 24 CFR 570.204 of the Community Development Block Grant regulations, dated March 1, 1978 as well as any other powers deemed necessary or appropriate for local economic development purposes. The composition of local economic development decisionmaking bodies should reflect the needs and established priorities of the locality. In many instances, local economic development corporations are governed by a board consisting of public and private members. Since the use of UDAG requires public hearings and local governing body approval for applications, public body approval is built in to the process when UDAG is used.

8. Do UDAG Projects Have to Comply with a City's Master Plan? Are There Public Hearings Apart from the UDAG Hearings?

Consistency with a city's master plan is a local determination. Apart from federally required public hearings for a UDAG application, local governments may wish to hold additional informational and public awareness workshops to assure a receptive and supportive constituency.

9. How Does One Quantify the Amount of Private Funds Leveraged When Many of These Funds Are Guaranteed by the Public Sector?

Generally, public guarantees of private financial commitments does not reduce the extent to which these funds are quantified for leveraging purposes. In some instances, private commitments which are publically guaranteed and enjoy a reduced interest rate may be discounted when establishing the ratio of private to public commitments.

10. Are Certain Cities or Certain Types of Projects Better Able to Leverage Funds Than Others?

Industrial projects in nonmetropolitan cities seem to enjoy higher leveraging ratios. Metropolitan cities appear to attract more commercial projects than any other types.

Bibliography

Alexander, Christopher (1964). *Notes on the Synthesis of Form.* Cambridge: Harvard University Press.

Banfield, Edward C. (1965). *Political Influence: A New Theory of Urban Politics* New York: The Free Press, Macmillan.

Federal Register (1978b). Subpart G, Vol. 43, No. 6, Urban Development Action Grant Regulations (January 10).

Federal Register (1978a). Subpart C, D, Vol. 43, No. 41, Community Development Block Grant Regulations (Wednesday, March 1).

Federal Register (1980). Vol. 45, No. 93, Proposed Rules, 24 CFR 570, Clarification and Changes To Urban Development Action Grant Requirements (May 12).

Goodman, Richard. *The Last Entrepreneurs.*

Jacobs, Susan S., and Roistacher, Elizabeth A. (1979). "The Urban Impacts of HUD's Urban Development Action Grant Program or Where's the Action in Action Grants?" in *The Urban Impacts of Federal Policies*, Norman J. Glickman, ed., Baltimore: Johns Hopkins University Press.

Jantsch, Erich (1975). *Design for Evolution.* New York: George Braziller.

A New partnership to Conserve America's Communities: The President's Urban and Regional Policy Group Report (March 1978).

New York State, Urban Development Corporation and Department of State (1980). *A Step-by-Step Guide to Resources for Economic Development*, 1515 Broadway, New York, NY.

Orlans, Harold (1975), "Neutrality and Advocacy in Policy Research". *Policy Sciences*, 6 (June 2).

U.S. Conference of Mayors, National Community Development Association, and the Urban Land Institute (1979a). "Economic Development: New Roles for City Government" (September).

U.S. Conference of Mayors, National Community Development Association, and the Urban Land Institute (1979b). "Local Economic Development Tools and Techniques: A Guide for Local Government" (September).

U.S. Department of Housing and Urban Development, (1978). *The President's* 1978 *National Urban Policy Report*. A Biennial Report to the Congress Submitted Pursuant to Sections 702 and 703(a), National Urban Policy and New Communities Development Act, as Amended in 1977 (August).

U.S. Department of Housing and Urban Development (1979). *Urban Development Action Grant Program*, First Annual Report. Washington, D.C.: HUD, (July).

U.S. Department of Housing and Urban Development (1980). Urban Development Action Grant Program, 2d Annual Report. Washington, D.C.: HUD, (July).

U.S. General Accounting Office (1979). *Improvements Needed in Selecting and Processing Urban Development Action Grants*, USGAO Report. (March 30).

"The Urban Development Action Grant Program: Despite Much Criticism, It's Been An Effective Tool," *The Daily Bond Buyer*, Special Conference Supplement, No. 1 (June 4, 1979).

XIV

Implementing the CRA: Innovative Steps in Constructing a New Relationship Between the Sectors

Eugene R. Eisman

Executive Summary

In 1977, the Congress passed legislation requiring federal regulatory agencies to assess the lending records of financial institutions in low- and moderate-income neighborhoods in reviewing applications for new branches, mergers or other structural changes. The legislation, known as the Community Reinvestment Act (CRA), has had significant impact on urban revitalization and public–private development finance by bringing together regulated local financial institutions, community groups, and local governments.

Vigorous enforcement of CRA by some of the four federal regulatory agencies charged with implementing it and aggressive participation in the CRA process by local community organizations (in the form of protesting applications by local financial institutions) have combined to create a new public–private "process." One result of CRA already visible is increased use of a public–private partnership technique called "leveraging," the combining of public and private funds to provide financing for housing rehabilitation or construction. Leveraging relies primarily on federal Community Development Block Grants and Urban Development Action Grants as the source of the public funds, and participation of local financial institutions for private capital.

Assessments of the impact of CRA vary. Activist community groups cite a lack of uniformity in enforcement by the four federal regulatory agencies, while the industry view is that CRA was not and is not needed, but does nonetheless have positive aspects.

Although the Reagan administration's attitude toward CRA is not clear, the process generated by this legislation has the potential to become a model for public–private cooperation in development finance.

Nearly four years ago, buried deep in a mammoth piece of legislation noted primarily for the billions of dollars it authorized for community development and housing programs, the U.S. Congress included a section entitled the "Community Reinvestment Act of 1077."* It differed from much of the remainder of the legislation in at least two ways: it was short—only a few paragraphs, as compared to other sections that ran for many pages—and it contained no authorization for federal expenditures.

Nonetheless, in its own way, the Community Reinvestment Act (CRA), which requires federal regulatory agencies to assess the lending records of financial institutions in low- and moderate-income neighborhoods, may, in the long run, have as much effect on urban revitalization as the direct expenditure of the federal funds for housing and community development.

Using the CRA itself and the regulations promulgated to implement it, neighborhood organizations in many parts of the country are challenging the performance of local financial institutions in meeting the credit needs, especially for home mortgages, of the communities they serve. Alleging failure to meet those needs, the challenges ask federal regulatory agencies to deny required approval of new branches, mergers, or other structural changes by local financial institutions.

The results of these protests have so far been a mixture of approvals, "conditional" approvals, and a few outright denials by the federal agencies, along with a great deal of negotiations between community groups and local lenders. But, there is little doubt that the battle has been joined, and that the issue of what constitutes adequate neighborhood access to home mortgage and home improvement financing and other forms of credit will be hard fought throughout the 1980s.

One result of the enactment of CRA is *already* visible: it has given a strong push to the use of a public–private partnership technique called leveraging. Leveraging, the technique of combining public and private dollars to provide a pool of funds for housing rehabilitation or construction, involves the use of limited public funds to "lever" private dollars, thereby producing a greater impact in the use of the public money.

Although there are additional reasons for its current popularity, leveraging is the revitalization technique many local governments and community groups are using to translate the CRA into real benefits for their cities and neighborhoods. Therefore, this chapter first explores CRA's impact on the new relationship between the public and private sectors, and then considers the role of leveraging.

As enacted by the U.S. Congress, CRA is basically a statement that "regulated financial institutions are required by law to demonstrate that their deposit facilities serve the convenience and needs of the communities in which

---

*The Community Reinvestment Act of 1977 is Title VIII of the Housing and Community Development Act of 1977 (Public Law 95–128).

they are chartered to do business," specifically including low- and moderate-income neighborhoods. The appropriate federal financial regulatory agencies are to use their authority to "encourage" financial institutions to meet the credit needs of the areas they serve, "consistent with the safe and sound operation of such institutions."

CRA applies to the lending institutions regulated by the Federal Deposit Insurance Corporation, The Federal Home Loan Bank Board, the Comptroller of the Currency and the Federal Reserve Board. These include commercial banks, savings and loan associations and savings banks. The appropriate federal supervisory agency is directed to "assess the institution's record of meeting the credit needs of the entire community, including low- and moderate-income neighborhoods" and to "take such record into account" before granting an application for a new branch, merger or other structural changes in the institution's operation.

The somewhat bland and vaguely bureaucratic language of the act does not reveal its near-revolutionary impact on financial institutions and the neighborhoods and communities they serve. For a number of years preceding passage of CRA, organized neighborhood and community groups in dozens of cities had literally "taken to the streets" to protest what they contended was the outright refusal of many financial institutions to make loans in certain sections of their communities.

Using a variety of techniques, including picketing, marches and massive withdrawals of funds, these local community organizations protested what they called "redlining" by some banks, savings and loans, mutual savings banks, and mortgage bankers. The focus of their protests was their allegation that some local lenders refused to make either home improvement or home mortgage loans in certain blue-collar and minority neighborhoods.

The result of this refusal, according to the protestors, was that these neighborhoods, cut off from bank credit, were doomed to deteriorate. They believed that these neighborhoods and their residents were credit-worthy, and charged that some local lenders were ignoring an "obligation" to make loans in neighborhoods where they actively solicited deposits from residents.

The financial institutions denied that they engaged in redlining or any other systematic form of economic or racial discrimination against either neighborhoods or individuals. They contended that their loan decisions were based strictly on objective considerations such as the value of the housing on which a mortgage was sought, and the ability of the borrower to repay the loan. They also cited an obligation to their shareholders and depositors to maximize return on assets and exercise prudence in granting loans.

The major neighborhood organizations joined forces at the national level, and in 1975 achieved a key national victory, passage of the Home Mortgage Disclosure Act (HMDA). It requires all insured commercial banks, savings and loan associations, savings banks, and credit unions to collect and make public, on an annual basis, data on the conventional and government insured and guaranteed home mortgage loans they make or purchase, including first mortgages, multifamily project loans and home improvement loans.*

Two years later, in 1977, the national and local neighborhood organizations were able to convince Congress that additional legislation was needed to enable them to hold financial institutions "accountable" for their neighborhood lending activities and to force the lenders into a "dialogue" with them. The U.S. Senate Housing, Banking and Urban Affairs Committee held hearings on the proposed CRA. Representatives of the federally regulated financial institutions opposed its enactment, contending that, consistent with good business practices, they were already meeting the credit needs of the neighborhoods in their service area, and that additional legislation was therefore neither necessary nor desirable.

Following enactment, the four federal financial supervisory agencies held public hearings and then published regulations to implement CRA. The final regulations took effect in November, 1978, and represented a compromise between the contending factions: the federally-regulated financial institutions and the neighborhood organizations.

It is these regulations which breathe life into the CRA itself, and a basic understanding of what they contain is essential to any assessment of the first two years of CRA implementation. Although each of the four federal financial supervisory agencies with CRA responsibilities issued its own regulations, all are virtually the same.

Purpose

The regulations seek to "Encourage (the regulated financial institutions) to help meet the credit needs of their local community or communities; to provide guidance to (the financial institution) as to how the (appropriate federal agency) will assess the records of (the financial institution) in satisfying their continuing and affirmative obligations to help meet the credit needs of their local communities, including low- and moderate-income neighborhoods, consistent with the safe and sound operation of those (financial institutions); and to provide for taking into account those records in connection with... applications" for the establishment of a new branch, the relocation of the main office or a branch, a merger or consolidation, or for a charter or deposit insurance.

Requirements

Each financial institution covered under CRA is required to prepare, and review at least annually, a "delineation" of the areas that comprise its "entire community" and to illustrate the "delineation" on a map. The community is

---

*Late in 1980, Congress extended HMDA until 1985, and added new provisions which will extend coverage of the act to include the release of data on FHA-insured mortgages made by mortgage bankers.

defined as the "contiguous areas surrounding each office or group of offices, including any low- or moderate-income neighborhoods in those areas." Each covered financial institution must also prepare a CRA "statement" for each local community in which it operates, including a list of specific types of credit it offers in each community, such as one- to four-family mortgage loans, housing rehabilitation and home improvement loans, small business, farm and community development loans, etc.

The financial institution is "encouraged" to include in the statement descriptions of its efforts to ascertain the credit needs of its community, and how its current efforts help to actually meet those needs. The CRA statement must be reviewed by the institution's board of directors at least annually, and the statement must be available for public inspection at the institution's head and branch offices.

Public Access and Notice

Each institution must maintain for public inspection files which include any signed comments from the public within the last two years relating to its CRA statement or performance in helping to meet the credit needs of its community, any responses the institution wishes to make, and any CRA statements in effect during the past two years.

Each covered institution must post in each of its offices a CRA notice stating the purpose of the act, the availability of the institution's CRA statement, and the public's right to comment on the CRA statement and see other comments and to receive notice of any applications covered by the act. If the bank involved is a subsidiary of a bank holding company, that fact must be indicated in the CRA notice.

Assessing the Record

As part of its regular examination of the institutions it regulates, each federal supervisory agency must assess the institution's performance in helping to meet the credit needs of its entire community. The examination will include review of the institution's CRA statement and any comments offered by the public.

The examiners will also consider 12 specific factors, including activities conducted by the institution to ascertain the credit needs of its community; to market the credit services it offers; the geographic distribution of its credit extensions, applications and denials, along with any practices intended to discourage applications for types of credit listed in the institution's CRA statement; and its record in opening and closing offices and providing services at offices.

Also considered are the institution's participation in local community development programs; its originations of residential mortgages, home improvement and housing rehabilitation loans and small business or small farm loans within its community; its participation in government insured, guaranteed or subsidized programs for housing, small businesses or small farms; and its ability to meet community credit needs based on its financial condition, size, and other factors.

Effect on Applications

In considering applications for establishment of a new branch, relocation of the main office or a branch, a merger or consolidation, or for a charter or deposit insurance, the appropriate federal agency will consider, "among other factors," the applicant's record of CRA performance. That record "may be the basis for the denial of the application."

The Record so Far

As mentioned earlier, the results of CRA are mixed. Each of the four federal regulatory agencies with CRA responsibilities has adapted its own strategies and policies in responding to protests filed under the act.

As of the fall of 1980, for example, two of the agencies, the Federal Reserve Board and the Federal Home Loan Bank Board, had not denied any applications covered under CRA. However, in addition to approvals, both had granted either "conditional" approvals or approvals only after lenders had committed to negotiate with community protestors or taken "independent" initiatives to improve their community lending record. These actions by the two federal agencies, while stopping short of outright rejection of an application, recognized that a problem existed and that corrective action was necessary.

The two other federal agencies with CRA responsibilities, the Comptroller of the Currency and the Federal Deposit Insurance Corporation, have denied a total of six applications based on failure to meet the requirements of the act. Of the two, FDIC has been the most active, denying five applications, although two were initially decided by state regulatory agencies which must approve applications before FDIC acts on them.

A total of 77 CRA protest cases had been decided by the four federal agencies as of October, 1980. Of these, 61 received approval or conditional approval.

FDIC, in the words of *The Wall Street Journal*, "shocked the banking industry" in April, 1979, by turning down an application by the Brooklyn-based Greater New York Savings Bank to open a branch office in Manhattan. In its written decision, the first denial under CRA, the FDIC board of directors said that the bank's mortgage lending in Brooklyn, compared to other areas it serves, "remains at a fairly low level." However, the board noted that Greater New York Savings was making a significant effort to improve its record, and that it should reapply at a later date.

Robert Cook, chief of the FDIC's Civil Rights Section, noted that the Greater New York Savings decision had a major impact on other financial institutions that were preparing applications covered under CRA.* "Many of them pulled back; they realized that their applications probably wouldn't succeed, and they went back and restructured them," he said.

"CRA has had a substantial impact beyond what was expected by the industry, some supporters of the legislation, and the regulators," Cook said. "CRA has had an invisible effect on applications filed with us."

He noted that there was "hostility toward CRA by the industry at first. The attitude of some people in the industry was that 'you are going to have to pull us in screaming and kicking,' and there was fear that CRA would lead to credit allocation." That attitude has altered over time, Cook said, and new "relationships with depositors and borrowers have substantially increased the number of good investments made by the banks, and resulted in new 'goodwill.'"

He said that a positive result of CRA was that many banks have changed their "approach to lending in low- and moderate-income neighborhoods. They now look at these areas on a case-by-case basis. Our goal is an end to literal redlining;" that is, the refusal to make loans in entire neighborhoods. Cook added that enactment of CRA has resulted in "a number of banks finding out that there are good loans out there to be made."

The federal regulatory agencies are attempting to assist local lenders in meeting CRA requirements by providing them with technical assistance and publications on federal housing and economic and community development programs in which they can become involved, Cook said.

He also noted that CRA has had more impact in older urban areas of the northeastern United States than in some other parts of the country, because of the concentrations of older housing stock, and the impact of the redlining issue there. "There is little or no CRA impact on the small rural banks, and it is difficult to assess their compliance because of an urban bias in the CRA criteria." He added, however, that at least one CRA protest had been filed in each of FDIC's 14 regions.

Community Groups

Community groups have brought about 70% of the protests under CRA (somewhat unexpectedly, about a quarter of the protests have originated with competing banks, with the remainder from individuals and other sources). One of the major sources of assistance for community groups involved in CRA issues is the Washington-based Center for Community Change (CCC), a nonprofit public interest group.

Allen Fishbein, a director of the CCC's Neighborhood Revitalization Project, said "there are real problems with CRA," and gives it only "mixed reviews." He said the act "is vague, and it is only as good as agency

---

*With the exception of the quotes on page 373 attributed to Mr. Donald Lasater, all quotes in this chapter are from interviews conducted by the author in late 1980.

enforcement is. It depends on strong, agressive enforcement by four separate agencies, and only such enforcement will lead to revitalization in neighborhoods."

He said that community groups had specific problems with CRA enforcement by the four federal agencies: assessments of individual lenders are "made in a vacuum; there is no comparison to what other lenders are doing," and there have been "too few denials and conditional approvals handed down under CRA; the industry will see this as a lack of commitment by the federal agencies."

Although there is no "typical" case of community group involvement in CRA issues, a recent FDIC denial of an application for a branch sought by Dauphin Deposit Bank and Trust company in Harrisburg, Pa., shows the impact such involvement can have.

Two community groups in the central Pennsylvania city contended in their successful protest that the bank "has not made sufficient funds available to rehabilitate and restore the inner-city of Harrisburg." Noting the requirements of CRA with regard to banks meeting the credit needs of their communities, the FDIC said in its denial that "there is little evidence that...the bank affirmatively attempted to identify and service the credit needs of that part of the local community which encompasses the residents of the inner-city of Harrisburg... or to communicate to this segment of the community the credit services it might provide."

Following release of the FDIC decision in June, 1980, the bank entered negotiations with the two protesting groups. In October, the bank and the community organizations agreed that Dauphin Deposit would make $700,000 in mortgages and home improvement loans immediately available to home-owners in low- and moderate-income neighborhoods in the city, at a rate 1% below market interest rates. The bank also established a lending goal of $5,000,000 for the same areas over the next three years. In addition, Dauphin Deposit agreed to undertake several other programs to increase credit availability in Harrisburg's inner-city neighborhoods.*

The Industry View

The industry assessment of CRA reflects two central themes: it was not, and is not, really necessary, but it nonetheless has some positive aspects.

Barry Tate, staff vice-president and director of Urban Affairs for the U.S. League of Savings Associations, said his organization opposed passage of

---

*In December 1980, citing "significant and substantial negotiations" between Dauphin Deposit and the protesting groups, and other measures taken by the bank, FDIC noted that the bank had agreed to participate in a city program to rehabilitate declining Harrisburg neighborhoods, had hired a full-time community relations specialist, and taken other steps to meet the credit needs of low-and moderate-income city neighborhoods. As a result of these activities, the FDIC noted, the protesting groups had withdrawn their objections and supported the application for the proposed new office in the Harrisburg suburbs.

CRA. "We felt it was not needed, and many still feel it is not needed," he said. "But many grudgingly accept it. It has resulted in (some League members) making loans they might otherwise have missed by calling their attention to good business opportunities in urban areas."

In the two years since its implementation, CRA has "become institutionalized. The 'scare factor' has been taken out of it by the regulatory agencies," Tate added. "The federal agencies view CRA as a positive tool, an educational tool, and it's working."

The American Bankers Association (ABA) has formed a Community Economic Development Policy Board to encourage and assist bank participation in neighborhood revitalization efforts. During a special session on community reinvestment at its annual convention last October in Chicago, a member of the Policy Board noted that neighborhood representatives the group had spoken with were concerned about "the general unwillingness of bankers to talk to community groups."

The comment was made by Donald Lasater, chairman of the board, and chief executive officer of Mercantile Trust Co., St. Louis, who added that this unwillingness was the "most critical element leading to CRA challenges. There was overall neighborhood group agreement that without CRA, most banks would have little incentive to establish a dialogue with them on community credit needs...."

The ABA Policy Board's chairman, Walter J. Connolly, Jr., chairman of the Connecticut Bank and Trust Co., Hartford, said that "bankers generally don't feel the need for this legislation. We're doing our job now (of providing adequate credit to neighborhoods) and have been doing the job (in the past)."

"The philosophy behind the CRA regulations is pretty good," Connolly said, but their implementation by the federal regulatory agencies "is a little paranoid... the regulators (come in to a bank) expecting to find intentional violations." He attributed these problems to the "tension (that) comes about in any break-in period."

He said he hoped that CRA would serve as a "catalyst" to bring community groups and bankers together. "Bankers may have been slow to learn of changes in their community... they may not have picked them up," Connolly said. "The feeling of community groups that there was a lack of communication between them and the banks should be eased by CRA."

Despite the conflicting assessments and attitudes among those impacted by the Community Reinvestment Act of 1977, there *does* appear to be one of agreement: The relationships between federal regulators, local lenders, and the residents of the neighborhoods they serve have been significantly altered, and it will be several years before the final form of a new relationship becomes clear.

However, as noted earlier, it's not too soon to take a look at one area where CRA is acting as a significant spur to the construction of new relationships between the public and private sectors: leveraging.

Of course, there are other reasons, besides CRA, for leveraging's increased use in large and small cities. In a time of reduced appropriations for many federal aid-to-cities programs, leveraging can increase the efficiency and impact of public dollars. It offers a cost effective way for local government to attract private resources and utilize the expertise of private lenders. At the same time, it frees public agency staff to focus on program controls and technical assistance to borrowers. Local lenders benefit because leveraging generates market-rate loans and, by lowering housing costs, makes it possible to serve those of low- and moderate-income. Finally, the U.S. Department of Housing and Urban Development (HUD), the source of nearly all public funds used for leveraging, has placed great emphasis on its use.

FNMA and Leveraging

The Federal National Mortgage Association (FNMA), a private, share holder-owned corporation, is the largest single investor in residential mortgages in the nation. It purchases mortgage loans from local lenders, including banks, savings and loan associations, and mortgage companies. The funds which lenders receive from FNMA replenish their resources for further lending.

Late in the last decade, FNMA launched an effort to acquaint more local governments and local lenders with the concept of leveraging and how to use it in their communities.

In 1977, as part of an increased commitment to urban revitalization, Fannie Mae (FNMA) created an Office of Urban Activities with several responsibilities, including: increasing FNMA's participation in urban mortgages, disseminating information on urban revitalization methods and programs, and exercising a leadership role in developing urban revitalization techniques and programs.

As a part of that commitment, the Office of Urban Activities has been encouraging an approach to leveraging that differs from most local efforts which utilize federal Community Development Block Grant (CDBG) funds. The majority of these local programs to date have been limited to home improvement loans made in the form of a second mortgage for rehabilitation in the $10,000 range for terms of from seven to ten years. The use of public dollars for this type of program appealed to communities for a number of reasons, including the practical and political need to use the limited CDBG funds to benefit as many low- and moderate-income families and neighborhoods as possible.

This type of publicly-funded program provided families in neighborhoods targeted for revitalization with below-market loans to improve their residences. Home improvement loans also minimized relocation problems by emphasizing help for current residents.

However, after several years of highly successful operation of such programs in cities all over the nation, there appeared to be a need for a program that went beyond home improvement loans. Generally, such programs were not large enough to pay for major structural rehabilitation.

The advent of the Urban Development Action Grant (UDAG) program late in the last decade, along with experience gained by operating CDBG programs, provided vehicles which enabled some communities to move beyond leveraged home improvement loans. UDAG applicants are required to show how the funds will be leveraged by private investment to stimulate economic development and neighborhood renewal, and the program offers great flexibility to recipient communities. As examples later in this chapter will illustrate, many communities are using UDAG and CDBG to undertake innovative housing programs.

Leveraging with a Difference

FNMA's efforts to encourage greater use of innovative leveraging techniques complement and supplement these local programs. While home improvement loans are a vital part of any community's neighborhood revitalization program, leveraging can also be used in conjunction with long-term, first mortgage financing to meet other revitalization needs. These include:

Substantial rehabilitation of older homes to "recycle" them by adding decades to their useful life.

Conversion of renters to homeowners at a price low- and moderate-income families can afford.

Refinancing the existing first mortgage to permit the owner to undertake *major* home improvements or substantial additions to the house.

Encouragement of homeownership to help stabilize or "anchor" neighborhoods targeted for revitalization.

Response to the problems caused by displacement in revitalizing neighborhoods.

There are, of course, various ways to use leveraging to increase homeownership. Information on three such methods has been developed and distributed by FNMA.

First mortgage supplements combine an unsubsidized, market-rate first mortgage with a subsidy of public funds to achieve an effective interest rate for the borrower which is below-market. The public subsidy, or supplement, which could come from UDAG or CDBG funds, can be in the form of low- or no-interest loan, a deferred payment loan or a grant. The size and terms of the first mortgage supplement are determined by local program considerations, including what income level the program is seeking to assist and the desired effective housing cost for the borrower.

A "write-down" of the property to be purchased and rehabilitated is a second type of leveraging technique for homeownership. The write-down combines a first mortgage with a public subsidy of the actual rehabilitation work done on the property. The goal is to lower the cost of the house to low- and moderate-income families, and thus qualify for mortgage financing families not otherwise eligible. As with first mortgage supplements, local program goals and considerations determine the amount of subsidy. (Although CDBG funds cannot be used to subsidize new construction, UDAG can be used for this purpose; therefore, the write-down technique can also be used for new construction in some instances.)

A third type of leveraging with long-term funds is the *first mortgage write-down*. Using this method, public funds are used to "buy-down" the interest rate on the first mortgage loan. Although this is, according to HUD, the most popular technique for leveraging home improvement loans, it is only beginning to be used to assist families in purchasing or refinancing a rehabilitated home.

During 1980, the Office of Urban Activities staff in FNMA's regional offices in Dallas, Los Angeles, Atlanta, Chicago, and Philadelphia have been working with local and state governments and local lenders to develop and implement first-mortgage leveraging programs. The results are several local programs already underway or in an advanced state of planning. Some example follow.*

Urban Loan Participations

In 1978, Fannie Mae began a program to make funds available for financing housing in urban areas where mortgage money is in short supply or available only on more stringent terms than elsewhere. The program was designed to encourage urban lending by institutions which need a secondary market to provide liquidity and thereby generate investment funds. The program allows local lenders to use their existing portfolio of conventional mortgages in urban areas to generate additional funds.

Eligible conventional mortgages—on both new and existing one- to four-family homes and single-family units in condominiums—are placed in mortgage pools by the local lender. If the loans meet FNMA yield and underwriting requirements, FNMA, at the local lender's request, buys a participating interest in the mortgage pool range (in 10% increments) from 60–90% of the pool's value. There is a $250,000 minimum on the amount Fannie Mae will invest in any pool, but no maximum. The local lender services the loans for FNMA.

Participating local lenders must agree to reinvest the amount paid by Fannie Mae for its share of the pool in similar urban areas. The reinvested funds may finance either residential or commercial construction or rehabilitation. Local lenders using this program are not required to be approved by FNMA if they are a federal- or state-insured and supervised institution.

Working with local lenders and government officials in three southern cities, the Urban Activities staff of Fannie Mae's Atlanta Regional Office developed a leveraging plan which would combine UDAG or CDBG funds and the Urban Loan Participation Program. One of the three, Orangeburg, South

---

*In December 1980, FNMA announced changes in its mortgage programs which affected at least some of the examples discussed. However, the examples are still useful in illustrating innovative public–private sector relationships and how they can benefit cities.

Carolina, has applied for a $604,200 UDAG to be used to assist in the construction of 13 new quadruplexes on scattered sites in a Neighborhood Strategy Area (NSA) that lies between the city's central business district and two liberal arts colleges. The UDAG funds include a number of programs related to construction of the quadruplexes, including CETA training for some of the construction workers, energy conservation, and counseling for both the tenants and owners of the structures.

The quadruplexes will be owner-occupied, and the three rental units in each will be available to persons or families possessing Section 8 eligibility certificates. Based on an average value of between $110,000 and $120,000 for each quadruplex, a total of between $1,430,000 and $1,560,000 in permanent financing will be needed for the project.

Orangeburg wants additional rental units in the NSA, as well as an increase in middle-income residents. Therefore, no income limits are planned for the owner-occupant of the quadruplexes. However, the city will make Section 8 rental subsidies available, and require, in return for a reduced interest rate on the mortgage, that the three rental units be occupied by Section 8 eligible persons.

Under the plan to use the Urban Loan Participation Program to leverage the UDAG, the city of Orangeburg would use UDAG funds to purchase 30% of the pool made up of the mortgages on the quadruplexes. A local lender would retain a 10% interest, and Fannie Mae would purchase the remaining 60%. In effect, the Orangeburg plan would expand the normal two-party Urban Loan Participation Program (Fannie Mae and the local lender) to a three-party participation by adding the city's involvement.

The city would not receive any interest on its part of the participation, but the principal would be returned to the city as the loans are amortized or paid in full. The participating local lender can use one of Fannie Mae's urban mortgage lending programs to obtain up to 95% mortgage financing for the quadruplexes, and would then sell a total of 90% of the mortgage pool to the city and Fannie Mae.

This leveraged participation plan would result in effective interest rates for the borrower substantially lower than market. Although market rates may well fluctuate by the time the program is actually implemented, an example prepared by FNMA's Atlanta Regional office will illustrate the possible savings:

Y = FNMA YIELD (Example: 12%)*

F = FNMA's INTEREST (60%)

S = SELLER's (LOCAL LENDER) INTEREST (10%)

C = CITY INTEREST (30%)

SF = SERVICING FEE (.00375)

*Gross yield including servicing fee.

$$N = \text{NOTE RATE TO BORROWERS}$$
$$(F+S) \times Y + (C \times SF) = N$$
$$(.6+.1) \times .12 + (.3 \times .00375) = N$$
$$(.7 \times .12) + (.3 \times .00375) = N$$
$$.084 + .001125 = .085125$$

INTEREST RATE TO BORROWER $= 8.5\%$

The seller (local lender) would receive the same interest as FNMA on their holding and, in addition, a servicing fee for the city's and FNMA's portion of the funds.

The leveraged participation plan is an example of the first mortgage write-down type discussed earlier.

Leveraging in Columbus

In Columbus, Ohio, Fannie Mae's Chicago regional office worked with local government and local lenders to develop a leveraging program to prevent the total gentrification of the renewing Near North/University neighborhood. The city was concerned that revitalization in the approximately 28 square-block area, near Ohio State University, would result in the displacement of low- and moderate-income families as middle-income groups moved in.

Using a portion of its $2 million Innovative Grant Program (part of Columbus' CDBG funds), the city developed a program aimed at providing home purchase opportunities for 120 low- and moderate-income families. The families are currently tenants in the neighborhood and would otherwise likely face displacement in the near future.

The city has entered a partnership with a neighborhood local nonprofit housing corporation and a private management company which owns most of the rental property in the area. The nonprofit housing group will acquire about 60 houses from the management firm and other property owners and rehabilitate them. The homes will then be sold to the current tenants. The nonprofit group will work with local lenders to secure construction and permanent financing for the tenant household.

CDBG funds would be used to subsidize the families in one of two ways: a $7,500 to $10,000 grant would be used either to write-down the rehabilitation work or to reduce the sales price of the home at the mortgage closing. This would represent use of the property write-down or first mortgage write-down leveraging techniques discussed earlier.

City officials asked FNMA to assist them in encouraging local lenders to participate in the program, with the aim of developing mortgages meeting FNMA's underwriting requirements so that the corporation can purchase them.

"Stabilization Grants" in Minneapolis

Minneapolis has begun operation of a complex leveraging plan aimed at "stabilizing" selected neighborhoods by converting tenants and contract for deed purchasers into owners. (Contract for deed purchases don't obtain title to the property until it is entirely paid for; they therefore buy the property under a contract).

The program, developed with the active assistance of Fannie Mae's Chicago regional office, is centered in 13 city-designated neighborhoods, and uses CDBG funds. It resulted from concerns that Minneapolis' five-year Housing Assistance Plan failed to meet adequately the need for family housing. The City Council responded to the concerns by incorporating the need for financing family housing in a formal "statement of credit needs" filed with local financial institutions under provisions of the Community Reinvestment Act. This meant that Minneapolis was asking local lenders to help it meet the need for additional family housing by offering mortgage financing.

At this point, FNMA became involved and brought together representatives of the city's Housing and Redevelopment Authority (MHRA) and local lenders to work out a plan acceptable to all parties. The idea was to develop a joint effort that would generate mortgages meeting FNMA's underwriting criteria and therefore eligible for purchase by FNMA.

The resulting program involves purchase by MHRA of homes in the target neighborhoods at current market value. The homes are rehabilitated and brought up to code standards while still occupied. They are then sold to the tenants or sold back to the previous contract for deed purchasers, who then become owners. The key to the program is a Stabilization Grant of up to $12,000 for eligible families (those with a maximum adjusted gross income of $16,000).

The size of the write-down, using CDBG funds, is based on how much the individual family can afford. This "affordability" factor means that the program is tailored to meet the needs of each participant. An example: the cost of acquiring a structure is $20,000, and the rehabilitation costs an additional $15,000, for a total of $35,000. The purchaser can afford only $20,000. MHRA provides a Stabilization Grant of $12,000, and a deferred payment, no-interest second mortgage of $3,000. A conventional mortgage, eligible for purchase by FNMA would provide the remaining funds.

Conclusion

This chapter has discussed the content and greater-than-expected impact of the Community Reinvestment Act of 1977 on public–private development finance. The CRA has served as a catalyst to bring together local financial institutions, local governments, and community organizations for a dialogue that had not previously existed. And, in some cases, discussions between the public and private sectors have moved beyond talk to action—to actual partnerships using financial leveraging to revitalize neighborhoods.

The brief history of the CRA indicates its potential as a "model" process for bringing together the two sectors for relationships that can produce meaningful results for both, and for cities themselves. It seems clear that continued vigorous enforcement of CRA by at least some of the federal regulatory agencies, combined with aggressive participation in, and monitoring of, the CRA process by local community groups and local government will produce salutary results for all participants.

Nonetheless, as of the spring of 1981, there is reason for caution: The changes sought by the new Reagan administration in programs and regulations *could* alter the entire public–private partnership equation, the enforcement of CRA, and the potential of leveraging. There will be new leadership at nearly all of the federal financial regulatory agencies that enforce the CRA, put in place by an administration stressing "less federal regulation;" major changes seem in store for HUD's UDAG program, and the new administration's attitude toward public-private partnerships as a concept is not clear. Realization of the potential impact of the CRA process must await a clearer definition of the new administration's policies and philosophies.

Bibliography

Background and Source Material

Aronsen, Leanne (1978). "Positive Urban Lending Strategies: Organizational Strategies to Curb Redlining", in *Mobilizing Capital for Urban Economic Development*, Bearse, P.J. ed. Princeton: Woodrow Wilson School of Public and International Affairs (August).

Assessing Community Credit Needs: A CRA Guidebook (1979). Washington, DC: U.S. Department of Housing and Urban Development.

Barton, Michael and Vitarello, James (1980). "Comptroller's Programs Encourage Public/Private Community Development Partnership." *Journal of Housing* (May), pp. 262–267.

CRA: Bridging Public/Private Partnerships, Office of Public/Private partnerships, U.S. Department of Housing and Community Development, Washington, DC (undated).

Eisman, Eugene R. (1980). "Leveraging Maximizes the Effectiveness of State and Federal Housing Program Funds." *Journal of Housing* (November), pp. 552–556.

Financial Leveraging In Community Development Rehabilitation: A Technical Assistance Guide (1979). Washington, D.C.: U.S. Department of Housing and Urban Development (July).

Gressel, David & Associates (1978). *Participation in Block Grant Rehabilitation Programs*. Special Management Bulletin, U.S. League of Savings Associations, Chicago (May).

Lender's Guide to Fair Mortgage Policies (1980). Washington, DC: The Potomac Institute (October).

Neighborhood-Based Reinvestment Strategies: A CRA Guidebook (1979). Washington, DC: U.S. Department of Housing and Urban Development.

Reports on Current CRA Developments

American Bankers Association. Urban and Community Economic Development, 1120 Connecticut Avenue, NW, Washington, DC 20036. Monthly newsletter containing summaries of CRA decisions as they are issued by federal regulatory agencies. Write for subscription information.

American Bankers Association (1980). "A New Frontier For Business Opportunities: A Handbook for Private Initiative In Community Revitalization."

American Bankers Association (1979a). "Assessment Guide For Compliance With The Community Reinvestment Act."

American Bankers Association (1979b). "Consumer Compliance: A Source Book of Materials and References."

American Bankers Association (1979c). "Consumer Compliance Seminar."

American Bankers Association (1979d). "Planning Guide For Consumer Compliance."

American Bankers Association (1978). "Bankers and Community Involvement: Profiles of Selected Bank Programs in Economic And Community Development," 1978.

Citibank, N.A. (1980). "What's Citibank Doing in Flatbush?" New York: Citibank Flatbush Project, 885 Flatbush Ave., Brooklyn, N.Y. 11226.

Federal Financial Institutions Examination Council. 490 L'Enfant Plaza, SW Eighth Floor, Washington, DC 20219. Composed of Federal regulatory agencies; issues periodic statements on CRA compliance.

Federal Home Loan Bank Board of New York (1980). "Progress Through Partnership", A Report on Community Investment Activity in District 2, June 1978–December 1979. New York: One World Trade Center.

The CRA Reporter. The Neighborhood Revitalization Project of the Center for Community Change, 1000 Wisconsin Avenue, NW, Washington, DC 20007. Occasional newsletter on CRA developments from neighborhood perspective.

Supplementary Readings

Bradford, Calvin, *et al.* (1980). "Community Development Policy Paper: Structural Disinvestment—A Problem in Search of a Policy." Washington, DC: Corporation For Enterprise Development (mimeo).

Goetz, Rolf (1979). *Understanding Neighborhood Change*. New York: Ballinger.

Hood, Edwin T., and Weed, Cynthia M. (1979). "Redlining Revisited: A Neighborhood Development Bank as a Proposed Solution." *Urban Lawyer*, 139, (No. 1, Winter).

XV

The Emerging Public–Private Partnership

David Jamison

"If it is not local, it is not real." That phrase, used to characterize the early attempts at getting national church institutions to work cooperatively, could well be used to describe the still-evolving partnership process between public and private institutions in this country.

The history of cooperation between the public and private sectors is best described as erratic. The concept seemed to flower briefly at the national level during the Carter administration. The practice is still seeking roots at the local level through a variety of ad hoc arrangements. Cooperation is still too often characterized by talk rather than action in an arena where "the action," according to those in both sectors with their eye on the "bottom line," is doing "a real deal."

The last few years have been witness to a number of successful attempts to engage the private sector in urban revitalization projects and to create public and private sector partnerships to accomplish this work. There are a number of reasons for this, beginning with the recognition that unlimited federal resources simply do not exist. Perhaps, more importantly, there is recognition that the ability of the federal government to realistically assess the needs and priorities of localities is also severely limited. This perception is matched by the growing initiative of state and local public bodies in economic development activities.

Recent years have seen a subtle shift in emphasis towards placing greater responsibility on state and municipal governments to solve urban problems, a shift which is likely to accelerate under the Reagan administration. Beginning with the 1970s, many businesses which have economic and traditional ties to cities have begun to recognize their own self-interest in helping to solve the problems that have tended to weaken the cities in which their plants are located. Thus the public–private partnerships that are just now beginning to emerge are rooted in the self-interest that actors in each sector have in protecting and enhancing their assets or bases of activity. A climate for meaningful and effective public–private partnerships at the local level has developed.

Recent Changes at the Public–Private Interface

A case for effective public–private partnerships has been demonstrated at the federal level by the Urban Development Action Grant (UDAG) program, which was enacted by Congress in 1977. Some $1.3 billion in federal money has leveraged more than $8 billion of firm, private sector investment. Compared to the urban renewal program, which resulted in an inverse ratio of more than two public dollars to each private dollar, the UDAG program has leveraged more than six private dollars for each public dollar. These statistics, however, say nothing of the dynamics of this effort to link public and private sector "enlightened self-interest" to contribute to urban revitalization projects, a topic which Chap. XIII treats in depth.

Throughout American economic history, relationships between the public and private sectors have undergone numerous shifts roughly associated with transitions between major stages in the nation's economic development. During the postwar decades these shifts have been intertwined with changes in views towards the problems of urban development. In the past four years a fundamental change in *attitude* of the federal government toward urban revitalization has taken place. This attitudinal change has resulted in numerous opportunities for the private sector to work in partnership with public bodies to develop projects where both public and private agencies profit. This change comes out of a realization on the part of the public sector that urban revitalization cannot succeed when the demands of entrepreneurial creativity and the burden of development and financing are left to government acting alone. It has also occurred because of fundamental population shifts adverse to cities' tax bases and finances.

Yet, something has been missing from this process, something so fundamental to urban development that both the public and private sector interests alike have taken it for granted. That missing element is the entrepreneur—the individual, group, or institution which could provide both the vision and the capital needed to get a "grand urban scheme" off the ground.* By entrepreneur is meant the developers, investors, and lenders who assume the financial risks of projects proposed by planners and public officials. Put more succinctly, these are the people who "make things happen." Until just recently, most of the entrepreneurial activity directed to urban development has been taking place in the more affluent and commercial segments of the marketplace found most often in suburban areas.

---

*The quoted phrase is borrowed from Doxiadis' *Ekistics.*

The incentives for urban revitalization projects, particularly those targeted on providing housing for lower- and lower-moderate-income groups of people, were simply not flexible enough for many entrepreneurs to risk their equity capital, and without that essential risk capital, the normal capital marketplace would not respond. Costs of land, construction, and financing were deemed too high, and the limits of return on investment implied by federal restrictions often mitigated against entrepreneurial activity in center city areas. Thus the past two decades have seen most center city development done by one of three groups:

1. private developers who brought large groups of wealthy investors together for the express purpose of building high-risk projects to which the federal government offered major tax incentives;
2. nonprofit, quasi-public organizations, many of whom had little or no experience in the field of real estate development, but who nevertheless developed sensitive neighborhood residential and commercial revitalization projects; or
3. the public sector itself through the urban renewal program, public housing authorities, and economic development vehicles.

Government at all levels, local, state, and federal, lacked the capital necessary to finance urban revitalization. It also lacked the incentives—the "carrots"—necessary to attract private capital to this effort. Government needed to develop a concept of "public entrepreneurship" backed by specific tools and resources which could attract the private sector and leverage its capital to finance urban revitalization projects.

There is an expression in many languages which says: "There is a time and a place for everything." During the past several years there has been a gradual shift in the attitude of the general public away from the notion that the government alone can (or should) work to ameliorate the economic and social problems plaguing cities. The shift seems rooted in a laissez-faire philosophy which dominated economic policy until Keynesian economic theories came into fashion and which, even then, was very much alive. The "new" attitude with old roots holds that government can do more to spur private development by seeing things from the private perspective and by providing those tools, programs, and resources which will stimulate private investment rather than supplant or thwart it.

The shift has not been lost on political leaders. Legislation such as the Tax Reform Act of 1969 led the way in stimulating urban reinvestment. The Revenue Act of 1978 reduced the maximum tax rate on capital gains to 28%, down from an effective rate of 48%. This latter change has been credited with tripling the amount of venture capital that the private sector has contributed to new business formations and expansions. Further changes in the tax code to spur capital formation are in store for 1981. The evolution of national economic and social priorities has also resulted in the development of a new attitude of public entrepreneurship within federal agencies, such as the Department of Housing and Urban Development (HUD) and the Economic Development Administration (EDA) in the Department of Commerce. The Urban Development Action Grant program, previously referred to, is a first, fledgling example of this new federal attitude which seeks to equip local municipalities with the resources to become public entrepreneurs and to catalyze private sector capital to rebuild cities' economic bases (see Chap. XIII).

Overhauling the scope, strategies, and modes of federal assistance has involved policy consultations with diverse interest groups, major legislative actions, and extensive initiatives by administrations led by both major parties. Yet the pace of change palpably accelerated during the last few years. More than 13 out of 19 bills submitted to Congress in 1977 and 1978 in the field of urban and economic development were enacted at the beginnning of fiscal year 1980. Perhaps as significant, during the same period, more than 100 administrative improvements in existing programs were made to cut red tape, increase local flexibility to carry out program initiatives, foster interagency coordination, target assistance priorities, and promote strategic planning.

Perhaps the most telling indication of the change in attitudes during these past few years has been the introduction of three new words into the governmental lexicon: "targeting," "leveraging," and "management reform."

Targeting

Targeting is the concentration of federal resources on places and people most in need, in contrast to prior tendencies to spread assistance all over the map. It connotes a commitment to "investing in distress," as in the case of economic development assistance directed to many older northeastern and midwestern cities. The initial focus on "distressed cities" was modified to recognize so-called "pockets of poverty" in otherwise strong economic growth areas, e.g., a run-down poverty neighborhood in Dallas, Texas. Some sample results of the new targeting policy include:

1. modification of the Economic Development Administration's original rural orientation to enable it to focus equally on urban and rural communities;
2. reorientation of HUD's Block Grant formula entitlement funds and the increased use of discretionary reserves for special cases of need or local initiatives;
3. aiming of HUD's Section 8 subsidies for housing assistance to developers who conform to local strategic plans; and
4. the serious consideration currently being given to "enterprise zones" which would entail a much more selective targeting of development incentives than any thing so far attempted. (See Heritage Foundation, 1980.)

Leveraging

Leveraging is the commitment of public resources to catalyze private investment. Quite simply it means government borrowing and adapting a concept from the private developer's dictionary. Many public agencies and authorities now seek, wherever possible, to engage private investment on a so-called multiplier ratio, to share risks and roll over funds for additional deals. Although federal investment must still fill gaps in the market place, there is increased recognition of the pitfalls of throwing money at completely unmarketable projects. Again, the UDAG program is a good example of the leveraging concept. Other incentives are found in tax-exempt industrial revenue bond financing for private construction as well as employment and rehabilitation investment tax credits for both commercial and industrial investment.

Management Reform

Management reform includes broad legislative and administrative initiatives to make programs work better, to improve federal coordination, to encourage joint public–private funding of projects at local levels, and to facilitate local public–private planning and use of federal assistance.

During the last few years, consortiums of federal agencies have created and implemented joint programs, including the Neighborhood Business Revitalization program sponsored by HUD, EDA, and the Small Business Administration (SBA), now active in more than 40 cities. EDA's imaginative pilot program in 37 cities known as Comprehensive Economic Development Strategies (CEDS), in which HUD and other agencies have cooperated, gives strong encouragement to coordinated and strategic local planning of public–private investments. Management reforms are being sought in the private sector as well. For example, the Community Reinvestment Act (CRA), described elsewhere in this book, focuses on financial institutions' lending practices in local areas of perceived high risk. Yet the overhaul of the federal apparatus is unfinished and is still going on in earnest as this chapter is being written.

Table 1 describes some of the assistance available from HUD and EDA to catalyze private investment capital.* It is organized by program areas in terms that investor/developers understand, namely the manner in which land is acquired and improved. This description by no means exhausts the federal resources available; it only illustrates those which have been developed in the two principal federal agencies concerned with the nation's economic development agenda.

The Economic Development Administration (EDA) was created under the Public Works and Economic Development Act of 1965. HUD's commitment to economic development began with the Urban Development Action Grant program in fiscal year 1977. During the same year, the potential uses of the multibillion dollar Community Development Block Grant program were broadened to include economic development and were clearly (re)specified to permit the dollars to leverage commercial and industrial development projects.

---

*The basic programs and categories still exist but the amounts of assistance have been severely cut back by the Reagan administration.

Table 1. Assistance Available From HUD and EDA for Investors & Developers[a]

| | HUD | | | | EDA | | | Development Finance | |
	CDBG	UDAG	312	108	Public Works	Revolving Loan Fund	Economic Adjustment Assistance	Loan Guarantee	Grant
Public Land Acquisition and Improvement[b]									
Land Acquisition	○	○		○	○	○	○		
Clearance & Relocation	○	□			○	○	○		
New Construction	□	□		○	○	○	○		
Building Rehabilitation	□	□	□		○	○	○		
Infrastructure	□	○		○	○	○	○		
Business Finance[b]									
Land		□				☆	☆	☆	□
Building Construction		□				☆	☆	☆	□
Equipment & Machinery		□	☆			☆	☆	☆	□
Rehabilitation		□				☆	☆	☆	□
Working Capital	□					☆			

Source: Office of Public-Private Partnerships (1980), Emerging Partnership Opportunities for Cities, Washington, D.C. (March).

[a] Key: ○ = City eligible applicant and user of funds; ☆ = Private developer eligible and user of funds; □ = City is eligible applicant to finance public and/or private portions of development.

[b] Location can be Central Business District. Neighborhood, and/or Industrial Park area.

(See Chap. XI for an assessment of this initiative, which has major implications for the Reagan administration's proposed greater reliance on block grant funding.)

As noted earlier, states and substate units have new and increasing roles in the delivery of tools and services to mobilize private capital for development projects. This amounts to a reversal of a long-term trend. From the post-Depression era through the decades following World War II, the role of the states was increasingly limited as the federal government created tools and programs and delivered them directly to cities. Part of the new federal attitude is to involve the states as significant actors in the delivery of services. Federal programs such as Revenue Sharing and HUD's Section 107 technical assistance program are designed to build state capacity and resources to enable them to become a public partner with federal and city public entrepreneurs in carrying out development projects. Although much remains to be done to enable the states to reclaim their rightful role in the delivery of resources for development, some attitudinal changes are at least now in place.

But what of private sector economic development? Has the private sector simply been a passive actor in the process described as urban revitalization? Part of the problem of answering questions such as these lies in the problem of defining just what we mean by the "private sector." Do we refer exclusively to business, and if so, then what types or sizes of businesses and at what level of management are they represented? Our definition must be inclusive, not merely denoting private, for-profit corporations. It must embrace the multitude of not-for-profit organizations that are now flourishing in the neighborhoods of our nation's cities, seeking to reclaim commercial and residential areas. Our definition must embrace eleemosynary nonprofit organizations, particularly the real estate development offices of hospitals, colleges, religious organizations, and the host of political and civic groups that comprise the voluntary "third" sector in our nation's cities. Our definition must also recognize the substantial differences between large businesses and small businesses. Perhaps the answer is that the definition of "private sector" is existential, that is to say, defined in the context of each given situation. The definition is necessarily fluid since the dynamics of the urban revitalization process seems to call forth creative responses from both the "public" and "private" sectors alike, leading to a host of institutional hybrids which are quasi-public or quasi-private. (Again, a reading of Chap. XIV would be helpful here.)

At least for the large private corporations, the day is most certainly over when the phrase "corporate social responsibility" draws a snort of disgust from the chief executive officer with an added retort that "the only responsibility of this corporation is to make a profit for its stockholders." It is not that "sweetness and light" have invaded the boardrooms of corporate America. The "bottom line" is still of primary importance; however, in this increasingly interdependent urban world, some of the very factors that nibble away at that bottom line can be ameliorated by corporate efforts that have come under the general heading of "corporate social responsibility." For example, it is poor corporate policy to make charitable donations to local causes while ignoring the poor state of a local educational system that may be costing higher than average turnover among skilled employees and middle managers.

The corporate role in public–private partnerships was recently the subject of a study done for HUD by the Stanford Research Institute International (SRI International) in cooperation with the Conference Board. The executive summary asserts the following:

> Corporate urban action is socially responsible action, but it is far wider in scope than philanthropy, although targeted philanthropy plays an important part.
>
> Both companies and governments have come to realize that, in an era of limits, there is still much work to be done in the public interest. There are areas of need in communities that government has never served and areas of need that government has served less well than imagined; and companies have some resources to meet those needs and some self-interest in having them met. The beneficiaries of corporate urban ventures can be the local government, the community, or private development and assistance agencies (SRI International, 1980, p.4).

The study goes on to suggest some definitional answers to the questions we have posed regarding the so-called private sector:

> The public sector differs from the private sector in important ways that corporate urban ventures must recognize. Local governments have assumed service delivery responsibilities that may be far more complex and have more demanding clients than a company may imagine. For this reason, some companies undertaking ventures have stayed away from service delivery programs and have concentrated on the internal management and financial functions of the government as a corporation.
>
> However, the most difficult client group for any corporate urban venture will be the communities involved. Companies can do themselves a great service by recognizing and incorporating into their approach, the need to respond to community-defined issues when both the community and the company can see clear benefits for both. The company will also profit by defining its role as one of the actors within the community and by being as serious about this process as about any other line of business that is an important profit center. Even though some corporate urban ventures may not make a direct short-term profit, they can be expected to provide a return (SRI International, 1980, p. 4).

In sum, it can be safely stated that there is now a new attitude on the part of the federal government that, to the maximum degree possible, federal agency discretionary program resources be used to catalyze private capital through local public–private partnerships.* It can also be apparent, however, that the federal government is not yet sufficiently encouraging public partnerships with state and substate units of government to enlist both their active assistance and their resources in the development process. With respect to the private sector, there is emerging both a dynamic definition of who the players are and more

---

*This statement pertained most strongly under the Carter administration and may need to be modified in light of subsequent changes in the new administration.

importantly what their self-interest is in linking up their entrepreneurial activities with those of the new public entrepreneurs.

From Dialogue to Action

The evolution of public–private partnerships in this country can be described as a cooperative effort which is moving from dialogue to action. The term "public–private partnership or cooperation" embraces a variety of arrangements and relationships. These have been described in numerous sources* and can be categorized and exemplified as follows:

Government Incentive for Business Involvement

Local governments traditionally have provided various kinds of incentives to retain or attract business. Typically these include tax abatements and loan assistance, although a variety of techniques has been tried with mixed success. In recent years state and local governments have increased the use of tax-free municipal bonds to provide financial assistance to business.

The Industrial Development Agency of New York, created in 1974, issues tax-free revenue bonds to assist industries in the acquisition, construction, and equipping of their facilities.

The Dayton, Ohio, Department of Development provides a number of services to businesses in an attempt to retain businesses located in the city.

The Urban Development Action Grant program developed by the U.S. Department of Housing and Urban Development, assists the private sector through loans and grants in such areas as construction, land acquisition, site improvements, development of water or sewer lines and housing.

Government Agencies for Economic Development

Many local governments have separate agencies whose purpose is to provide information and assistance to businesses wishing to locate or expand in their city, to develop coordinated plans for economic development, and to monitor and expedite implementation.

The Milwaukee, Wisconsin, Department of City Development, a line agency of the city government, combines the financial powers of a development

---

*Examples are taken from numerous sources including the following: *Business / Government Partnership in Local Economic Development Planning*, The Conference Board, Inc., New York, NY, 1976; *Response*, Clearinghouse on Corporate Social Responsibility, Washington, DC, Vol. VIII, No. 3, May 1979; *Coordinated Urban Economic Development*, National Council for Urban Economic Development, Washington, DC, March 1978; "Public–Private Partnerships for Revitalizing Urban Neighborhoods, in *Roundtable Proceedings*, The Academy for Contemporary Problems, Columbus, OH, April 1978; "More Clout for Tax Dollars," *Dun's Review*, New York, February 1979; *Detroit, Michigan: Economic Development System Options*, National Council for Urban Economic Development, Washington, DC, April 1977; "The Private Sector and Central Business Districts," Hart Schaffner & Marx, Chicago, IL, July 1977.

corporation, an urban renewal authority, an economic development agency, and a public housing authority.

The Chicago mayor's Council of Manpower and Economic Advisors, a public policy-making body made up of both public and private sector members, directly coordinates manpower, economic development, planning, urban renewal, and housing functions.

The Portland, Oregon, Office of Planning and Development, created by the mayor in 1973, oversees the activities of the Planning Bureau, the Building Bureau, the urban renewal authority, and the housing and community development agency.

Joint Development Projects

Local governments traditionally have provided basic infrastructure, including streets, water and sewerage, to support private investment. In certain cases special arrangements are made to accommodate large or otherwise unusual private development, including public participation in financing and direct public investment in new construction. Several downtown redevelopment efforts have involved the development of coordinated plans of public and private investment.

The Hartford, Connecticut, new Civic Center was cooperatively financed and constructed by the City of Hartford and the Aetna Life and Casualty Company. The land, owned by the city, was acquired through the urban renewal process.

Nicollet Mall in Minneapolis is a good example of a city government/downtown business partnership. The city was able to finance a special benefits assessment and contruct the Mall as a regular public works project due to the strong commitment of business leaders.

Two urban renewal projects in downtown Baltimore, Charles Center and Inner Harbor, were planned and executed jointly by the City of Baltimore and the local business community. Local business leaders, through the Charles Center-Inner Harbor Management, Inc., contributed strongly to the management and marketing of the projects, while the city served as master developer.

Development Institutions

A variety of quasi-public or limited-profit private organizations have been used to undertake specific development projects or to focus on the redevelopment of certain areas of cities.

The Philadelphia Industrial Development Corporation, a quasi-public, non-profit development corporation, was formed in 1958 to stimulate industrial development and retain jobs and tax base in the City of Philadelphia. It has served as a model for urban industrial development corporations throughout the country. Examples of its most recent programs include commercial development financing and market assistance, monitoring of city-sponsored economic development projects, and creation of new financing tools.

San Diego County's Economic Development Corporation is a nonprofit corporation which interacts with the public through its administration of an industrial attraction and retention program, aimed at creating a highly skilled business environment. It is primarily concerned with program implementation, as opposed to policy formulation, and attempts to create jobs and diversify employment opportunities for residents of the County.

The Dayton City-Wide Development Corporation, created in 1972 as a quasi-public, nonprofit real estate development corporation, attempts to stimulate new construction and rehabilitation in the city through the investment approach, rather than through the grant approach. The bulk of the investment the corporation has attracted is in residential facilities and the restoration of historic neighborhoods.

Private Spending for Public Purposes

Private companies traditionally have made contributions to support public programs.

One of the more extensive efforts has been that of a group of businesses in the Minnesota Twin Cities led by the Dayton Hudson Corporation to provide 5% of profits—which is tax deductible—for the support of a variety of public programs.

The Downtown Council, a private organization of business leaders in Minneapolis, assists in the financing of architectural planning for many public and private projects.

The Chicago Central Area Committee, a consortium of business leaders, in cooperation with Chicago's City Planning Department, financed the $350,000 Chicago 21 plan.

Business Expertise Applied to Government

Over the years numerous businesses and businessmen as individuals have given their time to assist local government in improving the management of public programs. Notable examples include:

The Economic Capital Corporation of New York City.

The City Management Advisory Board of the Society for the Promotion, Unification and Redevelopment of Niagara, Inc., Niagara Falls, New York.

The Committee for Progress in Allegheny County (COMPAC) of Pittsburgh, Pennsylvania.

Contracting Public Services to Private Firms

In the last several years there has been growing interest in contracting public services previously provided by government agencies to private businesses.

While most city governments contract for many privately produced goods and services, the new interest is in contracting what have generally been thought of as publicly provided services.

Rural/Metro Fire Department, Inc., provides fire services to the City of Scottsdale, Arizona.

Two years ago in Gainesville, Florida, the city's sanitation department was abolished and the job of refuse collection was turned over to Houston's Browning-Ferris Industries. As a result, costs have been cut and service complaints reduced.

The City of Gainesville, Florida, has also hired Philadelphia's ARA Services to maintain the city's vehicle fleet.

Joint Public – Private Promotional Efforts

Chambers of Commerce traditionally supported local boosterism programs, as have many city governments themselves. While often undertaken individually, they generally are seen by both business and government as serving the same purpose of creating a favorable image for the city in order to attract business and tourism. In some cases, jointly sponsored programs are developed.

Detroit Renaissance, Inc., a private organization consisting of top executives of Detroit's major businesses, has sponsored a nationwide image program designed to promote the positive features of the city.

The Port Authority of New York and New Jersey, in addition to its regular operations, carries on worldwide promotional efforts to attract shipping and cargo movement to New York.

Government Initiative to Help Solve Business Problems

Occasionally local political and governmental leaders will take the initiative to help solve private sector problems which affect the local economy.

The mayor of Jamestown, New York, promoted an effort to establish a productivity improvement program for the ailing manufacturing companies of the Jamestown area.

The Community and Economic Development Department of Detroit provides business liaison and assistance to firms operating in the city in an effort to develop, conserve, and promote use of Detroit's land and physical resources.

Political Organization and Relationships

One of the least tangible, and yet probably one of the most important approaches to public–private cooperation, is the development of constructive relationships among the various political interests in a community, often through a combination of formal and informal channels.

In Kansas City a reform movement which ousted the corrupt Pendergast machine gave rise to a strong professional city manager style of government and relatively harmonious political relationships between government and the private sector.

Improvement of Government Effectiveness in Assisting the Private Sector

One of the most common complaints of businesses is that government bureaucracies are difficult to deal with and have an antibusiness attitude. Some local governments have made conscious efforts to improve the ability and attitude of the various agencies of government that deal with the private sector: cutting red tape, simplifying application and permit procedures, encouraging helpfulness on the part of employees, etc.

In Chicago, government administrators and private developers have fostered working relationships that permit detailed problems of development and construction to be resolved with a minimum of red tape.

The State of New Jersey has established an "Office of Business Advocacy" which offers "one-stop shopping" for assistance to businesses which cuts red tape in dealing with regulatory and business expansion or location problems. Many other states have established similar agencies.

Creation of Committees or Task Forces

Business leaders frequently establish committees through their own initiative or at the behest of government officials and other representatives or in combination with government officials and other community representatives, to deal with perceived problems or needs.

In 1977 Mayor Coleman Young commissioned the Economic Growth Council of Detroit, Inc., made up of 50 of the city's leading corporate, labor, and community leaders, to recommend ways in which Detroit's declining economic and fiscal capacity and structural deterioration trends might be halted or reversed.

Chicago United, organized and supported by the private sector in Chicago, consists of chief executive officers of major businesses who discuss and attempt to deal with such social and economic problems as housing, job training, economic development, etc.

The Office of Public–Private Partnerships

To assist and replicate these local models of public–private arrangements, and to effect the new "attitude" articulated above, the federal government created, in 1979, an Office of Public–Private partnerships in the Department of Housing and Urban Development. This initiative proved to be short-lived: the

Office was in operation only two years before being abolished in the budget reconciliation act of 1981. Yet it is instructive to note some of the purposes and projects pursued during this brief history in order to see how small commitments of resources at higher levels of government can facilitate new public–private initiatives at lower levels.* The Office was established to encourage partnership efforts between the public, private and nonprofit sectors which would spur local efforts towards revitalization of economically depressed urban or rural communities. In addition, the Office acted as a broker within the federal government to foster interagency cooperation and coordination in support of local partnership initiatives. Its three divisions established liaison with business and trade groups, foundations, public interest groups and voluntary associations. In each of these areas, private efforts could be geared toward collaborative relationships with the public sector. The Office agenda focused on specific programs with achievable goals. The staff worked to develop a few demonstrations which would show the potential "leverage" or "multiplier" effect of local partnerships. The Office then aimed to provide technical assistance to local public and private organizations so that they could build on these early successes to create an ongoing, institutionalized national public–private sector network in support of economic revitalization.

Among the demonstration projects launched by the Office, the most important were the following:

Aetna Life and Casualty Company and the National Training and Information Center (NTIC)

In cooperation with the Department, Aetna provided $250,000 to support a technical assistance effort designed to build the capacity of neighborhood organizations in four cities to engage in neighborhood revitalization projects. OPPP provided $100,000 in matching funds. This project, now in its second year, has already generated some $8 million in permanent financing for projects with four of the six groups, with total development expected to exceed $20 million. This project also encouraged the development of reinvestment programs in a number of other major insurance companies.

National Main Street Project

Restoring the economic vitality of small towns is an important opportunity for partnership efforts. Under a contract between OPPP, the National Trust for Historic Preservation and the International Downtown Executives Association, a nationwide competition was conducted to select six States to participate in the National Main Street demonstration project. An Interagency working group coordinated by OPPP provided some $500,000 in funding to establish the National Main Street Center. The Center will provide technical assistance to some 30 small communities located in the six States, which were selected by

*The budget of the Office was about $1 million during FY 1980–1981.

State economic development offices. This project intended both to stimulate the creation of local public–private partnerships to revitalize small city main streets and to increase State capacity to deliver assistance. The National Main Street Center opened for business on October 1, 1980, on schedule. OPPP negotiated an innovative interagency agreement with seven federal agencies. The agreement was designed to facilitate the flow of resources to this effort and to uncover policy and program regulations which impede assistance efforts that support local public–private initiatives in revitalization. The seven agencies involved were the Departments of HUD, Commerce, Interior, Transportation, Agriculture, Small Business Administration, and the National Endowment for the Arts.

Community Reinvestment Act Workshops

To encourage private reinvestment, OPPP entered into a contract with the U.S. conference of Mayors and the Center for Community Change to develop Case Study materials and hold a series of regional workshops which provided public officials, voluntary association groups and private sector interests with information and strategies on local public–private partnerships for economic revitalization that have been stimulated by the Community Reinvestment Act.

New World Foundation Study

OPPP financed a research project with the New World Foundation which brought together over 50 leaders in the public–private–nonprofit sectors to look at the role of neighborhood- and community-based corporations in economic development and the ways in which public–private partnerships could enhance these efforts. A report entitled "Initiative for Community Self-Help: Efforts to Increase Recognition and Support" summarized the findings. This effort also led OPPP to create the Triangular Partnerships demonstration described below.

Triangular Partnerships Project

After the New World Foundation research project was completed, OPPP developed the concept of Triangular Partnerships and launched a demonstration project. Supported by a grant of $250,000 from the Charles Stewart Mott Foundation of Flint, Michigan, and $100,000 from HUD, this demonstration project, in three phases and involving participation in some eight to 12 medium and large cities, was designed to develop improved institutional mechanisms to spur private investment in neighborhood economic development. The project was focused on downtown development in cities where downtowns have become or are close to becoming competitive but where neighborhoods near downtown continue to stagnate or decline. The project provided linkages between the downtown area and the neighborhoods, with local governments and neighborhood development organizations (NDOs) acting as brokers for the arrangements. It further sought to develop models for sustained processes through which capital and other benefits could flow from successful downtown developments to low- and moderate-income residents. The second phase offers technical assistance in the development of institutional mechanisms, plus other financing and resource requirements needed to sustain ongoing partnerships among downtown and neighborhood groups. The linkages established by the Triangular Partnerships Project further demonstrate the need for a national public–private vehicle to provide support for these local partnerships.

Reflections and Directions for the Future

At the beginning of this chapter we noted that the still-evolving partnership process could be properly subjected to the injunction: "If it is not local, it is not real." As we reflect on the emerging partnership movement between public, private, and the voluntary sectors, that philosophical premise needs to be kept in view.

The Executive Summary of a Report on Business Roles in Economic Development, done for EDA by the Center for Public Resources (1980), makes some particularly helpful recommendations:

> For the most part, existing national forums tend to reflect either a public or a private orientation, most often the former. Existing effort has been limited largely to board policy recommendations and has not taken the next step of defining specific strategies to implement those recommendations. What is needed are multisectoral mechanisms at local, regional and national levels to involve public and private leadership in building strategies needed to realize policy objectives.
>
> The public sector needs to develop a better understanding of how to position itself as a resource to support existing, and stimulate additional, private sector initiatives. Viable private initiatives are seldom, if ever, created by government. Too often, government is not perceived by the business community as a resource. To build government resourcefulness, public policy issues, including regulatory requirements, should be analyzed by business and government professionals to determine the nature of opportunities and constraints at the national level. It is also necessary to expand city, state and regional government capacity to support local private initiatives.

The Center's report simply echoes the sentiments of those in both the public and private sector. The "laundry list" of complaints is lengthy. Without being exhaustive, let us illustrate some of the problems:

1. the lack of a meaningful match between legislation and resources at the federal level and public sector capacity at the local level, so that local actors can take advantage of the assistance available;
2. the age-old problem of "turfism" between federal agencies, federal–state and local public sector representatives—a jurisdictional battle that is compounded by a vast jumble of conflicting regulations and administrative requirements;
3. the continuing problem of defining the private sector and making certain

that the definition is broad enough to include all of the organizational players, including small business and the newer not-for-profit groups;

4. a very uneven pattern of "enlightened self-interest" on the part of the business community to engage in joint ventures with the public sector, in part based on the fear of red-tape entanglement and in part based on the vast differential in capacity between and among the public–private sector players;

5. the difficulty in moving from safe dialogue to a "real live deal" which obviously involves risk;

6. the problem of diminishing resources, a problem which both the public and private sectors share as the nation faces a likely continuation of many of the economic problems which arose during the latter half of the 1970s—economic dislocations, cutbacks in public programs, high unemployment and the high cost of money to finance new ventures; and

7. the problematic ability of federal and state programs to aid in the development and support of small businesses.

Yet this list of problems also provides us with opportunities. We have described a multitude of specific federal programs, as well as suggested some state, city and private sector programs that either attempt to improve the public sector at all levels, or attempt to improve financial and/or regulatory incentives that will catalyze public–private partnerships. However, there are few efforts directed at the formal recruitment of private and philanthropic sector organizations to participate in urban revitalization projects.

"Pump-priming" of the economy by government during the post-Depression era was supposed to work by funneling assistance to consumers, who would then stimulate the economy with their purchase activity. Budget deficits were created during national economic downturns and surpluses during boom times, yet these very "stop and go" tactics have resulted, according to some critics of so-called "demand side" economics, in a condition that was supposed to be impossible in Keynesian economic theory, namely, simultaneous high inflation and unemployment. Current federal efforts are labeled "supply-side" economics. Yet the "supply-side" concept driving current policy is too narrow. It denies both the necessity and the promise of the public–private institution-building efforts which this chapter has described. The aborted Office of Public–Private Partnerships, for example, focused on the supply-side by attempting to formally recruit and to improve the institutional capacity of the voluntary, public, and philanthropic sectors in our economy to engage in urban revitalization projects.

From Here to ... ?

This chapter has sketched an emerging framework, such as it is, for public and private partnership. It has described some of the relevant public sector economic incentive programs and private sector activities and some current models of public–private cooporation. The challenges we face in our current economic malaise are indeed great. So are the opportunities offered us. The public–private partnership vehicles now emerging may well hold the key to the way we as a nation move forward to rebuild the vitality of our cities and towns.

Bibliography

Butler, Stuart M. (1980). *Enterprise Zones: Pioneering in the Inner City*. The Heritage Foundation.

Center for Public Resources (CPR) (1980). *Business Roles in Economic Development — Executive Summary*, published under grant from the Economic Development Administration, U.S. Department of Commerce (July).

SRI International (1980). *Working and Measuring Corporate Urban Ventures — Executive Summary*, published in cooperation with the Conference Board under contract to U.S. Department of Housing and Urban Development (June).

U.S. Department of Housing and Urban Development (1980). *Emerging Partnership Opportunities for Cities — An Introduction to the Use of Federal Economic Development Tools and Techniques for Investors and Developers*. Washington, DC: Office of Public–Private Partnerships (March).

XVI

Targeted Development Finance: Lessons from European Experience

Peter J. Bearse and Arthur W. Bearse

The recent American experience with private–public sector cooperation in development finance has been limited to a few variations on traditional urban or rural development programs. Western Europe has a longer history of active public–private–labor cooperative involvement in encouraging the flow and amount of capital that is devoted to either specific industrial sectors or to designated geographic regions. Given U.S. governmental institutions and a long-standing tradition of separate public and private sector activities, it is understandable that the "mixed" economies of Western Europe would be more likely to adopt cooperative efforts among what, in the American setting, are usually competing groups or adversaries. The Western European attitude is one that accommodates the concept of "planned" economies as a way of life. The contrary U.S. tradition has been one where policies to foster competition are long-standing. The purpose of this chapter is to review the European experience with targeting development finance on a spatial and industrial basis, taking as examples Great Britain, France, and West Germany.[1] Then, recognizing the different U.S. attitude toward cooperative public–private sector programs and a different institutional and geographical setting, we will see if the United States can adopt or adapt certain aspects of the European experience. One difficulty at the start is that "targeting" or "discrimination" in development efforts seems to run contrary to U.S. democratic traditions.* As a practical matter, however, inner city economic problems and the differential

---

*This chapter uses "targeting" or "discrimination" as equivalent terms denoting efforts to allocate financial resources for development only to certain priority areas or industries. Targeting is the term commonly used in the United States.

growth characteristics of regional economies lead one directly into a search for better methods to promote domestic development. The most logical step is to look at cases where there is prior experience in the selective application of development finance tools. The European experience is apropos.

While the focus of this chapter is on three countries, one should recognize that there are other European economies that practice forms of mixed public–private sector financing and investment encouragement.[2] For example, Holland has a long tradition of including both social and private cost–benefit calculations in its macroeconomic planning function.[3] By concentrating on three countries, however, it is possible to see typical examples of processes at work in different governmental settings, geographical regions, and economic organizations.

If one was to examine the entire European Economic Community (EEC),, there would be diverse methods, policies, and unique situations for achieving public–private sector cooperation toward economic development objectives for specific areas or industries. In spite of this potentially large set of possible methods, there is an important group of common approaches. Some form of discrimination to allocate scarce resources must be followed. For instance, in Germany, designated "growth-points" are established. The direction of resource flow must be positive to some sectors and negative or held constant to other sectors.[4] A common technique is to grant interest rate subsidies or differentials to those industries or geographic regions where additional investment is desired. Tax breaks are given for similar reasons. A third method is to target infrastructure development—building structures,[5] roads, and utilities in designated underdeveloped regions. A fourth approach is to develop or encourage a shifting of the necessary labor pool through training and/or relocation grants, wage subsidies, and wage differentials.

Examples of targeted investment and infrastructure have by no means been absent from American experience, especially recently.[6] The main trend of the American experience, however, has been one where methods of discriminating by region or industrial sector have neither represented major economic tools nor avowed policy aims.[7] To the contrary, the American experience has been oriented to "more of the pie for all," macroeconomic growth *in toto* for the *entire* economy. Such a strategy was characteristic of the 1960s. With rare exceptions, such as the Appalachian Regional Commission, the "Great Society" represented development policy without discrimination. Money eventually filtered down to every town and village, even if only a few dollars. In an attempt to satisfy the conflicting needs of political representatives there was a failure to concentrate funds according to development needs. Another familiar nondiscriminatory program has been the universal provision of tax breaks for investment, such as accelerated depreciation allowances. American economic policy has been predominantly of a nondiscriminatory nature. This is understandable in light of a democratic tradition that looks with disfavor on favors for special groups. Also in the American experience, consistent long-term policies have been hindered by any consistent attitude (except suspicion) toward a governmental role in economic management [see Schonfield (1965)].

The 1970s have seen a number of pilot programs that have started to explore public–private cooperation to achieve domestic development goals. Urban Development Action Grants (UDAG), Economic Development Administration (EDA) programs, and recent proposals for a National Development Bank (NDB) are examples. In no sense, however, has the American experience attained the consistent policies, sectoral cooperation, and scope of the European programs. These programs have not yet reached a consensus on implementation. A major area of debate continues to be the extent to which financial incentives should be automatic, available to any business meeting certain criteria, or be discretionary, available only to certain businesses in certain areas. If the latter, they will need to be limited in scope and subject to bureaucratic control. Once a decision is made to follow discriminatory goals, another issue appears. On what basis to discriminate? By turning to the European experience with domestic development, one can look at practical cases where these issues have been faced.

Prior to addressing the lessons available to the United States from the European experience, the first order of business is to review the key features of the British, French, and German programs, along with an overview of the role of the European Economic Community (EEC) and some key concepts.

A Survey of the European Experience

In contrast to an American economic policy that relies relatively more on the indirect macroeconomic jobs effect of income increases, European policy depends *relatively* more on private industry subsidies, capital investment, and programs to provide plant and equipment from which jobs follow directly. European traditions of greater cooperation between labor, government, and industry are rather at odds with American traditions of an independent private sector and a strong American aversion to cooperative efforts that could lead to abuses of the doctrine of separation of powers.

The Role Played by the European Economic Community (EEC)

European countries face a constraint that does not exist for the United States. The economic role of the European Economic Community (EEC) includes a development role under EEC control as well. While EEC development programs are at a smaller level than those of individual countries, it is important to understand their role in order to get an overall view of development activities within the European countries.

An aspect of regional policy in Europe is that the European Economic Community imposes limits on the amount of regional aid which member nations can provide. The purpose of EEC limits is to prevent unfair competition and distortions of trade. The EEC ceiling is often described as 20% in "central" areas and 35% in "peripheral" areas, but its actual workings are complicated.

The EEC also operates its own Regional Development Fund, although its program is small relative to the regional policies of the member nations. The amount that the EEC spends annually in all nine member nations is less than one-third of the annual spending for comparable purposes by Great Britain alone. EEC Regional Development Funds are allocated by formula to the member nations and are often used by them to offset their own regional-policy expenditures. All nine member states receive allocations; even Germany gets 6.4% of the total. Allocations range from Italy, which receives 40% of the funds allocated, to Luxembourg, which receives 0.1%. Funds can only be spent in the nationally designated development areas. They can be used both for subsidies to private firms and for infrastructure development purposes.

The EEC also operates a European Investment Bank (EIB), which borrows funds outside of the community and makes loans primarily for infrastructure development. In 1976 the bank's outlays were at the level of $1 (U.S.) billion for infrastructure (72.6% of total) and private industry (27.4%) (European Investment Bank, 1976). Later on in this chapter the EIB is discussed as a role model for a U.S. National Development Bank.

The European Concept of Regional Policy and Its Relationship to Macro-Policy

The European Concept of Regional Policy

The European use of the term "regional policy"[8] is broader than the traditional American use. In American use the term is used to describe programs devoted to improve the economic indicators of a region such as New England. Often it refers to targeted infrastructure subsidies rather than subsidies to private industries.

European use of the term "regional policy" refers primarily to spatially targeted subsidies to private industry. In some countries the term also includes measures to provide new and expanded infrastructure in areas designated as development regions. Regional policy can also include the application of controls to prevent firms from locating or expanding in certain developed and/or congested areas. The emphasis, in this chapter, however, is on the "carrots" rather than the "sticks" of European regional policy.[9] Direct state investments can also contribute to regional policy. The location of state industries in development areas or the construction of factory space to be leased to firms locating or expanding in development areas are typical examples.

Regional policy in Europe tends to involve larger geographical areas than those which figure in U.S. urban policy. Yet the essential character of the two types of policy (European regional policy and American urban policy) is the same, to discriminate or "target" spatially in order to promote economic development. While the national government in the United States does provide some subsidies to employers who locate, expand, or modernize in designated geographical areas, such programs are much smaller in size and scope and much more specialized than their European counterparts. Spatially targeted programs for economic development in the United States have tended to be limited to infrastructure. (TVA and The Appalachian Regional Commission are examples.) The present programs of the Economic Development Administration include subsidies to private employers for economic development and adjustment. Subsidies are also provided for small businesses and trade adjustment purposes. The UDAG program ("Urban Development Action Grants") involves aid to private firms, too, though there is a significant degree of emphasis on infrastructure investments related to economic development and industrial siting. All of these various programs together are smaller and narrower in scope than the regional development programs of the European countries.

Regional policy in Western Europe typically involves a mixture of automatic and discretionary financial incentives* along with tax incentives to firms that locate, expand, or modernize facilities in designated development regions. Most assistance is for manufacturing firms, although assistance is also provided to large service firms where the firms involved have "a choice of location." (Banks, insurance companies, and mail order firms are examples of the latter.) The magnitude of the assistance provided tends to vary according to degree of "need" indicated by the development area designations. Britain and France, for example, have three gradations of regional designation, with the maximum package payable in the neediest areas and smaller amounts of assistance available in the lower gradations of development area.

Another important point about regional policy is that it is much more likely to be successful when jobs and GNP are *expanding* than in periods (like the present) of limited economic growth in Western Europe and the United States.

The three countries discussed below have designated areas containing about 35% of their population as eligible development areas. Politically there tends to be a rather consensual, approximate one-third ratio guiding development policy throughout Europe. It is interesting in this connection that the preliminary listing of areas eligible for assistance from the Carter Administration's proposed National Development Bank† accounted for about 35% of population in the United States.

Relationship to Macro-Policy

It is important to keep in mind what national macroeconomic goals are to be achieved by European regional policy programs in addition to their locational aims. A major aim of the regional policies studied is to increase total invest-

---

*See discussion below under implementation issues.

†The concept and design of a National Development Bank proposal are discussed in Chap. XVIII.

ment, both internal and external. Foreign investment (what the British call "inward investment") is especially important in this context. Sixteen percent of all manufacturing workers in Scotland (a priority development region in Britain) are employed by American firms. Scottish industrialists and development officials have aggressively promoted their region in the United States. The ratio is even higher in Ireland. This poses an interesting dilemma for regional development subsidies. They have grown to the point where large curtailments by any one country would be difficult to justify even if their basic redistributional purpose was eventually eliminated or significantly reduced. Unless some regions of a country are at or near the EEC ceilings, reduction of regional subsidies would undermine its competitive position in terms of inducements to foreign firms vis-à-vis its colleagues in the Common Market. This competitive problem is felt to be most serious by development officials in France, which is seen as having the weakest regional incentives among the three nations.

The Domestic Development Programs of Three European Countries*

In this section we turn to capsule descriptions of three countries (Great Britain, France, and the Federal Republic of Germany) in order to understand the mechanics of their programs. In order to facilitate comparison, the descriptions have been organized by (1) setting, (2) substance, and (3) process of regional policy. Additional information about European financial institutions is covered below under the section "Lessons for the United States." The three countries taken as a group provide a representative coverage of the European experience with domestic development programs.

Great Britain—Setting

The rationale for regional policy in Britain[10] is threefold: (1) to narrow the disparities in employment and growth rates between the developed and less-developed areas of the country; (2) to reduce congestion and avoid overheating the economy in the southeast (primarily the London metropolitan area); and (3) initially, to move industry out of London for military reasons. The first of these two objectives has been the most important. Dispersing population (second objective listed) entered the picture in the postwar period as an outgrowth of the Barlow Report. In recent years both disparities in employment levels and congestion in the southeast have abated somewhat. New policies to achieve other purposes may have somewhat weakened regional policy. In particular, the general slowdown in the economy and a new concern about "inner areas" (the core areas of central cities) have resulted in the adoption of grants to modernize industry generally and to aid inner areas,

---

*This section follows Nathan (1979) closely, since some of the observations evolved out of his personal contact with European officials.

including parts of London. Both programs diminish the relative advantage of the development areas, located in the north and west in the United Kingdom. In addition, one regional incentive, the Regional Employment Premium (REP), was recently repealed.[11] An important reason for the repeal was European Economic Community (EEC) pressures on the United Kingdom, claiming that its regional incentives are too strong and that the REP format, i.e., continuous assistance, is a violation of EEC policy.

Great Britain—Substance

The primary instrument of British regional policy is the regional Development Grant (RDG). The RDG is an automatic grant provided on an item-by-item basis to almost all manufacturing industries in the development regions for a variety of types of investments. This includes new plant and equipment, modernization and even the replacement of existing equipment on an item-by-item basis. It is the latter type of investment—replacement items—that is most controversial. The EEC is applying steady pressure, but not yet sanctions, to have the British modify this policy. The maximum level of the RDG is 22% in what are defined as "special development areas." It is 20% in the second and third levels of development areas, although only buildings are eligible for assistance in the third level of development area.

A distinctive feature of the RDG is its *automaticity*. Germany has a smaller automatic grant. France has a grant that is said to be discretionary, but in practice it also tends to operate on a quite automatic basis. The major development finance initiatives of the Carter administration envisioned all subsidies to employers made on a discretionary (or project) basis, an important departure from European practice.

The second instrument of British regional policy is discretionary, what are termed "selective financial assistance grants." These grants to "top off" the RDG vary in amount, the upper limit being a function of the EEC ceiling. Although these grants are discretionary, the policy appears to be that all qualifying industries which decide to build, expand, or modernize in development regions should be given some measure of additional assistance. Development officials appear to engage in what in the United States would be considered "outreach" activities. Recently, the inauguration of two forms of grants to promote industrial modernization on a generalized basis (Section 8 of the National Industrial Development Act of 1972 and National Enterprise Board programs) has produced a situation in which some employers qualify for a larger industrial development grant than they could receive under the "selective financial assistance" program. In such cases, British development officers interviewed in the field indicated that they see their role as ensuring that the employer applies for the largest grant possible. Subsidies to industry on a generalized development grant basis focus on industrial sectors not limited to a regional development area.

A third instrument of British development policy is the construction, leasing, and sale of "advance factories." Space in these factories can be rent-free for up to five years.

Still a fourth instrument of regional development policy in Britain is Industrial Development Certificates (IDC) to limit growth outside of the designated development areas.[12] Although required, such certificates are relatively freely granted at the present time. They are not an important instrument of British regional policy under current conditions of widespread unemployment and surplus labor even in the more prosperous areas.

Great Britain—Process

Several actors play a role in British development policy, but the leading role is that of the Department of Industry (formerly part of the Department of Trade and Industry). The Department has primary policy responsibility for all four development programs nationwide and directly administers them in England. Special arrangements apply for Scotland and Wales. The Secretaries of State for Scotland and Wales administer these programs in their region, but maintain close ties with the Department of Industry. Northern Ireland has its own Department of Commerce which administers a legally separate system, similar to Britain's, but more generous.

Other actors are the National Enterprise Board which, as noted above, has generalized nationwide industrial responsibilities, and the Department of Environment, the lead agency for implementing the new White Paper on "inner areas."[13] Both of these programs can get drawn into regional policy decision-making.

France—Setting

Like that of Great Britain, French regional policy seeks to stimulate industrial development in outlying areas to relieve congestion in the region of its capital city (the Paris Basin).[14] By contrast, however, France's development areas tend to contain fewer large cities. Much of the emphasis of French regional policy has been on agricultural conversion, especially in the western part of the nation where small and inefficient farms predominate and the percentage of the population engaged in agriculture is very high.

A common characteristic of the setting of regional policy in France and the United Kingdom is the tendency for currently lagging economic conditions nationwide to induce more generalized development initiatives that in relative terms undermine the role and effect of regional policy.

France—Substance

The most striking characteristic of the regional incentives provided in France is their explicit connection to job creation. Unlike the other two countries studied, the value of regional development subsidies in France varies according to the number of jobs added for each investment aided. A flat amount is provided per added employee, ranging from 25,000 francs in the highest gradation of development area to 15,000 in the lowest.[15] French officials maintain that this system puts them at a competitive disadvantage compared to other European countries, particularly Common Market nations, which provide development subsidies in relation to the amount of capital (rather than labor) added.

The use of negative sanctions (controls on location) was found to be more important in France than in Great Britain. Much of the controversy surrounding regional policy and the role of the French development agency relates to its lead responsibility in preventing firms from locating in the Paris Basin, a policy which has been progressively loosened in recent years in response to protests.[16]

France—Process

The primary agency responsible for administering regional policy in France is the *Délégation à l'Aménagement du Territoire et à l'Action Régionale* (DATAR). Although formerly part of a Cabinet agency, it is now an independent agency responsible directly to the Prime Minister. DATAR has a small staff—40 professionals—which only becomes directly involved in the processing of applications for the very largest regional grants, those exceeding 10 million francs. All other applications (in fact, 90% of the total) are processed by the Prefects, the senior officials of the national government in the 89 departments (administrative areas) of France.

In reviewing the applications considered centrally, DATAR is part of a three-member team consisting of its representative and representatives of the Department of Industry and the French national bank. Applications for regional development grants approved by these review teams are submitted to the minister of finance for final approval.

Although on the surface this process appears to be discretionary, studies have found that the award of these grants is essentially automatic for firms meeting the job-creation and other requirements of the program. In fact, the role of DATAR with respect to the larger grants appears to be analogous to the outreach activities described earlier for the Department of Industry in Britain. DATAR officials are described as "entering into a dialogue" with firms (both domestic and foreign) considering large investments in France, in order to be able to provide assurances that assistance will be forthcoming if they proceed with a particular project under consideration. This is said to be especially important for foreign investors where "a quick promise" is frequently needed. DATAR staff members are also involved in the national economic planning process which is unique to France among the countries studied.

The Federal Republic of Germany—Setting

The most prominent difference in the foundation of regional policy between Germany[17] and the two previous cases is demographic. Germany, unlike

Britain and France, does not have a single dominant population center; the congestion factor has been much less important as a rationale for regional policy. The generally stronger economic condition of Germany also tends to make regional policy less prominent in national policy than in France and Britain. Another factor that tends to reduce the visibility of regional policy in the Federal Republic is the federal arrangement itself. Rather than a single and cohesive regional policy, many decisions are made by the Land governments (analogous to state authorities in the United States), rather than the Bund (Federal level). Considerable tension exists currently between the two levels, and there has been discussion, much of it spirited, of plans to devolve this joint task and others to the Laender.

Germany—Substance

Under the basic law for the joint task of regional policy in Germany, a national Planning Council with two Bund and eleven Land members developed the designation system whereby some 300 communities in 21 regions (mostly small cities and towns called "growth points") are priority areas for development.[18] There are two gradations of development regions. The population of the development regions (including the "growth points") is equal to approximately 35% of the population of the Federal Republic.

Two basic instruments of regional policy are used in Germany: the Investment Allowance (IA) and the Investment Grant (IG). An Investment Allowance of 7.5% is available to all manufacturing (and some service) firms which establish new facilities, expand, or modernize their facilities in the growth points. Investment Allowances can also be paid to firms which expand or modernize in the development regions outside of the growth points; however, new establishments can only be aided if they are located in a growth point community.

The second instrument of regional policy in Germany—the Investment Grant—is administered on a discretionary basis by the Laender, though it is jointly funded (on a 50–50 basis) by the Bund and the Laender. The Laender have wide discretion within general guidelines in the award of an Investment Grant.

Special and higher priority under German regional policy is given to the areas which border East Germany. Combined incentives (the IA and IG) can equal 25% in the zonal border areas as compared to a 20% ceiling in the highest priority growth points in the other designated development regions.[19]

Generally speaking, development programs for infrastructure in the Federal Republic are separate from the programs to subsidize private employers. However, the Laender can use their Investment Grant funds for infrastructure *directly related* to industrial siting and expansion. Some do and some do not. North Rhine–Westphalia does not use any of its IG funds for infrastructure. Its regional development program is of special interest because North Rhine–Westphalia alone among the ten participating Laender (Berlin is treated as a special case) operates a Land-financed IA and IG system in its own designated development areas, although at lower levels of support than in the nationally designated development areas. One reason for this special program is a dispute involving the designation of new development areas. As a result of this dispute, North Rhine–Westphalia and two other Laender have taken the position publicly that this "joint task" should devolve to the Laender.

Germany—Process

For U.S. purposes, the most interesting institutional feature of regional development programs in Germany is the division of responsibilities between the Bund and the Laender. As indicated, the Planning Council, with two members from the Bund and one from each Land, has been stalemated on major changes in the designation system for eligible areas. As of this writing the original system is still in effect with only marginal changes. This system stands out among the three countries studied as having the most complex statistical base. When it was adopted in 1974, the criteria used were juggled several times in typical U.S. fashion to assure the inclusion of a sufficient number of "growth points" in Bavaria to win adoption.[20]

The Investment Allowance, which is automatic, is paid through the tax system in cash or as a tax credit. It is nationally administered by the Bund's Economic Ministry. The Investment Grant is administered by the economic ministries of the ten participating Laender. Within the guidelines of the Planning Council, they have considerable flexibility to allocate these funds between infrastructure and industrial subsidies, to add conditions, and to vary the amounts of the Investment Grant up to a ceiling figure.

Local governments in German domestic affairs are extensively regulated by the Laender. They do not have formal policy involvement in the matters handled by the Bund and the Laender in the field of regional development. This situation contrasts with that of the United States where in recent years the federal government has increasingly entered into direct financial and regulatory relationships with local governmental units for developmental and other purposes.

Lessons for the United States

Through the use of various incentives and financial mechanisms, the European experience demonstrates that public–private sector cooperation can achieve both spatial and industrial discrimination to the areas targeted for domestic development and growth. As a rule of thumb, about 35% of a country's population seems to fall within targeted areas. These programs, then, are much larger in scope than those currently under way in the United States.[21] As was pointed out above, Urban Development Action Grants and programs of the Economic Development Administration *started* to encourage private sector participation and incentives in urban development programs. If the United

States, however, is to proceed to undertake programs which, on the scope and scale of those in Europe, attempt shifts in the flows of capital and investment, it behooves us to understand the issues thereby posed for the United States. The United States has very different traditions and institutions, even vis-à-vis Britain.[22] In terms of size alone, the United States seems to face alternatives, both undesirable, either: (1) extremely costly programs if industries and geographic regions are to quality automatically under criteria as in Europe, or (2) a horrendous bureaucratic snafu while seeking to evaluate large numbers of proposals for funding on a discretionary basis. To extend the dilemma further, once a discretionary program is started, how does one insulate it from political pressures? At the risk of repeating some points, five program issues *any* U.S. program must face need to be summarized, given what we now know of the European experience.

Five Implementation Issues

1. The Automaticity Issue

This issue is how to strike an appropriate balance between the provision of development finance assistance on a virtually automatic basis and its provision according to a discretionary (project-by-project) review process.

Several premises or themes underlie European preference for automaticity. One is a concern about *uncertainty*. It is argued that if an employer is unsure about whether the firm will receive a grant, its value is likely to be discounted. Regional policy would tend to influence the firm's locational and investment behavior less strongly than would be the case if the receipt of a grant were assured and its value could be calculated in advance.

The second underpinning of automaticity in European regional policy is the *fairness* argument. This point is especially emphasized in Great Britain. The theory is that all firms should be able to receive a grant. None should be arbitrarily excluded. The boldest and strongest will then come forward and apply. In this way, problems that might occur as a result of state intervention in private-sector decisionmaking are minimized.

Still another advantage of an automatic program is that it can be administered more easily and with a smaller staff.

The automaticity issue will be extremely difficult to resolve in the United States. Assuming for the moment that the one-third ratio is a guiding rule of thumb in regional policy and that incentives above some threshold as high as 20% are needed to affect the behavior of private investors, the cost of an automatic regional development program in the United States would be many times that projected for a discretionary program. This cost constraint reinforces arguments for an independent entity with a strong staff as a condition necessary for successful implementation in the United States. It would also appear to support the idea of a two-tier approach (federal and state) as a means of taking some of the political pressure of operating a discretionary program off the central authorities.*

There is also a demographic dimension to the automaticity issue. To the extent that the urban problem of the United States consists of a fairly small number of poverty-impacted city cores, the test of implementation will be the capability to discriminate in favor of these areas. The relatively small number of cities facing these conditions and the regional concentration of these distressed core cities add to the challenge of operating a discretionary program in the U.S. context. Again, European experience suggests that the ability to perform this task effectively will require extremely careful institution building at the outset.

2. Eligibility Issues

A number of eligibility issues are suggested by the European experience:

What areas should be designated and how should they be selected? The German experience is most instructive with regard to the designation of eligible areas. Within the designated regions, priority is given to "growth points": small and medium-sized cities, 20,000 to 50,000 population. Incentive grants for new plants, although not expansion and modernization projects, are limited to these cities. This narrow definition of eligible areas is much closer to the targeting of urban areas in the United States than is the case of Great Britain where, for example, eligible areas tend to be quite large geographical areas, equivalent in size and population to three or four large counties in the United States.

A second and related aspect of the designation issue is whether there should be gradations of area eligibility. Such arrangements are characteristic of European regional development programs. For different levels of economic distress, the size of development incentives can be varied or, as in the German case, the type of qualifying investment can be differentiated. This might be an effective way to help target the most distressed communities in the United States.

What types of investment projects should be assisted? Basically, three types of projects can be identified from European experience—new plants (what the British call "setting up"), expansions, and modernization. Where priority is given according to project type, it is usually given to new plants. Again, this could be a basis for differentiation either as to eligibility or the amount of assistance. Such an approach, however, would create problems in helping "retain" existing industries in distressed areas. Retention investments, by definition, are of the expansion or modernization variety.

*These arguments and ideas are discussed further in Chap. XVIII, which deals directly with proposals for development banking in the United States.

A unique feature of the British system is that regional subsidies can be provided on an item-by-item basis and they can help pay for the replacement of equipment even if it is identical to existing equipment, i.e., if no modernization is involved. This policy has led to controversy with the EEC authorities, who maintain that the item-by-item approach for replacement expenditures constitutes "continuous" aid and violates EEC policy that regional development subsidies should be limited to one-time investment projects. The need to maximize the use of limited resources on the part of the United States calls for an approach which also limits aid to one-time projects, as opposed to the British replacement approach.

Should there be limits on the types of industries aided? The countries studied as a general rule do not limit or vary *regional* development subsidies by industry within the manufacturing sector.[23] By contrast, *national* industrial development programs may discriminate by industry or sector.[24] In Great Britain, for example, 40 industrial committees have been established to concentrate government policy on the promotion of particular industries and industrial processes with growth potential.

The most important question as to type of industry for regional policy relates not to manufacturing but to *services*. The countries studied tend to have special policies to determine whether service firms should qualify for aid. One basis for including service firms—an approach used in the United Kingdom—is that they have a "genuine choice of location." Another way of stating this criterion—used as a basis for policy in Germany—is whether they export their product out of the region, e.g., insurance companies, correspondence schools, most banks, and mail order companies.

Assuming that such tests make sense, the next question is: How should service firms be aided? Unlike manufacturing firms, the value of investment (plant and equipment) is usually not an appropriate benchmark for determining the level of aid to be provided. Service firms generally rent space and often have relatively limited equipment needs. Their principal expenditures tend to be for labor. It makes sense, therefore, to relate the level of incentive payments to service firms to the number of employees added by a locational decision.[25] The British, for example, provide a grant of £1,500 for each job created in a priority development area, with various minimums and maximums built into their program (e.g., a ten-job minimum for new establishments in a development area). The net effect of this approach (the concept and the limits applied) is that the service-industry component of British regional policy is much smaller and less important than for manufacturing industries. The same applies to the other two countries studied.

The main lesson for the United States in this area is the need to include service industries but to treat them somewhat differently. Currently, services industries are largely left out of development finance incentive programs in the United States. The "choice of location" criterion and the use of subsidies associated with labor intensity may lend themselves to U.S. needs. However, there is also a need, particularly in urban areas, to go beyond the European criteria in order to aid neighborhood shopping centers as well as smaller scale investments by service firms of various types. European policy does not offer lessons in this field.

What kinds of conditions should be applied to regional development subsidies? Many kinds of conditions can be attached to regional development subsidies. For U.S. purposes, one obvious type of condition is the employment of indigenous workers, particularly long-term unemployed or disadvantaged persons. So far as could be determined, none of the three European countries studied have established such labor-market requirements for regional development grants. They tend to look for fulfillment of two objectives: job creation and tax base expansion. Despite the more serious problems of structural and minority-group unemployment in distressed areas in the United States, the lesson of European experience is to caution against specific requirements for employing low-income persons or the disadvantaged as a condition of receiving assistance.[26] Other programs, such as education, employment and training, may be more appropriate to this goal. Successful implementation of new development finance initiatives for the United States is such a heady challenge that ancillary requirements which make the task more difficult should be resisted.

3. Instrument Issues

Several possibilities exist relating to the way in which investment subsidies can be provided. Outright grants equal to a fixed proportion of an investment are the most common approach in Europe. Alternatively, or as a supplement to a grant, interest-relief payments can be made. Under European regional development programs, interest-free periods are also provided in some cases along with interest-relief grants. This could result, for example, in an arrangement whereby, for the first year or two years of a loan, only payments of principal are made, and after that the interest rate is subsidized. Soft loans are also used, though more sparingly because they tie up more funds than grants or interest-relief payments. Selective financial assistance in the United Kingdom, for example, is provided in the form of a soft loan only if a qualifying investor is unable to obtain loan funds from other sources.

Closely related to the question of the instrument used is the issue of its *tax treatment*. Regional development grants are tax free income in Britain. In Germany, the investment allowance is tax free, but the investment grants administered by the Laender are not. Regional subsidies are taxable, but with special tax treatment, in France. The value of regional development grants is further enhanced if the assets created can be fully depreciated, which is the case for most of the subsidies provided in the countries studied.

Local tax abatements can also be provided in conjunction with regional policy. In France local tax relief is granted by a process similar to the award of investment grants, i.e., the national policy apparatus controls decisionmaking;

however, the revenue foregone locally is not reimbursed by the central government.

In sharp contrast to Europe, local property tax concessions are the most important subsidies to attract industry to both distressed and nondistressed communities in the United States. Unfortunately, little recent research has been done on the relative size and the effects of these tax concessions. It is a subject which requires careful scrutiny because the equity considerations (the most distressed areas being the least able to play the game) are so perverse.[27]

4. Timing Issues

In addition to their rate and tax treatment, the value of investment subsidies is affected by their timing. If grants are paid, as in Britain, very early in the process on submission of audited bills received, their value is enhanced vis-à-vis subsidies paid retrospectively. It is not surprising that the British system involves early payment. The more automatic the subsidy system, the more feasible it is to pay early.

Payment can be made at the time of approval of an application for expenses already incurred or on submission of proof of payment in the case of ongoing investment projects. The delayed-payment approach does not present any special problems. The timing issue is merely one, and not a critical one, of the valuation of a subsidy. The more critical aspects are its amount and tax treatment.

5. The Rationale for Regional Development Subsidies

The final category of program issue, and an important one, pertains to the rationale for a system of incentive payments to private employers to achieve spatial discrimination for public purposes.

Three basic options are available. One is the idea of *compensation* for the added costs of doing business in a development area. Another is the idea of a *stimulus*, in effect, a reward for a firm's willingness to operate in a development area. These two rationales can go together and, in fact, tend to be joined in European policymaking for regional development. A firm can be viewed as receiving compensation for the added costs of supporting regional policy objectives, and on top of that, an extra payment for good behavior supportive of national development policy.

A third possible rationale for regional development subsidies that is especially important in the European Economic Community relates to the international competitiveness of producers. Regional development subsidies can be viewed as a means of attracting foreign investments. This rationale has not been mentioned in the U.S. context. Presumably the justification for subsidies in the United States would be twofold: compensation and stimulus.

It is particularly important for a discretionary program in tune with U.S. traditions to articulate the *compensation* rationale. It will be needed to answer the complaints of non-aided firms who are concerned about competitive advantages being given to aided firms. In an automatic system where all firms are eligible if they invest in the designated areas, the government can respond to such complaints simply: If you want to play, you have but to come forward. In the case of the United States, on the other hand, one needs to be able to argue that participation in its carefully selected projects involves extra costs to employers which the government should compensate in exchange for their participation in desired domestic development projects.

Discussion and Summary of Findings

We have reviewed five major issues which need to be confronted in the design and implementation of a publicly initiated development finance system to engage private enterprise in the development of targeted areas. The next step should be to look specifically at what these issues imply for the design and implementation of policies and programs within the American setting. Chapter XVIII examines one type of proposal that has received serious attention in recent years—for a National Development Bank. Another proposal outlining a decentralized administrative arrangement for development finance programs, has been set forth elsewhere by Richard Nathan (1980). Both are designed to adapt the best features of the European experience to an American environment. One should realize, however, that a great deal of the requisite planning and research has not yet been done which would enable U.S. decisionmakers to come to grips, not merely with the major issues, but with a multitude of thorny issues of implementation and political palatability.[28]

In spite of constraints in the state of the art, let us take a moment to reflect further on some issues arising out of the discussion thus far.

The European experience makes a strong and logical case for automaticity—reduction of uncertainty, reduction of eligibility problems using fairness criteria, and reduction of transactions costs through smaller administrative staffs. Given the much greater size of the United States, American traditions of nondiscrimination in macroeconomic policy, and the potential costs involved if most eligible U.S. firms were to step forward to participate, the U.S. need is for *both* a degree of automaticity for administrative efficiency and a degree of discretion to reduce participation. The decentralization proposal cited above is designed to address these issues.

If one does not view approximately 35% coverage as a sacrosanct rule of thumb, significant narrowing of coverage through tightly drawn eligibility criteria becomes a real possibility. A good example of this is provided by the Kemp-Garcia bill now before the U.S. Congress, which would target financial incentives on narrowly drawn "enterprise zones" representing no more than 5% of the U.S. population. Completely apart from the other merits or demerits of this legislation, one should be skeptical because (1) the incentives in the political system are all one way—to broaden ("spread the goodies around") rather than narrow coverage— and (2) the quality of local data is generally not good enough to permit fine-grained targeting.

Political isolation is necessary to achieve two key objectives: (1) fairness in administration of eligibility standards and (2) professional business management of development finance programs. U.S. traditions of political involvement come into conflict with European models when one tries to achieve these goals.

The need for a *financial liquidity vehicle* is also apparent, given the long lags in awarding grant funds in the United States. Combined, these two considerations have resulted in proposals to involve U.S. financial markets, using commercial bank review and lending roles, creation of a secondary market, or to create a National Development Bank (NDB) with lending capability and directors who fill a nonpolitical role.

Within the content of a single chapter, it is impossible to examine all the institutional mechanisms and committee roles that underlie the European models. Should one wish to design a comprehensive U.S. program, it would be wise to probe much more deeply into these mechanisms. For France, Hackett and Hackett (1963) provide a detailed description. More of the German mechanisms are covered by Reuss (1963). For Great Britain, Fels (1972) and Ryder (1977) describe the inner workings of specific "Boards" (policy committees). Caution is necessary when drawing analogies from foreign experiences and administrative preferences. The European models also exist within institutional and political environments very different from those in the United States, some of whose machinery *might* or *might not* be called into play in daily administration of development finance programs. Even though debate on development banking and other development finance initiatives has subsided, it will surely arise again, and an understanding of the relevance of European experience will be needed. This chapter has tried to provide at least some of that understanding.

Notes

[1] The descriptions of the three main countries rely heavily on Nathan (1979). The bibliography includes additional references for the reader interested in delving further into the topic.

[2] See, for example, LaPalombara (1966), Nicol and Wettman (1978), Wellisz (1960), and Boudeville (1966).

[3] See Theil (1966) and Tinbergen (1969).

[4] While population shifts are not currently an object of policy in the U.S. policy, attempts to influence population growth by regions have been part of the European experience. See Sundquist (1975).

[5] Sometimes rent-free for a period of time.

[6] Cf., for instance, the targeting criteria in the "UDAG" program, described in Chap. XIII.

[7] Two exceptions come quickly to mind, oil depletion allowances and the defense contracts of the 1960s. Some defense contract awards were contingent on the winner agreeing to develop facilities in a specific region, e.g., Huntsville, Alabama.

[8] Continuing research on European Regional policy is being accomplished by the Center for the Study of Public Policy at the University of Strathclyde, Scotland, and the International Institute for Management's Science Center, Berlin.

[9] For additional discussion on restrictive controls, see Nicol and Wettman (1978).

[10] For additional information see Fels (1972), Ryder (1977), Stewart (1977), and Yuill (1978).

[11] The REP was enacted in 1967 and repealed in 1976. It involved a flat weekly payment to employers (£3 for full-time men, £1.50 for women and boys, and £0.95 for girls) and was viewed as a way of offsetting the standard capital orientation of regional incentives. The REP still exists in Northern Ireland. See Douglas Yuill (1978).

[12] See Sundquist (1975, pp. 42–46, 53–55) for a description of controls that evolved to prevent the "drift to the south" of British population.

[13] This program, announced in July 1978, has limited funding and all the earmarks of the U.S. Model Cities program. Its basic aim is to establish coordinating mechanisms to "bend" existing programs to conform to "comprehensive" plans for designated inner area locations.

[14] For additional information see Boudeville (1966), Hackett and Hackett (1963), Hull (1978), Kindleberger (1967), Massé (1963), Schollhammer (1969), and Wellisz (1960).

[15] For some large projects under current law, the authorities may award up to 25% of eligible expenditures irrespective of the cost-per-job limit. See Chris Hull (1978).

[16] See Sundquist (1975, pp. 138–142).

[17] For additional information see Arndt (1966), Casper (1978), Reuss (1963).

[18] The two Bund members have the same number of votes as the eleven Land representatives. Decisions are taken by a three quarters vote.

[19] A special depreciation allowance is provided in the zonal border areas.

[20] Bavaria is a large, traditionally independent, and generally conservative Land which plays a role in German federalism somewhat analogous to that of Texas in the United States.

[21] Note, however, that proposals for a U.S. National Development Bank (NDB) and for a large-scale development finance capability under Economic Development Administration auspices also targeted about 35% of the population (Nathan, 1979, p. 3).

[22] The essential details and implications of these differences for economic planning and development policy are nicely set forth in Schonfield (1965).

[23] In Germany, soft loans in the development areas are not provided to all manufacturing industries. (And, as referred to here and elsewhere, "soft loans" are those provided at below market rates and more flexible terms than in the private market.)

[24] In France, small firms are excluded from eligibility. Industrial growth rates can be encouraged or discouraged by the French *national* decisionmaking group.

[25] Whether such a policy will continue to make sense, i.e., whether service firms will continue to be "labor intensive," is an important question in itself. See Stanback and Bearse (1981) for some perspective on this question.

[26] This caution was also sounded in a January 1980 meeting of U.S. experts and officials from both the public and private sectors to discuss the implementation of the National Public Works and Economic Development Act of 1980 (NPWEDA). The private sector participants, especially, cautioned that too many "social" objectives would diminish private sector participation. See Public/Private Ventures (1981).

[27] Detroit Mayor Coleman Young was recently quoted as describing property tax concessions as "a suicidal cutthroat competition. It's too bad we have a competition system where dog eats dog and the devil takes the hindmost." Describing Detroit's abatement program, Young said, "I mean to compete... I'm tired of being the hindmost."

[28] Another important area of program design must consider accountability for use of funds to meet established goals. Audit techniques have an efficiency gain over detailed rules and regulations. [Cf. "Critical Issues in Development Finance" (Public/Private Ventures, 1981) for program implementation issues.]

420

Bibliography

Arndt, Hans-Joachim (1966). *West Germany: Politics of Nonplanning*. Syracuse: Syracuse University Press.

Boudeville, J-R. (1966). *Problems of Regional Economic Planning*. Edinburgh: The University Press.

Casper, Ullrich (1978). "Background Notes to Regional Incentives in the Federal Republic of Germany," prepared for the Atlantic Conference on Balanced National Growth, Racine, Wisconsin (January 4–6).

Downie, J. (1963). "What Can the U.S. Learn from Foreign Experience," prepared for the University of California Conference on Unemployment and the American Economy, Berkley, California (April 18–20).

European Investment Bank (1976). *Annual Report*.

Fels, Allan (1972). *The British Prices and Incomes Board*. Cambridge: Cambridge University Press.

Hackett, John, and Hackett, Anne-Marie (1963). *Economic Planning in France* (With a forward by Pierre Massé). London: George Allen & Unwin.

Hicks, Ursala K. (1965). *Development Finance: Planning and Control*. Oxford: Oxford University Press.

Hull, Chris (1978). "Background Notes to Regional Incentives in France," prepared for the Atlantic Conference on Balanced National Growth, Racine, Wisconsin (January 4–6).

Kindleburger, Charles P. (1967). "French Planning" (with comment by Stanilaw Wellisz), in *National Economic Planning*, edited by Max F. Millikan. New York: National Bureau of Economic Research, pp. 279–304.

LaPalombara, Joseph (1966). *Italy: the Politics of Planning*. Syracuse, NY: Syracuse University Press.

Massé, Pierre (1963). "The Guiding Ideas Behind French Planning," in *Readings in Comparative Economic Systems*, edited by Wayne A. Leeman. New York: Houghton-Mifflin.

Nathan, Richard P. (1979). *Lessons from European Experience for a U.S. National Development Bank*. The Council for International Urban Liaison (International Urban Reports), Washington, DC.

Nathan, Richard P. (1980). "A Proposal for the Decentralized Administration of the Development Finance Program," prepared for the Corporation for Public/Private Ventures Conference on Development Finance, Princeton, NJ (January 18–19).

National Council for Urban Economic Development Information Service (1977). "Update: States and Urban Development—Part II," 11 (August).

Nichol, Bill, and Wettmann, Reinhart (1978). "Background Notes to Restrictive Regional Policy Measures in the European Community," prepared for the Atlantic Conference on Balanced National Growth, Racine, Wisconsin (January 4–6).

Public/Private Ventures, Inc. (1981). "Critical Issues in Development Finance," Philadelphia; for the U.S. Economic Development Administration (January).

Reuss, Frederic (1963). *Fiscal Policy for Growth Without Inflation: the German Experiment*. Baltimore: The Johns Hopkins Press.

Ryder, Lord (1977). "The National Enterprise Board," in *The Individual, the Enterprise and the State*, edited by R.I. Tricker. New York: John Wiley, pp. 37–50.

Schollhammer, Hans (1969). "National Economic Planning and Business Decision Making-Making," in *California Management Review*, Vol. XII, No. 2 (Winter), pp. 74–78.

Schonfield, Andrew (1965). *Modern Capitalism: The Changing Balance of Public and Private Power*. New York: Oxford University Press.

Stewart, Michael (1977). *The Jekyll and Hyde Years: Politics and Economic Policy Since 1964*. London: J.M. Dent.

Sunquist, James L. (1975). *Dispersing Population: What America Can Learn From Europe*, Washington, DC: Brookings.

Theil, Henri (1966). *Applied Economic Forecasting*. Amsterdam: North-Holland.

Tinbergen, Jan (1969). "The Theory of the Optimum Regime," in *Economic Models, Estimation and Risk Programming: Essays in honor of Gerhard Tintner*, edited by K.A. Fox et al. Berlin: Springer-Verlag.

Wellisz, Stanislaw (1960). "Economic Planning in the Netherlands, France, and Italy," *Journal of Political Economy*, Vol. LXVII, No. 3 (June), pp. 252–283.

Yuill, Douglas (1978). "Background Notes on Regional Incentives in Britain," prepared for the Atlantic Conference on Balanced National Growth," Racine, Wisconsin (January 4–6).

XVII

Emerging Issues in Financing Basic Infrastructure

Richard J. Moore and Michael A. Pagano

One of the most traditional activities of urban and local governments—the construction, maintenance, and repair of infrastructure—has come under increasing scrutiny and criticism in the past decade. Caught between the Scylla of declining tax bases and the Charybdis of increasing costs, local governments have diverted maintenance funds to more visible operating expenses. Yet, recently, long-term neglect of the infrastructure and deferral of maintenance have raised the political awareness and importance of this issue in many cities. Mayor Richard Caliguiri of Pittsburgh, after assuming the temporary mayoral position when Pete Flaherty resigned in spring, 1977, bolstered his political appeal for the November elections by resurfacing almost 100 miles of Pittsburgh's 900 miles of street. He won the subsequent election without the endorsement of either political party by capitalizing on the fact that Flaherty's "austere" budgets of the previous six years had resulted in an alleged under-maintained and underrepaired infrastructure.

The problem of a deteriorating urban infrastructure has reached epidemic proportions nationwide. New York City only resurfaced 43 miles per year of the city's 5,300 miles of streets, implying a resurfacing cycle of 132 years (Grossman, 1977). New Orleans resurfaced 19 miles of street in 1977 for a resurfacing cycle of 84 years. Prior to 1977, the cycle was over 300 years (Moore and Pagano, 1979). While the deferral of street maintenance and resurfacing programs are reaching critical levels in many cities, the problem of ignoring other infrastructural categories becomes no less important. For example, the Federal Highway Administration issued a report which suggested that:

> America's bridges are falling down at an alarming rate of 150 a year. Eight to ten persons die annually in bridge collapses and 2000 more in accidents attributable

to obsolete bridge structures, dangerous approaches or poor alignment between the highway and bridge entrance. ...one-fifth of this country's 563,500 bridges are candidates for a fall (Abramson, 1979, p. 4).

Experts insist that billions of dollars should be spent in order to maintain urban infrastructure at adequate levels and to replace and reconstruct aging and neglected infrastructure. Countless newspaper reports and articles raised the same issue: Urban infrastructure is neglected and deteriorating at alarming rates [see *inter alia*, Peterson (1976, 1978)]. Furthermore, cities with a declining population cannot reduce expenditures on infrastructure in proportion to population decreases. In recent Congressional testimony, Sternlieb stated:

When you have few users and enormous fixed costs, and you have all the problems of the geriatric diseases: an aging bridge system, an aging street system, you can't cut back costs as casually as is sometimes thought. You cannot reduce your support as the number of users go [sic] down. In part, this is one of the dimensions of the urban problem (U.S. Congress, Joint Economic Committee, 1979b, p. 66).

Indeed, the problem of "geriatric diseases" become increasingly complex in an era of scarcer and scarcer resources as revenues are insufficient to cover the cities' infrastructural needs.

The academic literature on urban (and regional) economic growth and development places its emphasis on transportation, labor, and material costs. It places far less importance on infrastructure provision by the public sector. The assumption made by this body of literature is that requisite infrastructure will be provided in response to demands or in anticipation of such demands [see, e.g., Richardson (1979)]. But, the amount of public funds to be spent on the infrastructure is constrained by the tax base represented by central city residents. And their presence in the city is a result of their perceptions that both the benefits derived from public services and infrastructure are sufficient and that other potential locations (e.g., suburbs) are not perceived as providing a better mix of services at a lower cost (Tiebout, 1956). If costs (i.e., taxes) at one location exceed the benefits at the location, then they will "vote with their feet" by moving to other areas that provide a better "package" of services for an acceptable cost. In other words, the costs of publicly provided infrastructure is an element in the location decision of individuals (and firms). Although the public cost of infrastructure has been treated as an element in the decision to locate at a certain site, most of the urban economics literature gives shortshrift to the importance of the infrastructure as a critical element in economic growth.

If the urban and regional economics literature has slighted the role of infrastructure, the literature on economic development considers it crucial. Economic development consists of complex interactions among the industrial and agricultural sectors of an economy which can be stimulated or induced to grow through appropriate government policies [see, e.g., Myrdal (1957) and

Hirschman (1958)]. The public sector's role in promoting economic development can take the form of infrastructure-building (e.g., constructing and maintaining water and sewer systems, streets and highways, providing education, manpower training, etc.) and/or producing industrial and agricultural goods (e.g., automobiles, steel, fertilizer, grain, etc.). Hirschman has created a broad classification scheme for these kinds of activities. He defines infrastructure as Social Overhead Capital (SOC) and the production of industrial and agricultural goods as Directly Productive Activities (DPA):

> SOC is usually defined as comprising those basic services without which primary, secondary, and tertiary productive activities cannot function. In its wider sense, it includes all public services from law and order through education and public health to transportation, communications, power and water supply, as well as such agricultural overhead capital as irrigation and drainage systems (1958, p. 83).

By implication, DPA are those primary, secondary, and tertiary productive activities which Hirschman mentions. Holland goes one step farther than Hirschman and proposes that SOC should be separated into "economic overhead capital" (EOC) and "social overhead capital":

> If we are more specific in defining 'social' and 'economic' overhead capital, we could also make a clearer distinction between the two, and classify the former as including housing, health, education, welfare, social facilities (including cinemas, sport facilities and so on), and general infrastructure essential for domestic use, even if also used in directly productive activity, such as roads, power and water, communications facilities, sanitation services and sewerage. This would mean that the concept of '*economic overhead capital*' *would refer to that infrastructure essential for the directly productive activities of firms*, such as available land and buildings, access to transport routes (either urban or nonurban), on-site power and water supply, on-site communication facilities, sanitation and sewerage (1976, p. 214, emphasis added).

In American cities, the urban public sector—the states, counties, and special districts—are responsible for providing EOC.* If the public provision of EOC becomes an essential element in promoting economic development, then studies on public expenditures and revenue sources must distinguish between SOC and EOC. This study, while not denying the importance of SOC or "human capital," examines only the EOC activities of the urban public sector. In support of this approach, Holland remarks:

> In effect, however desirable it may be from a social welfare viewpoint to increase SOC in relatively backward areas, it is increasingly evident that SOC infrastructure is not essential for the efficient undertaking of directly productive activity, and *that the provision of EOC alone is a necessary condition for it.* (1976, p. 216, emphasis added).

*Historically, EOC was provided initially by the private sector in many instances. In almost all cases, these EOC activities reverted to public ownership or, at least, public regulation.

Holland's assertion that EOC is a necessary condition for economic development also finds support in the public finance and welfare economics literature. In order to pay for social welfare functions, society must be wealthy and productive enough to afford them. Furthermore, social welfare expenditures maintain or ensure certain income/quality of life levels; that is, they do not necessarily create wealth or contribute to economic growth to the degree that EOC or infrastructural expenditures can, except (possibly) in the sense of increasing aggregate demand. And welfare seldom provides revenues to the local government because it is usually tax-exempt.

In other words, social welfare expenditures do not have the growth promoting characteristics that the provision of infrastructure or EOC does. Indeed, Senator Daniel Patrick Moynihan has been voicing this concern for many years. Recently, he asserted that "It continues to be the case that New York receives more 'soft' money that 'hard' [from federal programs]. The faster growing regions of the country get infrastructure, we get food stamps" (Moynihan, 1979, p. 6). Moynihan's concern is consonant with the arguments presented herein. The primary *raison d'etre* for infrastructure, often, if not always, provided by the (urban) public sector, is to aid the capital accumulation/investment functions of the economy in order to promote economic growth and development. Hence, the perspective and underlying premise of this study, based on the preceding discussion, is that *urban economic development is dependent, to a substantial degree, on the existence of a viable, sufficient and well-maintained urban infrastructure.* Although this study's focus is not on urban economic development, per se, the emphasis is on a necessary condition for urban economic development to take place (i.e., on urban infrastructure).

In order to promote urban economic development, implementation of public policy requires that taxes or other public revenues be available for those activities. A variety of factors affect a city's ability to provide, maintain, and extend its infrastructure; a principal factor is the city's fiscal capacity to finance these activities.

In other words, the causes and consequences of differential performance of cities' EOC activities can be attributed to the varying degree by which cities generate sufficient revenue for infrastructural purposes. A principal failing of many conventional arguments related to fiscal crisis in cities is that little attention is paid to the role and needs of public infrastructure as factors exacerbating fiscal strain. Furthermore, arguments on urban fiscal stress, with few exceptions, have tended to gloss over the specific conditions of individual cities over time in the pursuit of static, macrolevel comparisons. Studies rarely have attempted to gain a longitudinal perspective on city fiscal performance. In the present essay, we attempt to overcome some of these deficiencies, focusing on one aspect of urban economic development and fiscal crisis: the relative performance and financing of public infrastructure.

As Steinlieb suggested above, a principal dilemma for older, "declining" cities is that earlier costs associated with growth do not experience a corresponding decline (Sternlieb, 1978). In fact, many of these costs of maintaining the urban network increase in spite of declining populations. Given this problem, we argue first that as cities are strained increasingly to generate additional own-source revenues, the maintenance of existing capital stock is adversely affected. The result is the physical deterioration of the urban public capital stock. Additionally, adequate maintenance expenditures are more likely to be realized if the principal finance mechanism is user charges rather than if it is taxation, irrespective of both the number of functions for which a central city is responsible and the degree of fiscal stress. Finally, we argue that intergovernmental transfers, and particularly Federal grants-in-aid, have not ameliorated the cost factor for older cities, but potentially have increased urban maintenance expenditures for the future.

Methodology

To analyze these issues, this study examines maintenance and capital expenditures and revenues for four major infrastructural categories for the 1957–1977 period in nine central cities. The study relies on *actual*, not *budgeted*, expenditures. Intensive, in-depth case studies were undertaken to determine the levels of maintenance and investment in urban public infrastructure. The primary reason for on-site research resides in the fact that maintenance expenditures are not reported by the Bureau of the Census or by other governmental agencies, and revenues for specific capital projects are not clearly delineated. Instead of examining all activities that cities undertake, EOC categories were selected which, while being common to all cities, were also significant in terms of total expenditures of all urban areas. The four functional categories selected were water systems, sewer systems, streets, and bridges. Together, these four represent 25% of total city expenditures for all activities for each of the past five years; furthermore, these EOC categories represented more than 50% of all cities' capital outlays for FY 1976–1977 (U.S. Bureau of the Census, 1978, pp. 5–6).

Selection of cities as research sites proceeded in two stages based on five selection criteria: regional location, population, age, fiscal condition, and jurisdictional responsibility. Twenty-one cities were selected for initial survey purposes using these five criteria (Pagano, 1980). The primary purpose of the survey was to ascertain the physical condition of the cities' infrastructure. From this survey, another variable—condition of the capital stock as determined in this initial survey—was added to the above list of variables for case study selection purposes. Since the "condition" of the capital stock in the 21 cities was ascertained by interviews with city officials,* the condition rating should be viewed only as a qualitative statement.

*For a more detailed description of the methodology employed in the broader study, see CONSAD Research Corporation, *A Study of Public Works Investment in the United States, Volume IV: Appendices*, prepared for the U.S. Department of Commerce, March, 1980.

From the initially surveyed cities, a cross-section of nine cities was selected and visited on the basis of the six selection criteria. Because the size of the sample was small due to budgetary constraints, statistical inferences may not always be appropriate to make from the findings presented below to comparable cities. However, it was our intent to select nine cities which were substantially different from one another so that a wide range of issues could be addressed. Hence, this study must be seen as exploratory, but hopefully provocative. The nine cities were Baltimore, Dallas, Des Moines, Hartford, Newark, New Orleans, Pittsburgh, St. Louis, and Seattle.

Analysis

Maintenance, Fiscal Stress, and Finance Mechanisms

One of the clear advantages possessed by older, large cities is the inherited capital stock. However, the installation of infrastructure at a given moment has implications for future costs of maintenance and repair. Although it is recognized as an "urban problem," the response to an aging infrastructure often is one of neglect because of low political visibility, especially for fiscally stressed cities. That is, maintenance needs increase while the costs to maintain become exorbitant; maintenance is postponed.

Maintenance activities usually are financed from the operating budget and own-source revenues. A city's inability to generate own-source receipts in order to prevent the deterioration of infrastructure is indicative of fiscal stress. The poorer the capacity to increase own-source revenues, the greater the degree of fiscal stress. This is evident in a variety of indicators applied to the nine cities studied (see Table 1). Low relative per capita income, high property taxes, declining population base, high incidence of poverty, declining manufacturing employment, and reliance on state and federal aid, all are indicative of fiscal stress. On a qualitative, summative index, described more fully in other work done by the authors (Moore and Pagano, 1979; Pagano, 1980), Dallas and Des Moines possessed "very good" capacities to augment own-source revenues compared to the other cities examined. Seattle's capacity rated as "good"; Pittsburgh and Baltimore rated "fair"; and Hartford, New Orleans, and St. Louis fell in the "poor" category. Finally, Newark's capacity to increase own-source revenues is "very poor."

An assessment was made of the condition of infrastructure in each of the cities. Table 2 presents a qualitative condition assessment of each function studied. The condition of the infrastructure for the two cities in very good fiscal condition, Dallas and Des Moines, ranks in the "good" range for all four selected functional categories. The fiscally stressed cities, on the other hand, appear to have trouble maintaining capital stock at adequate levels. However, one important exception appears in these comparisons: the water and sewer systems of all the cities (except Newark's and St. Louis's sewer systems) are in "fair" or "good" condition.

If constant or increasing funds for maintenance purposes are indicative of a well-maintained infrastructure, then those functions that are in relatively good

Table 1. Indicators of Capacity for Selected Cities to Increase Own-Source Revenues

City	1 — Change in Population 1960-1975	2 — Central City Income as Percentage of National Per Capita Income (1975)	3 — Central City Income as Percentage of SMSA Per Capita Income (1975)	4 — Poverty Rate	5 — Change in Manufacturing Employment Between 1958 and 1972	6 — Tax Rate for City Activities Per $1000 of Fair Market Value	7 — Intergovernmental Aid as Percent of General Revenues (1976-1977)	8 — Capacity to Increase Own Source Revenues[a]
Baltimore	− 9.3%	94.7%	86.6%	19.8%	−18.9%	$26.54	65.0%	Fair
Dallas	+19.6	115.6	107.4	13.4	+41.3	10.42	15.8	Very Good
Des Moines	− 7.1	108.8	98.0	10.4	+ 5.7	13.50	34.3	Very Good
Hartford	− 5.1	87.4	75.5	19.2	−50.4	54.73	43.8	Poor
New Orleans	−11.8	88.1	96.2	26.8	− 2.1	1.97	39.9	Poor
Newark	−16.2	73.2	59.3	25.6	−39.8	58.80	60.3	Very Poor
Pittsburgh	−24.1	96.8	94.6	17.4	− 3.9	27.50 (land) 13.75 (bldgs.)	41.6	Fair
St. Louis	−31.1	87.6	84.9	23.7	−28.6	27.40	28.9	Poor–Fair
Seattle	−12.6	126.8	141.8	10.9	−33.0	4.95	37.2	Good

Sources: For columns 1, 2, 3, and 5: U.S. Department of Commerce, Bureau of the Census, *County and City Data Book* (various years).

For column 6: *Annual Financial Reports* and *Official Bond Offering Statement* for each city (latest years, 1977 or 1978).

For column 7: U.S. Department of Commerce, Bureau of the Census, *City Government Finances, 1976-1977.*

For column 4: Private communications with John Magowski (October 1979), Data Systems and Statistics Division, Office of Management, Community Development and Planning, Department of Housing and Urban Development.

These poverty rates are based on 1970 Census Information and refined by HUD for purposes of distributing revenue to cities under General Revenue Sharing, Urban Development Action Grants and Anti-Recessionary Fiscal Assistance Programs.

[a]No attempt has been made to rank order cities based on the variables included (column 8). Instead, this is intended to be a qualitative summary variable.

Table 2. Comparative Condition Ratings[a] for Each Functional Area by City[b]

	Water System	Sewer System	Streets	Bridges
Poor and deteriorating rapidly				P, N
Poor		N (collection)		
Poor–Fair, but worsening			NO, H	H
Poor–Fair		N (treatment) SL	P, B, N, SL	NO, SL, B
Poor–Fair, but improving				
Fair, but worsening	N (city) SL		S	
Fair		P (collection)		S
Fair, but improving				
Fair–Good	NO, B, S N (regional)	B, S (collection)	D	
Good	D, H, P	DM, NO, D, H, S (treatment)	DM	D
Good–Very Good		P (treatment)		
Very Good	DM			DM

[a]The condition rating for all functional areas was based on the evaluation of various documents, information, and interviews in each city. This evaluation was performed by an engineer of the American Public Works Association. It is our belief that the ratings are at least comparative in that a "fair" rating for one city is similar to a "fair" rating in another. Absolute and generally recognized measures are lacking, and formulas to determine a quantitative "condition" assessment do not exist. Through the careful use and examination of city information, it is hoped that our estimated condition ratings are generally accurate.

[b]B = Baltimore; D = Dallas; DM = Des Moines; H = Hartford; NO = New Orleans; N = Newark; P = Pittsburgh; SL = St. Louis; and S = Seattle.

condition should be receiving adequate or increasing funds for maintenance. Constant dollar maintenance expenditures for the various cities and functions were compiled and compared across time. In general, those cities that are fiscally strained to generate sufficient revenues expend less for maintenance purposes on *tax-supported functions* (bridge and street systems) than fiscally healthy cities. However, user-charge supported activities (water and sewer systems) do not appear to be affected by the degree of fiscal stress experienced by a city. Water and sewer systems, even in those fiscally stressed cities studied (such as Hartford or New Orleans), are maintained at adequate levels.

City outlays for maintenance purposes that are financed from taxation decrease rather dramatically for Hartford, Newark, and St. Louis, but remain constant or increase for fiscally healthy cities, such as Des Moines. Two exceptions appear. One is Pittsburgh, which increased its street maintenance expenditures during the last two years of the study period. This is reflective of the higher needs of a city with very poor streets and many freeze–thaw cycles; it also reflects the Caliguiri Administration's political promises to increase pothole repairs. The other exception is Dallas which shows a decline in the last four years. This aberration is due to the unusual cold and icy winters of the past several years which required resurfacing jobs (a capital outlay) rather than simple patchwork (a maintenance outlay). Dallas, in fact, increased capital expenditures dramatically during the last two years, more than offsetting maintenance declines.

On the other hand, maintenance outlays for public services that relied on *user charges* (water and sewer) were considered to be adequate for all cities regardless of fiscal condition. Even where declines in maintenance expenditures were experienced, productivity increases offset the declines, resulting in good performance ratings for these systems. The implication is that, if increased costs can be passed on to the consumer in the form of higher prices and if differential quantities can be consumed and be paid for by the resident population, those public activities that are financed via a market-type mechanism (i.e., user charges) in general, will not contribute to the fiscal stress of cities. Furthermore, urban fiscal stress will not affect the pattern of maintenance expenditures for water and sewer systems; adequate maintenance outlays will be realized.

What we suggest here may be contrary to the idea, prevalent in the extant literature, that the *number* of functions for which a city is responsible results in high expenditures that contribute to fiscal crisis. Schultze et al. (1977, p. 199) argue that:

> Another factor responsible for the growth in big-city expenditures is the proliferation in the number and kind of services provided for the urban governments. For example, local programs for pollution control, consumer protection, drug rehabilitation, family planning, day care, and community colleges, were almost nonexistent a decade ago.

The implication is that it is the proliferation of urban functions which impinges on the city's capacity to be solvent.

The worsening condition of the infrastructure and declining maintenance expenditures appear to apply to those functions that *both* rely on taxation (as opposed to user charges) *and* are located in fiscally stressed cities. Therefore, those cities that are responsible for more activities may indeed experience greater fiscal stress than those that have lesser responsibilities, *but differential responsibility alone is not an indicator of fiscal stress*. Thus, while we do not disagree that proliferation of urban functions contributes to increased expenditures, we do challenge the implication that increased expenditures alone contribute to fiscal crisis. It is the *financing* mechanism that is important, not the *number* of functions or high expenditures per capita. For example, a city that increases its scope of responsibility to include sewer, water, electricity, and gas services—services that can be priced via the market mechanism—will be in better fiscal condition, *ceteris paribus*, than one that becomes responsible for drug rehabilitation, AFDC, and other social services that are financed out of higher tax rates.

The Role of Intergovernmental Aid

A number of authors point to federal responsibility for the current urban crisis, arguing that federal grant programs in some ways have inspired local patterns of expenditure. (Fainstein and Fainstein, 1976.) We agree, and further suggest that the pattern of intergovernmental (especially federal) transfers to cities may add to the differential cost of urban government.

First of all, federal largesse in earlier periods encouraged localities to expend out of proportion to their revenue-raising capacity. Property taxes provide the single largest source of income for local governments. While the property tax is less significant for large cities than for local governments in general—city income taxes have begun to play a larger role—it still remains the predominant tax form. Further, the proportion of revenue represented by property tax has decreased somewhat from 71 to 59% of total own-source receipts between 1957 and 1977; yet, the *burden* of that tax has become greater. In 1957, the property tax burden was $73 per capita in all localities; in 1977, it was a remarkable $279 per capita (U.S. Bureau of the Census, 1958 and 1978). Even among those few urban centers that have diversified the tax base, there still exists the inability to resolve the spatial problem of residents/workers/consumers "voting with their feet" and utilizing their "exit" option. During the past 20 years, burgeoning federal aid programs stepped in to fill the void created by own-source fiscal squeeze. Thus, while local revenues became increasingly scarce, expenditures continued to climb as the direct result of the growing participation of the federal government (Yin, 1979). Yet, by the mid-1970s the rate of growth of federal grants-in-aid had slowed. This slowdown is even more dramatic given the rate of inflation of the period.

The perspective of this changing role is especially clear in examining public *capital* investments. As a result of the "tightness" of bond markets and increasing federal "activism," cities have become very dependent on the federal government for aid in capital investments. While federal aid as a proportion of state and local capital expenditures in the 1960s was between 20 and 25%, in the 1970s it was as high as 45% (U.S. Budget, various years). This dependence has impacted those cities that are fiscally stressed more than healthy cities. This is clear in Table 3 for the nine cities studied. The fiscally stressed cities, such as Hartford, New Orleans, Newark, show high dependence on federal aid across all functions (except water, where federal aid was not significant for any city). The "healthy" cities, Dallas, Des Moines, and Seattle, show relatively low levels of federal dependence.

Coupled with the impact of federal aid on high-reliance cities in general, most Federal programs for *capital* expenditures formally exclude the use of funds for maintenance activities. While less money (relative to total grants) is in the form of capital grants today, those programs that remain in existence bias against maintenance expenditures. Examination of capital grants in the four functional areas of concern here yields the consistent finding that maintenance, even when not formally excluded from the use of funds, is rarely encouraged. In several programs (wastewater treatment, bridges, and until 1976 the Federal aid highway fund) no provisions are made for maintenance activities. In others, there are few incentives, and in some cases great disincentives, to maintain infrastructure. An extreme case of this disincentive concerns mass transit. Even though Urban Mass Transit Administration grants are for both capital and operating (maintenance) expenses, the capital grants are so lucrative (financing 80% of capital costs) that early replacement of buses (and trolleys, subway trains) is encouraged rather than encouraging maintenance of the existing fleet. Where federal programs exclude maintenance activities, the burden of future maintenance of the facility falls squarely on the shoulders of the local government. A recent *National Journal* article cites Kevin Shepard, director of Cincinnati's planning and management support system:

> The acceptance of federal money brings with it the responsibility to take care of the facility for a long, long time. We are beginning to take a hard look... to see whether we can afford the gift (Stanfield, 1980).

The incapacity or unwillingness to increase local revenues has meant that the local government must refuse millions of dollars for capital outlays.

We are not suggesting that capital grants produce negative or unintended results across all urban areas. In fact, in growing areas federal programs do correspond to city need in that capital expenditures are doubly advantageous. Newer and growing urban areas need to construct infrastructure. Ironically, however, it is not the growing cities that need aid, but rather the older cities that are experiencing outmigration and a declining revenue base which need

Table 3. Federal Contributions as Percent of Capital Outlays

Central Cities (listed according to fiscal stress condition)	Streets		Bridges		Water System		Sewer System	
	1957-1977	1968-1977	1957-1977	1968-1977	1957-1977	1968-1977	1957-1977	1968-1977
Dallas	3.9%	5.5%	14.1%	30.0%	[a]	[a]	21.3%	29.0%
Des Moines	3.8	5.2	11.9	20.3	0.0%	0.0%	24.1	34.8[b]
Seattle	1.7	2.7	combined with "streets"		18.5[b]	13.7[c]	NA	22.2[b]
Pittsburgh	8.1	11.2	combined with "streets"		9.9	9.1	NA	50.0
Baltimore	NA	69.1	combined with "streets"		NA	6.2	NA	51.2
St. Louis	4.6	23.9	10.2	36.0	0.0	0.0	36.9[b]	28.5[b]
New Orleans	NA	37.9	NA	0.0	NA	0.8	NA	56.7
Hartford	60.5	63.3	combined with "streets"		NA	6.4	NA	34.5
Newark	60.8	66.2	0.0	0.0	2.5	8.0	48.8	65.1[d]

[a] Negligible.
[b] Includes state contributions.
[c] 1957-1970.
[d] 1968-1970 only.

funds. Federal capital grants, then, are differentially advantageous to some (i.e., growing) cities with new infrastructural needs.

Urban Policy Alternatives to Improve EOC

Probably the most obvious, and most discussed, policy alternative to help alleviate the deteriorating condition of cities' infrastructure is to restructure federal aid programs and to accelerate federal involvement. However, too many federal grants are categorical *capital* grants which do not confront the maintenance needs of older, fiscally stressed cities. Other Federal programs become too uncertain for cities to rely on (e.g., witness the current attacks on the revenue-sharing program) such that urban planning becomes a risky undertaking. Furthermore, Federal grants-in-aid have not kept up with the cost of living in most cities, resulting in unintended cutbacks in service levels. A recent newspaper article drove home the point:

> ...Federal aid to states and localities ...suddenly slowed to 5.4 percent growth for the 1979 fiscal year and may increase only 1 percent in 1980. That's a fraction of the inflation rate and means a major cut. (Peirce, 1979)

The "major cuts" become acute for those fiscally stressed cities which are truly dependent on federal aid for their survival. Indeed, much has been written about the need for increased federal aid (see, for example U.S. President, 1978; CONSAD, 1980; Peterson, 1976). Although this strategy may be appropriate to pursue, here we prefer not to "beat a dead horse." Instead, we examine the potential of four alternative policies that cities might consider as "release valves" to their revenue-generating dilemma:

1. increasing city reliance on user charge mechanisms;
2. encouraging an expansion of the (property) tax base, principally through active annexation policies;
3. stimulating private investment through public subsidies;
4. utilizing public funds for public economic development.

User Charges as Escape Valve

Passage of the Jarvis–Gann Property Tax Initiative, commonly referred to as Proposition 13, has forced city administrators to rethink financial strategies and to come to grips with the reality of fiscal restraint. While the impact of this and similar measures has been differential, depending upon an area's reliance on property tax revenues, a clear change in philosophy for local officials has occurred. Two components of this changed approach to local finance are divestiture of public services and the increased application of a "pay-as-you-go", user-charge approach to the provision of public goods, many of which were formally financed from tax revenues. The application of user charges, however, it not equally viable for all functions, and, in fact, is contingent upon the relative divisibility of the good (or service). The standard response of public finance is that the key criterion for the possibility of user charges is excludability: the potential for excluding an individual from the benefits of a service for which he/she is unwilling to pay.*

As is clear, certain "public" goods—those that are nondivisible or for which no exclusionary principle can be applied—should not rely on other forms of finance than taxation. The more divisible publicly provided goods and services can be priced (and produced) much like private market goods. However, even some divisible goods are consumed by all city residents (such as water), while others (such as city-owned parking lots) are provided for only a portion of residents. In the former case, the rationale for public provision that encompasses all potential consumers is that negative externalities may occur from impure (or disease-infested) water, requiring that all consumers be provided with pure water. In the latter case, few negative externalities obtain from not providing parking spaces; and as price increases, aggregate consumption (theoretically) declines, and consumer surplus decreases.

By placing a price tag (user charge) on previously "free" (tax-supported) goods, consumption will decline, and those who cannot afford to pay for the goods and services will be the ones who "freely" decide not to consume the good. This will result unless an ability to pay provision is instituted or if an inelastic demand curve ensures that a particular consumption level will be maintained. Thus, the effect of the imposition of user charges is an equity question as well as efficiency question. If a change in price can be readily absorbed, then the equity-for-individuals issue is not critical; it is when changes (increases) cannot be absorbed that equity becomes a more relevant issue. We will discuss the ramifications of this equity concern more fully later. For the present, it is important to note that focusing on city fiscal health, the use of user fees, enterprise funds, or a pay-as-you-go strategy augurs well for city financial solvency. Not only does this approach ensure the availability of maintenance funds for public infrastructure, but, in the case of separately administered funds, the potential for improving the capacity for indebtedness of certain cities is advantageous. While the municipal bond market for cities (especially for larger cities) has improved dramatically in the past two years, it still remains true that statutory authority borrowing has seen the largest growth of any form of municipal borrowing as governments have utilized various mechanisms (other than short-term debt) to avoid limitations.

Evidence of the increasing appeal of utilizing user charges and market-oriented devices abound. For example, in recent months the Koch Administration in New York City has proposed a charge for street usage in the case of street fairs and block parties in the city (*The New York Times*, 4/17/80). The "street use fee" would allow the city to share in the profits obtained by merchants'

---

*Public goods, in the public finance literature, are those that meet several criteria—the internalization of externalities, the existence of nondivisible goods, and the lack of an exclusionary principle (Musgrave, 1969).

associations in the area. These funds, in turn, would support the city's General Fund. Other mechanisms, such as contracting for services and privatization of services, can be cited (Pascal, 1980).

However, the major implication of fiscal retrenchment as well as many of the potential applications of market-oriented devices is that those individuals least able to pay for "new" services will be excluded. The case of California, where much of the current mood began, provides clear evidence of the potential inequities. The "tax revolt" that has led to current interest in user charges is disadvantageous to the (nonpropertied) urban poor who gain nothing by reductions in property tax rates, especially if rate reductions are not reflected in rental rates. Recently, however, reports suggest that cities have applied user charges to museum and recreational facility admissions, and city parks in California increased collection of service charges by as much as 11% between 1977 and 1978 (Pascal, 1980). Those who traditionally made use of these facilities are the poor who lack open space of their own. Even here, then, the distributional impact of fees is considerable.

Concern for equity and the need for fiscal relief in cities need not be mutually exclusive alternatives. Several mechanisms exist to reduce the potentially regressive effects of user fees or similar mechanisms. The creation of user-fee services or autonomous funds operating on a for-profit basis, or even the privatization of existing services, can include mechanisms for differentially distributing the impact of costs. A recent proposal for introducing auto-use fees for the New York metropolitan region as a means for keeping down transit fares is an example (*The New York Times*, 1/8/80). Graduated charges and voucher systems offer other alternatives. Another option is to seek relief for cities through a restructing of financial responsibility, the metropolitanization of services. In continuation, we will examine the metropolitanization issue.

Metropolitanization as Escape Valve

Urban scholars long have debated the relative merits of metropolitanization schemes, in terms of the fragmenting consequences, the need for area-wide coordination, the geographical distribution of burden to consumers, and the need for central city relief [see, for example, Haar et al. (1972), Helfand (1976), and U.S. President (1978)]. The argument for metropolitanization of services rests on the logic of economics of scale and the perceived negative effects of balkanization of jurisdictions. In addition, recent times have seen central cities attempt to jettison functional responsibilities. However, the approach taken by many authors does not necessarily favor the central city in distress. We argue throughout the present paper that it is not the *number* of functions that a city performs that leads to fiscal stress, but rather that it is the finance mechanism utilized that is the critical fiscal matter. We suggested that fiscal crisis impinges on the central city's maintenance budget (in the case of tax-supported functions). Furthermore, user-charge financed maintenance activities suffer less than tax-supported functions. Thus, severing user-charge supported functions from the city's budget does little to relieve city fiscal stress (although the "economy and efficiency" arguments of special district creation may still be true). Instead, if one is concerned merely with the need to relieve city financial burdens, metropolitanization should be effectuated for those functions that are tax-supported, while user-charge supported functions should be retained. Not only does this approach augur well for providing for maintenance activities, but the ability of these functions to enter the municipal bond market on a performance basis is advantageous for capital investment purposes as well. Thus, consideration of the nature of the finance mechanism is important when discussions of service consolidation are conducted.

Annexation as Escape Valve

Annexation is perhaps the most dramatic form of the metropolitanization strategy, resolving both the problem of "voting with one's feet" and the need for an expanded tax base. Cities that have pursued vigorous annexation policies have been aided, in the short run, on several fronts. Federal capital grant programs that are aimed at new construction are ideally suited for this growth-oriented strategem. In addition, in some areas land developers in unincorporated sectors construct the infrastructure and, ultimately, these costs are passed on to the homeowner. This is particularly true in Texas, where the granting of extraterritorial jurisdiction (ETJ) powers has allowed cities to control contiguous unincorporated areas (Fleischman, 1977). An interesting pattern of public/private interaction is evident in the land developer–government relationship. Thus, through both forms of annexation the city gains a revenue base, new capital construction costs are kept to a minimum, and tax rates are kept low.

In Dallas, for example, annexation has proven to be a critical fiscal tool, and helps to explain why the central city per capita income is *higher* than that of the entire SMSA in 1975. From 1958 to 1977, the city grew from 266 square miles to 376 square miles.

Ironically, the use of annexation as a fiscal tool is limited to a rather exclusive club of (primarily) fiscally solvent areas, and most notably to the South and Southwest. Key examples would include most large Texas cities, San Diego, Phoenix, and Oklahoma City (Harrigan, 1976, p. 219). This is not an option readily available to older, fiscally stressed cities that find themselves boxed in by the historical development of autonomous suburban units.

The annexation strategy so actively pursued by a number of Sunbelt cities is already showing signs of wear. While obvious short-run advantages have resulted, the longer-run fiscal implications are not as healthy in appearance. Massive fringe infrastructure development (as has been true in Dallas, for example) implies tremendous increases in maintenance costs for the future. Barring any changes in the nature of federal grant programs, these costs will need to be absorbed locally and lead to increasing reluctance on the part of some officials to encourage new capital construction. Furthermore, while the strategy has aided in keeping taxes low, public services have been spread very thin in some areas.

The recognition of these inherent difficulties for a future not far away is evident in some areas today. The newly elected mayor of Houston, James McConn, had barely been inaugurated in January 1980 when he served notice that Houston's favorite means of keeping its tax base strong would probably be set aside (*The New York Times*, 1/9/80, p. A14).

It is unlikely, therefore, that this strategy will serve as model for developmental options for the future.

Private Investment Prodding

Most analysts and urban observers would agree that the fiscal health of a city is directly related to its economic health as a center of production, exchange and distribution. As jobs are lost to the suburbs and other areas, the taxable wealth of the city declines; this is especially true if the high-paying firms emigrate. Therefore, cities historically have attempted to attract new business or to entice business to expand through various *Locate Here!* campaigns. Initially, the postwar era witnessed renewed emphasis in the central city's economic activities by rebuilding the old, decaying central business districts. Pittsburgh's renaissance of the 1940s and the 1950s—probably the most noticeable because it required so few public monies—was followed in rapid succession by Detroit, Baltimore, and many other older, northeastern and midwestern cities. The premise upon which this strategy hinged was that if cities could modernize the central business district or create industrial parks, the private sector would take advantage of the public sector's commitment and commit investments to the city—and, they hoped, the consumer would be attracted to new, modern retail establishments. Indeed, this strategy is prevalent today, (e.g., Boston, Philadelphia).

This view was elevated to official status during the Carter Administration. A careful reading of *The President's 1978 Urban Policy Report* reveals that the most important urban policy issue is that urban economic development be stimulated; for without economic development, employment growth, poverty eradication, and the fiscal solvency of cities—i.e., those long awaited solutions to urban ills—will not be attained. Cities, particularly employment-losing cities, must stimulate private sector investment, subsidize private sector employment of "long-term unemployed and disadvantaged," and otherwise do everything in their power to promote private sector employment and productivity increases which will create an expanded and healthy urban economy that in turn will allow the revenue-generating capacity of city government to improve. [For a relevant statement concerning urban policy which addresses the fiscal crisis/job loss/unemployment problem, see Chinitz (1979).]

A variety of incentives are made available by public sectors for attracting and stimulating private investment funds, ranging from the assembly of land parcels in industrial parks to granting tax exempt status and low interest rate loans. [For a summary of these programs, see National Council for Urban Economic Development (1979).] Public funds should be used, it is argued, for stimulating economic development and creating an attractive environment for investment. Indeed, these uses of public monies have been (are) employed. For example, the City of Hartford granted a seven-year tax-exempt status to a major insurance company's 20- (or more) story building as part of a lucrative *locate here* package. Baltimore, Pittsburgh, and almost every other city in the country have relied on federal, state, and local funds for the express purpose of promoting private economic development.

The Federal UDAG (Urban Development Action Grant) program whose basic objective is "to use public funds in a manner which attracts private investment to revitalize severely distressed cities" (Comptroller General of the U.S., 1980, p. 1) rests on the proposition that public sector funds should be used to leverage private investment. And the CDBG (Community Development Block Grant) program, which consolidated seven categorical programs, increasingly is being utilized to entice private investment into distressed cities and neighborhoods. [See, e.g., National Council for Urban Economic Development (1980).] These and other state and local programs are predicated on the assumption that if urban economic development can be stimulated, then the economic and social ills of cities as well as the financial status of city budgets will be ameliorated. In other words, to paraphrase Perry and Watkins (1978), improving the city's "urban health" as measured by its rate of capital accumulation is the primary means by which urban problems and fiscal stress will be overcome. However, the current urban policy of improving "urban health" may not *resolve* the problem of urban fiscal crisis:

> To the extent [the President's urban policy] provides for business—even if only to promote employment in the cities—it simultaneously aggravates the problem, precisely by subsidizing business, which will sail away on the fresh breeze, leaving more unemployment and poverty in its wake when the wind dies down. To the extent that government responds to demands from the people and provides for direct needs of housing, education, health and social welfare, it must further tax business, which will then invest still less, move abroad more, and further squeeze wages. Either way, the urban policy fails (Goldsmith and Derian, 1979, p. 19).

The underlying theory to the current urban policy approach is to stimulate capitalist economic development by socializing excessive costs. Although the "people versus place" debate suggests that public policy should concentrate on bringing jobs to the people, or on stimulating migration of people to jobs, it seems that the former position is the formal policy but the latter position is more likely to be realized [see Pierce and Hagstorm (1978)]. The reasons are as follows: The creation of incentives and stimuli for private business expansion and relocation may promote economic development through raising employment, diminishing the exodus of firms and jobs, and providing a more healthy urban economic base, all within the conventional position of creating private rewards (i.e., profits). But as Goldsmith and Derian imply, businesses are *not* oriented to resolving community or city fiscal needs; that is a by-product of resolving profitability needs. Public aid seldom, if ever, is contingent upon remaining within the city or community. Hence, most policies which rely on the "leveraging" capacity of public funds accept as an underlying theory both that capitalist economic development provides the best hope for cities and that, since the pursuit of profit is not challenged, business and profit end up being more important than communities or neighborhoods. The policy of taking jobs to people only accentuates the competition among urban governments to provide a better "incentive package" [see Goodman (1978)]. Nowhere is receipt of government aid tied to remaining in a community. Indeed, private business may "sail away on the fresh breeze."

Public Economic Development

We have attempted to review three alternative revenue-generating mechanisms that would provide fiscal relief for cities. However, it is our contention that the application of user charges to cities' social services tends to be regressive; the use of annexation generally is unavailable to the fiscally stressed, older cities of the northeast and midwest; and public leveraging of private funds is nothing less than a massive subsidy to firms which need not remain at that particular location. Further, unless a major overhaul in the federal grant structure is undertaken, the infrastructural problems presented above will not be addressed and resolved adequately. Although increased federal aid may help to some extent, we would like to propose and recommend a fourth alternative approach to urban economic development. First, let us review the empirical findings of this research effort.

We began with the proposition that (urban) economic development depends on an adequate and well-maintained infrastructure. Through an analysis of the data compiled from the nine cities, we concluded that the condition of the tax-supported infrastructure was positively associated with the degree of fiscal stress which a city experiences. Furthermore, user-charge supported EOC categories apparently receive better maintenance care than tax-supported functions. And finally, the federal response has possibly exacerbated the problems of fiscally stressed cities by ignoring their maintenance needs and by placing them in a position of being highly dependent on (uncertain) federal largesse. Fiscally stressed cities, then, require additional revenues to address their growing EOC needs and simultaneously they need to promote urban economic development in order to stimulate employment and eradicate job losses.

The proposal discussed earlier to "metropolitanize" some city functions provides the initial impetus to develop an alternative way of thinking about resolutions to the urban crisis. Metropolitanization stops short of being a fiscal safety valve because many of the functions that have been metropolitanized were user-charge supported functions (e.g., sewer and water systems). We propose that the General Fund of cities could benefit by retaining those user-charge supported activities if:

1. A mechanism could be established to refund revenues to the General Fund;
2. a fair return on investment could be realized.

Since it is the cities' General Funds (that finance infrastructural and maintenance activities) which appear to be cut back when cities begin to feel fiscal stress, the proposal to retain these user-charge financed enterprises and revamp the fund structure so that cross-subsidization might be realized would be helpful to those cities' finances. This strategy would help cities hold down (usually high) taxes and possibly augment expenditure levels to be closer to the city needs level. Indeed, we would argue that metropolitanization of user-charge supported functions which enjoy a monopolistic or near-monopolistic position would provide a fiscal safety valve if those revenues could be transferred legally to the city's General Fund.

Furthermore, the urban public sector issues millions of dollars worth of revenue bonds for industrial parks, grants tax exemptions, and provides subsidies to the private sector in order to stimulate urban economic development. Goldsmith and Derian suggest that this policy "fails" if business decides to relocate, and the city again becomes a "reservation" for the poor, unemployed, aged. It fails if the remaining residents bear the costs of promoting this form of urban economic development. It fails if communities and neighborhoods are obliterated. The point is less that this approach must fail than it is that *there are no guarantees that it will succeed*. Private businesses attempt to maximize their own profit; they are not expected to be concerned primarily with job losses or fiscal crisis. Not that they would be averse to promoting employment or supporting fiscal soundness (i.e., Carter's "urban health"), but rather that their immediate concern is to stay in business and reap the benefits or profits.

If business is not oriented primarily toward promoting "urban health", the urban public sector does concern itself with seeking sufficient revenues, minimizing job losses, and promoting employment opportunities. One of the oldest city functions ensures, or helps to ensure, that jobs and businesses will expand or locate in the city (i.e., the urban public sector's provision of infrastructure, economic overhead capital). The costs of urban infrastructure are borne by the taxpayers, the residents of the political jurisdiction. The direct benefits or externalities of urban infrastructure become absorbed or captured by businesses which use infrastructure as a relatively costless input into their production process. And, to follow the argument presented above, infrastructure costs borne by the taxpayers may not necessarily mean that the businesses which rely on the infrastructure will continue to do business at that location. Our proposition goes beyond the recommendation of merely "metropolitanizing" user-charge functions. We propose that the city should undertake what

Hirschman calls directly productive activities which rely on user-charges or other revenue/market mechanisms that do not drain the resources of the city's treasury.

The public sector's role theoretically is discussed in terms of absorbing externalities, usually *negative* externalities (e.g., unemployment, pollution, etc.). But the recommendation that *positive* externalities resulting from the provision of infrastructure be internalized by a public sector organization (the city) may begin to confront two related issues: one of maintaining an infrastructure adequately, the other of promoting economic development. Furthermore, an added merit of this strategy might be that public enterprise will be creating externalities, or outputs, if the public enterprise produces a commodity for other public or private firms to take advantage of or to use as inputs into their own production processes.

If urban policy could be oriented toward encouraging publicly owned enterprises that "return" revenues to the city's General Fund, then to a certain degree we have discovered another revenue source for the city. The problems of older, fiscally stressed cities are at least two-fold: first, the city's revenue base and revenue-gathering capacity have diminished; second, infrastructural maintenance needs have grown. By establishing a productive public sector activity (e.g., electric utility, gas utility, glass factory, specialty steel mill), that would be required to refund a certain amount of revenues annually to the city, the financial status of the General Fund will be improved and the city would be in a better fiscal position to address the maintenance needs of its traditionally tax-supported EOC functions. In addition to addressing infrastructural and revenue-generating issues of the central city, this strategy may also allow central cities to address their social needs as well by creating a larger public "pie" to distribute.

Lest this begin to sound like a defense of wholesale introduction of user charges, a clarification is in order. We would agree that implementing user charges for all functions that respond to "market signals" probably would result in alleviating many cities' fiscal stress. However, that is not the thrust of our argument; indeed, it is diametrically opposed. We have not argued that, for example, central-cities' welfare responsibilities or higher education institutions should be eliminated in order to achieve fiscal solvency (although we have suggested that some tax-supported activities, such as welfare, should be "metropolitanized"). Nor have we argued that tax-supported activities now be financed via user charges. Our argument is nothing more than the following. Central cities should be able to continue (or expand) many of their activities, e.g., welfare, which may strain their fiscal resources. Publicly owned and profitable enterprises should be created which would subsidize (to a degree) these and other city activities, such as welfare, higher education, and maintenance of the city's infrastructure. In other words, the "profit" should be used for social or community purposes. This proposed city activity will not necessarily force higher taxes in order to afford it; it should be self-financing. The city's fiscal solvency, therefore, should not be threatened.

As Nove suggests, "One of the principal arguments for public operation and control of the economy is that is permits the *internalization of externalities*. Indeed, that is what 'taking the public interest into account' means" (1973, p. 17). If Nove is correct, then the public interest should be addressed through the proposal of stimulating *public* economic development.

The urban policy recommendation of city-owned enterprises should be viewed as a tentative proposal. Our focus has been on urban infrastructure and fiscal stress. The proposal was meant to deal with improving the financing and infrastructure position of older, declining cities in particular. However well these issues have been addressed, other "issues" have been ignored. Three critical issue areas deserve to be incorporated at this point to accentuate or deemphasize the recommendations—besides the obvious one of whether it will ever be acceptable to the city power structure. First of all, we have not considered the distributional (who benefits) dimension. This policy may, indeed, be regressive in the sense that those who cannot afford to pay the price, the user charges, are excluded from consuming the city-produced goods. Currently, some city-owned utilities, such as water supply, incorporate into their rate structures an ability-to-pay provision on the assumption that water is a vital good for survival. But, if a publicly produced commodity is not critical to an individual's life, the public sector may exclude a segment of the city population through its price mechanism. If public provision of a good traditionally was based on the notion of expanding "consumer surplus," the proposed urban policy may militate against the notion that no one can be excluded from consuming public goods. Depending on the commodity, this area of investigation should be pursued.

Another problem derives from an analysis by Roland Liebert. Liebert (1976), in his attempt to explain the effects of the structure of urban government, concluded that "broad-scope governments," city governments with many functional responsibilities, were more highly correlated with political participation than "narrow-scoped governments." In response to active political participation these "broad-scope governments" expanded their activities at a more rapid rate than "narrow-scope governments." Therefore, the following question becomes important: Will additional city responsibilities that are financially self-sufficient create greater or lesser political activism? If we assume that high levels of political participation should be encouraged in a democratic society, what impacts would a city-owned enterprise have on democracy? Numerous scenarios may be presented. The residents of the city may demand a voice in the affairs of the enterprise. A regulatory commission may be established to watch over its operations and keep the citizens' "best interests" uppermost in mind. Or, it may operate according to sound business principles by removing itself from public pressures. [For an interesting discussion of these questions in the Italian case, see Holland (1972).]

The last caveat centers on a major limitation of this study. Our whole emphasis has been on Economic Overhead Capital functions of cities; ignored were the Social Overhead Capital functions as defined by Holland (1976). In order to provide a more complete picture of city performance, an examination of SOC expenditures and needs should be undertaken. The conclusions regarding federal grants-in-aid, fiscal stress, and urban infrastructure refer only to EOC and not to the city's total activities. We purposefully excluded SOC activities because, as Holland suggests, EOC is a necessary condition for economic development, not SOC.

Because of the limited focus of the present study, the finding and policy recommendations must be tempered in light of the absence of SOC analysis. Cities expend according to a major constraint: revenues. If this constraint were absent, cities—especially fiscally-stressed cities—would not be forced to decide where to expend resources among competing alternatives. But, given that degrees of fiscal stress exist for many cities, urban government must choose and decide. The decisions are not only between maintaining or constructing a facility and doing nothing; they more importantly force cities to decide between spending for infrastructural needs and spending for social needs. Hartford's City Manager suggested that the Department of Human Resources received increasing amounts of funds from a shrinking pie, and Public Works received less. Pittsburgh, since 1977, began a vigorous campaign of increasing expenditures on the infrastructure after years of neglect. Although it is too early to tell whether SOC activities were short-changed since 1977, Pittsburgh adopted the posture that improved infrastructure together with active promotion of attracting businesses will create the environment for urban economic development.

Expenditure trends and analysis of the behavior of city officials should provide the data base from which an examination can be undertaken of what we perceive as the shifting emphasis between SOC and EOC functions. The unenviable position in which usually older, declining, fiscally stressed cities find themselves must be scrutinized and compared with the newer cities, that is to say, the position of having a shrinking revenue base against which both the *social* (SOC) needs of the residents and the *infrastructural* (EOC) needs of industry and commerce must compete. It is to an examination of these two conflicting sets of needs within the framework of scarce resources that future urban policies and research should be directed.

Bibliography

Abramson, Martin (1979). "Our Bridges Are Falling," *Parade* (January 7), pp. 4–7.

Chinitz, Benjamin, ed. (1979). *Central City Economic Development.* Cambridge: Abt Associates, Inc.

CONSAD Research Corporation (1980). *A Study of Public Works Investment in the United States* (4 volumes). Prepared for U.S. Department of Commerce, Pittsburgh, PA: CONSAD Research Corp.

Fainstein, Susan S., and Fainstein Norman I. (1976). "The Federally Inspired Fiscal Crisis," *Society*, Vol. 13, No. 4 (May/June), pp. 27–32.

Fleischman, Arnold (1977). "Sunbelt Boosterism: The Politics of Post-War Growth and Annexation in San Antonio," in *The Rise of Sunbelt Cities*, David C. Perry and Alfred Watkins, eds. Beverly Hills: Sage Publications.

Goldsmith, William W., and Derian Michael J. (1979). "Is There an Urban Policy?" *Journal of Regional Science*, Vol. 19, No. 1 (February), pp. 93–108.

Goodman, Robert (1979). *The Last Entrepreneurs: America's Regional Wars for Jobs and Dollars*. New York: Simon and Shuster.

Grossman, David (1977). *Capital Construction Needs of New York City in the 1977–1986 Period: A Preliminary Report*. New York: Twentieth Century Fund.

Haar, Charles, et al. (1972). *Metropolitanization and Public Services*. Baltimore: Johns Hopkins University Press, published for Resources for the Future.

Harrigan, John J. (1976). *Political Change in the Metropolis*. Boston: Little Brown and Company.

Helfand, Gary, ed. (1976). *Metropolitan Areas, Metropolitan Governments: A Reader*. Dubuque, Iowa: Kendal/Hunt.

Hirschman, Albert O. (1958). *The Strategy of Economic Development*. New Haven: Yale University Press.

Holland, Stuart, ed. (1972). *The State as Entrepreneur*. London: Weidenfeld and Nicolson.

Holland, Stuart (1976). *Capital Versus the Regions*. New York: St. Martin's Press.

Liebert, Roland J. (1976). *Disintegration and Political Action: The Changing Functions of City Governments in America*. New York: Academic Press.

Moore, Richard J., and Pagano Michael A. (1979). "Urban Functions, Federal Bias, and Fiscal Strain: Financing Urban Public Works." Paper presented at the Southern Political Science Association Meetings, Gatlinburg, TN.

Moynihan, Daniel P. (1979). "New York State and the Federal Fisc, III: Fiscal Year 1978." Statement by Senator Daniel P. Moynihan (June 10).

Musgrave, Richard A. (1969). *Fiscal Systems*. New Haven: Yale University Press.

Myrdal, Ginnar (1957). *Economic Theory and the Underdeveloped Regions*. London: G. Duckworth and Company, Ltd.

National Council for Urban Economic Development (1979). *Federal Programs for Urban Economic Development: A Summary of Available Assistance*. Washington, DC: National Council for Urban Economic Development.

Nove, Alec (1973). *Efficiency Criteria for Nationalized Industries*. London: George Allen and Unwin, Ltd.

Pagano, Michael A. (1980). "Fiscal Stress and the Financing of Urban Infrastructure." Ph.D. dissertation presented to the University of Texas at Austin.

Pascal, Anthony H. (1980). "User Charges, Contracting Out, and Privatization in an Era of Fiscal Retrenchment." The Rand Corporation, P-6471 (April).

Peterson, George (1976). "Finance" in *The Urban Predicament*, William Gorham and Nathan Glazer, eds. Washington, DC: The Urban Institute, pp. 35–118.

Peterson, George (1978). "Capital Spending and Capital Obsolescence: The Outlook for Cities." in *The Fiscal Outlook for Cities*, Roy Bahl, ed. Syracuse: Syracuse University Press.

Peirce, Neil R. (1980). "City Revival Rests Squarely on Public–Private Links," *Nation's Cities Weekly*, Vol. 3, No. 2.

Peirce, Neil R., and Jerry Hagstrom (1978). "The Growing Movement to Take the Jobs to the People." *National Journal*, Vol. 10, No. 13.

Richardson, Harry (1969). *Regional Economics*. New York: Praeger Publications.

Schultze, Charles L., et al. (1976). "Fiscal Problems of Cities," *The Fiscal Crisis of American Cities*, in Roger Alcaly and David Mermelstein, eds. New York: Vantage.

Sternlieb, George (1979). *Is the Urban Crisis Over?* Testimony before the Subcommittee on Fiscal and Intergovernmental Policy of the Joint Economic Committee. Washington, DC: U.S. Government Printing Office.

Tiebout, Charles M. (1956). "A Pure Theory of Public Expenditures." *Journal of Political Economy*, Vol. LXIV, No. 5 (October), pp. 416–424.

U.S. Bureau of the Census (various years.). *City Government Finances*. Washington, DC: U.S. Government Printing Office.

U.S. Bureau of the Census (various years). *Government Finances*. Washington, DC: U.S. Government Printing Office.

U.S. Comptroller General (1979). *Funding State and Local Government Pension Plans: A National Problem*. Report to the Congress. Washington, DC: U.S. Government Printing Office.

U.S. Congress, Joint Economic Committee (1979). *Deteriorating Infrastructure in Urban and Rural Areas*. Washington, DC: U.S. Government Printing Office.

U.S. President (1978). *The President's National Urban Policy Report*. A Biennial Report to the Congress prepared by the U.S. Department of Housing and Urban Development. Washington, DC: U.S. Government Printing Office.

XVIII

Regional Economic Development and Public Development Banking

Bruce W. Marcus

In 1938, William O. Douglas spoke before the Economic Club of Chicago on the problem of, and the need for, new structures for regional finance. Today, some 40 years later, we find ourselves addressing the same topic, and with even more intensive concern.

In over 40 years, has nothing changed? Have the needs discerned in 1938 been ignored all this time, or has the problem simply defied skill and imagination?

Obviously, at least in economic context, a great deal has changed. And yet the problem remains with us, as untouched by the passage of time as are the great pyramids of Egypt, except that its magnitude has increased.

The changes in the socioeconomic structure since World War II alone—the growth of industry and technology, urban shifts, the complete transition from an agricultural to an industrial society, inflation—have brought a complexity to the system that defies simple solutions. The shifts in the capital markets, inherent in the structure of the system, add to the complexity of the problem. As the economy has grown, so have the needs for vast pools of capital multiplied. But as the needs for new capital have multiplied so too have the sources. New giant pools of capital exist in insurance companies, in pension funds, and in other institutions. Even the American middle class has grown to become a source of capital, as unstable and as uncertain as it may be. At the same time the growth of both the needs for capital and the pools of capital have created their own instability, as witness the changes on Wall Street alone. For example, between the end of 1968 and the beginning of 1975 the number of major brokerage houses declined from 646 to 505, an average loss of more than 20 firms a year, this trend shows no sign of slowing down appreciably.

Nor has all the technology of recent decades contributed to the solution of regional and municipal problems. Quite the contrary. It has exacerbated the problem. Dislocations of population to the cities have placed the greatest burden for costly municipal services on those communities least able to afford them. The advantages of the city as communications, transportation, intellectual, and industrial centers have turned into disadvantages, as shifts in the economic winds create pockets of distress and pockets of prosperity in the same nation. At a time when the national unemployment rate hovers at 9%, the black unemployment rate hovers at 16%. The need of economic aid pits the urban center against the rural center, with both chasing the same dollar. And fanning the flame is the brisk constant wind of inflation.

We are a nation in which distress and prosperity are polarized within our national boundaries, and the regional problem as just a regional problem becomes blurred. In today's economy, what company can be said to be truly regional? In Belleville, New Jersey, there is a small printer who has a volume of about a million dollars a year, much of it from customers within a 50-mile radius of his plant. But he is also the regional printer for the promotional material for Chicago-based Encyclopedia Britanica. He prints material for national distribution for New York-based American Management Association. His company is publicly owned—a product of those horrible "go-go" years when so many companies went public irrationally, and while most of his shares are locally owned, some are owned by investors on the West coast. His bank is a local New Jersey bank, but his capital, to a degree, comes in part nationally. He is a local printer, but his customers and a portion of his source of capital are national. Should he need an additional $200,000 for a new press, he is too large for his local bank and too small for national help.

Moreover, his plant is located in one of those small decaying towns in which every other storefront on the main street is empty. Is he part of the town, or independent of it?

While no one company can be said to be typical of all local or regional companies, there are elements of his operation that indicate the complexity of viewing the regional company and its problems. The most significant, of course, and the one that concerns us here, is availability of capital. The local or regional company has more trouble getting capital for growth, expansion, or just normal operational needs than does the national company. And if the community in which the company resides is itself in trouble, then local banks and other sources of capital are incapable of meeting its needs. How separate then, is the industrial capital problem from the municipal capital problem? Can economic development problems be solved without solving municipal problems at the same time?

This paradox is at the heart of the persistent discussion about regional problems. The attempts to solve these problems have historically focused on these short-term answers—on existing institutions and programs: the banks, the government, the public sources of equity capital, venture capital from private sources, and federal programs that attempt to solve problems by putting money (usually not enough) into those areas that most loudly cry the greatest need at any given moment.

Perhaps the reason we find ourselves addressing the same concerns today as we did 40 years ago is because we are focusing on the needs themselves, and not on the nature of change. Needs change—institutions and programs don't. Perhaps, then, it is not just the needs that must be dealt with in seeking solutions, but the fact of constant flux in industry, finance, and the capital markets, and in society itself. Perhaps it's a matter of revising the structures to serve not the immediate needs, but the changes and the flux as well. It is only when we learn to do this that we shall have successfully attacked the problem.

Looking at the problem in this way, we see several things:

1. Basically, at the core, the problem is not money itself. What we call a capital shortage is not a shortage of money, so much as a feature of the capital markets, i.e. their inability to consistently put money where it's most needed. The economic history of the U.S. clearly indicates that, overall, the successful and growing economy breeds sufficient capital to fuel that growth—else there would have been no growth. On the other hand, the nature of the capital markets and of our economic system allows the capital to gravitate toward the larger and more successful companies, and away from the smaller, newer company. Money goes to the company that appears to have the greater capability to supply a return on the investment. It is usually the larger, more visible company. This fact alone offers the greatest potential danger to the American economy.

2. There is little flexibility in the financial institutions themselves and the structures for channelling capital. When smaller businesses most need capital, smaller banks are less able to lend it and the equities market is less able to support it. Banks are limited by such factors as legal loan–deposit ratios. With a responsibility to their depositors and shareholders, they must be extremely conservative.

   Venture capital structures are limited by external factors over which they have no control, such as the liquidity of the stock market. Currently, for example, vast investments of venture capital are frozen by the condition of the stock market, particularly as it pertains to the smaller company. Where there is little liquidity, the investor cannot realize his profits. Under the circumstances, there is not likely to be a tremendous rush for further investment.

3. Historically, there is no prolonged period of stability in the capital markets. Interest rates fluctuate. The equities market fluctuates. Capital shifts to larger, better established companies. Local and regional sources of capital become overextended.

   Perhaps one of the most significant examples of a shifting capital pool is seen in the effect of ERISA (Employee Retirement Insurance Securities Act) on pension fund investment. The anxiety caused by the widespread misunderstanding of ERISA caused a demonstrable shift of pension fund investment of the Fortune 500 stocks and to fixed income securities, thereby depriving small businesses of access to some $400 billion in equity capital.

In the equities market, the pools of capital from both institutions and the individual investor rise and fall with the market itself. In a down market the institutions move to strong cash positions or fixed income securities and the individual investor stays away. Then capital is there, but not available to smaller businesses. Is there, then, a shortage of capital, or is it the structures for channelling capital to the smaller companies that are the problem?

4. There is greater inherent risk in a small business. The larger national company has assets, track record, market momentum, visibility to the capital markets, and most importantly, the sophistication and expertise to use that capital effectively. Compare the risk in investing in this kind of company with that of investing in a smaller company, which has less flexibility in its assets, less control over its markets, is either too young to have a track record or, if it is established and still small, has a track record that highlights its limitations rather than its virtues. Its visibility to the capital markets is a function only of the manager's direct contact. And what is most significant, the small business can rarely demonstrate sophistication and skill in maximizing the use of capital. Obviously, the risk of investing in the small business is greater than in the larger business.

And if there is one thing that characterizes the local and regional business, it is size. Virtually by definition, a regional business is a smaller business, and becomes larger only when it can expand its market outside its own region. The problem of regional financing, then, evolves to the problem of financing the smaller, newer, thinly capitalized company.

Because of the risk inherent in investing in, or lending to, this kind of company, the sources of capital are fewer, and the size of the capital pool is smaller than for the blue chip company. The small company is lower on the totem pole, and the more scarce is capital, the less likely is capital to filter down to be available to the smaller, regional company.

5. While it is usually accepted, to some degree, that there is a direct relationship between municipal financing problems and the problems of financing the regional company, it becomes important to look beyond that to determine where the common thread lies.

Obviously, the region that is having trouble with industrial economic development will frequently be the region with municipal financial problems. Where there are no jobs there is no tax base, and yet the need for services increases. But the mechanism for channelling capital to both industry and the municipal structure are essentially the same. Just as a healthy company has less trouble getting capital for growth, so does the healthy municipality have less trouble getting money for its services and programs.

The question is the degree to which the same economic problems apply to both, and to which solutions they both respond. Municipalities, after all, are not financed by either the stock market or venture capital. Nor, essentially, is business directly financed by such federal programs as revenue sharing. However, both are served or hindered by the same general problems of prevailing economic conditions, the nature of the capital markets, and the limited structure of the institutions available to serve them.

6. Federal funds allocated to programs to help regional companies and municipalities are short-term amelioratives that work for a short time, that work for too small a portion of the economy, or that do not work at all. These programs address themselves to short-term needs rather than long-term solutions or vehicles for solutions. And most significantly, they address themselves only to needs, and not to the structure for change or changing needs.

Government programs can rarely serve better than existing institutions. Moreover, most government-sponsored programs suffer from a kind of public shackle. In order to avoid scandal or other basis for public attack, the rules under which they function must be clearly prescribed and rigid. Very little option is allowed for flexible decisions, and for this reason as well as many others, administration of these programs rarely attracts imaginative and flexible people. For most small companies, the red tape involved is strangling and, except in sheer desperation, most companies potentially eligible for public programs are reluctant to avail themselves of them. The very structure is self-defeating of the purpose.

7. Perhaps the one element most overlooked in any analysis of the capital problems of industry or municipalities is expertise. And yet this is the most important factor in the total problem.

The lack of expertise is inherent in both the sources of capital and in the company or municipal entity itself. It is usually seen in lack of knowledge of the sources of available capital, and in the financial skill necessary to adequately determine the entity's actual need for capital and the best ways to integrate it into the business for greater return, or into the municipal structure for greater effectiveness.

In competing for capital the company that has consistently demonstrated its ability to use that capital wisely is the company that wins. It is the company that invariably presents the best record to the financial community. As we have seen most recently in the case of New York City, the municipality that most flagrantly presents the face of mismanagement is the municipality that has the greatest trouble in using outside sources to solve its economic problems.

The market attends to the need for expertise by inverse proportion. The less expertise and capability in a company or municipality, the greater the need for capital. A badly managed company or municipality will not use its capital well, and will have, then, persistent capital problems.

At the same time, the smaller, newer company—the company that most needs help to overcome its fragility—is the one least likely to have the ability to compete successfully in all areas (markets, finance, etc.). And yet, this is the company the economy needs for vitality, for new industry, to bring new capability into the system, and for local and regional jobs.

It can be argued that, under a free enterprise system, only the most capable should be allowed to survive and thrive in the marketplace. But this is an argument of the 19th century, when the economy was simpler. The economy serving our population now demands a constant infusion of new enterprise. If entrepreneurs did not arise of themselves, our society would have to invent them.

One of the most serious defects of financial institutions has been the inability to bring that expertise to the companies they serve. Merely bringing money to a company will no longer suffice, particularly in a fluctuating and a capital-scarce economy. If the financial institution cannot supply expertise in determining the precise need for capital, and the techniques for maximizing return on it, it is merely dispensing money. And yet, is not that how most financial institutions function? They look at the current financial statements, and lend on what appears to be the ability to pay.

Nor do most businessmen have access, either in expertise or through information, to the varying and changing sources of capital. They must rely on their banker or investment banker, neither of whom may be willing or able to be flexible beyond his own capabilities. The banker may see only his own bank as a source. The investment banker may also be limited by his own regional experience.

The need for change in the institutions, even within current legal framework, is clear. Institutions must be more flexible, and do their jobs differently, better and more consistently with contemporary needs. They must supply greater expertise to the company. They must be more national in their view of the capital markets, more regional in their relationship with local business. They must funnel the national economic intelligence to the smaller company with the lesser informed management.

That this has been demanded of institutions for generations, and that this demand has been unmet, is both a symptom and a clue to the solution of the problem.

A bank must protect its depositors and stockholders, which may very well mean being fiscally conservative.

A venture capitalist cannot change the nature of the market, that makes it difficult for him to recoup the profits on his investments by increasing liquidity.

The regional investment banker cannot control the equities market nor can he gain ready access, for his smaller clients, to the large pools of private placement capital available to larger, better established companies.

If current institutions, because of structure or law, cannot change, then the answer must lie in new institutions. Not new programs that serve short-term needs without solving long-term problems. Not in changing the basic structure of existing institutions, clearly a legal, economic and competitive impossibility. Rather, a new kind of institution that's predicated on the fact that economic conditions change, that capital markets change, that urban and rural society changes. It must be flexible to the degree that it can cope with that change, and with long-range objectives as well as immediate needs. Its focus should be on expertise, and the ability to supply both information and technical financial skill to meeting the capital and management needs of small or emerging companies, as well as municipalities. It must be designed to meet the ever-changing problems caused by the volatile socioeconomic conditions of both the capital markets and the regions. Only in this way will it serve the long-term needs for regional economic development.

And ultimately, its major aim should be to serve as an element of stability in an otherwise unstable economy.

Moreover, the new institution should be self-sustaining without extensive support from either the Federal government or the private sector.

It must have at least the following capabilities:

1. It should be able to identify sources of capital and channel them, at reasonable rates, to industries and municipalities that can use the capital effectively.
2. It should be managed by people who have the training, skill, sophistication and capability to guide the companies and governments they serve in the best forms of capitalization, in getting the capital from many sources, and then in applying and managing new capital most effectively.
3. It should be an instrument of regional economic development, with the primary emphasis on creating jobs and producing goods and services that will enhance the economic well-being of the community. Its role in dealing with the municipality should be to enhance services effectively and efficiently.
4. It must be noncompetitive with commercial and private sources of capital, and should serve as a primary source only when the private sector cannot accommodate. It should, in fact, function in conjunction with private sources of capital as a supplement—and not as an alternative.

It must be, in other words, a development bank.

Although as a financial institution the development bank concept is relatively new it has been much discussed. A national urban development bank was proposed by the Carter Administration as part of its urban policy, and development banking exists in one form or another in some states and Canadian provinces. There is now enough experience with it to project its possibilities, its structure, its strengths and weaknesses, and its place in the American economy.

Its greatest value, and the objective of the development bank, is to channel funds, either supplied by the government or lent to the bank by the government as seed money, to industry and the municipalities. This is the concept upon which the old RFC functioned. It worked well during the depression when the shortage of capital was so acute that few small businesses had any viable alternative. This is not the case today. The problem we face is that capital does not sift down to smaller and more fragile businesses, and smaller municipalities are having trouble selling their bonds.

Under the proper circumstances the capital is available for the smaller business and the municipality. But there is a shortage of the expertise necessary to determine the circumstances under which that capital is allocated, and to assist with the best uses of that capital. And commercial institutions are concerned with either their own profitability (rightly so) or, in the case of the government agencies, with applying abstract and general criteria to specific situations.

Even in its short history, the development bank has shown that it can transcend these problems. It need not be profitable, in the sense of return on investment. It must be successful, in terms of meeting the needs of its constituency. It must take in more than it gives out, not in the sense of profits, but in that it generates its own capital for reinvestment in regional development.

In financing industry, the development bank does not serve as an alternative source of capital to the private sector, because if there were an alternative to the development bank in the private sector there would be no need for the development bank. Existing sources would be sufficient. It must, then, fill a niche not readily filled by the private sector.

This is also true in the case of municipalities. If the municipal bond market were holding firm consistently, there would be no need for the development bank as a source of capital.

The range and the number of plans now being discussed is extensive, and each has its merits and deficiencies. Rather than rehash existing and current arguments, I would like to look at several aspects of the concept from a different point of view.

Properly structured, a development bank must look to first principles. What is it trying to accomplish?

The most obvious answer is to foster economic development that will bring the business of the region it serves to a self-sustaining level and, concurrently, strengthen the municipalities within that region.

It is assumed in the first instance that a major criterion is jobs. Will aiding a business generate jobs within the community? Will it generate sufficient jobs to improve the tax base of a community, and thereby make the community more financially stable and more readily able to finance its services?

The relationship between the private and the public sectors in economic development is a very strong one on a highly pragmatic level. If any economic development program or structure is to strengthen a region economically, it becomes impractical to support the private without at the same time supporting the public sector.

But the needs of the public and private sectors would seem to be different, beyond the fact that they might both need money, one for capital and the other for the expenses of serving the community.

In fact they are not. What is missing in both cases is financial expertise. What is also missing is an awareness of the relationship between the two.

In the private sector, a company needs expertise in three areas—determining its real capital needs, raising the capital, and using that capital effectively. A municipality faces the same problem in expertise—accurately determining its capital needs, raising the capital and applying the capital effectively.

This was seen most clearly in New York City, where municipal ineptitude allowed the debt to rise to such proportions that a Federal bailout was required. During the course of determining the viability of Federal support it became abundantly clear that the major problem was indeed ineptitude in using the funds effectively.

Thus, the most important problem in devising the development bank is not a function of deciding whether the bank shall supply debt or equity, or whether it shall supply capital or just guarantees. In view of the larger problems in serving total needs, this kind of focus is too shallow.

The real problem is to structure the bank so that it has two basic elements:

First, it must be flexible, in that it is designed to meet not needs, but change. Short-term needs are classically attacked by programs which after a while cease to function effectively, because the conditions that warranted the program change. This leaves a program and a structure in place without a need for it. A development bank must attack the structure of change itself; must be flexible enough to be a stable force under unstable economic conditions.

Secondly, it must be structured to supply financial expertise.

A concrete example of how this can work effectively may be seen in one of the most successful examples in the country today of the development bank concept—the Government Development Bank for Puerto Rico.

Even allowing for the fact that the Government Development Bank for Puerto Rico functions in a context of a commonwealth rather than a state, its structure has proven successful.

It serves as the fiscal agent for the Government of Puerto Rico and its municipalities, and all municipal financial needs are channelled through the bank. It is the bank, and not the individual municipal authority, that arranges for the sale of bond issues. Its other major purpose, in conjunction with other specialized agencies, is economic development. It is a public corporation.

In serving municipal and Commonwealth needs, this has a number of distinct advantages.

1. It allows the sophisticated expertise of professional financial people to review and determine the financial needs of a particular municipal or

regional authority (e.g., Water Authority, Housing Authority, etc.) on professional, nonpolitical grounds.

2. It brings professional and sophisticated standards to the structuring of each bond issue.

3. The bank, by virtue of its position in representing all municipalities and authorities, is constantly in touch with the bond market—an absolute necessity in timing, negotiating interest rates, etc.

4. By virtue of its success and professionalism over a period of years the bank has taken on a credibility in its own right in the bond market, which enhances the sale of any individual bond issue.

5. And perhaps, most significantly the bank monitors fiscal performance of each of its Authorities. It knows that the money is being used properly. A computer early warning system keeps the bank informed of any problems that may arise in any of the Authorities, allowing broad-based financial skill to be brought into play before any problem becomes too acute.

6. It advances money to the Authorities in anticipation of bond sales to allow smooth and consistent Authority operation. This is particularly useful in preventing rushes to market under favorable conditions.

In other words, the bank functions as a kind of supermunicipal agency to maintain a high level of performance in all municipal agencies, which further enhances the ability of even the most troubled agency to be served by the capital market.

Another form of this kind of superagency structure is the Vermont Bond Bank.

Recognizing that small municipalities and districts were having trouble selling bonds at favorable rates, the state of Vermont, in conjunction with the investment banking firm of Goldman, Sachs, formed the Vermont Bond Bank. The participating municipalities sell their bonds to the Bond Bank. The Bond Bank then sells a master bond issue to cover the total debt, plus sufficient more for a contingency reserve. This process enables the district or municipality to sell its own bonds to the Bond Bank at rates and under conditions considerably more favorable than they might otherwise receive. In the several years of is existence it has proven to be quite effective.

The Puerto Rican Bank has been overwhelmingly successful in keeping municipal financing on an even keel, despite some serious national economic problems particularly felt by Puerto Rico from time to time. By monitoring the activities of the various authorities and municipalities the Bank assures itself that, within the framework of each Authority's responsibilities, it is fiscally sound. It supplies thoroughly professional expertise in an area that is not traditionally overwhelmed by financial sophistication. It deals professionally with the money markets, and therefore advantageously.

And at the same time, through a program of development lending to the private sector, it works with local business to enhance job-producing economic development.

The Puerto Rican Bank recognizes that highly volatile economic conditions require a flexibility that addresses itself specifically to that volatility. Basically, there are no limits or restriction on whether the aid shall be debt or equity, capitalization or guarantees. It does all of them as circumstances warrant. Moreover it avoids being competitive with local commercial banks by being a bank of last resort. It will lend only when all other possibilities have been exhausted and all other opportunities for the business foreclosed. It works closely with private sector banks on guarantees and joint financing.

Which is not to say that it lends arbitrarily. It's criteria are based on a business' potential for success. It recognizes that funds are frequently unavailable to perfectly sound companies because the commercial banks may require a somewhat lower degree of risk, or more collateral, than the business may be able to supply, or that local banks may be overlent in relation to assets. That still leaves a good deal of business that represents a sound investment. As a government development bank, with no shareholders other than the public, and no private depositors, the bank can accept a longer time span for return. And historically, its bad loan ratio has been at least as good as most commercial banks and probably better than some. It will help both local business, or mainland business locating in Puerto Rico.

While its board of directors is directly responsible to the Governor of Puerto Rico, it is highly visible to the public and financial community, and the question of accountability has never been a problem. What is most significant is that the bank is itself financially successful. If we avoid the term "profitable" the bank has consistently shown that it takes in more money each year than it pays out, it has a year-end-surplus, while at the same time it is highly successful in fulfilling its prescribed functions.

Granted that the context in which it functions, the Commonwealth of Puerto Rico, is unique. But even so, the success of the bank and its approach to its problems offer clear evidence that the concept can work successfully, and can be applied to a broad variety of regional situations.

In fact, a view of all existing development bank structures clearly indicates that the bank must indeed be regional, and not national. There are a number of reasons for this.

Primary, of course, is that the economic development needs of the nation are regional, not national. And even within a region, urban needs differ distinctly from rural needs. The economic development problems of a state like New Hampshire are not particularly urban problems—they are state-wide. New York City has different needs than does the rest of the state. The emerging economy of the South offers significantly different problems than the recovery problems of the Northeast.

And yet, to depend upon each state to develop its own bank is unrealistic. The concept is somewhat more sophisticated than can be grasped readily by a good many state governments, particularly those that are highly politicized. The great fear seems to be that the banks themselves will be politicized, thereby attacking their credibility and, ultimately, their value.

Perhaps the answer lies in a Federal agency that oversees and takes responsibility for the sound operation of state or regional development banks, but still leaves the operation of the bank to the state or region. Both the successes and excesses of the Port Authority of New York are cited as examples of pro and con for the development bank concept. Even given the veto power of the Governors of both New York and New Jersey, the Authority has become so totally independent that only under the rarest circumstances can public pressure be brought to bear to correct excesses. If, on the other hand, the Authority were to continue at its present functions, but were federally monitored, the likelihood is that it would function successfully in its mission, with most of the excesses eliminated. The form of federal monitoring might include a basic oversight that it fulfill its original mandate. The term is *monitoring*—not regulating.

A federal enabling statute, prescribing a model for the bank, would give impetus to each state's developing its own bank. There could still be flexibility enough to serve regional needs. The federal role would be to guide, advise, and monitor, with the monitoring provision being sufficient to circumvent regional political objection. It may even be feasible for the federal government to advance seed money for the start of the bank, or to purchase seed money bonds at favorable rates. Even here there are several options. It can be a grant, or a loan, or purchase of the bank's own debt instrument.

Another compelling reason for keeping the geographic jurisdiction smaller rather than larger is the ability to attract professional management on a competitive level—and professional management is absolutely crucial to the success of the concept.

Even in a national development bank the heaviest reliance would be on the local or regional manager. With a federal pay scale it's not likely that the managers for the larger urban centers could be paid enough to attract top-notch personnel from commercial banking, which is absolutely necessary. The manager of a New York State development bank would obviously have to be more highly paid than the manager of the Mississippi State bank. He would have to have a different kind of experience and a different kind of capability. To limit the management of local or regional banks to a uniform federal standard of qualification and compensation would clearly be disastrous, and deprive the total concept of the talent necessary to make it function.

The crucial question that must be resolved in any regional economic development program is the question of criteria for the private sector.

Beyond the judgment of whether a business applying for aid would supply jobs or otherwise enhance the community, there is the more serious question of the degree to which financing standards for the development bank should differ from those of the commercial bank. Obviously, the standards should be different, else why a development bank?

The difference lies in objectives and must be clearly delineated if the criteria for the development bank are to be meaningful.

The commercial source of capital has, as its primary objective, the appreciation of that capital, whether it's debt or equity. This is its perfectly legitimate function, and the economic system cannot be perverted to make it do what it was not devised to do. The commercial institution may see an ultimate advantage to its own profitability to sustain the economic strength of the region in which it functions and it would be shortsighted for such an institution not to recognize it. Nevertheless, there is a limit to which it can profitably support its future economic context without some short-term profitability to sustain it and to satisfy its own depositors and investors.

The economic development bank, on the other hand, has regional economic development as both its long-term and short-term goals. If the structure is self-sustaining then all the better. But the ultimate beneficiary must be the community it serves.

This is an important consideration in judging criteria for supporting a business. But at the same time, whether the development institution needs to be self-sustaining or not, it does not serve the economic well-being of any region to support a business that will not ultimately be able to sustain itself. Investing in a business that has not the slightest apparent chance of surviving on its own, sooner or later, solves no problem for the community and in fact, engenders false hope and ultimate disappointment and bitterness. No one—not the community nor the government nor the institution nor the business itself is helped by criteria that are so low that money is invested or lent to a business doomed to failure.

Nevertheless, there is a broad area between the business that is a poor risk for any institution, private or public, and the business that is sufficiently credit-worthy to warrant support from the private sector. There is, for example the business that supplies long-term training that's necessary before it can become profitable. Or the start-up business that has a somewhat longer than average period before it can become self-sustaining. Or the business that lacks only trained management, but is otherwise potentially sound. These are quite properly beyond the purview of the commercial institution, and quite properly within the purview of the development bank.

The line can sometimes be a delicate one, and even with the most rigidly defined formula the judgment, in the final analysis, becomes subjective. This is another reason why the bank requires people of greater skill and capability and experience than are likely to be found in a federally dominated institution, and another reason why a federally oriented institution is more likely to fall short.

The decisions necessary to genuinely serve small business go much beyond formulas, and this is perhaps why so few businessmen who are eligible to participate in some of the government programs consider them a viable source of capital. The criteria are too abstract, relative to the specific needs and potential of a company. The rules are too rigid, and thus decisions become immersed in the kind of red tape that the small businessman can least afford. To allow this to happen in a development bank would be disastrous.

To predetermine categorically that a bank shall operate with either debt or equity, or shall either capitalize or guarantee loans, or that it should or should not supply working capital as opposed to capital expenditures, is unrealistic, and defeats the purpose of development programs.

A major objective of the development bank is to foster business that contributes to the economic well-being of the community. The nature of business is that sometimes debt is needed and sometimes equity. Sometimes the capital to buy a new machine is crucial, and sometimes all that is needed is to guarantee a loan that may be marginal for a commercial bank but is otherwise sound. Sometimes a cash flow problem that is solved with an infusion of working capital can make the difference between success and failure of a business. If the bank is not structured to be flexible enough to meet any or all of these needs, it cannot function. The same holds true of venture capital, which in a development bank context has a slightly different meaning than it does in the private sector.

Venture capital, in the private sector, is capital infused into a business, usually a new or emerging business, to allow it to take advantage of market opportunities. The venture capitalist expects a large return on his money in the shortest possible time.

The development bank, infusing capital in the same business under the same circumstances, does not face the same needs for either the return on investment or short-term payout as does the private venture capitalist. It should be completely within the purview of the development bank to enter into situations that might normally be called venture capital investments, if all of the development bank's other criteria apply.

Nor is this kind of investment competitive to the private sector, since the government development bank is a lender of last resort and not an alternative. This venture capital role becomes extremely important to stabilize the ebb and flow of the capital markets. Private venture capital becomes plentiful when there are periods of good liquidity and scarce when liquidity is scarce. This puts the burden of economic development into a stream of uncertainty, subject to changing tides of economic conditions. It also defeats the purpose of economic development, which is most needed in periods of capital scarcity.

Looking at the development bank concept in a political context, the question of accountability becomes a serious one, and is perhaps one of the greatest obstacles in many states to development banks. But this need not be a problem since the development bank is itself apolitical in nature.

By federalizing its supervision, and by a federal enabling act that defines a basic structure and purpose, the political onus is removed from state legislatures for establishing and monitoring a development bank. The state legislature need only establish and empower the bank, structured within a predetermined framework, and modified in terms of regional needs. In conjunction with federal monitoring, the state's monitoring concern would be its normal banking oversight.

Secondly, the management of a development bank relies on the professionalism of its management, obtained in a competitive labor market. Presumably the best commercial bankers in the state, offered competitive salaries and opportunity, can be wooed into the bank's management structure.

Thirdly, the mechanics for public disclosure are very well known, and high visibility is the greatest deterrent to chicanery. Annual reports, quarterly reports, press releases, periodic Federal and state audits—all of these are tools of high visibility, and readily solve the problem of accountability.

At this stage in the economic history of the United States it should be clear that where existing institutions no longer serve to meet changing needs, new institutions must be developed that are capable of dealing with change and instability. There is sufficient experience in many states, as well as throughout Europe, to allow for the formulation of economic development banks that serve both the public and private sectors in a partnership to solve regional economic problems. It is only through such mechanisms, and not through short-sighted, short-termed federal programs, or dependence upon existing private sector structures, that capital can be properly channelled to those areas of our municipal and economic life that most need it.

Index